THE MUSIC
OF ANCIENT GREECE

AN ENCYCLOPAEDIA

THE MUSIC
OF ANCIENT GREECE

AN ENCYCLOPAEDIA

by

SOLON MICHAELIDES

D.C. Mus, Hon. FTCL, LENM (Paris)
Hon. Director-General, State Symphony Orchestra
and Conservatoire of Music, Thessalonike, Greece

FABER AND FABER LIMITED
IN ASSOCIATION WITH
FABER MUSIC LIMITED

3 QUEEN SQUARE
LONDON

First published in 1978
by Faber and Faber Limited
in association with
Faber Music Limited
3, Queen Square, London W.C. 1
Printed in Cyprus by
Zavallis Press Limited

ISBN 0 571 10021 X

FOREWORD

Solon Michaelides has for decades played a prominent part in the musical life of Greece and now, nominally retired, is still active as conductor and as adjudicator at musical festivals in many parts of Europe. A composer as well as a musicologist, in the course of a long and busy life he has never lost his intense interest in the music of ancient Greece but (while not professedly a classicist) has devoted his leisure to the compilation of this encyclopaedia, which is unique. No doubt much of its information can be found by delving into lexica and many-volumed encyclopaedias; but here within a brief compass the enquirer will find articles on poets and musicians and musical instruments, on theorists and technical terms of theory. Not only so, he will also find the epithets used in musical contexts by lyric poets, together with much recondite information. (What do we know about Amoebeus the citharode? What do b a l l i s m o s and g i n g r a s and o r s i t e s mean?) The subject abounds of course in controversial issues; and on these the writer wisely contents himself with lucid statements of received opinion while providing enough up-to-date bibliography to enable the student to pursue his own enquiries. There are few who will not find the exploration of this encyclopaedia a fascinating and rewarding pursuit.

R. P. WINNINGTON - INGRAM

PREFACE

This encyclopaedia is principally addressed to students of ancient Greek music; it is hoped however that it may be useful as a book of reference to those incidentally interested in the matter.

The main concern of the author has been to provide a comprehensive work embracing as many aspects and elements of Greek musical life as possible: musical terms (including words not of a specific musical meaning but closely related to Greek musical expression); musical instruments, and dances as well, musical theorists and writers on music, composers and executants; philosophers and poets—principally lyric—whose names have been associated either by historical evidence or by legend with Greek music, or with a certain musical event, innovation or invention of some importance.

The author was well aware of the vastness of the field to be explored but his conviction of the necessity and practical utility of such a work overcame his hesitations. It is hoped that the result will be a positive contribution to the study of Greek music.

The most difficult and disturbing problem has been Greek musical theory itself and the widely diverse opinions, ancient and modern, about its elements, character, and essence. I thought it was wise for a book of this kind to avoid controversy, and expound those views objectively, by citing only where necessary sources and select bibliography.

I also thought it more convenient and preferable to include in the text the references to various sources (instead of notes which in this case would be very obtrusive), and to use the terms and names, as far as possible, in Greek, e.g. aulos, harmonia, kithara, lyra, nomos, tonos etc. This will, I hope, help to prevent the usual confusion from the use of such terms or names as flute, harmony, harp etc. After each entry the pronunciation of the Greek word in modern Greek is added.

Finally, I want to express my grateful acknowledgment to the Loeb Classical Library (Harvard University Press: William Heinemann) for allowing me to quote a number of passages from the Loeb Athenaeus, Nonnos and Plut. Moralia, and to Professor R. P. Winnington - Ingram, Dr. E. K. Borthwick and Miss Mary Cosh for their very valuable advice and assistance in preparing the final text of the book.

Athens, March 1977   SOLON MICHAELIDES

ABBREVIATIONS

AC	= "L'Antiquité Classique" 1932-; Louvain-Bruxelles
adj.	= adjective
adv.	= adverb
Aesch.	= *Aeschylus*
Agiop.	= *Agiopolites,* ap. Vincent "Notices" p. 259 ff (Βιβλίον Ἁγιοπολίτης)
Alyp.	= *Alypius* Isagoge (Εἰσαγωγὴ Μουσική; ap. Meibom and C.v.Jan)
Anon. Bell.	= *F. Bellermann*: "De Anonymi Scriptio de Musica" («Ἀνωνύμου σύγγραμμα περὶ Μουσικῆς»; Berlin, 1841); new ed. D. Najock, Göttingen 1972
ap.	= apud
Apollod.	= *Apollodorus* Bibliotheca, ed. R. Wagner, Leipzig, 1894
Aristides	= *Aristides Quintilianus*: De Musica (ed. Meibom, see below; A. Jahn, Berlin, 1882; R. P. Winnington-Ingram, Leipzig, 1963)
Aristoph.	= *Aristophanes*: Neph. = Nephelae (Clouds)
"	" Av. = Aves (Birds)
Arist. Metaph.	= *Aristotle* : Metaphysica
" Polit.	= " : Politica
" Probl.	= " : Musical Problems
" Rhet.	= " : Rhetorica (Τέχνης Ρητορικῆς)
Aristox. Harm. or simply *Aristox.*	= *Aristoxenus*: Harmonic Elements (Ἀριστοξένου: Ἁρμονικὰ Στοιχεῖα)
Athen.	= *Athenaeus*: "Deipnosophistai" (Ἀθηναίου: Δειπνοσοφισταί; ed. G. Kaibel, 3 vols, Leipzig, 1887-90; Teubner Ed.) With an English translation by Charles Burton Gulick; London, and New York (vols. I-V, 1927-1933)—Cambridge, Mass. (vols. VI-VII, 1937-

1941). The Loeb Classical Library

b.	= *born*
Bacch. Isag.	= *Bacchius the Old :* Isagoge, or Introduction to the Art of Music (Βακχείου τοῦ Γέροντος: Εἰσαγωγὴ Τέχνης Μουσικῆς) ap. Meibom and C.v.Jan.
Bell. Anon.	= *F. Bellermann* (see above Anon. Bell.)
Bothe PSGF	= *Fr. H. Bothe :* Poetarum Scenicum Graecorum Fragmenta, Leipzig, 1844, 4 vols.
Brgk	= *Theodorus Bergk*
Brgk Anth. Lyr.	= „ : Anthologia Lyrica (Leipzig, 1897)
„ PLG	= „ : Poetae Lyrici Graeci (Leipzig, 4th ed. 1878-82)
Bull. de corr. hell.	= Bulletin de correspondance hellénique
Man. Bryen.	= *Manuel Bryennius :* Harmonica (Μανουὴλ Βρυεννίου: Ἁρμονικά; ed. J. Wallis, III, 1699); "The Harmonics of Manuel Bryennius" with an English translation by G. H. Jonker (Groningen, 1970)
Callim.	= *Callimachus*
cf.	= *confer ; compare*
Clem. Alex.	= *Clement of Alexandria* (Clemens Alexandrini: Opera; Τὰ εὑρισκόμενα, 1592). Protrept. = Protrepticus. Strom. = Stromateis
Cleon. Isag.	= *Cleonides* Isagoge, or Harmonic Introduction (Κλεονείδου Εἰσαγωγὴ Ἁρμονική; ap. C.v.Jan.)
contr.	= *contracted*
d.	= *died*
Dem.	= *D. Demetrakos* «Μέγα Λεξικὸν ὅλης τῆς Ἑλληνικῆς Γλώσσης», Ἀθῆναι, 1964; 9 vols. (Great Dictionary of all the Greek Language, Athens, 1964)
Dict. Ant. Gr. Rom. or DAGR	= *Dictionnaire des Antiquités grecques et romaines*, Ch. Daremberg et Edm. Soglio; Paris, 1877-1912, 10 vols.
E. Diehl Anth.Lyr.Gr.	= *Ernestus Diehl* "Anthologia Lyrica Graeca" (Leipzig, 1925)
„ Suppl. Lyr.	= Supplementum Lyricum; Bonn, 1910
dimin.	= *diminutive*
Dinse: De Antig. Theb.	= *L. M. Dinse :* "De Antigenide Thebano Musico" (Berlin, 1856)
Diod. Sikel.	= *Diodorus Sikeliotes* (Siculus; Διοδώρου Σικελιώτου: Βιβλιοθήκη Ἱστορική). T. ed. Dindorf, revised

	Fr. Vogel (vols. I-III, 1888-1893; vols. IV-V C. Th. Fischer, 1906)
Diog. Laert.	= *Diogenes Laertius*

Diog. Laert. = *Diogenes Laertius*

α) Διογένους Λαερτίου: «Περὶ βίων, δογμάτων καὶ ἀποφθεγμάτων».

β) Lives of Eminent Philosophers with an English translation by R. D. Hicks, 2 vols; London, 1925

Dio Chrys. = *Dio Chrysostomus*; ed. Guy de Budé; Leipzig, 1916, 1919

Dion. Hal. = *Dionysius Halicarnasseus*

A. B. Drachmann = Schol. Vet. in Pind. Carm. = Scholia Vetera in Pindari Carmina; 3 vols; Leipzig, 1903, 1910, 1927

E. M. = *Etymologicon Magnum* (ed. Thomas Gaisford; Oxford, 1848)

Eurip. = *Euripides.* Cycl. = Cyclops; Hippol. = Hippolytus, Phoen. = Phoenician women (Phoenissae)

Eust. ad Il. = *Eustathius*, Episcopus Thessalonicensis: "Commentarii ad Homeri Iliadem et Odysseam"; Leipzig, 1825-30; 7 vols. («Παρεκβολαὶ εἰς Ἰλιάδα καὶ Ὀδύσσειαν»)

F H G = *Carl O. Müller*: "Fragmenta Historicorum Graecorum"; Paris, 1841-70; 5 vols.

Gaud. Isag. = *Gaudentius :* "Isagoge" or "Harmonic Introduction" (Γαυδεντίου Φιλοσόφου: «Ἁρμονικὴ Εἰσαγωγή»; ap. Meibom and C.v.Jan)

Gev. = *F. A. Gevaert :* Histoire et Théorie de la Musique de l'Antiquité; Ghent, vol. I, 1875; vol. II, 1881

Gev. Probl. = *F. A. Gevaert et J. C. Vollgraf* "Les problèmes musicaux d'Aristote"; Ghent, 1903

Grove = *Grove's* "Dictionary of Music and Musicians"; 5th ed., London, 1954

Heracl. Pont. = *Heracleides Ponticus*

Herod. = *Herodotus*: Historiae (Leipzig, 1886-7., T., in 2 vols)

Hes. = *Hesychius* Lexicon (ed. M. Schmidt; Jena, 1858-68)

Hom. Il., Od. = *Homer* Iliad, Odyssey; English translation by A. T. Murray; Odys. 1919, Iliad 1924

I. D. = *Ingemar Düring*

J H S. = *Journal of Hellenic Studies*

C.v.J.	= *Carl von Jan* (Carolus Janus): Musici Scriptores Graeci; Leipzig, 1895 *Supplementum Melodiarum reliquiae;* Leipzig, 1899
Th. Kock Comic. Att. Fr.	= *Theodorus Kock :* Comicorum Atticorum Fragmenta; Leipzig, 3 vols, 1880, 1884, 1888
Laloy	= *Louis Laloy :* "Aristoxène de Tarente, disciple d'Aristote et la Musique de l'Antiquité"; Paris, 1904
L S J	= *H. G Liddell and R. Scott* "A Greek-English Lexicon". Revised and augmented by Sir Henry St. Jones; with a Supplement, Oxford, 1968; Reprint 1973
LS, Gr.	= *Henry S. Liddell and Robert Scott,* Greek edition (Μέγα Λεξικὸν τῆς Ἑλληνικῆς Γλώσσης; transl. into Greek by Xen. P. Moschos) with a Supplement, Athens, 1972
Luc. Orch.	= *Lucian* "On Orchestics" (or "On Dancing"; «Περὶ Ὀρχήσεως»)
Macran or H.S.M.	= *Henry S. Macran :* "The Harmonics of Aristoxenus" (Ἀριστοξένου: «Ἁρμονικὰ Στοιχεῖα»; Oxford, 1902)
Mart. Cap.	= *Martianus Capella,* ed. Adolfus Dick, ad. Jean Préaux; Stuttgart, 1969; Liber IX "De Harmonia" pp. 469-535
Mb.	= *Marcus Meibomius :* "Antiquae Musicae Auctores Septem, Graece et Latine"; Amsterdam, 1652
metaph.	= *metaphorically*
m. pr.	= *modern pronunciation*
Moeris Lex.	= *Moeridis Atticistae* Lexicon Atticum (Μοίριδος Ἀττικιστοῦ «Λέξεις Ἀττικῶν καὶ Ἑλλήνων»; Leyden, 1759)
Monro	= *D. B. Monro :* "The Modes of Ancient Greek Music"; Oxford, 1894
A.T.M.	= A. T. Murray; see Homer
Nauck Eurip. Perd. Fr.	= *Aug. Nauck :* Euripides Perditarum Fragmenta Tragoediarum (Leipzig, 1885)
,, *T G F*	= Tragicorum Graecorum Fragmenta (Leipzig, 1956); Supplementum... ed. Bruno Snell, 1964
Nicom. Ench.	= *Nicomachus of Gerase :* "Harmonic Manual" or

	"Enchiridion" (Νικομάχου Γερασηνοῦ: «Ἁρμο-νικῆς Ἐγχειρίδιον»; ap. Meibom and C.v. Jan)
Nicom. Exc.	= *Excerpta ex Nicomacho* (ap. Meibom and C.v. Jan)
Nonnos Dion.	= *Nonnos* "Dionysiaca" (Νόννου Διονυσιακά; with an English translation by W.H.D. Rouse, Harvard U.P., 1940)
op. cit.	= opere citato
oppos.	= opposite
G. Pach.	= *George Pachymeres* "On Harmonike" (Γεωργίου Παχυμέρη «Περὶ Ἁρμονικῆς»; ap. Vincent "Notices")
p. p.	= past participle
Page PMG	= *D. L. Page*: Poetae Melici Graeci; Oxford, 1962. Supplementum Lyricis Graecis, Oxford, 1974
Par. Chron.	= Parion Chronicon; ed. F. Jacoby, Berlin, 1904
Pauly's R.E.	= *Pauly-Wissowa* "Real Encyclopädie", Stuttgart, 1894-1967
Paus.	= *Pausanias the Traveller*: Description of Greece (Παυσανίου «Ἑλλάδος Περιήγησις»; with an English translation by W.H.S. Jones, 6 vols, London, 1918)
Philod. de Mus.	= *Philodemus* "De Musica"; ed. J. Kemke, Leipzig, 1884
Phot. Lex.	= *Photii Patriarchae* Lexicon; ed. S. A. Naber, Leyden, 1864-5
Phryn. Epit.	= *Φρυνίχου Ἐπιτομὴ* (Phrynichi Sophistae, Preparatio Sophistica; ed. Ioannes de Borries, Leipzig, 1911)
Plato	= Prot. = Protagoras, Rep. = Republic
PLG, see Bergk Th.	= Poetae Lyrici Graeci
Plut.	= *Plutarch*
„ An seni resp. ger. sit.	= An seni respublica gerenda sit
„ De adul. et am.	= De adulatore et amico
„ De anim. procr.	= De animae procreatione in Timeo
„ De aud.	= De audiendo (De recta ratione audiendi)
„ De E ap. Delph.	= De E(EI) apud Delphos
„ De Mus.	= De Musica
„ De Pyth. orac.	= De Pythiae oraculis
„ De virt. mor.	= De virtute morali

Plut. Praec. Ger. Reip.	= Praecepta Gerendae Reipublicae
„ Quaest. conv.	= Quaestiones convivales (Quaestionum conviva-lium)
„ Quaest. Gr.	= Quaestiones Graecae
„ Reg. et Imp. Apophth.	= Regum et Imperatorum Apophthegmata
Pollux	= Pollucis Onomasticon (ed. E. Bethe, Leipzig, T., **Lexicographi Graeci**, vol. IX, 1900)
Polyb.	= *Polybius* Histories
Porph. Comment.	= *Porphyrius*: Commentarius in Ptolemaei Harmo-nica (ed. I. Wallis, Oxford, 1699; I. Düring, Göteborg, 1932)
Procl. Chrest.	= *Proclus* "Chrestomatheia"; ed. Th. Gaisford, Leipzig, 1832
M. Psell.	= *Michael Psellus*: «Μουσικῆς Σύνοψις ἠκριβωμέ-νη»; Paris, 1545
PSGF	= See *Bothe*
Ptolem.	= *Ptolemaeus*: Harmonica (Πτολεμαίου Ἁρμονικὰ (ed. I. Wallis, Oxford, 1699; I. Düring, Göteborg, 1930)
Th. Reinach : La mus. gr.	= *La musique grecque*; Paris, 1926
Ruelle	= *Charles-Émile Ruelle*
Sachs : Hist. of Mus. Instr.	= *Curt Sachs*: The History of Musical Instruments (N. York, 1940)
Snell Pind. Carm.	= *Bruno Snell*: Pindari Carmina cum Fragmentis (Leipzig, 1964)
Strabo	= *Geographica* (ed. Aug. Meineke; Leipzig, 1852)
Suid.	= *Suidas* Lexicon (ed. A. Adler; Leipzig, 1928)
s.v.	= *sub voce, under the word*
synecd.	= *synecdochically*
T.	= Teubner Edition
Theocr.	= *Theocritus* "Bucolici"
Theon Smyrn.	= *Theon Smyrnaeus*: Περὶ Μουσικῆς («Τῶν κατὰ μαθηματικὴν χρησίμων...», book II; ed. Ism. Bullialdo; Paris, 1644)
Theophr. Hist. Pl.	= *Theophrasti* Historia Plantarum; ed. Fr. Wim-mer; Leipzig, (T.), 1854

	b) *Theophrastus* "Enquiry into Plants" with an English translation by Sir Arthur Hort, in 2 vols; London-N. York, 1916
Vincent "Notices"	= *A. J. H. Vincent* "Notices sur divers manuscrits grecs relatifs à la musique"; Paris, 1847
vb.	= *verb*
H. Weil et Th. Rein. : Plut. De la mus.	= *Henri Weil et Théodore Reinach*: "Plutarque De la Musique"; Paris, 1900
R.P.W.-I.	= *R. P. Winnington-Ingram*
Xen. Oecon.	= *Xenophon* "Oeconomicos"
„ Symp.	= „ "Symposium"
(*)	= The asterisk refers to the entry under that word

MODERN GREEK PRONUNCIATION

After each entry the pronunciation of the word in modern Greek is added in brackets.

Letters are pronounced as follows:

a as in the word *last ;*

d as *th* in *that ;*

e as e in *end ;*

g with e or i as *y* in *yes* or *yield ;*

  with a or o very light g;

i as in *pit ;*

o as in *hot ;*

s as *s* in *sun* or *ss* in *assist ;*

ch as *h* in *harmony ;*

th as *th* in *theory ;*

the diphthongs: *ou* as *oo* in *foot ;*

      oi as i above;

      ai as *e* above;

all the other letters (b, c, f, k, l, m, n, etc.) as in English.

A

achordos (ἄχορδος); without strings. Theognis (ap. Nauck TGF, p. 769, Fr 1) «ἄχορδος φόρμιγξ» (achordos phorminx) = phorminx without strings.

Metaph. unmusical, discordant; e.g. ἄχορδον μέλος (achordon melos) = unmusical (unpleasant) song (Dem.).

Arist. Rhet., book III, ch. 6, § 7, 1408A: «ὅθεν καὶ τὰ ὀνόματα οἱ ποιηταὶ φέρουσι, τὸ ἄχορδον καὶ ἄλυρον μέλος» ("poets also make use of this in inventing words, as a *melody without strings* or *without the lyre*"; transl. J. H. Freeze, London, 1926, p. 376). According to Dem. "unmusical melos".

achoreutos (ἀχόρευτος; m. pr. achóreftos); untrained in dancing and singing; without choir-training; also not accompanied by dancing. Plato Laws (Book II, 654 A-B): «Οὐκοῦν ὁ μὲν ἀπαίδευτος ἀχόρευτος ἔσται, τὸν δὲ πεπαιδευμένον κεχορευκότα θετέον;» ("Shall we assume that the uneducated man is *without choir-training*, and the educated man fully choir-trained?"; transl. R. G. Bury, London, 1926, vol. 1, p. 93). Metaphor. joyless, sad, mournful.

achoros (ἄχορος); the same as achoreutos. Pollux IV, 81: «ηὔλουν δὲ τὸ ἄχορον αὔλημα, τὸ πυθικὸν» ("they played on the aulos the Pythian aulema (solo) which is *without dancing*", or "the mournful Pythian aulema". Θυσία ἄχορος, a sacrifice performed without dancing.

Note: Used as an epithet of god Mars (Ares) it signified metaphorically horrible, terrible, terrifying.

adein, ado (ᾄδειν, ᾄδω; m. pr. ádin, ádo), in poetic language ἀείδειν, ἀείδω (aeidein, aeido), to sing. It was also used with the meaning: to relate, to narrate (often by singing); Homer, Il. A «μῆνιν ἄειδε, θεά» ("The wrath do thou sing, O goddess'"; transl. A. T. Murray Il. p. 1.).

It meant also: to praise (a person; a hero).

ᾄδειν πρὸς (αὐλὸν or λύραν) = to sing to aulos or to lyra accompaniment; to sing in concord with aulos or lyra.

The opposite of adein was λέγειν (legein) = to speak; cf. Aristox. Harm. I, Mb. 9, 24. The verb ᾄδειν (adein) was used by extension also in the case of birds etc. Timaei Fragmenta in FHG, I p. 207, Fr. 64 «οἱ τέττιγες ᾄδουσιν» ("the crickets sing"). In a contest between two kitharodes, Eunomus the Locrian and Ariston of Rhegium, while the first was performing "*a cricket* flew

1

onto his lyra and *sang*" («τέττιξ ἐπὶ τὴν λύραν ἐπιπτὰς ᾖδεν»). Strabo (VI, p. 260), in relating this story, says that "one of the strings (of Eunomus' kithara) having been broken a cricket flew over the instrument and filled up the note".

(Cf. FHG I p. 207, Fr. 65; Paus. VI, 6, 4 and Strabo; Clem. Alex. Protrepticus, ch. I, § 2).

Adonia, Adonidia (ἀδώνια, ἀδωνίδια).

1. *ἀδώνια* (plur. of ἀδώνιον, Adonion) was a) a lament for Adonis; b) a ceremony in honour of Adonis.

2. *ἀδωνίδια* (plur. of ἀδωνίδιον, Adonidion) were the funeral songs sung by women at a sacred procession in honour of Adonis. At a ceremony for Adonis called ἀδώνια (Adonia), in which only women took part, the women carrying images of Adonis made of wax or baked clay held a procession through the streets of the city, and with an expression of the utmost grief and dolour beating their breast, they sang and danced to the aulos gingras* (γίγγρας) accompaniment.

3. *Ἀδώνια* were also the name of the images of Adonis made of wax or baked clay carried by the women at the funeral procession mentioned above.

4. *ἀδωνιασμὸς* (*Adoniasmós*) was another term for the lament in honour of Adonis; Hes. «Ἀδωνιασμὸς ὁ ἐπὶ τῷ Ἄδωνι θρῆνος» ("Adoniasmos, the lament in honour of Adonis").

5. *ἀδώνιον* (*Adonion*) signified also a kind of war-march played on the aulos; Hes. «Ἀδώνιον τὸ παρὰ τοῖς Λάκωσιν αὐληθὲν ἐπιβατήριον» ("Adonion was the epibaterion melos [a marching melody] played on the aulos among Laconians").

The women who were taking part in the procession were called *Ἀδωνιάζουσαι* (*Adoniazousai*) from ἀδωνιάζειν = to take part in the Adonia ceremony.

aedon (ἀηδών; m. pr. aïdón); nightingale. But also metaphorically the reed of the aulos, and the aulos itself. Hes. «ἀηδόνα· γλωσσίδα μεταφορικῶς Εὐριπίδης Οἰδίποδι» ("Euripides in Oedipus [called] metaphorically the reed [of the aulos], *aedon*"). Also «καὶ τοὺς αὐλοὺς δὲ *λωτίνας ἀηδόνας* που ἔφη (Εὐριπίδης)» ("and he [i. e. Euripides] also somewhere called the auloi, lotus-made aedons")

Cf. Aug. Nauck: Euripidis Perdit. Fragm. Fr. 560, p. 149 and Fr. 923, p. 261 (Fabularum fragm.) and note.

aelinos (αἴλινος; m. pr. élinos); a mournful exclamation; also a fierce lament, a mournful song, a dirge.

Aesch. Agam. 121 (139, 159) «αἴλινον, αἴλινον εἰπὲ» ("chant a strain of woe, a strain of woe". As an adj. it means "mournful, plaintive" (LSJ). Cf. *linos*.

2

The vb aelinein (αἰλινεῖν; m. pr. elinín); to sing an aelinos, a mournful song; to sing a lament, a dirge.

Aeolia harmonia (αἰολία, -ιϰή ἁρμονία; m. pr. eolía, -ikí armonia); so was called, by some writers before Aristoxenus, the octave series (διὰ πασῶν, octave species):

a-g-f-e-d-c-b-a (Diatonic genus).

It was usually called αἰολὶς ἁρμονία or αἰολιστὶ (Aeolis, Aeolisti).

According to Heracleides Ponticus (ap. Athen. XIV, 624 C-D, ch. 19) the Aeolia Harmonia was one of the three Greek Harmoniai (the other two being the Dorios* and the Ionios*) after the three main Greek tribes (Δωριεῖς, Αἰολεῖς, Ἴωνες; Dorians, Aeolians and Ionians). It expressed the character (ethos*) of the Aeolians: the haughty and pompous («γαῦρον καὶ ὀγκῶδες») as also the lofty and confident ethos («ἐξηρμένον καὶ τεθαρρηκός»). The Aeolian was later replaced by the Hypodorian Harmonia.

The Aeolios tonos (τόνος αἰόλιος) held the 7th place in the table of the neo-Aristoxenean system of 15 tonoi; see under *tonos*.

Aeolios nomos (αἰόλιος νόμος); a kitharodic nomos. Lysias (ap. Plut. De Mus. 1132D, ch. 4) includes this nomos among those kitharodic nomoi invented and named by Terpander («οἱ δὲ τῆς κιθαρῳδίας νόμοι πρότερον πολλῷ χρόνῳ τῶν αὐλῳδικῶν κατεστάθησαν ἐπὶ Τερπάνδρου· ἐκεῖνος γοῦν τοὺς κιθαρῳδικοὺς νόμους πρότερος ὠνόμασεν, Βοιώτιόν τινα καὶ Αἰόλιον...» = "the kitharodic nomoi were initiated by Terpander much earlier than the Aulodic nomoi; and were called by him Boeotian, *Aeolian*...").

Hesychius calls this kitharodic nomos αἰολὶς (*Aeolis*); «αἰολίς· κιθαρῳδικὸς νόμος, οὕτω καλούμενος» = "Aeolis; a kitharodic nomos, so called".

Aeolis (αἰολίς; m. pr. eolís);
See above, under *Aeolios nomos*.

aeolomolpos (αἰολόμολπος; m. pr. eolómolpos);
See below, under *aeolophonos*.

aeolophonos (αἰολόφωνος; m. pr. eolóphonos), from αἰόλος (aeolos; nimble, impetuous; metaph. changeable) and φωνὴ (phone*; voice, sound); having or producing a varied, colourful voice. Αἰολόφωνος ἀηδὼν = colourfully singing nightingale.

In Nonnos (Dionys. 40, 223) αἰολόμολπος (*aeolomolpos*) of varied (colourful) singing; «Μυγδονὶς αἰολόμολπος (ἐπέκτυπε αἴλινα) σῦριγξ»; "the melodious Mygdonian syrinx (sounded their dirge)"; transl. by W. H. D. Rouse, vol. III, p. 169).

aeora (αἰώρα; m. pr. eóra) and *eora* (ἐώρα);
See under *aletis*.

Aeschylus (Αἰσχύλος; m. pr. Eschílos); b. Eleusis, 525 B.C.; d. Gela Sicily, 456 B.C.

Of the music of this great tragedian nothing unfortunately survives. We know from ancient sources that his musical style was simple, austere and majestic; his melodic language was imbued with lyrical impulse, but was plain and diatonic, carefully avoiding the chromatic genus (cf. Plut. De Mus. 1137E, ch. 20; also Phrynichus*). The music in his dramatic works is principally concentrated in the choral parts; his choral music and that of Phrynichus represent, for Aristoxenus, the "real models" of dramatic music. His lyricism however is not confined only to the choral parts; it spreads throughout the whole drama.

Aeschylus wrote, according to Suidas, 90 plays; 79 are known by name. Seven of them survive: Persians, Seven against Thebes, Supplices (Suppliant Women), Prometheus Bound and the trilogy Oresteia (Agamemnon, Choephori and Eumenides). They survived complete; but their music still escapes us. We must have recourse to the rhythmopoeia and the poetic language, often exalted, sublime and grandiloquent, to imagine what the character of the melopoeia might be. Indeed various scholars tried, through the rhythmical structure of his works, to bring to light the secrets of the Aeschylean melos. Such poetic creations of incomparable lyrical beauty as the "commos" of Xerxes and the chorus in the "Persians" or that in "Choephori" between Electra, Orestes and the chorus might perhaps justify the opinion of some scholars that "though these products of the musical genius of ancient Greece survive only in one of their two factors, the rhythmopoeia, they appear to us as aesthetic creations which, by their power of expression, stand equal to the melodic marvels of the 19th century" (Gev. II, p. 529, on "Oresteia").

Aeschylus, a powerful genius of imposing poetic stature, of ennobled and lofty inspiration, "full of gods",[1] creator of new and great words,[2] creator of the European drama,[3] excelled also as a melodic composer. Together with his mele he invented new figures of dancing, and took personal interest in teaching them to the chorus.

He composed also Elegeia, and even competed with Simonides on Elegy. He was crowned 13 times at dramatic contests (Suidas says 28).

Cf. Brgk Anth. Lyr., p. 124, four fragments of Elegeia. Aug. Nauck TGF, pp. 3-128, various fragments from his lost plays. O. Schroeder: Aeschylus, Cantica, 2nd ed., T., 1916.

1. "Plein des dieux"; P. Girard "Les Tragiques grecs"; Paris, 1914, p. XII.
2. "He built great words into towers"; Gilbert Murray "Aeschylus, the creator of tragedy"; OUP, 1962, p. 32.
3. J. T. Sheppard "Aeschylus and Sophocles, their work and influence"; New York, 1963, p. 5.

The following, among others, may be consulted with regard to Aeschylus' rhythmopoeia and music:

J. H. Heinrich Schmidt: "Die Kunstformen der griechischen Poesie"—"Die Eurhythmie in den chorgesängen der Griechen"; Leipzig, 1868. See esp. "Text und Schemata" of Aeschylus' "chorika", pp. 146-381.

F. A. Gevaert: "Histoire et Théorie de la Musique de l'antiquité"; Ghent, vol. II 1881; pp. 522-531.

Evanghélos Moutsopoulos: "Une philosophie de la musique chez Eschyle" in "Revue des Études grecques"; vol. 72, Paris 1959, pp. 18-56.

Agathocles ('Αγαθοκλῆς; m. pr. Agathoclís); c. end of the 6th cent. B.C., Athenian sophist and musician. He was a pupil, for music, of Pythocleides*, and teacher of Lamprocles*; and, according to some writers, also of Pindar. He belonged to the Athenian School established by Pythocleides.

Plato (Protag. VIII, 316E) speaks of Agathocles as of a "great sophist" who, like Pythocleides and many others, out of fear for other people's envy used music as pretence and screen («μουσικὴν δὲ 'Αγαθοκλῆς τε ὁ ὑμέτερος πρόσχημα ἐποιήσατο, μέγας ὢν σοφιστής, καὶ Πυθοκλείδης ὁ Κεῖος καὶ ἄλλοι πολλοί. Οὗτοι πάντες, ὥσπερ λέγω, φοβηθέντες τὸν φθόνον ταῖς τέχναις ταύταις παραπετάσμασιν ἐχρήσαντο»).

Agathon ('Αγάθων; m. pr. Agáthon); b. 5th cent. B.C., d. c. 400 B.C.; Athenian tragedian and composer, son of Teisamenus, generally considered as the most important dramatic poet after the three great tragedians.

He was credited with the introduction of the chromatic genus to tragedy (Plut. Quaest. conviv. book III, I, 11-12; «πρῶτον εἰς τραγῳδίαν φασὶν ἐμβαλεῖν καὶ ὑπομῖξαι χρωματικόν»).

His name was given to a kind of aulesis* ('Αγάθωνος or ἀγαθώνειος αὔλησις; "Agathon's or Agathoneios aulesis') which, according to Suidas, was "soft (effeminate) and voluptuous: neither loose, nor bitter, but tempered and most pleasant" («'Αγαθώνειος αὔλησις· ἡ μαλακὴ καὶ ἐκλελυμένη· ἢ ἡ μήτε χαλαρά, μήτε πικρά, ἀλλ' εὔκρατος καὶ ἡδίστη»). Agathon was the first to introduce to the drama the so-called embolima* choral songs which had no direct connection with the main theme of the drama (Aristotle "Poetike, 1456A, ch. 18 «ἐμβόλιμα ᾄδουσι πρώτου ἄρξαντος 'Αγάθωνος τοῦ τοιούτου»).

When very young he first took part in the dramatic contest Lenaea (Λήναια) in Athens in 416 B.C., and won the first prize. He was one of the principal interlocutors in Plato's "Symposium".

He became very popular in Athens for his dramatic works, and his sociability, his pleasant company and his somewhat effeminate beauty. Aristophanes bitterly satirized him in the "Thesmophoriazousae".

5

Agathon died probably in 401 or 400 B.C. in Macedonia where he had been invited in 407 B.C. by king Archelaus (413-399 B.C.).

Only a few verses of his survived.

Th. Bergk Anth. Lyr., p. 132; PLG II, p. 593.

Agathoneios aulesis (ἀγαθώνειος αὔλησις; m. pr. agathónios ávlisis);
See *Agathon*.

agechoros (ἀγέχορος; m. pr. agéchoros), also *hegechoros* (ἠγέχορος; m. pr. igéchoros); the leader of the chorus. Cf. Aristoph. Lys. 1281. The words *agesichoros* and *hegesichoros* (ἀγησίχορος, ἡγησίχορος) have the same meaning. Cf. Dem. s.v. *agechoros, agesichoros*.

See *choregos*.
Note: The term agechoros has been disputed by some scholars.

Agelaus of Tegea (Ἀγέλαος ὁ Τεγεάτης; m. pr. Agélaos Tegeátis); 6th cent. B.C. kitharist from Tegea (Τεγέα; hence his surname Tegeates).

He was crowned at the 8th Pythian Games (558 B.C.) as a kitharist, when, according to Pausanias (book X, ch. 7, § 7), the kitharistike (solo kithara playing) was first introduced.

See under *kitharisis-kitharistike* the text of Pausanias.

Agenor of Mytilene (Ἀγήνωρ ὁ Μυτιληναῖος; m. pr. Agínor Mitilinéos); c. 4th cent. B.C., well-known musician of his time. He was one of the successors to Lasus' teaching, and a contemporary of the famous orator Isocrates (436-338 B.C.).

His School of music is mentioned by Aristoxenus (Harm. II, Meib. 36, 35 to 37, 1) together with that of Pythagoras of Zante*, and by Porphyry* (Wallis, III, p. 189). Among his pupils were included the grandchildren of Isocrates who out of respect to his teaching pleaded in a specific letter to the governors of Mytilene to allow his return home from exile (Isocr. Letter, VIII, 1 "To the governors of Mytilene"; «Τοῖς Μυτιληναίων Ἄρχουσιν»).

agoge (ἀγωγή; m. pr. agogí).

1. ἀγωγή was the term for the progression of the melody in stepwise order. Cleonides (Isag. § 14; Meib. p. 22; C.v.J. p. 207) says "*agoge* is the progression of the melody by consecutive notes" («ἀγωγὴ μὲν οὖν ἐστιν ἡ διὰ τῶν ἐξῆς φθόγγων ὁδὸς τοῦ μέλους»).

Aristoxenus (I, p. 29, 32 Mb) goes further, specifying that each of these consecutive notes is preceded and succeeded by a simple interval.

Arist. Quintilianus (Mb pp. 19 and 29, RPW-I, pp. 16, 29) distinguishes three species of agoge: a) εὐθεῖα (direct), ascending in stepwise order; b) ἀνακάμπτουσα (coming back), descending in stepwise order; c) περιφερής (revolving, circular), ascending and descending in stepwise order. But in the circular

the tetrachord ascends by conjunction and descends by disjunction or vice versa
(«περιφερὴς δὲ ἡ κατὰ συνημμένων μὲν ἐπιτείνουσα, κατὰ διεζευγμένων
δὲ ἀνιεῖσα, ἢ ἐναντίως» (p. 29); it is therefore modulating («μεταβολική»).

See also Bell. Anon. Note pp. 86-87, and p. 82, § 78; Gev. I, p. 378.

2.   The term ἀγωγὴ is also used in the general sense of progression,
sequence; Aristox. (Harm. II, 53, 8 Mb) «ἐκεῖνοι μέν γὰρ ὀλιγωρεῖν φαίνονται
τῆς τοῦ μέλους ἀγωγῆς» ("those [theorists] seem to disregard the *progression*
of the melody").

3.   *Agoge* was also used to mean the rate of movement; the equivalent of
tempo in modern music; Aristox. I, 12, 29 and II, 34, 15. Arist. Quint. (Mb p.
42, RPW-I, p. 39) defines the «ρυθμικὴ ἀγωγὴ» (rhythmical motion) as "the
rapidity or the slowness of times" («Ἀγωγὴ δὲ ἐστι χρόνων τάχος ἢ βραδύ-
της»).

4.   Method, style; Plut. De Mus. (1141C, ch. 29) «εἰς τὴν διθυραμβικὴν
ἀγωγὴν μεταστήσας (ὁ Λᾶσος) τοὺς ρυθμοὺς etc.» ("[Lasus of Hermione]
changed the rhythms into the dithyrambic style etc.").

See *Lasus of Hermione**.

agonistes (ἀγωνιστής; m. pr. agonistís); combatant, competitor. Also
experienced (or professional) artist. Cf. Arist. Probl. XIX, 15.

akariaeos (ἀκαριαῖος; m. pr. akariéos);

ἀκαριαῖος τόπος (locus), a very small, imperceptible locus in which the
extremes of concords may move. Aristox. (II, p. 55, 3-8 Mb): "When we consider
the magnitudes of intervals we find that while the concords either have no locus
of variation... or have an *inappreciable* locus"; transl. H.S.M., p. 206 («Ἐπεὶ
δὲ τῶν διαστηματικῶν μεγεθῶν τὰ μὲν τῶν συμφώνων ἤτοι ὅλως οὐκ ἔχειν
δοκεῖ τόπον... ἢ παντελῶς ἀκαριαῖόν τινα»).

Note: ἀκαριαῖος is derived from ἀκαρής=brief, short, momentary; used with the word
χρόνος (time), as in «ἀκαρὴς χρόνος» or as an adverb «ἀκαριαίως» (or «ἐν ἀκαρεῖ») = in a
very short time, instantly.

akinetoi phthongoi (ἀκίνετοι φθόγγοι; m. pr. akíniti phthóngi); immovable notes.

See under *hestotes* (ἑστῶτες).

aklineis (ἀκλινεῖς; m. pr. aklinís); fixed, unmoved.

See under *hestotes* (ἑστῶτες).

akoe (ἀκοή; m. pr. akoï), from ἀκούειν (akouein)= to hear, to listen; the sense

7

of hearing.   Also what is being heard (word or sound); the act of hearing, and sometimes the ear itself.

The verb ἀκούειν was used to signify also: to follow (to hear) the lessons or courses of a master.   In this respect it is a synonym of «ἀκροᾶσθαι» (akroasthai = to hear, to follow lessons).   Hense «ὁ ἀκούων» (the hearer) = the pupil, the disciple, the follower of a course.   Aristox.   Harm. (II, 30, 18) «τοὺς πλείστους τῶν ἀκουσάντων παρὰ Πλάτωνος» = "most of those who attended Plato's courses"; Ibid (II, 31, 13 «τοῖς μέλλουσιν ἀκροᾶσθαι παρ' αὐτοῦ (τοῦ Ἀριστοτέλους)» = "to those intending to become his (Aristotle's) pupils".

akousma (ἄκουσμα, τό; m. pr. ákousma); everything heard; sound or by ext. music; a rumour.   Also an akroama*.

akousmation (ἀκουσμάτιον, τό; dimin.); a short (little) song or story.

akroama (ἀκρόαμα), from ἀκροᾶσθαι (akroasthai) = to hear especially with attention; a musical performance; everything to which one listens, esp. with pleasure, a song, a recitation, etc..   The term was taken to signify all kinds of entertainments, offered especially during the symposia.   Xen. Symp. (2, 2) «οὐ μόνον δεῖπνον ἄμεμπτον παρέθηκας, ἀλλὰ καὶ θεάματα καὶ ἀκροάματα (pl) ἥδιστα παρέχεις» ("You did not only serve an impeccable dinner, but you offer too most delightful spectacles and *entertainments*").   The principal entertainments at banquets were singing and dancing, since Homer's time; «Μολπή τ' ὀρχηστύς τε, τὰ γὰρ τ' ἀναθήματα δαιτὸς» ("Both the song and the dance are the embellishments of the symposium").

But besides singing and dancing there were many other kinds of entertainment: comic monologues, mimic actions, juggling etc; and musicians were engaged for this purpose (especially women, auletrides* and psaltriai), mimes, jugglers, buffoons, even ribald jokers.   The "akroamata" were of such extent during the symposia that they had the character of a mixed, musico-theatrical, performance.

2.   The word «ἀκρόαμα» (especially in plur. ἀκροάματα) signified, synecdochically, also the executants themselves; Athen. XII. 526: «αὐλητρίδας καὶ ψαλτρίας καὶ τὰ τοιαῦτα τῶν ἀκροαμάτων» ("auletrides and psaltriai and the similar *entertainments*" or "*entertainers*").

akroasis (ἀκρόασις); the act of hearing, of perceiving by the ear, of listening especially with attention; from ἀκροᾶσθαι (see under akoe).   Akroasis was also the following of lessons given orally by teachers; also a lesson, a course, a recitation, a narration which can be followed by ear; an entertainment (as akroama).   Synecdochically: the audience and the auditorium. Plut. "De adulatore et amico" (58 C, § 15): «ὅθεν ὁρᾶν τις ἐστιν αὐτοὺς ἕδρας τε τὰς πρώτας ἐν ἀκροάσεσι καὶ θεάτροις» ("this is the reason why such persons are

8

to be seen taking possession of the front seats at *entertainments* and theatres";
transl. Fr. C. Babbitt, vol. I, p. 313). Aristox. (Harm. II, 30, 18-19) «Καθάπερ
᾽Αριστοτέλης ἀεὶ διηγεῖτο τοὺς πλείστους τῶν ἀκουσάντων παρὰ Πλάτωνος
τὴν περὶ τἀγαθοῦ ἀκρόασιν παθεῖν» ("Such was the condition, as Aristotle used
often to relate, of most of the audience that attended Plato's *lectures* on the
Good"; transl. H.S. Macran, p. 187). «Τοὺς πλείστους τῶν ἀκουσάντων»
may be translated also "most of those who attended the courses".

(See *akoe*).

akroaterion (ἀκροατήριον; m. pr. akroatírion); the part where lectures, musical or other performances took place; auditorium. Synecd. the public that follows
or listens to a speech, a musical performance etc. Plut. "De audiendo" «Περὶ
τοῦ ἀκούειν» (45 F, § 15): «οἱ δὲ τὰς ξένας φωνὰς τοῖς ἀκροατηρίοις νῦν
ἐπεισάγοντες οὗτοι» ("those who nowadays introduce into our *auditoriums*
strange expessions").

akroates (ἀκροατής; m. pr. akroatís); a listener.   One who follows a course (a
pupil or disciple) or listens to a public speech, a musical performance etc. Plato,
Laws II, 668C «ποιηταί τε καὶ ἀκροαταὶ (pl.) καὶ ὑποκριταὶ» ("poets and
listeners and actors").

akros (ἄκρος); extreme; akroi (ἄκροι, pl.) = the extreme notes (or strings) of a
tetrachord or system.   Those in between were called μέσοι (intermediary).
The extreme notes of the tetrachord were immovable (see *hestotes*).

akrotetos (ἀκρότητος; m. pr. akrótitos); in the case of an instrument, not
struck, not played; hence which has not produced a sound.   By extension, not
sounding together or euphoniously; sounding discordantly, out of tune, out of
rhythm.   «Μέλη πάραυλα κ᾽ ἀκρότητα κύμβαλα» = "Mele (songs) out of
tune, and *cacophonous* (or not synchronized) cymbals"; Trag. Adesp. 93 (in
Aug. Nauck TGF, p. 857).

aleter (ἀλητήρ; m. pr. alitír); a kind of dancing native to Sicyon (in Peloponnesus) and the island of Ithaca.

Cf. Athen. XIV, 631D, ch. 30 (see the text under the word *kidaris*); see also FHG II
p. 284, Aristox. «Συγκρίσεις».

aletis (ἀλῆτις; m. pr. alítis) fem. of aletes (ἀλήτης) = wanderer.

1.   a song sung on a swing, while swinging.   Pollux, IV, 55 «῏Ην δὲ καὶ
ἀλῆτις ᾆσμα ταῖς αἰώραις προσᾳδόμενον» ("There was also a song [called]
aletis sung on the swings").   It was believed to be a song in honour of Erigone
(᾽Ηριγόνη; see Note below); Athen. XIV, 618E, ch. 10 "there was also a song
sung at the Swing-festival, in memory of Erigone, which they call the wanderer's
song" (transl. by Ch. B. Gulick, vol. VI, p. 333).

2. Thus also a feast in Athens; Hes. «Ἀλῆτις, ἑορτὴ Ἀθήνησιν, ἡ νῦν Ἐώρα λεγομένη, καὶ ἡμέρας ὄνομα, ὡς ὁ Πλάτων ὁ Κωμικὸς» = "*Aletis*, a feast at Athens, the so-called Eora (or Αἰώρα = swing); the name also of this day (is Eora), according to Plato the comic poet".

Note. Erigone (Ἠριγόνη) was the daughter of Icarius an Athenian, to whom Dionysus taught the cultivation of the vine and the production of wine. She gave birth, by Dionysus, to a son, called Staphylos (staphyle, σταφυλὴ=grape).

Her father offered some of the wine to some shepherds who got drunk, and thinking that they were given poison killed Icarius. Erigone, with the help of her father's dog Maira, found the body, and in despair she hanged herself; but before dying she put the maidens of Attica under a curse to hang themselves too. Their fathers, advised by oracle, established a feast in honour of Erigone in which the maids of Attica hung swings, and while swinging they used to sing the song called "aletis".

See, among others, Nonnos Dion. book XLVII, 34ff.

Also: *George K. Spyridakes* "On the Spring-Swing among the Greek and other peoples of the Balkan peninsula" (Γεωργίου Κ. Σπυριδάκη: «Περὶ τῆς κατὰ τὸ ἔαρ αἰώρας εἰς τὸν Ἑλληνικὸν καὶ τοὺς λοιποὺς λαοὺς τῆς Χερσονήσου τοῦ Αἵμου») in "Epeteris tou Kentrou Erevnes tes Ellenikes Laographias", vol. XXII, 1969-72; Athens, 1973, pp. 113-130; with a Summary in French, pp. 131-134. The author also refers in some detail to the "aeora" in ancient Greece, p. 121ff (in the French summary pp. 132-133).

Alkaeus, or **Alcaeus** (Ἀλκαῖος; m. pr. Alkéos); end of 7th to 6th cent. B.C., lyric poet and composer, from Lesbos or Mytilene (surnamed Λέσβιος or Μυτιληναῖος, Lesbios or Mytilenaeos). He was active during the 45th Olympiad (598 B.C.), and was a contemporary of Sappho.

His life was very turbulent owing to his taking part in the struggles against the tyrants of Lesbos; he lived a long time in exile, wandering from one part to another. Eventually he returned home where he died. He was known as a lover of good-living and drinking; in Athen. (X, 29 A, ch. 33) we read that "both Alcaeus, the lyric-poet (melody maker; μελοποιός, composer) and Aristophanes, the comedian, used to write their poems while getting drunk" («καὶ Ἀλκαῖος δὲ ὁ μελοποιὸς καὶ Ἀριστοφάνης ὁ κωμῳδοποιὸς μεθύοντες ἔγραφον τὰ ποιήματα»).

As a poet Alcaeus held a high position, and was considered, with Sappho, as the chief representative of the Aeolian poetry. His muse derived its source from an ardent and sprightly nature, noble and glowing. He wrote patriotic and war-songs, Hymns, Erotica, and especially Scolia* (drinking-songs), of which some fragments survive.

See in Brgk PLG, III, pp. 147-197 Hymns, Stasiotica (Στασιωτικά, Rebellious Songs), Scolia, Erotica etc.; also in Brgk Anthol. Lyr. pp. 183-193, and Athen. XIV, 627A. Also Page "Sappho and Alcaeus", Oxford 1959.

Alcaeus is credited with the introduction of a metrical schema known as "Alcaic strophe" ("metron").

Alkeides or **Alceides** ('Aλκείδης; m. pr. Alkídis); 2nd to 3rd cent. A.D. A musician from Alexandria, one of the Deipnosophists of Athenaeus; book I, 1F «μουσικὸς δὲ παρῆν ᾿Αλκείδης ὁ ᾿Αλεξανδρεὺς» ("and the musician Alkeides of Alexandria was also present").

The name of Alkeides appears also twice in Book IV, 174B, ch. 75; when from a neighbouring house a very sweet and pleasant sound from a hydraulis was heard, Ulpianus, another Deipnosophist, turning "to the musician Alkeides" drew his attention to that harmonious sound («συμφωνίας», or «εὐφωνίας», according to various editions) so different in character from that "of the single-pipe (monaulos) so common among you Alexandrians, which causes pain to the listeners rather than any musical enjoyment". This observation gave the opportunity to Alkeides to defend the achievements in music of the Alexandrians, and to deliver a long and informative speech on musical instruments extending to the whole of Book IV (174B, ch. 75 to 185A, ch. 84).

His time is unknown but it may be supposed that he was a contemporary of Athenaeus (2nd to 3rd cent A.D.)

Alkman or **Alcman** ('Aλκμάν; m. pr. Alkmán); 7th cent. B.C. lyric poet and composer. According to Suidas he was born at Messoa (Μεσσόα, a part of Sparta according to Strabo), but it was more generally believed that he was born at Sardes of Lydia, in Asia Minor. Sold as a slave in Sparta, Alcman was later emancipated and settled there. Suidas gives as his time around the 27th Olympiad, i.e. 672-668 B.C., and that he lived during the reign of Ardys (῎Αρδυς), king of the Lydians; modern scholars place him later than this time, towards the end of the 7th cent. Alcman was the founder of the Spartan classical style of choral song. He used himself to write both the poetic text and the music of his Hymns, Hymenaeoi, Partheneia, Hyporchemata, Paeans and Scolia, and even defined, where necessary, the movements and figures of the dances. For him poetic text (λόγος), music and dance formed a living unity. Holding the post of chorus master he composed Hymns, Partheneia etc. for the public festivities.

For his "aulodic nomoi" he used three Phrygian auletes (see under *aulodia**). According to Himerius "he knew how to combine the Dorian lyra with the Lydian melos". Aristoxenus in his second book "On Music" (ap. Plut. De Mus. 1136F, ch. 17) praises his Partheneia written in the Doristi Harmonia.

Many verses of Alcman have survived.

Cf. Brgk PLG, III pp. 14-78 and Anth. Lyr. pp. 166-181.
Also Page PMG Frgs 1-177, pp. 1-91, and "The Partheneion", Oxford 1951.

alogos (ἄλογος); alogía (ἀλογία).

See *rheton-alogon; chronos.*

alopex (ἀλώπηξ; m. pr. alópix); fox. Hes. "a kind of dance" («ὄρχησίς τις»).
Cf. L. B. Lawler "The dance in Ancient Greece" (London, 1964) p. 69.

Alypius (Ἀλύπιος; m. pr. Alípios); 3rd or 4th cent. A.D. theorist. His time is placed by Meibom in the 2nd cent. A.D., and by Carl v. Jan ("Philologus" vol. 30, p. 402, 4) after Ptolemy.

Nothing is known of his life. His "Introduction to Music" («Εἰσαγωγὴ Μουσική»), which consists entirely of tables of the Greek scales (15 tonoi, τόνοι) in the three genera with their notation, is the principal source of our knowledge of ancient Greek notation and scales (see *Parasemantike*).

The "Introduction" was first edited at Leyden (Ed. Elzevir) with commentary by Joannes Meursius, together with Aristoxenus' Harmonic Elements and Nicomachus' Manual of Harmonics or Enchiridion ("Aristoxenus, Nicomachus, Alypius, auctores Musices antiquissimi"; Lugduni, Ed. L. Elzevir, 1616, pp. 95-124). Athanasius Kircher published in his "Musurgia Universalis" (Rome, 1650; vol. I, facing p. 540) Tables of the Greek notation after Alypius.

But the first reliable edition of Alypius' Introduction (or Isagoge) was made by Marc Meibom, with Latin translation in his "Antiquae musicae auctores septem, Graece et Latine" (Amsterdam, 1652; vol. I, iv, pp. 1-65).

A more recent and very commendable edition of the Greek text is found in Carl v. Jan's (1836-1898) "Musici scriptores Graeci" (Leipzig, 1895; VIII, pp. 367-406). The "Isagoge" was translated into French by Ch. Émile Ruelle after the text of Meibom and published (without the Greek text) with commentary in "Alypius, Gaudence et Bacchius l'Ancien" (Paris, 1895, pp. 1-48; pp. 141-2 a complete table of the Greek notation; No. V in his "Collection des auteurs grecs relatifs à la musique", 1870-1895).

Note: Alypius' name is mentioned in Eunapius' "Lives of sophists" (Loeb, p. 373 ff). in connection with Iamblichus; also by Cassiodorus (Migne P. L. vol. 70, p. 1272).

See E. Graf.: Alypios in Pauly's R. E., II, col. 1710-1711 (Stuttgart, 1894).

alyros (ἄλυρος; m. pr. áliros); without the lyra, unaccompanied by lyra (LSJ). *Alyron melos* (ἄλυρον μέλος); a tune not accompanied by the lyra. Metaphor. alyros signified sad, mournful, melancholic.
See *achordos*.

amelodetos (ἀμελῴδητος; m. pr. amelóditos); unmelodic, also unsingable, a very small interval which cannot be sung. Aristox. (Harm. I, 21, 25-28 Mb) "semitones, thirds of tone and quarter-tones can be sung but intervals smaller than these are *unsingable*" (ἀμελῴδητα). According to Aristoxenus these intervals cannot be used in a system or scale: Harm. I, 25, 24-25 Mb: «ἀμελῴ-

12

δητον γὰρ λέγομεν ὃ μὴ τάττεται καθ᾽ ἑαυτὸ ἐν συστήματι» ("*amelodeton,* we call that (interval) which cannot be itself placed in a system"). See under *dodecatemorion.*

b) *amelodetos* also signified not sung; not praised by singing; he who was not praised in melody.

ametabolos (ἀμετάβολος; m. pr. ametávolos); unchangeable, not modulating. Ἀμετάβολον σύστημα (neut., ametabolon systema) = immutable system.

See "Perfect Immutable System" under *systema* (σύστημα).

ἁρμονία ἀμετάβολος (*harmonia ametabolos*); Plut. "De Defectu Oraculorum" 437D, § 50.

Amoebeus (Ἀμοιβεύς; m. pr. Amivéfs); well-known Athenian kitharode of the 3rd cent. B.C. Aristeas in his book "On kitharodes" («Περὶ κιθαρῳδῶν») says that Amoebeus lived in Athens "residing near the theatre, and that whenever he came forth to sing he received a fee of one Attic talent (τάλαντον) a day" (Athen. XIV, 623D, ch. 17).

Plutarch also mentions him (in De virtute morali, Περὶ ἠθικῆς ἀρετῆς, 443A, ch. 4) saying that the philosopher Zeno urged his pupils to listen "to Amoebeus' inspired playing and singing"; «ὅπως καταμάθωμεν οἵαν ἔντερα καὶ νεῦρα καὶ ξύλα καὶ ὀστᾶ λόγου καὶ ἀριθμοῦ μετασχόντα καὶ τάξεως ἐμμέλειαν καὶ φωνὴν ἀνίησιν». ("Come, let us observe what harmony and music gut and sinew, wood and bone, send forth when they partake of reason, proportion and order"; transl. W. C. Helmhold Moralia, vol. VI, p. 31).

amousos (ἄμουσος); not trained in the muses, uneducated, unrefined, without taste, rude. Also not trained in music, not knowing music or not having a taste or inclination for music. Plato (Rep. 455E) says: «ἀλλ᾽ ἔστι καὶ γυνὴ μουσική, ἡ δ᾽ ἄμουσος φύσει».

Pl. Laws (Book III, 700C) «ἄμουσοι βοαὶ πλήθους» ("*unmusical* (rude) cries of the crowd"); Eurip. Alcestis 760 «ἄμουσ᾽ ὑλακτῶν» ("*unmusically* (rudely, dissonantly) howling").

amousia (ἀμουσία); the lack of education or culture; also the fact of being unmelodious, unmusical.

Opp. eumousos (εὔμουσος) and eumousia (εὐμουσία).

Plato Laws, book II, 670A «ψιλῷ δ᾽ ἑκατέρῳ αὐλήσει καὶ κιθαρίσει πᾶσά τις ἀμουσία καὶ θαυματουργία γίγνοιτ᾽ ἂν τῆς χρήσεως» ("the use of both aulesis and kitharisis (without orchesis and singing) is a specimen of *unmusicality* and juggling").

The adj. *apomousos* (ἀπόμουσος) is also met, with the same meaning.

Eurip. Phoen. v. 815 «ἀπομουσοτάταισι» (in Bernardakis' ed. «ἀμουσοτάταισι») σὺν ᾠδαῖς» ("with unattuneable [rude, cacophonous] odes").

13

ampeira (ἄμπειρα; m. pr. ámpira); poetic form of ἀνάπειρα (anapeira), test.

The second section of the kitharistic Pythian nomos was so named, according to Strabo (IX, 3, 10, c. 421).

Hes. «ρυθμὸς αὐλητικός» ("auletic rhythm").

Amphion ('Αμφίων); famous mythic kitharode, son of Zeus and Antiope. Several legends were created around his name, and were preserved by many writers. According to one tradition he was the first lyra-player and was taught by Hermes or Zeus himself. He learned from the Lydians the Lydian harmonia, and was credited with the invention of the kitharodia* and the kitharodic art, and the addition of three strings to the four old ones of the lyra.

(Heracl. Pont. ap. Plut. 1131F, ch. 3; Paus. book II, ch. 6, § 4 and IX, ch. 5, §§ 7-9).

His name was connected with the construction of Thebes' walls; according to the legend his twin-brother Zethus (Ζῆθος) by his legendary strength transported bulky stones from the mountains, while Aphion by his lyra and his singing charmed them so that they placed and adjusted themselves on the walls. Thus Thebes' walls with seven gates (Heptapylos) were constructed; "Heptapylos" owing to Aphion's Hepta (Seven-) stringed lyra (Hesiod, FHG I, p. 204; Excerpta ex Nicom. Meib. p. 29, C.v.Jan p. 266; etc.). Eur. Phoenician women vs 823-4.

The poet of "epi to Europa" («ὁ τὰ ἔπη ἐς Εὐρώπην ποιήσας») says that Amphion's songs drew even stones and beasts after him (in Paus. ibid.).

According to Pausanias (IX, ch. 17, § 7) the common tomb of the twin-brothers was placed on the "Ampheion" ('Αμφεῖον), a hill NE of Cadmeia, and the Thebans used to show "the stones placed by themselves following Amphion's singing". Amphion was married to Tantalus' daughter Niobe; and, according to a legend, he was killed by Apollo (Luc. "On Orchestics" 44).

anabasis (ἀνάβασις; m. pr. anávasis); ascension. In music the ascending succession of notes; ascending scale. Also called *anagoge** (ἀναγωγή).

anabole (ἀναβολή; m. pr. anavolí), also *ambole* or *ambola* (ἀμβολὴ or ἀμβολά, in poetic language).

An instrumental prelude; a dithyrambic innovation ascribed to Melanippides* according to which the dithyramb is not divided into strophes-antistrophes but follows the free melodic form of the nomos and the hyporchema.

See Melanippides* and Aristotle Probl. XIX, 15.

Notes: a) The verb ἀναβάλλομαι (anaballomai) in music signified to start playing or singing.

b) Ingemar Düring ("Studies in Musical Terminology in 5th Century Literature", Eranos, vol. 43, 1945, p. 183) holds that "the usual translation of ἀναβολὴ as 'musical prelude' is insufficient; it also stands for the new dithyramb as a whole".

14

Anacreon ('Ανακρέων); 6th cent. B.C. lyric poet. He lived between 563 and 478 B.C. (he died at the age of 85). Anacreon was born at Teos (Τέως, hence his surname Τήϊος, Teïos) on the Ionian coast of Asia Minor. Very few facts are known about his life; when his native-town fell under the Persian domination (545 B.C.), Anacreon went and lived in Samos at Polycrates' court. After the assassination of that tyrant (522) he took refuge with Hipparchus ("Ιππαρχος), son of Peisistratus (Πεισίστρατος), in Athens. When Hipparchus was also assassinated (514) Anacreon left Athens, probably for Thessaly; after that time nothing definite is known about the rest of his life.

Of his music we do not know much.

Critias (ap. Athen XIII, 600 D, ch. 74) calls Anacreon "the enchantment of banquets, women's infatuation, aulos' adversary, *friend of barbiton*; sweet, sorrowless" («συμποσίων ἐρέθισμα, γυναικῶν ἠπερόπευμα, αὐλῶν ἀντίπαλον, φιλοβάρβιτον, ἡδύν, ἄλυπον...»). He was even accredited with the invention of the instrument barbiton* (cf. the Historian Neanthes of Kyzikos ap. Athen. IV, 175E, ch. 77).

Anacreon was the first to use the Ionian metres in anaklastic schema (Ionians alternating with trochaic dipodies); see below, *"Anacreonteion metron"*. He used also the Glyconic systema (three Glygonic lines with a Pherecratean at the end). Cf. *Glyconeios** and *Pherecrateios** (stichos).

For the accompaniment of his songs he never used the aulos but preferred the magadis and pektis; one of his verses, preserved by Athen. (XIV, 635C, ch. 37), runs as follows: "I play on a twenty-stringed magadis, O Leucaspis" («Ψάλλω δ᾿ εἴκοσι χορδαῖσι μάγαδιν ἔχων»; see *psallein*). Further in the same text of Athenaeus (635D) the Alexandrian author Poseidonius says that Anacreon made use only of three harmonias, namely the Dorian, the Phrygian and the Lydian.

See Brgk III pp. 296-338; Page PMG Frgs 346-505, pp. 171-235.

Anacreonteion metron (ἀνακρεόντειον μέτρον; m. pr. anacreóntion métron); acatalectic Ionian dimetron (Ionian a minore with trochaic dipody; anaklasis*).

$$\cup \; \cup \; \underline{\mid} \; \cup \mid \_ \; \cup \; \_ \; \underline{\cup}$$
$$\cup \; \cup \; \underline{\mid} \; \cup \; \underline{\mid} \; \cup \; \underline{\mid} \; \underline{\cup}$$

It was so named because Anacreon made extensive use of it in Erotica and Convivial songs (συμποτικά). The Anacreonteion metron was later used by the poets of the "Anacreonteia"; even Christian poets made use of it (Synesius, Gregorius Nazianzenus and others).

anadosis (ἀνάδοσις); heightening of a note; a synonym of the more frequently used term, ἐπίτασις (*epitasis**).

15

Anon. Bell. (§ 4, p. 22): «Πρόληψίς ἐστιν ἐκ τοῦ βαρυτέρου φθόγγου ἐπὶ τὸν ὀξύτερον κατὰ μέλος ἐπίτασις, ἤτοι ἀνάδοσις» ("Prolepsis is the motion from a lower note to a higher one in vocal melody; that is *anadosis*"). M. Bryen. (Wallis; sect. III, p. 479): «ἐπίτασις ἤτοι ἀνάδοσις» = "epitasis that is *heightening*" (*anadosis*).

See under *epitasis*.

anadrome (ἀναδρομή; m. pr. anadromí); a repeat. Repetition of a section of a musical composition.

anagoge (ἀναγωγή; m. pr. anagogí); leading up. Another term for anabasis*.

anaklasis (ἀνάκλασις; m. pr. anáklasis); in music, reflection of sound, re-echoing. From vb anaklan (ἀνακλᾶν), to reflect (sound, light); to resound; to reverberate. In metric, mixing of trochaic dipodies with Ionian feet (Dem.).

In anaklasis the Ionian (a majore or a minore) alternates with trochaic or iambic dipody. *Anaklasmos*, in metre, overlapping (LSJ).

anaklesis (ἀνάκλησις; m. pr. anáklisis).

See *anesis* (ἄνεσις) and *analysis*.

anakrousis, or **anacrusis** (ἀνάκρουσις; m. pr. anákrousis); prelude, introduction, prooemion; the beginning of an instrumental melody. The term ἄγκρουσις (*ankrousis* or *agkrousis*), poet. form, is also used. According to Strabo (IX, 3, § 10, 421) ἄγκρουσις or ἀνάκρουσις was the first part of the kitharistic Pythian nomos.

Note: The verb ἀνακρούω (*anakrouo*), and poet. ἀγκρούω (*agkrouo*, *ankrouo*) in music signified to begin, to start playing.

See *anabole* (ἀναβολή).

analysis (ἀνάλυσις; m. pr. análisis); separation into constituent elements, resolution of a compound into its elements etc. In Anon. Bell. (§ 78, p. 82) it is met with the meaning of anesis*: "Agoge is the progression, step by step, from lower loci (while *analysis* is the contrary) or a run of notes from a lower to a higher locus; and *analysis* is the contrary" («ἀγωγὴ προσεχὴς ἀπὸ τῶν βαρυτέρων ὁδὸς (ἀνάλυσις δὲ τὸ ἐναντίον) ἢ κίνησις φθόγγων ἐκ βαρυτέρου τόπου ἐπὶ ὀξύτερον· ἀνάλυσις δὲ τοὐναντίον»). The words in brackets are omitted in A.J.H. Vincent's edition of the same book (in "Notices", Paris, 1847). Vincent uses in the second place the word «ἀνάκλησις». It is used also in the meaning of the inverse of synthesis*; in § 81, p. 85 of the Anon. (Bell.) an example is given of analysis of the interval of the 4th («ἀνάλυσις τοῦ διὰ τεσσάρων») as the inverse of synthesis (see under *synthesis c′*). The analysis is a melodic figure consisting of a tetrachord taken alternately by an ascending leap of a fourth followed by a series of four contiguous notes (a), and then

16

repeated in contrary motion (b); the analysis should proceed downwards by stepwise degrees, e, d, c etc.

anamelpein (ἀναμέλπειν; m. pr. anamélpin); to sing; to praise in song.
Theocr. 17, 113 «ἀναμέλψαι ἀοιδὰν» ("to sing a song").
Anacreontea 36,2 «ἀναμέλψομεν Βάκχον» ("let us sing praises to Bacchus").

anaminyrizein (ἀναμινυρίζειν; m. pr. anaminirízin);
See under *minyrismos.*

anapaestos (ἀνάπαιστος; m. pr. anápestos); the well-known metrical foot consisting of two short syllables and one long ʋʋ- (a reversed dactyl).
anapaestic metre (ἀναπαιστικὸν μέτρον); consisting of anapaests; Arist. Quint. (De Mus. Meib. p. 50, RPW-I p. 45): «Τῶν δὴ μέτρων πρωτότυπα μέν ἐστι καὶ ἁπλᾶ τὸν ἀριθμὸν ἐννέα· δακτυλικόν, ἀναπαιστικόν...» etc. ("Of the metres nine are original and simple; the dactylic, *anapaestic* etc.").

anapale (ἀναπάλη; m. pr. anapáli): a very ancient dance similar to the gymno-paedike* (γυμνοπαιδική), danced by naked boys (or youths) imitating gym-nastic movements and figures.
Athen. (XIV, 631B, ch. 30): «ἔοικε δὲ ἡ γυμνοπαιδικὴ τῇ καλουμένῃ ἀναπάλῃ παρὰ τοῖς παλαιοῖς· γυμνοὶ γὰρ ὀρχοῦνται οἱ παῖδες πάντες». ("the gymnopaedike resembles the dance called by the ancients *anapale*; for all the boys use to dance it naked").

anapeira (ἀνάπειρα; m. pr. anápira);
Hes. "an auletic rhythm".
See *ampeira.*

anaphysesis (ἀναφύσησις; m. pr. anaphísisis); (LSJ) prelude in aulos-playing. (Dem.) "the first blowing (lesson) or a prelude in aulos-playing". Cf. Eust. 1406, 50, Hes. s.v., and *gronthon*.*

anaploke (ἀναπλοκή; m. pr. anaplokí); a progression of ascending (rapid) notes; Ptol. Harm. II, ch. 12.
(See the text in *syrigmos**).
Opp. *kataploke** (καταπλοκή).

anarmostos or **anharmostos** (ἀνάρμοστος); not hermosmenos*, not regu-lated according to the laws of music (of harmonia), discordant; almost the same as ekmeles.

17

Opp. of euhármostos and hermosmenos. «Ἐκμελὴς τε καὶ ἀνάρμοστος (φωνὴ)» = "unmelodious and discordant (voice)".

See under *ekmeles*; also Aristox. Harm. I, p. 18, 24; II, p. 52, 25 Mb.; Aristotle Probl. XIX, 20 and 36.

anatretos tropos (ἀνάτρητος τρόπος; m. pr. anátritos trópos); bored-through style. Cf. E. K. Borthwick, "Myrmekia, myrmekos atrapoi" in Hermes 96 (1968), 69 ff.

anaulos (ἄναυλος; m. pr. ánavlos); without the aulos.
Metaph. unmusical.
Eurip. Phoen. women, 791 «κῶμον ἀναυλότατον προχορεύεις» ("As thou leadest the dance of a revel accurst, Where no *flutes* (*auloi*) *ring*"; transl. A.S. Way "Euripides", London, 1912; vol. III, p. 412).

Andreas of Corinth (᾿Ανδρέας ὁ Κορίνθιος; Andréas Corínthios); Corinthian composer of unknown date. He is mentioned by Soterichus (in Plut. De Mus. 1137F, ch. 21), with Tyrtaeus* of Mantineia and Thrasyllus* of Phlious, as examples of composers keeping the ancient tradition, and by preference avoiding the chromatic genus, modulation, the use of many strings and other innovations in rhythmopoeia, melopoeia and interpretation.

aneimenos (ἀνειμένος; m. pr. animénos);
See *chalaros*.
Also *epaneimenos* (ἐπανειμένος; epaniménos); e.g. «ἐπανειμένη λυδιστί» ("loose, slack Lydian"; see *harmonia*).

anekoos (ἀνήκοος; m. pr. aníkoos); incapable of hearing, deaf; not having heard (or attended) lessons (courses); metaph. ignorant (of education, of music). Not having learned (or been taught or informed). Also, not heard.
anekoia (ἀνηκοΐα, m. pr. anikoîa); inability to hear, deafness; metaph. ignorance.

anesis (ἄνεσις), from the verb ἀνιέναι = to relax, to loosen; relaxation of a string. Hence the motion from a higher position to a lower one.
Opp. *epitasis** (ἐπίτασις).
Aristox. (Harm. I, 10 Mb) «ἡ δ᾿ ἄνεσις ἐξ ὀξυτέρου τόπου εἰς βαρύτερον» ("*anesis* [is the motion] from a higher locus to a lower one"). Arist. Quint. (Meib. II, p. 8, RPW-I pp. 6-7) «ἄνεσις μὲν οὖν ἐστιν ἡνίκα ἂν ἀπὸ ὀξυτέρου τόπου ἐπὶ βαρύτερον ἡ φωνὴ χωρῇ» ("*anesis* is when the voice proceeds from a higher locus to a lower one"). Bacch. (Isag., Mb. p. 12; C.v.Jan p. 302) «κίνησις μελῶν ἀπὸ τοῦ ὀξυτέρου φθόγγου ἐπὶ τὸ βαρύτερον» ("a melodic motion from a higher note to a lower").
Anon. Bell. uses too the term anesis (§ 21, p. 30), but also the term *ana-*

18

*lysis** (§ 78, p. 82). Vincent ("Notices") uses the word *anaklesis* (ἀνάκλησις) instead.

2. Aristoxenus (Harm. I, p. 10 Mb) says that many people identify *epitasis** (ἐπίτασις) with height of pitch, and *anesis* (ἄνεσις) with depth of pitch.

angelike (ἀγγελική; m. pr. angelikí); a kind of pantomimic dance performed during a banquet in Syracuse.

Athen. (XIV, 629E, ch. 27) «καὶ τὴν ἀγγελικὴν δὲ πάροινον ἠκρίβουν ὄρχησιν» ("and [the Syracusans] perfected another dance, the *angelike*, danced at banquets").

Pollux (IV, 103) says that it imitated angelic figures («τὸ δὲ ἀγγελικὸν ἐμιμεῖτο σχήματα ἀγγέλων»); ἄγγελος (angel) = messenger.

anisotonoi (ἀνισότονοι);
See *isotonia-isotonoi*.

ankones (ἀγκῶνες, pl. of ἀγκών; m. pr. angón or agkón, agkónes); term used for the parts (ribs) of the kithara supporting its arms (πήχεις, pecheis*) (Hes. «καὶ τῆς κιθάρας δὲ τὰ ἀνέχοντα τοὺς πήχεις ἀγκῶνες λέγονται»).
Cf. Athen. XIV, 637D, ch. 42.
Note: ἀγκὼν = elbow, and by extension the end, the angle of various objects.

anomos (ἄνομος); against the nomos, not following (violating) the nomos.* Hence unmusical, unmelodious.

anomia (ἀνομία); violation of the nomos (music), the act of not keeping the nomos.

antapodosis (ἀνταπόδοσις); the result of touching or striking a string; the sound which the string produces in response to touching it.

antechema (ἀντήχημα; m. pr. antíchima); echo, *antechesis**.

antechesis (ἀντήχησις; m. pr. antíchisis) from ἀντηχεῖν (antechein), to sound in reply, to resound; resonance, re-echoing.

Also, echo. Arist. Probl. XIX, 24.

antechos (ἄντηχος; m. pr. ántichos); resounding.

antepirrhema (ἀντεπίρρημα; m. pr. antepírrima); the seventh and last part of the parabasis* (παράβασις). It corresponded to the fifth part which was called epirrema* (ἐπίρρημα), and it was composed of trochaic tetrameters and recited directly to the audience by the leader (coryphaeus) of the chorus.

anthema (ἄνθεμα, pl. of ἄνθεμον, τό); an alert and gay folk-dance to celebrate the coming of the spring and the blooming of flowers. It was performed with some mimic action by two groups of men dancing and singing at the same time.

In the "Deipnosophists" (Athen. XIV, 629E, ch. 27) we find the following

19

words sung during the dancing, as they have been preserved, «ποῦ μοι τὰ ῥόδα, ποῦ μοι τὰ ἴα, ποῦ μοι τὰ καλὰ σέλινα;» «ταδὶ τὰ ῥόδα, ταδὶ τὰ ἴα, ταδὶ τὰ καλὰ σέλινα» ("where are my roses, where are my violets, where is my beautiful parsley?" "Here are thy roses, here are thy violets, here is thy beautiful parsley").

Note: The word ἄνθεμον is derived from the verb ἀνθεῖν (anthein) = to bloom.

Anthes of Anthedon (Ἄνθης ὁ ἐξ Ἀνθηδόνος; m. pr. Anthis of Anthidón); mythical minstrel from the little town Anthedon (Ἀνθηδὼν) in Boeotia. He is cited by Heracl. Ponticus (ap. Plut. De Mus. 1132A, ch. 3) as a composer of Hymns, and contemporary of Linus*, Pierus* of Pieria, and Philammon* of Delphi.

His name, Anthes, as that also of Pierus, may have been created from the name of the city itself.

(Cf. Gev. I, p. 41).

Anthippus (Ἄνθιππος; m. pr. Ánthippos); mythico-historical poet and musician, to whom the invention of the Lydian harmonia was ascribed by Pindar (cf. Plut. De Mus. 1136C, ch. 15; «Πίνδαρος δ᾽ ἐν Παιᾶσιν ἐπὶ τοῖς Νιόβης γάμοις φησὶν Λύδιον ἁρμονίαν πρῶτον ὑπ᾽ Ἀνθίππου διδαχθῆναι»; "Pindar in his Paeans on Niobe's wedding ascribes the invention of the Lydian harmonia to *Anthippus*"). Cf. also Pollux IV, 78 («λυδιστὶ [ἁρμονία] ἣν Ἄνθιππος ἐξεῦρε »=« (and) the Lydian [harmonia] which *Anthippus* invented"). Others ascribed the invention of the Lydian harmonia to Torebus*.

antichordos (ἀντίχορδος); a) being in concord; Hes. «ἀντίχορδα (pl. neut.) σύγχορδα, ἰσόχορδα»; b) also in the contrary sense, in discord with another sound. Plut: Quaest. convivialium, IV, 1, 663F; «καὶ ταῦτα μὲν ὡς ἀντίχορδα κείσθω τοῖς ὑπὸ σοῦ πεφιλοσοφημένοις» ("let this be my response in opposition to your speculations"). See also *antiphonos* and *antiphthongos*.

Antigenidas or -ides (Ἀντιγενίδας, Ἀντιγενείδας or Ἀντιγενίδης; m. pr. Antigenídis); c. end of 5th to 4th cent. B.C. aulete and composer of repute from Thebes, son of Dionysius. He was considered the chief of the auletic School of Thebes of his time. According to Suidas he was engaged for some time as aulete accompanist of the famous dithyrambic poet Philoxenus* («αὐλῳδὸς Φιλοξένου»).

He is cited as an innovator, and both he and his school were opposed to the school of Dorion*, another well-known aulete of the time (Plut. 1138B, ch. 21).

He was one of the artists invited to the banquet held on the occasion of the marriage of the Athenian orator and general Iphicrates to the daughter of king Kotys (Κότυς) of Thrace; this symposium became celebrated for its

20

extravagance and was scorned by the comedian Anaxandrides in his "Protesilaus" («Πρωτεσίλαος»; ap. Athen. IV, 131B, ch. 7). He left many disciples and his school continued to flourish long after his death.

Antigenidas was known for his disdain of the applause of the crowd; it is said that when once he heard the uproar of the crowd for an aulete, he said "it must be something very bad otherwise the public would be less lavish in acclamations" (P. J. Burette "Remarques sur le dialogue de Plutarque" in "Mémoires de Littérature" No. VII, CXLV, CXLIV, CXLIII).

Bibliography: *H. L. M. Dinse* "De Antigenida Thebano musico" (Berlin, 1856).

antimolpos (**ἀντίμολπος**) from ἀντὶ = against, instead of, and μολπὴ (molpe; song); being in contrast (or discord) with the molpe or another sound; see *antiphthongos.* Also: performed or sung instead of (LSJ).

antiphonon (**ἀντίφωνον**) neut., τό; the octave, sounding in answer. Also ἀντίφωνος (ὁ, ἡ) and ἀντιφωνία (antiphonía). The verb «ἀντιφωνεῖν» (antiphonein) to sing in reply, to sing on the octave.

Arist. Probl. XIX, 39 «Διὰ τί ἥδιόν ἐστι τὸ ἀντίφωνον τοῦ ὁμοφώνου; ῍Η ὅτι τὸ μὲν ἀντίφωνον σύμφωνόν ἐστι (τῷ) διὰ πασῶν»; ("Why is the *antiphonon* more pleasant than the homophone? Is it because the *antiphonon* is in concord (with) the octave?"); see also Probls. XIX, 16, 17, 18.

Gaud. (Isag. § 20, C.v.Jan p. 348; Mb p. 21) «τὴν μέσην τὴν νῦν ἀντίφωνον τῷ προσλαμβανομένῳ» ("the mese which is now the 8ve of the proslambanomenos*):

antiphthongos (**ἀντίφθογγος**); a) being in concord with another sound, of answering sound; the octave of another sound, antiphonos.

Pindar (PLG, Fr. 102 [91]; Athen. XIV, 635B, ch. 36) in his scolion to Hieron of Syracuse calls the magadis «ψαλμὸν ἀντίφθογγον» ("plucking [soundding] at the 8ve").

b) being in contrast or in discord with another sound, contradictory; «ἀντίφθογγον τὴν γλῶτταν τοῖς νοήμασι πλουτεῖν» ("to enrich the language *with contradictions* as to the meaning").

Another word for this is *antimolpos*.

antipsalmos (**ἀντίψαλμος**); being in concord at the octave (the song with the accompanying kithara, played directly by the fingers); struck at the octave of the song.

21

antipsallein (ἀντιψάλλειν), vb; to play a stringed instrument (without a plectrum) as accompaniment to a song.

Aristoph. Aves (Birds) v. 218-219 «τοῖς σοῖς ἐλέγοις ἀντιψάλλων ἐλεφαντόδετον φόρμιγγα» ("[Phoebus] playing an accompaniment to thy elegies on his phorminx inlaid with ivory").

antispastos (ἀντίσπαστος); a metrical foot consisting of an iambus and a trochee ᴜ--ᴜ. In music, antiphthongos, plucking at the octave. Phrynichus in "Phoenician women" (ap. Athen. XIV, 635C, ch. 36; also A. Nauck Trag. Gr. Fr. Phrynichus Fr. 11 [ed. 1956 Fr. 12 p. 560]) says «ψαλμοῖσιν ἀντίσπαστ' ἀείδοντες μέλη» ("with plucking of the strings *they sing* their songs in *octaves*"). Ἀντίσπαστα μέλη = mele in antiphthongic concord. Ἀντισπαστικὸν μέτρον (*antispastic metre*); a metre consisting of antispastic feet; cf. Arist. Quint. (De Mus. Meib. II, p. 50; R.P.W.-I. p. 45).

antistrophe (ἀντιστροφή; m. pr. antistrophí); the turning of the chorus to the opposite direction (from right to left) during the dramatic performance; the contrary of the strophe*. The ode sung during this turning was also called, by extension, antistrophe. The second part of the lyric songs in ancient dramas corresponding to the schema strophe-antistrophe. See *strophe*.

antistrophos (ἀντίστροφος, fem. ἡ); the sixth part of the Parabasis* corresponding to the fourth which is called strophe (Pollux IV, 112). Also used in the sense of antistrophe*.

antyx (ἄντυξ; m. pr. ántix); the circumference of a circular body. The bridge of the lyra or, in some writers, another word for the zygon* (ζυγόν), cross-bar of the lyra.

Eur. Hippol. 1135 «μοῦσα δ' ἄυπνος ὑπ' ἄντυγι χορδᾶν» ("the incessant singing of the strings which are found under *the antyx* [the cross-bar of the lyra"]);
Cf. Dem.; N. Bernardakis Euripides, vol. II, Hippol. v. 1135 (Athens, 1888).

aoede (ἀοιδή; m. pr. aïdí) from ἀείδειν-ᾄδειν = to sing; Ionian type of ᾠδή, met very often in Homer. a) Its first and principal signification was song; but it signified also: b) the art of song (Hom. Od. VIII, 498; «ὡς ἄρα τοι πρόφρων θεὸς ὤπασε θέσπιν ἀοιδὴν» = "that the god has a ready heart granted thee *the gift of divine song*"; transl. A.T. Murray, Od. vol. I, p. 295); c) the act of singing; Hom. Il. XVIII, 304-5 («οἱ δ' εἰς ὀρχηστύν τε καὶ ἱμερόεσσαν ἀοιδὴν τρεψάμενοι τέρποντο»; "but the wooers turned to dance and gladsome song, and made them merry"; A.T.M., vol. II, p. 219); d) the subject or theme of the song; the story sung.

22

aoedimos (ἀοίδιμος; m. pr. aídimos); that which is sung or is subject of a song. Herod. (book II, ch. 79) «Λίνος, ὅσπερ ἕν τε Φοινίκῃ ἀοίδιμός ἐστι καὶ ἐν Κύπρῳ καὶ ἄλλῃ» ("*linos* which is sung in Phoenicia, in Cyprus and elsewhere").

aoedos (ἀοιδός; m. pr. aïdós); also ᾠδός, contr. form (odos); epic singer, minstrel; very often poet-composer-singer. The aœdoi (pl. minstrels) were professional poets-composers-singers invited or engaged by a palace; they used to sing, to phorminx* accompaniment, epic songs and the exploits of heroes. Renowned aoedoi were Demodocus*, who lived at king Alkinoos' palace in the island of the Phaeacians, Phemius*, who lived at Ulysses' palace in Ithaca, and Thamyris* from Thrace.

The aoedos was highly respected by all and was often surnamed "divine"; Hom. Od. IV, 17 «μετὰ δέ σφιν ἐμέλπετο θεῖος ἀοιδὸς φορμίζων» = "and among them a *divine minstrel* was singing to the phorminx"). Also, Od. VIII, 479-480 «τιμῆς ἔμμοροί εἰσι καὶ αἰδοῦς»; "for among all men that are upon the earth minstrels win honour and reverence"; transl. A.T.M.).

The aoedos was also a dirge singer, a mourner; Hom Il. XXIV, 720 «παρὰ δ' εἶσαν ἀοιδοὺς θρήνων ἐξάρχους, οἵ τε στονόεσσαν ἀοιδὴν οἱ μὲν ἄρ' ἐθρήνουν, ἐπὶ δὲ στενάχοντο γυναῖκες» = "and by his (Hector's) side set *singers, leaders of the dirge,* who led the song of lamentation, they chanted the dirge, and thereat the women made lament"; transl. A. T. Murray, Il. vol. II. p. 617).

Ἀοιδὸς signified also incantator, enchanter, a charmer who cured by singing epodes (incantations).

aoedos, fem.; songstress; aoedos Mousa (ἀοιδὸς Μοῦσα).
As an adj., musical, melodious.

apadein, vb (ἀπᾴδειν; m. pr. apádin);
See *apodos*.

apechema (ἀπήχημα; m. pr. apíchima); echo, antechema*.
apechesis (ἀπήχησις; m. pr. apíchisis); resounding, re-echoing, resonance. From vb *apechein* (ἀπηχεῖν; m. pr. apichín); to sound in answer, to re-echo.
Cf. *antechesis*; Arist. Probl. XI, 6 and XIX, 11.

aphonos (ἄφωνος); voiceless. In music, without words, *aphona kroumata* = pieces without singing; see under *kitharistike*. Also, kakophonos or with a poor voice; Suid. (s.v. Κόννου ψῆφον) «Ὁ δὲ Κόννος λυρῳδὸς ἦν, ὥς τινες φασιν, τῶν ἀφώνων». Dion. Thrax (631,21) «ἄφωνος τραγῳδός».

aphormiktos (ἀφόρμικτος); without the phorminx, unaccompanied by the

23

phorminx. Metaphor. sad, melancholic.

Cf. *alyros*.

aplastos (ἀπλάστως) adv.; naturally, in a simple, unaffected way; e.g. «αὐλεῖν ἀπλάστως» = to play naturally (in a simple way) on the aulos.

Theophr. Hist. Plant., book XI, 4 «ηὔλουν ἀπλάστως» = "they played the pipe in the simple style"; transl. Sir A. Hort, Theophr. "Enquiry into plants", vol. I, p. 371.

aplates (ἀπλατής; m. pr. aplatís); without breadth (a sound without breadth). Aristoxenus was the first to contend that sounds have no breadth; in his Harm. Elem. (I, p. 3, 21-25 Mb), he writes that one "must avoid the blunder of Lasus and some of Epigonus' School who thought that sound has breadth" («ἀναγκαῖον τὸν βουλόμενον μὴ πάσχειν ὅπερ Λᾶσος τε καὶ τῶν Ἐπιγονείων τινὲς ἔπαθον, πλάτος αὐτὸν [τὸν φθόγγον] οἰηθέντες ἔχειν»). Many followed his view. Cleon. Isag. (Mb p. 2; C.v.Jan p. 180, § 1) «τόνος δέ ἐστι τόπος τις τῆς φωνῆς δεκτικὸς συστήματος, ἀπλατὴς» ("tonos is a locus of the voice apt to receive a system; it is *without breadth*"). Exactly the same definition is given by M. Bryennius (Harm. sect. III; Wallis III p. 389). Nicom. (Enchir. § 4, Mb p. 7, C.v.Jan pp. 242-3) «φθόγγον δὲ [εἶναι] φωνῆς ἐμμελοῦς ἀπλατῆ τάσιν» ("sound is a tension [pitch] *without breadth* of a melodious voice"). And Porphyry (Commentarius on Ptolemy's Harm.; Wallis ed., III p. 258; I.D. p. 82, 4-5) «λέγεται δὲ τόνος καὶ ὁ κατὰ τὸ σύστημα τόπος, κατὰ Ἀριστόξενον, δεκτικὸς ὢν τελείου συστήματος, ἀπλατὴς» ("tonos is also said as to the system, according to Aristoxenus, apt to receive a perfect system, [and] *without breadth*").

apochordos (ἀπόχορδος); out of tune; unattuned. Cf. Clem. of Alexandria Stromateis, book II, 123.

(See the text under *ektonos*).
See also *apodos ; parachordos*.

apodos (ἀπῳδὸς) from apodein, or apadein, vb (ἀπῳδεῖν, ἀπάδειν), in music, to sing [or to be] out of tune; sounding or singing out of tune; discordant. Plato Laws (VII, 802E) «δεινὸν γὰρ ὅλῃ τῇ ἁρμονίᾳ ἀπάδειν ἢ ῥυθμῷ ἀρρυθμεῖν» ("it is a terrible experience *to sing out of tune* in the whole scale or out of time in rhythm"). Arist. Probl. XIX, 26: «διὰ τί ἐπὶ τὸ ὀξὺ ἀπάδουσιν οἱ πλεῖστοι;» ("Why is it that most people *sing out of tune* on the high pitch?"); also, XIX, 46.

Eurip. Cyclops, v. 490 «σκαιὸς ἀπῳδὸς» ("rude [inelegant] singing out of tune"). Suidas «ὁ κακόηχος, ὁ ἀπὸ τῆς ᾠδῆς» ("ill-sounding; that which is out of the ode [tune]"); «ἀπῳδὸν μέλος (apodón melos) τὸ μὴ ἀρέσκον» ("displeasing tune").

apokinos (ἀπόκινος); a kind of erotic dance, danced by women with rotary motion of the belly. Pollux IV, 101 «Βακτριασμὸς δὲ καὶ ἀπόκινος καὶ ἀπόσεισις ἀσελγῆ εἴδη ὀρχήσεων ἐν τῇ ὀσφύος περιφορᾷ» ("Baktriasmos*, and *apokinos* and aposeisis*, lustful kinds of dances because of the rotation of the waist"). Athen. (XIV, 629C, ch. 26) «Τὴν δ᾽ ἀπόκινον καλουμένην ὄρχησιν ... ἣν καὶ πολλαὶ γυναῖκες ὠρχοῦντο, ἅς καὶ μακτροκτυπίας (or μακτριστρίας) ὀνομαζομένας οἶδα» ("and there is the so-called *apokinos* dance... which many women too used to dance, who were called maktroktypiai [or maktristriai], as I know"). Further, in Athen. (629F) the *apokinos* is included in a number of ludicrous dances.

apolelymena (ἀπολελυμένα, ᾄσματα; m. pr. apoleliména), pl. of p.p. of ἀπολύομαι = to be free, liberated; free (in form) songs. These songs were composed of various sections different from each other in character, and without strophic responsion.

apomousos (ἀπόμουσος);
See *amousos*.

apopsalma (ἀπόψαλμα, neut. τὸ) from apo-psallein (ἀποψάλλειν)=to pluck off, to pull (the strings or the hair); the part of the string which is touched or plucked by the performer. Porphyry (in Commentarius to Ptol. Harm.; ed. Wallis III, p. 295): «καθ᾽ ὃ τοὺς ἤχους αἱ χορδαὶ ἀποδιδοῦσι» ("the part where the strings produce the sounds"). Also Ptol. Harm. I, 8.

aposeisis (ἀπόσεισις, fem; m. pr. apósisis); licentious dance. Aposeisis is included by Pollux with apokinos* in lustful and licentious dances (IV, 101).

apostolika, mele (ἀποστολικά, μέλη; pl. of ἀποστολικόν, τό); 1. messengers' songs; songs composed for a special mission, sung on departure.
   Procl. Chrest. «ἀποστολικὰ δέ, ὅσα διαπεμπόμενοι πρός τινας ἐποίουν» ("and [there were] messengers' songs which they composed on sending a message to certain people").
   2. Ἀποστολικοί, τρόποι (pl. of ἀποστολικός, masc.); kinds of poetry which were danced. Athen. (XIV, 631D, ch. 30): «βέλτιστοι δὲ εἰσι τῶν τρόπων οἵτινες καὶ ὀρχοῦνται. Εἰσὶ δὲ οἴδε· προσοδιακοί, ἀποστολικοὶ (οὗτοι δὲ καὶ παρθένιοι καλοῦνται) καὶ οἱ τούτοις ὅμοιοι» ("the best varieties [of lyric poetry] are those which are danced as well. They are these: prosodiakoi [processional hymns], *apostolikoi* (also called parthenioi) and the like".

apostrophos (ἀπόστροφος); "turning away of chorus from stage in comic parabasis" (LSJ); in Dem., on the contrary, the discourse addressed to the audience by the chorus in ancient drama, "the parabasis".
   Cf. *parabasis**.

apothetos (ἀπόθετος, νόμος); an aulodic nomos, the invention of which was attributed to Clonas* (Κλονᾶς). Nothing is known about its character.

See Plut. De Mus. (1132D, ch. 4 and 1133A, ch. 5) and Pollux IV, 79.

apotome (ἀποτομή, ἡ; m. pr. apotomí; from ἀποτέμνειν [apotemnein] = to cut off); a term by which the Pythagoreans called the major semitone.

Gaud. (Harm. Isag.; § 14, C.v.Jan p. 343; Mb p. 16) «Τοῦ δὲ λείμματος τὸ λεῖπον εἰς συμπλήρωσιν τόνου καλεῖται ἀποτομή· κοινῶς δὲ καὶ αὐτὸ ἡμιτόνιον, ὥστε ἔσται τῶν ἡμιτονίων τὸ μὲν μεῖζον, τὸ δὲ ἔλαττον» ("The remainder of the leimma* to complete the tone is called *apotome*; commonly this is also a semitone. Therefore one of the semitones will be the major [i.e. the apotome], and the other one the minor [leimma]").

Philolaus divided the tone into two unequal parts, the diesis (13/27) and the *apotome* (14/27). He took the 3 to the third power, i.e. 27, then he divided the 27 into two, inevitably unequal, parts and called the minor part (13) diesis and the major (14) *apotome*.

(Cf. A. E. Chaignet: "Pythagore et la Philosophie Pythagoricienne"; Paris, 1873; vol. I, p. 231; see also under *Philolaus*).

apycnon, systema (ἄπυκνον, σύστημα; neut; m. pr. ápicnon); 1. a system not pycnon, not dense. The opposite of pycnon.

Aristox. (Harm. I, p. 29, 2 Mb) «μετὰ τὸ πυκνὸν ἢ τὸ ἄπυκνον... σύστημα» ("after the pycnon or the *apycnon*... system").

2. *apycnos* (ἄπυκνος, masc.) was also the term for any note which did not belong or enter into any relation with the pycnon. Thus only three notes were apycnoi, the Proslambanomenos and the two Netai (Nete Synemmenon and Nete Hyperbolaeon).

See under *Pycnon*. Also: Cleon. (Isag. 4, C.v. Jan p. 186; Mb p. 7); Bacch. (Isag. C.v. Jan p. 300; Mb 9); Alyp. (Isag. C.v.Jan p. 368; Mb p. 2); Arist. Quint. (Meib. II p. 12; R.P.W.-I. p. 9).

arche (ἀρχή, ἡ; m. pr. archí); Dorian type ἀρχὰ (archá); beginning, commencement. The first part of the kitharodic nomos* was so called.

ἀρχὴ was also the first note (the root) of the tetrachord (taken in a downward motion); the last one was called τελευτὴ (teleute; end, opp. of arche). Arist. Probl. XIX, 33 «Διὰ τί εὐαρμοστότερον ἀπὸ τοῦ ὀξέος ἐπὶ τὸ βαρὺ ἢ ἀπὸ τοῦ βαρέος ἐπὶ τὸ ὀξύ; Πότερον ὅτι τὸ μὲν ἀπὸ τῆς ἀρχῆς γίγνεται ἄρχεσθαι; ἡ γὰρ μέση καὶ ἡγεμὼν ὀξυτάτη τοῦ τετραχόρδου· τὸ δὲ οὐκ ἀπ' ἀρχῆς ἀλλ' ἀπὸ τελευτῆς;» ("Why is the succession of sounds better adjusted from high to low than from low to high? Is it because in the first case we start from the beginning? since the mese and principal note is the highest note of the tetrachord, while in the second case we start from the end rather than from the beginning?"): a - g - f - e

    ↑   ↑
  arche teleute

Archilochus (’Αρχίλοχος; m. pr. Archílochos); b. c. end of 8th cent. B.C.; d. 645-640 B.C. Elegiac and satirical poet from the island of Paros in the Cyclades.

To Archilochus were attributed many innovations in the rhythmopoeia (the trimeter, the alternative use of unequal metres etc); the word ρυθμὸς [ρυσμὸς in its Ionian form] appears for the first time in Archilochus though not in the more modern sense that it has in classical times. See *rhythmos*.

He was considered the first to introduce the parakataloge* (a kind of accompanied recitative), and the free accompaniment of song on the kithara («κροῦσιν ὑπὸ τὴν ᾠδὴν») instead of the instrumental doubling of the vocal part. Archilochus also initiated alternate singing and reciting with instrumental accompaniment in the iambic verses.

See Plut. De Mus. 1140F-1141B, ch. 28; also *Fr. Lasserre*: Les épodes d'Achiloque; Paris, 1950, and *Proschordos**.

In Athenaeus (XIV, 627C, ch. 23) we read that Archilochus' participation in civic rivalries (or war struggles; «πολιτικῶν» or «πολεμικῶν» ἀγώνων in different editions), took pride of place over his poetic talents.

See Brgk PLG II, 383-440, 199 Frgs and Anth. Lyr. pp. 2-16, Elegeia, Iamboi, Epodoi, Iobacchoi, Epigrams. Also M.L.West: Iambi et Elegi Graeci, 2 vols., Oxford 1971-2.

Cf. *Giovanni Tarditi*: Archiloco; Roma, 1968, with 291 various Frgs.

Archytas (’Αρχύτας; m. pr. Archítas).

1. Pythagorean philosopher, mathematician and perhaps the most important acoustician of ancient Greece. He lived in the first half of the 4th cent. B.C. in Tarentum. Diog. Laertius ("Lives of Eminent Philosophers", book III, ch. 4, § 79) speaking about his life says that he was admired by most people for his eminence in every field. As a statesman he was highly respected and was seven times elected governor, and governed Tarentum for many years, while it was not allowed by law for anyone to be "general" (governor) for more than one year («Ἐθαυμάζετο δὲ καὶ παρὰ τοῖς πολλοῖς ἐπὶ πάσῃ ἀρετῇ· καὶ δὴ ἑπτάκις τῶν πολιτῶν ἐστρατήγησε, τῶν ἄλλων μὴ πλέον ἐνιαυτοῦ στρατηγούντων διὰ τὸ κωλύειν τὸν νόμον»).

His researches on musical sound led him to the discovery that sound was produced by vibrations of the air, and that its pitch depended on the rapidity of the pulsations; higher sounds are produced by more rapid pulsations and lower sounds by slower pulsations (cf. Porph. Comment., ed. I. Düring, pp. 56-57). Archytas worked out the ratios of the intervals of the tetrachord in the three genera, diatonic, chromatic and enharmonic. He also discovered the ratio of the major third in the enharmonic genus (e - e $\frac{1}{4}$ - f - a).

Archytas was a contemporary and friend of Plato whom he received at Tarentum, and helped to face the hostility of Dionysius, the tyrant of Sicily. He became moreover famous for his many mechanical discoveries. According to a tradition he was drowned in a shipwreck near Italy.

Bibliography:

Giuseppe Navarro : Testamen de Archytae Tarentini vita atque operibus etc. 4o, Hafniae 1819.

J. C. von Orelli : Archytae ... Fragmenta quae supersunt. Gr. et Lat. 1821.

Political Fragments of Archytas, Charondas, Zaleucus and other ancient Pythagoreans ...preserved by Stobaeus. Translated from the Greek by Thomas Taylor. London, 1822.

E. Egger : De Archytae vita, operibus etc. (Paris, 1833).

A. E. Chaignet : "Pythagore et la philosophie Pythagoricienne" (2 vols., Paris, 1873), etc.

2. A musician from Mytilene of unknown date mentioned by Athenaeus (XIII, 600F) as one of the Harmonists, who wrote a book on music in which he claimed that Alcman was the leader in the field of erotic songs.

Diog. Laertius (XVIII, ch. 4, § 82) relates of this Archytas that when at a contest he was reproached for not being heard, he replied "my instrument shall speak for me and win".

Cf. Hesychius Milesius ap. FHG IV, p. 159.

Ardalus ("Αρδαλος; m. pr. Árdalos); musician from Troezen (Τροιζὴν) in Peloponnesus, of unknown date. He is placed by some before Clonas* (7th cent. B.C.) while others consider him a mythic personality. Plutarch (De Mus. 1133A, ch. 5) says that according to some writers Ardalus composed aulodic music before Clonas. To him is attributed the establishment in Troezen of an altar in honour of the Muses who were called Ardalides after his name ('Αρδαλίδες; Paus. II, ch. 31, § 3). Some writers however derive the surname Ardalides from ἄρδειν (ardein) = to irrigate; metaph. to entertain, to offer recreation.

Argas ('Αργᾶς); 4th cent. B.C. kitharode and composer.

According to Suidas Argas was a composer of spiteful and difficult nomoi («'Αργᾶς τοὔνομα ποιητὴς ὢν νόμων πονηρῶν καὶ ἀργαλέων»). Phaenias of Eresus in his book "Against the Sophists' "(ap. Athen. XIV, 638C, ch. 42) speaks of Argas as follows: "Telenicus of Byzantium, and Argas as well, who were composers of immodest nomoi, were successful in their own type of poetry, but they could not in the slightest degree approach the nomoi of Terpander or Phrynis".

See also Dinse "De Antigen. Theb." p. 13, and Athen. IV, 131B.

Aríon (Ἀρίων); born c. 625 B.C.; d. ? Mythico-historical lyric poet.

Arion was born at Methymne (Μηθύμνη) of Lesbos, the son of Cycleus (Κυκλεύς). His life is surrounded by legends; even his existence was disputed by Alexandrian philologists.

Suidas gives the following information: "Arion; from Methymne, lyric poet, Cycleus' son; he lived in the 38th Olympiad (around 625 B.C.). Some writers believe that he was a pupil of Alcman. He wrote songs, prooemia in two epe (ἔπη). It is said that he was the inventor of the tragic style, and that he was the first to station a chorus and sing a dithyramb, with satyrs expressing themselves in verse (metrically)". Arion was considered the best kitharode of his time and exercised an influence on the development of the kitharodic nomos. Herodotus (I, ch. 23) says that as a kitharode he was second to none, and attributes to him the invention of the dithyramb which he taught in Corinth. Herodotus relates too (I, 24) the well-known and charming legend according to which Arion, when on his way back to Corinth from Sicily, was thrown by pirates into the sea and was saved by a dolphin. Arion lived most of his time at the court of Corinth's tyrant Periandrus (625-585 B.C.). Suidas says that his father's name Cycleus due to the circular (κύκλιος) chorus placed by Arion around the altar.

See Brgk PLG III, pp. 79-81 a Hymn to Poseidon with praise to the fond of music dolphins («φιλόμουσοι δελφῖνες»). Also Page PMG p. 507, frgt 939.

Aristides Quintilianus (Ἀριστείδης Κου(or Κο-)ϊντιλιανός; m. pr. Aristídis Koïntilianós).

Writer on music. His time is not known but it is supposed that he lived between the 1st and the 3rd cent. A.D.

He is the author of an important treatise on music («Περὶ μουσικῆς») divided into three books. The first deals in detail with definitions of theory, rhythm and metre, and follows the Aristoxenean theoretical principles. In the second he deals with the educational value of music in which Aristides is mainly interested. The third deals with the relationship of music to natural phenomena as expressed by number; in this book he follows the Pythagorean doctrines.

A. Jahn calls him a "Pythagorean Platonean".

His treatise was edited (Greek text with Latin translation) by Marc Meibom ("Antiquae musicae auctores septem, Graece et Latine" vol. II, pp. 1-164); Meibom found important parts of this treatise in Martianus Capella's "De Nuptiis Philologiae et Mercurii". Also by Albert Jahn (Albertus Iahnius "Aristidis Quintiliani: De Musica, Libri Tres"; Berlin 1882), and recently by R.P. Winnington-Ingram (Aristidis Quintiliani: De Musica, libri tres; Lipsiae, 1963). A German translation, without the Greek text, was published by Rudolf Schäfke

('Aristides Quintilianus Von der Musik'; Berlin, 1937, pp. 366, 8o) with an introduction and commentaries (transl. pp. 157-366).

Ariston (᾽Αρίστων), a kitharode from Rhegium in Italy of unknown date.
See under *Eunomus* and *adein*.

Aristonicus of Argos (᾽Αριστόνικος ὁ ᾽Αργεῖος; m. pr. Aristónicos Argíos); 8th to 7th cent. B.C. kitharist from Argos (῎Αργος). According to Menaechmus (ap. Athen. XIV, 637F, ch. 42) he was the first to introduce the "psili kitharisis"* (ψιλὴ κιθάρισις, solo kithara playing). Aristonicus was a contemporary of Archilochus*, and lived in Kerkyra (or Korkyra; Corfu).

Aristophanes (᾽Αριστοφάνης; m. pr. Aristophánis); b. c. 450 B.C.; d. 385 B.C.

He was born in the Athenian deme of Kydathenaeon (δῆμος Κυδα-θηναίων) but the date of his birth is uncertain. We know only that in 427 B.C., still very young, he produced his first comedy "Daetales" («Δαι-ταλῆς»; Banqueters) which won a second prize. Of his private life very little is known; it is probable that he passed his boyhood in the country, hence his affection for country life.

Of his comedies eleven survive complete: Acharnians (᾽Αχαρνῆς, 425), Knights (῾Ιππῆς, 424), Clouds (Νεφέλαι, 423), Wasps (Σφῆκες, 422), Peace (Εἰρήνη, 421), Birds (῎Ορνιθες, 414), Lysistrata (Λυσιστράτη, 411), Thesmo-phoriazousae or Women at the Thesmophoria (Θεσμοφοριάζουσαι, 411), Frogs (Βάτραχοι, 405), Ecclesiazousae or Women in Assembly (᾽Εκκλησιά-ζουσαι, 392), and Plutus (Πλοῦτος, 388).

Unfortunately nothing of his music survives, and we must have recourse to his rich and varied rhythmopoeia, and his poetic language, often full of sparkling spirit, to imagine what the character of his melopoeia might be. Gevaert in an enthusiastic appreciation of Aristophanes' musical abilities (vol. II, p. 556; "Aristophane musicien") holds that he shows an incomparable facility for assimilating the technique of his predecessors. Many of the existing forms of lyric composition and of traditional music (such as Archilochus' epodes, folk songs, hymns, scolia, orchestic strophes etc.) are met in his works, and are imitated and cultivated "with a rare perfection". In his first comedies the choral part prevails. Lyric stanzas sung to music are given to the chorus but sometimes also to leading characters alone, or in lyric dialogue with the chorus (cf. K. J. Dover: Aristophanic Comedy, London 1972, p. 68). For Gevaert and other scholars the middle group of his comedies, including especially the Birds and the Frogs, represent the summit of his art. The Frogs are perhaps the richest and most musical of all his comedies. Special mention may be made of the lyric dialogue of the first parodos between Dionysus and the chorus, and of the fine and impressive four hymns (2nd parodos) to Dionysus, to Pallas Athena, to Demeter and to Iacchus with well-calculated aesthetic contrast between the enthusiastic and joyful songs to Dionysus and Iacchus on the one hand, and the subjective hymn to Athena and the rustic song to Demeter on the other hand. But one cannot fail to mention also the beautiful lyrics of the Clouds («'Αέναοι νεφέλαι», "Eternal Clouds" vs. 275-290, and «Παρθένοι ὀμβροφόροι», "Maidens who bear the rain", vs. 298-313; cf. Dover op. cit., p. 71). In the last two comedies the purely musical element is greatly reduced while dancing became the principal factor in the interludes.

In conclusion it may be said that Aristophanes was a conservative musician, and believed in musical tradition. He often scorns and satirizes the innovations and musicians of the 5th century "avant-garde". He highly praised Sophocles' mele, but showed unjustified enmity towards Euripides' music. As a lyric composer he knew how to reconcile idealism with realism, and his comedies reflect faithfully the Hellenic reality of his time, both in life and in music. See O. Schroeder, Aristophanes, Cantica, 2nd ed., T., 1930.

Aristoteles, Aristotle ('Αριστοτέλης; m. pr. Aristotélis); b. Stagira (Στάγιρα or Στάγειρα) in Chalkidike (Χαλκιδικὴ) 384 B.C.; d. Chalkis (Χαλκὶς) in Euboea (Εὔβοια) 322 B.C. Aristotle was a pupil of Plato at the "Academy" in Athens where he later became a teacher; he stayed at Plato's side for about 20 years until his master's death in 347. In 343 at the invitation of Philip of Macedonia he became Alexander's teacher. He returned to Athens in 335 and founded his School, the "Lyceum" (Λύκειον), later called "Peripatos" (Περίπατος). In 323 he retired at his estate in Chalkis where he died a year later in 322.

Though the great philosopher was well acquainted with the theory and practice of music, he did not write a treatise on music; but he refers very often to music in his writings.

Like Plato, he professes the ethical value of music and discusses in detail its importance in the education of youth in the "Politics" (book VIII, 1339A to 1342B, ch. V § 3 to ch. VII § 11). Aristotle discusses three possible views about the purpose for which music ought to be studied: a) that its purpose is "amusement and relaxation" («παιδιᾶς ἕνεκα καὶ ἀναπαύσεως»); b) that music may exercise an influence on the shaping of our character by habituating us to being able to rejoice in the right way («... πρὸς ἀρετὴν τείνειν τὴν μουσικήν... καὶ τὸ ἦθος ποιόν τι ποιεῖν»); c) that music can contribute to intellectual entertainment and culture («πρὸς διαγωγὴν καὶ πρὸς φρόνησιν»). Aristotle follows the same line of thought as Plato. but his views are more liberal and less intransigent.

To Aristotle are attributed the "Problems", the authenticity of which is disputed by many and ascribed to a Pseudo-Aristotle; but most agree that the material of the Problems is derived from Aristotle and his School. The Problems concerning music (in the form of dialogue) deal with acoustics, consonances, philosophy, musical aesthetics etc. and are divided into two large sections: "On voice" («Ὅσα περὶ φωνῆς»; most of part XI) and "On Harmonia" («Ὅσα περὶ ἁρμονίαν»; the whole of part XIX, Problems 1-50).

The Musical Problems were edited with the Greek text and a French translation and commentaries by F. A. Gevaert and J. C. Vollgraf ("Les problèmes musicaux d' Aristote", Ghent, 1903) classified in order of the subject dealt with: "Acoustique", "Consonnances" etc. Ch. Ém. Ruelle published also a French translation ("Problèmes musicaux d' Aristote", Paris, 1891, with an "Avertissement" (pp. 1-3) in which he supports the view that the "Musical Problems" are a genuine work of Aristotle; he refers to Diogenes Laertius' catalogue of Aristotle's writings in which a book on Problems («Περὶ Προβλημάτων») is included, and to the fact, as he says, that Aristotle himself often refers to it. A more recent edition of the Greek text with an Italian translation was published by Geraldo Marenghi (Florence, 1957, pp. 137). Only the Problems "On Harmonia" («Ὅσα περὶ ἁρμονίαν») XIX, 1-50, are included and translated in this edition (pp. 26-83), together with Notes (pp. 85-119), Bibliography (pp. 123-125) and a glossary of musical terms met in the text (glossario dei termini musicali; pp. 127-133).

There is also an English translation by E. S. Forster (vol. VII of the Oxford translation of "The Works of Aristotle"; Oxford, 1927; "Problemata", book XI "The Voice" 898b-906a and book XIX "Music" 917-923a. Another English transl. is by W. S. Hett, London 1936-7 (Aristotle: Problems, vol. I, pp. 252-295 Probls. XI.; vol. I pp. 378-415 Probls. XIX connected with Harmony).

The Greek text of the Musical Problems is included in C.v.Jan's "Musici scriptores graeci" (Leipzig, 1895; pp. 60-111) under the title "Ps-Aristotelis 'Problemata', Ἀριστοτέλους προβλήματα". C.v.Jan has also published a collection of Aristotle's writings on music including the whole part of the "Politics" dealing with the ethical importance of music in education, VIII, 1339A to 1342B ("Mus. script. gr." pp. 3-35, under the title "Aristotelis Loci de musica").

Besides the above mentioned, the following bibliography may be consulted:

E. Fred. Bojesen "De Problematis Aristotelis", Hafniae 1836.

C. Prantl : 'Über die Probleme des Aristoteles' in "Abhand. d. philos.-philol. Klasse d. Bayer. Akad. VI (1851) pp. 339-377.

E. Richter : 'De Aristotelis Problematis'; Bonnae 1885.

C.-Ém. Ruelle : "Corrections anciennes et nouvelles dans le texte des Problèmes d' Aristote", in "Revue de Philologie" XV, 1891, pp. 168-174.

C. Stumpf "Die pseudo-aristotelischen Probleme über Musik" in "Abhand, d. Berliner Akad." III, 1896, pp. 1-81.

E. d'Eichthal et Th. Reinach "Nouvelles observations sur les Problèmes musicaux" in 'Revue des Études grecques' XIII, 1900, pp. 18-44.

See also: *Lukas Richter :* Zur Wissenschaftslehre von der Musik bei Platon und Aristoteles, Berlin, 1961; pp. XI, 202; 8°.

Aristoxenus ('Αριστόξενος; m. pr. Aristóxenos);

Philosopher and musical theorist; he was born between 375 and 360 B.C. at Tarentum (Τάρας, hence his surname Ταραντῖνος) and died in Athens. He was the most important and influential figure in the field of theory of music in ancient Greece, generally known in ancient times as "the Mousikos" («ὁ Μουσικός»; "the Musician"). According to Suidas, the principal source for his life, Aristoxenus lived during and after Alexander's time, c. the 111th Olympiad (around 333 B.C.); he was the son of Mnesias (Μνησίας) otherwise called Spintharus (Σπίνθαρος), a musician from Tarentum. A pupil first of his father, he studied afterwards with Lamprus of Erythrai ('Ερυθραί; Λάμπρος ὁ 'Ερυθραῖος) in Mantineia where he passed a part of his youth. On his return to Italy he studied under the Pythagorean philosopher Xenophilus of Chalkis (Ξενόφιλος ὁ Χαλκιδεὺς) with whom he developed a friendship. For some time later he was in Corinth where he met with the exiled Dionysius, tyrant of Syracuse. At last he became a pupil of Aristotle at the Lyceum in Athens; it seems that he held an important position among the pupils of Aristotle, and expected to be named as his successor. But Theophrastus having been selected as the head of the Lyceum, Aristoxenus deeply disappointed used disrespectful language against his dead master (Suid. «εἰς ὃν ['Αριστοτέλη] ἀποθανόντα ὕβρισε, διότι κατέλιπε τῆς σχολῆς Θεόφραστον, αὐτοῦ ['Αριστοξένου] δόξαν μεγάλην ἐν τοῖς ἀκροαταῖς τοῖς 'Αριστοτέλους ἔχοντος»).

Aristoxenus was a most prolific writer; his books on music, philosophy, history and on every kind of education reach the number of 453 volumes, according to Suidas («συνετάξατο δὲ μουσικά τε καὶ φιλόσοφα καὶ ἱστορίας καὶ παντὸς εἴδους παιδείας, καὶ ἀριθμοῦνται αὐτοῦ τὰ βιβλία εἰς 453»).

Among his works the following are treatises on various musical subjects:

1. "Harmonic Elements" («ʿΑρμονικὰ Στοιχεῖα») in three books, mostly preserved (see below);
2. "Elements of Rhythm" («Ρυθμικὰ στοιχεῖα) of which an important fragment survives;
3. "On Music" («Περὶ μουσικῆς»);
4. "On melopoeia" («Περὶ μελοποιΐας»);
5. "On tonoi" («Περὶ τόνων»);
6. "On musical hearing" («Περὶ τῆς μουσικῆς ἀκροάσεως»);

7. "On the time-unit" («Περὶ τοῦ πρώτου χρόνου»);
8. "On instruments" or "On auloi and instruments" («Περὶ ὀργάνων» ἢ «Περὶ αὐλῶν καὶ ὀργάνων»);
9. "On piercing of auloi" («Περὶ αὐλῶν τρήσεως»);
10. "On auletai" («Περὶ αὐλητῶν»);
11. "On the tragic orchesis" («Περὶ τραγικῆς ὀρχήσεως»);
12. A work from which the rhythmical fragment of Oxyrhynchus is derived.

Most of the above mentioned books have been lost but we know extracts of them through frequent references by Plutarch, Athenaeus, Porphyry and other writers. Valuable details of his theoretical doctrines and teaching are found principally in Cleonides'* "Isagoge" and Arist. Quintilianus'* treatise on Music; and partly in Gaudentius' "Harmonic Introduction" and Bacchius' "Introduction to the art of Music".

The "Harmonic Elements" («Ἁρμονικῶν Στοιχείων βιβλία τρία») have been published several times:

1. First edition in 1542 by Antonius Gogavinus in a Latin translation without the Greek text (Ant. Gogavino Graviensi: "Aristoxeni musici antiquissimi"; Venetiis, 1542; Latin transl. pp. 7-45).
2. First edition of the Greek text with commentary by Johannes Meursius ("Aristoxenus, Nicomachus, Alypius, auctores Musices antiquissimi"; Lugduni, Ed. L. Elzevir, 1616; pp. 3-59; Notes p. 125 ff).
3. Next edition of the Greek with a Latin translation by Marc Meibom (Marcus Meibomius "Antiquae musicae auctores septem, Graece et Latine"; Amsterdam, 1652; vol. I, pp. 1-74).
4. Greek text with a German translation and a Supplement including the Fragments on Rhythm, by P. Marquard (Pavlus Marquardii: "De Aristoxeni Tarentini Elementis Harmonicis"; Berolini, 1868; pp. XXXVII + 415); Appendix with the Rhythmical Elements, pp. 409-415.
5. French translation by Charles Émile Ruelle ("Eléments Harmoniques d' Aristoxène", traduits en français pour la première fois; Paris, 1870), based on Meibom's Greek text.
6. Greek text with an English translation, notes, introduction and index of the Greek words, by Henry S. Macran (Ἀριστοξένου Ἁρμονικὰ Στοιχεῖα; The Harmonics of Aristoxenus; Oxford, 1902).
7. A recent edition of the Greek text with Commentary, Testimonia etc. by Rosetta da Rios ("Aristoxeni Elementa Harmonica"; Romae, 1954).

Several MSS of the Elements have been preserved in many Codices (see H. S. Macran pp. 90-91, R. da Rios pp. 3-4).

The Rhythmical fragments were first published in Venice by Morelli in

1785; then with a German translation by Feussner (Hanau, 1850), P. Marquard (1868; see above 4), and by R. Westphal ("Aristoxenus von Tarent, Melik and Rhythmik"; vol. II, Leipzig, 1893).

The most authoritative and thorough study of Aristoxenus so far is published by Louis Laloy ("Aristoxène de Tarente"; Paris, 1904; with a valuable "Lexique d'Aristoxène" at the end).

See also in FHG, II, pp. 269-292 various fragments (especially pp. 285-288 "Musica Fragmenta").

Other bibliography:

W. L. Mahne : Diatribe de Aristoxeno philosopho; Amsterdam, 1793.

Ch. Ém. Ruelle : Étude sur Aristoxène et son école.
    Rev. arch. 14, 1858, pp. 413-422; 528-555.

R. Westphal : Aristoxenos von Tarent, Melik und Rhythmik des classischen Hellenentums, Bd I-II, Leipzig, 1883-93.

C. v. Jan : Realencyclopaedie; Pauly-Wissowa (1896), Bd II, p. 1057 ff.

R. P. Winnigton-Ingram : "Aristoxenus and the Intervals of Greek music"; Cl. Q 26 (1932) pp. 195-208.

K. Schlesinger : Further Notes on Aristoxenus and Musical Intervals"; Cl. Q 27 (1933) pp. 88-96.

Fritz Wehrli : Die Schule des Aristoteles; Aristoxenos, Heft II (a) Aristoxenos Texte, b) Kommentar. Basel, 1945.

arrhythmos (ἄρρυθμος; m. pr. árrithmos); unrhythmical, lacking in rhythmical co-ordination. The opposite of ἔνρυθμος or εὔρυθμος (enrhythmos*; eurhythmos*).

ἀρρυθμία (*arrhythmia*; m. pr. arrithmía); lack of rhythm, of rhythmical co-ordination. Ptolemy (C.v. Jan "Excerpta Neapolitana", in "Mus. script. gr." p. 414) calls «ἄρρυθμοι» (pl.) those times (χρόνοι) which have not the least rhythmical co-ordination between themselves.

arsis-thesis (ἄρσις - θέσις).

arsis (ἄρσις, from αἴρειν = to lift, to raise); upbeat.

thesis (θέσις, from τίθημι = to put, to place); downbeat.

Arist. Quint. (Meib. p. 31, RPW-I p. 31) «ἄρσις μὲν οὖν ἐστι φορὰ μέρους σώματος ἐπὶ τὸ ἄνω, θέσις δέ, ἐπὶ τὸ κάτω ταυτοῦ μέρους» ("*arsis* is an upward motion of a part of the body, and *thesis* a downward motion of the same part").

The thesis was also in old times called βάσις (*basis*; from βαίνειν = to walk); a rhythmical "step".

Aristoxenus used the term «ὁ ἄνω χρόνος» (the up-time, the up-beat) or simply «τὸ ἄνω» (the up), instead of the arsis, and «ὁ κάτω χρόνος» (the downtime, down-beat) or «τὸ κάτω» ('the down') instead of the thesis. The terms were ultimately reversed when the Greeks referred to raising (arsis) and lowering (thesis) of the voice (stress).

asigmos (ἄσιγμος); without the letter sigma (*S*). *"Ασιγμος* ᾠδή, an ode in which on musical and aesthetic grounds the letter sigma was avoided. Athen. (X, 455C) «Λάσου τοῦ Ἑρμιονέως τὴν ἄσιγμον ᾠδήν».

See under *Lasus* of Hermione.*

askaros (ἄσκαρος; usually in pl. ἄσκαροι); a kind of krotala, clappers or castanets. Hes. «γένος ὑποδημάτων ἢ σανδαλίων· οἱ δὲ κρόταλα» ("a kind of shoe or small sandal; some say *krotala**"). Askaros was by some people considered to be the same as or similar to another percussion instrument, the psithyra*; Pollux IV, 60 «ἔνιοι δὲ τὴν ψιθύραν τὴν αὐτὴν εἶναι τῷ ἀσκάρῳ ὀνομαζομένῳ νομίζουσι» ("some people believe that the *psithyra* is the same as what is called *askaros*").

Ἀσκαροφόρος (*askarophóros*) was the term for the man holding and playing the askaros.

askaules (ἀσκαύλης; m. pr. askávlis); bag-piper. The word appears in Roman times; Martialis (1st cent. A.D.) 10, 3 (LSJ).

Asklepiadeios stichos (ἀσκληπιάδειος στίχος; m. pr. asklipiádios stíchos); Asklepiadic line, verse; so called after the name of Asklepiades (Ἀσκληπιά-δης). There were two kinds:

1) The "*minor* Asklepiadic line" («ἐλάσσων ἀσκληπιάδειος στίχος»), consisting of two kolons: ˈ‿ ¯ ‿ ‿ ‿ ⌞ | ˈ‿ ‿ ‿ ‿ ‿ ⋀

2) The "*major* Asklepiadic line" («μείζων ἀσκληπιάδειος στίχος»), consisting of three kolons: ˈ‿ ¯ ‿‿ ‿ ⌞ | ˈ‿ ‿ ‿ ⌞ | ˈ‿ ‿ ‿ ‿ ‿ ‿. Alcaeus and Sappho made use of both Asklepiadic lines.

asma (ᾆσμα), Ionian and poetic ἄεισμα (aeisma, áisma), song, principally the lyric song, or ode. Suidas «ᾆσμα· τὸ μέλος, ἡ ᾠδὴ» ("*asma*: the melos, the ode").

asmatopoeos (ᾀσματοποιός); the composer of songs; Athen. V, 181E («ὁ γοῦν Ὀδυσσεὺς προσέχει τοῖς τῶν Φαιάκων ᾀσματοποιοῖς»).

asmatokamptes (ᾀσματοκάμπτης; m. pr. asmatokámptis); (LSJ) twister of song. This is said of those dithyrambic poets who by various anti-aesthetic devices distorted the melodic line (cf. Pollux IV, 64; Aristoph. Neph. 333). *Καμπὴ* (kampe); twisting. Pherecrates in his comedy "Cheiron" (Χείρων; Plut. De Mus. 1141E-F, ch. 30) scorns the Athenian dithyrambic poet Kinesias in these words «Κινησίας, ὁ κατάρατος Ἀττικός, ἐξαρμονίους καμπὰς ποιῶν... ἀπολώλεκέ με [τὴν Μουσικὴν]» ("Kinesias, the cursed Attic, by composing antiharmonic (distorting) twistings ... destroyed me [Music]").

See *Kinesias*.*

asymmetros, -on (ἀσύμμετρος, -ον; m. pr. asímmetros); incommensurable, disproportionate (LSJ).

ἀσύμμετρον διάστημα = incommensurable interval; Aristox. (Harm. I, p. 24 Mb): «Τὸ μὲν οὖν διὰ τεσσάρων ὃν τρόπον ἐξεταστέον, εἴτε μετρεῖταί τινι τῶν ἐλαττόνων διαστημάτων, εἴτε πᾶσίν ἐστιν ἀσύμμετρον» ("The proper method of investigating whether the [interval of the] Fourth can be expressed in terms of any lower [smaller] intervals, or whether it is *incommensurable* with them all"; transl. H. S. Macran, p. 182).

ἀσυμμετρία (asymmetría); want of symmetry, of harmony; incommensurability, disproportion.

asymphonos (ἀσύμφωνος; m. pr. asímphonos); not concordant, a sound which is not in concord with another one; discordant, not harmonious.

The lack of concord, or the fact of not being concord was ἀσυμφωνία (asymphonia). Plato's Rep. book III, 402 D «Εἰ δ᾽ ἀξύμφωνος εἴη, οὐκ ἂν ἐρῴη» ("if there were *disharmony* he would not love this"; transl. P. Shorey vol. I, p. 263.

Cf. Aristox. Harm. II p. 54,10 Mb.

Opp. σύμφωνος - συμφωνία (*symphonos** - *symphonia*).

asynthetos, neut. **-on** (ἀσύνθετος, -ον; m. pr. asínthetos); not compound, simple.

a) ἀσύνθετον διάστημα; a simple interval; that which can not contain other notes between its constituent ones in the same genus. Thus e-f (as also f-g and g-a) is a simple interval in the Diatonic genus because no other note can be inserted between them (in the same genus): a)

But the interval e-f is compound in the Enharmonic genus because (ex. b) between these two notes there exists the note *e ¼ b)

In the same way the interval f-a is compound in the Diatonic (a) and simple in the Enharmonic (b). Thus generally speaking ἀσύνθετον is an interval which cannot be subdivided [in the same genus] into smaller ones. Aristox. (Harm. III, p. 60, 10 Mb) «ἀσύνθετον δ᾽ ἐστὶ διάστημα τὸ ὑπὸ τῶν ἑξῆς φθόγγων περιεχόμενον» (= "*simple* is the interval contained by contiguous notes").

b) ἀσύνθετος χρόνος = indivisible time.
See *chronos.*

c) ἀσύνθετον μέτρον = a simple metre.
See *pous**.

Athena (’Aθηνᾶ; m. pr. Athiná);

1. a kind of aulos mentioned by Pollux (IV, 77) without any information regarding its construction; «καὶ ’Aθηνᾶ δέ, εἶδος αὐλοῦ, ᾗ μάλιστα Νικωφελῆ τὸν Θηβαῖον εἰς τὸν τῆς ’Aθηνᾶς ὕμνον κεχρῆσθαι λέγουσι» ("*Athena*, a species of aulos, which Nicopheles of Thebes used for the Hymn to Athena [Minerva], as they say").

2. ’Aθηνᾶς νόμος (nomos of Athena); a nomos to goddess Athena (Minerva) attributed to Olympus of which a description is found in Plut. De Mus. (1143 B-C, ch. 33).

Athenaeus (’Aθήναιος; m. pr. Athíneos); 2nd to 3rd cent. A.D. grammarian and sophist. He was born at Naucratis (Ναύκρατις) in Egypt, and lived between 160 and 230 A.D.

His principal work is the monumental "Deipnosophistai" («Δειπνοσοφισταί») written probably after the death of Emperor Commodus (Κόμμοδος, 180-192 AD) who in the XIIth Book (537) is ridiculed. In books I, IV, XIV and XV there is ample information on ancient Greek music; books IV (from 174A to 185) and XIV (616E to 639) especially contain information on musical instruments (IV), and on dances, on various professions, kinds of odes, genera, harmonias etc. (XIV). Much musical material of the "Deipnosophists" is derived from Heracleides Ponticus, Douris, Aristoxenus and many other older sources.

The work is divided into 15 books but has not survived intact; parts of books I, II, III, XI, and XV have been lost.

The first edition was published under the supervision of the eminent Cretan philologist Marcus Musurus (Μᾶρκος Μουσοῦρος; see under Hesychius) in Venice, 1514, from the Codex Marcianus. Since then several editions of the Greek text and translations (of parts or of the whole) into other languages have been made, including that of the Greek text by G. Kaibel (in Teubner, Leipzig, 1887-90) and with English translation by Prof. Ch. B. Gulick (London, N. York-Cambridge Mass., 1927-41), in the Loeb Classical Library, to which reference is often made in this encyclopaedia.

athlothetes (ἀθλοθέτης; m.pr. athlothétis); adjudicator, judge at the Games. As the Games included musical contests the athlothetes also judged competitions in music. Cf. Plato Laws, VI 764E (see the text under "*monodia*").

Attis (”Aττις); God of the Phrygians approximately equivalent to Adonis.

38

He is credited with the invention of the shepherd's syrinx, made of ten pipes.

Cf. Agiopolites ('Αγιοπολίτης), 2nd Fragment, ed. by A. J. H. Vincent in "Notices", p. 264.

aude (αὐδή, ἡ; m. pr. avdí), and αὐδὰ or αὔδα (auda); sound, voice, talk; also a hymn or ode in honour of somebody.

«σάλπιγγος αὐδὴ» = trumpet's sound.

The verb αὐδεῖν (audein) = to talk; to praise.

aulema, aulesis (αὔλημα, αὔλησις; m. pr. ávlima, ávlisis):

aulema, a melody played on the aulos, an aulos solo.

aulesis (αὐλεῖν, to play the aulos), the act of aulein, of playing on the aulos.   By usage it became a synonym of aulema.

Ψιλὴ αὔλησις (*psile aulesis*) was a specific term for solo aulos playing without words (singing); see under *psilos*.   Generally speaking the word aulesis was used in the sense of solo playing (on the aulos) in contradistinction to aulodia* (αὐλῳδία) which was a song to aulos accompaniment. The performer on the aulos was called αὐλητὴς or αὐλητὴρ (auletes*, auleter*). Pollux (IV, 78-83) mentions various kinds of auleseis, pl. (εἴδη αὐλήσεων); the Alexandrian lexicographer Tryphon in his second book of Denominations gives a catalogue of names of various auleseis (ap. Athen., XIV, 618c, ch. 9): "komos, boucoliasmos, gingras, tetrakomos, epiphallos, choreios, kallinikos, polemikon, hedykomos, sikinnotyrbe, thyrokopikon or krousithyron, knismos, mothon.   All these were played on the aulos with dancing."

See each of these auleseis under their own name.

auleter (αὐλητήρ; m. pr. avlitír); a synonym of *auletes**, aulos player. Nonnos Dion. (40, 224) «καὶ Φρῦγες αὐλητῆρες (pl.) ἀνέπλεκον ἄρσενα μολπὴν» ("and Phrygian *auletai* [pipers] entwined a manly tune"); Theognis (E. Diehl; T., 1925) p. 144, v. 533 «χαίρων δ' εὖ πίνων καὶ ὑπ' αὐλητῆρος ἀείδων» ("I rejoice at drinking well and singing accompanied by an aulete").   Archilochus (ap. FHG II, p. 718, Frg. 123 [106]) «...ᾄδων ὑπ' αὐλητῆρος» ("singing accompanied by *aulete*").

auletes, auletike (αὐλητής, αὐλητική; m. pr. avlitís, avlitikí).

a) *αὐλητής*, aulos player, usually a professional; he was also sometimes called αὐλητὴρ (auleter*). Fem. αὐλητρὶς (*auletris*; avlitrís) and αὐλήτρια (*auletria*; avlítria); often a professional player of aulos engaged to play at banquets.

b) *αὐλητική*, the art of the aulete, of aulos playing.

In the beginning auletai (αὐληταί, pl.) simply accompanied the song (αὐλῳδία, aulodia*) sung by the aulodos* (αὐλῳδός).   The function of the

39

aulete at that remote time was of secondary importance; at contests it was the aulodos who was crowned, not the aulete (Athen. XIV, 621B, ch. 14 "and the wreath is given to the hilarodos* (ἱλαρῳδός) and the aulodos, neither to the player of a stringed instrument (ψάλτης), nor to the aulete"). The first accompanist auletai came from Phrygia and Mysia (Athen. Ib. 624B, ch. 18) and had names of slaves; a number of them are given in Athenaeus (taken from Alcman and Hipponax).

The Phrygian auletai contributed greatly to the development of the auletic art which from the 6th cent. B.C. evolved into an independent and important, purely musical art. In the 3rd year of the 48th Olympiad (586 B.C.) the auletike was first introduced into the contests of the Pythian Games at Delphi. Sakadas* (Σακάδας), the most famous aulete and composer of his time, was the first winner with his celebrated Pythikos nomos*; he won also at the next two Pythians.

The School of Argos, after Sakadas, and later that of Thebes particularly contributed to the expansion and flourishing of the auletic art, which reached its culmination in the 5th and the 4th centuries B.C. with a number of reputable performers.

Note: Pindar in the 12th Pythian Ode (vs 11-13) refers to the attribution of the invention of the auletike to Athena («τὰν ποτε Παλλὰς ἐφεῦρε θρασειᾶν [Γοργόνων] οὔλιον θρῆνον διαπλέξαισ᾽ Ἀθάνα»; "the art which Pallas Athena invented when she wove in music the sinister dirge of the Gorgons".

See also A.B. Drachmann Schol. Vet. in Pind. Carm., Leipzig 1910, Vol. II p. 265.

aulodia, aulodikoi nomoi (αὐλῳδία, αὐλῳδικοὶ νόμοι; m. pr. avlodía, avlodikí nómi).

a) *αὐλῳδία*, singing to aulos accompaniment; a song with aulos accompaniment. While in the kitharodia* (κιθαρῳδία) only one executant was needed (singing and accompanying himself on the kithara), in the aulodia two executants were indispensable, the singer (αὐλῳδός, aulodos*) and the aulos-player, the piper (aulete*); the more important of the two was the aulodos to whom the prize was given at the contests. Usually the aulos part was confided to a Phrygian aulete; Alcman used three such Phrygian slaves as auletai (named Sambas, Adon and Telos), and Hipponax three others (Kion, Kodalus and Babys);.

See Athen. XIV, 624B, ch. 18.

b) *αὐλῳδικοὶ νόμοι*.

According to Plutarch's De Musica (1132C. ch. 3, and 1133A, ch. 5) Clonas* (Κλονᾶς) was the first to initiate the aulodic nomoi; he was followed by Polymnestus* (Πολύμνηστος): «Ὁμοίως δὲ Τερπάνδρῳ Κλονᾶν τὸν πρῶτον συστησάμενον τοὺς αὐλῳδικοὺς νόμους καὶ τὰ προσόδια...» ("And like

Terpander, Clonas was the first to establish the aulodic nomoi and the prosodia").

Some writers attributed the introduction of the aulodic nomoi to Ardalus* from Troezen.

There were several types of aulodic nomoi; the following were generally known: Apothetos* ('Απόθετος):, Elegoi* ("Ελεγοι), Komarchios* (Κωμάρχιος), Schoenion* (Σχοινίων), Kepion* (Κηπίων), Deios* (Δεῖος) and Trimeles* (Τριμελής). To them the Polymnasteia (Πολυμνάστεια) were later added (Plut. 1132D, ch. 4). According to various writers Clonas was the inventor of the Apothetos and the Schoenion; Pollux (IV, 79) «καὶ Κλονᾶ δέ, νόμοι αὐλητικοί, ἀπόθετός τε καὶ σχοινίων» ("and the auletic nomoi Apothetos and Schoenion were both invented by Clonas"). Pollux writes by mistake auletic instead of aulodic. Two others, the Kommarchios and Elegos, also were attributed to Clonas. The aulodia never became so popular as the kitharodia. According to Pausanias (X, ch. 7, § § 4-5) the aulodia, introduced with the auletic by the Amphictyons ('Αμφικτύονες; the delegates forming the council of the confederation of states) in the third year of the 48th Olympiad (586 B.C.), was soon withdrawn.

See *Echembrotus*.

auloboas (αὐλοβόας; m. pr. avlovóas); aulos-playing; sounding the aulos.

aulodoke and **aulotheke** (αὐλοδόκη, and αὐλοθήκη; m.pr. avlodóki, avlothíki); aulos-case. Also *sybene** (συβήνη) and *auleteria** (αὐλητηρία).

aulodos (αὐλῳδός; m. pr. avlodós); a musician singing to aulos accompaniment. In a competition of aulodia or of aulodic nomos, where two executants taking part were indispensable (the aulodos and the aulete), the aulodos was considered the principal competitor, and it was he who won the prize and was crowned. Athen. (XIV, 621B, ch. 14): «δίδοται δὲ ὁ στέφανος τῷ ἱλαρῳδῷ καὶ τῷ αὐλῳδῷ, οὐ τῷ ψάλτῃ, οὐδὲ τῷ αὐλητῇ» ("and the wreath is given to the hilarodos* and to the aulodos, neither to the psaltes (= player on a stringed instrument without plectrum), nor to the aulete").

Αὐλῳδὸς was often used for the composer of aulodiai.

Note: αὐλῳδεῖν, vb (aulodein) = to sing to aulos accompaniment.

aulopoeos (αὐλοποιός; m. pr. avlopiós); aulos-maker. Pollux (IV, 71) «ὁ δὲ τοὺς αὐλοὺς ἐργαζόμενος, αὐλοποιός»; Plut. 1138A, ch. 21.

aulopoeia (αὐλοποιΐα; m. pr. avlopiía); the making of auloi; Aristox. Harm. II, p. 43, 24 Mb. The aulopoeia developed greatly during the 5th cent. B.C., especially in Thebes. The vb *aulothetein* (αὐλοθετεῖν); to make auloi.

aulos (αὐλός; m. pr. avlós).

The principal and most important wind instrument of ancient Greece. Alone or combined with the voice or with stringed instruments, especially the kithara, it played a very prominent part in the social life of Greece. It was used in many ceremonies, especially those in honour of Dionysus, in processions, in the drama, at the National Games, at the banquets; it accompanied most of the dances (sacred, social or folk), it regulated the movements of rowers (see *trieraules*) and the marching of soldiers (embaterion* melos).

History. The origin of the aulos is not clearly elucidated. According to many ancient sources it came from Asia Minor, and specifically from Phrygia. The name of the aulos (as a musical instrument) appears twice in Homer's Iliad, the first as an instrument of the Trojans (X, 12, «θαύμαζεν [Ἀγαμέμνων] πυρὰ πολλὰ τὰ καίετο Ἰλιόθι πρό, (13) αὐλῶν συρίγγων τ᾽ ἐνοπὴν ἵμαδόν τ᾽ ἀνθρώπων»; "He [Agamemnon] marvelled at the many fires that burned before the face of Ilion, and at *the sound of 'flutes' (auloi) and pipes*, and the din of men"; transl. A. T. Murray, vol. I, p. 437).

The second time, together with phorminxes (S, XVIII, 495), in the description of Achilles' shield: «κοῦροι δ᾽ ὀρχηστῆρες ἐν δ᾽ ἄρα τοῖσιν (495) αὐλοὶ φόρμιγγές τε βοὴν ἔχον» ("And young men were whirling in the dance, and in their midst *'flutes' (auloi)* and lyres sounded continually"; transl. A. T. Murray Ibid; vol. II, p. 325). One of the oldest sources on the origin of aulos is perhaps the "Parion Chronicon*" or "Marble"; it says (v. 10; F. Jacoby ed.; Berlin, 1904) that "Hyagnis the Phrygian first invented the aulos at Kelaenai [of Phrygia] and played on it the Phrygian harmonia". According to the writer Alexander (ap. Plut. De Mus. 1132F, ch. 5) "Hyagnis was the first to play the aulos («Ὕαγνιν δὲ πρῶτον αὐλῆσαι»), and after him his son Marsyas, and then Olympus" (Plut. Ibid 1133F, ch. 7).

According to another legend it was the goddess Athena (Minerva) who invented the aulos, but seeing in the reflection of the waters that her face was deformed, she threw it away; it fell in Phrygia and was found by Marsyas. This legend tending to establish a Greek origin for aulos was most probably created later than the legend of the Apollo-Marsyas combat (cf. Plut. De Cohibenda ira, 456 B-D, chs. 6-7; Pind. 12th Pythian ode, and A.B. Drachmann: Scholia Vetera in Pind. Carmina, Leipzig 1910, p. 265).

In all probability, however, the aulos in some form was known in Greece from very remote times, but the auletic art evolved under the influence and impulse of Phrygian auletai.

Construction. The main body of the aulos was a pipe called bombyx* (βόμβυξ) of a cylindrical shape, leading sometimes at the end to an open, slightly widened, bell. The pipe was made of reed, or of box or lotus-wood, of bone, of horn, of ivory or of beaten brass, and had a number of lateral finger-holes, called *trémata* or *trypémata* (τρήματα, or τρυπήματα); Pollux (IV, 71) says: «Ἡ δὲ ὕλη τῶν αὐλῶν κάλαμος, ἢ χαλκός, ἢ πύξος ἢ λωτὸς ἢ κέρας ἢ ὀστοῦν ἐλάφου ἢ δάφνης τῆς χαμαιζήλου, τὴν ἐντεριώνην ἀφῃρημένος» ("And the material of the aulos [was] reed or brass or box-tree, or lotus, or horn, or bone of deer, or branch of shrubby laurel with the pith extracted"). The earlier pipes had four or even three holes. Later the number was increased up to 15, so that the range of pitch of the aulos reached two octaves. The holes being more than the nine or eight fingers available for covering and uncovering (the thumb of the left hand was used to close the upper hole (behind) and that of the right hand was used to hold the instrument) the Theban School (headed by Pronomus*) invented special metal collars or rings made of brass or bronze (see "*bombyx*"*). The length of the pipe was also extended by the Theban School which greatly contributed to the expansion of the auletic art in the 5th-4th cents. B.C.; generally speaking the length varied according to the range of pitch and the species of aulos. At the top of the pipe the mouth-piece was inserted; it was formed of the *holmos** (ὄλμος) and the *hypholmion** (ὑφόλμιον) which supported the holmos. In the holmos the reed was inserted and affixed.

The question of whether the reed was single or double is a problem which caused much discussion among specialists. Most of them hold that the reed was double; others claim that the double reed was in use up to the time of Antigenidas* (5th-4th cent. B.C.), and then gave way to the single or beating-reed (K. Schlesinger "The Greek aulos"; London, 1939, p. 45 ff.).

So it seems most probable that the Greeks knew both the double and the single reed (double-reed as in the oboe family, single or beating-reed as in the clarinet family).

The reed was called *glottis** or *glossis* (γλωττίς, γλωσσίς), or *glossa* (γλῶσσα) and was made of reed, cane (see *synkrotetikai glottai**). It seems that a certain force was required to blow the aulos, and the auletai used to wear a leather band, called *phorbeia** (fem. φορβειά); it passed over the cheeks, leaving a hole in front of the mouth to permit the insertion of the mouth-piece, and was fastened behind the head. It is often seen on vase-paintings.

Usually the aulos was used in pair; the two auloi were called δίδυμοι αὐλοί (twin auloi), also δικάλαμος (double-pipe) and δίζυγες αὐλοί; each one had its own mouth-piece. Sometimes the pipes of the two auloi were of equal length, sometimes one was longer than the other. Pollux (IV, 80) writes: «Καὶ τὸ μὲν γαμήλιον αὔλημα δύο αὐλοὶ ἦσαν, μείζων ἅτερος, συμφωνίαν ἀποτελοῦντες, οἱ δὲ παροίνιοι, σμικροὶ μὲν ἴσοι δ᾽ ἄμφω» ("And the nuptial aulema** [was played on] two auloi, of which one was longer, and they constituted a concord; and those auloi played at banquets [are] small but both equal in length").

The question of the use of the double-aulos is another unsolved problem. Some have suggested that either they played in unison (when their length was equal). or one played the melody while the other kept a drone (in the case of unequal pipes).

Species. There were several species of aulos which might be classified into categories or classes according to the range of pitch, the origin, character etc.

a) *Division according to pitch-range.*

According to the grammarian Didymus of Alexandria (1st cent. A.D.; ap. Athen. XIV, 634 E-F, ch. 36 and FHG p. 286, Fr. 67) Aristoxenus in his lost book "On piercing of auloi" («Περὶ αὐλῶν τρήσεως») recognized five γένη of aulos (genera, kinds or classes):

1. The Παρθένιοι (*parthenioi**; virginal);

2. The Παιδικοὶ (*paedikoi**; infantine, or boys' pipes);

3. The Κιθαριστήριοι (*kitharisterioi**; accompanying the kithara);

4. The Τέλειοι (*teleioi**; perfect);

5. The Ὑπερτέλειοι (*hyperteleioi*; super-perfect).

If we take into consideration: a) that the ensemble of the last two classes are called ἀνδρεῖοι (masculine), b) that Aristoxenus writes that the highest of the wind instruments were the parthenioi (No. 1 above) and the lowest the hyperteleioi (No. 5), and c) that between the two extremes there was a distance of three octaves (Aristox. Harm. p. 20-21 Mb) we can fairly safely conclude that the above division was made according to the pitch-range. Thus, the first (No. 1) could correspond to the soprano, the second to the mezzo-soprano, the third to the alto, the fourth to the tenor, and the fifth to the bass. Cf. Athen. IV, 176F, ch. 79; Gev. I, p. 235, II, p. 272 ff.

b) *Division according to origin.*

1. Phrygian aulos; also called elymos* (ἔλυμος);

2. Lydian aulos (Λυδὸς μάγαδις* αὐλός);

3. Libyan aulos (Λίβυς* αὐλός);

   also Tyrrhenian, Theban, Thracian, Boeotian, Cretan etc.

   (Pausanias book IV, ch. 27, § 7: «εἰργάζοντο δὲ καὶ ὑπὸ μουσικῆς ἄλλης μὲν οὐδεμιᾶς, αὐλῶν δὲ Βοιωτίων καὶ Ἀργείων»).

c) *Division according to the material used.*

1. *calaminos* or simply *calamus*, made of reed; the "Tityrinos" was a variation of this.

2. *pyxinos* (πύξινος; made of box-wood);

3. *lotinos* (λώτινος; made of lotus-wood); also called photinx* (φῶτιγξ);

4. *keratinos* (κεράτινος; made of horn);

5. *elephantinos* (ἐλεφάντινος; made of elephant-bone).

6. *chalkelatos* (χαλκήλατος; forged from brass).

    d) *Division according to the character.*

Several kinds of aulos belong to this class; to mention some of them, discussed elsewhere, *gingras** (γίγγρας), *kitharistérios** (κιθαριστήριος; see also class a), *embaterios** (ἐμβατήριος);

    e) *Division according to form and sound production.*

1. *monaulos* (μόναυλος; *single-pipe*); *monocalamos* (μονοκάλαμος);

2. *double-aulos* (δίαυλος);

3. *transverse* (πλαγίαυλος).

Various epithets were given to aulos, such as: *diopos* (δίοπος; having two holes); *hemiopos* (ἡμίοπος; having half the number of holes); *hypotretos* (ὑπότρητος; pierced from below); *kalliboas* (καλλιβόας; with fine tone); *mesokopos* (μεσόκοπος; of middle size); *paratretos* (παράτρητος; sideways pierced); *polytretos* (πολύτρητος; having many holes). Pollux (IV, 67) mentions a whole and interesting series of epithets: *polykampes* (πολυκαμπής; much twisted); *polykompos* (πολύκομπος; loud sounding, sonorous), *polymekes* (πολυμήκης, with great length), *polymeles* and *polymelpes* (πολυμελής, πολυμελπής; many-toned, capable of many melodies), *polyphthongos* and *polyphonos* (πολύφθογγος, πολύφωνος; producing many tones, sounds). Plato called the aulos, by extension from stringed instruments, *polychordos* (πολύχορδος = having many strings; in this case giving many notes).

Other epithets used: *barybromos* (βαρύβρομος; with deep, strong sound); τέρην, *teren* (= tender; Anacr. ap. Athen. IV, 182C, ch. 79), *threnodes* (θρηνῴδης), *aeazon* (αἰάζων) etc. In conclusion it may be said that the aulos was more confined to Dionysus' cult than to Apollo's, for which Greek music had the lyra. For this reason and owing to its character, the aulos was not considered fitted for educational purposes. Most of the ancient writers and philosophers, including Plato and Aristotle, recommended avoidance of its use for the education of youth. But nevertheless the auletic art was held in high esteem as a musical art, and was much sought-after. Athenaeus (IV, 184C-F, chs. 83-84) says that all the Lacedaemons and Thebans learned to play the aulos, and that many important people, including many Pythagoreans, practised this art.

Notes: a) The denomination αὐλός (*aulos*) was a generic designation of various wind instruments (especially the reed-blown ones) used by the Greeks, except the *salpinx** (σάλπιγξ, trumpet) which was not used for purely musical purposes. b) The vb aulein (αὐλεῖν), to play the aulos, was often used in the sense of playing any wind instrument. Cf. *salpinx**. c) Some auloi, complete and in parts, have survived, discovered in Pompeii, Herculaneum, Athens, etc. and are now at the Museum of Naples, the National Archaeological Museum of Athens, the Danish National Museum in Copenhagen etc.

Bibliography:

A. A. Howard: The αὐλός or tibia. Harvard Studies in Classical Philology, vol. IV, Boston, 1893, pp. 1-60.

C. v. Jan: "Aulos = Tibia" in Pauly's R. E., vol. II$_2$ (1896), col. 2416-22.

Th. Reinach: "Tibia" in D.A.G.R., vol. IX, 1919, pp. 300-332.

H. Huchzermeyer: "Aulos und Kithara in der griechischen Musik"; Münster-Westph. 1931.

W. Vetter: "Monaulos" in Pauly's R.E.; vol. 31, 1933, col. 74-75.

Kathleen Schlesinger: The Greek Aulos, London, 1939.

C. Sachs: The History of Musical Instruments; N. York, 1940, pp. 138-142.

Nicholas B. Bodley: The auloi of Meroë, American Journal of Archaeology, vol. L, 1946, pp. 217-240.

Max Wegner: a) "Das musikleben der Griechen"; Berlin 1949, p. 52 ff.

b) "Griechische Instrumente und Musikbräuche " in Fr. Blume's "Die Musik in Geschichte und Gegenwart" vol. V, Kassel 1956, col. 865-881.

c) Musikgeschichte in Bildern, vol. II (Musik des Altertums-Griechenland) Leipzig 1963.

A. Baines: "Aulos" II; Grove, London 1954; vol. I, pp. 263-4.

J. D. Landels: a) The Brauron aulos. Annual of the British School at Athens, No. 58, London 1963, pp. 116-119; description of an ancient aulos discovered at Brauron (Βραυρὼν) on the east coast of Attica in Aug. 1961, during excavations by the Greek archaeologist I. Papademetriou.

b) A newly discovered aulos. Ann. of the Brit. Sch. at Athens, No. 63, 1968, pp. 231-238; "a full descriptive account" of an aulos acquired in 1967 by the Museum of Greek Archaeology in Reading University.

Despina Mazaraki: The aulos of the Karapanos collection (Ὁ αὐλὸς τῆς συλλογῆς Καραπάνου καὶ ἡ σύγχρονη πράξη; «Λαογραφία» ("Laographia"), vol. XXVIII, Athens 1972).

See Plates I, II.

aulotrypes (αὐλοτρύπης; m. pr. avlotrípis); maker of the finger-holes of the aulos; aulos-borer.

Arist. Probl. XIX, 23 «οἱ αὐλοτρῦπαι» (plur.); Pollux IV, 71.

See *trema*.

autokabdalos (αὐτοκάβδαλος; m. pr. aftokávdalos); improviser, popular mime, buffoon.

See under *iambus*.

B

baccheios (βακχεῖος; pr. vacchíos); a metrical foot consisting of three syllables, two long and one short, in the following form --υ or υ--; also a foot consisting of four syllables as in the form -υυ- (called βακχεῖος ἀπὸ τροχαίου, baccheios beginning from trochee*, -υ), or υ--υ (called βακχεῖος ἀπ' ἰάμβου, baccheios beginning from iambus*, υ-).

Bacchius the Old (Βακχεῖος ὁ Γέρων; m. pr. Vacchíos Géron); musical theorist of the time of Constantine; he lived after Ptolemy (2nd cent. A. D.), and probably in the 3rd or 4th century. Nothing is known about his life.

He is known for his "Introduction (or Isagoge) to the Art of Music" («Εἰσαγωγὴ Τέχνης Μουσικῆς»). Bacchius' Isagoge was first published in 1623 with a Latin translation by Fed. Morellus who calls him "physician-mathematician", confusing him probably with his synonym from Tanagra (3rd cent. A. D.), editor and commentator of Hippocrates' works. The title of this rare edition is as follows: "BACCHII SENIORIS, iatromathematici, Εἰσαγωγὴ sive Introductio Methodica ad Musicam per Dialogismum" (Lutetiae [Paris], 1623; 8°, pp. 24). The same year (1623) the same Greek text was published by Marine Mersenne in the "Paralipomena" of his "Quaestiones Celeberrimae in Genesim" (Lutetiae Parisiorum, 1623; 4°, pp. 1887-1891); the Latin translation by Fed. Morellus was included.

The Isagoge was later published also with a Latin translation by Meibom (Marcus Meibomius "Antiquae musicae auctores septem, Graece et Latine"; Amsterdam, 1652; vol. I, vi, pp. 1-25). The Greek text appears also in C.v. Jan's "Musici scriptores graeci" (ed. Teubner, Leipzig, 1895; VI, pp. 292-316).

A French translation, after the text in Meibom, was published with commentary by Ch. Ém. Ruelle (in "Collection des auteurs grecs etc."; V "Alypius, Gaudence et Bacchius l'Ancien"; Paris, 1895, pp. 103-140).

The Isagoge is written in the form of dialogue, and mostly follows the Aristoxenean School.

Fr. Bellermann in his edition of an Anonymous book on Music ("Anonymi scriptio de musica"; Berlin, 1841) includes also (pp. 101-108) another "Introduction to the Art of Music" by Bacchius (Bacchii senioris "Introductio artis musicae"), a text completely different from that published as above by Meibom and Jan. This Greek text, which is much shorter and not in dialogue form, was taken, as Bellermann says, from five other codices, two of Naples (262, 259) and three of Paris (2458, 2460, 2532).

The same text as in Bellermann's edition is also published by A.J.H. Vincent in his "Notices sur divers manuscrits grecs relatifs à la musique" (Paris,

1847; p. 64 ff). This Isagoge is attributed by some scholars to a Dionysius.

See *C. v. Jan*: Bakcheios Geron, in Pauly's R.E., vol. III, cols 2790-2792.

Bacchylides (Βακχυλίδης; m. pr. Vacchilídis); b. c. 520 or 518 B.C.; d. c. 450 B.C. He was born at Ioulis of Keos (Ἰουλίς, Κέως), and his mother was Simonides'* sister. He is considered as one of the principal representatives of choral poetry, and is placed in importance after Pindar and Simonides.

He composed Partheneia, Prosodia, and Paeans (Plut. 1136F, ch. 17); also Hymns, Erotic songs, Epigrams, Hyporchemata.

See Bruno Snell: Bacchilidis Carmina cum Fragmentis (Leipzig, 1934; T.; 10th edn, enlarged, 1970); also "Lyra Graeca" ed. and transl. by J. M. Edmonds, vol. III, pp. 80-223, 75 Frgs (Loeb Cl. Libr., 1931, repr. 1952). Cf. *A. Körte*: Bacchylidea, in Hermes, 53, 1918, pp. 113-147, and *A. Severyns*: Bacchylide, Essai biographique. Liège-Paris 1933.

baktriasmos (βακτριασμός; m. pr. vaktriasmós); for maktrismós* (μακτρισμός). It is included by Pollux (IV, 101) in a number of lustful dances, with apokinos* and aposeisis*. It was danced by women rotating the belly. Athenaeus used the word μακτρισμός.

bakylion or **baboulion** (βακύλιον or βαβούλιον; m. pr. vakílion, vavoúlion); according to lexicographers a synonym of κύμβαλον (cymbal*). Hes. «κύμβαλον· βακύλιον, βαβούλιον, εἶδος ὀργάνου μουσικοῦ» ("cymbal; bakylion, baboulion, a kind of musical instrument").

balaneon ode (βαλανέων ᾠδή); a song of bath-attendants.

βαλανεὺς (*balaneus*; m. pr. valanéfs) was the bath-man or the bath-keeper; also the servant who assisted those bathing in the bath-room.

Cf. Athen. XIV, 619A, ch. 10.

ballismos (βαλλισμός; m. pr. vallismós); a kind of hopping dance with twistings (jumping about) in use in Sicily and Magna Graecia (S. Italy).

The verb βαλλίζειν (*ballizein*) was used in the sense to leap, to jump, to dance, to move the feet here and there. Athen. VIII, 362A «βαλλίζουσιν οἱ κατὰ τὴν πόλιν ἅπαντες τῇ Θεῷ», and in a further paragraph (362B-C), Ulpianus disputing the authenticity of the verb «βαλλίζω», Myrilus cites various examples of its use in the Greek language in the sense of "dancing".

barbitos or **barbiton** (βάρβιτος ὁ, masc. and ἡ, fem. more often; and βάρβιτον, τό, neut; m. pr. várvitos, -on); a variety of the lyra. It was narrower than the lyra and longer; concequently its strings were longer and its range of pitch lower. The barbitos was a very old instrument. In Athenaeus there are two different explanations of its invention. According to Pindar (ap. Athen. XIV, 635D, ch. 37) "Terpander was the inventor of the barbitos" («Πινδάρου λέγοντος τὸν Τέρπανδρον ... εὑρεῖν ... τὸν βάρβιτον»); according to Neanthes, the historian from Kyzikos, on the other hand, it was Anacreon's invention («καὶ Ἀνακρέοντος [εὕρημα] τὸ βάρβιτον»; Athen. IV, 175E, ch. 77; also FHG III p. 2, fragm. 5). It was an instrument in great honour in the School of Lesbos (Terpander, Alcaeus, Sappho, Anacreon).

The number of the barbiton's strings is not known. Theocritus (Idyll XVI, «Χάριτες ἢ Ἱέρων», V, 45) says it was "a polychord instrument" («βάρβιτον ἐς πολύχορδον»), while the comic poet Anaxilas in his "Lyra-maker" («Λυρο- ποιός», Lyropoeos; ap. Athen. IV, 183B, ch. 81) speaks of *trichord barbitoi* («ἐγὼ δὲ βαρβίτους τριχόρδους»).

Other names, such as βάρμος (*barmos*), βάρωμος (*baromos*) and βαρύμιτον (*barymiton*), for barbitos are also met. Athen. XIV, 636C, ch. 38: «καὶ γὰρ βάρβιτος ἢ βάρμος» ("and *barbitos* or *barmos*"); Pollux IV, 59: «Τῶν μὲν κρουομένων εἴη ἂν λύρα, κιθάρα, βάρβιτον. Τὸ δ᾽ αὐτὸ καὶ βαρύμιτον» ("[The names] of the stringed instruments are lyra, kithara, *barbiton*; the same as *barymiton*").

Barymiton from βαρύς, low, grave, and μῖτος (*mitos*), thread, string. In Athenaeus, however, (IV, 182F, ch. 80) the *baromos* was mentioned as a dis- tinctly different instrument («τὸν γὰρ βάρωμον καὶ βάρβιτον, ὧν Σαπφὼ καὶ Ἀνακρέων μνημονεύουσι»; "the *baromos* and *barbiton* which [plur.] Sappho and Anacreon mention").

For playing the barbitos the verb «βαρβιτίζειν» (barbitizein) was used. Th. Kock "Comic. Attic. Fragm.", Leipzig 1880, vol. I, p. 571, Aristoph. Fr. 752, and Pollux IV, 63. *Barbitistes* (βαρβιτιστὴς) was the performer, and *barbitodos* (βαρβιτῳδὸς) the singer accompanying himself on the barbiton.

For Bibliography see under *enchorda, lyra* and *mousike.*

Fig. 1. Barbitos

See PLATE III.

baromos (βάρωμος; m. pr. váromos).

See *barbitos,* above.

baryaches and **baryeches** (βαρυαχὴς and βαρυηχής; m. pr. variachís, variichís); low sounding; with deep or strong sound; also sorely lamenting or sighing; bellowing.

barychordos (βαρύχορδος; m.pr. varíchordos); deep-toned, deeply sounding (stringed instrument); also the deep (low) sound of a stringed instrument («βαρύχορδος φθόγγος», barychordos phthongos = a deep sound, note).

baryllika pl., τὰ (βαρύλλικα; m. pr. varíllika); a kind of sacred dance for women in honour of Apollo and Diana. Pollux (IV, 104): «καὶ βαρύλλικα, τὸ μὲν εὕρημα Βαρυλλίχου, προσωρχοῦντο δὲ γυναῖκες ᾿Απόλλωνι καὶ ᾿Αρτέμιδι» ("The dance baryllika too, the invention of Baryllichus, which women used to dance in honour of Apollo and Diana").

barypycnos (βαρύπυκνος; m. pr. varípicnos); the lowest note of the pycnon*. Barypycnoi (pl.) were five: namely, the Hypate Hypaton (b), the Hypate Meson (e), the Mese (a), the Paramese (b_1) and the Nete Diezeugmenon (e_1). All of them were invariable notes of the tetrachord.

For more details see the article on *pycnon;* also *mesopycnos* and *oxypycnos.*

barys, barytes (βαρύς, βαρύτης; m. pr. varís, varítis).

a) βαρύς; low in pitch (Aristox. Harm. I, p. 3, 11 and p. 14 Mb etc.).

opp. ὀξὺς (*oxys*).

Also strong (sound). Of a syllable, unaccented.

b) βαρύτης; depth in pitch. It is the result of relaxation of a string (of anesis*, ἄνεσις). Aristox. (Harm. I, p. 10, 28 Mb: «βαρύτης δὲ τὸ γενόμενον διὰ τῆς ἀνέσεως» ("*depth* is the result of relaxation"); see also Anon. Bell. § 37, p. 50.

Aristotle (in Probl. XIX, 49) says that the lower sound (note) of an interval is the more melodic, and that the low (pitch) is more important than the high (Cf. Probl. XIX, 8). In prosody bareia, grave accent.

See *anesis, epitasis, oxys.*

basis (βάσις; m. pr. vásis) from βαίνειν = to walk, to step (on foot); the first or downbeat. This term was used in ancient times and was later superseded by the term "thesis" (θέσις) and by the Aristoxenean «ὁ κάτω χρόνος» or «τὸ κάτω» (the downbeat).

See *arsis - thesis.*

batalon (βάταλον; m. pr. vátalon) neut.; kroupeza, kroupezion*. Clapper of wood or metal pressed by an aulete with his foot to mark the rhythm (LSJ Suppl. s.v. βάταλον, κρούπεζαι 2). Cf. Phot. s.v. κρούπεζαι.

bater (βατήρ; m. pr. vatír); 1) same as *chordotonon**; board to which the strings were attached. Also a kind of peg. Nicom. Enchir. (ch. 6, C.v.J. p. 248, Mb p. 13) «μετέθηκεν εὐμηχάνως τὴν μὲν τῶν χορδῶν κοινὴν ἀπόδε-σιν ἐκ τοῦ διαγωνίου πασσάλου εἰς τὸν τοῦ ὀργάνου βατῆρα, ὃν χορδότονον ὠνόμαζε» ("he [Pythagoras] skilfully changed the common tying of the strings from the diagonal peg to the *bater* of the instrument, which he called *chordo-tonon*"); 2) a part of the aulos, probably the lowest section.

Cf. Nicom. op. cit. (ch. 10, C.v.J. p. 255, Mb. p. 19).

Bathyllus (Βάθυλλος; m. pr. Váthillos); 1st cent. B.C. to 1st cent. A.D., famous mime from Alexandria (known as ὁ Ἀλεξανδρεύς, the Alexandrian).

He introduced, with Pylades, the pantomimic art to the Roman Theatre in about 23-22 B.C. He wrote a book "On Orchesis" («Περὶ ὀρχήσεως») in which he treats of the Italian orchesis, constituting a mixture of kordax*, emmeleia* and sikinnis* (cf. Athen. I, 20D, ch. 37). At the begin-ning he collaborated with Pylades* but later the differences between them deepened to such a degree that serious disturbances were caused in the theatre among their followers; this state led to a temporary exile of Pylades by Emperor Augustus (17 AD). Bathyllus' art was differentiated from that of Pylades in being more hilarious and cheerful, nearer to the kordax; as Plutarch says (Sympos. VII, Probl. 8, § 3) "I prefer [accept] the Bathyllean [orchesis] as it approaches the kordax" («δέχομαι τὴν Βαθύλλειον [ὄρχησιν] τοῦ κόρδακος ἁπτομένην»). That of Pylades was described thus (Plut. Ibid.) «ἀποπέμπω τὴν Πυλάδειον ὀγκώδη καὶ παθητικὴν καὶ πολύκοπον οὖσαν»; "I reject the Pyladean as it is pompous, pathetic and tiresome (or bewailing")".

batrachiskoi, pl. (βατραχίσκοι; m. pr. vatrachíski; pl. of βατραχίσκος). Hes. "a part of the kithara" («μέρος τι τῆς κιθάρας») not defined.

baukalema (βαυκάλημα; m. pr. vafkálima); lullaby. From the verb βαυκα-λᾶν (also βαυκαλίζειν; *baukalan, baukalizein*) = to lull to sleep by singing. Suidas «τιθηνεῖσθαι μετ᾽ ᾠδῆς τὰ παιδία» = "to lull children with song"; also Moeris Attic Lex. p. 102. βαυκάλησις = lulling (a child) to sleep.

See also *katabaukalesis*.

baukismos (βαυκισμός; m. pr. vafkismós); a kind of Ionian dance of a Bacchic character, named after the dancer Βαῦκος (*Baukus*; m. pr. Vafkos).

Pollux (IV, 100) «καὶ βαυκισμός, Βαύκου ὀρχηστοῦ κῶμος ἐπώνυμος, ἁβρά τις ὄρχησις καὶ τὸ σῶμα ἐξυγραίνουσα» ("*Baukismos* [is] a carousal dance named after Baukus the dancer, a gentle dance making the body supple").

According to Hesychius so also was called a kind of a lyric song (ᾠδή) adapted to the dance; «Ἰωνικὴ ὄρχησις καὶ εἶδος ᾠδῆς πρὸς ὄρχησιν πεποιη-μένον» ("An Ionian dance and a kind of song adapted to dancing").

bechia (βηχία, ἡ, fem. and βηχίας, ὁ, masc.; m. pr. vichía); hoarseness, a hoarse sound; unmusical voice or sound.

Excerpta ex Nicomacho (C.v.Jan p. 274; Mb. p. 35) «βυκανισμοὺς καὶ *βηχίας*»; see the full text under *bycane*.

bibasis (βίβασις; m. pr. vívasis); a kind of Laconic dance, danced especially in Sparta. It was also a sort of dance competition in which boys and girls were allowed to take part. According to Pollux (IV, 102) the competitors had to jump (sometimes alternatively on each foot, sometimes on both feet) and touch the breech with the feet. The number of jumps was counted, and a prize was given to the winner. Pollux quotes an Epigram about a maiden prize-winner who succeeded in making one thousand jumps.

blityri (βλίτυρι; m. pr. vlítiri); LSJ, twang of a harp-string, hence a meaningless sound.

Cf. *tenella**, *threttanelo**, *torelle**.

Boeotios nomos (Βοιώτιος; m. pr. Viótios); Boeotian nomos; A kitharodic nomos initiated and named by Terpander. Cf. Plut. De Mus. 1132D, ch. 4 (see the text under Aeolios nomos*).

bombos (βόμβος; m. pr. vómvos); booming sound, e.g. of wind (LSJ). Also of aulos.

bombykias (βομβυκίας; m. pr. vomvikías).

See *calamus**.

bombyx (βόμβυξ; m. pr. vómvix);

a) the whole pipe, the principal body of the aulos. b) In pl. bombykes (βόμβυκες) were called "collars" (or wide rings) "that had corresponding holes and could be turned to cover or uncover the pipe holes";

(C. Sachs: Hist. of Mus. Instr., p. 139).

According to the grammarian Arcadius (4th cent. A.D.?; ed. E. H. Barker, Leipzig, 1820, p. 186) "they were turned up and down, and inside and outside" («ἄνω καὶ κάτω, καὶ ἔνδον τε καὶ ἔξω στρέφοντες»);

ap. D. Mazaraki: "The aulos of the Karapanos Collection" in "Laographia", vol. XXVIII, Athens, 1972, pp. 257-8).

Pollux IV, 70 «Τῶν δὲ ἄλλων αὐλῶν τὰ μέρη, γλῶττα, τρυπήματα καὶ *βόμβυκες*» ("The parts of the other auloi [are] the reed, the holes, the collars").

c) the aulos itself, especially the deep-toned aulos; Pollux (IV, 82): «τὸ δὲ τῶν *βομβύκων* ἔνθεον καὶ μανικὸν τὸ αὔλημα» ("and the piping on (solo of) the deep-toned auloi [was] enthusiastic (inspired) and passionate").

d) the lowest note produced by the aulos when all the holes were closed, i.e. by the entire length of the air-column.   Arist. Metaph. (1093B, 2; C.v.Jan p. 35): «καὶ ὅτι ἴσον τὸ διάστημα ἔν τε τοῖς γράμμασιν ἀπὸ τοῦ Α πρὸς τὸ Ω καὶ ἀπὸ τοῦ βόμβυκος ἐπὶ τὴν ὀξυτάτην νεάτην ἐν αὐλοῖς» = "and that the interval in the letters from A to Ω [the last letter of the Greek alphabet] equals from the *bombyx* (the lowest note) to the highest nete on the auloi").

Cf. Nicom. (Ench. ch. 5; C.v.Jan p. 245; Mb. p. 10) «*βομβυκέστερος*» (τόνος) = lower (tonos); comparative.

borimos (βώριμος; m. pr. vórimos)

1. *βώριμος*, also *βῶρμος* (vórmos); a folk-song of a mournful character sung by Mariandynian farmers to aulos accompaniment. It was a kind of dirge, like the Egyptian maneros* and was sung in memory of Borimos (Βώριμος), son of king Upius and brother of Mariandynus and Iollus, who died young while hunting in summer. Pollux who relates the story (IV, 54) adds «τιμᾶται δὲ [Βώριμος] θρηνῴδει περὶ τὴν γεωργίαν ᾄσματι» ("and he [Borimos] is honoured by a lamenting pastoral song").

This story is also related, with some variations, by Nymphis;

(Ap. Athen. XIV, 619E-F, ch. 11). Cf. also *linos,* and *maneros.*

2. *Βώριμος* was also the name for a kind of aulos; «Μαριανδυνοὶ κάλαμοι».

boucoliasmos, boucolismos (βουκολιασμὸς and βουκολισμός; m. pr. voucoli[a]smós); singing or playing pastoral tunes; by extension:

1. a shepherd's song; *βουκόλος* (boukolos) = shepherd.

Athen. (XIV, 619A, ch. 10) «ἦν δὲ καὶ τοῖς ἡγουμένοις τῶν βοσκημάτων ὁ βουκολιασμὸς καλούμενος. Δίομος δὲ ἦν ὁ βουκόλος Σικελιώτης ὁ πρῶτος εὑρὼν τὸ εἶδος» ("and there was also a song of the shepherds called *boucoliasmos*; Diomus, a shepherd from Sicily, was the inventor of this kind of song").

2. an aulesis (aulos solo) of a bucolic character; a pastoral melody played on the aulos.   Boucoliasmos is one of the auleseis (pl.) included in the catalogue of kinds of auleseis of the Alexandrian lexicographer Tryphon (ap. Athen. XIV. 618C, ch. 9).   See also under *aulesis.*

brachys (βραχύς; m. pr. vrachís); short.   In prosody:

βραχεῖα συλλαβὴ = short syllable, expressed by the sign ‿.

bromos (βρόμος; m. pr. vrómos);

strong sound, clamour; «βρόμος αὐλῶν» = "strong sound of auloi". From the verb «βρέμειν» (bremein; m. pr. vrémin) = to produce a strong sound or noise; in music, to sound strongly, to emit a strong sound.

Some derivatives met with:

a) βρόμιος (bromios); causing clamour, loud-sounding, sonorous, noisy. Pind. Nemean IX, 18a «βρομίαν (fem.) φόρμιγγα» ("*sonorous* phorminx"). Bromios was a name of Bacchus.

b) ἄβρομος (*abromos*) = soundless, noiseless, voiceless; but also in exactly the opposite sense = with much noise, noisy, loud-sounding.

Il. XIII, 39-41 «Τρῶες δὲ φλογὶ... Ἕκτωρ... ἕποντο... ἄβρομοι, αὐΐαχοι» ("But the Trojans like flame... were following after Hector... with *loud shouts and cries*"; tr. A. T. Murray, vol. II, p. 5).

c) ἀλίβρομος (*halibromos*); loudly sounding; producing a clamour, like the sea (ἅλς = sea); Nonn. Dion. 43, 385: «ἀλίβρομος σῦριγξ» (strongly sounding, *sonorous* syrinx". In LSJ: "murmuring like the sea".

d) μελίβρομος (*melibromos*) = with sweet, pleasing sound.

bryallicha (βρυαλλίχα, ἡ, fem.; m. pr. vriallícha); also *bryllicha* or *brydalicha* (βρυλλίχα, βρυδαλίχα). A kind of Laconic dance in honour of Apollo and Diana. It was performed by women wearing men's dress or by men wearing women's dresses, dancing with lewd movements of the hips.

The word βρυλλίχα (bryllicha) or βρυδαλίχα (brydalicha) signified, according to Hesychius, a person wearing feminine dresses. Also the word «βρυλλιχίδει» (bryllichidei) = (Hes.) "a person wearing feminine mask and dress".

βρυαλιγμὸς (bryaligmos); Hes. "noise, sound".

βρυαλ[λ]ίκτης (bryaliktes); war-dancer.

Bryennius, Manuel (Βρυέννιος, Μανουήλ; m. pr. Vriénnios Manouíl); 14th cent. A.D. Byzantine theorist and writer on music. He lived during the reign of Michael Palaeologus (1285-1320), and he may descend from the noble Byzantine family of Bryenni. He left an important work on music entitled "Harmonica" («Ἀρμονικά») published in Greek and Latin by I. Wallis in the third volume of his "Opera Mathematica" (3 vols., Oxford, 1699) pp. 359-508, together with Ptolemaeus' Harmonica (pp. 1-152) and Porphyrius' Commentary on it (pp. 189-355). Bryennius' Harmonica, divided in three books, is a compilation from older Greek music treatises, such as those by Aristoxenus, Aristides, Nicomachus, Ptolemaeus, Theon of Smyrna and others. This is the last of the works containing information on ancient Greek music.

A new edition of "The Harmonics of Manuel Bryennius" with an English translation was published as Thesis (Proefschrift) by Goverdus Henricus Jonker in 1970 (Wolters-Noordhoff Publishing; Groningen, The Netherlands). This important edition (8°, pp. 454) contains a Select Bibliography (pp. 9-15), a comprehensive Introduction on a) M. Bryennius and his work, and b) the

54

manuscript tradition (pp. 17-47); and the Greek text with English translation (pp. 50-375), followed by Notes (376-403), Indices and an Appendix (pp. 404-454).

See also: *W. Vetter*: 'Manuel Bryennios' in Pauly's R. E., Stuttgart, 1930; vol. XIV, cols 1362-1366.

Maria Stöhr: 'Bryennios, Manuel' in Fr. Blume's 'Die Musik in Geschichte und Gegenwart''; vol. II, Kassel, 1952, cols. 411-415.

bycane (βυκάνη; m. pr. vikáni); originally a horn in use by shepherds. A curved or spiral trumpet, made of horn or brass; it was used in armies and also as a hunting horn.

Suidas says simply "a musical instrument".

Polybius (Historiae, XV, 12,2) mentions the bycane in the following passage ''ἅμα δὲ τῷ πανταχόθεν τὰς σάλπιγγας καὶ τὰς βυκάνας (pl.) διαβοῆσαι τινὰ μὲν διαταραχθέντα τῶν θηρίων ὥρμησε..» ("as soon as from all quarters the trumpets and the *bycanai* loudly sounded some of the beasts were disturbed and rushed on").

βυκανητὴς or βυκανιστὴς (*bycanetes* or *bycanistes*), the player of the bycane; Polyb. (Hist. II, 29,6): «ἀναρίθμητον μὲν γὰρ ἦν τὸ τῶν βυκανητῶν καὶ σαλπιγκτῶν πλῆθος (Κελτῶν)» ("innumerable was the crowd of the *bycanetai* (horn-players) and trumpeters [Celts]").

βυκάνημα (*bycanema*), the sound of the bycane; generally a trumpet-call. Also βυκανισμὸς (*bycanismos*) which signified also a deep, bass, strong, note; Excerpta ex Nicom. (ch. 4; C.v.Jan p. 274; Mb. p. 35) «βυκανισμοὺς καὶ βηχίας, φθέγματα ἄσημα καὶ ἄναρθρα καὶ ἐκμελῆ» ("*bycanismoi* [sounds of bycane] and hoarsenesses, trivial sounds, inarticulate and unmelodious").

βυκανάω = to play the bycane, the trumpet.

C

calamaules and **calamauletes** (καλαμαύλης and καλαμαυλητής; m. pr. calamávlis, calamavlitís); an aulete who played on a reed-made aulos, a reed-piper.

Hedylus ap. Athen. (IV, 176D, ch. 78) «ἀλλὰ Θέωνα τὸν καλαμαυλητὴν εἴπατε «χαῖρε Θέων», ὥσπερ οὖν τοὺς τῷ καλάμῳ αὐλοῦντας καλαμαύλας λέγουσι νῦν» ("but you greeted Theon the *reed-piper*, 'Farewell, Theon'; precisely, then, as they call those who play on a calamus-made aulos, *calamaulai*".

See also *rapaules*.

calamus (χάλαμος; m. pr. cálamos); in a general sense the plant "calamus", reed; also various objects made of it were called "calamoi" (pl.). Thus, calamus was a name for the aulos, as made of reed; especially the shepherd's aulos.

calamóphthongos (καλαμόφθογγος); of sounds or tunes played on a reed-made aulos; Aristoph. Frogs 230 «Πάν, ὁ καλαμόφθογγα παίζων» ("Pan, who plays melodies on *a reed-made aulos*").

The vb *calamizein* (καλαμίζειν), to blow on a reed, to play the calamus (aulos). The best calamus came from the lake Kopais of Boeotia (now dried up) and supplied the best material for the Theban auletai.

Scholia Vetera in Pind. Carm. (ed. A. B. Drachmann, 1910; vol. II, p. 268): «τοὺς δόνακας, οἳ παρὰ τῷ Ὀρχομενῷ φύονται, ἐξ ὧν αἱ αὐλητικαὶ γλωσσίδες γίνονται» ("*the donakes* [see *donax**; cane, calamus], which grow near Orchomenos and from which the auletic reeds are made").

Note: Orchomenós was an ancient town on the western part of lake Kopais.

The "auletic calamus" (reed) was called, according to Theophrastus (Hist. Plant. IV, 11, 3), *zeugites* (ζευγίτης) when it stayed in the lake "until the next year and became mature" («μείναντα δὲ τὸν ἐπιόντα ἐνιαυτὸν ἁδρύνεσθαι· καὶ γίνεσθαι τὸν μὲν ἁδρυθέντα ζευγίτην»); it was used for the making of the mouthpiece of the aulos. It was called *bombykias* (βομβυκίας) when it did not stay in the water; from this "calamus" the pipe was made.

canon (κανών; m. pr. canón); in Porphyry's words "the measure of accuracy of the symmetries" (Commentary; ed. J. Wallis, III, p. 207). By the canon the ratios of the intervals were determined.

Ptolemaeus (ed. Wallis; book I, ch. 8, p. 18; ed. I Düring, p. 18) gives the following diagram of the canon:

Note: αβγδ   is the straight line of the canon («εὐθεῖα τοῦ κανόνος»)
αεηδ   the string («χορδή»)
αε, ηδ   the "dependants" («τὰ καὶ ἐξάμματα»)
εβ, ηγ   upright bridges («κάθετοι μαγάδες»)
κκ, λλ   small movable bridges («μαγάδια κινούμενα»)

See Nicom. Ench. (ch. 10; C.v.Jan p. 254; Mb. p. 18); Gaud. Isag. (§ 11; C.v.J. p. 341; Mb. p. 14). Also *Eucleides**.

The canon is often taken for the monochord* (μονόχορδον).

Canonion; dim. of canon.

56

chalaros, adj. (χαλαρός); loose, slack. A term met especially in Plato; ἁρμονία χαλαρά (harmonia chalará) not syntonos, loose; effeminate as to the ethos*.

Aneimenos (ἀνειμένος; p.p. of ἀνίημι = to loosen) was also used with the same meaning. Plato Rep. (III, 398E): «'Ιαστί, ἦ δ' ὅς, καὶ Λυδιστί, αἵτινες χαλαραὶ καλοῦνται»; "The Ionian, said he, and Lydian harmoniai which are called *chalarai,* loose").

Arist. (Polit. VI (IV), 3, 1290A, 20 «τὰς δ' ἀνειμένας [ἁρμονίας] καὶ μαλακὰς δημοτικάς» ("those that are low in pitch and slack being of the nature of democracy"; transl. H. S. Macran, Aristox. p. 72). H. Rackham (Politics London, 1932 in the Loeb Cl. Libr. Ed.; p. 289) translates "the *relaxed* (ἀνειμένας) and soft ones democratic".

cheirokalathiskos (χειροκαλαθίσκος; m. pr. chirokalathískos);
See *kalathiskos.*

cheironomia (χειρονομία; m. pr. chironomía); a pantomimic movement of the hands performed in rhythm, either while dancing or during a theatrical performance; it was used to express by the movements of the hands various meanings or thoughts. Pollux II, 153 «χειρονομῆσαι (verb) δέ, τὸ ταῖν χεροῖν ἐν ρυθμῷ κινηθῆναι. Ἡρόδοτος δὲ εἴρηκεν ἐπὶ Ἱπποκλείδου τοῦ Ἀθηναίου τοῖς ποσὶν ἐχειρονόμησεν» ("*cheironomesai* is to move the hands in rhythm. And Herodotus said that the Athenian Hippocleides expressed himself by movements of the feet"); Cf. Herod. VI, 129. See also Plut. "De esu carnium oratio (Περὶ σαρκοφαγίας, λόγος β') Moral. 997C («μὴ πυρρίχαις χαίρειν, μηδὲ χειρονομίαις, μηδ' ὀρχήμασι»; Luc. "On orchesis" § 38.

b) Χειρονομία was a kind of (or another name for) pyrrhiche; Athen. (XIV, 631C) «καλεῖται δ' ἡ πυρρίχη καὶ χειρονομία» ("the pyrrhiche was also called *cheironomia*").

cheironomos (χειρονόμος); the performer of cheironomia, also the dancer who at the same time danced and performed cheironomiai; Hes. «χειρονόμος· ὀρχηστὴς» ("*cheironomos*; a dancer").

cheirourgia (χειρουργία; m. pr. chirourgía); handicraft.

The adj. *cheirourgikos* (χειρουργικός; m. pr. chirourgikós) is used in the sense of technical dexterity (LSJ), also of practical, instrumental. Plut. De Mus. (ch. 13, 1135D): «ἡμεῖς γὰρ μᾶλλον χειρουργικῷ μέρει τῆς μουσικῆς ἐγγεγυμνάσμεθα» ("as to myself [Lysias] I have rather studied the practical part of music [i.e. execution]").

chelidonisma (χελιδόνισμα; m. pr. chelidónisma); swallow-song. Name for a song which boys in Rhodos went round from house to house in the month of Boedromion singing and collecting small gifts or money (Dem.).

Boedromion (βοηδρομιών; m. pr. voïdromión) was the name of a month corresponding to about 15 September to 15 October.

chelidonismos (χελιδονισμός; m. pr. chelidonismós); singing of the swallow-song (LSJ).

chelidonistes (χελιδονιστής; m. pr. chelidonistís); singer of the swallow-song. Usually in plur. (χελιδονισταί) the boys who sang the swallow-song.

chelidonizein (χελιδονίζειν; m. pr. chelidonízin) vb; to sing the swallow-song (chelidonisma). Athenaeus says (VIII, 360B) that chelidonizein was among the Rhodians "another kind of agermos" (ἀγερμὸς = collection), and preserves such a song (360C) mentioned by Theognis in his Second Book of Sacrifices in Rhodos (FHG IV, 514). Cf. *koronisma**.

chelys (χέλυς; m. pr. chélis); χελώνη, tortoise. The primitive lyra; so called because its sound-box was a tortoise-shell. Hes. «χέλυς· χελώνα, λύρα, μηχανημα» ("*chelys*; a tortoise, a lyra, a machine"). Pollux (IV, 59) includes chelys in the list of the stringed instruments.

Philostr. 777 (ap. Dem.) «τῆς λύρας τε σόφισμα πρῶτος Ἑρμῆς πήξασθαι λέγεται κεράτων δυοῖν, κατὰ ζυγοῦ καὶ χελύος» ("the invention of the lyra is due to Hermes who first fastened two horns against a cross-bar and a tortoise").

A description of the construction by Hermes of the first chelys (lyra) is found in Homer's Hymn to Hermes (Mercury; vs 24-25, 47-51). vs *24-25*: "There found he a tortoise, and won endless delight, for lo, it was Hermes that first made of tortoise a minstrel"; vs *47-51*: "He cut to measure stalks of reed, and fixed them in through holes bored in the stony shell of the tortoise, and cunningly stretched round in the hide of an ox, and put in the horns of the lyre, and to both he fitted the bridge, and stretched seven harmonious chords of sheep-gut"; transl. by Andrew Lang "The Homeric Hymns", London, 1899.

b) χέλους (*chelous*); Hes. «μουσικὸν ὄργανον» ("a musical instrument").

For bibliography see under *lyra*.

chiazein (χιάζειν; m. pr. chiázin); to use or perform pretentious (affected) melodies. This expression was derived from the name of Democritus' native island of Chios (Χίος); Pollux (IV, 65): «τὸ μέντοι σιφνιάζειν καὶ χιάζειν, τὸ περιέργοις μέλεσι χρῆσθαι, ἀπὸ Δημοκρίτου τοῦ Χίου καὶ Φιλοξένου τοῦ Σιφνίου, ὃς καὶ Ὑπερίδης ἐκαλεῖτο» ("indeed [the expressions] siphniazein and *chiazein*, i.e. the using of strange [affected] melodies [were derived] from Democritus of Chios [chiazein] and Philoxenus of Siphnos [siphniazein], who was also called Hyperides").

choliambos (χωλίαμβος; m. pr. cholíambos); a lame iambus; a verse which consisted of an iambic trimeter with a spondee (or trochee) at the last foot: ℧-℧--- or ℧-℧- -℧. It was invented by Hipponax (Ἱππῶναξ; a satirical poet, 6th cent. B.C.). The choliambos was also called «σκάζων» (skázon*; σκάζειν, skázein = to limp).

chora (χώρα); space, place. In music the position on a scale; the position (locus) where a note is situated.

Aristox. (Harm. III, p. 70, 20 Mb.) «χῶραι (pl.) φθόγγων» ("positions of the notes").

See also *topos* (locus).

choraules (χοραύλης; m. pr. chorávlis); the aulete who accompanied the chorus on the aulos; a theatrical aulete; the aulete of the dance-group. Plut. (Antonius, 24) «Ἀναξήνορες δὲ κιθαρῳδοὶ καὶ Ξοῦθοι χοραῦλαι (pl.)» ("Anaxenores kitharodes and Xouthoi *choraulai*").

χοραυλεῖν, vb (*choraulein*; choravlín) = to accompany the chorus on the aulos. Strabo XVII, ch. 1, §11 «καὶ ὁ ὕστατος, ὁ Αὐλητής, ὃς χωρὶς τῆς ἄλλης ἀσελγείας χοραυλεῖν ἤσκησε...» ("and the last [Ptolemaeus], Auletes, who, apart from his other licentiousness, practised the *accompaniment of choruses with aulos*").

chorde (χορδή; m. pr. chordí); originally gut, also a string of gut which stretched can produce a sound. Hence a string of a musical instrument. In this sense it appears in Homer's Hymn to Hermes (Mercury) v. 51 «ἑπτὰ δὲ συμφώνους ὀΐων ἐτανύσσατο χορδάς» pl. ("and stretched seven harmonious *strings* of sheep-guts").

Also in Odyss. XXI 406-407: «ὡς ὅτ' ἀνὴρ φόρμιγγος ἐπιστάμενος καὶ ἀοιδῆς ῥηϊδέως ἐτάνυσσε νέῳ περὶ κόλλοπι χορδὴν» = "even as when a man well-skilled in the lyre and in song easily stretches the *string* about a new peg"; transl. A. T. Murray vol. II, p. 333. Hes. «χορδή· νευρὰ κιθάρας» ("*chorde*; a string of the kithara"); also Pollux (IV, 62) on parts of the instruments.

The strings were made of gut or sinew (of sheep or kid); «χορδαῖς ὀπταῖς ἐριφείοις» = of baked strings of kid; cf. Pherecr. Persai, ap. Kock. Com. Att. Fr., vol. I, p. 182, Frg. 130. The word χορδή (chorde, string) became a synonym of sound, note. Plato, e. g., called the aulos «πολύχορδος» (polychord; first meaning = having many strings, but here having [producing] many notes). Later it was also used in the case of the vocal cords: φωνητικαὶ χορδαὶ (phonetic chordai, strings, cords).

The word νευρὰ (*neura**) was often used for χορδή. The maker of strings was called χορδοποιὸς (*chordopoeos*). The string-twister was called χορδοστρόφος (*chordostrophos*); in a sense he was a string-maker, also a string tuner.

chordotonos, chordotonion (χορδοτόνος, χορδοτόνιον); a small board at the lower part of the sound-box of the lyra and the kithara, on which the strings were attached by a knot. Artemon (ap. Athen. XIV, 637D, ch. 41) writes, speaking about the instrument tripous*: «ὑπερθεὶς ἑκάστῃ [χώρᾳ] πῆχυν καὶ κάτω προσαρμόσας χορδοτόνια» ("at the top of each [space] he fixed a cross-arm and below he adjusted the *chordotonia*"). Man. Bryen. (Harm.; ed. Wallis III, p. 417) «ἡ ὑπὸ τὰς χορδὰς ὑποκειμένη σανὶς χορδο-τόνος ὀνομάζεται» ("the wooden board which is found below (under) the strings is called *chordotónos*"); cf. *Nicom*. Enchir. (ch. 6; C.v.J. p. 248; Mb. p. 13). χορδότονον, neut. (*chordótonon*), but also χορδότονος (masc.) was the peg (kollops*, kollabos*; κόλλοψ, κόλλαβος) by which the strings were tuned. *Chordótonos* of an instrument, having stretched string (or strings); chordótonos lyra (Plut. "De cohibenda ira" (Περὶ ἀοργησίας) 455D.

See also *epitonion* (ἐπιτόνιον).

choregos (χορηγός; m. pr. chorigós): the leader of the chorus, later called koryphaeus* (κορυφαῖος).

In Athens the choregos was also the person who paid the expenses for the organization of the chorus and of the dramatic performance. Ἀγέχορος (*agechoros**) or ἡγέχορος (*hegechoros*) was another word for choregos; also *choregetes* (χορηγέτης), *hegemon* (ἡγεμὼν τοῦ χοροῦ; Poll. IV, 106). Plato Laws (book II, 665A) «Θεοὺς δέ, ἔφαμεν, ἐλεοῦντας ἡμᾶς συγχορευτάς τε καὶ χορηγοὺς ἡμῖν δεδωκέναι τόν τε Ἀπόλλωνα καὶ Μούσας, καὶ δὴ καὶ τρί-τον, ἔφαμεν, εἰ μεμνήμεθα Διόνυσον» ("and, as we said, Gods out of pity for us have granted to us dancer-mates and chorus-leaders Apollo and the Muses, and, as we said, a third one if you remember, Dionysus").

Demetrius of Byzantium in the fourth book of "On Poetry" (ap. Athen. XIV, 633A-B, ch. 33) says «ἐκάλουν δὲ καὶ χορηγοὺς οὐχ ὥσπερ νῦν τοὺς μισθουμένους τοὺς χορούς, ἀλλὰ τοὺς καθηγουμένους τοῦ χοροῦ, καθάπερ αὐτὸ τοὔνομα σημαίνει» ("and they used to call *choregoi* (*chorus-leaders*), not as nowadays those who hire the choruses, but the leaders of them, as the etymology of the word denotes"). See also *chorostates* (χοροστάτης).

choregema (χορήγημα; m. pr. chorígima); the expenditure for the organ-ization of a chorus. *choregesis* (χορήγησις); m. pr. chorígisis); the defraying of the expenses of the chorus.

choregia (χορηγία; m. pr. chorigía); office, function of the choregos.

choregeion (χορηγεῖον); the place where the members of the choruses were assembled and trained by the choregos. Phryn. Epitome (Ἐπιτομή, Sophistae Preparatio [Σοφιστικὴ Προπαρασκευὴ] ed. Ioannes de Borries, T.; 1911) p. 126 «χορηγεῖον (Demosth. XIX, 200) ὁ τόπος, ἔνθα ὁ χορηγὸς τοὺς τε χοροὺς καὶ τοὺς ὑπηρέτας συνάγων συνεκρότει».

choreia fem. (**χορεία**; m. pr. choría); a) a kind of sacred dance performed in front of sanctuaries during the procession of Eleusinia; generally, a choral dance; also a cyclic dance with singing; and choir-training.

Plato (Laws, book II, 654A «χορεία γε μὴν ὄρχησίς τε καὶ ᾠδὴ τὸ ξύνολόν ἐστι» ("but *choreia* of course is the ensemble of dance and song"); see also book II, 665A. Suidas «χορείαν, τὴν μετὰ ᾠδῆς ὄρχησιν» ("*choreia*; dancing with song").

b) χορεία (*choreia*); also a dance-melody; Pratinas ap. Brgk III, p. 1219, Fr. 1, v. 17 «κισσοχαῖτ᾽ ἄναξ ἄκουε τὰν ἐμὰν δώριον χορείαν» ("ivy-crowned lord listen to my Dorian *choreia*").

c) χορεῖα, τὰ (*choreia*; pl. of χορεῖον, choreion); LSJ "thank-offerings for victory of a chorus".

choreios (**χορεῖος**; m. pr. chorios); a) a kind of aulesis, a solo for aulos. As such it is included in Tryphon's catalogue of Denominations of auleseis (ap. Ath., XIV, 618C, ch. 9).

See the full catalogue of Tryphon under the word *aulesis*.

b) *choreion*, neut. (χορεῖον); dancing place; the place where the dance took place. Choreion was also an aulema (αὔλημα), a melody for aulos; also the dancing-school. Hes. gives many meanings to the word: «Χορεῖον· διδασκαλεῖον καὶ βωμός τις καὶ αὔλημά τι καὶ μέρος τι χωρίου (prob. μέλος χορικὸν)» = "*Choreion*; a dancing-school, and an altar, and a melody for aulos and a choral-song".

Suidas: «ἡ χόρευσις» = "the dancing".

c) *choreios*; also the well-known poetic foot trochee.
See *pous*.

choreuma (**χόρευμα**; m. pr. chórevma); choral-dance; a dance. Eurip. Phoenician women 655 «Βάκχιον χόρευμα» ("Bacchic *dance*").

choreus (**χορεύς**; m. pr. choréfs); a member of the chorus, singer or dancer.
Hes. «χορεύς, μελῳδεῖ· βακχεύς, ὀρχεῖται» ("the *choreus* sings; the baccheus dances").

choreusis (χόρευσις); dancing, orchesis. Suidas under word choreia. Pind. Paean 6, v. 9 (Ernst Diehl: Suppl. Lyr., Bonn 1910, p. 31; Br. Snell Pind. Carm., T., 1964, p. 27): «ὀρφανὸν ἀνδρῶν χορεύσιος ἦλθον».

61

choreutes (χορευτής; m. pr. choreftís); dancer; principally choral-dancer; member of the chorus in the drama.

choreuein, vb (χορεύειν; m. pr. chorévin); to dance a choral-dance; to dance with accompaniment of singing (or instrumental music); to take part in a chorus, dance group; to celebrate or honour by choral-dance; to incite to dancing; to move in a circle, in a circular movement.

choriambos (χορίαμβος; m. pr. choríamvos); a metrical foot consisting of a trochee and an iambus -υυ-; the reverse was called antispastos* (ἀντίσπαστος).

χοριαμβικὸν μέτρον (*choriambic metre*); a metre consisting of choriambi; Arist. Quint. (De Mus. I, p. 50 Mb, RPW-I p. 45) includes the choriambic in the nine simple metres.

chorikos (χορικός); choral.

chorikon melos (χορικὸν μέλος, neut.); a choral song.

As a kind of composition it originated from the ancient orchesis. During the dancing the ancients used to express their feelings first by exclamations, then by whole phrases and then by songs. The choral song developed in connection with sacred ceremonies in honour of various deities, and included some mimic dancing. It became and remained a basic element of the dithyramb and the drama. Choral songs were the embateria* (ἐμβατήρια), the partheneia* (παρθένεια), the hyporchemata* (ὑπορχήματα), the paeans* etc.

chorikón (χορικόν; as a substv.); the choral part in the drama (see *parodos*, *stasimon*, *epiparodos*, *exodion*).

chorikós aulos (χορικὸς αὐλός; m. pr. chorikós avlós); often in pl. chorikoi auloi, the auloi used at the dithyramps.

Pollux (IV, 81) «οἱ δὲ χορικοὶ διθυράμβοις προσηύλουν» ("*the choral auloi accompanied the dithyrambs*").

chorikai odai, plur. (χορικαὶ ᾠδαί; m. pr. choriké odé); choral songs; esp. those choral songs in the ancient drama.

chorike mousa (χορικὴ μοῦσα; m. pr. chorikí mousa); choral muse.

chorodia (χορῳδία; m. pr. chorodía); choral song, choral singing. Plato in Laws (VI, 764 D-E) distinguishes between monodia and chorodia, suggesting that different judges should be set for those competing in "monody" and for those competing in choral singing. See the text under *monodia*.

The vb chorodein (χορῳδεῖν), to sing in chorus or to a chorus, appears in later times; Dio Cassius (Historicus) 61, 19 (LSJ, Dem.)

chorodidascalos (χοροδιδάσκαλος); chorus-teacher; also the chorus-trainer who trained and prepared the chorus for dramatic performance. In the beginning the training of the chorus was the responsibility of the dramatic poet himself. On one such occasion while Euripides was teaching the chorus, he noticed a member deriding him, and turning to him Euripides said in anger "if you were not insensible and ignorant you would not have laughed when I was singing in the Mixolydisti harmonia" («εἰ μή τις ἦς ἀναίσθητος καὶ ἀμαθὴς οὐκ ἂν ἐγέλας ἐμοῦ μιξολυδιστὶ ἄδοντος»).

Cf. Plut. De audiendo [Περὶ τοῦ ἀκούειν], 46B § 15.

chorokale (**χοροκάλη**; m. pr. chorokáli); probably a wrong expression for «χορῷ καλὴ» (LSJ and Dem.); Hes. «καλῶς χορεύουσα» ("dancing nicely [well]").

Il. XVI, 180 «τὸν τίκτε χορῷ καλή, Πολυμήλη, Φύλαντος θυγάτηρ» ("and him [Eudorus] did Polymele *fair in the dance*, daughter of Phylas, bear"; transl. A. T. Murray Il., vol. II, p. 177).

chorokithareus (**χοροκιθαρεύς**; m. pr. chorokitharéfs) and *chorokitharistes* (*χοροκιθαριστής*; m. pr. chorokitharistís); a kitharist accompanying (or playing for) the chorus. The verb χοροκιθαρίζειν (*chorokitharizein*) = to play the kithara to the chorus. C. Suetonius Tranquillus (Τράγκυλλος ὁ Σουητώνιος) in Domitianus, ch. 4, § 4: "*citharaoedos, chorocitharistae* (pl. of choroc[k]itharistes) et *psilocitharistae*".

chorolectes (**χορολέκτης**; m. pr. choroléctis); chorus-elector; one who selected the members of a chorus. Pollux IV, 106. Also *choropoeos* (*χοροποιός*; m. pr. choropiós); one who formed the chorus.

chorostates (**χοροστάτης**; m. pr. chorostátis); one who formed a chorus; who brought together the members of a chorus (chorolectes*). Also leader of a chorus (*choregós**).

Hes. «χοροστατῶν· χοροῦ κατάρχων» ("*chorostatón*: leader of a chorus"). The verb *chorostatein* (χοροστατεῖν) = to lead the chorus; to form the chorus; to select its members.

chorostasia (*χοροστασία*); formation of a chorus; also the performance of dancing, hence orchesis, dance.

Hes. «χοροστασία· χορὸς» ("*chorostasia*; dance").

chorostás, fem. (χοροστάς, -αδος; pl. χοροστάδες; *chorostádes*); usually in pl.; feasts celebrated with choral dances (LSJ).

choropsaltria (*χοροψάλτρια*; fem. of choropsaltes, χοροψάλτης, which is more modern); the woman kitharist who accompanied the chorus [by playing usually without plectrum];

See *psallein*.

chorus, choros (**χορός**; m. pr. chorós);

a) dance; an ensemble of rhythmical movements of the body, of the hands and the feet.   Another word for orchesis* (ὄρχησις);

b)   choir; ensemble of singers and dancers; the chorus in ancient drama.

c)   the place where the orchesis took place, especially in Homer; Od. VIII, 260 «λείηναν δὲ χορὸν, καλὸν δ᾽ εὔρυναν ἀγῶνα» "they levelled a *place for the dance*, and marked   out a fair wide ring" (transl. A. T. Murray: Od. vol. I, p. 277). Also Od. XVIII, v. 590 «ἐν δὲ χορόν, ποίκιλλε» ("therein he wrought a *dancing-floor*"; transl. A.T.M.).

In Sparta the *agorá* (ἀγορά; public square, meeting-place in ancient Greek cities) was called χορὸς; because youths used to dance therein the gymnopaedias; Paus. (III, ch. 11, § 9 «Σπαρτιάταις δὲ ἐπὶ τῆς ἀγορᾶς Πυθαέως τέ ἐστιν Ἀπόλλωνος καὶ Ἀρτέμιδος καὶ Λητοῦς ἀγάλματα· χορὸς δὲ οὗτος ὁ τόπος καλεῖται πᾶς, ὅτι ἐν ταῖς γυμνοπαιδίαις.....οἱ ἔφηβοι χοροὺς ἱστᾶσι τῷ Ἀπόλλωνι». ("At their meeting-place the Spartans have statues of Apollo Pythaeus, of Artemis and of Leto.   The whole of this place is called   *chorus* because at the gymnopaedias...youths perform dances in honour of Apollo").

chreon apocope (χρεῶν ἀποκοπή; m. pr. chreón apocopí); debt-cancelling. A kind of dance included (ap. Athen., XIV, 629 F, ch. 27) in a list of ludicrous dances; no information as to its figures and way of performance is given.   Cobet suggests that the expression is «κρεῶν ἀποκλοπή» = "meat theft"; this has some connection with a dance mentioned by Pollux (IV, 105): «μιμητικὴν δὲ ἐκάλουν δι᾽ ἧς ἐμιμοῦντο τοὺς ἐπὶ κλοπῇ τῶν ἑώλων μερῶν [κρεῶν] ἁλισκομένους» ("they called mimetic dancing that by which they imitated those arrested for stale-meat theft").

chresis (χρῆσις; m. pr. chrísis); according to Arist. Quint., one of the three parts of the melopoeia by which the melody is completed or realized (Mb p. 29, RPW-I p. 29): «χρῆσις δέ, ἡ ποιὰ τῆς μελῳδίας ἀπεργασία. Ταύτης δὲ πάλιν εἴδη τρία, ἀγωγή, πεττεία, πλοκή» ("*chresis* is a form of completion of the melody.   And there are three species (kinds) of it, agoge*, petteia*, ploke*).

chresmodos (χρησμῳδός; m. pr. chrismodós); one who delivers an oracle in song or in verse; singer of oracles.   An epithet of Apollo «Λοξίας ὁ χρησμῳδός» (for the double meaning of his oracles).   By extension chresmodos was applied to a prophet; one who prophesied.

chresmodia (χρησμῳδία; m. pr. chrismodía); the answer of an Oracle (μαντεῖον) delivered in song or in verse.   Also *chresmodema* (χρησμῴδημα), but principally the oracle.

The verb *chresmodein* (χρησμῳδεῖν; chrismodín) = to deliver an oracle in song (or in verse); to sing an oracle.

chroa, chroea (χρόα, χροιά;   m. pr. chróa, chriá); shade, nuance; a term signifying the particular division in each genus; it defines the variety of intervals composing the genus in each case.

Aristoxenus (Harm. II, pp. 50-52 Mb) recognizes six chroai (shades, divisions) in all three genera, namely two in the Diatonic (a) μαλακόν, Soft; b) σύντονον, Tense, one in the Enharmonic, and three in the Chromatic (Soft, Hemiolic and the Toniaeon or Tense). More details are given in each case separately: see under Diatonon*, Enharmonion* and Chromatikon*.

Cleon. (Isag. ch. 6, C.v.Jan p. 190; Mb p. 10): «Χρόα δέ ἐστι γένους εἰδικὴ διαίρεσις· χρόαι δέ εἰσιν αἱ ρηταὶ καὶ γνώριμοι ἕξ, ἁρμονίας μία, χρώματος τρεῖς, διατόνου δύο» ("Chroa is a specific division of the genus; and the chroai are six, precise and known; one of the Enharmonic, three of the Chromatic and one of the Diatonic").

Ptolemaeus recognized eight chroai: five in the Diatonic, one in the Enharmonic and two in the Chromatic; Porph. Comment., ed. I.D. p. 157, 21-29; (see also G. Pachymeres Harm. in Vincent "Notices" pp. 422-3).

Chroea is met also in the sense of tone-colour, "timbre". Gaud. (Isag. § 2, C.v.Jan p. 329; Mb I, p. 4): «χροιὰ δέ ἐστι, καθ' ἣν διαφέροιεν (ἂν) ἀλλήλων οἱ κατὰ τὸν αὐτὸν τόπον ἢ χρόνον φαινόμενοι, οἷον ἡ τοῦ λεγομένου μέλους φύσις ἐν φωνῇ καὶ τὰ ὅμοια» ("chroea is [the quality] by which notes [sounds] appearing [heard] on the same locus [pitch] or time differ from each other, as the vocal nature of the melos and the like").

See also Plut. De Mus. 1143E, ch. 34.

Chromatikon genos (Χρωματικὸν γένος) or simply Chroma (Χρῶμα).

The genus in which an interval of one tone and a half is used; thus the chromatic tetrachord would proceed by semitone, semitone, and one tone and a half, as follows: e - f - f$\sharp$ - a.

The names of the constituent notes of the chromatic tetrachord should be taken in accordance with their general order in the tetrachord (the interval between the Lichanos and the Mese considered as a simple one, not as a compound or as a leap); compare, in the following example, the names in both the Diatonic and the Chromatic tetrachords:

There were three divisions (chroai) of the Chromatic Genus: a) the μαλακὸν (Soft), b) the ἡμιόλιον (Hemiolic) and c) the τονιαῖον or σύντονον (Tense).

According to Anon. Bell. (§ 53, p. 57-59): a) the Soft is that in which the pycnon* (i.e. when the sum of the two small intervals (e-f-f♯ above) is less than the remainder of the tetrachord, (f♯-a above) is equal to three enharmonic dieseis minus one twelfth, i.e. the enharmonic diesis being $\frac{1}{4}$ of the tone, the chromatic pycnon will be equal to $3 \times \frac{1}{4} = \frac{3}{4}$ or $\frac{9}{12}$ minus $\frac{1}{12} = \frac{8}{12}$ of the tone. Thus the Soft Chromatic would proceed as follows:

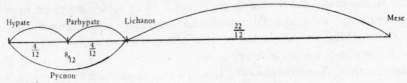

b) *The Hemiolic* was that in which the pycnon is equal to a semitone and one enharmonic diesis, i. e. $\frac{1}{2} + \frac{1}{4} = \frac{3}{4} = \frac{9}{12}$ of the tone:

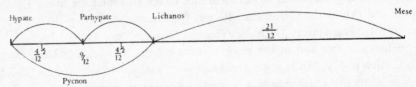

c) *The Tense* (*Syntonon*) is that in which the pycnon consists of two semitones (e-f-f♯) and the remainder is one and a half tones (f♯ - a). These definitions originated with Aristoxenus. Indeed, Aristoxenus (Harm. II, pp. 50-51 Mb) defines: a) The *Soft Chromatic* is that in which the pycnon consists of two minim chromatic dieseis («ἐκ δύο χρωματικῶν διέσεων ἐλαχίστων»), i.e. $\frac{4}{12} + \frac{4}{12} = \frac{8}{12}$ and the remainder of a semitone taken thrice (i.e. $\frac{1}{2} \times 3 = \frac{3}{2}$ or $\frac{18}{12}$) plus one chromatic diesis ($\frac{4}{12}$), i.e. $\frac{18}{12} + \frac{4}{12} = \frac{22}{12}$. Thus Aristoxenus' Soft Chromatic is the same as that of Anon. Bell. above, $\frac{4}{12} + \frac{4}{12} + \frac{22}{12}$.

b) *The Hemiolic* is that in which the pycnon is one and a half times the enharmonic pycnon ($\frac{1}{4} + \frac{1}{4} = \frac{1}{2} = \frac{9}{12}$ enh. pycnon; plus $\frac{3}{12}$, half of it), i.e. $\frac{6}{12} + \frac{3}{12} = \frac{9}{12}$; and each (Chromatic) diesis is one and a half times the enharmonic diesis, i.e. $\frac{3}{12} + 1\frac{1}{12} = 4\frac{1}{12}$. Thus the first two intervals of the Chromatic tetrachord (e - f - f♯) taken as a pycnon would be, according to Aristoxenus, $\frac{9}{12}$ of the tone, exactly as that of Anon. Bell. above.

c) *The Toniaeon* is the Tense of Anonymous. The Tense is defined by Anon. Bell. (p. 59) as "that in which the pycnon is a semitone"; this is an evident error, as the pycnon in the Tense is two semitones. Cleonides (Isag. ch. 7, C.v.J. p. 190; Mb p. 10) defines the three chroai of the Chromatic tetrachord in exactly the same sense though the phrasing differs slightly.

Arist. Quint. (Meib. II, i p. 18, RPW-I, p. 16) says that the Chroma (Χρῶμα, Colour) is so-called "because it is stretched by semitones" («τὸ δι᾿ ἡμιτονίων συντεινόμενον»).

Anon. Bell. (§ 26, pp. 30-31) on the other hand holds that "the Chroma is so-called either because it somewhat deviates from the Diatonic, or because it colours the other systems; and that it is sweetest and most plaintive" («Χρῶμα δέ, ἤτοι παρὰ τὸ τετράφθαι πως ἐκ τοῦ διατονικοῦ, ἢ παρὰ τὸ χρώζειν μὲν αὐτὸ τὰ ἄλλα συστήματα... ἔστι δὲ ἥδιστόν τε καὶ γοερώτατον»).

chronos (χρόνος); in a general sense, the time.

In poetry and metrics it was the duration, the quantity (in time) of a syllable. In music, the basic element of rhythm, the element of measuring.

According to Bacchius (Isag.; C.v.J. p. 313; Mb. p. 23) the chronoi were three:

a) the *short* (βραχύς; «ὁ ἐλάχιστος καὶ εἰς μερισμοὺς μὴ πίπτων» = "the smallest and indivisible");

b) *the long* (μακρός; «ὁ τούτου διπλάσιος» = "long, its double");

c) the *alogos, irrational* («ἄλογος; ὁ τοῦ μὲν βραχέος μακρότερος, τοῦ δὲ μακροῦ ἐλάσσων ὑπάρχων· ὁπόσῳ δέ ἐστιν ἐλάσσων ἢ μείζων διὰ τὸ λόγῳ δυσαπόδοτον, ἐξ αὐτοῦ τοῦ συμβεβηκότος ἄλογος ἐκλήθη» = "that which is longer than the short, and shorter than the long; and as it cannot be proved how much shorter or longer, it was called *irrational*").

Ἄλογος (irrational) time, according to Aristoxenus, is that which can be conceived and expressed by fractions of the first time (χρόνος πρῶτος, otherwise βραχύς, ἐλάχιστος). "First time is that which cannot be divided by any rhythmical way and on which are not placed two sounds, nor two syllables or two orchestic movements; the time-unit; chrónos δίσημος (double) that which contains twice the first; τρίσημος (triple) that which contains thrice the first; τετράσημος (τετράσημος; quadruple) that which contains four times the first; πεντάσημος (pentasemos; quintuple) five times". (Aristox. Rhythm, ed. Feussner, ch. 3; Anon. Bell. (§ 1, § 3). Thus, first time is indivisible (ἀσύνθετος, simple, not compound); all the others are compound (σύνθετοι).

The time of silence was called «χρόνος κενὸς» (*time empty* or *void*). Arist. Quint. (Mb. pp. 40-41, RPW-I pp. 38-39) admits two void times: the *leimma* (λεῖμμα), the short or simple silence, and the *prosthesis* (πρόσθεσις, addition) the long silence, double the first one. The end of a section was noted by a sign (‖ :) called (*diastole**, διαστολή; see also *parasemantike*); this signified a rest of indefinite duration.

See *rhythmos*.

Cleonides (Κλεονείδης, Κλεονίδης, or by some **Κλεωνίδης;** m. pr. Kleonídis).

Musical theorist placed in the 2nd cent. A.D.; nothing is known of his life. To him is now attributed the "Harmonic Introduction" (or Isagoge;

«Εἰσαγωγὴ 'Αρμονικὴ») which was before usually attributed to Euclid (Meibom "Ant. mus. auct. sept., gr. et lat.", vol. I, ii, pp. 1-22), or to the mathematician Pappus* of Alexandria, or to Zosimus (Ζώσιμος).

Ch. Ém. Ruelle in the Introduction ("Avertissement") to his translation of the Isagoge (pp. 1-15) discusses in detail the question of its authorship. The name of Euclid, he says, as author of the Isagoge appears in a MS in Venice of the 12th cent., and in many codices of the 14th-15th cents., probably from the same prototype. Other MSS give the name of Pappus, and many others that of Cleonides (Barberine II 86, Paris 2535 16th cent., Vatican 221, Florence). One MS of the National Library of Madrid gives the name of Zosimus, while that in the "Codex Vulganis" of Leyden attributes the authorship to an Anonymous. Various scholars of the 19th cent. do not agree as to the authorship; Vincent ascribes it to Pappus, while Westphal to a Pseudo-Euclid. Carl v. Jan attributes it to Cleonides for convincing reasons, now generally accepted.

First edition of a Latin translation (without the Greek text) was published by *Georgio Valla* under the name of Cleonides ("Cleonidae harmonicum introductorum"; Venice, 1497).

Carl v. Jan was the first to present the Greek text under the name of Cleonides in his "Mus. script. gr." (Leipzig, 1895; pp. 179-207).

A French translation with an interesting Introduction ("Avertissement") and commentary was published by *Ch. Ém. Ruelle* in his "Collection des auteurs grecs relatifs à la musique" (Paris, 1883; vol. III, pp. 16-41).

Cleonides' Isagoge is based on Aristoxenus' doctrines, and is considered as an important source of information regarding Aristoxenus' theoretical concepts and teaching.

Clonas (Κλονᾶς); 7th cent. B.C. aulete and composer.

He was born at Tegea of Arcadia in Peloponnesus (Τεγέα; hence his surname Tegeates, Τεγεάτης); but the Boeotians claimed that he was born at Thebes.

He lived soon after Terpander*, whose invention of the kitharodikos* nomos he followed by initiating the aulodikos* nomos (Heracl. ap. Plut. De Mus. 1132C, ch. 3; see also 1133A, ch. 5). He also introduced the prosodia*, and invented two aulodic nomoi, called Apothetos* and Schoenion* (Plut. Ibid.; Pollux IV, 79); see under *aulodia*. Clonas composed elegies and epic songs.

comma (κόμμα, τό, neut.); a) the difference between seven octaves and twelve fifths. This was the Pythagorean comma or diatonic comma. The comma of Didymus or Didymean comma, also called syntonic or simply "comma", was the difference between a major tone (9:8) and a minor tone (10:9), i.e. 81:80, or between a diatonic semitone (16:15) and a Pythagorean limma (256:243), i.e. 3888:3840, or 81:80.

b) *comma* (from κόπτω = to cut off) was also a poetic or melodic section. The cómmata (κόμματα; pl.) were small sections which followed each other during the nomos.

The adj. *κομματικὸς* (*commatikós*) was used for the song which was divided into sections. The neut. form, however (*κομματικόν*; *commatikón*) together with the word melos was a synonym of *commós**.

commos (**κομμός**; from κόπτω = to cut off); stroke, beat; beating of the head and the breast while lamenting; hence, lamentation. Commos was the lamentation, the dirge in classical drama; it was sung alternately by the actors and the chorus. Arist. (Poetics, 1452B, ch. 12,9): «*κομμὸς δὲ θρῆνος κοινὸς χοροῦ καὶ ἀπὸ σκηνῆς*» ("*commós* is a common lamentation of the chorus and those [the actors] on the stage").

The commos was also called *κομματικὸν μέλος* (*commatikón melos*).

composition types (εἴδη συνθέσεως)

The principal types of musical composition were the following:

a) the *kitharodía** (*κιθαρῳδία*); singing to kithara accompaniment; this was the most ancient kind of (mixed) musical composition.   A variety of it was the *lyrodía* (*λυρῳδία*), which never became popular;

b) the *aulodia** (*αὐλῳδία*); singing to aulos accompaniment;

c) the *psile kitharisis** (*ψιλὴ κιθάρισις*), kithara solo;

d) the *psile aulesis** (*ψιλὴ αὔλησις*), aulos solo;

e) the *enaulos kitharisis** (*ἔναυλος κιθάρισις*) kithara solo with aulos accompaniment; a variety of this was the pariambis* (*παριαμβίς*);

f) the *nomos** (*νόμος*); the most important type of composition;

g) various *choral, lyrical* and *dramatic* compositions.

Of the above, those under c, d, e and certain classes of nomos (f) were purely musical (instrumental) compositions. Many other compositions are treated under their special headings.

Corinna (**Κόριννα**); lyric poetess of the 6th cent. B.C. She was born in Boeotia (at Tanagra or at Thebes), and was a pupil of Myrtis*. According to Suidas she defeated Pindar five times at lyric contests. She composed lyric nomoi and epigrams totalling five volumes (Suid. «ἐνίκησε δὲ πεντάκις ὡς λόγος Πίνδαρον. Ἔγραφε βιβλία πέντε (ε) καὶ ἐπιγράμματα καὶ νόμους λυρικούς»).

See Brgk PLG, III pp. 543-553 and Anth. Lyr., pp. 269-271, small fragments.
Also Page PMG Frgs. 654-695A, pp. 325-358.

cyclios (**κύκλιος**; m. pr. kíklios); circular, round in a general sense (from κύκλος = circle).

κύκλιος χορὸς (cyclios, *circular chorus*): a dance in circular formation of the dancers; especially danced around the altar (chiefly of Dionysus); the dithyramb. Callimachus Hymn to Delos, v. 313 «...περὶ βωμὸν κύκλιον ὠρχήσαντο, χοροῦ δὲ ἡγήσατο Θησεύς» ("they danced the *circular* dance around the altar, and Theseus led the chorus").

κύκλιοι αὐληταὶ (*cyclioi auletai*; pl.); the auletai who played the aulos at circular dances.

κύκλια μέλη (*cyclia mele*; cyclic songs); lyric and chiefly dithyrambic songs (having the same subject). Pollux (IV, 78) mentions «κύκλιοι νόμοι», "*cyclic nomoi*" («οἱ δὲ Εὐΐου νόμοι, κύκλιοι»; "and the nomoi of Euius* are *cyclic*"); but no explanation is given as to their character.

Generally speaking the cyclic dances and songs were connected chiefly with the dithyramb and with Dionysus.

cymbala, cymbals (κύμβαλα, pl.; m. pr. kímvala); percussion instrument consisting, like modern cymbals, of two hollow hemispheric metal plates. The cymbals were of Asiatic origin, and were first used in the orgiastic cults of Cybele and later of Dionysus (Bacchus). Plut. Coniugalia Praecepta (Γαμικὰ Παραγγέλματα) 144E «οἱ δὲ κυμβάλοις καὶ τυμπάνοις ἄχθονται» ("and they are annoyed by the *cymbals* and the tambours").

Another word for cymbal was βακύλλιον (bakyllion*) or βαβούλιον (baboulion);

The cymbals, for the Greeks, were devoid of any real musical value.

The verb κυμβαλίζειν (*cymbalizein*) = to play the cymbals.

Κυμβαλιστὴς (*cymbalistes*) and κυμβαλοκρούστης (*cymbalokroustes*), the player of cymbals; fem. κυμβαλίστρια (*cymbalistria*);

κυμβαλισμὸς (*cymbalismos*), the playing of cymbals;

κυμβάλιον (*cymbalion*), dimin. of κύμβαλον; a small cymbal.

D

dactylikos (δακτυλικός; m. pr. dactilikós).

a) a kind of aulos used for the hyporchema*, or also a kind of melos (song); Pollux (IV, 82): «καὶ δακτυλικοὺς (pl.) τοὺς ἐπὶ ὑπορχήμασιν [αὐλούς], οἱ δέ, ταῦτα οὐκ αὐλῶν ἀλλὰ μελῶν εἴδη εἶναι λέγουσιν» ("they call *dactylic* those [auloi] played at the hyporchemata; but others say that these are not kinds of aulos but of tunes"). See embaterios* aulos; also Athen. IV, 176F, ch. 79.

b) *dactylikon* (δακτυλικόν; neut.); a stringed instrument, probably a kind of kithara.

Pollux (IV, 66) «τὸ μέντοι τῶν ψιλῶν κιθαριστῶν ὄργανον, ὃ καὶ πυθικὸν ὀνομάζεται, δακτυλικόν τινες κεκλήκασι» ("the instrument of the kithara-soloists, which is also called pythic, was by some people called *dactylikon*").

Note. Some scholars consider the word "dactylikos", as above, as an adjective (from dactylos, finger), and interpret it as meaning "played by the fingers"; this however would not make any sense since all instruments are mostly played by using the fingers (dáctyloi). Perhaps it would make more sense if "dactylikos" (aulos) was interpreted as "having the width of a finger".

dactylos (δάκτυλος; m. pr. dáktilos); finger.

a) In plur. *dactyloi* (*δάκτυλοι*); a kind of simple and static but varied dance.

Athen. (XIV, 629 D, ch. 27): «τὰ δὲ στασιμώτερα καὶ ποικιλώτερα καὶ τὴν ὄρχησιν ἁπλουστέραν ἔχοντα καλεῖται δάκτυλοι, ἰαμβική...», etc. ("those kinds of dance, more static and varied but simpler in dance-figures, are called *dactyloi*, iambike...", etc.).

Note: The word «ποικιλώτερα» in the text is read by some «πυκνότερα» (in closer order) or «ἀποικιλώτερα» (less varied).

b) *dactylos* (*dactyl*); the well-known metrical foot, consisting of one long and two short syllables, -υυ.

Dactylic genus was the genus in which the relation between thesis and arsis was 2 to 2.

Iambic dactylos (δάκτυλος ὁ κατὰ ἴαμβον); a metrical foot consisting of the following schema υ-υ-, otherwise diiambus (διίαμβος); Arist. Quint. De Mus., Mb p. 48, RPW-I p. 45.

Dactylic metre (*δακτυλικὸν μέτρον*); a metre consisting of dactyls; Arist. Quint. op. cit., Mb p. 50, RPW-I p. 45.

Dactylic hexameter (*δακτυλικὸν ἑξάμετρον*); a rhythmic section consisting of six dactylic feet; also called "Heroic hexameter".

Damon (Δάμων); 5th cent. B.C. philosopher and theorist; he was born at Athens (commune of Oa), and lived around 430 B.C. One of the most important musical theorists of the Pre-Aristoxenean period. He was a pupil of the sophist Prodicus and of the musician Lamprocles*, and teacher of the musician Dracon* and, as it is said, of Pericles himself; according to Diog. Laertius (II, ch. 5, § 19) he was a teacher of music to Socrates too.

Being highly educated he exercised a great influence, and Plato mentions him with particular esteem and respect. In his Republic (IV, 424C) Damon is cited by Socrates in a phrase which shows deep respect for his views on the ethical value of music: "because nowhere could the styles of music be changed without shaking the fundamental laws of society, *as Damon says*

71

and I agree" («οὐδαμοῦ γὰρ κινοῦνται μουσικῆς τρόποι ἄνευ πολιτικῶν νόμων τῶν μεγίστων, ὡς φησί τε Δάμων καὶ ἐγὼ πείθομαι»). Damon's name is mentioned by Plato also in Laches III, 180D, XXVI 197D, XXIX 200A.

Damon's views regarding the inner relation of the soul to music (song and dance) are expressed in Athenaeus (XIV, 624C, ch. 25). It seems also that Aristides owes to Damon much of his conception of the educational value of music (see esp. Ar. Quint. II, 14, Mb p. 94, RPWI p. 80, where Damon and his School is cited).

Damon became an intimate friend of Pericles to whom he used to submit daring political suggestions; owing to these political activities he was ostracized.

Cicero considered him the first and most original of all the musicians of the Pre-Aristoxenean time.

Of Damon's writings only some fragments from a work entitled "Areopagos" (Ἀρεόπαγος), on Rhythm and on the ethical value of music, have been preserved.

Cf. *Fr. Lasserre*: Plutarque de la Musique, chs. 6-7, pp. 53-95 "Damon à Athènes" and "La postérité de l'éthique damonienne"). *Ev. Moutsopoulos*: "La Musique dans l'oeuvre de PLATON" IIIe partie, ch. II, 1) "L'ère pré-damonienne" pp. 175-185; 2) "L'ère damonienne et post-damonienne", pp. 185-197.

daphnephorika mele; pl. (**δαφνηφορικὰ μέλη**; m. pr. daphniphoriká méli) from δαφνηφορεῖν = to bear branches or crowns of laurel; songs sung to dancing in honour of Daphnephoros (Δαφνηφόρος) Apollo. The dancers used to bear branches of laurel; Pollux IV, 53.

According to Proclus (Chrest. 26) the "daphnephorika" belonged to a class of the Partheneia*: «δάφνας γὰρ ἐν Βοιωτίᾳ δι' ἐννεατηρίδος εἰς τὰ τοῦ Ἀπόλλωνος κομίζοντες οἱ ἱερεῖς, ἐξύμνουν αὐτὸν διὰ χοροῦ παρθένων» ("because in Boeotia every nine years the priests of Apollo carrying laurels glorify him with a chorus of maidens").

δαφνηφορία, ἡ, fem. (*daphnephoria*); the carrying of laurels. Proclus (Ib.) «ἡ δὲ δαφνηφορία, ξύλον ἐλαίας καταστρέφουσι δάφναις καὶ ποικίλοις ἄνθεσιν» ("the *daphnephoria* is [when they] decorate [or crown] with laurels and various flowers").

deikelistes (**δεικηλιστής**; m. pr. dikilistís) Dor. type deikeliktas (δεικηλίκτας); a comedian or mime who imitated various comic characters; an actor, buffoon especially in Laconia. EM., 260, 42 «δεικηλισταί, μιμηταὶ παρὰ Λάκωσιν» ("*deikelistai* [pl.]; mimes among Lacedaemons").

Athenaeus (XIV, 621F, ch. 15) says that there were many other designations («προσηγορίαι») in various parts for the deikelistai; so, the Sicyonians call them *phallophoroi* (φαλλοφόροι; phallus-bearers), others [call them] *autokabdaloi** (*improvisers*) and others *phlyakes*, φλύακες (Dorian type of φλύαροι;

72

nonsense-utterers, clowns, buffoons), while the Thebans, "who use to give special names for many things", call them *ethelontai* (ἐθελονταί; volunteers). Most people called them sophists (σοφισταί) too.

The *autokabdaloi* (αὐτοκάβδαλοι), as Semus of Delos says in his book "On Paeans" (ap. Athen. Ib. 622B, ch. 16), were also called *iamboi** (ἴαμβοι) like their poems.

deikelistike (δεικηλιστική; m. pr. dikilistikí); a kind of pantomimic dance, performed in popular fairs by masked mimes who imitated various comic characters (deikelistai).

demetroulos (δημήτρουλος; m. pr. dimítroulos); a hymn to Demeter.

See under *ioulos* (ἴουλος).

Demodocus (Δημόδοκος; m. pr. Dimódocos); one of the oldest epic singers. He was blind, and lived in the palace of Alkinoos, king of the Phaeacians (Φαία-κες). He is mentioned in Homer's Odyssey (IX, 44 ff). When Ulysses, after his last shipwreck, took refuge in the island of the Phaeacians, his last stop before the end of his Odyssey, he was given a feast of honour by king Alkinoos. During the banquet, Demodocus, at Ulysses' insistance, sang his exploits which led to the capture of Troy, causing him great emotion.

(See also Paus. III, ch. 18, § 11).

Heracl. Pont. (ap. Plut. 1132B, ch. 3) in his "Collection" mentions Demo-docus of Kerkyra (Δημόδοκον Κερκυραῖον) among the oldest musicians, and as having sung the capture of Troy, and the marriage of Aphrodite and Hephae-stus (Vulcan).

2. Another epic singer (ἀοιδός) with the same name is mentioned by Demetrius Phalereus (Δημήτριος Φαληρεύς). He was left by Agamemnon to protect Clytemnestra, but he was taken by Aegisthus to a deserted island and left there as prey to wild beasts or vultures.

Cf. Sextus Empir. Book VI, § 12.

According to a legend he was a brother of Phemius*.

3. A gnomic (didactic) poet (not to be confused with Nos. 1 and 2 above) of the 6th c. B.C. from the island of Leros. Some short fragments of his Epi-grams and Iambuses have been preserved.

Bergk PLG II, pp. 442-3, and Anth. Lyr., pp. 47-48.

dendryazousa (δενδρυάζουσα; m. pr. dendriázousa); a term used by singing teachers (phonaskoi) for a certain kind of tone (perhaps veiled tone [?], sug-gested by Dr E. K. Borthwick). Ael. Dion. 119: «φωνήν τινα καλοῦσιν οἱ φωνασκοὶ δενδρυάζουσαν».

diaeidein (διαείδειν; m. pr. diaïdin) and **diadein** (διάδειν);

    a)   to sing for prize, or to compete in singing;

    b)   to be dissonant, oppos. *synadein* (LSJ and Dem.).

Diagoras (Διαγόρας); c. middle of 5th cent. B.C. (Suidas says 78th Olympiad, i.e. 468-465 B.C.). Poet-composer and philosopher from Melos (Μῆλος), surnamed the Atheist because of his atheistic works where he ridiculed the Phrygian cult and gods. Suidas says that he was a slave, and was bought by the philosopher Democritus of Abdera (Δημόκριτος ὁ Ἀβδηρίτης) for ten thousand drachmas and became his pupil. He lived after Pindar and Bacchylides, and was older than Melanippides.

Because of his atheistic ideas and the disclosing of the secrets of the mysteries, he was sentenced to death; he was saved by flight. According to a legend he died in a shipwreck, while Suidas says that he settled and died in Corinth.

See Brgk PLG III, pp. 562-563 and Anth. Lyr., p. 274 two small fragments without title.

diagramma, diagram (διάγραμμα); a plan, a drawing, a figure, used to help students to visualize the acoustical differences in all genera.

Bacch. (Isag. § 62; C.v.J. p. 305, Mb p. 15) «*Διάγραμμά ἐστι σχῆμα ἐπίπεδον εἰς ὃ πᾶν γένος μελῳδεῖται. Διαγράμματι δὲ χρώμεθα ἵνα τὰ τῇ ἀκοῇ δύσληπτα πρὸ ὀφθαλμῶν τοῖς μανθάνουσι φαίνηται*» (= "*Diagram* is a flat figure through which every genus can be sung. The purpose of the diagram is to help pupils to visualize what is difficult to perceive by hearing").

Cleon. (Isag. ch. 14, C.v.J. p. 207; Mb p. 22): «*Διάγραμμα δὲ σχῆμα ἐπίπεδον τὰς τῶν μελῳδουμένων περιέχον δυνάμεις*» ("*Diagram* is a flat figure containing [defining] the functions of notes in a system"; see *dynamis*).

According to Phaenias it was Stratonicus the Athenian who first introduced the diagram (Athen. VIII, 352C, ch. 46; FHG II, 298). The subdivision of the intervals into quarter-tones on the diagram was called "katapycnosis of the diagram" («καταπύκνωσις τοῦ διαγράμματος»); Aristoxenus (Harm. I, p. 28, 1 Mb): «ἐν ταῖς τῶν διαγραμμάτων καταπυκνώσεσιν» ("in the subdivisions [compressions] of the diagrams"); see also Ib. I., p. 7, 32.

    See *katapycnosis**.

diagyios, foot (διάγυιος; m. pr. diágios); paeon diagyios consisting of a long thesis and a short and a long arsis (-υ-).

    Cf. Aristides De Mus., Mb p. 38, RPW-I p. 37 and *pous**.

diakteria (διακτηρία; m. pr. diaktiría); a doubtful word met in Theophr. Hist. Plant IV, 11,5, meaning probably the passing through of the air. Sir A. Hort translates as "accompaniment" (Enquiry into Plants, vol. I, p. 372 "the opening of the reed-tongues is well closed, which is a good thing for the purpose

74

of *accompaniment*"; «συμμύειν δὲ τὸ στόμα τῶν γλωττῶν, ὃ πρὸς τὴν διακτη- ρίαν εἶναι χρήσιμον»). The word appears in some editions as «διακτορία»; it might be perhaps *διατορία*.

(See under *diatoria*).

dialectos (**διάλεκτος**; m. pr. diálectos); in a general sense, discourse, conver- sation, speech, language; the language of a country (Dem., LSJ). In music it is met with the meaning of style; mode of expression; phrasing (Th. Reinach: "phrasé"; H. Weil et Th. Rein. Plut. De la Mus., Note 359, p. 140). Krouma- tike dialectos (ap. Plut. De Mus., 1132B, ch. 21) = musical (or intrumental) style. Th. Reinach translates "le dessin mélodique exécuté sur l'instrument" (Ibid, Note 202, p. 85).

On musical instruments: quality, timbre.

See *krouma**.

dialepsis (**διάληψις**; m. pr. diálipsis); a term according to which a string of the kithara or of the lyra was slightly touched at the middle of its length and produced the 8ve (harmonic).

Cf. Th. Reinach "Lyre" (in D.A.Gr. R., vol. VI, pp. 1437-51).
See *syrigmos*.

dia pason (**διὰ πασῶν**); through all strings. The complete expression would be «ἡ διὰ πασῶν τῶν χορδῶν συμφωνία» = concord through all notes; the concord between the first and the last note. Hence the interval of the octave. Bacch. (Isag. § 11; C.v.J. p. 294; Mb p. 3): «τὴν δὲ διὰ πασῶν [δηλοῦσι] προσλαμβανόμενος καὶ μέση» ("and [they define] the "dia pason" [octave] as the interval between the proslambanomenos* and the mese*", i.e. the octave).

The octave was the most perfect concord (see *symphonia**);

Arist. Probl. XIX, 35a «ἡ διὰ πασῶν καλλίστη συμφωνία».

Ptolemaeus considers the interval of the octave as the best and most unify- ing of the *homophones**. The "*dis dia-pason*" (δὶς διὰ-πασῶν) was the double-octave; as Bacchius says (Ib.) the interval between the proslambanomenos and the nete hyperbolaeon:

See also Arist. Probl. XIX, 14.

b) The term «διὰ πασῶν» (dia pason) replaced, after Aristoxenus' time,

75

the term *harmonia**. Nicom. (Enchir. ch. 9; C.v.J. p. 252, Mb p. 16) «ἁρμονίαν μὲν καλοῦντες [οἱ παλαιότατοι] τὴν διὰ πασῶν» (="the *dia pason* was called [by the most ancients] *harmonia*").

dia pente (διὰ πέντε); «ἡ διὰ πέντε χορδῶν συμφωνία», "concord through five strings"; the interval of the perfect 5th. By the Pythagoreans it was called *δι' ὀξειῶν χορδῶν* (= through *high-pitched* strings) or *διοξεῖα (dioxeia**)*.

Nicom. (Enchir. ch. 9; C.v.J. p. 252; Mb p. 17) quoting Philolaus' definition: "the size of harmonia is equal to one syllaba* (a 4th) and one di' oxeion (a 5th); because from Hypate to Mese it is a 4th, and from Mese to the Nete it is a 5th".

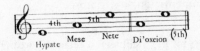

"And the 5th is greater than the 4th by one tone" («τὸ δὲ δι' ὀξειῶν μεῖζον τᾶς συλλαβᾶς ἐπογδόῳ»).

See *symphonia-symphonoi*, and *homophonia-homophonoi*.

diaphonia (διαφωνία); discord.

Cleonides (Isag. ch. 6; C.v.J. p. 188; Mb p. 8) defines diaphonia as the refusal of two notes to combine (or to unite, to amalgamate) so that they grate on the ear («διαφωνία δὲ τοὐναντίον δύο φθόγγων ἀμιξαὶ [Mb «ἀμιξία»], ὥστε μὴ κραθῆναι, ἀλλὰ τραχυνθῆναι τὴν ἀκοήν»).

diaphonoi phthongoi (διάφωνοι φθόγγοι); discordant notes or sounds; those which do not blend.

Gaudentius (Isag. ch. 8; C.v.J. pp. 337-8; Mb p. 11) gives the following definition of "diaphonoi": "but when discordant sounds are struck or blown at the same time («ἅμα κρουομένων ἢ αὐλουμένων») there seems to be nothing of identity in the relation of the lower note to the higher, or of the higher to the lower"; transl. H. S. Macran (in Aristox. Harm. p. 235).

See also Bacch. Isag. § 59 (C.v.J. p. 305; Mb. p. 14); Arist. Quint., Mb. p. 12, RPW-I p. 10. As the ancient Greeks recognized as concords the intervals of the 8ve, the 4th and the 5th, all the rest were discords.

Note: The verb διαφωνεῖν (diaphonein) signified to disagree; speaking of intervals, to be in discord, not to blend.

diapsalma (διάψαλμα); **diapselaphema (διαψηλάφημα**; m. pr. diapsiláphima); an instrumental interlude between two parts of a vocal (or choral) piece. From the verb διαψηλαφεῖν = to touch.

76

As diapsalma is derived from the verb διαψάλλειν (as ψάλλειν in a stronger sense) which means to play on a stringed instrument with the fingers (without plectrum), the term should be interpreted as an interlude on the kithara or another stringed instrument; this same view stands too for the diapselaphema. Hesychius says that diapsalma is a change or variation of the vocal melody or rhythm («μουσικοῦ μέλους ἢ ρυθμοῦ...ἐναλλαγή»). Also Suidas says «μέλους ἐναλλαγή» ("a change of melody"). Anon. (Bell. § 3, p. 22) calls *diapselaphemata* (pl.) those irregular mele which are performed on instruments.

See *kechymena mele;* also *diaulion.*

diaschisma (διάσχισμα) was by ancient theoreticians used for the distance which is equal to half of the minor semitone, or the difference between four perfect fifths and two major thirds on one hand, and three octaves on the other hand (or otherwise the interval by which the three octaves exceed the ensemble of four perfect fifths and two major thirds); or the interval by which two diatonic semitones exceed a major tone.

diastasis (διάστασις); interval, the distance between two sounds different in pitch. This term is used by Aristoxenus; in Harm. El. (I, p. 3,35 Mb) he says «Περὶ τῆς τοῦ βαρέος τε καὶ ὀξέος διαστάσεως» ("about *the interval* between the low and high [in pitch]").

See also Ibid I p. 13, 32; p. 14, 9; 18, 30 etc.

diastema (διάστημα; m. pr. diástima); the distance between two notes of different pitch; interval.

Cleon. (Isag. ch. 1; C.v.J. p. 179; Mb 1) «διάστημα δὲ τὸ περιεχόμενον ὑπὸ δύο φθόγγων ἀνομοίων ὀξύτητι καὶ βαρύτητι» ("*interval* is what is bound by two notes differing as to height and depth"). Same definition in Bacchius' Isagoge.

Anon. (Bell. § 22, p. 30): «διάστημα δ' ἐστὶ τὸ περιεχόμενον ὑπὸ δύο φθόγγων ἀνομοίων τῇ τάσει, τοῦ μὲν ὀξυτέρου, τοῦ δὲ βαρυτέρου» ("*interval* is what is contained between two notes different in pitch, of which one is higher and the other lower"). In a Fragment of a MS (ed. by Vincent in "Notices" p. 234) the definition is as follows «Διάστημα δ' εἶναι μέγεθος φωνῆς ὑπὸ δυοῖν περιεχόμενον φθόγγων» ("*Interval* is the extent [space] of voice contained between two notes").

Nicomachus (Ench. ch. 12; C.v.J. p. 261; Mb p. 24) employs the term «μεταξύτης» (fem. ἡ; *metaxytes*, m. pr. metaxítis) = that which is in between; «Διάστημα, he writes, δ' ἐστὶ δυοῖν φθόγγων μεταξύτης» ("*Interval* is that which is between two notes").

There were various differences between the intervals;

a) as to the size; b) as to the genus; c) as to concord and discord; d) between the compound and simple (σύνθετα, ἀσύνθετα); e) between reta (ρητά, rational) and aloga (ἄλογα, irrational); Cf. Aristox. Harm. I. p. 16, 22-30; Cleon. op. cit., ch. 5, C.v.J. p. 187, Mb p. 8; Anon. Bell. § 58, pp. 71-72 etc.

The intervals were called ἄρτια (even) and περιττὰ (odd) in relation to the number of dieseis they contained; e.g. the semitone and the tone are even as they contain two and four dieseis ($\frac{1}{4}$ tone each) respectively. The interval between the Parhypate and the Lichanos in the Soft Diatonon* is odd as it contains three dieseis.

diastematike kinesis (διαστηματικὴ κίνησις; m. pr. diastimatikí kínisis), melodic motion by intervals; opp. συνεχὴς κίνησις = continuous motion.

Aristox. (Harm. I., p. 8, 18-19 Mb: «δύο τινές εἰσιν ἰδέαι κινήσεως, ἥτε συνεχὴς καὶ ἡ διαστηματικὴ»* ("the species of motion are two, the continuous and that *by intervals*"). Further, Aristoxenus (Ibid p. 10, 9) calls the diastematic motion, melodic (μελῳδική), i.e. employed in singing.

See the same expression about the «συνεχὴς τε καὶ λογικὴ» ("the continuous motion of speech") and the «διαστηματικὴ τε καὶ μελῳδικὴ» ("the diastematic and melodic") motion, in Cleon. op. cit., ch. 2 (C.v.J. p. 180; Mb p. 2); also under the word *syneches*.

diastole (διαστολή; m. pr. diastolí); the clear and distinct enunciation of the successive notes in a song or an instrumental piece. Also a rest, pause, interruption of an indefinite duration; it was marked by a double vertical line with two dots to the right II:. Man. Bryen. (Harm., sect. III p. 480; ed. Wallis) "the *diastole* is used in both the singing (ode) and notation of music; it asks for a rest and separates those preceding from those which follow" («ἡ δὲ διαστολή, ἐπί τε τῆς ᾠδῆς καὶ τῆς κρουματογραφίας παραλαμβάνεται, ἀναπαύουσα καὶ χωρίζουσα τὰ προάγοντα ἀπὸ τῶν ἐπιφερομένων»).

Sergius (p. 1836, ap. A. J. H. Vincent's "Notices" p. 221) says "*Diastole est nota contraria hyphen*" = "The diastole is a sign opposite to the hyphen*" (which is a tie joining two notes).

Man. Bryennius includes the diastole in the twelve schemata (figures) of melos and discusses it as the last of them (pp. 479-480).

dia tessaron (διὰ τεσσάρων); «ἡ διὰ τεσσάρων χορδῶν συμφωνία», "concord through four strings"; the interval of the perfect 4th; called by the Pythagoreans *syllabe** or *syllaba*. Ratio 4:3.

Arist. Quint. (Mb p. 17, RPW-I p. 15) «παρὰ μὲν τοῖς παλαιοῖς τὸ μὲν διὰ τεσσάρων ἐκαλεῖτο συλλαβὴ» ("by the ancients the interval of the fourth was called *syllabé*"). Ἐπιδιατεσσάρων was called the higher fourth, and ὑποδιατεσσάρων the lower fourth.

See *dia pente, symphonia* and *homophonia*.

diatome (διατομή; m. pr. *diatomí*): perforation, finger-hole of aulos or syrinx. See under *trema*.

Diatonon genos (διάτονον γένος); the genus* in which use was made of tones and semitones. *Διάτονος* (from the verb diateinein, διατείνειν = to stretch, to distend) = tense. Nicom. Ench., ch. 12 (C.v.J. p. 262; Mb. p. 25): "it is called *diatonic* because alone out of all the other genera it proceeds by tones" («διατονικὸν καλεῖται ἐκ τοῦ προχωρεῖν διὰ τῶν τόνων μονώτατον τῶν ἄλλων»). Anon. Bell. (§ 25, p. 30): "if the melody proceeds by semitone and tone, it creates the so-called *diatonon* genus" («εἰ μὲν πρὸς ἡμιτόνιον καὶ τόνον προκόπτοι τὰ τῆς μελῳδίας, τὸ καλούμενον διάτονον ποιεῖ γένος»).

There were two varieties or divisions (chroai) of the Diatonic, the *μαλακὸν* (*soft*, mild) and the *σύντονον* (*tense*, sharp); a) *the Soft* is that in which the order and species of intervals (from low to high) are as follows: Hypate, ½ tone-Parhypate, ¾ or 9/12 of tone [three dieseis] —Lichanos, 5/4 or 15/12 of tone [five dieseis] —Mese (see ex. a below);

b) the *Tense* is that in which the intervals are: semitone, tone, tone (b). etc. Anon. Bell. (§ 54, pp. 59-61) defines the intervals of the Soft as semitone, nine twelfths (9/12) [and consequently 15/12 for the remainder]. Both intervals of the Soft should be considered as simple intervals (not compound) in the sense that between each two notes no other note intervenes in the same genus (Cf. *σύνθετος, ἀσύνθετος; synthetos, asynthetos**).

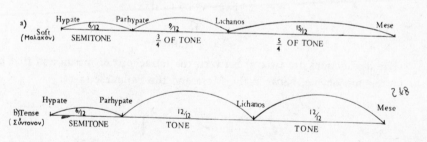

The Diatonic genus was the oldest of the three genera and was considered as simpler, more natural, as also "more masculine and austerer" (Anon. Bell. § 26, p. 30).

Aristides says that the voice in the Diatonic is more forcefully distended («ἐπειδὴ σφοδρότερον ἡ φωνὴ κατ᾽ αὐτὸ διατείνεται»; Mb. p. 18, RPW-I pp. 15-16).

Διατονικὸν μέλος (*Diatonic melody*) is the melody which uses the Diatonic genus (Cleon. op. cit., ch. 6, C.v.J. p. 189; Mb., p. 9; «Διατονικὸν [μέλος] μὲν οὖν ἐστι τὸ τῇ διατονικῇ διαιρέσει χρώμενον»).

diatoros (διάτορος); of sound, piercing, high-pitched. Suid. «διάτορον, ἐξά-κουστον, ὀξύτερον, μεγαλόφωνον» ("*diatoros*; distinctly heard, high-pitched, loud-voiced"). *diatoría* = piercing music; "high-pitched music" (LSJ).

diaulia (διαυλία; m. pr. diavlía); an aulos duet (Hes.).

diaulion (διαύλιον; m. pr. diávlion); an interlude for solo aulos performed between two parts of the choral song, during a pause of the chorus. Cf. *diapsalma*. The word appears also as διαύλειον (diauleion) in Suidas.

diaulos, or **didymoi auloi** (δίαυλος, δίδυμοι αὐλοί; m. pr. díavlos, dídimi avlí); double-aulos, twin-auloi. Also called δικάλαμος (*dicálamus*, double pipe) and *dizyges auloi* (δίζυγες αὐλοί; double-auloi, pipes).

Nonnos Dion. (XL, 227-8 «καὶ Κλεόχου Βερέκυντες ὑπὸ στόμα δίζυγες αὐλοὶ φρικτὸν ἐμυκήσαντο Λίβυν γόον» ("*the double* Berecyntian *pipes* in the mouth of Cleochos droned a gruesome Libyan lament"; transl. W.H.D. Rouse, v. III, p. 171).

Cf. *aulos; dizygoi auloi.*

See PLATES I + II

diazeuxis (διάζευξις; m. pr. diázefxis); disjunction. A term to designate the disjunction of two tetrachords, i.e. when a whole tone separated the end of a tetrachord and the beginning of the next one,

e.g.   e - f - g - a - b - c - d - e
↑
disjunction

The disjunctions are two: a) between the tetrachord of meson and that of the diezeugmenon, i.e. between the Mese and the Paramese (a-b):

b) between the tetrachord of synemmenon and that of the hyperbolaeon (i.e. between the nete synemmenon and the nete diezeugmenon, d-e; cf. Bacch. Isag. § 39, C.v.J. p. 301, Mb p. 10).

See also: *hypodiazeuxis, paradiazeuxis* and *hyperdiazeuxis.*

80

dichordos (δίχορδος) Adj., having two strings. Sopater: "dichordos pektis" ("two-stringed pektis"); see the text under *pektis**.

dichordon, n. neut.; an instrument with two strings. Euphro (Εὔφρων): "Brothers" («Ἀδελφοί», ap. T. Kock Com. Att. Frg., vol. III, p. 318) v. 34 «καὶ πρὸς τὸ δίχορδον ἐτερέτιζες» ("you were humming [a tune] to the accompaniment of the *dichordon*")

dichoria (διχορία); subdivision of a chorus into two parts. Pollux IV, 107 (see the text under *hemichorion**).

Didymus (Δίδυμος; m. pr. Dídimos); b. c. 63 B.C.; d. 10 A.D.; grammarian from Alexandria (Ἀλεξάνδρεια, surnamed «ὁ Ἀλεξανδρεύς», Alexandréfs). He was surnamed also "Chalkénteros" («Χαλκέντερος»=having copper-intestines, hard-working, indefatigable, untiring) "for his tenacity on books" (Suid.), and "Bibliolathas" («Βιβλιολάθας»; forgetting the books) because having written a very great number of books (according to Suidas, 3500!) he could not remember them (Athen. IV, 139C, ch. 17). He wrote a theoretical work on music, which is lost, mentioned by Ptolemy and Porphyry, in which he discussed the theories of Pythagoras and Aristoxenus. He was credited with the definition of the so-called Didymean comma, or comma of Didymus (see comma), which is the difference between a major tone (9:8) and a minor tone (10:9), i.e. 81:80.

See *diesis*.

diesis (δίεσις) from the verb διίημι (diíemi) = to pass, or allow something to pass through; to throw something through etc.; in general use: the passing through.

In music it is a term with various meanings. For most theoreticians it signified the quarter-tone, called δίεσις τεταρτημόριος (*diesis tetartemorios*). Theon of Smyrna (ch. 12, p. 87) says "*Diesis* according to the school of Aristoxenus is the quarter-tone, while the Pythagoreans [called *diesis* the semitone, $\frac{1}{2}$ of a tone"; see also M. Psellus "Syntagma" «Μουσικῆς Σύνοψις ἠκριβωμένη» (Paris, 1545; p. 22). By many writers diesis was generally used for any interval smaller than the semitone, or the smallest possible interval. According to Aristoxenus (Harm. I, p. 14, Mb) "the voice cannot differentiate, nor can the ear discriminate, any interval smaller than the smallest *diesis*"; (transl. H. S. Macran, p. 175); this means that, in Aristoxenus' view, diesis is the smallest interval that the voice can produce, and the ear perceive.

Arist. Quint. Mb. p. 14, RPW-I p. 12): "diesis was the smallest interval of the voice". In a musical Fragment (Vincent "Notices" pp. 235-6) the diesis is defined as follows: "the minimum interval which can be conceived is *diesis*, about a quarter-tone, but it numbers in the value of $\frac{33}{32}$; and it is an interval extremely difficult («χαλεπώτατον») to be sung and not by everybody". According to Didymus' evaluation it would be something between $\frac{32}{31}$ and $\frac{31}{30}$.

Ἐναρμόνιος δίεσις (*Enharmonic diesis*); that which is used in the Enharmonion* genus; according to Nicom. (Ench., ch. 12, C.v.J. p. 262; Mb. p. 26) it is the half of the semitone («ἐναρμόνιος δίεσις, ὅπερ ἐστὶν ἡμιτονίου ἥμισυ»); also Gaud. (Harm. Isag. § 5, C.v.J. p. 331; Mb. 5) says that the Enharm. diesis is equal to $\frac{1}{4}$ of a tone; and other theoreticians agree to that.

Χρωματικὴ δίεσις (*Chromatic diesis*); that which is used in the Chromatikon* genus. Gaud. (Ib.), following Aristoxenus, evaluates the *minima chromatic diesis* (δίεσις χρωματικὴ ἐλαχίστη) as equal to $\frac{1}{3}$ of the tone (δίεσις τριτημόριος, diesis tritemorios); see in the article on *Chromatikon genus* Aristoxenus' views; also Harm. II p. 50 Mb.

Ἡμιόλιος δίεσις (*Hermiolic diesis*) is that which is used in the Hemiolic Chromatic genus; equal to one and a half Enharmonic diesis, i.e. the Enharmonic diesis being $\frac{1}{4}$ of a tone, the Hemiolic would be $\frac{1}{4} + \frac{1}{8} = \frac{3}{8}$ or $\frac{4\frac{1}{2}}{12}$ of a tone.

Mart. Cap. (De Mus., Mb p. 179) also says that the Hemiolic diesis is equal to $\frac{1}{4}$ of a tone plus half of it ($\frac{1}{8}$); i.e. $\frac{3}{8}$ or $\frac{4\frac{1}{2}}{12}$ or $\frac{9}{24}$ of a tone.

Cleonides (Isag. ch. 7; C.v.J. p. 192; Mb p. 11) says: "it is supposed that the tone is divided into twelve minima molecules, each of which is called a twelfth ($\frac{1}{12}$)... the semitone is six twelfths ($\frac{6}{12}$), and the *diesis*, the [so-called] tetartemorios (one-fourth of a tone) has three twelfths ($\frac{3}{12}$), and the tritemorios diesis (one-third of a tone) has four twelfths ($\frac{4}{12}$)".

Diktaeos hymnos (Δικταῖος ὕμνος; m. pr. Diktéos ímnos); a famous hymn of the Kouretes addressed to Zeus, discovered at Palaeocastron in Crete (text only).

Diocles (Διοκλῆς; m. pr. Dioclís); b.? d.?

Athenian musician to whom, according to Suidas, was attributed the invention of a "Harmonia" (series of notes) produced from a series of shell-pots struck by a small wooden stick. Suidas, however, wrongly attributes this invention to the comedian Diocles.

Cf. *oxybaphoi*.

Diodorus (Διόδωρος; m. pr. Diódoros); see under Pronomus*.

Dionysius (Διονύσιος; m. pr. Dionísios);

1. Lyric poet and musician from Thebes; end of the 5th to beginning of the 4th cent. B.C.

He is mentioned by Aristoxenus (ap. Plut. De Mus. 1142B, ch. 31) among the distinguished lyric poets and musicians, together with Pindar*, Lamprus* and Pratinas*.

As a musician he was considered equal to Damon*; according to Th. Reinach he probably taught Epameinondas the kitharistike and the kitharodia (cf. H. Weil et Th. Reinach: Plut. De la Mus., p. 128, note on § 317).

2. Another *Dionysius* of uncertain date to whom are attributed the Hymns to the Muse (Calliope) and to Helios, the composition of which is placed in the 2nd cent. A. D. (Fr. Bellermann: "Die Hymnen der Dionysius und Mesomedes"; Berlin, 1840; pp. 68-78).

See under *"Remains of Greek Music"* (Nos 8, 9).

3. *Dionysius of Halicarnassos* (Διονύσιος ὁ ᾿Αλικαρνασσεύς; m. pr. Dionísios Alicarnaséfs); 1st cent. B.C. historian and teacher of rhetoric. Among his many and important writings on various subjects (Ρωμαϊκὴ ἀρχαιολογία, Περὶ τῶν ἀρχαίων ρητόρων etc.) his "De compositione verborum" («Περὶ συνθέσεως ὀνομάτων») contains rich musical material.

See Pauly's R.E. V(IX) s.v. Dionysios (No. 113, cols 934-971, article by Radermacher). Cf. *Euripides*.

4. Another *Dionysius of Halicarnassos* (Διονύσιος ᾿Αλικαρνασσεύς).

Sophist and musician who lived during the reign of Hadrian (117-138 A.D.) known as Dionysius the Musician. According to Suidas he wrote a History of music (in 36 vols.) in which he mentions the names of auletai, kitharodes and poets of all sorts; also "On Musical Education" (vols. 22); "On what is said about music in Plato's Republic" (vols. 5); "About similarities". All these books are lost. To Dion. Halicarnaseus are attributed by R. Westphal and others the two Hymns mentioned above (Dion. 2), or the Hymn to the Muse only. The name of "Dionysius the Old" is mentioned in some MSS.

See Pauly's R.E. V(IX) s.v. Dionysios (No. 142).

5. *Dionysius the Iambus* (Διονύσιος ὁ ῎Ιαμβος); 3rd cent. B.C. grammarian and poet. According to Soterichus (ap. Plut. 1136C, ch. 15), he attributed the invention of the Lydian Harmonia to Torebus*.

Dionysodorus (Διονυσόδωρος; m. pr. Dionisódoros); 4th cent. B.C. composer and aulete of repute. He was a contemporary and rival of Ismenias*, another well-known aulete.

Diog. Laertius (book IV, ch. IV, § 22) says that Dionysodorus boasted that "no one ever heard his (instrumental) melodies (κρούματα), as those of Ismenias were heard, either on shipboard or at the fountain" (transl. R. D. Hicks "Diog. Laert. Lives of Eminent Philosophers", vol. I, p. 399).

Dionysodotus (Διονυσόδοτος; m. pr. Dionisódotos); lyric poet and composer of paeans from Laconia. According to Athenaeus (XV, 678C, ch. 22) paeans of Dionysodotus were sung at the gymnopaedias* in Sparta, together with songs of Thaletas and Alcman, by choruses of boys and men.

diorismenoi, phthongoi (διωρισμένοι, φθόγγοι; pl.; m. pr. diorisméni phthóngi); not consecutive notes; opp. συνεχεῖς. Porphyry (Comment.; ed. Wallis, III, p. 285; ed. I. Dür. p. 112) commenting on Ptolemy's isotonoi* and anisotonoi sounds, defines those of the anisotonoi (=sounds having different pitch) «others are consecutive (contiguous; συνεχεῖς, synecheis) and others are not consecutive, discontiguous (διωρισμένοι)».

The verb διορίζειν generally signified to draw a boundary through, to separate (LSJ).

dioxeia, and **dioxeion** (διοξεῖα, δι' ὀξειῶν; m. pr. dioxía, dioxíon); the interval of the perfect 5th, so-called by the Pythagoreans. The 5th was generally known as dia pente*.

diploun, systema (διπλοῦν, σύστημα; m. pr. diploún sístima); double system. In juxtaposition to the simple system, the "double system" would be considered as a "modulating system". According to Cleonides (Isag., ch. 11; C.v.J. p. 201; Mb p. 18) double systems were those which were tuned to two Meses («διπλᾶ [συστήματα] τὰ πρὸς δύο [μέσας ἡρμοσμένα]»). Aristoxenus (Harm. II, p. 40, 20 Mb) uses the term μετάβολον (metábolon; μεταβολὴν ἔχον) for the system which is not simple.

Also Ib. II, 38, 8 Mb. Cf. *haploun*, and *systema*.

dipodia (διποδία) and **dipodismos** (διποδισμός); two-step, a kind of Laconic dance. Pollux (IV, 102) «καὶ διποδία δέ, ὄρχημα Λακωνικὸν» ("and *dipodia* [two-step] which is a Laconic dance"). Hes. «διποδία· εἶδος ὀρχήσεως, οἱ δὲ διποδισμὸς» ("*dipodia*; a kind of dance, which others call *dipodismos*").

See also Athen. XIV, 630A, ch. 27.

The verb διποδιάζειν (*dipodiazein*) is met with the meaning: to dance the two-step dance.

b) *dipodia* in a general sense was the union of two metrical feet; also the fact of having two feet.

discos (δίσκος); gong. A disk of metal with a hole in the middle, suspended by a cord and struck with a hammer. Cf. Sext. Empir. Adversus Mathematicos, V, § 28. Hippasus of Metapontium (Ἵππασος Μεταπόντιος), the Pythagorean philosopher, invented a disc-chime consisting of four discs of the same diameter but of different and well-calculated thickness, by which he produced the 4th, the 5th and the 8ve.

Cf. Sachs Hist. of Mus. Instr. pp. 149-150.

disemos (δίσημος; m. pr. dísimos); χρόνος (chronos) =double time; time which contains twice the first time (otherwise, twice the time-unit, the short time).

Cf. *chronos*.

84

distichía (διστιχία); ensemble of two poetic verses (στίχος, stichos = verse), distich.

Also *distichon* (δίστιχον).

dithyrambos (διθύραμβος; m. pr. dithíramvos); a lyric song of an enthusiastic character sung in honour of Dionysus; its theme was originally the birth of Bacchus, but later the scope became wider. The word «διθύραμβος» appears for the first time in a fragment by Archilochus (Brgk PLG II, Fragm. 77 [38], p. 704 and E. Diehl: Anthol. Lyr. Gr., Fr. 77, p. 233):

«ὡς Διώνυσ' ἄνακτος καλὸν ἐξάρξαι μέλος οἶδα διθύραμβον ("for I know how to lead off, in the lovely song of lord Dionysus, the *dithyramb*"; Athen. XIV, 628A, ch. 24; transl. Ch. B. Gulick, vol. VI, p. 387).

Dithyrambein (verb διθυραμβεῖν) = to sing dithyrambs; Athen. Ibid. «οἱ παλαιοὶ σπένδοντες οὐκ αἰεὶ διθυραμβοῦσιν» ("the ancients do not always sing dithyrambs while pouring libations"). In the beginning the dithyramb was improvised during the spring ceremonies of Dionysus in Attica, Sicyon, Corinth and elsewhere.

Arion was the first to regulate the dithyramb in strophes and antistrophes, choruses and solos (of the choregoi or koryphaeoi); see *anabole*. The etymology of the word is not known. Proclus (Chrest. XII) claims that the dithyrambos takes its name from "Dithyrambos" Dionysus; the epithet "Dithyrambos" was given to Dionysus because he was twice born, once from Semele and the second time from Zeus' thigh; it is also suggested that the word was derived from: δίς, θύρα, βαίνω (dis = twice, thyra = door, baeno = to go).

The poet-composer of dithyrambs was called *dithyrambopoeos* and *dithyrambographos* (διθυραμβοποιὸς καὶ διθυραμβογράφος), and the art of composing dithyrambs: *dithyrambopoeetike* (διθυραμβοποιητική). *Dithyrambic eidos* (διθυραμβικὸν εἶδος) was the poetic kind of dithyramb, as also the "dithyrambic poetry" («διθυραμβικὴ ποίησις»).

Dithyrambodidáscalos (διθυραμβοδιδάσκαλος) dithyrambic poet trainer of his own chorus.

Cf. *O. Crusius*: "Dithyrambos" in Pauly's R. E. (1903), vol. V(IX), cols 1203-1230.

Helmut Schönewolf: "Der jungattische Dithyrambos"; Giessen, 1938.

Sir Arthur W. Pickard-Cambridge: "Dithyramb, Tragedy and Comedy"; Oxford, 1927.

ditonon (δίτονον); an interval consisting of two tones. Also *dítonos* (δίτονος). The ditonon was a simple interval in the Enharmonic genus:

a) e-¼ e - f - a

in the sense that no other note in this genus can exist between the two notes, as they are contiguous; the ditonon in the Diatonic genus is a compound interval

b)   e - f - g - a

Δίτονος λιχανὸς (*dítonos Lichanos*); the Lichanos of the Enharmonic genus which is in the distance of two tones from the Mese; Aristox. (Harm. I, p. 23,4 Mb): «῞Οτι δ᾿ ἔστι τις μελοποιῖα *διτόνου λιχανοῦ* δεομένη...» ("that there is a kind of melopoeia which demands a Lichanos at a distance of two tones from the Mese"; transl. H. S. Macran p. 181). See ex. a above.

dizygoi, or **dizyges auloi** (**δίζυγοι, δίζυγες αὐλοί**, pl.; m. pr. dízigi, díziges); double aulos; twin-auloi. The word *δίζυξ* (*dizyx*; sing. of dizyges) meant that which is yoked together with another, hence double-yoked; double.

Nonnos (Dion., book VIII, 17): «εἰ κτύπος οὐρεσίφοιτος ἀκούετο *δίζυγος αὐλοῦ*...» ("if the mountain-roaming tones of the *double* aulos...").

Cf. *diaulos* and *aulos*.

Note: In sing. *διζυγής, δίζυγος, δίζυξ* (*dízyges, dízygos, dízyx*); all three have the same sense.

Dizyx brass (*δίζυξ χαλκὸς*); pair of cymbals or castanets.

dochmios (**δόχμιος**); in ancient prosody a pentasyllabic foot, principally of the kind υ - - υ -. So called for its diversity and dissimilarity in the rhythmopoeia.

dochmios rhythmos (*δόχμιος ρυθμός*; dochmiac rhythm); Bacch. (Isag. §§ 100-1; C.v.J. pp. 314, 315 and 316; Mb pp. 24-25) considers the dochmiac rhythm as compound, and composed "of iambus, anapaestos and paean".

Cf. Aristides, Mb. p. 39, RPW-I p. 37.

dodecachordon, systema (**δωδεκάχορδον σύστημα**); a system with twelve strings or notes.

See *systema**.

dodecatemorion (**δωδεκατημόριον**; m. pr. dodecatimórion); one twelfth of the tone. It was a theoretical interval. Cleonides (Isag. ch. 7; C.v.J. p. 192; Mb p. 11): "it is supposed that the tone is divided into twelve minima molecules each one of which is called a *twelfth of the tone*" («ὑποτίθεται γὰρ ὁ τόνος εἰς δώδεκά τινα ἐλάχιστα μόρια διαιρούμενος, ὧν ἕκαστον *δωδεκατημόριον* τόνου καλεῖται»; see the full text of Cleonides under "diesis").

The dodecatemorion is the difference between the chromatic diesis ($\frac{1}{3}$ of the tone) and the enharmonic diesis ($\frac{1}{4}$ of the tone); Aristox. (Harm. I, p. 25, 15 Mb) «ἡ χρωματικὴ δίεσις τῆς ἐναρμονίου διέσεως δωδεκατημορίῳ τόνου μείζων ἐστὶ» ("the chromatic diesis is greater than the enharmonic diesis by one twelfth of the tone"). Cf. *Chromatikon* (Soft) *genus**.

The dodecatemorion ($\frac{1}{12}$ of a tone) is unsingable, ἀμελῴδητον (*amelodeton**).

donax (**δόναξ**); a kind of small slender reed. Pieces of donax were used inside the tortoise-shell (sound-box) of the lyra to support the membrane (Cf. *lyra*); this donax was called donax hypolyrios (hypo = under); Pollux (IV, 62) «καὶ δόνακα δέ τινα ὑπολύριον οἱ κωμικοὶ ὠνόμαζον, ὡς πάλαι ἀντὶ κεράτων ὑποτιθέμενον ταῖς λύραις» ("and the comedians called a certain *donax* (reed) *hypolyrian,* as in old times it was placed under the lyras in place of horns"). Hes. «δόνακα ὑπολύριον, πάλαι γὰρ ταῖς λύραις κάλαμον ἀντὶ κέρατος ὑπετίθετο» ("*donax* [reed] *hypolyrian;* the reed which in old times they used to place under the lyras instead of horn").

Aristoph. Frogs 232-3 «ἕνεκα δόνακος, ὃν ὑπολύριον ἔνυδρον ἐν λίμναις τρέφω» ("because of the *hypolyrian reed* which, growing in water, I nourish in marshes").

b)   The slender reed used, it is said, for the making of syrinxes. Eust. Il. 1165,23 «καὶ δοκοῦσιν ἐκ δονάκων μὲν σύριγγες γίνεσθαι, αὐλοὶ δέ ἐκ καλάμων» ("and they believe that the syrinxes were made *of donax*, and the auloi of reed [calamus]").   From donax the auletic reeds (γλωσσίδες) were made; cf. Schol. Pind. Pythian XII (A.B. Drachmann vol. II, p. 268); see *calamus**.

c)   Hence donax was called the syrinx or shepherd aulos.

Himerius (Speeches, Λόγοι 15,674) «αὐλοῖς ἐπηχῶν ἢ δόναξι» ("playing on auloi or on *donakes*").   Athen. (III, 90D «οἱ δὲ σωλῆνες... πρός τινων δὲ αὐλοὶ καὶ δόνακες» ("and the pipes... called by some people auloi and dónakes").   Also Hes. at the word «δονάκων».

Dorion (Δωρίων); 4th cent. B.C. aulete, chief of an auletic School rival to that of Antigenidas*.

Plutarch (De Mus. 1138B, ch. 21) writes about this rivalry: "those of Dorion's School disdaining the Antigenidian style never use it, and those of Antigenidas' School do exactly the contrary for the same reason".

Dorion's name is also met with in Athenaeus (VIII, 337B, ch. 18, and X, 435B-C, ch. 46), and in Theopompus (FHG, I, 323).

Dorios or **Doristi harmonia** (δώριος ἢ δωριστὶ ἀρμονία); generally accepted as the octachord (διὰ πασῶν, dia pason):

e - d - c - b - a - g - f - e (Diatonic genus).

Cleon. Isag. (ch. 9, C.v.J. pp. 197-8; Mb p. 15): «Τέταρτον [εἶδος τοῦ διὰ πασῶν] ἔστι ἀπὸ ὑπάτης μέσων ἐπὶ νήτην διεζευγμένων, ἐκαλεῖτο δὲ δώριον» ("The fourth [species of dia pason] is from Hypate Meson to Nete Diezeugmenon, and was called *Dorion*").   Same expression in Bacchius' Isag. § 77 (C.v.J. p. 309; Mb p. 19).

The Dorian Harmonia was considered as the "pre-eminently Greek harmonia".   Plato in Laches (XIV, 188D) says that a true musician is he who has regulated his life in words and deeds, "not according to the Ionian, nor the Phrygian nor the Lydian, but according to the *Dorian harmonia* which is the *only Greek harmonia*" («... δωριστί, ἀλλ' οὐκ ἰαστί, οἴομαι δὲ οὐ δὲ φρυγιστί, οὐδὲ λυδιστί, ἀλλ' ἥπερ [δωριστί] μόνη Ἑλληνική ἐστιν ἁρμονία»).

Heracl. Pont. in his third book "On Music" (ap. Athen. XIV, 624D, ch. 19) writes that "the *Dorian harmonia* expresses the masculine and the majestic ethos" («ἡ μὲν δώριος ἁρμονία τὸ ἀνδρῶδες ἐμφαίνει καὶ τὸ μεγαλοπρεπές»); also "the sombre and the powerful" («σκυθρωπὸν καὶ σφοδρόν).

Cf. *ethos**.

Dracon (Δράκων); c. end of the 5th or beginning of the 4th cent. B.C. Athenian musician, pupil of Damon and cited as one of Plato's music teachers (Plut. De Mus. 1136F, ch. 17). Nothing else is known about his life.

dynamis (δύναμις; m. pr. dínamis); in a general sense power, might. In music it signified a special virtue of the notes; a function which a note fulfils in relation to the other notes of the scale. It was a virtue quite different from the pitch of the note (sound) and in some way it corresponded to the tonal function of a degree in a modern scale.

Cleon. Isag. (ch. 14; C.v.J. p. 207; Mb p. 22): "*Dynamis* is a function of a note in a system; or a function by which we know [conceive] each of the notes" («Δύναμις δέ ἐστι τάξις φθόγγου ἐν συστήματι, ἢ δύναμίς ἐστι τάξις φθόγγου, δι' ἧς γνωρίζομεν τῶν φθόγγων ἕκαστον»).

Aristoxenus (Harm. II, p. 33, 8-9 Mb) says that "by the hearing we judge the magnitudes of the intervals while by the intellect we contemplate the *functions* of the notes" («τῇ μὲν γὰρ ἀκοῇ κρίνομεν τὰ τῶν διαστημάτων μεγέθη, τῇ δὲ διανοίᾳ θεωροῦμεν τὰς τῶν φθόγγων δυνάμεις»); also Ibid III, p. 69, 9 Mb.

Ptolemaeus distinguished the «κατὰ δύναμιν» (in respect to function) from the «κατὰ θέσιν» (in respect to position) with regard to the denominations of the notes; (book II, ch. 5; ed. I. Dür. p. 51).

Cf. *onomatothesia** (*nomenclature*).

dysaulia (δυσαυλία; m. pr. disavlía); Dem. "bad or difficult aulesis" (aulos-solo).

dysaulos (δύσαυλος; m. pr. dísavlos) ἔρις (eris; quarrel); unsuccessful contest of aulos (LSJ).

dyseches (δυσηχής; m. pr. disichís); unpleasantly sounding; or hardly sounding (of a body which hardly produces a sound owing to thickness).

Hes. «νάβλας, εἶδος ὀργάνου μουσικοῦ δυσηχοῦς» ("nablas*; a kind of *unpleasantly sounding* musical instrument").

E

echeion (ἠχεῖον; m. pr. ichíon), from echos (ἦχος, sound); the word is met with in various meanings:

1. In principle it signified an object which when struck or set in motion creates a sound. Hence, echeion was a percussion instrument, in metal. In Demeter's cult the word echeion (ἠχεῖον) was the mystical name for the cymbal which played an important part in the cult.

2. *echeion* was also used for the sound-plate (or sound-box) of stringed instruments.

3. *echeia* (ἠχεῖα, plur.) were hemispheric vases used in different sizes in order to produce different sounds; they were played by a small stick.

4. *echeia* were also vessels placed in hollow parts of the ancient theatres for transmission of sounds to the public, like the bronteion (βροντεῖον) which was a mechanical construction used in the theatres for imitation of thunder (βροντή, bronte).

Hes. says that "the echeion was made of brass, and that for some people it meant the brass-made sound-plate of the magadis" («ἠχεῖον· τὸ χαλκόν· οἱ δέ, μουσικὸν τὸ πρὸς τῇ μαγάδει χάλκωμα»).

The word ἠχεῖον as an adj. with the word ὄργανον (instrument, vessel) meant a sounding vessel.

Echembrotus (Ἐχέμβροτος; m. pr. Echémvrotos); aulode from Arcadia, b. c. end of the 7th cent. B.C., and flourished in the 6th cent. B.C.

He competed and won the first prize at the aulodic competitions held at the Pythian Games at Delphi in 586 B.C.; this was the first time that competitions for both auletai and aulodoi were admitted by the Amphictyons (3rd year of the 48th Olympiad, 586 B.C.). The first prize for the auletic was won by Sakadas* of Argos, and that for the kithara by Melampous* of Cephalonia. But at the next Pythians the aulodic contest was withdrawn, because, as Pausanias says (book X, ch. 7, § 5), the tunes of the aulos were adjudged most depressing, and the words sung to them, of a lamenting character («Ἡ γὰρ αὐλῳδία μέλη τε ἦν αὐλῶν τὰ σκυθρωπότατα καὶ ἐλεγεῖα [θρῆνοι] προσᾳδόμενα τοῖς αὐλοῖς»). Thus, Echembrotus became the first and last victor in aulodic at the Pythians; in remembrance of his victory he dedicated to Heracles at Thebes a bronze tripod with the following inscription (Paus. ibid):

> "Echembrotus of Arcadia dedicated this
> votive offering to Heracles
> When he won a victory at the Amphictyonic
> Games, by singing melodies and elegies
> for the Greeks".

See PLG III, p. 203 a small fragment by Echembrotus.

echos (ἦχος; m. pr. íchos); sound in the general sense. For musical sound the terms φωνή (*phone**) and φθόγγος (phthongos*) were generally used.

Sometimes the word ἠχώ (*echo*) was used for echos (sound), see below; also in the Attic dialect the word ἠχή (*eche*; Dor. type ἀχά, acha) meant, according to Moeris (Lexicon p. 175), ἦχος (echos, sound). But usually tumultuous noise. Arist. Probl. XIX, 50 «Διὰ τί ἴσων πίθων καὶ ὁμοίων ἐὰν μὲν ὁ ἕτερος κενὸς ᾖ, ὁ δὲ ἕτερος εἰς τὸ ἥμισυ διάμεσος, διὰ πασῶν συμφωνεῖ ἡ ἠχώ;» ("Why is it that if we take two similar vessels of the same size, if the one is empty and the other is half full, the (combined) *sound* gives an octave consonance?" transl. by W.S. Hett, p. 415).

Note: ἠχεῖν (echein, verb) = to produce a sound, to sound. Some derivatives often met with were: ἠχήεις (echeeis; m. pr. ichíis), sonorous; ἤχημα (echema; íchima), sound, also, by extension, song; ἠχέτης and ἠχητής (echetes) clear-sounding, musical (LSJ); cf. Pind. Threnoi (ap. PLG I, p. 335, Fr. 116); κακοηχὴς (kakoeches; kakoichís) cacophonous, disagreeably sounding; πολυηχὴς (polyeches: poliichís), very sonorous, also sounding with rich diversity of tone («πολυηχὴς φωνὴ ἀηδόνος» = "richly diverse voice [song] of the nightingale").
See also *eueches* (εὐηχής).

eidos (εἶδος; m. pr. ídos); species, form.

Εἶδος τετραχόρδου = species of tetrachord; the form the tetrachord takes by the disposition of its constituent parts. Aristoxenus (Harm. III, 74,18) says that "there are three species of the Fourth" («τοῦ διὰ τεσσάρων τρία εἴδη»), i.e. a) that in which the pycnon* lies at the lower part, b) that in which a diesis lies on either side of the ditone, and c) that in which the pycnon lies above the ditone (III, 74, 19ff).

Aristoxenus (Ibid, 74, 11) also considers the term eidos, species (εἶδος) as a synonym of figure (σχῆμα): «διαφέρει δ' ἡμῖν οὐδὲν εἶδος λέγειν ἢ σχῆμα, φέρομεν γὰρ ἀμφότερα τὰ ὀνόματα ταῦτα ἐπὶ τὸ αὐτὸ» ("for us the words 'species' and 'figure' do not differ at all, therefore we shall apply both these terms to the same phenomenon").

«τὸ τοῦ συστήματος εἶδος» (Aristox. ibid, III, 69,16) = the form of the system.

The term *eidos* is met also in the sense of style; Cf. Plut. De Mus. (1110E, ch. 27) «τὸ τῆς διαφθορᾶς εἶδος» (="the style of decadence [of degeneracy]").

eiresia (εἰρεσία; m. pr. iresía); a song of rowers; a song rhythmically accompanying the rowing. The word eiresia principally signified "rowing".

eiresione (εἰρεσιώνη; m. pr. iresióni). a branch of olive-tree or laurel wreathed with wool and fruit carried by boys who went from house to house singing during certain celebrations, like the Thargelia (Θαργήλια) held in honour of

Apollo in the eleventh month of the Athenian year (called Thargelion, Θαργη-λιών). Offerings were made to Helios (Sun) and the Orae ("Ωραι, Hours), and the branch was hung on the door of the house until next year.

Synecd. *eiresione* was also the song itself; Plut. Theseus (22, 10B): «τὴν δὲ εἰρεσιώνην ἐκφέρουσι, κλάδον ἐλαίας ἐρίῳ μὲν ἀνεστεμμένον.... ἐπᾴδοντες «Εἰρεσιώνη, σῦκα φέρειν» etc. ("[The Athenians] also carry the *eiresione* which is an olive-branch wreathed with wool... singing 'Eiresione brings us figs' " etc.

Later, the word eiresione was used for all the songs of beggars.

ekbole (ἐκβολή; m. pr. ekvolí); a term signifying the raising of a note by five dieseis ($\frac{5}{4}$ of a tone).

Arist. Quint. (I, Mb and RPW-I p. 28) "*ekbole* is the raising by five dieseis" («ἐκβολὴ δέ, πέντε διέσεων ἐπίτασις»). Bacch. Isag. § 42 (C.v.J. p. 302; Mb p. 11) "*ekbole* is when from one note of the enharmonic genus we raise by five dieseis, as e.g. from e$\frac{1}{4}$ to g" («ὅταν ἀπό τινος φθόγγου ἁρμονίας ἐπιταθῶσι πέντε διέσεις, οἷον ἀπὸ EΠ ἐπὶ ΠΖ»): e* - f - g.

$$\underset{\underline{\quad\quad\quad}}{\tfrac{1}{4}}$$

See Enharmonion Genus*.

According to Plutarch (De Mus. 1141B, ch. 29) Polymnastus* (Πολύμνα-στος) was the first to introduce into practice the *ekbole* and the eklysis*.

ekchordos (ἔκχορδος); without strings. From the vb ekchordousthai (ἐκχορ-δοῦσθαι), to be deprived of strings (LSJ); to send forth or to utter from the vocal cords (Dem.).

Sopater (ap. G. Kaibel, Comic. Gr. Fr., p. 195, Fr. 16; and Athen. IV, 175C, ch. 77).

«οὔτε τοῦ Σιδωνίου νάβλα λαρυγγόφωνος ἐκκεχόρδωται τύπος» ("nor has the deep-toned thrum of the Sidonian nablas passed from the strings"; transl. Ch. B. Gulick, Athen. vol. II, p. 295). In Kaibel p. 195 it is noted "chordis exutus est", «ἔκχορδος πεποίηται».

ekkrousis-eklepsis (ἔκκρουσις, ἔκληψις; m. pr. ékkrousis, éklipsis). "Εκ-κρουσις signified the proceeding from a higher note to a lower one in instrumental melody; the equivalent in vocal melody was called ἔκληψις (*eklepsis*).

This could be done either directly (ἀμέσως), i.e. by step (ex. a) or indirectly (ἐμμέσως), i.e. by a leap (ex. b) of a 3rd, 4th or 5th. When the notes were tied, this was called "Hyphen from outside" («ὑφὲν ἔξωθεν»; ex. c):

Cf. Anon. Bell. (§ § 7,89 and note, p. 24); Man. Bryen. (ed. Wallis, III, p. 479) and A. J. H. Vincent (Notices, p. 53).

The ekkrousis and eklepsis were schemata of the melos.

See also under prokrousis—prolepsis, prokrousmos—prolemmatismos, ekkrousmos —eklemmatismos, kompismos—melismos, teretismos and diastole.

ekkrousmos-eklemmatismos (ἐκκρουσμός, ἐκλημματισμός; m. pr. ekkrousmós-eklimmatismós).

Ἐκκρουσμὸς (*ekrousmos*) was a term signifying the intercalation of a lower note between two enunciations of the same note, in instrumental melody; the equivalent in vocal melody was called ἐκκλημματισμὸς (*eklemmatismos*).

This could be done either directly (ἀμέσως), i.e. by step (ex. a), or indirectly (ἐμμέσως), i.e. by a leap of a 3rd, 4th or 5th (ex. b).

Both the ekkrousmos and the eklemmatismos were schemata of the melos.

Cf. Anon. Bell. (§§. 8 and 90, p. 25), Man. Bryen. Harm. (ed. Wallis, III, p. 480) and A.J.H. Vincent (Notices p. 53).

See also under ekkrousis—eklepsis for other schemata.

eklaktisma (ἐκλάκτισμα; usually in plur. ἐκλακτίσματα, eklaktísmata); a kind of feminine dance in which the women dancers (ὀρχηστρίδες, orchestrides) had to kick the feet high up and over the shoulder.

Pollux (IV, 102) "*eklaktísmata* were feminine dances [so-called] because they had to kick over the shoulder"; («τὰ δὲ ἐκλακτίσματα, γυναικῶν ἦν ὀρχήματα· ἔδει γὰρ ὑπὲρ τὸν ὦμον ἐκλακτίσαι»).

Hes. defines *eklaktismós* (ἐκλακτισμὸς) as "an intense figure of dancing".

eklelymena mele pl. (ἐκλελυμένα μέλη; m. pr. ekleliména meli), perf. partic. pass. of eklyein (ἐκλύειν), to release, to relax etc.; slack, loose tunes; melodies lacking in vigour of style.

Phryn. Epit. (p. 79): «ὅτι τὰ ἐκλελυμένα τῶν μελῶν καὶ ἀδόκιμα πρὸς τὰ ὄστρακα ᾖδον, οὐχὶ πρὸς λύραν ἢ κιθάραν» ("that *the loose* and unacceptable [unsatisfactory, not genuine] mele were sung 'to ostraka accompaniment', not to the lyra or the kithara").

See *ostrakon**, for Euripides' music (schol. Aristoph. Frogs 1305); also *Agathon*.

eklysis (ἔκλυσις; m. pr. éklisis); the lowering of a note by three dieseis (i.e. by ¾ of a tone); oppos. spondeiasmos.

Arist. Quint. (I, Mb and RPW-I p. 28) "*eklysis* was the lowering of a note by three uncompound dieseis" («ἔκλυσις μὲν οὖν ἐκαλεῖτο, τριῶν διέσεων ἀσυνθέτων ἄνεσις»).

Bacch. Isag. § 41 (C.v.J. pp. 301-2; Mb. p. 11) *eklysis* is "when from a certain note of the Enharmonic genus three dieseis are lowered, as from e¼ to e flat (E⅃ to H⟩)" («ὅταν ἀπό τινος φθόγγου ἁρμονίας ἀνεθῶσι τρεῖς διέσεις· οἷον ἀπὸ E⅃ ἐπὶ H⟩"):

According to Plutarch (De Mus. 1141B, ch. 29) Polymnastus* (Πολύμναστος, or Polymnestus) was the first to introduce into practice *the eklysis* and the *ekbole**.

ekmeles (ἐκμελής; m. pr. ekmelís); contrary to the laws of melos; violating these laws; unmelodious.   Unmelodious should be distinguished from amelodetos* (ἀμελῴδητος) which meant unsingable.   Timaeus (the Locrian) 101B «ἁ δὲ ἄτακτός τε καὶ ἄλογος (φωνὴ) ἐκμελὴς τε καὶ ἀνάρμοστος» ("the unruly and irrational [voice] is *ekmeles* and discordant").

᾿Εκμελῶς (*ekmelos*, adv.) in a way violating (or contrary to) the laws of melos.

᾿Εκμελὲς (*ekmelés*, neut.), the quality of being against the laws of melos.
See Aristox.   Harm. II 36, 27; 37, 2 Mb.

According to Ptolem. (Harm. I, iv, 7) ekmele were the intervals of the seventh (major and minor); the sixth (major and minor), and the tritone with its inversion, the "minor" or "imperfect" fifth.

Cf. *emmeles*.

ekpyrosis (ἐκπύρωσις; m. pr. ekpírosis), conflagration. With the word «κόσμου» («κόσμου ἐκπύρωσις» = *world-conflagration*), mentioned in Athen. (XIV, 629F, ch. 27) as a kind of dance; «καλεῖται δέ τις καὶ ἄλλη ὄρχησις κόσμου ἐκπύρωσις ἧς μνημονεύει Μένιππος ὁ κυνικὸς ἐν τῷ Συμποσίῳ» ("and another dance is called *world-conflagration*, of which mention is made by the cynic Menippus in his Banquet").   No indication is given as to its character.

ekrhythmos (ἔκρυθμος; m. pr. ékrithmos); out of rhythm; unrhythmical; oppos. *enrhythmos**.

ektonos (ἔκτονος); out of tune.
Clement of Alexandria: Stromateis (book II, ch. XX, 123) «ἵνα μή τινες τῶν ζηλούντων ἔκτονον καὶ ἀπόχορδον ᾄσωσιν» ("in order that some zealots do not sing *out of tune*").

elegeia, fem. (ἐλεγεία; m. pr. elegía), also *elegeion*, neut. (ἐλεγεῖον; m. pr. elegíon); a small lyric poem of a rather melancholic and mournful character. It consisted of distichs composed of a hexametric and a pentametric verse alternately following each other. The recitation was accompanied by the aulos. In later times elegeia (elegy) was a song of a threnetic character, a lament; Schol. Plato «ἐλεγεῖα, ᾠδαί, θρῆνοι» ("*elegies*, odes, threni").

The first mentioned elegiac poet was Kallinus (or Callinus) of Ephesus (Καλλῖνος ὁ Ἐφέσιος; 8th or 7th cent. B.C.).

See R. Westphal: Scriptores Metrici Graeci (Leipzig, 1866) vol. I, p. 242 (from Procl. Chrest. B); also Brgk PLG II, p. 391; Anth. Lyr. pp. 1-2; E. Diehl Anth. Lyr. I2 p. 3.

elegos (ἔλεγος, masc.); a mournful song, usually accompanied by aulos; Eustath. p. 1372, 28 «καὶ οἱ Ἑλληνικοὶ δὲ ἔλεγοι, ὅ ἐστι θρῆνοι, μετ᾽ αὐλοῦ, φασιν, ἤδοντο ("and the Greek *elegoi*, that is to say lamentations, were sung, as they say, with aulos").

Procl. Chrest. (ap. R. Westphal Scriptores Metr. Gr., vol. I, p. 242) «Τὸ γὰρ θρῆνος ἔλεγον ἐκάλουν οἱ παλαιοὶ καὶ τοὺς τετελευτηκότας δι᾽ αὐτοῦ εὐλόγουν» ("The lamentation was called by the ancients *elegos* and by this they blessed [praised] the dead").

In plur., Ἔλεγοι (*Elegoi*) was the name of one of the aulodic nomoi attributed to Clonas*; Plut. De Mus. 1132D, ch. 4.

See also under *aulodia - aulodikoi nomoi*.

elymos (ἔλυμος; m. pr. élimos); a kind of Phrygian aulos made of box-wood; it had two pipes of unequal length of which the longer one (that on the left) was curved, and ended in a bell; cf. Athen. (IV, 185A, ch. 84). The horn of its bell corresponded to that of the trumpet. Pollux (IV, 74) says that its material was box-tree, its invention Phrygian, and its horned end (bell) was recurved (ἀνανεῦον). The bore (see koelia*) was narrow; cf. Aelianus ap. Porphyr. Comment. I.D., p. 34.

According to Hesychius *elymos* was also the upper part of the aulos where the reed was placed; also the box where the kithara was placed («ἔλυμοι, τὰ πρῶτα τῶν αὐλῶν, ἐφ᾽ ὧν ἡ γλωσσὶς... καὶ ἡ τῆς κιθάρας...θήκη»). The elymos aulos was closely connected with Cybele's cult (Pollux IV, 74).

It was also known in Egypt, especially in Alexandria, and in Cyprus (Athen. IV, 176F, ch. 79 and 177A, ch. 79; «χρῆσθαι δ᾽ αὐτοῖς καὶ Κυπρίους, φησὶ Κρατῖνος ὁ νεώτερος» = "and use was made of them [the elymoi auloi] by the Cypriots as well, says Kratinus the younger").

See *engeraules* and *kerastes*.

embaterion melos (ἐμβατήριον μέλος; m. pr. emvatírion); a marching-song; a song accompanying a military march. It seems that the melody itself was played on the aulos while the words were more recited, and the rhythm was marked by the feet of the soldiers. It was also called *enoplion melos* (ἐνόπλιον μέλος).

94

Famous "embateria" were those of Tyrtaeus sung in Sparta, and generally in Laconia, and those of Ibycus in Crete.

Athen. (XIV, 630F, ch. 29): "For the Spartans [Laconians] are warlike, and their sons adopt the *marching-songs* which are also called *enoplia*. And the Laconians themselves in their wars recite from memory the poems of Tyrtaeus as they march forward rhythmically").

Embaterion melos was also a term for the aulema (the melody played on the aulos); Hes. «εἶδος αὐλήματος» ("a kind of aulema", aulos-solo). See *Kastorion* melos.

b) *embaterios rhythmos* (ἐμβατήριος ρυθμός); marching-rhythm; the rhythm of the embateria mele, based on anapaestic feet (υυ-). Plut. Instituta Laconica (Laconic apophthegms), 238B, ch. 16: "And the marching-rhythms incited to bravery, to courageousness and disdain of death; they were used in dances as well and to aulos accompaniment to stimulate the warriors" («Καὶ οἱ ἐμβατήριοι δὲ ρυθμοὶ παρορμητικοὶ ἦσαν πρὸς ἀνδρείαν καὶ θαρραλεότητα καὶ ὑπερφρόνησιν θανάτου, οἷς ἐχρῶντο ἔν τε χοροῖς τε καὶ πρὸς αὐλόν, ἐπάγοντες τοῖς πολεμίοις»).

c) *embaterioi kineseis* (ἐμβατήριοι κινήσεις; marching movements); a kind of dancing.

embaterios aulos (ἐμβατήριος αὐλός; m. pr. embatírios avlós); the aulos playing the embaterion* melos; also the aulos accompanying the prosodion* (προσόδιον). Pollux (IV, 82) "some people called also *embaterioi auloi* those used in prosodia" («ἔνιοι δὲ καὶ ἐμβατηρίους αὐλοὺς ὠνόμαζον τοὺς ἐπὶ τοῖς προσοδίοις»).

embolimon (ἐμβόλιμον; m. pr. emvólimon), intercalary; embolima (plur., ἐμβόλιμα) were choral songs intercalated in the drama between the *epeisodia*, and had no direct connection with the main theme of the drama. They were introduced by Agathon*. Arist. Poetics 1456A, ch. 18.

emmeleia (ἐμμέλεια; m. pr. emmélia); the dance of the chorus in ancient tragedy. In comparison to the war-dance (πυρρίχη, pyrrhiche*) and the satiric dances (σίκιννις, sikinnis*, and κόρδαξ, kordax*) the emmeleia was distinguished by its lofty, dignified and restrained character.

Athen. (XIV, 630E, ch. 28); "The gymnopaedike* resembles the tragic dance which is called *emmeleia*; in either of them the grave and the dignified (solemn) may be seen" («ἐν ἑκατέρᾳ δὲ ὁρᾶται τὸ βαρὺ καὶ τὸ σεμνόν»). Further (XIV, 631D, ch. 30) Athenaeus adds that "among the Greeks kordax is vulgar, while the *emmeleia* is dignified [serious]" («ὁ μὲν κόρδαξ παρ' Ἕλλησι φορτικός, ἡ δὲ ἐμμέλεια σπουδαία»).

Cf. also Luc. "On dancing", § 26.

b) *emmeleia* was also used for the melody which accompanied the dance. Herod. (book VI, ch. 129); «τὸν αὐλητὴν αὐλῆσαι ἐμμελείην» ("[he ordered] the aulete to play the *emmeleia* on the aulos").

c) *emmeleia* meant also the quality of being emmeles* (ἐμμελής, melodious, tuneful); tunefulness.

emmeles (**ἐμμελής**; m. pr. emmelís); that which is in accordance with the laws of melos; melodious, tuneful.

Aristox. (Harm., I, p. 9,10 Mb) «...τὸ χωρίσαι τὴν ἐμμελῆ κίνησιν τῆς φωνῆς ἀπὸ τῶν ἄλλων κινήσεων» ("...the distinction between the *melodious* motion of the voice and its other motions"; also I, p. 27,9 («ἐμμελὲς τετράχορδον» = "melodious tetrachord").

Bacchius Isag. § 69 (C.v.J. p. 307; Mb. p. 16) "*emmeleis* (plur.) are those sounds of which use is made by singers and players on instruments" («ἐμμελεῖς [φθόγγοι], οἷς οἱ ᾄδοντες χρῶνται καὶ οἱ διὰ τῶν ὀργάνων ἐνεργοῦντες»).

Ptolemaeus (I, ch. 4; ed. I. Dür. p. 10, 24-25) gives the following rule for emmeleis: «εἰσὶ δὲ ἐμμελεῖς μὲν ὅσοι συναπτόμενοι πρὸς ἀλλήλους εὔφοροι τυγχάνουσι πρὸς ἀκοήν, ἐκμελεῖς δὲ ὅσοι μὴ οὕτως ἔχουσι» ("*emmeleis* are those [sounds] which are easily [agreeably] accepted by the ear [acceptable to hearing], and *ekmeleis* the contrary"). Emmeleis notes and intervals were, according to Ptolemaeus, the following: the semitone (ratio 16:15), the tone, major and minor (9:8 and 10:9), and the major and minor third (5:4 and 6:5 respectively); cf. I, ch. 7, ed. Wallis, III, p. 16; I. Dür. p. 15, 15-16. Also Porph. Comment.; Wallis p. 292, and Cleon. Isag. ch. 13 (C.v.J. p. 205; Mb. 21).

ἐμμελὲς (*emmelés*, neut.); the quality or virtue of being in accordance with the laws governing the melos; Aristox. Harm. II, p. 37,2 («ἡ περὶ τὸ ἐμμελές τε καὶ ἐκμελὲς τάξις» = "the order concerning the *melodious* and the unmelodious").

See also *hermosmenos**.

emmelós (ἐμμελῶς, adv.); in a manner agreeing with the laws of melos; tunefully; «πάνυ ἐμμελέστατα» (superlat.) = "most melodiously" (Athen. XIV, 623C, ch. 17).

emmetros (**ἔμμετρος**); metrical, pertaining to metre. In poetry, composed in metre, in verse. Ἔμμετροι (pl.) ποιηταί, the Epic and Tragic poets; those who used metres suitable for recitation, in contradistinction to the Lyric poets who used metres suitable for singing.

ἔμμετρον μέλος (*émmetron melos*), a melody composed in metre.

emphysomena (**ἐμφυσώμενα**, pl.; emphisómena); the wind instruments Also ἐμπνευστὰ (*empneusta*; m. pr. empnevstá); Athen. XIV, 636C, ch. 39.

Pollux (IV, 58) enumerates the following denominations of the wind instruments: *empneómena* (ἐμπνεόμενα), *katapneómena* (καταπνεόμενα), *epipneómena* (ἐπιπνεόμενα), *emphysomena* (ἐμφυσώμενα).

The first three denominations are derived from the verb: pnéein (πνέειν) = to blow; hence, to produce a sound by blowing. The emphysomena is derived from physan (φυσᾶν), which also means to blow.

empneomena, (ἐμπνεόμενα) pl.;
See *emphysomena* and *empneusta*.

empneusta, empneustika (ἐμπνευστά, ἐμπνευστικά, m. pr. empnefstá, empnefstiká) pl. organa; wind instruments. Also *epipneómena* (ἐπιπνεόμενα). Pollux (IV, 67) «Περὶ ἐμπνευστῶν ὀργάνων. Τὰ δὲ ἐπιπνεόμενα ὄργανα, τὸ μὲν σύμπαν, αὐλοὶ καὶ σύριγγες» ("*About wind instruments.* The wind instruments are on the whole auloi and syrinxes").

The wind instruments in use in ancient Greece, except the salpinx (trumpet) and the horns (kerata, bycanai) which were not used for purely musical purposes, could be divided into two main categories, the reed-blown instruments, and those producing the sound by direct blowing, without the aid of a reed.

The ancient writers generally used for the first class the word "aulos" and for the second the word "syrinx". All particular varieties are examined under separate entries; cf. aulos, bombyx, borimos, calamus, dactylikos, dizygoi auloi, elymos, embaterios aulos, gingras, hippophorbos, iobas, Libys aulos, magadis (b), monaulos, niglaros, paedikoi auloi, parthenioi, photinx, plagiaulos, syrinx, thereios, threnetikos, Tityrinos aulos, Tyrrenos aulos.

For bibliography see under *aulos** and *mousike**.

enaulos kitharisis (ἔναυλος κιθάρισις; m. pr. énavlos kithárisis); playing the kithara to aulos accompaniment. According to Philochorus (FHG I, p. 395, Frg. 66; Athen. XIV, 637 F, ch. 42) the enaulos kitharisis was first introduced by the School of Epigonus*; «Λύσανδρος ὁ Σικυώνιος [φησὶ Φιλόχορος] πρῶτος μετέστησε..... καὶ τὴν ἔναυλον κιθάρισιν ᾗ πρῶτοι οἱ περὶ Ἐπίγονον ἐχρήσαντο» ("Lysandrus of Sicyon [says Philochorus] was the first to institute too the kithara solo to aulos accompaniment, which those around Epigonus adopted first").

Note: The word "enaulos" used metaphorically meant:
sounding like the aulos, i.e. having a lively, distinct sound, like that of the aulos. The enaulos kitharisis in the above fragment of Philochorus is translated by some scholars "giving that flute-like tone to strings [harmonics]" (Ch. B. Gulick, vol. VI, p. 443). Other scholars, however, interpret the "enaulos kitharisis" as above (cf. Gevaert, II, p. 359, "musique de cithare accompagnée

d'un instrument à vent"; Th. Reinach "La musique grecque", p. 144 "duo d'aulos et de cithare").

"Εναυλος λόγος, ἔνηχος (enaulos logos, word; sounding).

Cf. Timaeus the Sophist from Plato's words in C. Fr. Hermann's Appendix Platonica, T, 1920, p. 399.

enchorda, organa (ἔγχορδα, ὄργανα; m. pr. énchorda, órgana); stringed instruments.

The stringed instruments in use in ancient Greece were numerous; they differed in form, size, pitch-range and in name. The basic principle governing almost all of them was that the strings are stretched and touched (or struck) in the void (without neck), and each of them gives one sound. The Greeks did not know the use of the bow; the sound was produced by striking either directly with the fingers, or by the use of a plectrum. Some instruments with a neck, like the monochord*, were used for scientific purposes; others, like the pandoura* or trichordon* were better known in Alexandria.

There were various denominations for the stringed instruments: besides enchorda, *krouómena* (κρουόμενα, from krouein = κρούειν to strike), *entatá* (ἐντατά, stretched); Athen. IV, 174E, ch. 75. Pollux (IV, 58) gives also the following: *plettómena* (πληττόμενα, struck; from πλήττειν, plettein = to strike) and *epiplettómena* (ἐπιπ ληττόμενα; struck upon, from ἐπὶ-πλήττειν, epi-plettein = to strike upon).

The stringed instruments could be divided into various categories, the main being:

a) that of the lyra* and kithara*, to which belonged also the phorminx*, the kitharis* and the barbitos*. These instruments used strings equal in length, but different in thickness, bulk and tension. They varied slightly between themselves as to the pitch-range, the construction of the sound-box etc., and were played either by the fingers or with the aid of a plectrum.

b) that of the *psalterion* family. The instruments of this family were of foreign origin, and were played by direct touch of the fingers; hence their generic denomination "psalterion" (ψαλτήριον, from ψάλλειν, psallein* = to strike with the fingers.) They were also called *"epipsallómena"* (ἐπὶ-ψαλλόμενα) and *psaltiká* (ψαλτικά).
See *psallein*.

To this family belonged mainly, besides the psalterion itself, the magadis*, the pektis*, the sambyke* and the phoenix* or phoenikion or lyro-phoenix*. It seems that these instruments did not substantially differ from each other, and this is why they are often mixed up by many ancient writers. To this class belonged also two instruments Greek by invention, the epigoneion* and the simikion*. In this category belonged also a variety of instruments with strings of different length, such as the trigonon*. The lute family (instruments with a neck) is represented only by the trichordon* - pandoura* which constitutes a rather isolated case.

Many scholars prefer the classification: lyra (and kithara) family, harp family, lute family.

The instruments of the *lyra-kithara* family had a rather limited number of strings, rarely exceeding twelve (see *lyra*), while those of the psalterion family had always a great number of strings (up to forty). These last instruments were called *polychords** (πολύχορδα), especially by Plato, who condemned their use (Rep. III, 399D). Aristoxenus (ap. FHG II, p. 286, Fr. 64; Athen. IV, 182F, ch. 80) calls "foreign instruments" («ἔκφυλα ὄργανα») the phoenix, the pektis, magadis, sambyke, trigonon, klepsiambos, skindapsos and the nine-chord.

Note: C. Sachs (Hist. of Mus. Instr., p. 137) believes that a few passages in Aristotle, Pollux and Juba possibly suggest the existence of zithers in Greece. Such instruments with a great number of strings, as the simikion and the epigoneion, might be board-zithers (see *Epigoneion**), he suggests.

Bibliography:

> H. *Abert*: "Saiteninstrumente" in Pauly's R. E., Stuttgart 1920; 2nd series I, cols 1760-1767.

> M. *Wegner*: "Das Musikleben der Griechen"; Berlin 1949; "Saiteninstrumente" p. 28ff.

> M. *Wegner*: "Griechische Instrumente und Musikbräuche" in "Die Musik in Gesch. k. Gegenw."; Kassel 1956, vol. V, col. 865 ff.

For other bibliography see under *lyra* and *mousike*.

endrome (ἐνδρομή; m. pr. endromí), from endromein (ἐνδρομεῖν), to run through, or inside something.

This was the name of an instrumental melody played during the Pentathlon contest. An "endrome" composed by Hierax,* the 7th cent. B.C. aulete and composer, became famous, and continued to be played for centuries at the Olympic Games during the Pentathlon contest.

Cf. Plut. De Mus. 1140D, ch. 26.

enechos (ἔνηχος; m. pr. énichos); sounding; having the property of producing a sound.

In the neut., plur., ἔνηχα ὄργανα (*enecha instruments*) are taken by some to be "wind instruments", and by others "percussion instruments". Athen. (XIV, 636C, ch. 38) «καὶ ἄλλα πλείονα, τὰ μὲν ἔγχορδα, τὰ δὲ ἔνηχα κατεσκεύαζον» ("and many other [instruments], of which some were stringed, and others *enecha* instruments".

99

Gulick and Schweighäuser translate "percussion instruments"; LSJ and Dem. "wind instruments";

See also Anon. Bell. note 17, pp. 27-28.

energmos and **enerxis** (ἐνεργμός, ἔνερξις); a) method or way of playing the kithara; b) according to Euphronius, a peg for tuning the strings. E. M. p. 340,3 «ἐνεργμὸς τὸ δ᾽ αὐτὸ καὶ ἔνερξις, κροῦμα κιθαριστικόν. Εὐφρόνιος δὲ τὸν ἐν μέσῃ τῇ κιθάρᾳ πασσαλίσκον, δι᾽ οὗ ἡ χορδὴ διήρτηται» ("*energmos*, and *enerxis* as well, a piece for kithara. But, according to Euphronius, the little peg, found inside the middle, from which the string is attached").

Cf. also Th. Kock Comic. Att. Fr., vol. I, p. 371; Fr. 6 (Phryn. Konnus) «τί, δαί; τὸν ἐνεργμὸν» ("what? the *energmos*").

enerxis (ἔνερξις, and ἔνειρξις);

See above, *energmós*; E. M.; p. 540, 2.

Enharmonion genos (ἐναρμόνιον γένος; m. pr. enarmónion génos); the genus in which use was made of quarter-tones. The tetrachord in the enharmonic genus proceeds as follows: e - e* - f - a.

$$\tfrac{1}{4} \quad \tfrac{1}{4} \quad 2\,\text{t}.$$

The interval of the ditone (f-a) must be seen as a simple interval (not compound, not a leap), because no other note is understood, in the Enharmonic, between the third (f) and the fourth (a) notes of the tetrachord. The names of the notes (or strings) remain the same, as in the diatonic, in accordance with their order in the tetrachord:

The Enharmonic genus was the last of the three genera to come into use, and Olympus was accredited with its invention. Plut. De Mus. (1134F, ch. 11): "Olympus, as Aristoxenus says, was considered by the musicians as the inventor of the Enharmonic genus, because all before him were diatonic and chromatic"; cf. FHG, II, 287, Fr. 69.

Arist. Quint. (I Mb p. 19; R.P.W-I p. 16) defines the Enharmonic as more precise (or accurate; ἀκριβέστερον) and that "it has been accepted by the most distinguished men in music" («παρὰ γὰρ τοῖς ἐπιφανεστάτοις ἐν μουσικῇ τετύχηκε παραδοχῆς»); and as difficult to be performed for many people. The term «ἁρμονία» (harmonia) very often replaced the term enharmonic from Aristoxenus' time onwards (Aristox. Harm. I, p. 2, 9; p. 23, 21 etc; Cleon. Isag. ch. 3, C.v.J. p. 181, Mb p. 3). Often both terms are used in the same text

100

(Aristox. Harm. I, Mb p. 2, 9; 12, 17 etc.; Arist. Quint. (I Mb p. 18 and p. 19; R.P.W-I pp. 15-16).

Note: The adj. ἐναρμόνιος (*enharmonios*) was often used to signify melodious, emmeles*; e.g. enharmonion asma (ἐναρμόνιον ᾆσμα), melodious song; enharmonios phthongos (ἐναρμόνιος φθόγγος; Theon Smyrn. De sono, p. 47).

Also in the sense of "concerted", adjusted together, e.g. in chorus; Athen. (XIV, 628A, ch. 24) «ἐναρμονίων γὰρ ὄντων τῶν ᾀσμάτων» ("the songs being sung in chorus [concerted, in 'harmony']"); "since the songs are sung *in concert* (i.e. in chorus)" as transl. by Ch. B. Gulick, vol. vi, p. 385).

enharmonios (ἐναρμόνιος; m. pr. enarmónios);
See Note to *Enharmonion genus** and *enharmosis**.

enharmosis (ἐνάρμοσις; m. pr. enármosis), from vb enharmozein or enharmottein (ἐναρμόζειν, ἐναρμόττειν; m. pr. enarmózin, enarmóttin) to fit in, to tune an instrument to a certain harmonia (esp. Med. enharmottesthai, ἐναρμόττεσθαι; cf. Aristoph. Equites, Ἱππῆς, v. 989); tuning of an instrument to a certain harmonia.

enharmostos (ἐνάρμοστος; m. pr. enármostos) Adj., harmonious, concordant (Dem., LSJ).
See *harmosis** and Note to *Enharmonion genus**.

enkeraules (ἐγκεραύλης; m. pr. engerávlis, or egkerávlis); the aulete who played on a double Phrygian aulos, the so-called elymos*.

Hes. «ὁ τοῖς Φρυγίοις αὐλῶν· ἔχει γὰρ ὁ ἀριστερὸς προκείμενον κέρας» ("the player of the double Phrygian aulos, of which the left one has at the end a horned bell"). The verb enkeraulein (ἐγκεραυλεῖν) signified, according to Hes., "to play the Phrygian aulos".

enkomion (ἐγκώμιον; m. pr. engómion); encomium; an ode praising a victor at one of the athletic games. It was sung during the festival procession of the victors.

Athen. (XIII, 573F) «Πίνδαρός τε τὸ μὲν πρῶτον ἔγραψεν εἰς αὐτὸν (Ξενοφῶντα) ἐγκώμιον» ("And Pindar wrote for him [Xenophon the Corinthian, victor at the Olympic Games] the first *enkomion*").

The *enkomion* is distinguished from the epinikion* in that the first was sung by the komos* (κῶμος, the festival group in procession) while the epinikion was performed by the chorus in the temple.

enneachordon (ἐννεάχορδον); a nine-stringed instrument, hence its name. It was of Asiatic origin, and became known to Greece from early times; for some scholars it resembled the lyra.

The nine-chord, together with the klepsiambos*, the trigonon* and the

101

elymos* aulos fell into oblivion from Apollodorus' time (2nd cent. B.C.); Athen. XIV, 636F, ch. 40.

See the text under *klepsiambos.*

The nine-chord was included in the group of instruments called by Aristoxenus "degenerate" or "foreign" (see *enchorda*).

enneaphthongon melos (ἐννεάφθογγον μέλος); having nine notes. Also *enneaphonos* (ἐννεάφωνος, -ον).

Aug. Nauck Trag. Graec. Fragm. (Leipzig, 1926) Adesp. No 419, p. 920 «τὸν γὰρ Ὀρφέα λαβὼν αὐτῶν τε μουσῶν ἐννεάφθογγον μέλος».

enodos (ἔνῳδος or ἐνῳδός; ἐν-ῳδή); melodious; musical. Nicom. (Harm. Enchir. ch. 2; C.v.J. p. 240, Mb p. 5) «τοῦ τῆς ἐνῳδοῦ φωνῆς τόπου» ("of the locus of the *musical* voice [sound]").

Ἐνῳδῶς (adv. *enodós*) or ἐνῳδῶς; melodiously.

Nicom. (Ibid.) «δι᾽ ἐμμελείας καὶ ἐνῳδῶς προχωρεῖ» ("it proceeds *melodiously*").

enoplios (ἐνόπλιος);

a) *enóplios rhythmós* (ἐνόπλιος ῥυθμός); war- (or martial-) rhythm; rhythm of war-melodies.

Xen. Anabasis (VI, I, 11) "After that the Mantineans (Μαντινεῖς) and some of the Arcadians stood up armed as best as they could, and sang to the *enoplios* rhythm played by the aulos, and sang paeans, and danced as in the processions in honour of Gods". Cf. *pous*.

b) *enóplios orchesis* (ἐνόπλιος ὄρχησις); war-dance, danced on the enoplios rhythm. The "enoplios" dancing was also called *kouretike* (κουρητικὴ) from the Kouretes by whom it was danced in Crete; Dio Chrys. "On reigning II Β" § 61 (Περὶ Βασιλείας, Β) "the *kouretike enoplios* [dance], which was a local dance among the Cretans" («τὴν ἐνόπλιον κουρητικήν, ἥπερ ἦν ἐπιχώριος τοῖς Κρησί»).

c) *enóplion melos* (ἐνόπλιον μέλος); war-tune; martial melody.

d) *enoplios nomos* (ἐνόπλιος νόμος); an auletic nomos; a solo for aulos inciting to war, usually combined with dancing. Epicharmus in his "Muses" (ap. Athen. IV, 184F, ch. 84) says that "Athena (Minerva) played on the aulos the *enoplios nomos* to the Dioscuri [Castor and Pollux]" («καὶ τὴν Ἀθηνᾶν δέ, φησὶν Ἐπίχαρμος ἐν Μούσαις, ἐπαυλῆσαι τοῖς Διοσκούροις τὸν ἐνόπλιον»).

enrhythmos, and **errhythmos** (ἔνρυθμος, and ἔρρυθμος; ἐν-ρυθμός; m. pr. énrithmos, érrithmos); rhythmical. Athen. (XIV, 631B, ch. 30) «γυμνοὶ γὰρ ὀρχοῦνται οἱ παῖδες πάντες ἐρρύθμους (or ἐνρύθμους) φοράς τινας ἀποτελοῦντες» ("for all the boys use to dance naked performing certain *rhythmical movements*").

ἐνρύθμως, and *ἐρρύθμως* (enrhythmos, errhythmos) adv., rhythmically, in rhythm. Athen. (Ibid) «κινοῦντες ἐρρύθμως (or ἐνρύθμως) τοὺς πόδας» ("moving the feet *rhythmically*").

The enrhythmos (rhythmical) should be distinguished from eurhythmos* (eurhythmic).

entasis (**ἔντασις**); tension; the same as tasis* (τάσις). From vb. enteinein (ἐντείνειν; m. pr. entínin) = to stretch (a string); also to tune a string.

entaton, organon (**ἐντατόν, ὄργανον**); stringed instrument.
See *enchorda*.

eora (**ἐώρα**; m. pr. eóra); see under *aletis*.

epadein, vb (**ἐπᾴδειν**; m. pr. epádin); to sing in accompaniment; to sing as an incantation (LSJ). Cf. Plato Laws II, 666c.
See *epode**.

epankonismos (**ἐπαγκωνισμός**); a kind of dance mentioned in Athen. XIV, 630A with other dances (kalathiskos, strobilos, etc.).

epaulein (**ἐπαυλεῖν**; m. pr. epavlín) vb.; to accompany by the aulos; to play the aulos together with a vocal melody.
Paus. (book VI, ch. 14, § 10) «Πυθόκριτος ὁ Σικυώνιος... ἐπηύλησεν ἑξάκις τῷ πεντάθλῳ» ("Pythocritus of Sicyon ... accompanied the pentathlon by the aulos six times"). Sextus Empir. ("Against Musicians"; «Πρὸς μουσικούς»; book VI, § 8): «παρήνεσε [Πυθαγόρας]...τῷ αὐλητῇ τὸ σπονδεῖον αὐτοῖς [τοῖς μειρακίοις] ἐπαυλῆσαι μέλος» ("[Pythagoras] advised the aulete to play for them [i.e. the youths] the spondeion* tune").
epaulema (ἐπαύλημα; m. pr. epávlima); the melody or tune itself, played on the aulos as above.

epeisodion (**ἐπεισόδιον**; m. pr. episódion); episode. That part of the ancient tragedy which is found between the choral mele (Arist. Poet. 1452B, ch. XII). In the ancient comedy an interpolated comic melos (tune) was so called.

ephymnion (**ἐφύμνιον**; m. pr. ephímnion); a song sung after a hymn; an epode to a hymn.
Suid. «τὸ ἐπὶ ὕμνῳ ᾆσμα» ("the song [which comes] after the hymn").

epibemata (**ἐπιβήματα**; pl. of ἐπίβημα; m. pr. epivímata); kinds of choral dancing (Hes: εἴδη χορικῆς ὀρχήσεως).

103

Epigoneion (ἐπιγόνειον; m. pr. epigónion); a stringed instrument of the psalterion family, i.e. of those played directly by the fingers without the aid of a plectrum. It had 40 strings and was one of the largest "polychord" instruments used in ancient Greece. It is not exactly known what was its range, how many notes it gave and what was its character. If the Epigoneion was tuned either diatonically or chromatically (by semitones), its range would surpass five or three octaves respectively; i.e. beyond the range in practice according to the evidence of Aristoxenus (Harm. I, p. 20, 27-29 Mb; "... the largest consonant interval is two octaves and a fifth, because we do not reach the compass of three octaves"). Some scholars suggest that the strings of the Epigoneion were in pairs as in the magadis*; thus the sounds would really be 20.

Others, like Gevaert (Hist. et Théor., II, p. 247), suggest that the Epigoneion made use of intervals smaller than the semitone. As to its character some suggest that it might be like a harp, horizontally placed, as the Viennese zither (Th. Rein. "La m. grecque", p. 126).

According to ancient sources the Epigoneion was invented by Epigonus* from whom it took its name. C. Sachs (Hist. of Mus. Instr., p. 137) proposes another etymology for the Epigoneion: from epi (ἐπὶ) = on, upon, and gony (γόνυ) = knee. He suggests that the epigoneion (and the simikion as well) might be a board-zither, placed on the knees of the player.

Athen. (IV, 183C-D, ch. 81): "Iobas (Jubas) mentions also the lyrophoenix* and the *Epigoneion* which, now re-modelled into an upright psalterion, still preserves the name of its inventor; and Epigonus was by birth an Ambraciot, but by citizenship Sicyonian, and being most musical he played with the bare hand without a plectrum". See also Pollux (IV, 59) on the same text, with the addition that "the Epigoneion has 40 strings".

Epigonus (Ἐπίγονος; m. pr. Epígonos); 6th cent. B.C. musician of repute. Born at Ambracia (Ἀμβρακία, hence his surname Ambrakiotes, Ἀμβρακιώτης) he lived in Sicyon; Athen. (IV, 183D, ch. 81); «ἦν δ᾽ Ἐπίγονος φύσει μὲν Ἀμβρακιώτης, δημοποίητος δὲ Σικυώνιος» ("Epigonus was by birth an Ambraciot, but by citizenship a Sicyonian").

To Epigonus was attributed the invention of the forty-stringed instrument called Epigoneion* after his name (Pollux IV, 59).

He was considered an excellent performer, playing without the aid of a plectrum («μουσικώτατος δ᾽ ὢν κατὰ χεῖρα δίχα πλήκτρου ἔψαλλεν»; Athen. Ibid.). To him and his School was also attributed the initiation of the "enaulos kitharisis", i.e. solo kithara playing to aulos accompaniment (Athen. XIV, 637F, ch. 42; see the text under *enaulos kitharisis*).

His School and his disciples generally were known as Epigoneioi, Epigoneans (Ἐπιγόνειοι) or "those around Epigonus" («οἱ περὶ τὸν Ἐπίγονον»). Their interest extended beyond the practical side of music (performance) to the theory of music. Aristoxenus criticizes some of them who, with Lasus, attributed breadth to notes (Harm. I, p. 3, 23-24; see the text under *platos*, breadth).

epikedeion, melos (ἐπικήδειον, μέλος; m. pr. epikídion); a song sung at a funeral; a mournful tune. Procl. Chrest. *"the epikedeion* is sung at the funeral while the body is still lying exposed" ("...τὸ μὲν *ἐπικήδειον* παρ' αὐτό τε κῆδος, ἔτι τοῦ σώματος προκειμένου, λέγεται»).

As an adj. *epikedeios* masc. (ἐπικήδειος) signified *funeral*; epikedeios aulos (ἐπικήδειος αὐλός), funeral aulos. Plut. Quaest. Conv. (book III, Quaest. 8, § 2, 657A) «ὥσπερ [γὰρ] ἡ θρηνῳδία καὶ ὁ *ἐπικήδειος* αὐλὸς ἐν ἀρχῇ πάθος κινεῖ καὶ δάκρυον ἐκβάλλει» ("because, like the dirge, the *funeral aulos* at first rouses grief and causes tears").

Lamentations were sung in Greece at funerals from remotest times. In Homeric times there were the so-called "leaders of the dirge" («θρήνων ἔξαρχοι») who first began the singing, followed by the others (Il. XXII, 408ff; XXIV, 695). Around the mortuary bed relatives and friends of the dead were seated, and lamented. The procession was accompanied by auletes and mourners; after the burial funeral dinners were held during which lamentations were sung to aulos accompaniment.

See also *threnos-threnodia*.

epikredios (ἐπικρήδιος; m. pr. epikrídios); a kind of Cretan war-dance (pyrrhiche). Athen. (XIV, 629C, ch. 26): «ὅθεν ἐκινήθησαν αἱ καλούμεναι πυρρίχαι καὶ πᾶς ὁ τοιοῦτος τρόπος τῆς ὀρχήσεως· πολλαὶ γὰρ αἱ παρονομασίαι αὐτῶν, ὡς παρὰ Κρησὶν ὀρσίτης καὶ *ἐπικρήδιος*». ("there came into practice the so-called pyrrhichai*, and every such kind of dancing; numerous indeed are their denominations, as e.g. among Cretans the orsites and the *epikredios*").

Nothing definite is known about its characteristic features.

epilenios, dance (ἐπιλήνιος, χορός; m. pr. epilínios); a kind of folk-dance which originated from (and imitated) the movements of people while pressing grapes. Ληνὸς (lenos) was the trough in which the grapes, after having been collected, were pressed by the feet to produce wine.

b) *epilenia*, pl. of epilenion (ἐπιλήνια; m. pr. epilínia) were the songs sung during the actual pressing of the grapes. So too was called the festival of the vintage.

epilogos (ἐπίλογος); the last part of the drama (or of a speech, of a book etc.). According to Pollux (IV, 66) *epilogos* was the last (sixth) part of the kitharodikos* nomos; also called exodion* (ἐξόδιον).

epimelodema (ἐπιμελῴδημα; m. pr. epimelódima); what is sung afterwards (after something) like an epodos. Refrain (LSJ).

epinikion, melos (ἐπινίκιον, μέλος); a song composed to praise a victory, after a battle in war, or after an important poetic, musical or athletic contest. A triumphal ode, usually for victors at one of the four National Games (Olympic, Pythian, Isthmian and Nemean). In pl. *τὰ ἐπινίκια* (*epiníkia*) signified also the celebrations held to commemorate the victory, and the sacrifice as well, offered on the occasion of the victory. Also the prizes (ἐπινίκια ἆθλα).

The word *epínikos*, or *epiníkios* (masc.) hymn or (fem.) ode (ἐπίνικος; ἐπινίκιος masc. ὕμνος, fem. ᾠδή) was used in the same meaning as epinikion (neut.). The lyric poets, such as Simonides, Bacchylides and above all the greatest lyric poet of ancient Greece, Pindar, composed epinikioi (victorious, triumphal) hymns or odes.

epiparodos (ἐπιπάροδος).
See *parodos*.

epiphallos (ἐπίφαλλος); a kind of aulesis with dancing.
The epiphallos is included in Tryphon's catalogue of Denominations of auleseis (αὐλήσεις, plur.), ap. Athen. XIV, 618C, ch. 9.
See the full catalogue under *aulesis*.

epipneomena (ἐπιπνεόμενα) pl.; wind instruments.
See *emphysomena* and *empneusta*.

epiporpema, and **epiporpama** (ἐπιπόρπημα, and ἐπιπόρπαμα; m. pr. epipórpima, epipórpama); the special dress of the kitharode; a sort of mantle clasped on the shoulder. Pollux (X, 190): «ἐπιπόρπαμα δὲ κιθαρῳδοῦ σκευή» ("*epiporpama* [is] the kitharode's dress").

epipsalmos (ἐπιψαλμός); an accompaniment on a stringed instrument struck by the fingers.
Ptolem. Harm. (II, ch. 12; ed. Wallis vol. III, p. 85; I.D. p. 67, 7).
See *psallein* and *psalmos*.

epiptaesma (ἐπίπταισμα; m. pr. epíptesma); playing a string by the fingers; otherwise *psalmos*. Also, according to Pollux, called "ptaesma" (πταῖσμα). Th. Kock Comic. Att. Frg. (Aristoph. Incerta) p. 574, Frg. 773 «ἐπιπταίσματα»

106

(pl., *epiptaesmata*); Pollux II, 199 «τὰ δέ ὑπὲρ τοὺς δακτύλους κρούματα, πταίσματα· Ἀριστοφάνης δὲ καὶ *ἐπιπταίσματα* αὐτὰ καλεῖ» ("the performances by the fingers were called *ptaesmata* (pl.); Aristophanes calls them also *epiptaesmata*").

Cf. Bothe PSGF, II, p. 179.

epirrhema (ἐπίρρημα; epírrima); the fifth part of the *parabasis** (παράβασις).

It was composed (Pollux, IV, 112) of trochaic tetrameters, and was recited by the koryphaeus (the leader of the chorus) directly to the public.

epistomís (ἐπιστομίς);   another word for *phorbeia** (φορβειά).

episynaphe (ἐπισυναφή; m. pr. episinaphí); the conjoining of three conjunct tetrachords, i.e. when three tetrachords were conjoined to each other by a conjunction.

Bacch. Isag. (C.v.J. p. 311; Mb p. 21) *"episynaphe* is when three tetrachords are sung conjointly one after the other; as for instance the tetrachords of hypaton, meson and synemmenon" («ἐπισυναφὴ δέ ἐστιν, ὅταν τρία τετράχορδα κατὰ συναφὴν ἑξῆς μελῳδηθῇ· οἷον ὑπατῶν, μέσων, συνημμένων»).

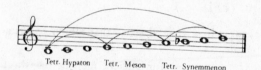

Tetr. Hypaton   Tetr. Meson   Tetr. Synemmenon

See also Man. Bryen. Harm., Sect. XI (ed. Wallis, vol. III, p. 506).

epitasis (ἐπίτασις; from epiteinein, ἐπιτείνειν = to stretch); tension, stretching of a string.   Hence the motion from a lower note to a higher one; this applied metaph. to wind instruments and the voice as well.

Oppos. *anesis** (ἄνεσις).

According to Aristoxenus (Harm. I, Mb p. 10, 24-25) *"epitasis* is the continuous motion of the voice from a lower position to a higher one" («ἡ μὲν οὖν *ἐπίτασίς* ἐστι κίνησις τῆς φωνῆς συνεχὴς ἐκ βαρυτέρου τόπου εἰς ὀξύτερον»).

Bacch. Isag. § 45 (C.v.J. p. 302, Mb p. 12): *"epitasis* is the motion of melodies from a lower note to a higher" («*ἐπίτασίς* ἐστι κίνησις μελῶν ἀπὸ τοῦ βαρυτέρου ἐπὶ τὸ ὀξύτερον).   Arist. Quint. (Mb. p. 8, RPW-I p. 7) *"epitasis* is when [the voice] proceeds from a lower (locus] to a higher" («*ἐπίτασις* δέ, ὅταν ἐκ βαρυτέρου [τόπου] μεταβαίνῃ [ἡ φωνὴ] πρὸς ὀξύτερον»).   Aristoxenus (Harm. I, p. 10,35) says that many people identify epitasis with height of pitch, and anesis with depth of pitch.

In Man. Bryen. Harm. (Sect. III; ed. Wallis vol. III, p. 479) and Anon. Bell. (§ 4, p. 22) epitasis is explained as *"anadosis (ἀνάδοσις* = heightening, raising), and is called by some people "Hyphen from inside" («ἐπίτασις ἤτοι ἀνάδοσις· ἥν τινες καλοῦσιν ὑφ᾽ ἕν ἔσωθεν»).

Cf. *ekkrousis*.

epithalamion (ἐπιθαλάμιον); neut., melos; or *epithalámios, ode (ἐπιθαλά-μιος, ᾠδή)*. A nuptial song sung by a chorus of maidens and youths in front of the bridal-chamber.

There were two kinds: a) the *katakoemetikon (κατακοιμητικόν*, from κατακοιμᾶν = to lull) sung in the evening, and b) the *diegertikon (διεγερτικόν*; lit. awakening) in the morning.

See also *hymenaeos (ὑμέναιος)*.

epitonion (ἐπιτόνιον); a) thong or peg by which the strings were tuned; kollabos.

b) Also, mouthpiece of an aulos (Dem.); handle of a syrinx (turncock or stopcock, Dem., LSJ).

Cf. Vitruvii: De Architectura (ed. F. Krohn, Leipzig, 1912) book X, ch. 8, § 5, English transl. by Frank Granger 1931-4, Loeb Class. Libr. vol. II, p. 319).

c) a small aulos (αὐλίσκος) used for tuning instruments, used as pitch-pipe for the chorus (LSJ).

epitritos (ἐπίτριτος); in a general sense that which consists of a whole and one third of the whole.

epitritos foot (ἐπίτριτος πούς) in ancient metrics was the foot which consisted of three long and one short syllables. The short syllable could be placed at the beginning, in the middle or at the end: a) ᴗ---; b) -ᴗ--; c) --ᴗ-; d) ---ᴗ.

epitritos lógos (ἐπίτριτος λόγος); the ratio 4:3 by which the dia tessaron (διὰ τεσσάρων; the interval of the 4th) is expressed.

epitymbios, nomos (ἐπιτύμβιος, νόμος; m. pr. epitímvios nomos); a sepulchral (epitaphial) auletic nomos. Pollux (IV, 79) «καὶ Ὀλύμπου, ἐπιτύμβιοι (νόμοι)» ("and the *sepulchral* [nomoi] of Olympus").

epode (ἐπῳδή; m. pr. epodí); a magical song. Also, as *epodos** (a).

epodos (ἐπῳδός; from ἐπί and ᾠδή) had various meanings.

a) That part of a lyric poem which was performed (sung) after the strophe and the antistrophe. Usually the strophe and the antistrophe were sung by two sections of the chorus alternately, while the epodos was sung by the whole body of the chorus.

b) A verse (or a whole strophe) repeated several times after a strophe, like the refrain in the rondo form.

c) That which is suitable for singing or which is "sung to music" (LSJ).

d) *epodos,* masc. (ἐπὶ-ἀοιδός, ἐπῳδός) signified also the man who by singing or reciting magical odes tried to enchant, and especially to cure or appease pains of the body (enchanter). Also fem. epode (ἐπῳδή); Plato Laws (book X, 903B) «ἐπῳδῶν γε μὴν προσδεῖσθαί μοι δοκεῖ μύθων ἔτι τινῶν» ([Athenaeus speaking] "but still he needs also, as it seems to me, *some words of counsel to act as a charm* upon him"; transl. R.G. Bury, vol. II, p. 363).

e) *epodon* (ἐπῳδόν) neut.; it appears once in neut. in Plut. De Mus. (1141A, ch. 28). According to Reinach (Plut. De la Mus., note 278, p. 108) it was a poem in distichs, with the second verse shorter than the first.

epogdoos (ἐπόγδοος); in a general sense that which consists of a whole and one eighth of the whole.

epogdoos logos (ἐπόγδοος λόγος) in music, the ratio 9:8; the major tone; the interval by which the 5th exceeds the 4th (Nicom. Enchir. ch. 6; C.v.J. p. 247; Mb p. 12; «ᾧ ὑπερέχει ἡ διὰ πέντε τῆς διὰ τεσσάρων, ἐβεβαιοῦτο ἐν ἐπογδόῳ λόγῳ ὑπάρχειν»).

Hence, *epogdoos* (or *epogdoon,* neut.) was the interval of a tone.

Hes. "*epogdoon;* a musical tone" («ἐπόγδοον· τόνος μουσικός»).

Eratocles (Ἐρατοκλῆς; m. pr. Eratoclís); 5th cent. B.C. harmonist, one of Aristoxenus' precursors. He and his School are mentioned by Aristoxenus among the "Harmonists" (Ἀρμονικοί, Harmonikoi) who preceded him; he discusses and refutes their views. For Eratocles, see Harm. Elem. I, Mb p. 5, 9-10 and p. 6, 13 and 21-22.

Eratosthenes (Ἐρατοσθένης; m. pr. Eratosthénis); b. Cyrene (Κυρήνη) 275 B.C.; d. Alexandria, 195 or 194 B.C. Scholar and scientist of great repute, considered as the most erudite man of letters and science of Alexandria. After studying first in Alexandria, and then in Athens, he returned and settled in Alexandria where he became administrator of the famous Library.

He was the first to be surnamed "Philologus" (Φιλόλογος, Philologist), and by many he was generally called "B" (Βῆτα, Beta), i.e. Second in every subject of general knowledge.

Among his numerous works on philosophy, geography, history, mathematics, astronomy etc. there are references to music.

Bibl. *G. Bernhardy:* Eratosthenes (Berlin, 1822); *G. Pachymeres* ap. A.J.H. Vincent: Notices, pp. 392-3; *C.v.J.* Excerpta Neapolitana, pp. 416-7.

eribremetes (ἐριβρεμέτης; m. pr. erivremétis), from ἐρι- (Hes.) very big, strong; and βρέμειν (bremein = to sound loudly); loud-sounding. «Αὐλὸς ἐριβρεμέτης» = a loud-sounding aulos. Also *eribromos* and *eribremes* (ἐρίβρομος, ἐριβρεμής).

erigerys (ἐρίγηρυς; m. pr. erígiris); loud-sounding. Hes. "loud-voiced" or "loud-speaking" («μεγαλόφωνος»).

Erigone (Ἠριγόνη; m. pr. Irigóni).
    See *aletis.*

escharinthon (ἐσχάρινθον; m. pr. eschárinthon); a Laconic dance mentioned by Pollux (IV, 105), so named after its inventor («ἐσχάρινθον μὲν ὄρχημα, ἐπώνυμον δ' ἦν τοῦ εὑρόντος αὐλητοῦ»).

ethos (ἦθος; m. pr. íthos); in a general sense, principally the moral character of a person (e.g. «πρᾶος τὸ ἦθος» = mild or gentle in character). In music ethos signified the moral character which the music tends to inspire in the soul. The notes, the harmoniai, the genera, the melos in general, and the rhythms had, in the view of many ancient Greek writers, ethical strength and purpose. For this reason they ascribed to music a most important educatioal role.

Plutarch (De Mus. 1140 B-C., ch. 26) writes "It is evident from the above that, reasonably, the early Greeks gave their best attention to the musical education. Because they believed that they ought to shape and attune the souls of Youth to decent morals by Music, as Music is beneficial at every time and for every virtuous action."

Plato, to quote one of his innumerable philosophical expressions on this matter, says in "Protagoras" (326 A-B) that the teachers of the kithara try to inspire wisdom in the boys "...and they insist on familiarizing the boys' souls with the rhythms and scales (harmoniai), that they may gain in gentleness, and by advancing in rhythmic and harmonic grace may be efficient in speech and action; for the whole of man's life requires the graces of rhythm and harmony"; «πᾶς γὰρ ὁ βίος τοῦ ἀνθρώπου εὐρυθμίας καὶ εὐαρμοστίας δεῖται» (transl. by W.R.M. Lamb, p. 144).   And in the "Republic" (Book III; Socrates speaking) "Is it not for this reason, dear Glaucon, that education in music is most important because rhythm and harmonia penetrate deeply into the inmost soul and exercise strongest influence upon it, by bringing with them and imparting beauty, if one is rightly trained, or the contrary?".

Arist. Quint. (De Mus. p. 65 Mb) "there is no human action which is done without music" («οὐκ ἔστι πρᾶξις ἐν ἀνθρώποις, ἥτις ἄνευ μουσικῆς τελεῖται»).

a) ETHOS OF NOTES AND PITCH

Aristides (op. cit. Mb. p. 13, RPW-I p. 10), speaking on the differences between the musical sounds (see under *phthongos**), defines as the fifth difference that of the *ethos*. The ethos varies according to the pitch of the sounds; "one, he says, is the ethos of higher notes, another of lower notes, and another when they are in the region of the parhypate or of the lichanos" («ἕτερα γὰρ ἤθη τοῖς ὀξυτέροις, ἕτερα τοῖς βαρυτέροις ἐπιτρέχει, καὶ ἕτερα μὲν παρυπατοειδέσιν, ἕτερα δὲ λιχανοειδέσιν»).

b) ETHOS OF MELOS

The ethos in the melopoeia is distinguished in three different ways of expression (cf. Cleon. Isag. ch. 13; C.v.Jan p. 206; Mb p. 21).

1. the *diastaltic* (διασταλτικὸν) which expresses the majestic and a manly disposition of the soul («μεγαλοπρέπεια καὶ δίαρμα ψυχῆς ἀνδρῶδες»); it incites to heroic actions, and is used in tragedy;

2. the *systaltic* (συσταλτικὸν) by which the soul is led to humbleness and want of manly disposition («εἰς ταπεινότητα καὶ ἄνανδρον διάθεσιν») This is suited to love feelings, lamentations, compassion and the like; and

3. the *hesychastic* (ἡσυχαστικὸν) which brings to the soul calm and peace. "It is suitable for hymns, paeans, encomiums, counsels and the like".

Arist. Quint. (p. 30 Mb and RPW-I) also distinguishes the same three kinds of ethos in the melopoeia, the systaltic, the diastaltic and the medium (cf. *melopoeia**).

c) ETHOS OF HARMONIAI

Each harmonia is expressive of ethos.

1. The ethos of *Doristi* or *Dorian* harmonia was described as manly and majestic (ἀνδρῶδες, μεγαλοπρεπές; Heracl. Pont. ap. Athen. XIV, 624D, ch. 19); sombre and impetuous («σκυθρωπὸν καὶ σφοδρόν»; Heracl. Pont. ap. Athen. ibid); distinguished and dignified («ἀξιωματικόν, σεμνόν»; Plut. De Mus. 1136D & F, chs. 16 & 17); steadiest and masculine (Aristotle Polit. VIII, ch. 7 § 10 «περὶ δὲ τῆς δωριστὶ πάντες ὁμολογοῦσιν ὡς στασιμωτάτης οὔσης καὶ μάλιστ᾽ ἦθος ἐχούσης ἀνδρεῖον»; "and about the Doristi harmonia all agree, as being steadiest and having above all masculine ethos").

2. The ethos of *Hypodoristi* or *Hypodorian* harmonia (or old Aeolian) was described as "haughty, pompous and somewhat conceited", also "lofty and confident" («γαῦρον καὶ ὀγκῶδες, ἔτι δὲ καὶ ὑπόχαυνον», «ἐξηρμένον καὶ τεθαρρηκός»; Heracl. Pont. ap. Athen. ibid); deep-toned («βαρύβρομον»; Lasus of Herm. ap. Athen. ibid); majestic and steady (Arist. Probl. XIX, 48 «ἡ δὲ ὑποδωριστὶ [ἦθος ἔχει] μεγαλοπρεπὲς καὶ στάσιμον, διὸ καὶ κιθαρῳδικωτάτη ἐστὶ τῶν ἁρμονιῶν» = "the Hypodoristi [has ethos] majestic and steady, and for this it is the harmonia which is most suitable to kitharodic music").

3. The ethos of *Phrygisti* or *Phrygian* (or Iasti) harmonia was described as inspired («ἔνθεον»; Luc. "Harmonides" I, 10), enthusiastic, also violently

111

exciting and emotional (Arist. Polit. VIII, 5, 9 and 7, 8, 1340B, and 1342B «ὀργιαστικὴ καὶ παθητική»). Suitable for the dithyramb.

4. The ethos of *Hypophrygisti* or *Hypophrygian* harmonia was described by Heracl. Pont. (ap. Athen. 625B, ch. 20) as "hard and austere" («σκληρὸν καὶ αὐστηρόν»), and by Lucian (Harmonides I, 10-12) as elegant («γλαφυρόν»).

5. The ethos of *Lydisti* or *Lydian* harmonia was described by many writers as mild and agreeable; by Plato as "convivial" and "slack" («συμποτικὸν καὶ μαλακόν»; Rep. III). Aristotle on the other hand (Polit. VIII, ch. 7, § 11, 1342B) finds the Lydian most suitable of all harmonias for the age of boyhood as it is decent and educative («διὰ τὸ δύνασθαι κόσμον τ᾿ ἔχειν καὶ παιδείαν»).

6. The ethos of *Hypolydisti* or *Hypolydian* harmonia was generally described as bacchic, voluptuous, intoxicating («βακχικόν, ἐκλελυμένον, μεθυστικόν»).

7. The ethos of *Mixolydısti* or *Mixolydian* harmonia, as passionate («παθητικόν», Plut. 1136D, ch. 16); as plaintive and restrained («ὀδυρτικωτέρως καὶ συνεστηκότως»; Arist. Polit. VIII, 5,8 1340B); as lamenting («θρηνῷδης», Plato Rep. III, 398E). See under *chorodidaskalos* the story of Euripides severely reproving a member of the chorus who mocked during the actual practice of the chorus in the Mixolydian.

d) ETHOS OF GENERA

1. The ethos of the *Diatonon* genus was described as more natural, masculine and more austere («φυσικόν», «ἀρρενωπόν» καὶ «αὐστηρόν»; Aristides Quint. I p. 19 and II p. 111 Mb, RPW-I pp. 16 and 92 respectively); as serious and vigorous («σεμνὸν καὶ εὔτονον»; Theon of Smyrn. "On Music", ch. 9, p. 85); as simple, brave and more natural («ἁπλοῦν τε καὶ γενναῖον καὶ φυσικώτερον»; M. Psellus p. 27).

2. The ethos of the *Chromatic* was described as most sweet and plaintive («ἥδιστόν τε καὶ γοερώτατον»; Anon. Bell. § 26, p. 31; also Aristides II, p. 111 Mb); and passionate («παθητικόν»; G. Pachym. p. 428).

3. The ethos of the *Enharmonic* was described as exciting and gentle («διεγερτικὸν καὶ ἤπιον»; Aristides ibid). RPW-I (Arist., Note p. 93) suggests «ἠθικὸν» (ethical) instead of «ἤπιον».

e) ETHOS OF RHYTHMS

Aristides (p. 97 Mb; RPW-I p. 82) holds that "those rhythms which start from thesis are quieter as they appease the intellect, while those starting from arsis are agitated". Also that the rhythms which are co-ordinated by regular relations («ἐν ἴσῳ λόγῳ τεταγμένοι») are more pleasant (graceful) while the hemiolic are more agitated. The dactyl from its majestic character is suited to the epic poetry, while the anapaest is more suitable for the embateria (marching tunes); the trochee, nimble and alert, is suitable for dancing melodies, etc.

Generally speaking the ethos was, according to many ancient writers and theorists, an important power in music; human morals were dependent upon the ethos of music. Philosophers, principally Damon, Plato and Aristotle, stressed that importance in their writings.

Bad music might exercise a very serious and destructive influence on the individual character and the morality of people. Plutarch (De audientis poetis, 19F) expresses this view: "Wicked music and evil songs create licentious morals and corrupt lives, and men loving voluptuousness and indolence, and submission to women" («Μουσικὴ φαύλη καὶ ἄσματα πονηρά, ἀκόλαστα ποιοῦσιν ἤθη καὶ βίους ἀνάνδρους καὶ ἀνθρώπους τρυφὴν καὶ μαλακίαν καὶ γυναικοκρασίαν»).

But there have been, especially in later times, different views concerning the moral influence of music, even contrary to the above. Mention should be made of the 5/4th c. "Hibeh" diatribe on music (Hibeh Papyri, 1906) transl. by Warren D. Anderson (pp. 147-9 of his book mentioned below, in the Bibliography), and of Philodemus (esp. book IV; see pp. 152-176 of Anderson). Sextus Empiricus (c. 3rd cent. A. D.) is another example; in his "Against Musicians" (VI, § 19ff) he discusses these views, severely criticizes and refutes them, by denying such a moral or social power to Music.

Bibliography:
Paul Girard: "L'Éducation athenienne"; Paris, 1891.
H. Abert: "Die lehre vom Ethos in der griechischen Musik"; Leipzig, 1899.
L. P. Wilkinson: "Philodemus on Ethos in Music"; Cl. Q 32 (1938), pp. 174-81.
E. A. Lippman: "The Sources and Development of the Ethical View of Music in Ancient Greece"; Mus. Quarterly XLIX, 1963.
W. D. Anderson: "Ethos and Education in Greek Music"; Cambridge, Mass., 1966.
For other bibliography see under mousike.

euchordos (εὔχορδος; m. pr. éfchordos); well-strung (LSJ), melodiously sounding (Dem.). "Euchordos lyra"; Pind. Nem. X, v. 21 «ἀλλ᾽ ὅμως εὔχορδον ἔγειρε λύραν» ("but he waked up the melodious lyra").

Eucleides, Euclid (Εὐκλείδης; m. pr. Evclídis); b. c. 350 or 330 B.C.; d. c. 275-270 B.C. Great mathematician and geometrician. It is not known where he was born; according to some sources he was born at Gela (Γέλα) in Sicily, hence his surname Gelóos (Γελῷος) or Sikelós (Σικελός); while others say he was born at Tyros in Syria of a Greek father (Naucrates, Ναυκράτης) from Damascus.

113

Euclid lived and taught in Alexandria at the invitation of the first king of Alexandria, Ptolemaeus I (323-284 B.C.).

To him was first attributed the "Isagoge" ("Introduction to Harmonike"); his name as its author appears in MSS of the 12th to 15th cents., and in Meibom's Ant. Mus. Auct. Sept. (vol. I, pp. 1-22). The "Isagoge" is now ascribed to Cleonides*.

Under his name now remains the "Division of the Canon" («Κατανομή Κανόνος, θεωρήματα μουσικά») published by Meibom (op. cit. pp. 23-40), and by C.v.Jan in Mus. Script. Gr. ("Sectio canonis", «Κατανομὴ Κανόνος», pp. 148-166).

The "Division of the Canon" was translated into French by Ch. Ém. Ruelle in his "Collection des auteurs Grecs relatifs à la musique", after the "Introduction harmonique" of Cleonides (Paris, 1883; "La division du canon d' Euclide le Géometre", pp. 42-59).

eueches (εὐηχής, εὖ-ἦχος; m. pr. evichís); sounding well or agreeably; producing a melodious or pleasant sound; melodious; euphonious.

Plut. "De Defectu Oraculorum", 437D, «ὥσπερ ὄργανον ἐξηρτυμένον καὶ εὐηχὲς» ("like an instrument set in good order and well-sounding [euphonious]").

Also *euechos* (εὔηχος; m. pr. évichos) and *euechetos* (εὐήχητος, evíchitos).

euepes (εὐεπής, εὖ-ἔπος; m. pr. evepís); melodious, euphonious, pleasing in tone. Xen. Cynegeticos (Κυνηγετικός; ch. XIII, 16) «φωνὴν δὲ οἱ μὲν εὐεπῆ ἴασιν, οἱ δ' αἰσχράν» ("some emit a *melodious* [pleasing] voice, while others a bad [displeasing] voice").

eugerys (εὔγηρυς, from εὖ and γῆρυς=voice, sound; m. pr. évgiris); having a sweet, agreeable tone; tuneful.

Aristoph. Frogs (v. 213) «εὔγηρυν ἐμάν ἀοιδάν» ("my *sweet-sounding* [tuneful] song").

euharmostos (εὐάρμοστος; m. pr. evármostos) from εὖ = well, and ἁρμόζειν (vb. harmozein) = to tune an instrument, to regulate according to the laws of music; well-regulated, well-tuned, well hermosmenos*. Oppos. anharmostos*.

Plato Laws (book II, 655A) «εὔρυθμον καὶ εὐάρμοστον, εὔχρων δὲ μέλος» ("eurhythmic and *harmonious*, and colourful melody").

euharmostia (εὐαρμοστία; m. pr. evarmostía), n.; good, harmonious tuning or regulation.

Plato Protag. (326B) «πᾶς γὰρ ὁ βίος τοῦ ἀνθρώπου εὐρυθμίας τε καὶ εὐαρμοστίας δεῖται» ("for the whole of man's life requires good rhythmical

114

and *harmonious* regulation [the graces of rhythm and harmony]'').

See *hermosmenos.*

euhymnia (εὐυμνία; m. pr. evimnía) from εὖ = well, and hymn; melodiousness. A synonym of eumolpia; Hes. «εὐμολπία, εὐυμνία».

The adj. *euhymnos* (εὔυμνος; évimnos) usually signified much praised; also, praised by (or in) many hymns.

Euius (Εὔϊος; m. pr. Évios); 4th cent. B.C. aulete and composer, from Chalkis (Χαλκὶς) in Euboea (Εὔβοια), surnamed Chalkideus (Χαλκιδεύς). He is mentioned (Athen. XII, 538F, ch. 54) as having participated in the brilliant festivities held by Alexander the Great on the occasion of his marriage at Sousa in Persia, together with a multitude of other well-known artists of the time (psilokitharists, kitharodes, aulodes and auletes).

Cf. Dinse: De Antigen. Theb., p. 27.

euktika, mele (εὐκτικά, μέλη; m. pr. efktiká) pl.; songs by which a wish or request was submitted to a god. Procl. Chrest., 29, «εὐκτικὰ δὲ μέλη ἐγράφετο τοῖς αἰτουμένοις τι παρὰ θεοῦ γενέσθαι» (*"invocatory* songs were composed for those wishing to solicit that something be done by a god").

Also *euktikoi hymnoi* (εὐκτικοὶ ὕμνοι); hymns expressing an earnest request.

eulyros (εὔλυρος; m. pr. évliros); skilled player of the lyra. Aristoph. Frogs (v. 229) «εὔλυροί τε Μοῦσαι» ("Muses skilled in lyra-playing").

eumeles (εὐμελής; m. pr. evmelís), from εὖ = well, and μέλος (melos); melodious; having an agreeable or graceful melodic line.

Arist. Polit. (book VIII, ch. 7, § 2; 1341B) «πότερον προαιρετέον μᾶλλον τὴν εὐμελῆ μουσικὴν ἢ τὴν εὔρυθμον» ("which of the two is preferable to choose, *the melodious* music or the eurhythmic").

eumelos (εὐμελῶς; evmelós) adv., melodiously, gracefully, euphoniously.
eumeleia (εὐμέλεια; evmélia), euphony; agreeableness in melody.

eumetros (εὔμετρος; m. pr. évmetros); well-proportioned, symmetrical. Also used in the sense of eurhythmic.

eumolpos (εὔμολπος; m. pr. évmolpos); he who sings melodiously. Also melodious, melodiously sung; *eumolpos ode* (εὔμολπος ᾠδή), melodious tune.

eumolpia (εὐμολπία; m. pr. evmolpía); melodiousness, tunefulness, euphony.
eumolpein, vb (εὐμολπεῖν; m. pr. evmolpín) = to sing melodiously.

Eumolpus (Εὔμολπος; m. pr. Évmolpos); a) mythical epic poet-musician of the pre-Homeric time. According to Suidas he was a native of Eleusis (Ἐλευσίς; hence surnamed Eleusinios, Ἐλευσίνιος); son of Musaeus* and pupil of

115

Orpheus*. For others he was the father of Musaeus (Diog. Laert., book I, Prooemion, § 3). Suidas says also that he won a prize with his lyra at the Pythian Games, and that he composed "three thousand epic songs"; also ceremonial songs for Demeter and for the Eleusinian mysteries.

b) *Eumolpus* is the name of the legendary king to whom Demeter taught the mysteries (Homer: Hymn to Demeter, 154), and who became the first hierophant of the Eleusinian mysteries. The priests of the mysteries considered themselves as descendants of Eumolpus and were called Eumolpidai (Εὐμολπίδαι) after his name. Hes: «*Εὐμολπίδαι· οὕτως οἱ ἀπὸ Εὐμόλπου ἐκαλοῦντο, τοῦ πρώτου ἱεροφαντήσαντος*» ("*Eumolpidai*; so named after Eumolpus, the first hierophant").

Par. Chron. (v. 15) refers to Eumolpus, son of Musaeus, who at the time of Erechtheus (Ἐρεχθεύς), king of Athens, established the mysteries in Eleusis.

As both "Eumolpoi" are connected with Eleusis and the initiation of the Eleusinian mysteries, it may be supposed that the question is whether there was one Eumolpus.

eumousos (εὔμουσος; m. pr. évmousos); musical; experienced in the arts, especially in poetry and music.

eumousia (εὐμουσία) n.; the sense of good in music and in art; skilfulness in music; also the melodiousness of a song.

eumousos (εὐμούσως; m. pr. evmoúsos) adv.; melodiously; gracefully.

Plut. Adversus Coloten («Πρὸς Κολώτην»; 1119D) «ὅτι παίζοντός ἐστιν εὐμούσως» ("of him who plays *gracefully*").

Eunides (Εὐνίδης; m. pr. Evnídis).

Name of an ancient Athenian family of kitharists "devoted from father to son to the cult of the kithara" (Dinse: De Antig. Theb., p. 27).

Eunomus (Εὔνομος; m. pr. Évnomos); Locrian kitharode of unknown date. His name survived in a well-known legend according to which, competing at Delphi against Ariston, a kitharode of Rhegium, one of his lyra's strings broke and then a cricket flew over his instrument and sang the missing note. See under *adein*. It is said that his statue at Locri, his native town in Italy, showed him with his kithara and a cricket sitting on it.

euodos (εὔῳδος; m. pr. évodos); pleasingly sounding.

euphonos (εὔφωνος; m. pr. éphonos) from εὖ = well, and φωνὴ (phone; voice, sound); euphonious; having a good, sweet and agreeable voice; on instruments with sweet tone.

Euphonos was used also to signify the man who has a strong, powerful voice; «εὔφωνος κήρυξ» a herald with a powerful voice.

116

euphonia (εὐφωνία; m. pr. ephonía); melodiousness, tunefulness; also sonorousness; brilliance in tone quality.

See also *eugerys*.

euphorminx (εὐφόρμιγξ; m. pr. ephórminx); he who plays skilfully on the phorminx. In lyric poetry it signified that which was accompanied well by the phorminx; hence very melodious.

Oppianus (3rd cent. A.D.) in his writings on fishing (*Ἁλιευτικά*; v. 618) writes: «μολπῆς εὐφόρμιγγος» ("*of a very melodious* song").

euphthongos (εὔφθογγος; m. pr. éphthongos); euphonious; producing pleasant, melodious sound.

euphthongos lyra (εὔφθογγος λύρα); "euphonious lyra"; Theognis (ap. E. Diehl Anth. Lyr. Gr. p. 144; v. 144) «χαίρω δ' εὔφθογγον... λύρην».

eurhythmos (εὔρυθμος; m. pr. évrithmos); in music, having good rhythmical structure; rhythmical.

eurhythma krousmata (εὔρυθμα κρούσματα; neut. pl.) rhythmical musical pieces; *eurhythmon* melos (εὔρυθμον μέλος), rhythmical, graceful tune. Plato Laws (II, 655A): see under *euharmostos**; also Arist. Polit. VIII, ch. 7, § 2, 1341B (*eumeles**).

Ptolem. (C.v.J. Excerpta Neapolitana, Πτολεμαίου μουσικά; Mus. Script. Gr. p. 414) "*eurhythmoi* [times] are those which keep good rhythmical order exactly between themselves" («εὔρυθμοι μὲν [χρόνοι] οἱ διαφυλάττοντες ἀκριβῶς τὴν πρὸς ἀλλήλοις εὔρυθμον τάξιν»).

eurhythmia (εὐρυθμία; evrithmía), n.; eurhythmy. It signified also, among others, symmetry, graceful movement; Luc. "On dancing", 8 «ἑώρων [Τρῶες]... τὴν ἐν τῷ πολεμεῖν αὐτοῦ κουφότητα καὶ εὐρυθμίαν ἣν ἐξ ὀρχήσεως ἐκέκτητο» ("they [i.e. the Trojans] saw his (Meriones') lightness [nimbleness] and *eurhythmy* in fighting which he acquired from dancing").

eurhythmos (εὐρύθμως; m. pr. evríthmos) adv.; rhythmically; in good rhythmical order; by extension, gracefully.

Euripides (Εὐριπίδης; m. pr. Evripídis); b. 480 (?) B.C.; d. 406 B.C. in Macedonia at king Archelaus' Court. Euripides was born at Salamis but the date of his birth is not certain. According to Par. Chron. (ed. F. Jacoby, § 50) he was born "when Aeschylus won for the first time in tragedy", i.e. 485 B.C. ("during Philocrates' governorship"). Suidas on the other hand says that "he was born on the day the Greeks defeated the Persians" (at Salamis), i.e. 480 B.C. An old legend well-spread, it appears, in antiquity and not completely unfounded, connected the three great tragedians with the victorious sea-fight of Salamis;

according to it on the day Aeschylus was fighting against the Persians at Salamis Euripides was born, and soon after Sophocles led the procession at the celebrations for the victory.

Of Euripides' music two small and mutilated fragments have survived so far: 1) a part of the first stasimon of "Orestes" (vs 338ff); it was found in 1892 on a Rainer papyrus and published in "Pap. Erzherzog Rainer" in 1894. It was first transcribed into modern notation by Carl Wessely ("Der Pap. Erzh. Rainer", vol. V; Wien, 1892); 2) a fragment from "Iphigenia in Aulis" discovered in December 1972 by Mrs Denise Jourdan-Hemmerdinger on a papyrus of the University of Leyden (Inv. No 510) and published in the "Comptes Rendus des Séances de l'année 1973" (p. 295) of the "Académie des Inscriptions et Belles-Lettres" (Paris).

See more details about both these fragments under "Remains of Greek music", Nos. 1 and 15.

These fragmentary and incomplete melodies cannot give us any idea of Euripides' music. It is known however from ancient sources that in spite of Aristophanes' unjust enmity and scorn[1] his music had many admirers, and several of his melodies became popular during his life-time and after his death. Plutarch in "Nicias" (§ 29) relates that after the disastrous Athenian campaign against Syracuse (415-413 B.C.) several Athenians were saved thanks to Euripides whose music ("muse") was loved in Sicily; "others straggling after the fight got food and water by singing some of his lyrics" («τῶν μελῶν ᾄσαντες»). In Lysandrus (§ 15) also Plutarch relates another characteristic anecdote: at a meeting of the allies to consider the terms of surrender to be imposed on besieged Athens (404 B.C.) some of Sparta's allies proposed that the Athenians be sold as slaves and the city be pulled down and destroyed; "but afterwards when at a party of the commanders a Phocian sang the first choral song (parodos) of Euripides' Electra which begins 'Oh! Electra, Agamemnon's daughter, I came unto your deserted home' («᾿Αγαμέμνονος ὦ Κόρα,/ἤλυθον, ᾿Ηλέκτρα», etc.) they were all moved to compassion and it seemed to them a cruel deed to destroy so famous a city which produced such men". Axionicus, a 4th cent. B.C. comic poet, in his play "Fond of Euripides" («Φιλευριπίδης»; ap. Athen. IV, 175B; Th. Kock Com. Att. Fr. II, 412) says "For both have such a morbid passion for

---

1. Aristophanes often scornfully calls Euripides' melodies "epyllia" (ἐπύλλια = versicles, chansonnettes). In "Peace" (vs 531-2) Aristophanes makes an intentional contradistinction between melodies of Sophocles and Euripides by referring to Sophocles' *mele* and Euripides' *epyllia* («Σοφοκλέους μελῶν, κιχλῶν, | ἐπυλλίων Εὐριπίδου»).

In the "Acharnians" (vs 398-400) he says with cruel mockery (through Euripides' Servant) that "His [Euripides'] mind is outside compiling versicles («ξυλλέγων ἐπύλλια») while he himself is inside lying down with his feet up and composing a tragedy".

the lyrics of Euripides, that everything else in their eyes seems the wail of a scrannel pipe and a mighty bore" (transl. by Ch. B. Gulick, vol. II, p. 295).

Some of his tunes survived and were sung for centuries. Dionysius of Halicarnassos* (1st cent. B.C.) bears witness; in "De compositione verborum", XI, "Which are pleasant to the hearing" («Ἀκοαῖς ἡδέα τίνα») he undertakes a detailed musical analysis of Euripides' melody which Electra sings to the chorus in "Orestes" («Σῖγα, σῖγα, λευκὸν ἴχνος ἀρβύλης...»).

Euripides wrote 92 plays of which 78 were known by the Alexandrians; of them the following 19 survive complete: Alcestis, Medea, Heraclidae, Hippolytus Crowned, Hecuba, Supplices (Suppliant Women), Andromache, Hercules Furens, Troades (Trojan Women), Electra, Ion, Iphigenia in Tauris, Helena, Phoenician Women (Phoenissae), Orestes, Bacchae, Iphigenia in Aulis, Cyclops (a satirical play) and Rhesus (authenticity doubtful).

Many fragments of other plays have been preserved.

He won five times at dramatic contests, of which once posthumously (Suid.). He composed also a Funeral Elegy (Ἐπικήδειον) for Nicias and the Athenians who perished in the disastrous war with Syracuse (413 B.C.), and an Epinikion to Alcibiades.

Cf. Brgk Anth. Lyr. pp. 130-131; two fragments and the Epinikion. Aug. Nauck T.G.F. pp. 363-716. O. Schroeder: Euripides, Cantica, 2nd ed., T., 1928.

With regard to his music the following, among others, may be consulted:

F. A. Gevaert: "Histoire et Théorie de la Musique de l'Antiquité"; Ghent, 1881, vol. II, esp. pp. 214-240, and 538-550.

Evanghélos Moutsopoulos: "Euripide et la Philosophie de la Musique" in "Revue des Études grecques", vol. 85, Nos 356-358; juillet-décembre 1962, Paris; pp. 396-452.

euthys (εὐθύς; m. pr. efthís); direct.

eutheia (fem.) *agoge* (εὐθεῖα ἀγωγή; efthía agogí); progression of the melody in stepwise order in the same direction; Aristox. Harm. (I, p. 29, 31 Mb): «ἀγωγὴ δ' ἔστω ἡ διὰ τῶν ἑξῆς φθόγγων...· εὐθεῖα δ' ἡ ἐπὶ τὸ αὐτό» ("agoge* is the progression by consecutive notes...; and *direct agoge* (progression) is that which maintains the same direction").

According to Aristides (I, pp. 19 and 29 Mb.; RPW-I. pp. 16 and 29) "*direct agoge* is the ascending progression in stepwise order" («ἡ διὰ τῶν ἑξῆς φθόγγων τὴν ἐπίτασιν ποιουμένη»).

eutonos (εὔτονος; m. pr. éftonos); well-pitched (LSJ); having a good, agreeable tone. Otherwise *eueches**, *eugerys**.

exarchos (ἔξαρχος); leader of the chorus; coryphaeus.

Also *hegemon* (ἡγεμὼν) of the chorus. In a general sense also, leader. See under *threnodia*.

119

exaulos (ἔξαυλος; m. pr. éxavlos); an aulos worn out; which became out of use. The verb ἐξαυλοῦμαι (exauloumai) used on aulos reeds signified to become worn out; or out of use.

Pollux (IV, 73) «ἐξηυλημέναι (fem. pl. of perf. tense part.) γλῶτται, αἰ παλαιαὶ» ("*exeulemenai* reeds [were] the old ones [those worn out]").

Exekestides (Ἐξηκεστίδης; m. pr. Exikestídis); c. end of the 4th cent. B.C. celebrated kitharode of the Athenian School. He won prizes at the Pythian contests, the Panathenaea and the Carnean.

His name is mentioned by Aristophanes (Birds, v. 764) in this phrase «εἰ δὲ δοῦλός ἐστι καὶ Κὰρ ὥσπερ Ἐξηκεστίδης» ("if some one is a slave and a Carian, like *Exekestides*").

exharmonios (ἐξαρμόνιος; m. pr. exarmónios); discordant (Dem., LSJ). Appears only in Pherecr. "Cheiron" (ap. Plut. De Mus. 1141E, ch. 30); «Κινησίας δὲ μ' ὁ κατάρατος Ἀττικὸς, ἐξαρμονίους καμπὰς ποιῶν» ("Kinesias, the cursed Athenian, by composing *discordant* modulations [sudden changes]").

exodion (ἐξόδιον); exodium.

a) *exodion aulema* (ἐξόδιον αὔλημα); aulos-solo played at the end of the dramatic performance during the exit of the chorus. Also *exodioi nomoi* (ἐξόδιοι νόμοι); Suid. «Ἐξόδιοι νόμοι· αὐλήματα, δι' ὦν ἐξῆεσαν οἱ χοροὶ καὶ οἱ αὐληταί» ("*exodioi nomoi*; aulos-solos by which the choruses and the auletes were led out of the stage [the orchestra]").

b) *exodion melos* (ἐξόδιον μέλος); the song which was sung at the end of the performance while going out. Pollux (IV, 108) «καὶ μέλος δέ τι ἐξόδιον ὃ ἐξιόντες ἦδον» ("and there was an *exodium* song which they sang while going out [of the orchestra]").

c) *exodion* or *epilogos* was also the last part of the kitharodikos* nomos; Pollux IV, 66.

Note: The exit of the chorus was called *exodos* (ἔξοδος); also hte las episode of the ancient drama which took place after the last stasimon*and thet exit of the chorus; Arist. (Poet. ch. XII; "*exodos* is the whole part of the tragedy after which there is no choral song").

G

gamelion (γαμήλιον; m. pr. gamílion); nuptial, *gamelion aulema* (γαμήλιον αὔλημα); aulos-solo played at the marriage ceremony. Pollux (IV, 80) «καὶ τὸ μὲν γαμήλιον αὔλημα δύο αὐλοὶ ἦσαν» ("and the nuptial aulema [was played on] two auloi");

See the full text under *aulos*.

gamelion or *gamikon* melos (γαμήλιον, or γαμικὸν μέλος); a nuptial or marriage song. Phryn. Epitome (ed. de Borries, p. 58) «γαμικὰ μέλη (plur.)· τὰ ἐπὶ τοῖς γάμοις λεγόμενα ὑμνικὰ» ("*nuptial tunes*; those songs sung at the marriage").

See also *hymenaeos**.

Gaudentius the Philosopher (Γαυδέντιος ὁ φιλόσοφος; m. pr. Gavdéntios); musical theorist of uncertain date, probably of the 2nd or 3rd cent. A.D.; some place him even later, in the 5th cent. He is surnamed "the philosopher", and is known for his "Harmonic Introduction" («Ἁρμονικὴ Εἰσαγωγή»).

This is an eclectic work which deals with the sounds, intervals, systems, genera etc., following partly the Aristoxenean and partly the Pythagorean doctrines.

The work was first translated into Latin by Lutianus (6th cent. A.D.). The Greek text, with a Latin translation, was published by Marc Meibom (Ant. Mus. Auct. Sept., Gr. et Lat.; Amsterdam, 1652; vol. I, v, pp. 1-29), and by C.v.Jan (Mus. Script. Gr., Leipzig, 1895; VII, pp. 327-355).

A French translation (after Meibom's text) was published, with commentaries and an attempt to reconstitute Tables left blank in the MSS of Gaudentius, by Ch. Ém. Ruelle, in his "Collection des auteurs grecs relatifs à la musique" (V, "Alypius, Gaudence et Bacchius l'Ancien", Paris, 1895; pp. 53-91 translation, and 93-102 reconstitution of the Tables).

genus, genos (γένος; m. pr. génos); a term signifying the different disposition of the intervals used in the constitution of a tetrachord or in a larger system, of which the tetrachord was a constituent part.

All the ancient theorists define the genus in almost exactly the same words: Aristides (I, p. 18 Mb; R.P.W-I. p. 15) «Γένος δέ ἐστι ποιὰ τετραχόρδου διαίρεσις» ("Genus is a certain division of the tetrachord"). Cleon. Isag. (C.v.J., p. 180; Mb., p. 1) "Genus is a certain division of four notes". Cf. Bacch. Isag. (C.v.J., p. 298; Mb., p. 8); Ptolem. (I, ch. 12).

There were three genera: the *Diatonikon* or *Diatonon* (διατονικόν, διάτονον), the *Chromatikon* or *Chroma* (χρωματικόν, χρῶμα), and the *Enharmonion* or *Harmonia* (ἐναρμόνιον, ἁρμονία). Each of them is discussed separately (under *Diatonon, Chromatikon* and *Enharmonion*).

The *Diatonic* was the first to be introduced into practice; it was considered as the more natural, and that it could be sung even by those wholly uneducated (Aristides p. 19 Mb; R.P.W-I, p. 16). The *Chromatic* came next into use, and was considered as the most technical (τεχνικώτατον) and performed by only educated people.

It was never used in tragedy; but was largely used in music for kithara. Plut. (De Mus. 1137E, ch. 20) "and the kithara, older by several generations than the tragedy, used [the Chromatic genus] from the beginning. And that the chroma [chromatic] is older than the Enharmonic is also well-known".

The *Enharmonic* genus was the last to be introduced, and, according to Aristoxenus, Olympus was its inventor (Plut. ibid, 1134F, ch. 11). It was considered extremely difficult, needed considerable practice («δυσμελῳδικώτατον, πολλῆς τριβῆς δεόμενον»; M. Psellus p. 27), and was almost impossible for most people.

For the ethos of the genera, see under *ethos*.

The genera in Rhythmic (Ρυθμική, the science of rhythm) are defined, according to Aristoxenus, by the relation of thesis to arsis (down-beat to up-beat). There were three rhythmic genera: the dactylic (relation 1 to 1, or 2 to 2, equal thesis to arsis), the iambic (1 to 2, arsis to double thesis), and the paeonic (3 to 2). According to Aristides (Mb p. 35, RPW-I p. 33) some add also a fourth rhythmic genus, the epitriton (4 to 3).

Sometimes the word "genus" (γένος) is used in the sense of style, like the word *tropos*; e.g. Plut. De Mus. (1142C, ch. 31) «καὶ διαπειρώμενον ἀμφοτέρων τῶν *τρόπων*, τοῦ τε Πινδαρείου καὶ Φιλοξενείου, μὴ δύνασθαι κατορθοῦν ἐν τῷ Φιλοξενείῳ *γένει*» ("and [Telesias] attempting to compose in both *styles*, that of Pindar and that of Philoxenus, he failed in the Philoxenean *style*").

georgika, mele (γεωργικά, μέλη) pl.; folk-songs of farmers; Procl. Chrest., 34.

geranos (γέρανος; m. pr. géranos); a kind of dance invented, according to a legend, by Theseus; he danced it for the first time in the island of Delos in the company of seven youths and seven maidens he had rescued from the Minotaur in Crete. The movements of the dance sought to express the intricate windings leading out of the Minotaur's home, the labyrinth. Pollux (IV, 101): "they used to dance *the geranos* in great numbers, each one after the other in a row, the extremities on each side being taken by the leaders around Theseus; [they danced it] first around the Delian altar, imitating the coming out of the labyrinth".

The leader of the geranos was called *geranoulkós* (γερανουλκός); Hes. «ὁ τοῦ χοροῦ τοῦ ἐν Δήλῳ γερανουλκός».

b) *geranós* was also a dance imitating the flight of cranes in line (in Greek γερανοί, pl. of γερανός). Cf. Luc. "On dancing" § 34.

ginglaros (γίγγλαρος; m. pr. gínglaros or gígklaros); a kind of small aulos of Egyptian origin.

Pollux (IV, 82): «γίγγλαρος δὲ μικρός τις αὐλίσκος, αἰγύπτιος, μοναυλίᾳ πρόσφορος» ("*ginglaros* [was] a very small aulos, Egyptian in origin, suitable for the monaulia*").

gingras (γίγγρας; m.pr. gíngras or gígkras); a word with various meanings.

a) *Gingras* (Γίγγρας); the name of Adonis in the Phoenician language.

b) A small aulos (αὐλίσκος) of Phoenician origin, with a piercing tone, and of a lamenting and mournful character; it took its name from Adonis. Pollux (IV, 76): «γίγγρας δέ τις αὐλίσκος, γοώδη καὶ θρηνητικὴν φωνὴν ἀφίησι, φοῖνιξ μὲν ὢν τὴν εὕρεσιν, πρόσφορος δὲ μούσῃ τῇ Καρικῇ· ἡ δὲ Φοινίκων γλῶττα Γίγγραν τὸν Ἄδωνιν καλεῖ καὶ τούτῳ ὁ αὐλὸς ἐπωνόμασται» ("*gingras* was a small aulos with a lamenting and mournful tone; it was of Phoenician origin and suited the Carian muse [i.e. lamenting muse]. In the Phoenician language Adonis was called *Gingras*, and from him the aulos took its name."

Athen. (IV, 174F, ch. 76): «γιγγραίνοισι γὰρ οἱ Φοίνικες, ὥς φησιν Ξενοφῶν, ἐχρῶντο αὐλοῖς σπιθαμιαίοις τὸ μέγεθος, ὀξὺ καὶ γοερὸν φθεγγομένοις· τούτοις δὲ οἱ Κάρες χρῶνται ἐν τοῖς θρήνοις ... Ὀνομάζονται δὲ οἱ αὐλοὶ γίγγροι ὑπὸ τῶν Φοινίκων ἀπὸ τῶν περὶ τὸν Ἄδωνιν θρήνων· τὸν γὰρ Ἄδωνιν Γίγγρην καλεῖτε ὑμεῖς οἱ Φοίνικες, ὡς ἱστορεῖ Δημοκλείδης» ("The Phoenicians, as Xenophon says, used span-long auloi [pipes], which give a piercing and lamenting tone; these are also used by the Karians in lamentations. ... And these auloi are called *gingrai* by the Phoenicians, from the laments for Adonis; because you, Phoenicians, call Adonis *Gingras*, as Democleides records").

c) *gingras* was also the name of an aulema (aulos-solo) for the instrument gingras; Tryphon (ap. Athen. XIV, 618C, ch. 9) in his book II, on Denominations, includes "gingras" among the aulos-solos. Cf. *aulesis**.

d) *gingras* was a kind of dance accompanied by the aulos gingras. Pollux (IV, 102) «ἦν δὲ καὶ γίγγρας πρὸς αὐλὸν ὄρχημα, ἐπώνυμον τοῦ αὐλήματος» ("and there was also a dance called *gingras*, danced to the aulos, so-called after the aulos–melody itself").

e) According to Hesychius *gingras* was an exclamation at carousals; «ἐπιφώνημά τι ἐπὶ κατὰ κώμων λεγόμενον· καὶ εἶδος αὐλοῦ» ("a certain exclamation declaimed at carousals; and a kind of aulos").

The tone produced by the gingras was called γιγγρασμὸς (*gingrasmos*; Hes.).

Glaucus of Rhegium (Γλαῦχος ὁ Ρηγῖνος; m.pr. Gláfkos Rigínos); c. 5th to 4th cent. B.C., grammarian and musicographer from Rhegium (Ρήγιον, hense his surname Ρηγῖνος, Rheginus). He was one of the first musicographers of ancient Greece. He wrote (c. 420 B.C.) a book "On ancient poets and musicians, («Περὶ τῶν ἀρχαίων ποιητῶν τε καὶ μουσικῶν») in which he gives ample information regarding ancient musicians, mythical and historical. He also speaks of the initiation and evolution of the kitharodic and aulodic art. His book was lost, but much information in Plutarch's De Musica is derived from it (1132D, 1133F, 1134D; chs. 4, 7, 10 respectively).

See also FHG II, pp. 23-24.

glaux (γλαύξ; m. pr. gláfx); a kind of comical or ludicrous dance mentioned in Athen. XIV, 629F, ch. 27, together with other ludicrous dances («γελοῖαι ὀρχήσεις»).

The word *glaux* (γλαὺξ) means *owl*.

See *skops*.

glottis, Attic form of *glossis*, and *glótta* or *glóssa* (γλωττίς, γλωσσίς; γλῶττα, γλῶσσα); the reed of the aulos; it was made of reed, cane. The cane used for making the reed was of a special quality (see *calamus* and *donax*).

The maker of reeds was called γλωττοποιὸς (*glottopoeos*), Pollux II, 108; Hes. «ὁ τὰς αὐλητικὰς γλωσσίδας ποιῶν»; ("the maker of auletic reeds"); EM p. 235, 44.

See *exaulos*, and *synkrotetikai glottai*.

glottokomeion (γλωττοκομεῖον; m. pr. glottokomíon); also *glossokomeion*, *glossokómion* and *glossókomon* (γλωσσοκομεῖον, γλωσσοκόμιον, γλωσσόκομον); the box in which the reeds of the aulos were kept.

Hes. «ἐν ᾧ οἱ αὐληταὶ ἀπετίθεντο τὰς γλωσσίδας» ("in which the auletes placed the reeds"). EM p. 235, 45.

See above, *glottis*.

Glyconeion, metre (γλυκώνειον, μέτρον; m. pr. glicónion, métron). Also Glyconeios stichos (Glyconic line, verse), so-called after the name of Glycon (Γλύκων; a poet of unknown date). A logaoedic (mixed) tetrapody consisting of three trochees and one dactyl. There were three kinds of Glyconeion depending on the place of the dactyl:

A_1 : ⏑⏑ — ⏑ — ⏑ — ⏑ (*acatalectic*; ἀκατάληκτον μέτρον)
A_2 : ⏑⏑ — ⏑ — ⏑ — ∧ (*catalectic*; καταληκτικὸν »)
B_1 : ⏑ — ⏑⏑ — ⏑ — ⏑ (acatalectic)
B_2 : ⏑ — ⏑⏑ — ⏑ — ∧ (catalectic)
C_1 : ⏑ — ⏑ — ⏑⏑ — ⏑ (acatalectic)
C_2 : ⏑ — ⏑ — ⏑⏑ — ∧ (catalectic)

124

Glyconeion systema: union of three (or more) Glyconic lines with a Pherecratean line at the end.

The Glyconeion was extensively used by lyric and dramatic poets. Cf. Anacreon*.

Notes: 1) For acatalectic and catalectic metres, see under *metron**.

2) The Λ is the sign for leimma (short empty time; chronos kenos brachys); see under *leimma** and *parasemantike**.

gnomologika, mele (**γνωμολογικά**, μέλη); songs of a paraenetic character. Procl. Chrest., 33 «τὰ δὲ γνωμολογικὰ δῆλον ὅτι παραίνεσιν ἠθῶν ἔχει» ("and *the paraenetic* [songs] evidently have [contain] a moral paraenesis").

gronthon (**γρόνθων**; m. pr. grónthon); first lessons on the aulos (Pollux IV, 83), or type of aulos composition. Hes. «ἀναφύσησις, ἥν πρῶτον μανθάνουσιν αὐληταὶ καὶ κιθαρισταὶ» ("the first lesson [or composition] that auletai and kitharistai learn to play"). Cf. *anaphysesis**.

gymnopaedia, usually in pl. **gymnopaediai** (**γυμνοπαιδία, γυμνοπαιδίαι**; m.pr. gimnopedía, gimnopedíe); an annual ceremony or festival of ten days' duration, held at Sparta in honour of Apollo; it was originally consecrated in memory of the Spartans who fell at the battle of Thyrea.

During the ceremony naked boys and youths performed gymnastic exercises and dances around the statues of Apollo, Diana and Leto; by their rhythmical movements they imitated wrestling and the pankration (cf. *gymnopaedike*). The verses and music were composed by famous poet-composers of the time, such as Thaletas and Alcman*.

The character of the dances and the ceremony in general was extremely serious, decent and majestic.

gymnopaedike (**γυμνοπαιδική**; m. pr. gimnopedikí); a kind of dance, similar to anapale*. It was danced by naked boys or youths imitating wrestling and the pankration (a mixed contest of wrestling and boxing) with rhythmical movements; Athen. XIV, 630 D-E, ch. 28 (see the text under "emmeleia").

The gymnopaedike was one of the three dances of the lyric poetry, the other two being the pyrrhiche and the hyporchematike. It was danced in honour of Dionysus and had two forms: the oschophoric (in honour of Athena) and the Bacchic.

See *oschophorika*.

gypones (**γύπωνες**; m. pr. gípones); dancers in Sparta who mounted on wooden stilts, and wearing feminine dress, used to dance by leaps. Pollux (IV, 104): «οἱ δὲ γύπωνες, ξυλίνων κώλων ἐπιβαίνοντες, ὠρχοῦντο διαφανῆ τὰ ταραντίδια ἀμπεχόμενοι» ("*the gypones* danced, mounted on wooden stilts and wearing transparent feminine dresses").

H

haploun (ἁπλοῦν; m.pr. aploún) neut.; simple.

haploun systema (ἁπλοῦν σύστημα), simple, non-modulating system.

Cleon. Isag. ch. 11 (C.v.J.p. 201, p. 18 Mb): "The difference between the modulating and non-modulating systems is the difference between simple and not-simple systems; *simple* are those which are tuned to one Mese, double those tuned to two Meses, triple those tuned to three, multiple those tuned to several Meses" («ἁπλᾶ μὲν οὖν ἐστι τὰ πρὸς μίαν μέσην ἡρμοσμένα "etc.). Arist. Quint. (I, p. 16 Mb; RPW-1 p. 13) says that simple are those composed in one mode («καθ' ἕνα τρόπον ἔκκειται»), and not-simple those in several modes («τὰ δὲ οὐχ ἁπλᾶ, ἃ κατὰ πλειόνων τρόπων τὴν πλοκὴν γίνεται»).

Aristoxenus had already distinguished between the haploun, the double and the multiple systems (Harm. I, p. 17, 32 Mb; «τὴν τ' εἰς ἁπλοῦν καὶ διπλοῦν καὶ πολλαπλοῦν διαίρεσιν»; also II, p. 40, 20).

The adj. ἁπλοῦς, masc. (haplous) is used in contradistinction to διπλοῦς (double) and πολλαπλοῦς (pollaplous; multiple).

See under *metabole* and *diploun*.

harmateios, nomos (ἁρμάτειος, or ἁρμάτιος, νόμος; m. pr. armátios). An auletic nomos performed at a battle with war-chariots or at a chariot race, with the purpose of inspiring the enthusiasm of those taking part. It is said that it was first established by Olympus; Plut. (De Mus. 1133E, ch. 7) «τὸν δὲ καλούμενον ἁρμάτιον νόμον λέγεται ποιῆσαι ὁ πρῶτος Ὄλυμπος» ("the so-called *harmatios* nomos is said to have been invented by the first Olympus*"). See also further in Plut. ibid, ch. 7 on the harmatios nomos.

b) *harmateion, melos* (ἁρμάτειον, μέλος); a mournful song, a lament. Eurip. Orestes (vs 1378-80) «ὡς δ' ὀλόμενον στένω ἁρμάτειον μέλος» ("how I lament over the destroyed with a *mournful* tune").

harmoge (ἁρμογή; m. pr. armogí) from ἁρμόζειν or ἁρμόττειν (harmozein. or harmottein), to fit together; method of tuning (LSJ); tuning; harmonia*.

According to Phrynichus, re-adjustment of tuning from one tone to another; but the correct term for re-tuning should be metharmoge* (μεθαρμογή). The text of Phrynichus (ed. I. de Borries, pp. 24-25) is the following: «ἁρμογὴ μουσικὸν τὤνομα, τιθέμενον ἐπὶ τῶν ἁρμόσεων, ἃς ποιοῦνται οἱ μουσικοί,

126

ἐπειδὰν ἐξ ἁρμονίας εἰς ἑτέραν ἁρμονίαν μετίωσι, φέρε ἐκ Δωρίων εἰς Ὑπο-δώρια (in Bekker Anecd. 15,20 «Ὑπιώνια») ἢ ἐκ Φρυγίων εἰς Ὑπερμιξολύ-δια, ἢ ὅλως ἐκ τινος τόνου εἰς ἕτερον τόνον, οὐ ταὐτὸν οὖσα ἡ ἁρμογὴ τῆς μεταβολῆς.... Ἁρμογὴ δέ ἐστιν, ὅταν αὐλήσας τὸν Φρύγιον τόνον καὶ ἐκτε-λέσας τό τε ᾆσμα καὶ τὰ κρούματα τελέως, μεθαρμόττηται εἰς ἕτερον τό-νον, Ὑποφρύγιον ἢ Λύδιον ἤ τινα τῶν τρισκαίδεκα ἁρμονιῶν· δύναται δ᾽ ἂν καὶ ἡ μεταβολὴ ἁρμογὴ καλεῖσθαι» ("*Harmoge* is a musical term used of the tunings which the musicians make when they move from one harmonia to another, as from Dorian to Hypodorian, or from Phrygian to Hypermixo-lydian, or generally speaking from one tonos to another, the harmoge not being the same as the metabole* ... *Harmoge* is when, after having played on the aulos in the Phrygian tonos and completely performed the song and the inter-ludes [instrumental parts] we re-adjust the tuning of the instrument to another tonos, for instance the Hypophrygian or Lydian or some other of the thirteen 'harmonias' [tonoi]; the metabole can also be called harmoge").

Cf. Th. Kock Comic. Att. Frg. (vol. I, p. 260 and note; Eupolis Frg. 11) "ταύτην ἐγὼ ζητῶν πάλαι τὴν *ἁρμογὴν*» ("this is the *harmoge* I am asking for"). Also Pollux IV, 57 and Suidas on the word "harmoge" (*ἁρμογή*).

See *harmonia, harmosis, hermosmenos.*

harmonia (**ἁρμονία**; m. pr. armonía; from the verb ἁρμόζειν or ἁρμόττειν, harmozein or harmottein = to fit or bind or fasten together, to join, to adapt); joining or fitting together, adjustment; also joint and means of joining (LSJ). Originally the word was used in this sense; Hom. Odyss. V, 248, 361, cf. Dem. and LSJ. It is also met with the same meaning later («αἱ τῶν λίθων ἁρμο-νίαι», "the joints of the stones" ap. Diod. Sikeliotes 2, 8).

In music, besides its simple signification of "tuning", it signified for the "most ancient" («οἱ πάνυ παλαιότατοι», as Aristides calls them in De Mus., Mb p. 21, RPW-I p. 18) the octave, and the different disposition of the notes in the octave or in a system with its parts adjusted so as to form a perfect en-semble. This was, according to Aristoxenus, the signification given to the term by the Harmonists (the Ἁρμονικοὶ) before him (Harm. Elem., II p. 36, 30 Mb «ἀλλὰ περὶ αὐτῶν μόνον τῶν ἑπτὰ ὀκταχόρδων, ἃ ἐκάλουν ἁρμονίας, τὴν ἐπίσκεψιν ἐποιοῦντο» = "but they [i.e. the Harmonists, 'our forerunners', «οἱ πρὸ ἡμῶν»] confined their attention only to the seven octachords which they called *Harmonias*"). Also writers of the 5th and 4th cent. B.C., including Plato, Aristotle and Heracleides Ponticus, used the term in the same sense.

Plato in the Rep. (III, 617B) says «ἐκ πασῶν ὀκτὼ οὐσῶν (χορδῶν, φωνῶν) μίαν *ἁρμονίαν* ξυμφωνεῖν» ("from all eight [strings] one *harmonia* is formed").

Aristotle (Polit. IV, 3, 1290A) also says "it is the same also in the case of the harmoniai as some people say; and there are two species, the Dorian and the Phrygian; all the other systems are classed either in the Dorian or in the Phrygian" («ὁμοίως δ' ἔχει καὶ περὶ τὰς ἀρμονίας, ὡς φασί τινες» etc.). Heracl. Ponticus in his third book "On music" (ap. Athen. XIV, 624C, ch. 19) speaks about the three "Greek harmoniai", the Dorian, the Aeolian and the Ionian (excluding the Phrygian and the Lydian as foreign) in analogy with the three Greek tribes.

The harmoniai mentioned by the above and other writers are the following seven octave-species, as generally accepted:

1.	Mixolydian	(Μιξολυδιστὶ)	b-b
2.	Lydian	(Λυδιστὶ)	c-c
3.	Phrygian	(Φρυγιστὶ)	d-d
4.	Dorian	(Δωριστὶ)	e-e
5.	Hypolydian	(Ὑπολυδιστὶ)	f-f
6.	Ionian, Hypophrygian	(Ἰαστὶ, Ὑποφρυγιστὶ)	g-g
7.	Aeolian, Hypodorian	(Αἰολιστὶ, Ὑποδωριστὶ)	a-a

These names differed from time to time and from one author to another.

In Aristoxenus' time and after him the term *harmonia* was very often used to signify the Enharmonic genus, together with the term Enharmonios (Aristox. Harm. I, pp. 2; 23 etc; Cleon. Isag. C.v.J. ch. 3, p. 181, Mb p. 3). On the other hand, after Aristoxenus' time, the term "dia-pason" (διὰ-πασῶν) replaced the term harmonia in many texts (Cleon. Isag. and Bacch. Isag. C.v.J. pp. 197 and 308 respectively; «τοῦ δὲ διὰ-πασῶν εἴδη ἐστὶν ἑπτὰ» = "and of the dia-pason there are seven species"). The term harmonia was used sometimes in the sense of "music" generally. See also under *tonos**.

Bibliography: Among the many contributions to the study of "harmonia" the following may be mentioned in chronological order:

D.B. Monro: The Modes of Ancient Greek Music (Oxford, 1894; esp. pp. 47-65, §§ 21 to 25).

R. P. Winnington-Ingram: Mode in ancient Greek music; Cambridge, 1936.

G. Reese: Music in the Middle Ages, N. York, 1940; p. 38 ff.

M. I. Henderson: The growth of the Greek ἀρμονία, Classical Quarterly 1942, 36; pp. 94-103.

Curt Sachs: The rise of music in the Ancient World, East and West, (N. York, 1943; pp. 216-238).

M. I. Henderson: The Growth of Ancient Greek Music, The Music Review, vol. IV, No. 1, 1943; pp. 4-13.

Matthew Shirlaw: The music and tone systems of Ancient Greece, The Music Review, vol. IV, No. 1, 1943; pp. 14-27.

M. Shirlaw: The music and tone-systems of Ancient Greece, Music & Letters 32, 1943; pp. 131-139.

Kathleen Schlesinger: The harmonia, Creator of the Modal System of Ancient

Greek Music, The Music Review, vol. V, 1944; pp. 7-39; 119-141.

Antoine Auda: Les gammes musicales; Ixelles, Belgium, 1947 (esp. pp. 49-77).

O. J. Gombosi: Key, mode, species; Journal of the American Musicological Society 4, 1951; pp. 20-26.

J. Chailley: Le mythe de modes grecs; Acta Musicologica 28, 1956; pp. 137-163.

Riemann: Music Lexikon, Sachteil (1967), s.v. Harmonia & Systema teleion, pp. 361 & 929 resp.

See also *harmoge, harmosis, hermosmenos*.

harmonia of the spheres (ἀρμονία τῶν σφαιρῶν); according to a conception attributed to the Pythagorean School, the planets while revolving produce different musical sounds, unheard by us, the ensemble of which create the "harmonia of the spheres". For Pythagoras and his School music was above all a mathematical science; its essence was number and its beauty was the expression of the harmonious relations of the numbers. Music was, too, the image of a celestial harmony; the harmonious relations of numbers were transferred to the planets. As Plato says, astronomy and music are sister sciences. Plinius (Naturalis Historia, II, 22) says that Pythagoras called the distance Earth-Moon a tone, the distance Moon-Hermes a semitone, from Venus to Sun a tone and a half etc. Arist. Quint. (III p. 145 Mb) says that the diapason expresses the "harmonious" movement of the planets («τὴν τῶν πλανητῶν ἐμμελῆ κίνησιν»).

Nicomachus (Enchir. ch. 3, C.v.J. pp. 241-2; Mb pp. 6-7) says that the names of the musical notes were derived from the seven planets and their place in relation to the earth. "Owing to the movement of Kronos (Saturn), which is the planet highest from us, the lowest note in the diapason was called Hypate (Ὑπάτη), because hypatos (ὕπατος) is the highest. And owing to the movement of the Moon which is the lowest of all, and the nearest to the Earth, the Neate (Nete) was so called; because néaton is the lowest".

To Zeus (Ζεύς), which is below Kronos, corresponds the Parhypate, and to Venus, which is above the Moon, corresponds the Paranete. And after the Sun, found in the middle, fourth from each side of the seven planets, the Mese was named, which is the note found in the middle, an interval of a fourth from each end of the heptachord. After Mars (Ἄρης), found between Zeus and Sun (Helios), the Hyper-mese or Lichanos was named, and after Hermes, found in the middle of Venus and Sun, the Paramese.

Thus the table of both harmoniai is as follows:

Harmonia of the Spheres		*Diapason*
Kronos	(Saturn)	Hypate
Zeus	(Jupiter)	Parhypate
Mars	(Ares)	Lichanos (or Hypermese)
Sun	(Helios)	Mese

Hermes		Paramese
Venus	(Aphrodite)	Paranete
Moon		Nete

Ptolemaeus (C.v. Jan, Excerpta Neapolitana, § 24, pp. 418-9) gives the following table: Ὅροι συστήματος κοσμικοῦ:

Φθόγγοι ἑστῶτες (Immovable notes)	Numbers		Spheres
Nete Hyperbolaeon	32	of	Kronos
Nete Diezeugmenon	24	„	Jupiter
Nete Synemmenon	21	„	Mars
Paramese	18	„	Sun
Mese	16	„	Venus
Hypate Meson	12	„	Hermes
Hypate Hypaton	9	of	Moon
Proslambanomenos	8	„	Fire, Air; Water, Earth

See also among others, Ch. Ém. Ruelle: Deux Textes grecs Anonymes, concernant le Canon Musical (Paris, 1878) p. 5.

harmonike (ἁρμονικὴ ἡ, fem.; m. pr. armonikí); according to Aristoxenus an important branch of the science of Melos. Its main object was to treat of everything regarding the "harmonia", and especially "of the theory of systems and the keys" (Aristox. Harm. I, p.1, 20-21).

Anon. Bell. (§ 19, p. 29) also describes the Harmonike as "the first and most essential part of music" («τῶν δὲ τῆς μουσικῆς μερῶν κυριώτατόν ἐστι καὶ πρῶτον τὸ ἁρμονικὸν» and in § 31, p. 46 «πρωτεῦον δὲ μέρος τῆς μουσικῆς ἡ ἁρμονική ἐστί»).

The Harmonike, according to Cleonides (Isag.; ch. 1, C.v.J. p. 179; Mb p. 1) is a theoretical and practical (in the sense of action) science; its subject matters are seven: the sounds (φθόγγοι), the intervals, the genera, the systems, the tonoi, the modulation (metabole) and the melopoeia.

Pachymeres (ap. Vincent "Notices", p. 401) calls the music itself Harmonike («ἡ μουσική, ἣν καὶ ἁρμονικὴν λέγομεν» = "the music which we also call Harmonike").

The Harmonike is expressed also by the term «τὸ ἁρμονικὸν» neut. (μέρος; "harmonikón"; see above Bell. Anon.), and in plur. «τὰ ἁρμονικὰ» (harmoniká). Aristox. Harm. (II, p. 31, 20 Mb) «μουσικοὶ ἀκούσαντες τὰ ἁρμονικὰ» ("[they think that] after having followed a course in Harmonike they will become musicians").

b) Harmonikos, (ἁρμονικός; m. pr. armonikós); a theorist dealing with the science of Harmonike. Aristoxenus calls his forerunners in the science of Harmonia «ἁρμονικοὶ» pl. (harmonikoi; harmonists).

See: Plut. De Mus. (1142F, ch. 33); Ptolem. Harm. (Wallis III, p. 1); Alyp. Isag. (C.v.J. p. 367; Mb p. 1); Mart. Cap. De Mus. (IX, p. 182 Mb).

harmosis (ἅρμοσις; m. pr. ármosis); from ἁρμόζειν or ἁρμόττειν (harmozein or harmottein) = to fit together; the tuning of an instrument (actually the act of tuning, and synecdoch. the result of tuning).

See *harmoge, harmonia, hermosmenos;* and for the tuning of the lyra and the kithara see *lyra**.

harp (ἅρπα; pr. árpa).

The harp, as an instrument, was known in Greece from quite remote times; but the name itself was unknown. The Greeks gave it the name *trigonon* (τρίγωνον) from its triangular form.

See under *trigonon.*

harpalyke (ἁρπαλύκη; m. pr. arpalíki); a song based on Harpalyke's legend, so-called after her name. Harpalyke, a nymph or maiden, fell in love with a young man called Iphiclus who treated her with despite; this led her to death, and a song competition among maidens was established in her honour.

(Aristox. ap. Athen. XIV, 619E, ch. 11; also FHG, vol. II, p. 287, Frg. 72).
See *kalyke.*

hectemorion, of tone (ἑκτημόριον, τόνου; m. pr. ektimórion); one sixth of the tone. It is, like the dodecatemorion*, a hypothetical and purely theoretical interval. The hectemorion is the interval by which two chromatic dieseis exceed two enharmonic ones; Aristox. (Harm. Mb I, p. 25, 15-21) «ἐπειδήπερ ἡ χρωματικὴ δίεσις τῆς ἐναρμονίου διέσεως δωδεκατημορίῳ τόνου μείζων ἐστί ... αἱ δὲ δύο χρωματικαὶ τῶν ἐναρμονίων δῆλον ὡς τῷ διπλασίῳ· τοῦτο δὲ ἐστὶν ἑκτημόριον, ἔλαττον διάστημα τοῦ ἐλαχίστου τῶν μελῳδουμένων» ("since the chromatic diesis is greater than the enharmonic by one-twelfth of a tone... the two chromatic dieseis evidently exceed the two enharmonic ones by double that interval, i.e. *the one-sixth*, an interval smaller than the smallest admitted in melody"; H.S.M. p. 183).

The hectemorion therefore was an "amelodeton"* interval, i.e. unsingable.

hedykomos (ἡδύκωμος; m. pr. idíkomos); a) a kind of dance mentioned by Pollux in his chapter "On kinds of dancing" (IV, 100) without any indication as to its character.

b) *hedykomos* is mentioned by Tryphon in the second book of Denominations (ap. Athen. XIV, 618C, ch. 9) among other names of aulos-solos (auleseis, αὐλήσεις), all of which were performed with dancing.

hegemon of the chorus (ἡγεμὼν χοροῦ); see *exarchos* and *koryphaeus.*

Hegemon, in the sense of chief, principal note, was called the Mese;

Cf. Arist. Probl. XIX, 33 (see under *arche*) ; also Plut. De Mus. 1135A, ch. 11.

For the metrical foot hegemon (=pyrrhic), see under *pyrrhiche** *(pyrrhichios)* and *pous**.

hekateris fem; **hekaterides** pl. (ἑκατερίς, ἑκατερίδες; m. pr. ekaterís, eka-terídes); a kind of lively hopping dance in which the dancers used to leap and beat the hips alternately with either of the heels (or the hands).

Pollux (IV, 102): «ἑκατερίδες δὲ καὶ θερμαστρίδες, ἔντονα ὀρχήματα· τὸ μὲν χειρῶν κινοῦν, ἡ δὲ θερμαστρὶς πηδητικὸν» ("*hekaterides* and therma-strides were lively dances; in the first they move the hands, while in the ther-mastris they leap"). See also Athen. XIV, 630A, ch. 27. Hes. «ἑκατερεῖν (verb) τὸ πρὸς τά ἰσχία πηδᾶν ἑκατέραις ταῖς πτέρναις» ("*hekaterein* (verb), to kick up to the hips alternately with either of the heels").

helicon (ἑλικών; m. pr. elikón).

An instrument by which they could measure the consonances (see *canon* and *monochord*).

Ptolemaeus describes the helicon in Harm. (II, ch. 2; I.D. p. 41 «Περὶ χρήσεως τοῦ κανόνος παρὰ τὸ ὄργανον ἑλικών», "On the use of the canon on the instrument *helicon*"). It was called *helicon* in a figurative sense from "*Helicon*, the mount of the Muses" («ὃ δὴ ῾Ελικῶνα φασιν ἀπ᾽ ὄρους ῾Ελικῶ-νος, ὅπου Μοῦσαι μυθεύονται χορεύειν»; Porph. Comment., ed. I.D., p. 157; also G. Pachym. ap. Vincent "Notices" pp. 477 and 479). Ptolemaeus gives the following diagram of helicon (ed. I.D. p. 46):

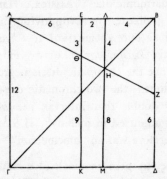

Note: The helicon is the square ΑΒΓΔ. We divide the lines ΑΒ and ΒΔ into two equal parts at points Ε, Ζ. We join ΑΖ and ΒΗΓ; then we take two lines parallel to ΑΓ, ΕΘΚ and ΛΗΜ. If the line ΑΓ is 12, then ΘΚ is 9, ΗΜ 8, ΖΔ 6 (also ΑΕ and ΕΒ), ΛΗ 4, ΕΘ 3, ΕΛ 2.

In this way we can take all the symphonies and the tone (epogdoos).

Cf. Aristides pp. 117-8 Mb, 98-99 RPW-I.

132

hemichorion (ἡμιχόριον; m. pr. imichórion); semi-chorus, half-chorus. Pollux (IV, 107): "when the chorus is divided into two parts this is called *dichoria* (διχορία), while each of the two parts [is called] *hemichorion*" («ὁπόταν γὰρ ὁ χορὸς εἰς δύο διαιρεθῇ, τὸ μὲν πρᾶγμα καλεῖται διχορία· ἑκατέρα δὲ μοῖρα, ἡμιχόριον»).

hemiolios (ἡμιόλιος; m. pr. imiólios) from ἡμι–, half, and ὅλος, a whole; in a general sense that which consists of a whole and one half of the whole. *Hemiolios logos* (ἡμιόλιος λόγος); hemiolic ratio, i.e. 3 to 2 (or 6 to 4). *Hemiolic pycnon* in the Chromatic genus was that shade (chroa, χρόα) in which the pycnon was equal to one semitone and a half, i.e. three-eighths of the tone;
Cf. Aristox. Harm. I, p. 25, 1 Mb.
See *diesis*.

hemitonion (ἡμιτόνιον; m. pr. imitónion); semitone. Also called *hemitoniaeon* (interval; ἡμιτονιαῖον διάστημα);
Cf. Aristox. Harm. II, p. 51, 25 Mb. The tone was divided into two unequal semitones, the major (μεῖζον) and the minor (ἔλαττον). According to Aristides (p. 114 Mb, 95 RPW-I) in order to find the ratio of the semitone, since between the numbers 9 and 8 (epogdoos 9:8) no other number existed, the ancients doubled both these numbers (18:16) and took the one which is found in between (i.e. 17); and defined the first semitone as 17:16, and the other as 18:17. See also Ptolem. Harm. (ed. Wallis, p. 48). Aristoxenus, however, divided the tone into two equal semitones.
Cf. Harm. II, p. 57, 10-11 Mb.

hendekachordon (ἐνδεκάχορδον; m. pr. endekáchordon); a system with eleven strings. It consisted of three tetrachords of which the two lower were conjunct and the third disjunct.

Cf. Ptolemaeus II, ch. 4.
The eleventh string was added by Timotheus* of Miletus. Ion of Chios (ap. Brgk PLG, vol. II, p. 427, Frg. 3): «ἐνδεκάχορδε λύρη δεκαβάμονα τάξιν ἔχουσα» ("*eleven-stringed* lyra with ten intervals").

heptachordos, masc. and fem. (ἑπτάχορδος; m. pr. eptáchordos); having seven strings. *heptachordos lyra* (ἑπτάχορδος λύρα); seven-stringed lyra.
heptachordon, neut. (ἑπτάχορδον); a scale consisting of seven notes. *heptachordon systema* (ἑπτάχορδον σύστημα); see *lyra*.
heptachordon was a musical instrument with seven strings.

133

Th. Kock Comic. Att. Frg. (Aristoph. Incerta; vol. I, p. 555, Frg. 659): «οὐχ οἷα πρῶτον ᾖδον ἑπτάχορδα πάνθ᾽ ὁμοῖα».

hendekakroumatos (ἐνδεκακρούματος; m. pr. endekakroúmatos); employing eleven notes. Timotheus Persae, 230, ap. Page PMG Fr. 791, p. 413 («ρυθμοῖς τ᾽ ἐνδεκακρουμάτοις»).

heptaglossos (ἑπτάγλωσσος; m. pr. eptáglossos); an epithet of the phorminx or of the lyra; having seven strings. Synonym of heptaphthongos.

Pind. (PLG I, p. 207; Nemean V, verse 24) «ἐν δὲ μέσας φόρμιγγ᾽ Ἀπόλλων ἑπτάγλωσσον χρυσέῳ πλήκτρῳ διώκων» ("in the midst of the Muses' chorus Apollo playing with golden plectrum *the seven-stringed* phorminx").

heptagonon (ἑπτάγωνον; m. pr. eptágonon); a septangular (?) instrument mentioned by Aristotle (Polit. VIII, ch. 6, §7; 134IA «ἑπτάγωνα καὶ τρίγωνα καὶ σαμβῦκαι καὶ πάντα τὰ δεόμενα χειρουργικῆς ἐπιστήμης» ("the *septangles*, the triangles and the sambykae and all the instruments requiring manual skill").

heptaktypos (ἑπτάκτυπος; m. pr. eptáktipos); of phorminx and lyra, the same as *heptachordos, heptaglossos, heptatonos, heptaphthongos.*

Pind. (PLG I, p. 112; Pythian II, v. 70-71) «χάριν ἑπτακτύπου φόρμιγγος» ("for the sake [or in honour] of the *seven-voiced* (*seven-toned*) phorminx").

heptaphonos (ἑπτάφωνος; m. pr. eptáphonos); seven-voiced.
See *heptaphthongos* (below).

heptaphthongos (ἑπτάφθογγος; m. pr. eptáphthongos); having or producing seven notes. *heptaphongos kithara* or *lyra*; *seven-stringed* kithara or lyra; Eurip. Ion v. 881.
The same as *heptaphonos* (ἑπτάφωνος).

heptasemos, chronos (ἑπτάσημος, χρόνος; m. pr. eptásimos); consisting of seven time-units.
See *chronos.*

heptatonos (ἑπτάτονος; m. pr. eptátonos); having seven (hepta) "tones" (= notes, strings). Synonym of *heptaphthongos* and *heptachordos.*

Eurip. Heracles, v. 683-4 «παρά τε χέλυος ἑπτατόνου μολπὰν» ("and where *the seven-toned* (seven-stringed) chelys sounds").

Also Ion of Chios (Brgk PLG, II, p. 428, Frg. 3).
See under *tetragerys.*

Heracleides, Heraclides, Ponticus (Ἡρακλείδης ὁ Ποντικός; m.pr. Iraclídis Ponticós); 4th cent. B.C. writer born at Heracleia (Ἡράκλεια) of Pontus in Asia Minor (hence his surname Ponticus).

A pupil and disciple of Plato, he was appointed, according to Suidas, as his substitute during his Master's absence in Sicily. Later he became a disciple of Aristotle. Among his many writings (classified by Diogenes Laertius in ethica, physica, grammatica, historica, etc.), there are also writings on music, which are cited by Plutarch and Athenaeus. Plutarch (De Mus. 1131F, ch. 3) mentions a «Συναγωγὴ τῶν ἐν μουσικῇ» ("Collection of facts concerning music"), and Athenaeus (XIV, 624C, ch. 19) a work "On Music" («Περὶ μουσικῆς»).

The authorship of some of his works—on other subjects than music— is ascribed by certain historians to other writers of the same name.

Cf. FHG vol. II (1848) pp. 197-224; *Fr. Wehrli*: "Die Schule des Aristoteles": Herakleides Pontikos, Heft VII, Basel, 1953 (especially pp. 46-50).

hermosmenos (ἡρμοσμένος; m. pr. irmosménos) from ἁρμόζειν (harmozein) = to fit together; in music, to regulate in accordance with the laws of music. Hermosmenos, p.p. = regulated in accordance with the laws of music, emmeles.

hermosmenon melos: melos (tune) obedient to the laws of melody.

Aristoxenus (Harm. I, p. 18, 18ff Mb) explains that "the hermosmenon melos is not constituted only by intervals and notes. A collocation upon a definite principle is also necessary—because as is obvious, the anharmoston* (melos violating the laws of harmony) is also constituted by intervals and notes; it follows therefore that the most important factor in the right constitution of the melos is the collocation in general and its peculiar nature in particular".

Cleonides (Isag. ch. 1, C.v.J. p. 179; Mb p. 1) defines the *hermosmenon* as "that which is constituted by notes and intervals having a certain order" («ἡρμοσμένον δὲ τὸ ἐκ φθόγγων τε καὶ διαστημάτων ποιὰν τάξιν ἐχόντων συγκείμενον»). In a more general sense the "hermosmenos" signified harmonious, harmonized; Sext.Empir. (VI, § 13) «οἵ τε μέγα δυνηθέντες ἐν φιλοσοφίᾳ, καθάπερ καὶ Πλάτων, τὸν σοφὸν ὅμοιόν φασιν εἶναι τῷ μουσικῷ, τὴν ψυχὴν ἡρμοσμένην ἔχοντα» ("those also who have been men of great ability in philosophy, such as Plato, say that the sage resembles the musician as he has his soul *harmonized*"; transl. by R.G. Bury, vol. IV, p. 379). Hippocrates Regimen («Περὶ διαίτης») I, § 18; «καλῶς δὲ ἡρμοσμένης γλώσσης τῇ συμφωνίᾳ τέρψις, ἀναρμόστου δὲ λύπη» ("when the tongue is well in tune [harmonized] the concord causes pleasure, while when it is out of tune it causes grief" [pain]).

The verb ἁρμόττεσθαι (*harmottesthai*; pass.) signified also to tune an instrument; Plato Rep. 349E «ἁρμοττόμενος λύραν» ("*tuning* the lyra") and

135

in Phaedon, 85E «ἡ μὲν ἁρμονία … θεῖόν τι ἐστὶν ἐν τῇ ἡρμοσμένη λύρᾳ» ("harmonia … is something divine in the *well-tuned lyra*").

Aristoxenus (Harm. I, p. 11,5) «τί ποτ' ἐστὶν ὃ ποιοῦμεν ὅταν *ἁρμοττό-μενοι* τῶν χορδῶν ἑκάστην ἀνιῶμεν ἢ ἐπιτείνωμεν» ("what is it that we are doing [what takes place] when in tuning we tighten or relax each of the strings").

Harmottesthai (ἁρμόττεσθαι) signified also to adapt verses to an already existing melody; Simonides (PLG III, p. 186, Frg. 184 [171]) «τὸν γλυκὺν ἐς παίδων ἵμερον *ἡρμόσατο*».

hestotes-kinoumenoi phthongoi (ἑστῶτες-κινούμενοι φθόγγοι; m. pr. estótes, kinoúmenoi).

a) *hestotes* (from ἵστημι, to stand, to stay) were those notes of a tetrachord which were immovable; i.e. unchanged in spite of any change in the genus of the tetrachord. Hestotes therefore were the extreme notes of the tetrachord, e.g.

Nicom. Enchir. (C.v.J.p. 263; Mb p. 26): "the extreme notes of a tetrachord are called *hestotes* (*immovable*) because they never change in any of the genera". Aristoxenus uses the term ἀκίνητοι (*immovable*) in place of hestotes (Harm. I, p. 22, 11; III, p. 61, 23 Mb). Alypius calls the hestotes also ἀκλινεῖς (steady, fixed, unmoved, unshaken); Isag. C.v.J. p. 368, Mb p. 2 «ἑστῶτες καὶ ἀκλινεῖς».

Among the hestotes the proslambanomenos* is also included as it is unchanged in the Greater Perfect System (in any genus).

b) *kinoumenoi* (κινούμενοι, movable; from κινοῦμαι = I move) were the notes found between the two extremes of a tetrachord.

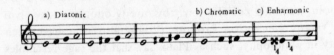

By Bacchius (Isag. § 36, C.v.J. p. 300; Mb p. 9) the movable notes are called *pheromenoi* (φερόμενοι; from φέρεσθαι = to be led or brought or moved from one place to another). Cf. Aristides (De Mus. Mb p. 12, RPW-I p. 9).

Note: the extreme notes of a tetrachord, or of a system or group of intervals, were called ἄκροι (pl., *extremes*) while those in between were μέσοι;

136

Aristox. Harm. II, p. 46, 20-22 and I, p. 29, 32 Mb.

Cf. Cleon. Isag. ch. 4 (C.v.J. pp. 185-6; Mb. pp. 6-7); Bacch. Isag., §§ 35-36 (C.v.J. p. 300; Mb p. 9); Alyp. Isag. (C.v.J. ch. 4, p. 368; Mb p. 2); Nicom. Enchir. ch. 12 (C.v.J. p. 263; Mb pp. 26-27).

Hesychius (Ἡσύχιος; m. pr. Isíchios); 5th cent. A.D. grammarian and lexicographer from Alexandria known as "Hesychius Alexandreus" (Ἡσύχιος Ἀλεξανδρεύς). His dictionary is considered one of the most important sources of information on the Greek language, history, life and arts. Among the rich material of the Lexicon we find much information regarding the meaning and use of ancient musical terms, instruments etc.

The full title of the Lexicon in Greek was «Ἡσυχίου γραμματικοῦ Ἀλεξανδρέως συναγωγὴ πασῶν λέξεων κατὰ στοιχεῖον ἐκ τῶν Ἀριστάρχου καὶ Ἀπίωνος καὶ Ἡλιοδώρου» ("Hesychius, grammarian of Alexandria's Collection of all words in alphabetical order according to those of Aristarchus, Apion and Heliodorus").

The first edition of the Lexicon was published in 1514 by Aldus Manutius, in Venice under the supervision of the Cretan philologist Marcus Musurus (Μᾶρκος Μουσοῦρος, 1470-1567), who also edited many other Greek works (of Athenaeus, Plato, Aristophanes, Euripides, etc.).

Other editions followed; by *A. Francino* (Florence, 1520); *C. Schrevelio-J. Pricaei* (Leyden, 1668); *Johannes Alberti* (Leyden, 1746-1766); *Mauricius Schmidt* (Iena, 1858-68); *K. Latte* (Copenhagen 1953, in progress).

heterophonia (ἑτεροφωνία; m. pr. eterophonía); heterophony. This term was used by Plato in the Laws (VII, 812 D); speaking about the education of youth, he says "the master of the lyra and his pupil should use this instrument in such a way that the melody be simply reproduced on the lyra note by note. But as to the *heterophony* and variety of the lyra, when the strings sound one tune and the composer of the melody another ... it is not necessary to exercise the boys in such things" («... τὴν δ᾽ ἑτεροφωνίαν καὶ ποικιλίαν τῆς λύρας, ἄλλα μὲν μέλη τῶν χορδῶν ἱεισῶν, ἄλλα δὲ τοῦ τὴν μελωδίαν ξυνθέντος ποιητοῦ ...»).

The question whether or not ancient Greeks had a kind of polyphony raised long and often passionate discussions among scholars, especially in the last century. The problem has not been definitely solved. What is rather more generally accepted is that in choruses the voices sang in unison or in parallel octaves (cf. Aristotle Problems XIX 17, 18, 39b). In the case of instrumental accompaniment of vocal pieces, the accompanying instrument (while playing the same melody at the octave) might use here and there some ornamental elaboration or some interval other than the octave. In instrumental music also something similar might have been in use. In all cases the accompaniment was placed above the main melody; cf. Arist. Problem XIX, 12 «διά τί τῶν [δύο] χορδῶν ἡ βαρυτέρα ἀεὶ τὸ μέλος λαμβάνει;» ("why is it that the lower of the [two] strings always has the melody?").

hexachordon (ἑξάχορδον; m. pr. exáchordon); a system of six strings. According to Boethius the sixth string was added to the pentachord by Hyagnis*.

For a hypothetical hexatonic (i.e. hexaphone, having six notes) scale as having preceded the heptatonic, see *J. Chailley*: L' hexatonique grec d' après Nicomaque", in Revue des Études grecques, LXIX, 1956, pp. 73-100. See also Note 2, under *systema**, where this question is referred to.

hexasemos (ἑξάσημος; m. pr. exásimos) chronos; consisting of six time-units.

See *chronos*.

hexatonos (ἑξάτονος; m. pr. exátonos); having six tones. Hexatonos was the diapason (octave) as containing six tones in all. Plut. De Animae Procreatione in Timaeo («Περὶ τῆς ἐν Τιμαίῳ ψυχογονίας») 1028E, ch. 31 «ὥσπερ τινὰ συμφωνίαν ἐν ἐξατόνῳ διὰ πασῶν ἀποδίδωσι» ("in the same way as the diapason makes a consonance (concord) by *six tones*").

hexes (ἑξῆς; m. pr. exís); contiguous. *Hexes phthongoi*, notes following each other in pitch; contiguous notes.

Bacch. Isag. § 26 (C.v.J. p. 298; Mb p. 7) «Τετράχορδον· τάξις φθόγγων ἑξῆς μελῳδουμένων» ("Tetrachord is a series of notes sung one after the other [contiguously]»).

ἑξῆς τετράχορδα (*hexes tetrachorda*); contiguous tetrachords, either conjunct or disjunct.

ἑξῆς διαστήματα (*hexes intervals*); the intervals which follow each other in pitch; those whose extremities are "hexes", i.e. contiguous.

Cf. *syneches*.

hierakion, melos (ἱεράκιον μέλος; m. pr. ierákion); a melody played on the aulos by young men during a procession in honour of Hera, in Argos; the procession, held by girls carrying flowers (ἀνθεσφόροι), was a part of the feast of the sacred marriage of Zeus and Hera.

Pollux (IV, 78): «ἱεράκιον τὸ Ἀργολικόν, ὃ ταῖς ἀνθεσφόροις ἐν Ἥρας ἐπηύλουν» ("the Argolic *hierakion* [melos] which was played on the aulos [accompanying] the flowers-carrying girls celebrating Hera").

b) *hierakios nomos* (ἱεράκιος νόμος; m. pr. ierákios nomos); an auletic nomos, so called after Hierax*, a pupil of Olympus, from Argos (c. 7th cent. B.C.) who died very young. Pollux (IV, 79): "And there was a nomos [called] hierakios, from Hierax* who died young, and was Olympus' suppliant (protégé), pupil and lover".

See also Athen. XIII, 570B, ch. 26 («αὗται αὐλητρίδες δὲ μόνον αὐλοῦσιν Ἱέρακος νόμον» = "these auletrides play only the nomos of Hierax").

Note: Probably the hierakion melos and the hierakios nomos were one and same thing·

hieraoedos (**ἱεραοιδός**; m. pr. ieraïdós); sacred epic singer, minstrel.

See *ἀοιδός (aoedos)*.

hieraules (**ἱεραύλης**; m. pr. ierávlis); aulete performing during the sacred ceremonies and the sacrifices. In the Eleusinian mysteries he was the head of the sacred music, and the chief of the Hymnodes (Ὑμνῳδοί).

Hierax (**Ἱέραξ**; m. pr. Iérax); 7th cent. B.C. aulete and composer from Argos. According to Pollux (IV, 79) he was a protégé (or suppliant), disciple and lover of Olympus*, and died very young. His name is connected with the hierakios nomos* or hierakion melos, explained above under its name. To him was also attributed a melody for aulos-solo called *endrome** which was played at the Olympic Games during the pentathlon contest.

hierosalpiktes and **hierosalpinktes** (**ἱεροσαλπικτὴς** and **ἱεροσαλπιγκτής**; m. pr. ierosalpiktís); the player of the salpinx (trumpet) at sacrifices. Pollux (IV, 86): «ὁ δὲ ἐπὶ τοῖς ἱεροῖς, ἱεροσαλπιγκτὴς» ("and the player of the salpinx at sacrifices was called *hierosalpinktes*"). Pollux adds that «ἱερὸς σαλπιγκτὴς» ("sacred salpinktes") is a more appropriate expression.

hilarodia, hilarodos (**ἱλαρῳδία, ἱλαρῳδός**; m. pr. ilarodía, ilarodós).

a) *hilarodia*; the singing of cheerful and joyful songs. Also the art of the hilarodos.

b) *hilarodos*; a singer of cheerful and merry songs. He was considered a serious artist, and was crowned at the competitions.

Athen. (XIV, 621B, ch. 14): "More serious than these poets is the so-called *hilarode*, because he does not make indecent gestures; he adopts a man's white gown, and is crowned with a golden crown ... he is accompanied, as the aulode, by a kitharist male or female; and the crown is presented to the hilarode and the aulode, but not to the 'psaltes' [the kitharist or player of a stringed instrument by bare fingers] nor to the aulete".

Sometimes the hilarodos was wrongly confused with the simodos*, a singer of indecent songs.

himaeos (**ἱμαῖος**; m. pr. iméos); a folk-song of the millers. Himaeos is mentioned (ap. Athen. XIV, 618D, ch. 10) among other folk-songs, in these words, «ἱμαῖος ἡ ἐπιμύλιος καλουμένη [ᾠδὴ] ἦν περὶ τὰς ἀλέτους ᾖδον» ("*himaeos*, the so-called 'epimylios' [mill-song] which they sang while grind-

139

ing". Also Aristophanes the grammarian (ap. Athen. 619B, ch. 10: «ἱμαῖος ᾠδὴ μυλωθρῶν» ("himaeos, a song of the millers"). Plutarch (in Septem Sapientum Convivium, 157D-E, ch. 14) has preserved the verses of the refrain (burden) of a charming mill-song of Mytilene, of the time of Alcaeus and Sappho:

«῎Αλει, μύλε [μύλα], ἄλει   "Grind, mill, grind,
καὶ γὰρ Πιττακὸς ἄλει,   because Pittacus grinds too,
μεγάλας Μυτιλάνας βασιλεύων»   the Governor of great Mytilene"

(Pittacus, considered as one of the seven wise men of ancient Greece (7th to 6th cent. B.C.), had been Governor [αἰσυμνήτης, aesymnetes, elected governor] of Mytilene for ten years.)

Note: himaeos was called after himalis (ἱμαλὶς) which, as is explained in Athen. (618D, ch. 10), among the Dorians meant the product (νόστος) and the measures (ἐπίμετρα) of wheat-flour.

hippophorbos (ἱπποφορβός; m. pr. ippophorvós); a kind of aulos used by the horsebreeders.

Pollux (IV, 74): "hippophorbos; it was invented by Libyan nomads, who use it for horses' pasturage. Its material was laurel denuded of the bark, with the pith extracted; it produces a piercing sound, which affects the horses by its acuteness".

Note: The word hippophorbos (ἱπποφορβός) principally meant horse-breeder. Hes. «ἱπποφορβός· ἱπποτρόφος» ("hippophorbos = horse-breeder").

Histiaeus (῾Ιστιαῖος; m. pr. Istiéos); end of 5th to 4th cent. B.C. musician fron Colophon (Κολοφῶν; hense his surname Κολοφώνιος, Colophonius).

He is credited by Nicomachus with the addition of the 10th string (Excerpta ex Nicomacho; ch. 4, C.v.J. p. 274, Mb p. 35). His time may be placed between Prophrastus* (middle of the 5th cent.), who added the 9th string, and Timotheus* (450-360 B.C.), who added the 11th string. No other information regarding his life or his career is known.

hodos (ὁδός; m. pr. odós); road, route, street. In music it was used in the meaning of a course or a progression from a certain point upwards or downwards. Aristox. Harm. (III, p. 66, 27-28 Mb): «᾿Απὸ δὲ τοῦ διτόνου δύο μὲν ὁδοὶ (plur.) ἐπὶ τὸ ὀξύ, μία δ᾿ ἐπὶ τὸ βαρὺ» ("From the ditone there are two [possible] progressions one upwards and one downwards").

holmos (ὅλμος; m. pr. ólmos); the upper part of the mouthpiece in which the reed was inserted and which was put between the lips. With the hypholmion* it formed the mouthpiece of the aulos. Both were attached at the extreme upper end of the aulos.

140

Phot. Lex. «ὅλμοι (plur.) καὶ ὑφόλμια, ἐπὶ αὐλῶν» ("*holmoi* (pl.) and hypholmia, on auloi"). Th. Kock Comic. Attic. Frg. (Eupolis Φίλοι; vol. I, p. 331, Fr. 267) «ῥέγκειν δὲ τοὺς ὅλμους» = "to blow the *holmoi*".

Cf. Pollux, IV, 70; and *lyra*.

homoeotropos (ὁμοιότροπος; m. pr. omiótropos); similar, of the same style. Plut. De Mus. (1137B, ch. 18) «μαρτυρεῖ γοῦν τὰ Ὀλύμπου τε καὶ Τερπάνδρου ποιήματα καὶ τῶν τούτοις ὁμοιοτρόπων (pl.) πάντων» ("as testify the compositions of Olympus and Terpander and all [other compositions] of the same style").

homophonia-homophonoi phthongoi (ὁμοφωνία-ὁμόφωνοι φθόγγοι; m. pr. omophonía, omóphoni phthóngi);

homophonia (homophony) is the unison and by extension the octave, double-octave etc. Bacch. Isag. § 60 (C.v.J. p. 305; Mb p. 15): «ὁμοφωνία· ὅταν ἅμα δύο φθόγγοι τυπτόμενοι μήτε ὀξύτεροι, μήτε βαρύτεροι ἀλλήλων ὑπάρχωσι» ("*homophony* [is] when, of two sounds struck together, neither is higher or lower than the other").

Ptolemaeus (Harm. I, ch. VII; ed. Wallis III, p. 15; ed. I.D. p. 15) defines the *homophones* as "those sounds which played together give acoustically the impression of one sound, like the diapasons (octaves) and those which are composed of them" («Ὁμόφωνοι μέν, οἱ κατὰ τὴν σύμψαυσιν ἑνὸς ἀντίληψιν ἐμποιοῦντες ταῖς ἀκοαῖς, οἷον οἱ διὰ-πασῶν καὶ οἱ ἐκ τούτων συντιθέμενοι»). Homophones therefore are, according to Ptolemaeus, the octave, the double-octave etc. («ὅ τε πρῶτος πολλαπλάσιος καὶ οἱ ὑπ' αὐτοῦ μετρούμενοι»). Porphyrius in his Commentarius (Wallis III, p. 292; ed. I.D. p. 118, 18ff) defines as "first the octave, and then the double-octave and the triple-octave".

Ptolemaeus (ibid) divides the intervals into three categories; first the homophones, secondly the symphones and thirdly the emmeleis. "First because of its superiority comes the class of *homophones*" («Προηγούμενον μέν, ἀρετῆς ἕνεκα, τὸ τῶν ὁμοφώνων»). And of the homophones the most unified and the best is for him the octave («Τῶν δὲ ὁμοφώνων ἑνωτικώτατον καὶ κάλλιστον τὸ διὰ πασῶν»).

For Gaudentius (Isag. § 8, C.v.J. p. 337; Mb p. 11) "*homophones* are those emmeleis* sounds (ἐμμελεῖς φθόγγοι) which do not differ in pitch" («οἳ μήτε βαρύτητι, μήτε ὀξύτητι διαφέρονται ἀλλήλων»). Aristides (De Mus. Mb p. 12; RPW-I p. 10) defines as *homophones* the notes which differ in function but have the same pitch" («ὁμόφωνοι δὲ οἵτινες δύναμιν μὲν ἀλλοίας φωνῆς, τάσιν δὲ ἴσην ἐπέχουσιν»). The terms *isotonia-isotonoi** (ἰσοτονία-ἰσότονοι), and *homotonia-homotonoi** (ὁμοτονία-ὁμότονοι) were also used

141

for homophonia-homophonoi.

See also under *symphonia-symphonoi*.

homotona σημεῖα, (ὀμότονα; m. pr. omótona) signs.

See below, *homotonoi phthongoi*.

homotonoi phthongoi (ὁμότονοι φθόγγοι; m. pr. omótoni); notes having the same pitch; a synonym of isotonoi.

Cf. Porph. Comment. (ed. Wallis, III, p. 258; ed. I.D. p. 82, 19). Gaudentius (Isag. § 21 C.v.J.p. 350; Mb p. 23) calls *homotona* (neut. pl.; ὁμότονα) the signs used for the homotonoi phthongoi.

hormos (ὅρμος; m. pr. órmos); a kind of cyclic dance. According to Lucian's description of it ("On dancing" § 12) it was performed by a mixed group of maidens and adolescents, dancing in a formation resembling a necklace. Leading the dance an adolescent imitated war-figures with youthful movements. A maiden followed with modest and reserved movements. So, as Lucian concludes, wisdom and bravery were combined in hormos.

horos (ὅρος; m. pr. óros); in Aristoxenean terminology the limit, the boundary of an interval; Harm. (II, Mb p. 49,20): «τοὺς τῶν διαστημάτων ὅρους» (pl.) = "the boundaries of the intervals". Also II, p. 56, 1 & 18, and especially III, p. 59, 15-19.

In Anon. Bell. (§ 12, p. 27) the term *horos* (ὅρος) is used in the sense of *definition*; «ὅρος μουσικῆς· μουσική ἐστιν ἐπιστήμη etc." ("*definition* of music: music is a science etc.").

Hyagnis (Ὕαγνις; m. pr. Íagnis); mythical musician from Kelaenai in Phrygia. According to a legend he was a pupil of Mariandynus (Μαριανδυνὸς) "the inventor of the threnetic aulody". To Hyagnis were attributed the invention of the aulos (single and double-piped) and of the auletic art (Plut. De Mus. 1133F, ch. 7). In the "Parion Chronicon*" (ed. Jacoby F.; v. 10) we read that "*Hyagnis* of Phrygia first invented the aulos at Kelaenai, and first played on it the harmonia called Phrygian and other nomoi of the Mother (Cybele) of Dionysus and Pan" («Ὕαγνις ὁ Φρὺξ αὐλοὺς πρῶτος ηὗρεν ἐν Κελαιναῖς καὶ τὴν ἁρμονίαν τὴν καλουμένην Φρυγιστὶ πρῶτος ηὔλησε καὶ ἄλλους νόμους Μητρὸς Διονύσου, Πανός»).

Alexander in his "Collection concerning Phrygian history" («Συναγωγὴ τῶν περὶ Φρυγίας») ap. Plut. op. cit. (1132F, ch. 5) says that "first Hyagnis played the aulos («Ὕαγνιν δὲ πρῶτον αὐλῆσαι»), and after him his son Marsyas and then Olympus".

The introduction and propagation in Greece of the aulos and the auletic art, and the Phrygian harmonia as well, were generally ascribed to Phrygian musicians, and by legend to the first "Phrygian triad" Hyagnis, Marsyas* and Olympus*.

Anon. Bell. (§ 28, pp. 34-35) says that "the Phrygian harmonia sounds better on the wind instruments; witness the first inventors Marsyas, Hyagnis and Olympus, the Phrygians" («ἡ Φρύγιος ἁρμονία πρωτεύει ἐν ἐμπνευστοῖς ὀργάνοις· μάρτυρες οἱ πρῶτοι εὑρεταί, Μαρσύας καὶ Ὕαγνις καὶ Ὄλυμπος, οἱ Φρύγες»).

hydraulis, hydraulos, hydraulikon organon (ὕδραυλις, ὕδραυλος, ὑ-δραυλικὸν ὄργανον; m. pr. ídravlis, ídravlos, idravlikón órganon) from ὕδωρ, water, and αὐλός, aulos; a water (hydraulic) organ in which the sound was produced by hydraulic air compression. The principle of the hydraulis (also called hydraulos and hydraulikon organon) is based on the syrinx polycalamus or Pan-pipes. The invention of the hydraulis has been attributed to Ktesibius*, a Greek mechanician of Alexandria; Alkeides (ap. Athen. IV, 174B, ch. 75) describes him as a "barber", while Tryphon in the Third book of Denominations (ap. Athen. ibid) clearly speaks of him as "Ktesibius the mechanician".

It seems that the principle of producing sounds by hydraulic air compression was an idea which Plato adapted on a night-clock like a very large clepsydra (κλεψύδρα), in which the hours were sounded by hydraulic air compression on pipes; Athen. (ibid): "it is said that Plato gave a small idea (hint) of its construction by having a night-clock made: similar to the hydraulic organ, like a very large clepsydra" («λέγεται δὲ Πλάτωνα μικράν τινα ἔννοιαν δοῦναι τοῦ κατασκευάσματος νυκτερινὸν ποιήσαντα ὡρολόγιον ἐοικὸς τῷ ὑδραυλικῷ, οἷον κλεψύδραν μεγάλην λίαν»).

Archimedes was also accredited with the hydraulis' invention by some writers.

Select bibliography:

Hero: "The Pneumatics of Hero"; translated and edited by Bennet Woodcroft (London, 1851)

J. Tannery et Carra de Vaux: "L' invention de l' hydraulis"; "Revue des Etudes Grecques" XXI, Paris 1908; pp. 326-332 (I,J.T.), 332-340 (II, C.d.V.)

Tittel: "Hydraulis" in Pauly's RE(1914), vol. XVII, col. 60-77.

H.G. Farmer: "The Organ of the Ancients: from Eastern Sources"; London 1931.

G. Bédart: Note sur "L'Hydraulis"; "Monde Musical" 44, Paris 1933, p. 225.

A. Cellier: "L'Orgue hydraulique d'Aquincum"; "Monde Musical" 44, Paris 1933, p. 190.

C. Sachs: The History of Musical Instruments; N. York, 1940, pp. 143-145.

J. W. Warman: "The Hydraulic Organ"; Grove (1954), vol. IV, pp. 442-3.

W. Walker-Mayer: "Die romische Orgel von Aquincum", 1970.

J. Perrot: "The Organ from its invention in the Hellenistic period", 1971.

hymenaeos (ὑμέναιος m. pr. iméneos); a nuptial or bridal song. It was sung by friends accompanying the bride from her parents' house to that of the bridegroom. Hes. «Ὑμεναίων· γαμικῶν ᾀσμάτων, μέλος ᾠδῆς» ("*Hymenaeoi* [pl.]; nuptial songs; melodies"); also Athen. XIV, 619B, ch. 10.

The melody was also played on the aulos; Pollux (IV, 75) «αὐλεῖ δὲ ὁ μόναυλος μάλιστα τὸν γαμήλιον» ("the nuptial song is played chiefly on the monaulos").

Anaxandrides in "The Treasure" («Θησαυρὸς», ap. Athen. IV, 176A, ch. 78) says "picking up the monaulos (single-piped aulos) I played *the nuptial song*" («ἀναλαβὼν ηὔλουν τὸν ὑμέναιον»).

See also *gamelion*.

hymnos (ὕμνος); m. pr. ímnos); principally a sacred ode addressed to a god or a hero; Plato Laws (book III, 700B) «καί τι ἦν εἶδος ᾠδῆς εὐχαὶ πρὸς θεούς, ὄνομα δὲ ὕμνοι ἐπεκαλοῦντο» ("and a kind of ode, prayers to the gods which were called *hymns*"). As poets of hymns in remote times, almost mythical, there were cited Olen* (Ὠλὴν) from Lydia, Orpheus*, Eumolpus* and Musaeus*. Such hymns were the well-known "Homeric Hymns" («Ὁμηρικοὶ Ὕμνοι»), of which 33 in dactylic hexameters have been preserved; they were epic songs recited by rhapsodes in feasts.

Sacred odes inserted in tragedies were also hymns;

Cf. Aeschylus' Agamemnon, verses 160ff, the Hymn to Zeus by the chorus. Among surviving hymns there are also interesting fragments with musical notation; see *Remains of Greek Music*.

hymnodos (ὑμνῳδός; m. pr. imnodós); singer of hymns.

hymnodia (ὑμνῳδία; m. pr. imnodía); the singing of hymns.

hymnodein, vb (ὑμνῳδεῖν; m. pr. imnodín), to sing a hymn; to praise by singing. Also *hymnein* (ὑμνεῖν; m.pr. imnín).

hypagogeus (ὑπαγωγεύς; m. pr. ipagogéfs); a movable underprop made of wood in hemispheric form, used to shorten the length of the strings; a sort of fret for stringed instruments.

Cf. Nicom. (Harm. Ench. ch. 10; C.v.J. p. 254; Mb 18); Ptolem. Harm. (I, ch. 3; II, chs. 2 and 12 etc; ed. I.D. pp. 9, 2; 48, 6; 66, 29 respectively).

hypate (ὑπάτη; m. pr. ipáti) = highest; the lowest note or string; it was so called (highest) because it was placed at the farthest end of the strings. Aristides Quint. (I, p. 10 Mb; R.P.W-I p. 8) says that "hypate hypaton was the first note of the first tetrachord, because the ancients used to call hypaton (ὕπατον) the first" («ὑπάτη δὲ ὑπάτων, ὅτι τοῦ πρώτου τετραχόρδου πρώτη τίθεται· τὸ γὰρ πρῶτον ὕπατον ἐκάλουν οἱ παλαιοί»).

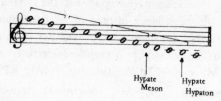

See *onomatothesia*.

hypatoeides, topos (ὑπατοειδής, τόπος; m. pr. ipatoïdís tópos); the region of the hypate; the lower region of the voice; Cf. Anon. Bell. §§ 63-64, pp. 76-77 and Note on §§ 63, 64.

hypatoeides phthongos (ὑπατοειδὴς φθόγγος) was the lowest note of the pycnon; the note produced by the string parhypate. Cf. Bacch. Isag. § 43 (C.v.J. p. 302; Mb p.11).

hypatoeides tropos (ὑπατοειδὴς τρόπος); a kind (style) of the melopoeia (of the composition of melos). One of the three "tropoi" (kinds, styles) of composition discussed by Aristides (Mb p. 30; R.P.W-I p. 30); the hypatoeides coincides with the tragic style of composition.

hypaulein (ὑπαυλεῖν; m. pr. ipavlín); to accompany (a song or a dance) by aulos; in this sense it is a synonym of "prosaulein"*. Epicharmus (ap. Athen. IV, 183C, ch. 81): «καὶ ὑπαυλεῖ σφιν σοφὸς κιθάρᾳ παριαμβίδας» ("and a skilful kitharist plays for them pariambides to *aulos accompaniment*"; see the full text under *pariambis*). This sentence however presents some difficulties, and it has been translated in different ways; Ch. B. Gulick ("Deipnosophistae" London, 1928; vol. II p. 309) translates "and one skilled in the cithara pipes for them harp airs in accompaniment". F. A. Gevaert (Hist. et Théor. de la Mus. de l'Ant., vol. II, p. 360, note 2) translates "tandisque sur la flûte, qui se joint à la cithare, un habile musicien *joue* (ὑπαυλεῖ) des pariambides" ("while on the flute, which joins the kithara, a skilful musician *plays* pariambides").

Dem. and LSJ: ὑπαυλέω = play on the "flute" in accompaniment.

hypechein (ὑπηχεῖν; m. pr. ipichín) vb; to echo, to sound in answer (LSJ, Dem).

Cf. Arist. Probls. XIX, 24 and 42.

Hyperaeolios tonos (ὑπεραιόλιος τόνος; m. pr. ipereólios tónos); the second tonos in the series of 15 tonoi of the neo-Aristoxenean system. Cf. the Table under *Tonos*.

145

hyperbaton (ὑπερβατόν; m. pr. ipervatón); transilient; oppos. of hexes. *Hyperbaton systema* (ὑπερβατὸν σύστημα) was the system in which the progression was made by transilience instead of by contiguous degrees. Aristox. (Harm. I, p. 17, 30 Mb) "for every system is either continuous or transilient" («πᾶν γὰρ σύστημα ἤτοι συνεχὲς ἢ ὑπερβατόν ἐστι»). Cf. Cleon. Isag. ch. 10 (C.v.J. p. 199; Mb p. 16-17); Aristides (p. 16Mb; RPW-I p. 13).

hyperbaton diastema (ὑπερβατὸν διάστημα); transilient interval; any interval bigger than the second in the Diatonic genus. The verb "hyperbaenein" (ὑπερβαίνειν; m.pr. ipervénin) in music signified to leap, to pass over (or sing) by leaps, or to leap the distance between two notes.

hyperbolaeoeides (ὑπερβολαιοειδής; m. pr. ipervoleoïdís) locus (τόπος); the region of the voice comprising all notes above the netoeides locus; the region of hyperbolaeon, i.e. the region after the nete synemmenon (cf. Bell. Anon. § 64, p. 77).

hyperbolaeon, tetrachordon (ὑπερβολαίων, τετράχορδον; m. pr. ipervoléon); the highest tetrachord in the Greater Perfect System and the Immutable System (cf. *systema*).

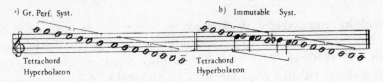

The notes of the tetrachord of hyperbolaeon taken upwards were called; Trite hyperbolaeon (f), Paranete hyperbolaeon (g) and Nete hyperbolaeon (a). The note e (last note of the tetrachord diezeugmenon, and first of the tetrachord hyperbolaeon) was called Nete diezeugmenon.

hyperdiazeuxis (ὑπερδιάζευξις; m. pr. iperdiázefxis), from hyper (ὑπέρ; above, beyond) and diazeuxis (disjunction). It is formed when two tetrachords are separated by an octave (dia-pason). Hyperdiazeuxis is found between the tetrachord of hypaton (b-c-d-e) and the tetrachord of hyperbolaeon (8ve e-f-g-a).

Cf. Bacch. Isag. § 87 (C.v.J. p. 312; Mb pp. 21-22) and Man. Bryen. Harm. (Wallis III, p. 506).

146

Hyperdorios tonos (ὑπερδώριος, τόνος; m. pr. iperdórios); the fifth tonos in the series of 15 tonoi of the neo-Aristoxenean system; it was the Mixolydian tonos of the Aristoxenean system of 13 tonoi (No 3 in the appropriate table).

Cf. *tonos*.

hyperhypate (ὑπερυπάτη; m.pr. iperipáti); Aristides calls hyperhypatai (pl.) the notes (or strings) lower than hypate meson which are movable (kinoumenoi) and change according to the genus (Cf. De Mus. Mb p. 10, RPW-I p. 8 «αὗται γενικῶς ὑπερυπάται καλοῦνται»).

Hyperiastios or **Hyperionios** tonos (ὑπεριάστιος, or ὑπεριώνιος, τόνος; m.pr. iperiástios, iperiónios); the fourth tonos in the series of the 15 tonoi of the neo-Aristoxenean system. It was the Higher Mixolydian (Μιξολύδιος ὀξύτερος, No 2) of the Aristoxenean 13 tonoi.

Cf. *tonos*.

Hyperlydios, tonos (ὑπερλύδιος; τόνος; m. pr. iperlídios); the first tonos in the series of the 15 tonoi of the neo-Aristoxenean system.

Cf. *tonos*.

hypermese (ὑπερμέση; m. pr. ipermési); the string "above" the mese as regards its place on the lyra or the kithara, but lower in pitch than the mese by a second. The hypermese was afterwards usually called "lichanos".

Cf. *G. Pachymeres* (ap. Vincent "Notices", p. 406); *Ch. Ém. Ruelle :* "Deux Textes grecs Anonymes" (Paris, 1878) p. 5; Nicom. Enchir. ch. 3 (C.v.J. p. 242, Mb p. 7).

See also *lyra* and *lichanos*.

Hypermixolydios, tonos (ὑπερμιξολύδιος, τόνος; m. pr. ipermixolídios); the highest tonos (No 1) in the Aristoxenean system of 13 tonoi, and the third (under the name of Hyperphrygios*) in the neo-Aristoxenean system of 15 tonoi.

Cf. *tonos*.

Hyperphrygios, tonos (ὑπερφρύγιος, τόνος; m. pr. iperphrígios); the third tonos in the series of the 15 tonoi of the neo-Aristoxenean system, and the highest tonos in the Aristoxenean system of 13 tonoi, under the name Hypermixolydios*.

Cf. *tonos*.

hypertonos (ὑπέρτονος; m. pr. ipértonos); Dem. & LSJ: strained to the utmost; exceedingly sharp or loud.

hypertonon salpisma (ὑπέρτονον σάλπισμα); very loud (or high pitched) trumpet-call.

hyphen (ὑφ᾽ἕν, later ὑφέν; m. pr. iphén); a tie joining two consecutive notes; it was expressed by a slur, e.g.   Γ‿L, L‿F, F‿C etc.

When the first note was lower the phenomenon was called by some «ὑφ᾽ ἕν ἔσωθεν» (*hyphen from inside*; see *epitasis*) and when the first note was higher it was called «ὑφ᾽ ἕν ἔξωθεν» (*hyphen from outside*; see *ekkrousis-eklepsis*).

The hyphen was the contrary of diastole*; Sergius (p. 1836 ap. Vincent "Notices", p. 221, note Q) says: "*Hyphen* est contraria diastole".

Cf. Anon. Bell., §§ 4 and 86-87, pp. 22-23: Vincent "Notices" pp. 53, 221.

hypholmion (ὑφόλμιον); the lower part of the mouthpiece which supported the *holmos** (from hypo [ὑπό, under] and holmos). It was attached to the bombyx* of the aulos, and had the form of a bulb. Both the holmos and the hypholmion formed the mouthpiece of the aulos.

Cf. Pherecrates (ap. Phot. Lex., ed. G. Hermann, 1808; p. 464). Pollux IV, 70 «τῶν δὲ ἄλλων αὐλῶν τὰ μέρη ... ὅλμοι καὶ ὑφόλμια» ("and the parts of the other auloi [are] ... holmoi and *hypholmia*" plur.).

Hypoaeolios, tonos (ὑποαιόλιος τόνος; m. pr. ipoeólios tonos) or lower Hypolydios; the 10th tonos of the 13 tonoi of the Aristoxenean system, and the 12th tonos of the 15 tonoi of the neo-Aristoxenean system.

See *tonos*.

hypodiazeuxis (ὑποδιάζευξις; m. pr. ipodiázefxis); formed when two tetrachords are separated by an interval of the fifth, and their extreme notes are at a distance of an octave.

Man. Bryen. Harm. (ed. Wallis III; sect. XI, pp. 505-6): "*Hypodiazeuxis* is when between two tetrachords the interval of the fifth is placed, and their extreme notes are in concord with the octave between each other. There are two hypodiazeuxeis, a lower and a higher. The first is formed when the tetrachord of *Hypaton* is separated from the tetrachord of *Diezeugmenon* by the tetrachord of Meson (e-f-g-a) and one tone, between the Mese and the Paramese (a-b¹); the second is formed when the tetrachord of *Meson* is separated from that of the *Hyperbolaeon* by the tone between Mese and Paramese (a-b¹) and the tetrachord of Diezeugmenon (b¹-c¹-d¹-e¹)." Between the extreme notes, b-b¹ and e-e¹, there is a distance of an octave.

See also Bacch. Isag. § 83 (C.v.J. p. 311; Mb. p. 21).

148

Hypodorios, harmonia (ὑποδώριος; m. pr. ipodórios) or *hypodoristi* (ὑποδωριστί; m.pr. ipodoristí); the octave series (διὰ πασῶν, octachord) a-a; in the diatonic genus:

$$a - g - f - e - d - c - b - a$$
$$1 \quad 1 \tfrac{1}{2} \quad 1 \quad 1 \quad \tfrac{1}{2} \quad 1$$

This harmonia was known first as the Aeolia (or Aeolisti) but after the time of Aristoxenus the term Hypodorios was generally used.

The expression "Hypo-Dorios" (hypo = under) is explained in Athenaeus (XIV, 625A, ch. 19) as used by analogy with other similar expressions; "as we call what is near to (resembles) the white, whitish, and what is not sweet, yet near to it, sweetish, in the same way we call Hypo-dorios that which is not quite Dorios".

b) *Hypodorios*, tonos (ʽΥποδώριος, τόνος); the lowest of the 13 tonoi in the Aristoxenean system, and of the 15 tonoi of the neo-Aristoxenean system.

Cf. *tonos.*

hypogypones (ὑπογύπωνες; m. pr. ipogípones) pl.; dancers who carried sticks (or walking-canes) and used to dance imitating old people.

Pollux (IV, 104) «οἱ δὲ ὑπογύπωνες, γερόντων ὑπὸ βακτηρίαις τὴν μίμησιν εἶχον» ("the *hypogypones* with the aid of sticks imitated the old").

Their dance was also called *hypogypones.*

Hypoiastios, tonos (ὑποϊάστιος, τόνος; m. pr. ipoiástios), or *Hypoïonios, Hypoionian* (ὑποϊώνιος; m. pr. ipoiónios); the 14th in the series of the 15 tonoi of the neo-Aristoxenean system.

Cf. *tonos.*

hypokitharizein, v. (ὑποκιθαρίζειν; m. pr. ipokitharízin); to accompany the song with the kithara.

Cf. Hom. Il. XVIII, v. 570 and "Scholia in Homeri Iliadem" by Gul. Dindorf, Oxford 1875, vol. II, p. 177.

hypokrekein, hypoteretizein (ὑποκρέκειν, ὑποτερετίζειν; m. pr. ipokrékin, ipoteretízin); LSJ, of stringed instruments, to "answer in harmony with". Suid. «ὑποκρεκόντων, κρουόντων, ἐγγιζόντων, τερετιζόντων». Cf. Pind. Ol. 9, 38 and schol. See the article of Dr E. K. Borthwick in Cl. Rev. 79 (1965), 252 ff.

Hypolydios, harmonia (ὑπολύδιος, ἁρμονία; m. pr. ipolídios) or *Hypolydisti* (ὑπολυδιστί; m. pr. ipolidistí); the octave series (octachord) f-f; in the diatonic genus:

$$f - e - d - c - b - a - g - f$$
$$\tfrac{1}{2} \quad 1 \quad 1 \quad \tfrac{1}{2} \quad 1 \quad 1 \quad 1$$

This octave species was called by Plato "Chalará Lydistí" («Χαλαρὰ λυδιστί»; Slack Lydian), by Plutarch "Aneimene or Epaneimene Lydisti" («Ἀνειμένη or Ἐπανειμένη Λυδιστί»; Slack, loose Lydian), while in Aristides Quintilianus it appears as Lydian; cf. *harmonia*.

The invention of the Hypolydian was attributed to Polymnestus (end of 6th cent. B.C.).

b) *Hypolydios*, tonos (ὑπολύδιος, τόνος); the 9th tonos of the 13 tonoi of the Aristoxenean system, and the 11th tonos of the 15 tonoi of the neo-Aristoxenean system.

Cf. *tonos*.

hypolyrios (ὑπολύριος; m. pr. ipolírios); placed "under" the lyra.

See *donax*.

Hypophrygios, harmonia (**ὑποφρύγιος**, ἁρμονία; m. pr. ipophrígios); the octave series (διά-πασῶν; octachord) g-g; in the Diatonic genus:

$$g - f - e - d - c - b - a - g$$
$$1 \; \tfrac{1}{2} \; 1 \; 1 \; \tfrac{1}{2} \; 1 \; 1$$

Before Aristoxenus it was generally known as *Iasti* (ἰαστὶ) or Chalara Iasti (Plato), i.e. Slack Ionian.

b) *Hypophrygios*, tonos (ὑποφρύγιος, τόνος); the 11th tonos of the 13 tonoi of the Aristoxenean system, and the 13th of the 15 tonoi of the neo-Aristoxenean system.

Cf. *tonos*.

hyporchema, hyporchematike (**ὑπόρχημα, ὑπορχηματική**; m.pr. ipórchima, iporchimatikí).

a) *hyporchema* was a melos sung with dancing in honour of Apollo. Hyporchema was also the dance itself. Lucian ("On dancing", § 16): "In Delos not even the sacrifices were performed without dancing, but with this and with music ... the songs composed for these dances were called *hyporchemata*" (pl.). Procl. Chrest., 17: "*Hyporchema* was a song sung with dancing" («Ὑπόρχημα δέ, τὸ μετ' ὀρχήσεως ᾀδόμενον μέλος»).

Etym. Magnum (ed. Th. Gaisford; p. 690): "*Hyporchemata* [were] those songs which they used to sing while dancing and running around the altar, during the burning of the sacrifices" («Ὑπορχήματα δέ, ἅτινα πάλιν ἔλεγον ὀρχούμενοι καὶ τρέχοντες κύκλῳ τοῦ βωμοῦ, καιομένων τῶν ἱερείων»).

The hyporchema had three forms (or figures); in the first all the members of the chorus were dancing and singing at the same time; in the second, the chorus was divided into two groups, of which one was dancing and the other was singing; in the third the coryphaeus (the leader of the chorus) sang while all the rest danced.

The hyporchema was at first accompanied by the phorminx, and later by the aulos and the kithara (or lyra; Lucian, op.cit., § 16 «καὶ ἐμπέπληστο τῶν τοιούτων ἡ λύρα»; "and the lyra filled up all these").

Pollux (IV, 82) says that the dactylic* aulos was used at the hyporchemata.

b) *hyporchesis* (ὑπόρχησις; m. pr. ipórchisis); another word for hyporchema.

c) *hyporchematike* (adj.) *orchesis* (ὑπορχηματικὴ ὄρχησις; m. pr. iporchimatikí órchisis); according to many writers a kind of playful dancing accompanied by song.   It was one of the three dances of lyric poetry (the other two being the pyrrhiche* and the gymnopaedike*), and was connected with the comic dancing, kordax* (cf. Athen. XIX, 630D-E, ch. 28).   According to Pindar it was danced by the Laconians; and it was danced by men and women as well (ap. Athen. op. cit., 631C, ch. 30; «ὀρχοῦνται δὲ ταύτην παρὰ τῷ Πινδάρῳ οἱ Λάκωνες, καὶ ἐστὶν ὑπορχηματικὴ ὄρχησις ἀνδρῶν καὶ γυναικῶν»).

hyposynhaphe (ὑποσυναφή; m. pr. iposinaphí) from hypo-(ὑπό, under) and synhaphe (συναφή, conjunction); a term which is used when between two similar tetrachords is placed the interval of the fourth.   Hyposynhaphe is formed when between the tetrachord of hypaton and the tetrachord of synemmenon is placed the tetrachord of meson.

Cl. Bacch. Isag. § 85 (C.v.J. p. 311; Mb p. 21); Man. Bryen. Harm., Sect. XI (ed. Wallis III, p. 506).

hypotheatroi, auloi (ὑποθέατροι, αὐλοί; m. pr. ipothéatri) pl.; this word appears in Pollux IV, 82, with the explanation that these auloi were used for playing the auletic nomoi («ὑποθεάτρους δὲ αὐλούς, ἐπὶ τοῖς νόμοις τοῖς αὐλητικοῖς»).

In Dem. Lex. the word ὑπότρητοι (*hypotretoi*) = pierced from below, is suggested in the place of "hypotheatroi"; in LSJ the word *hypothetron*, sing. neut. (ὑπόθετρον; "a kind of musical performance") is suggested instead.

151

I

ialemos (ἰάλεμος); a plaintive, mournful song; a dirge.

Moeris (Attic Lex.; p. 190) in the Attic dialect means "the dirge, and the cold man".

Aristophanes (the grammarian, 257-180 B.C.; the surnamed "Byzantios") in his Attic Lex. (Ἀττικαὶ Λέξεις) says that "ialemos was sung at mournings" (ap. Athen. XIV, 619B., ch. 10). The verb ialemizein (ἰαλεμίζειν) signified to lament, to bewail.

iambike (ἰαμβική; m. pr. iamvikí); a kind of dance, mentioned in Athen. (XIV, 629D., ch. 27) as one "of the more static (less animated), more varied and simpler dances".

iambikon (ἰαμβικόν; m. pr. iamvikón); a) the third section or part of the Pythikos* nomos (πυθικὸς νόμος), in which the combat between Apollo and the dragon is going on. During this part the aulos-soloist had to imitate the trumpet-calls and the grinding of the dragon's teeth (the so-called "odontismos", ὀδοντισμός). Cf. Pollux, IV, 84 («ἐν δὲ τῷ ἰαμβικῷ μάχεται [ὁ Ἀπόλλων] ἐμπερείληφε δὲ τὸ ἰαμβικὸν καὶ τὰ σαλπιστικὰ κρούσματα καὶ τὸν ὀδοντισμόν»).

b) *iambikon*, as an adj., signified that which consisted of iambuses, e.g. *ἰαμβικὸν μέτρον* (iambic metre).

iambic genus (ἰαμβικὸν γένος); that in which the arsis and thesis were to the relation of 1 to 2.

iambis (ἰαμβίς; m. pr. iamvís);

See *pariambis*.

iambus, iambos (ἴαμβος; m. pr. íamvos).

a) a satirical, witty song. The iambuses (iamboi, ἴαμβοι) were improvised at a ceremony in honour of Demeter. It is said that this custom originated from Iambe (Ἰάμβη), a daughter of Pan and Echo (Ἠχὼ) and maid to Metaneira (Μετάνειρα), wife of the king of Eleusis, Keleos (Κελεός); Iambe entertained Demeter by her jokes during a visit of the goddess to Metaneira at Eleusis. According to another legend (Procl. Chrest. B, ap. R. Westphal Script. Metr. Gr., p. 242), when Demeter, angry and in distress at her daughter's abduction, came to Eleusis and sat on the so-called "Agelastos stone" (Ἀγέλαστος, sullen), Iambe entertained her by jokes and led her to a cheerful disposition.

Semus of Delos in his book "On Paeans" (ap. Athen. XIV, 622 B, ch. 16) says that iamboi (pl.) were masked mimes, previously called "autokabdaloi"*, and their songs as well («ὕστερον δὲ ἴαμβοι ὠνομάσθησαν αὐτοί τε καὶ τὰ ποιήματα αὐτῶν»).

The singer of iamboi was called *iambistes* (ἰαμβιστής).

Iambizein (vb., ἰαμβίζειν) = to abuse, to scoff («καὶ γὰρ τὸ ἰαμβίζειν κατά τινα γλῶσσαν λοιδορεῖν ἔλεγον»; R. Westphal op. cit., p. 242).

b) *iambus* was principally the term for the well-known metrical foot (υ-). Aristides (p. 38 Mb; R.P.W-I p. 36) says that "iambus was named from the verb iambizein, which means to abuse (to laugh at)"; because of the inequality of its parts.

iambikon metron (ἰαμβικὸν μέτρον); iambic metre; a metre consisting of iamboi. Cf. Aristides p. 50 Mb; p. 45 R.P.W.-I).

c) *iamboi* and dactyloi (ἴαμβοι καὶ δάκτυλοι); according to Strabo (IX, 3, 10) the fourth part of a kitharisterios Pythikos nomos*; this was the section of the Pythian nomos containing the triumphant hymn on God's victory.

iambyke (ἰαμβύκη; m. pr. iamvíki); a stringed instrument of triangular form. It seems that its name came from "iamboi", because as some sources say, it accompanied these songs. Phillis of Delos in his second book "On music" (ap. Athen. XIX, 636B, ch. 38) says that "iambykai (pl.) were those instruments to which they sang the iamboi" («ἐν οἷς γὰρ τοὺς ἰάμβους ᾖδον ἰαμβύκας ἐκάλουν»); also Hesychius, "musical instruments to which they sang the iamboi".

Pollux simply mentions the name of the instrument among the stringed ones («κρουόμενα»).

Ibycus (Ἴβυκος; m. pr. Ívikos); 6th cent. B.C. lyric poet and musician, born in Rhegium (Ρήγιον) in S. Italy (hence his surname, Ρηγῖνος). He lived a wanderer's life. Suidas relates that he went to Samos and passed some time at the court of Polycrates (532-523 B.C.). As a musician Ibycus was accredited with the invention of the sambyke* (cf. Suidas; Neanthes the historian, ap. Athen. IV, 175E, ch. 77). He composed choral epinikia and enkomia.

The legend about his death is known from Suidas and other sources; Ibycus was killed by brigands near Corinth, but at the moment of the murder he invoked the evidence (or the revenge) of some cranes flying over the place. Some time after one of the brigands walking in Corinth noticed cranes above, and cried out "here are the avengers of Ibycus"; this led to the discovery of the murder and the punishment of the murderers.

See Brgk PLG, III, pp. 235-252. Also Page PMG, Frgs 282-345, pp. 143-169.

idouthoi, pl. (ἰδοῦθοι; m. pr. idoúthi); a kind of aulos. The word is met only in Pollux (IV, 77) who simply writes "a kind of auloi" («αὐλῶν εἶδος») without giving any details.

ígdis (ἵγδις); a kind of ludicrous (or humorous) dance in which the dancers used to beat continuously on the ground imitating the pounding of a pestle. The word "igdis" meant a mortar for pounding. The dance is mentioned in Athen. (XIV, 629F, ch. 27) among other ludicrous dances.

Antiphanes, the comic, mentions it too in his "Koroplathos" (ap. Th. Kock Comic. Attic. Fr., vol. II, p. 62; Fr. 127) «γύναι πρὸς αὐλὸν ἦλθες· ὀρχήσει πάλιν τὴν ἵγδιν» ("woman, you came [to dance] to the aulos; you will again dance the *igdis*". And further «τὴν θυΐαν [θυείαν] ἀγνοεῖς; τοῦτ᾽ ἔστιν ἵγδις» ("don't you know the mortar? that is *the igdis*"). Cf. Pollux X, 103.

The word *igdisma* (ἵγδισμα = pounding with a pestle) is also met for the same dance. Etym. M. (p. 464,51); "*igdisma*, a kind of dance in which they twisted similar to the pestle" («ἵγδισμα· εἶδος ὀρχήσεως ἐν ἦ ἐλύγιζον ἐμφερῶς τῷ δοίδυκι»).

iobacchos (ἰόβακχος; m. pr. ióvacchos); a hymn to Bacchus beginning with the words «Ἰὼ Βάκχε» ("Oh! Bacchus"). In the plural "iobacchoi" (ἰόβακχοι) was a group in Athens whose main purpose was the worship of Dionysus, with drinking and singing. The temple of worship was called Baccheion (Βακχεῖον), and their songs were also called "iobacchoi".

Ἰοβάκχεια (*Iobaccheia*) was a festival held in Attica in honour of Iobacchus Dionysus.

Procl. Chrest., 16 «Ἤιδετο δὲ ἰόβακχος ἐν ἑορταῖς καὶ θυσίαις Διονύσου, βεβαπτισμένος πολλῷ φρυάγματι» ("The *iobacchus* was sung at celebrations and sacrifices of Dionysus, with much drinking and screaming").

Ion of Chios (Ἴων ὁ Χῖος; m. pr. Íon Chíos); b. c. 490-480 B.C.; d. c. 422 B.C. Lyric poet, author and composer of tragedies. He composed elegies, hymns, dithyrambs and love-songs.

Cleonides in the Isagoge (ch. 12, C.v.J. p. 202; "Eucl." p. 19 Mb) says that Ion used the 11-stringed lyra.

Cf. FHG, II p. 44; Brgk PLG, II pp. 251-257, and Anth. Lyr., pp. 125-128. Page PMG 383-5, Frgs 740-6.

Ionikon (Ἰωνικόν); a kind of dance in honour of Diana in Sicily. Pollux (IV, 103) "the Sicilians (Sikeliotai) above all danced *the Ionikon* (Ionian dance) in honour of Diana" («τὸ δὲ ἰωνικόν, Ἀρτέμιδι ὠρχοῦντο Σικελιῶται μάλιστα»).

Ionikon metron (Ἰωνικὸν μέτρον; Ionian metre); a metre consisting of Ionic feet (Aristides p. 50 Mb; p. 45 R.P.W-I). The Ionic foot consisted of four syllables (either two long and two short, Ionic a majore, Ἰωνικὸς ἀπὸ μείζονος; or two short and two long, Ionic a minore, Ἰωνικὸς ἀπ᾽ ἐλάσσονος).

Ionios, harmonia, usually **Iasti** or **Ias** (Ἰώνιος, ἁρμονία, or ἰαστί, or ἰάς, fem.; m.pr. iónios, iastí, iás); term used by many writers before Aristoxenus for the octave series (diapason, octachord): g-g. In diatonic genus:

$$g - f - e - d - c - b - a - g.$$
$$1 \; \tfrac{1}{2} \; 1 \; 1 \; \tfrac{1}{2} \; 1 \; 1$$

Plato called it the "Chalara Iasti" (χαλαρὰ ἰαστί; Slack Ionian).
Cf. *harmonia.*

The Ionian was so called after one of the Greek tribes, the Ionians (Ἴωνες), and, according to Heraclid. Pont. (ap. Athen. XIV, 624 C-D, ch. 19), was one of the three Greek harmonias (the other two being the Dorian and the Aeolian).

The Ionian was later replaced by the Hypophrygios*.

b) *Iónios* or *Iástios*, tonos (Ἰώνιος, or ἰάστιος, τόνος); the 9th tonos in the series of the 15 tonoi of the neo-Aristoxenean system.
Cf. *tonos.*

ioulos (ἴουλος); a hymn to Demeter.

According to Semus of Delos (ap. Athen. XIV, 618 D-E, ch. 10) *iouloi* (pl.) and *ouloi* (οὖλοι) were the sheaves or bundles of barley and the products as well; *iouloi* and *ouloi* also were names for the hymns to Demeter, who was surnamed Iouló (Ἰουλώ). Other names for the same hymn were *demetroulos* (δημήτρουλος) and *kallioulos* (καλλίουλος; καλός, ἴουλος).

b) *ioulos* was what some people called the song of wool-spinners or wool-carders. Cf. Tryphon (ap. Athen. 618 D, ch. 10).

Ismenias (Ἰσμηνίας; m. pr. Isminías); 4th cent. B.C. aulete of repute and composer. He lived during the reign of Philip of Macedonia (359-336 B.C.), the father of Alexander the Great, and became known as a virtuoso of the aulos. Diogenes Laertius refers to Ismenias (Book VII, ch. 1, § 125) in the following praising words: "The wise man does all things well, just as we say that *Ismenias* plays well all the melodies (the aulemata) on the aulos" («Πάντα τ᾽ εὖ ποιεῖν τὸν σοφόν, ὡς καὶ πάντα, φαμέν, αὐλήματα εὖ αὐλεῖν τὸν Ἰσμηνίαν»).

Ismenias was taken prisoner by the king of the Scyths, Anteas (Ἀντέας).

Plutarch (in "Reg. et Imp. Apophthegmata", «Βασιλέων Ἀποφθέγματα καὶ Στρατηγῶν» 174 E-F, §3) relates the following charming anecdote: "When Anteas took as prisoner the excellent aulete Ismenias, he ordered him to play; and while the others were admiring, he swore that it was more pleasant for him to listen to a horse neighing" («Ἰσμηνίαν δὲ τὸν ἄριστον αὐλητὴν λαβὼν (ὁ 'Αντέας) αἰχμάλωτον ἐκέλευσεν αὐλῆσαι· θαυμαζόντων δὲ τῶν ἄλλων, αὐτὸς ὤμοσεν ἥδιον ἀκούειν τοῦ ἵππου χρεμετίζοντος»).

Cf. *Dinse*: De Antig. Theb., pp. 57-59.

isochordos (ἰσόχορδος); having strings of equal number or length.

isophthongos (ἰσόφθογγος); having the same sound (phthongos) or sounding equally with another one.

Cf. Nonn. Dion. VI, 202   (W.H.D. Rouse translates "in echo" vol. I, p. 229.).

isotonia, isotonoi (ἰσοτονία, ἰσότονοι; m. pr. isotonía, isótoni). *Isotonia* was unison; a term used by some writers as a synonym of homophonia*.

isotonoi, phthongoi (ἰσότονοι, φθόγγοι; notes) were two or more notes (sounds) having the same "tonos" (tension, pitch). Ptolemaeus (Harm. I, ch. 4; ed. Wallis III, p. 8; ed. I.D. p. 10) says that *"isotonoi* are those sounds which are exactly the same in pitch" («ἰσότονοι μὲν οἱ ἀπαράλλακτοι κατὰ τὸν τόνον»).   Porphyrius (in Comment.; Wallis III, p. 258; ed. I.D. p. 82), defines that Ptolemaeus used here the term "tonos" in the sense of pitch («τάσις»), and that *"isotonos* is the sound which has the same pitch as another one, as the nete (νήτη) synemmenon (ex. a below) is to the paranete (παρανήτη) diezeugmenon" (b):

Nete   Paranete
Synemmenon   Diezeugmenon

He prefers the term *homotonos** to isotonos («τὸν δέ, οὕτως, ἰσότονον ψόφον, κυριώτερον ὁμότονον καλοῦσι»).   The opposite of isotonos is *anisotonos* (ἀνισότονος); Ptolem. (I, ch. 4), «and anisotonoi (pl.) are those sounds which differ [in pitch]" («ἀνισότονοι δέ, οἱ παραλλάσοντες [κατὰ τὸν τόνον]»); Cf. also Porphyr. Wallis III, pp. 285-6).

Isotonos is also a sound which is equal to another one at its inner parts throughout all its duration; Porphyrius prefers to isotonos the term *homoeomeric* (ὁμοιομερὴς) as more appropriate in this case.

ithymbos (ἴθυμβος; m. pr. íthimvos); a Bacchic dance and song.   Pollux (IV, 104) «καὶ ἴθυμβοι ἐπὶ Διονύσῳ» ("and [among other dances] *ithymboi* in honour of Dionysus").   Hesychius defines *ithymbos* as a buffoon («γελοιαστής»).

Phot. Lex. (ed. S.A. Naber, 1864; I, p. 291) «ᾠδὴ μακρὰ καὶ ὑπόσκαιος» ("a long song with innuendoes").

ithyphalloi, pl. (ἰθύφαλλοι; m. pr. ithíphalloi); the superintendents of Dionysus who, dressed in feminine clothes, followed the procession of the phallus. So also were called the songs with dancing performed during the procession.

Suidas defines: "*Ithyphalloi*; the superintendents of Dionysus following the phallus and wearing a feminine dress. Phallus is the erect male organ; and the poems were sung with dancing to the uplifted phallus" («᾿Ιθύφαλλοι· οἱ ἔφοροι Διονύσου καὶ ἀκολουθοῦντες τῷ φαλλῷ γυναικείαν στολὴν ἔχοντες. Λέγεται δὲ φαλλὸς ὀτὲ μὲν τὸ ἐντεταμένον αἰδοῖον, καὶ ποιήματα δὲ καλεῖσθαι, ἃ ἐπὶ τῷ ἱσταμένῳ φαλλῷ ᾄδεται μετ᾽ ὀρχήσεως»).

Cf. Phot. Lex. (ed. S. A. Naber, 1864; I, p. 291).

Semus of Delos in his book "On Paeans" (ap. Athen. XIV, 622B, ch. 16) relates that the ithyphalloi at their entrance into the theatre have masks representing drunken men, are crowned with wreaths and have brilliantly coloured sleeves; they have tunics with white stripes and are belted with a Tarentine apron covering them down to the ankles. And after entering in silence, when they reach the centre of the orchestra they recite to the audience "Give way, give way! make room for the god; for the god wishes to pass through..." («᾿Ανάγετ᾽ ἀνάγετ᾽, εὐρυχωρίαν ποιεῖτε τῷ θεῷ· θέλει γὰρ ὁ θεὸς ... διὰ μέσου βαδίζειν»).

K

kalabrismos or **kolabrismos** (καλαβρισμός, or κολαβρισμός; m. pr. kalavrismós or kolavrismós); a kind of wild war-dance of Thrace, and Karia in Asia Minor.

Pollux (IV, 100) «κολαβρισμός, Θράκιον ὄρχημα καὶ Καρικὸν» ("*kolabrismos*, a dance of Thrace and Karia").

Cf. Athen. XIV, 629D, ch. 27, where *the kalabrismos* is mentioned among the dances which were "less animated, more varied and simpler".

The melody to which the "kolabrismos" was danced was called *kólabros* (κόλαβρος); Athen. XV, 697C «Κτησιφῶν ὁ ᾿Αθηναῖος ποιητὴς τῶν καλουμένων κολάβρων» ("Ktesiphon the Athenian poet of the so-called *kolabroi*").

The word "kolabros" meaning also "a little pig" (Suid.), the dance kolabrismos might be called a "pig-dance". The verb "kolabrizein" («κολαβρίζειν») signified to dance the kolabrismos; Hes. "to leap".

kalathiskos (καλαθίσκος) and **cheirokalathiskos** (χειροκαλαθίσκος; m. pr. chirokalathískos); a kind of dance or dance-figure. Pollux (IV, 105) includes *cheirokalathiskos* among the figures of tragic dancing («καὶ σχήματα μὴν τραγικῆς ὀρχήσεως σίμη, χειροκαλαθίσκος»). In Athenaeus (XIV, 629F,

157

ch. 27) the *kalathiskos* or *kalathismós* is mentioned among the dance-figures.

The word "kalathiskos" meaning originally a "small basket", the dance itself might be called "basket-dance".

kallabis or **kalabis**, usually in plur. **kallabides** (καλλαβίς, καλαβίς, καλλαβίδες; m. pr. kal[l]avís,-vídes); hip-dance, a kind of violent and wanton dance in which they used to rotate the hips. It was danced by Lacedaemons. Hes. "*kalabis*; the rotating of the hips, or a kind of dance [in which] the hips were indecently curved [or bent]"; («καλαβίς· τὸ περισπᾶν τὰ ἰσχία· ἢ γένος ὀρχήσεως ἀσχημόνως τῶν ἰσχίων κυρτουμένων»).

Eupolis mentions the kallabides in his "Flatterers" («Κόλακες») in these words (ap. Athen. XIV, 630A, ch. 27):

«καλλαβίδας δὲ βαίνει
σησαμίδας δὲ χέζει»

("His walk is a hip-dance, his excrement is sesame-cake"; transl. by Ch. B. Gulick; vol. VI, p. 399).

Kallabides are mentioned (in Athen. XIV, 629F) among the dance-figures («σχήματα ὀρχήσεως»).

kallichoros (καλλίχορος); LSJ: "with fair dancing-grounds"; "beautiful in the dance" (of Apollo).

kallinikos, in neut. **kallínikon** (καλλίνικος, καλλίνικον);

a) a kind of aulos-melody; Tryphon in his second book of Denominations (ap. Athen. XIV, 618C, ch. 9) includes kallinikos among the various auleseis (aulos-solos; see under *aulesis*).

b) a kind of dance; Pollux in his chapter "On kinds of dancing" (IV, 100; «Περὶ εἰδῶν ὀρχήσεως») includes kallinikos among the dances ("and *kallinikos*, [a dance] in honour of Heracles").

Hesychius also says: "*Kallinikos*; a proper name, and a kind of dance".

c) As an adj. means "praising a victory": "*kallinikos* hymn". Pind. Nemean IV, verse 16 («ὕμνον κελάδησε καλλίνικον»).

kallioulos (καλλίουλος); a hymn to Demeter.

See also *ioulos*.

kalyke (καλύκη; m. pr. kalíki); a folk-song sung by women. It took its name from Kalyke, a maiden who unhappy in her love committed suicide by falling into a precipice. Aristoxenus in his fourth book "On Music" (ap. FHG II, p. 287, Fr. 72; Athen. XIV, 619D, ch. 11) relates the sad story of Kalyke. "The song was composed by Stesichorus, and in it a maiden named Kalyke (Calyce), in love with a young man, Euathlus, prudently prays to Aphrodite that

she may be married to him. But when the young man treated her with disdain, she threw herself over a precipice. The tragic event occurred at Leucas".
See *harpalyke*.

kampe (καμπή; m. pr. kampí); Dem. and LSJ = turn, sudden change.
See *exharmonios*.

Karikon, melos (**καρικόν**, μέλος); a kind of funeral song; a dirge. Also a kind of aulos-solo (-melody). Its name came from the country of its origin, Karia, in the SW of Asia Minor. Pollux (IV, 75): "because lamenting is the *Karian* aulema (aulos-solo)"; («θρηνῶδες γὰρ τὸ αὔλημα τὸ Καρικόν»).

Aristoph. Frogs, v. 1302 «Καρικὰ αὐλήματα» ("Karian aulos-solos"). Plato, the comic (ap. Th. Kock Comic. Att. Fr.; vol. I, p. 620, Fr. 69, vs. 12-13): «αὐλοὺς δ᾽ ἔχουσά τις κορίσκη καρικὸν μέλος τι μελίζεται τοῖς συμπόταις» ("a little girl performs with the aulos a lamenting tune to the drink-companions"). See also Suidas.

Eust. Scholia to Iliad («Παρεκβολαὶ εἰς τὴν Ἰλιάδα») p. 1372, 27-28 «καὶ ᾠδαὶ θρηνητήριοι· ὁποῖα ὕστερον καὶ τὰ λεγόμενα μέλη καρικὰ» ("and lamenting songs; such as those called, later on, Karian songs").

Karike mousa, Karian muse (*Καρικὴ* μοῦσα); lamenting muse (music). Plato Laws, 800E «καρικῇ τινι μούσῃ προπέμπουσι τοὺς τελευτήσαντας» ("by a kind of *Karian* muse [funeral music] they accompany the deceased").

Karikós, was also in ancient metrics a rhythm consisting of alternate trochee (-υ) and iambus (υ-) -υυ-; another expression for choriambus.

karpaea (**καρπαία**; m. pr. karpéa); a folk or war-dance danced by Aenianians and Magnesians (Αἰνιᾶνες, and Μάγνητες), old Greek tribes in Thessaly.

This dance became known from an interesting and detailed description by Xenophon in his Anabasis (book VI, I, § § 7-8). The dance was danced by two persons, and was meant to describe by its intricate movements the fight between a farmer and a robber. According to Xenophon's description the first dancer, the farmer, after putting aside his arms, imitates with his dancing the movements of sowing and ploughing, while turning about like one in fear. The second dancer, the robber, seizes the arms and attacks the farmer. The fight continues for some time, and concludes either by the robber's victory who binds the farmer and seizes the oxen, or by the farmer's victory who captures the robber, binds him and then yokes him alongside the oxen and drives off.

The dance was performed in rhythm to aulos accompaniment («καὶ οὗτοι ταῦτ᾽ ἐποίουν ἐν ρυθμῷ πρὸς τὸν αὐλόν», "and they were doing all these things in rhythm to the aulos").

159

The word *karpea* (κάρπεα) is also met; Hes. «κάρπεα· ὄρχησις Μακεδονικὴ» ("*karpea*, a Macedonian dance").

Karyatis (**καρυᾶτις**; m. pr. kariátis); a kind of dance in honour of Diana, danced in Karyai of Laconia. The name of the dance was evidently derived from Karyai where every year the festival Karyatea (or Karyateia) in honour of Diana, the Karyatis, took place.

Cf. Pollux ("On kinds of dancing"; IV, 104).

The verb karyatizein (καρυατίζειν) signified, to dance the Karyatis dance, or to dance in honour of Diana, surnamed Karyatis.

Lucian ("On dancing", § 10) said that "the Lacedaemons, the best of the Greeks, believe that they learned to *karyatizein* (i.e. to dance the Karyatis dance) from Pollux and Castor, and they do everything with music even fighting in war to aulos and rhythm" («Λακεδαιμόνιοι μὲν ἄριστοι Ἑλλήνων εἶναι δοκοῦντες παρὰ Πολυδεύκους καὶ Κάστορος καρυατίζειν μαθόντες... ἄπαντα μετὰ μουσικῆς ποιοῦσιν ἄχρι τοῦ πολεμεῖν πρὸς αὐλὸν καὶ ῥυθμόν»).

Note : Karyatis was also a surname of Diana, as seen above.

kastorion, or **kastoreion** melos (**καστόριον**, or **καστόρειον**); a Laconic marching melody performed on the aulos in battle. Plut. (De Mus. 1140C, ch. 26) «καθάπερ Λακεδαιμόνιοι, παρ᾽ οἷς τὸ καλούμενον καστόρειον ηὐλεῖτο μέλος, ὁπότε τοῖς πολεμίοις ἐν κόσμῳ προσῄεσαν μαχεσόμενοι» ("like the Lacedaemons among whom the so-called *kastoreion* [melos] was performed on the aulos, when they advanced in order to battle").

Pollux (IV, 78) «μέλος δέ, καστόρειον μέν, τὸ Λακωνικὸν ἐν μάχαις, ὑπὸ τὸν ἐμβατήριον ῥυθμὸν» ("and the Laconic *kastoreion* tune [performed] in battle, in the military rhythm").

Cf. Pind. Pythian II, epode 3, v. 69 (ap. Brgk PLG, I, p. 112).

Kastorion, or **Castorion**, of **Soli** (**Καστορίων ὁ Σολεύς**); 4th cent. B.C. lyric poet, born at Soli (Σόλοι) in Cyprus. He lived in Athens during Demetrius Phaleraeus' governorship (317-308 B.C.; cf. "Par. Chron.", ed. F. Jacoby, v. 20, p. 23).

Fragments of his poems have been preserved in Athen. (X, 454F, and XII, 542E); one is addressed to Pan, and another was sung by chorus (during the procession of Dionysia) in honour of Dem. Phaleraeus, whom Kastorion calls in it "sunlike" in beauty («ἐξόχως δ᾽εὐγενέτας ἡλιόμορφος ζαθέοισ᾽ ἄρχων σε τιμαῖσι γεραίρει»; "the governor (archon), pre-eminently noble, 'sunlike' in beauty, celebrates thee with divine honours").

Cf. Brgk PLG III, pp. 634-6; E. Diehl Anth. Lyr. Gr., pp. 260-1; Page PMG p. 447, Fr. 845.

katabaukalesis (καταβαυκάλησις; m. pr. katavafkálisis); the act of lulling; a lullaby; usually the lullaby of wet-nurses.

Athen. (XIV, 618E, ch. 10): "the songs of wet-nurses are called *lullabies*" («αἱ δὲ τῶν τιτθευουσῶν ᾠδαὶ καταβαυκαλήσεις ὀνομάζονται»).

Tittheuousai (τιτθεύουσαι or τίτθαι) = nurses, wet-nurses. The verb *katabaukalan* (καταβαυκαλᾶν; m. pr. katavafkalán) signified to lull to sleep, either by singing or by the music of some instrument. Pollux (IV, 127): «τὸ σεῖστρον ᾧ καταβαυκαλῶσιν αἱ τίτθαι ψυχαγωγοῦσαι τὰ δυσυπνοῦντα τῶν παιδίων» ("the sistrum by which the wet-nurses *lull to sleep* by entertaining those children who do not easily fall asleep").

See also *baucalema*.

katachoreusis (καταχόρευσις; m. pr. katachóreusis); the fifth and last part of the Pythikos* nomos; celebration with dancing; the triumphal dance of the god (Apollo) on his victory over the monster.

From the verb *katachoreuein* (καταχορεύειν; m. pr. katachorévin), to dance triumphantly, to celebrate a victory or to express a very strong joy.

katadein, vb (κατάδειν; m. pr. katádin); to charm by song; to sing an epode, a magical ode.

Phryn. Epitome (ed. de Borries; p. 79) «γοητεύειν καὶ πείθειν» ("to charm and appease").

See also *katepadein*.

katakeleusmos (κατακελευσμός; m. pr. katakelevsmós); from the verb katakeleuein (κατακελεύειν), to order, to command; incitement, command, provocation. So was called the second part of the Pythikos* nomos, in which the god challenges the monster. According to Strabo (IX, 3, 10) it was the third part of a kitharisterios Pythikos nomos.

katalepsis (κατάληψις; m. pr. katálipsis); of stopping strings in lyra-playing. Cf. Schol. Aristoph. Clouds 318, («καὶ κρούσιν καὶ κατάληψιν»). See E. K. Borthwick "Κατάληψις: A neglected term in Greek music"; Cl. Quart. 53 (1959), pp. 23-29.

katalexis (κατάληξις; m. pr. katálixis); metrical term for cadence or close of a period; also the final syllable (LSJ).

kataloge (καταλογή; m.pr. katalogí); recitation without music.
Cf. *parakataloge**.

katapeplasmenon (καταπεπλασμένον); style of aulos playing. LSJ, "the artificial sound produced by stopping the higher notes in a 'flute' ".

kataploke (καταπλοκή; m. pr. kataplokí); a progression of rapid descending notes.   Opposite of *anaploke**.

Cf. Ptolem. Harm. book II, ch. 12 (ed. Wallis III, p. 85; ed. I. D. p. 67, 7).

katapneomena (καταπνεόμενα) pl.; wind instruments.

See *emphysomena* and *empneusta.*

katapycnosis (καταπύκνωσις; m. pr. katapícnosis); the subdivision of the intervals of the scale into quarter-tones. The verb katapycnoun (καταπυκνοῦν), to subdivide into small intervals, is also met with, in the expression «καταπυκνοῦν τὸ διάγραμμα» = to subdivide the diagram, the scale, into quarter-tones. Aristox. Harm. (I, p. 28, 1 Mb) «οὐχ ὡς οἱ ἁρμονικοὶ ἐν ταῖς τῶν διαγραμμάτων καταπυκνώσεσιν ἀποδιδόναι πειρῶνται» ("not as the Harmonists try to do *in the subdivisions* of the diagrams").

Aristoxenus (op. cit., II p. 38 Mb) considers *the katapycnosis*, i.e. arrangement in quarter-tones, as unmelodious; «ὅτι δέ ἐστιν ἡ καταπύκνωσις ἐκμελὴς καὶ κατὰ πάντα τρόπον ἄχρηστος, φανερὸν ἐπ᾽ αὐτῆς ἔσται τῆς πραγματείας» ("and that *the katapycnosis* is unmelodious and in every way useless, will be clear in the course of this essay").

kataspasmata (κατασπάσματα); pl. of katáspasma; vibrations of the reed of the aulos (Dem. LSJ).

Cf. Theophr. Hist. Nat. IV, ch. 11 § 5 «καὶ κατασπάσματα τὰς γλώττας ἴσχειν [«ἔχειν»]» ("and that the reed-tongues have ample vibrations"; transl. by Sir Arthur Hort "Enquiry into Plants" London, 1916, vol. I, p. 373; see also note 1, p. 373. K. Schlesinger ("The Greek Aulos", p. 66) interprets "kataspasmata" as "beatings" ("that the tongues curb the beatings"). She holds (note 2, p. 66) that "if κατασπάσματα refers to the action of the lips on the reed tongue, brought about by the pulling down of the Syrinx, then... the pitch would be raised, not lowered".

kataspasmos (κατασπασμός); lowering of the voice (Dem. and LSJ). From "kataspan ten phonen" («κατασπᾶν τὴν φωνήν») = to lower the voice.

For "kataspan ten syringa", see under *syrinx.*

katastrophe (καταστροφή; m. pr. katastrophí); end, conclusion; return of a vibrating string to its axial position (Dem., LSJ). Arist. Probl. XIX, 39 «τῶν μὲν ἄλλων συμφωνιῶν ἀτελεῖς αἱ θατέρου καταστροφαί (pl.) εἰσιν» ("as regards other consonances *the endings* of one of their elements are incomplete").

katatropa (κατατροπά); the third part of the kitharodic nomos.

See under *kitharodia - kitharodikos nomos.*

kataulesis (καταύλησις; m. pr. katávlisis); playing the aulos; entertaining by aulos-playing.

From the verb *kataulein* (καταυλεῖν; m. pr. katavlín), to play the aulos for someone else, to entertain by aulos-playing or even by singing. Plato Laws, book VII, 790E: "when mothers want to lull to sleep those children who cannot easily fall asleep, they sing [or play] a certain tune to them" («μελῳδίαν τινὰ καταυλοῦσι»).

See *metroa* («κατηύλησε τὰ μητρῷα»; "he played the metroa on the aulos").

kateches (κατηχής; m. pr. katichís); sonorous; loudly sounding.

katechesis (κατήχησις; m. pr. katíchisis); enchantment through musical sound; teaching by live, strong voice; instruction in general.

Dem.: accompaniment of the monochord by louder sounds which drown its sound.

Cf. Ptolem. Harm. II, ch. 12 (ed. I. D. p. 67, 19-20).

katepadein (κατεπάδειν; m. pr. katepádin); to charm by song or spell. Plato Meno, 80A (Meno to Socrates): "and now you seem to me to be simply bewitching me with spells and incantations" («καὶ νῦν, ὥς γε μοι δοκεῖς, γοητεύεις με φαρμάττεις καὶ ἀτεχνῶς κατεπάδεις»).

kathapton (καθαπτόν), órganon (ὄργανον); a term for a percussion instrument, played by touching by the hand, like the tympanum*. Alkeides of Alexandria (ap. Athen. IV, 174C) speaking about the hydraulis cites Aristocles who says that "it could be considered neither a stringed nor a percussion instrument" («ἐντατὸν οὖν καὶ καθαπτὸν οὐκ ἂν νομισθείη»).

kathaptein, vb. (καθάπτειν; m. pr. katháptin), to put or place upon something, to fix on.

kattyma (κάττυμα; m. pr. káttima); in pl. kattýmata = patchwork-pieces, patchings. Cf. Plut. De Mus. 1138B, ch. 21 «σχεδὸν γὰρ ἀποπεφοιτήκασιν εἴς τε τὰ καττύματα καὶ εἰς τὰ Πολυείδου ποιήματα [ποικίλματα]» ("as they have almost departed from *the patchings* and Polyeidus' compositions [embroideries]";

Cf. H. Weil. and Th. Reinach.: Plut. De la Mus., p. 85.

kechymena, mele (κεχυμένα, μέλη; m. pr. kechiména méli); pl. of kechymenon (κεχυμένον) p.p. of cheomai (χέομαι) = to flow. Flowing melodies, in the sense of being in a fluid state; not strictly measured, like a recitative.

Anon. (Bell. § 95, p. 93) «κεχυμέναι ᾠδαὶ καὶ μέλη λέγεται τὰ κατὰ χρόνον σύμμετρα, καὶ χύδην κατὰ τοῦτον μελῳδούμενα» (*"kechymenai* odai and mele are those which are regular in time, and are performed fluidly"). (Gevaert, I, note 1 p. 390, suggests that «σύμμετρα» should be corrected to «ἀσύμμετρα», irregular).

The term "kechymena" is used by Anon. Bell. (§§ 3 and 85) only for those melodies to be sung; for instrumental melodies the term "diapselaphemata"* («διαψηλαφήματα») is used.

Aristides (De Mus. I, p. 32 Mb; p. 31 R.P.W-I) uses the terms "kechymena asmata" and "ataktoi melodiai" («ἄτακτοι μελῳδίαι» not measured melodies; not rigidly in time).

keklasmena, mele (**κεκλασμένα**, μέλη); "broken" melodies, mostly using leaps; or melodies varied by modulation (LSJ), or with leaps and many rapid notes (melismatic). Keklasmenos is p.p. of "klan" (κλᾶν), to break. Plutarch (De Mus. 1138C, ch. 21) says that the ancients deliberately, and not by ignorance, avoided the use of "*keklasmena* ("broken" or too melismatic) mele" («δῆλον οὖν ὅτι οἱ παλαιοὶ οὐ δι' ἄγνοιαν, ἀλλὰ διὰ προαίρεσιν ἀπείχοντο τῶν κεκλασμένων μελῶν»).

Sextus Empir. ("Against musicians", VI, § 15): «ὅθεν εἰ καὶ κεκλασμένοις τισὶ μέλεσι νῦν καὶ γυναικώδεσι ῥυθμοῖς θηλύνει τὸν νοῦν ἡ μουσικὴ» ("íf therefore music effeminizes the mind by *melismatic* melodies and womanish rhythms").

keklasmene phone (κεκλασμένη φωνή): moving by intervals; cf. Excerpta Neapolitana, C.v.J. p. 413 (Ptolem. Musica) and Porphyr. Comment., p. 262 Wallis. "The voice standing on the same note is straight and 'unbroken', while curved and 'fallen' becomes melodic".

Ρυθμὸς κεκλασμένος (*keklasmenos rhythmos*), interrupted rhythm.

Note: "keklasmenos" is interpreted by many scholars metaph., "effeminate"; cf. LSJ p. 956 (κλάω, 3); Dem. Lex. p. 3957.

keklasménos (κεκλασμένως) adv., Suid. "effeminately". In this sense "keklasmena mele" should be interpreted as "effeminate mele" or "enervated".

kelados (**κέλαδος**); sound; clear, mighty tone. Eurip. "Iphig. in Tauris" v. 1129 «κέλαδον ἑπτατόνου λύρας» ("*sound* of the seven-toned lyra"); also Bacchae v. 578.

Pind. (ap. PLG, I, p. 348, Fr. 159) «νόμων ἀκούοντες θεοδμάτων κέλαδον» ("listening to *the voice* of divine nomoi").

keladeinos (κελαδεινός; m. pr. keladinós); tumultuous, noisy. E. M. «παρὰ τὸ κέλαδος γίνεται, ὃ σημαίνει τὸν θόρυβον καὶ τὴν ταραχὴν» ("it is derived from *kelados* which means noise [tumult] and disturbance").

keleustou orchesis (**κελευστοῦ ὄρχησις**; m. pr. kelefstoú órchisis); boatswain's dance (keleustes, κελευστής = boatswain).   It is mentioned in Athenaeus (XIV, 629F, ch. 27) as one of the dances to aulos accompaniment.

See also *pinakis*.

Kephisodotus (Κηφισόδοτος; m. pr. Kiphisódotos);   4th cent. B.C. Athenian kitharist, born at Acharnai (Ἀχαρναὶ) of Athens.   He is mentioned in Athenaeus (IV, 131B, ch. 7) as one of the virtuosi who were invited to the extravagant symposium (banquet) held at the palace of Kotys, the king of Thrace, on the occasion of his daughter's marriage with Iphicrates.

We know no other details of his life, except that he was a prominent member of the Stratonicus* School.

Cf. Dinse De Antig. Theb., p. 13; see also under *Antigenidas*.

kepion (κηπίων; m. pr. kipíon); an aulodic and/or kitharodic nomos.   The word is met twice in Plut. De Mus. (1132D, ch. 4); in the first case it is mentioned among the aulodic nomoi attributed to Clonas, while in the second it is mentioned among the kitharodic nomoi attributed to Terpander.

Its name came from Kepion (Κηπίων), the most important of Terpander's disciples (Plut. op. cit., 1133C, ch. 6).

keras (κέρας); horn. Cf. *bycane**, *salpinx**.

kerastes (κεράστης; m. pr. kerástis); made of horn; horned.
kerastes aulos; horn-made aulos.
Nonnos Dionys. XLV, v. 43 «αὐλὸς ... κεράστης».

keratophonos (κερατόφωνος); having or producing a sound similar to a horn-made trumpet (keras).
See *salpinx*.

keratourgos (κερατουργός); the maker of horns; especially of the horns of the kithara.
Hes. "*keratourgos*; the maker of the kithara's horns" («κερατουργός· ὁ ταῖς κιθάραις κερατοποιός»).
Besides keratourgos, the following words are also met with for the maker of horns: *keratoxóos* (κερατοξόος), *keraoxóos* (κεραοξόος) from keras (horn) and vb. xeein (ξέειν) to scrape. Also *keratopoeos* (κερατοποιός; from keras and poeein, to make) and *keratoglyphos* (κερατογλύφος; glyphein, γλύφειν =to carve).

keraules (κεραύλης; m. pr. kerávlis); player of a horn-made aulos. Luc. "Tragopodagra", vs 33-35 «πρὸς μέλος κεραύλου Φρυγίου ... κῶμον βοῶσι Λυδοὶ» ("to the melody of a Phrygian *keraules* ... the Lydians cry out (sing loudly) a komos* [a lustful song]»).

The playing of a horn-made aulos was called *keraulia* (κεραυλία; m. pr. keravlía).

kernophoros (κερνοφόρος).

a) The priest who carried the kernos (see Note below) in which they used to put fruits, oil etc. during ceremonies (kernos-pherein, κέρνος-φέρειν = to carry the kernos).

b) A sort of passionate dance; cf. Athen. (XIV, 629D, ch. 27) "and the *kernophoros*, the mongas and thermastris are passionate (μανιώδεις, furious) dances". See the Greek text under *mongas*.

Pollux (IV, 103) says that the "*kernophoron* orchema" (κερνοφόρον ὄρχημα) was danced by men carrying "kerna" or chafing-dishes (ἐσχαρίδες) which were also called kerna.

Note: The *kernos*, or *kernon*, both neut., was a sacred vessel or plate used in ceremonies, and especially at the Eleusinian mysteries; it was made of baked clay and had two ears and small cotyles around, and was used to hold oil, wine, milk, honey, fruits, etc. The kernos was carried during the ceremony by the priest or the priestess. The importance of the kernos is shown in the well-known symbolic formula «ἐκ τυμπάνου ἔφαγον, ἐκ κυμβάλου ἔπιον, ἐκερνοφόρησα, ὑπὸ τὸν παστὸν ὑπέδυν», ("I ate from a tympanum, I drank from a cymbal, *I carried the kernos*, I entered under the nuptial bed"; Clem. of Alex., Protrept. II, p. 14, ed. Pottec).

kidaris (κίδαρις); a kind of serious Arcadian dance, mentioned in Athen. (XIV, 631D, ch. 30): «ἡ δ' ἐμμέλεια σπουδαία, καθάπερ καὶ ἡ παρ' Ἀρκάσι κίδαρις, παρὰ Σικυωνίοις τε ὁ ἀλητήρ» ("the emmeleia is serious, like the *kidaris* among the Arcadians and the *aleter* among the Sicyonians"). The word "kidaris" signified also the head-dress of the ancient Persian Kings (tiara).

kindapsos, and **skindapsos** (κινδαψός, σκινδαψός); a big four-stringed instrument of a lyroid form, played with a plectrum like a feather. We read in Athen. (IV, 183A, ch. 81) that "*skindapsos* is a four-stringed instrument" («ἔστι δ' ὁ σκινδαψὸς τετράχορδον ὄργανον»), and that, according to Theopompus, the epic poet from Colophon, it was a big instrument of lyroid form («σκινδαψὸν λυρόεντα μέγαν χείρεσσι τινάσσων, οἰσύϊνον [or ὀξύϊνον] προμάλοιο τετυγμένον αἰζήοντος»; "holding in his arms a mighty lyre-like *scindapsus* made of withes of the lusty-willow (or of beech)"; transl. by Ch. B. Gulick, vol. II, p. 309).

Kinesias (Κινησίας; m. pr. Kinisías); 5th cent. B. C. Athenian composer of dithyrambs. He lived between 450 and 390 B.C.; his father, Meles (Μέλης), was a kitharode. Kinesias was considered one of the worst musicians and poets

of his time. He introduced new dancing-figures, and among his "innovations" was the abolition of the chorus in comedy, which he was able to
impose (in 400 B.C.) through a decision of the Athens Commune; for this he was
surnamed "chorus-killer" ("χοροκτόνος») by the comedian Strattis (Στράττις).
It has been suggested that he was so surnamed because of difficulty of singing
his music. See FHG II, p. 185, Fr. 272. His melodies were judged as lacking in
good taste and distinction. Suidas says that he was reputed for impiety and ille-
gality («οὗτος ἐπ᾽ ἀσεβείᾳ καὶ παρανομίᾳ διετεθρύλητο»); in fact his im-
pertinence, and disrespect to the Gods was such that, with friends, he used to
foul the statues of gods. His grotesque appearance (he was tall, lean and lame)
together with his general behaviour and his peculiar musical style were the
target of the comedians. Pherecrates in his comedy "Cheiron", through
Music — personified as a woman protesting to Justice — calls him "the cursed
Attic" («ὁ κατάρατος Ἀττικός»), and severely criticizes him. Aristophanes
also scorns him (or perhaps some other Kinesias) in the "Birds" (vs 1372-4)
and in the "Frogs" (vs 153-4).

He died in great poverty and misery.

Cf. Plut. 'De Gloria Atheniensium', ch. V, 348B. See in Brgk PLG (Cinesias) vol. III,
pp. 593-4, three small fragments. Also Page PMG Frgs. 774-776, pp. 398-9.

kinesis (κίνησις; m. pr. kínisis); motion; movement; change of a position.
κίνησις τῆς φωνῆς; motion of the voice.

Κατὰ τόπον κίνησις τῆς φωνῆς; the change of the voice as to locus
(position; voice in the sense of vocal and also instrumental sound); cf. Aristox.
Harm. (I, p. 3, 5-8 Mb). Aristoxenus (op. cit., p. 8, 18-19 Mb) distinguishes
two species of motion of the voice, the continuous (συνεχὴς) and the *diastematike* (by intervals; διαστηματική). He calls the first, λογικὴ (motion
of speech) and the second μελῳδικὴ (musical); cf. ibid p. 9, 20-25 and p.
10, 10. The same distinction is made by Cleonides (Isag. § 2, C.v.J. p. 180;
Mb p. 2). Ptolemaeus (Musica, in C.v.J. "Excerpta Neapolitana", p. 413)
uses the expression «χρῆσις διαστηματικῆς κεκλασμένης φωνῆς», for melodic motion; see *keklasmena mele*. Nicomachus (Enchir. ch. 2, C.v.J. pp. 238-
240; Mb pp. 3-5) calls the two species (γένη) of motion of the human voice:
a) *diastematic* and *énodon** (melodious), and b) *continuous* («συνεχές, καθ᾽
ὃ ὁμιλοῦμέν τε ἀλλήλοις καὶ ἀναγινώσκομεν»; *continuous* by which we
speak to each other, and we read").

See also *diastema, keklasmena mele*, and *syneches*.

b) ἔνρυθμος κίνησις; rhythmical movement (e.g. of the body, in dancing).

kinoumenoi, phthongoi (κινούμενοι, φθόγγοι; m. pr. kinoúmeni phthóngi)
pl.; movable notes of the tetrachord.

See under *hestotes-kinoumenoi*.

kinyra (κινύρα; m. pr. kiníra); a stringed instrument with ten strings, like the kithara, played with a plectrum, or directly with the fingers. It was associated with mournful music; the verb "kinyrein" («κινύρειν») or *kinyromai* signified to mourn, to wail (Hes. «κινύρειν· θρηνεῖν, κλαίειν»).

Suidas associates the name kinyra with the mythical king Kinyras of Paphos in Cyprus; as Suidas says, the king having competed unsuccessfully against Apollo at a musical contest, was given the nickname Kinyras from the instrument kinyra.

The kinyra was of Asiatic or Jewish origin; the Jewish kinnor, a kindred name, was a kithara with ten strings, and was played with a plectrum (cf. C. Sachs, Hist. of Mus. Instr., p. 107). Suidas simply says *"kinyra*; a musical instrument, or a kithara; from [the verb] to set the strings in motion [in vibration]" («κινύρα· ὄργανον μουσικὸν ἢ κιθάρα· ἀπὸ τοῦ κινεῖν τὰ νεῦρα»). Hesychius also writes *"kinyra*; a musical instrument, a kithara" («κινύρα. ὄργανον μουσικόν, κιθάρα»).

The word *kinyrós* (κινυρὸς) signified plaintive, doleful; cf. Suid. s.v. "kinyra" (κινύρα; κινυρόμεθα; κινυρομένη).

kithara (κιθάρα).

A more perfected and elaborate stringed instrument than the lyra. It differed from th lyra as to the sound-box, size and sonority. The sound-board was wooden, and much larger than that of the lyra. The two arms were strong and compact. The size was much bigger, and the tone more sonorous and ampler. On the whole the kithara was heavier and more strongly built, and the performer had to keep it almost upright, in an almost vertical position, even somewhat inclined towards the performer who was usually standing, while the lyra, being much lighter, was held aslant.

Apart from these differences the kithara was closely akin to the lyra in all respects; in fact, it might be said that it was a more perfected type of lyra, and what is said of the lyra* on construction, sound-production etc., applies to the kithara as well. But, while the lyra remained restricted to the amateurs, the kithara was largely the instrument of the professionals; Aristotle calls the kithara a "professional" instrument («ὄργανον τεχνικόν»; Polit. book VIII, ch. 6, 1341A «οὔτε γὰρ αὐλοὺς εἰς παιδείαν ἀκτέον, οὔτ' ἄλλο τεχνικὸν ὄργανον, οἷον κιθάραν» = "neither auloi, nor any other *professional* instrument [needing professional skill], like the kithara, should be used in education"). While the lyra was held in great respect as the national instrument "par excellence" for the education of youth, the kithara was held in great honour at the National Games (Olympic, Pythian etc.) and Contests.

Both the *kitharodia** and the *kitharistike** were arts practised, developed and glorified by ancient musicians of repute. In pre-classical times the kithara had three to seven strings; the seven-chord kithara was an innovation of Terpander (7th cent. B.C.). In the 6th cent. an 8th string was added, and in the 5th cent. kitharas appear with 9, 10, 11 and 12 strings.

(See this evolution in detail, under *lyra*).

According to Plutarch (De Mus. ch. 6, 1133C) "the form [of the kithara] was first fixed by Kepion, Terpander's pupil, and the kithara was called Asiatic probably because it was used by the Lesbian Kitharodes living near Asia" («ἐκλήθη δ' Ἀσιὰς διὰ τὸ κεχρῆσθαι τοὺς Λεσβίους αὐτῇ κιθαρῳδοὺς πρὸς τῇ Ἀσίᾳ κατοικοῦντας»), or from its Asiatic origin. Hesychius calls it "Asiatic" (Ἀσιὰς) as having been invented in Asia («διὰ τὸ ἐν Ἀσίᾳ εὑρῆσθαι»). The epithet "Asiatis" (Ἀσιᾶτις) is also met with for the kithara and for the whole of music (Strabo X, ch. 3, § 17: «καὶ ἡ μουσικὴ πᾶσα Θρᾳκία καὶ Ἀσιᾶτις νενόμισται»; "and hence the whole of music was believed to be of Thracian and Asiatic origin", or "all Thracian music was considered to be of Asiatic origin").

Note : For the tuning of the kithara, and other technical points see under *lyra*. For the origin of the kithara see among others:

M. Guillemin and *J. Duchesne :* "Sur l'origine asiatique de la cithare grecque"; AC, 4th year, vol. IV, Bruxelles 1935, pp. 117-124, with 8 Plates, 35 figures.

M. Wegner : a) Das Musikleben der Griechen, Berlin 1949, pp. 31-37, 46-47.
  b) Die Musikinstrumente des alten Orients, Münster, 1950.
  c) Griechische [Antike] Instrumente und Musikbräuche in Fr. Blume's "Die Musik in geschichte and gegenwart". vol. V, pp. 865-881.

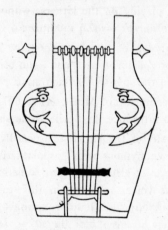

Fig. 2. Kithara

See PLATES IV and V.

kitharis (**κίθαρις**); a primitive stringed instrument which many historians identify with the lyra or the phorminx; others, however, identify kitharis with the kithara (C. Sachs, Hist. of Mus. Instr. p. 130).

The name kitharis, like that of phorminx, is often met in Homer; Odyss. I, vs. 153-4 "and a herald put the beautiful *kitharis* in the hands of Phemius" («κῆρυξ δ' ἐν χερσὶν κίθαριν περικαλλέα θῆκεν Φημίῳ»).

According to Aristoxenus (in his book "About instruments", FHG II, p. 286, Fr. 63) "the kitharis is the lyra" («κίθαρις γὰρ ἐστὶν ἡ λύρα»). The word itself is Ionian.

The verb «κιθαρίζειν» (kitharizein), to play the kithara or the kitharis, was generally used in the sense of playing also the lyra or the phorminx or any stringed instrument; Xen. "Oeconomicos" (ch. II, § 13) «οἱ δὲ δήπου τὸ πρῶτον μανθάνοντες *κιθαρίζειν* καὶ τὰς λύρας λυμαίνονται» ("Beginners, I fancy, are apt to spoil the lyres they learn on"; transl. E.C. Marchant, London, 1923, p. 379).

See also under *synhermosmenos*.

The verb "phormizein" («φορμίζειν») was also used in the same meaning; cf. *phorminx**.

kitharisis, kitharistike (κιθάρισις, κιθαριστική; m. pr. kithárisis, kithari-stikí).

a) *kitharisis*; playing the kithara (or the kitharis). From the verb "kitharizein" (κιθαρίζειν) = to play the kithara, or any other stringed instrument (see *kitharis*).

In the case of solo playing on the kithara, without any connection with singing, the term *psile kitharisis* («ψιλὴ κιθάρισις») was used.

Plato (Laws, 669E): «μέλος δ' αὖ καὶ ρυθμὸν ἄνευ ρημάτων *ψιλῇ κι-θαρίσει* καὶ αὐλήσει προσχρώμενοι ...» ("and again using the melody and the rhythm without words in the *solo-kithara* and aulos playing").

According to Menaechmus (ap. Athen. XIV, 637F, ch. 42) Aristonicus* of Argos was the first to introduce the "psile kitharisis".

b) *kitharistike*; the art of the kitharist; especially the art of solo kithara playing; a term almost synonymous with "psilokitharistike" («ψιλοκιθαριστι-κή»; see *psilos*). The pieces of kitharistike were sometimes called *aphona kroumata* (aphona = without voice, voiceless; in this case "without singing"): Paus. (X, ch. 7, § 7) «ὀγδόῃ δὲ Πυθιάδι προσενομοθέτησαν κιθαριστὰς τοὺς ἐπὶ κρουμάτων τῶν ἀφώνων καὶ Τεγεάτης ἐστεφανοῦτο 'Αγέλαος» ("they added by legislation at the eighth Pythiad the kitharists, those who played solo without singing; and Agelaus of Tegea was first crowned").

kitharisterios aulos, nomos (κιθαριστήριος αὐλός, νόμος; m. pr. kitha-ristírios avlós, nómos).

a) *kitharisterios aulos*; the aulos accompanying the kithara playing. Pollux (IV, 81) "and the *kitharisterioi* [pl. auloi] were so called because they accompanied the kitharas" («κιθαριστήριοι δὲ τοὔνομα, διότι κιθάραις προσῇδον»).

b) *kitharisterios nomos*; a kind of kitharistikos nomos (solo-kithara) with aulos accompaniment. It was called *pariambis*.

See also, Pollux IV, 83; and under *enaulos kitharisis*.

kitharistes (κιθαριστής; m. pr. kitharistís); a kithara player; one who plays only the kithara without singing, in contradistinction to "kitharodos"* who plays and sings at the same time.

kitharístria, and *kitharistris* (κιθαρίστρια, κιθαριστρίς) Fem. of kitharistes. The term usually applies to the solo performer.

kitharodia, kitharodikos nomos (**κιθαρῳδία, κιθαρῳδικὸς** νόμος).

a) *kitharodia* and *kitharódesis* (κιθαρῴδησις); singing to kithara accompaniment.

The kitharodia was the oldest and most respected kind of musical composition and performance. It needed only one executant, the singer and player of the kithara. Very often, almost always, the composer himself was also the "kitharodos".

According to Heracleides (ap. Plut. De Mus. 1131F, ch. 3) "Amphion*, the son of Zeus and Antiope, was the inventor of the kitharodia and the kitharodic poetry".

b) *kitharodikos nomos* (κιθαρῳδικὸς νόμος); an extended song with kithara accompaniment, like a modern concert aria. The nomos was dedicated to Apollo, and was invented by Terpander* in about 675 B.C. (cf. Plut. De Mus. 1132C, ch. 3). Clonas* and Polymnestus* followed Terpander's example with the aulodic nomos.

The kitharodikos nomos was composed of seven parts or sections (Pollux IV, 66):

1. *Archá* ('Αρχά; Dorian form of ἀρχὴ = beginning, introduction); also *Eparchá* ('Επαρχά);

2. *Metarchá* (Μεταρχά; the part after the beginning);

3. *Katatropá* (Κατατροπά; κατατροπὴ = change);

4. *Metakatatropá* (Μετακατατροπά; the part after the katatropá);

5. *Omphalós* ('Ομφαλὸς = navel; the central section);

6. *Sphragis* (σφραγίς; confirmation, final part);

7. *Epilogus* or *Exodion* ('Επίλογος, 'Εξόδιον; epilogue).

171

There were various kitharodic nomoi; Terpander was accredited with the denomination of many of them, such as the Boeotian, Aeolian, Trochaeos, Oxys (Acute), Kepion, Terpandrian and the Tetraoedian (Cf. Plut. ibid, 1132D, ch. 4).

The kitharodia and the kitharodikos nomos flourished especially in Lesbos from Terpander (c. 675 B.C.) to Pericletus (c. 560 B.C).

kitharodos; poetic form **kitharaoedos** (κιθαρῳδός; κιθαραοιδός); a musician who sang and accompanied himself on the kithara. The kitharodos appeared before the public wearing a long gown and crowned with a wreath of laurel. He began with the prooemion*, an instrumental prelude; then he proceeded to the main part of the kitharodia, singing and accompanying himself. Between the verses he played short interludes.

klepsiambos (κλεψίαμβος);

a) a stringed instrument of ancient origin with nine strings, as is said. It was used to accompany the "parakataloge"*, which was a declamation with instrumental accompaniment; in particular, it accompanied the "iamboi" of Archilochus*.

Its use became in time somewhat restricted; Athen. (XIV, 636F, ch. 40): "and the so-called *klepsiambos*, as also the trigonos*, the elymos* and the nine-chord, (enneachordon*), have become rather obsolete in use" («ἀμαυρό-τερα τῇ χρείᾳ καθέστηκε»). Pollux (IV, 59) merely mentions the klepsiambos with other stringed instruments ("krouomena").

b) *klepsiamboi* (pl.) were also a kind of songs, or verses; Hes. «κλεψίαμβοι· Ἀριστόξενος, μέλη τινὰ παρὰ Ἀλκμᾶνι» ("*klepsiamboi*; Aristoxenus [says] that they are certain tunes by Alcman").

knismos (κνισμός);

a) a kind of dance mentioned by Pollux (IV, 100) in his chapter "On kinds of dancing" («Περὶ εἰδῶν ὀρχήσεως»), without any indication as to its character.

b) a kind of aulos-melody included in Tryphon's catalogue of various kinds of auleseis, in his second book of Denominations (ap. Athen. XIV, 618 C, ch. 9). "All these melodies, it is added, were performed on the aulos with dancing."

kochlos (κόχλος); Dem. and LSJ: shell-fish with a spiral shell. It was used as a trumpet; Eurip. Iphig. in Tauris, v. 303 «κόχλους (pl.) τε φυσῶν» ("and blowing *the trumpets*").

172

kodon (κώδων; pl. κώδωνες, kódones); bell in the form of an inverted cup. There were two types, the simple and the compound. The simple was a metallic bell suspended and struck with a hammer or by a clapper inside (tongue). The compound was a chime of bells struck with a wooden stick. The bells were usually made of beaten brass (χαλκήλατοι κώδωνες) or sometimes of baked clay. Kodon was also used for the bell of the trumpet, and for the trumpet itself. Cf. *Diocles, discos.*

koelia (κοιλία; m. pr. kilía); bore, cavity. In music the cavity or bore of the aulos or of a wind instrument in general. Aristox. (Harm. II, p. 41, 34 Mb): «... ὁ αὐλὸς τρυπήματά τε καὶ *κοιλίας* (pl.) ἔχει» ("... the aulos has finger-holes and *bores* (pl.)").

Theon Smyrn. (ch. XII, p. 89) «ἐπὶ δὲ τῶν ἐμπνευστῶν καὶ διὰ τῆς εὐρύτητος *τῶν κοιλιῶν*...» ("on the wind instruments [the pitch is regulated] also by the width of *the cavities*").

The word *koeliosis*, or *koelosis* (κοιλίωσις, κοίλωσις), which means "hollowing out", "making hollow", was also used in the sense of bore or cavity of the aulos and wind instruments; Nicom. Ench. ch. 10 (C.v.J. p. 255; Mb. pp. 19-20) «κἀπὶ τῶν συρίγγων παραπλήσιόν τι τὰ μήκη ἀπεργάζεται καὶ αἱ τῶν *κοιλιώσεων* (pl.) εὐρύτητες, ὥσπερ αἱ τῶν χορδῶν παχύτητες» ("and on the syrinxes [wind instruments] the breadths of *the cavities* produce different effects just as do the different thicknesses of strings").

kok[k]ysmos (κοκκυσμός, or κοκυσμός; m. pr. kokismós); sharp, unaesthetic sound. Excerpta ex Nicom. (ch. 4; C.v.J. p. 274; Mb p. 35); «διὰ τὸ μὴ ἐπιδέχεσθαι τὴν ἀνθρώπων φωνήν... τούς τε *κοκκυσμοὺς* (pl.) καὶ τοῖς τῶν λύκων ὠρυγμοῖς φθόγγους παραπλησίους» ("the human voice cannot accept... *kokkysmoi* and such sounds similar to the howls of wolves").

Note : kokkysmos from kokkyzein (κοκκύζειν) = to croak like the bird κόκκυξ (cuckoo), to produce a hoarse sound. Also of the cock, to crow.

kollabos and **kollops**, pl. **kollopes** (κόλλαβος, κόλλοψ; m. pr. kóllabos); the thong or peg by which the strings were tuned. The word "kollops" was Attic and Homeric, while kollabos was a more common word.

In the more primitive lyras use was made of thongs of ox-leather to which the end of the strings was attached; by turning the thongs around the cross-bar the strings were tuned. This technique was improved by the use of pegs of wood, metal or ivory. The pegs had a little round head, were fixed accross the cross-bar, and by a rotary motion the strings were tightened.

Hes. «κόλλοπες, οἱ κόλλαβοι περὶ οὓς αἱ χορδαί» ("*kollopes* [were] the *kolloboi* [pegs] around which the strings [were turned]"). Theon. Smyrn.

p. 57, «ἔτι δὲ τῆς τάσεως γινομένης κατὰ τὴν στροφὴν *τῶν κολλάβων*» ("and the tightening is made by turning the pegs").

Cf. Pollux, IV, 62; Ptolem. III, 1; I. D. p. 85, 32.
See also *epitonion*.

kollobos, more correct **kolobos** (**κολοβός**; m. pr. kolovós); mutilated, curtailed, short-sized. Also a kitharodic nomos mentioned by Hesychius; «*κολλοβός·* κονδός, σμικρός, ὀλιγοστὸς ἢ ἐστερημένος, καὶ *νόμος τις κιθαρῳδικὸς*» ("*kollobos*; short-sized, small, petty or maimed [deprived of a limb], and a certain *kitharodic* nomos").

kolon (**κῶλον**); member, limb; a short sentence; a section of a period. In musical texts it is used in the sense of an instrumental passage, in contradistinction to singing parts.

Anon. (Bell. § 68, p. 78) «καὶ ὅτι ἐν τοῖς ᾄσμασί ποτε μεσολαβεῖ καὶ *κῶλα*» ("as in vocal tunes sometimes *instrumental passages* are intercalated").

See under *lexis*.

komarchios nomos (**κωμάρχιος νόμος**); one of the principal aulodic nomoi attributed to Clonas*. It was a song for the table sung to aulos accompaniment at banquets.

The word is derived from komos* (κῶμος) which was a merry symposium followed by a riotous procession, with singing to aulos, through the streets.

komastike, orchesis (**κωμαστική**, ὄρχησις; m.pr. komastikí órchisis); a kind of Bacchic dance connected with komos* (κῶμος).

Cf. Pollux (IV, 100).
Also *komastika mele* (pl.), tunes sung at komos.

kommation (**κομμάτιον**); a small piece, dimin. of komma, the first of the seven parts of the comic parabasis*. It consisted of a short song; Pollux (IV, 112) «ὧν τὸ μὲν *κομμάτιον* καταβολή τις ἐπὶ βραχέος μέρους» ("of which [i.e. the seven parts of the parabasis] the *kommation* is a certain introduction [beginning] of short duration").

Schol. Aristoph. "the *kommation* consists of two or three verses, never four".

kommos (**κομμός**);
See *commos*.

komos (**κῶμος**);
a) a kind of Bacchic dance performed at Dionysiac ceremonies; Pollux (IV, 100) "and there was also *komos*, a kind of dancing" («εἶδος ὀρχήσεως»).

174

b) also a merry symposium followed by a riotous procession through the streets, usually by young people, masked and crowned, carrying torches, singing to aulos and dancing.

Komos was also the name of the public procession in honour of Dionysus.

c) *komoi* (pl., κῶμοι) were the songs sung with aulos accompaniment during the komastic procession. Hesychius says that these songs were "lustful and libertine" («ἀσελγῆ ᾄσματα, πορνικά..»).

d) a kind of aulesis (aulos-solo); Tryphon in his second book of Denominations includes komos in the catalogue of auleseis (pl., aulos-solos; ap. Athen. XIV, 618C, ch. 9).

e) *komos* was also the group of those who in procession and with songs accompanied the victors at the athletic games.

See *enkomion*.

kompismos - melismos (κομπισμός - μελισμός);

kompismos was the term for the repetition of the same note in instrumental melody; *melismos* was the equivalent in vocal melody.

Man. Bryen. (ed. Wallis III, p. 480): "*kompismos* is when in the instrumental melody we repeat the same note more than once" («ὅταν τὸν αὐτὸν φθόγγον πλεονάκις ἢ ἅπαξ *κατὰ μέλος ὀργανικὸν παραλαμβάνωμεν*»); p. 482: "and *melismos*, when we repeat the same note more than once in the vocal melody with an articulate syllable" («ὅταν τὸν αὐτὸν φθόγγον πλεονάκις ἢ ἅπαξ, κατὰ μουσικὸν μέλος, μετά τινος ἐνάρθρου συλλαβῆς παραλαμβάνωμεν»).

Cf. Bell. Anon. p. 25, § 9a, b.

A. J. H. Vincent (Notices, p. 53) gives the following interpretation of kompismos and melismos which is basically different from that of Bryennius (c) and Bellermann (d).

Cf. *hyphen*.

Konnus (Κόννος; m. pr. Κόννos); 5th cent. B. C. Athenian kitharist who was a teacher of Socrates. Plato Euthydemus (272C; Socrates speaking) "as upon *Konnus*, the son of Metrobius, the kitharist who is still teaching me

175

to play the kithara' («ὃς ἐμὲ διδάσκει ἔτι καὶ νῦν κιθαρίζειν»); "so when the boys, my school-fellows, see us they laugh at me and call him old-men's teacher" («ἐμοῦ τε καταγελῶσι καὶ τὸν Κόννον καλοῦσι γεροντοδιδάσκαλον»).

He competed successfully at the Olympic Games. He lived in complete poverty; hence the proverb "Konnus' thrion" («Κόννου θρῖον») altered by Aristophanes to "Konnus' ballot" («Κόννου ψῆφος») meaning "nothing" or "naught".

Konnus has been identified with the aulete Konnás (U.v. Wilamowitz-Moellendorf "Plato" II, Berlin, 1920, 2nd ed. p. 139) mentioned by Aristophanes in the Knights, v. 533-4: «ἀλλὰ γέρων ὢν περιέρρει, ὥσπερ Κοννᾶς, στέφανον μὲν ἔχων αὖον» etc.; "but being an old man he wanders about like Konnas, bearing a withered crown" etc.

kordax (κόρδαξ); a comic dance; also a dance of the ancient comedy. It was considered as humorous, and sometimes common or vulgar, or even indecent.

Athen. (XIV, 630E, ch. 28): "the hyporchematike is related to the comic [dance] which is called kordax; both are humorous [playful]" («παιγνιώδεις δ᾽ εἰσὶν ἀμφότεραι»). Athen. (ibid, 631D) "the kordax among the Greeks is vulgar [or common]" («ὁ μὲν κόρδαξ παρ᾽ Ἕλλησι φορτικός»). Pollux (IV, 99): «εἴδη δὲ ὀρχημάτων, ἐμμέλεια τραγική, κόρδακες κωμικοί, σικιννὶς σατυρική» ("and the kinds of dances are emmeleia for the tragedy, kordakes (pl.) for the comedy, and sikinnis satirical").

Suidas: «κορδακίζειν (verb)· αἰσχρῶς ὀρχεῖται. Κόρδαξ γὰρ εἶδος ὀρχήσεως κωμικῆς» ("kordakizein (vb), to dance indecently. Because kordax is a comic dance"). Kordakismós was the dancing of the kordax; Hes. "kordakismoi (pl.), the jokes and plays (comic manners) of the mimes". Kordakismos and kordákisma were generally used in the sense of indecent dancing.

kordakistes (κορδακιστὴς) was the dancer of the kordax. See also for the kordax: Lucian "On dancing" § 22; Aristoph. Neph. 540; Paus. VI, ch. 22, § 1 etc.

koronisma (κορώνισμα); (LSJ) crow-song, a begging song sung by strollers. Cf. Hagnocles (Ἁγνοκλῆς) ap. Athen. VIII, 360B: «τὰ ᾀδόμενα δὲ ὑπ᾽ αὐτῶν (i.e. τῶν κορωνιστῶν) κορωνίσματα καλεῖται».

korone (κορώνη,; koróni); a kind of crow.

koronistes (κορωνιστής; m. pr. koronistis); singer of the crow-song (koronisma). The koronistai (pl.) used to walk about carrying a crow on their hand, and singing the koronisma for collecting money. Cf. Athen. VIII, 359E. "Koronistai", title of a work by Hagnocles.

koronizein (κορωνίζειν; m. pr. koronizin); to walk about carrying the crow and collecting money by singing the crow-song.

Cf. *chelidonisma**; (Athen. 360B: «καὶ χελιδονίζειν δὲ καλεῖται»).

Korybantes (Κορύβαντες; m. pr. Korívantes) pl. of Korybas; Corybants, priests of Cybele (or Rhea) in Phrygia, also associated with Dionysus. Their ritual performances were accompanied with orgiastic and frenzied dancing, and tumultuous and most exciting music.

Korybas (κορύβας; m. pr. korívas) as a n., enthusiasm.

Korybanteios (κορυβάντειος; m. pr. Korivántios) Adj., Corybantian. Κορυβάντεια ρόπτρα (Korybanteia roptra), Corybantian tambourines (see roptron*).

Korybanteion (κορυβαντεῖον; m. pr. korivantíon); the temple of the Corybants.

Korybantikos (κορυβαντικός; m. pr. korivantikós); Corybantic.

Korybantismos (κορυβαντισμός; m. pr. korivantismós); purification by Corybantic rites (Dem., LSJ).

Korybantizein (κορυβαντίζειν; m. pr. korivantízin) vb, to purify by Corybantic rites.

Korybantian (κορυβαντιᾶν; m. pr. korivantián) vb, to become possessed by Corybantian frenzy, to be somewhat mad (παρεμμαίνεσθαι, paremmaenesthai; Timaeus Lexicon Platonicum); LSJ: to "celebrate the rites of the Corybants".

koryphaeus (κορυφαῖος; m. pr. koriphéos); coryphaeus; the leader of the chorus in the ancient play.

Also called *"hegemon** of chorus" («ἡγεμὼν χοροῦ»), and *exarchos** (ἔξαρχος).

Pollux (IV, 106) «ἡγεμὼν χοροῦ· κορυφαῖος χοροῦ» (= "hegemon [leader] of chorus; coryphaeus of chorus").

korythal[l]istriai, fem. pl. (κορυθαλ[λ]ίστριαι; m. pr. korithalístrie); girls dancers who used to dance in honour of Diana during the celebration of a marriage, and in festivals of adolescents. They wore men's dresses and wooden masks, and their movements were not always very decent. Their dance was connected with the worship of fertility.

Note: *korythalia* or *korythale* (κορυθαλία, κορυθάλη) was an invocation in Sparta to Diana, protector of fecundity and fertility. So also was called a branch or wreath of olive-tree used during these festivities.

kradias, nomos; and **kradies** (κραδίας, κραδίης; m. pr. kradías, kradíis); an

177

ancient auletic nomos performed at the whipping of the scapegoats.

Hes. "*kradies* nomos; a certain nomos which they play on the aulos at the whipping, by branches of fig-tree and ropes, of the magicians" («κραδίης νόμος· νόμον τινὰ ἐπαυλοῦσι τοῖς ἐκπεμπομένοις φαρμακοῖς, κράδαις καὶ θρίοις ἐπιρραβδιζομένοις»).

Plut. De. Mus. (1133F, ch. 8) "and there is another ancient nomos called *kradias*, which, as Hipponax says, Mimnermus played on the aulos" («καὶ ἄλλος δ' ἐστὶν ἀρχαῖος νόμος καλούμενος Κραδίας, ὅν, φησιν Ἱππῶναξ, Μίμνερμον αὐλῆσαι»).

Notes: a) *krade* (κράδη); the end of a branch, especially of a fig-tree; a fig-branch.

b) *pharmakós* (φαρμακός); magician, sorcerer, impostor. By extension criminal. Suid. "pharmakos: one who is sacrificed for the purification of a city, otherwise an outcast, a criminal sacrificed for the expiation of others" («φαρμακός· ὁ ἐπὶ καθαρμῷ πόλεως ἀναιρούμενος, ἄλλως κάθαρμα, κακοῦργος, θυσιαζόμενος πρὸς ἐξιλασμὸν ἄλλων»). The pharmakos was also called kradesites (κραδησίτης), because he was whipped by krades (fig-branches); (Hes. «κραδησίτης· φαρμακὸς ὁ ταῖς κράδαις βαλλόμενος»).

Krates (Κράτης; m. pr. Krátis); 7th cent. B.C. aulete and composer. Nothing is known about his life. He is mentioned as a disciple of Olympus*, and as inventor of an auletic nomos called polyképhalos* ("many-headed") which other sources attributed to Olympus the elder or even to Athena (cf. Plut. De Mus. 1133D-E, ch. 7).

kregmos (κρεγμός; m. pr. kregmós); see *krekein* below.

krekein (κρέκειν; m. pr. krékin) vb; to strike the strings with the aid of a plectrum. "Krekein magadin" or "kitharan" («κρέκειν μάγαδιν ἢ κιθάραν») = to play the magadis or the kithara by striking the strings with a plectrum. In that respect the verb "krekein" was synonym to "plessein" (πλήσσειν; to strike) from which the word "plectron" (πλῆκτρον) was derived. The term used in the case of wind instruments signified "to play". Aristoph. Birds, v. 682 «ἀλλ' ᾦ καλλιβόαν κρέκουσ' αὐλὸν» ("but to which she *played* the tuneful [melodious] aulos").

Suidas writes «κρέκειν καὶ κρεκόντων, κρουόντων τὴν κιθάραν» ("krekein ... striking the kithara") and also «κρέκουσα· αὐλοῦσα» (fem. "playing the aulos"); and «κρέκω· τὸ ἠχῶ ... πλάκτρῳ Λοκρὶς ἔκρεξε», ("*kreko* to sound ... the Locrian girl played with the plectron").

The verb "krekein" signified also "to make a noise"; Aristoph. Birds, vs. 771-2 «συμμιγῆ βοὴν ὁμοῦ πτεροῖσι κρέκοντες ἴαχον Ἀπόλλω» ("rousing [i.e. the swans] at the same time a mingled clamour with their wings as a song in honour of Apollo").

Hesychius gives the meaning of "krekein" as simply "to play the kithara" («κρέκειν· κιθαρίζειν»).

178

kregmós (κρεγμός); the sound produced by striking a stringed instrument; Epicharmus (ap. Athen. IV, 183C, ch. 81) «πυκινῶν κρεγμῶν ἀκροαζομένα [Σεμέλη]» ("[Semele] listening to incessant *sparkling* sounds"; see the whole text under *pariambis*).

Note: The verb *anakrekesthai* (ἀνακρέκεσθαι; reflex.) is also met with the meaning of krekein.

krembalon (κρέμβαλον; m. pr. krémvalon), usually in pl. krembala (κρέμβαλα);

See *krotala*.

Kretikos, pous (κρητικός, πούς; m. pr. kritikós); Cretan poetic foot -υ-, called also ἀμφίμακρος (having long syllables at both ends).

The adj. Kretikos (Cretan) is often met with rhythm, metre, melos; κρητικὸς ρυθμὸς (Cretan rhythm), κρητικὸν μέτρον (Cretan metre), κρητικὸν μέλος (Cretan melos).

Krexus (Κρέξος); c. 450-400 B.C., poet and composer of dithyrambs.

He was considered the first to introduce into the dithyramb the «κροῦσιν ὑπὸ τὴν ᾠδὴν» ("krousin hypo ten oden"; the accompaniment of the song on the kithara by different notes). Before him the practice was to play on the kithara the same notes as the song («πρόσχορδα κρούειν»; "proschorda krouein"; to double in unison the vocal part on the instrument).

He also introduced into the dithyramb the alternate recitation or declamation and singing to the kithara accompaniment, an innovation that Archilochus* had initiated with iambic verses (ἰάμβεια).

Cf. Plut. 1141A-B, ch. 28; also *proschordos*.

krotala, (κρόταλα); a percussion instrument consisting of two hollow pieces of shell, wood or metal in various forms; clappers. The krotala were used, like the castanets, to keep the rhythm of the dancers, especially in ceremonies in honour of Cybele and Dionysus. They were usually fastened one on each hand.

Eust. (Il. II, XI, 160) «σκεῦός τι ἐξ ὀστράκου ἢ ξύλου ἢ χαλκοῦ ὃ ἐν χερσὶ κρατούμενον θορυβεῖ» ("a utensil [instrument] of shell or wood or copper which, kept in the hands, produces a noise [sound]").

The krotala were very often used by women; Herod. II, 60 «αἱ μέν τινες τῶν γυναικῶν κρόταλα ἔχουσαι κροταλίζουσι» ("some of the women holding *krotala* clap away".

The verb krotalizein (κροταλίζειν) meant to clap with the krotala; cf. Iliad XI, v. 160.

The word *krembalon* (κρέμβαλον) is often met for krotalon, and the

179

verb κρεμβαλι[ά]ζειν (*krembali[a]zein*); to shake the krembala, for krotalizein; Athen. XIV, 636D, ch. 39 «τὸ τούτοις [κρεμβάλοις] κρούειν κρεμβαλιάζειν εἴρηκεν [Ἕρμιππος]» ("the clapping of the krembala was called [by Hermippus] krembaliazein"). Cf. also Athen. ibid 636C, D, E. The clapping of the krembala was called *krembaliastys*, n. (κρεμβαλιαστύς; m. pr. krembaliastís).

The sound produced by the clapping of the krotala was called "rhymbos" (ρύμβος) or rombos* (ρόμβος).

krouma (κροῦμα), also **krousma** (κροῦσμα) from krouein (κρούειν; to strike); in principle the result of striking; stroke, beat. In music the term (usually in pl., kroumata) signified:

a) the sound produced by striking with a plectrum the strings of stringed instruments; and in general the sound of the stringed instruments. Hippocr. Regimen (Περὶ διαίτης) book I, § 18 «κρούεται δὲ τὰ *κρούματα* ἐν μουσικῇ τὰ μὲν ἄνω, τὰ δὲ κάτω» ("the notes produced by striking in music are some high, some low").

b) By extension also the sound of the wind instruments; Pollux (IV, 84) «τὰ σαλπιστικὰ *κρούματα*» ("the sounds of the trumpet").

c) In a broader sense a musical composition or piece of music; Plut. De Mus. (1142B, ch. 31) «καὶ τῶν λοιπῶν, ὅσοι τῶν λυρικῶν ἄνδρες ἐγένοντο ποιηταὶ *κρουμάτων* ἀγαθοὶ» ("and of all the other lyric poets those who have been meritorious creators of musical compositions"). Cf. Dio Chrys. "On reigning" I, § 4, p. 1. The adj. *kroumatikós* (κρουματικὸς) is also met with; *kroumatike* mousike (κρουματικὴ μουσική) kroumatic music; string-music, but sometimes also music of wind instruments.

Kroumatike dialectos (κρουματικὴ διάλεκτος); instrumental or generally musical dialect, style. Plut. ibid (1132B, ch. 21): «καὶ τὰ περὶ τὰς *κρουματικὰς* δὲ *διαλέκτους* τότε ποικιλώτερα ἦν» "and *the musical style* was more varied then [than it is now]".

See *krousis*, and *dialectos*.

kroupezion, pl. **kroupezia** (κρουπέζιον, -ια) dimin. of kroupeza (κρούπεζα); wooden shoe used to beat the time. Usually a small piece of metal was attached below so that the beating of time would be clearer and stronger.

Pollux (VII, 87) «τὰ δὲ *κρουπέζια*, ξύλινον ὑπόδημα, πεποιημένον εἰς ἐνδόσιμον χοροῦ. *Κρουπεζοφόρους* δ᾽ εἶπε τοὺς Βοιωτοὺς Κρατῖνος διὰ τὰ ἐν αὐλητικῇ κρούματα» ("the *kroupezia* [were] wooden shoes [sandals] used for beating the time in dancing. And Kratinus called the Boeotians *kroupezophoroi* [carrying wooden-shoes] for clapping at the auletic performances [i.e. beating the time to help the playing on the aulos]").

The words *kroupeza,* fem. (pl. kroupezai; κρούπεζα) and *kroupalon* neut. (κρούπαλον) are aslo met with the same meaning. Cf. Phot. s.v. κρούπεζαι.

The kroupezia or kroupala were worn by the coryphaeus (the chorus leader) who led the dance by also beating the time. Those who carried these wooden shoes were called *kroupezophoroi* (κρουπεζοφόροι; see above). The term *podopsophos** (ποδοψόφος) was also used for the man beating the time with his foot.

krousis (κροῦσις; from κρούειν, krouein = to strike); the act of striking, also the stroke. The striking of a stringed instrument, and synecdoch. string-music.

Philod. De Mus. (IV, p. 13, ed. J.K. 1884) «κρούσεις καὶ ᾠδαὶ» ("string and vocal music").

The term «κροῦσις ὑπὸ τὴν ᾠδὴν» ("krousis hypo ten oden"; playing a stringed instrument in accompaniment of a song) is generally interpreted as meaning "accompanying a song by a stringed instrument playing different notes from those of the vocal part"; cf. *proschorda krouein.* When the krousis accompanied the song it took the higher part; cf. Arist. Probl. XIX, 12 ("why is it that the melody is always given to the lower of the two strings?" «Διὰ τί τῶν χορδῶν ἡ βαρυτέρα ἀεὶ τὸ μέλος λαμβάνει;»)

Cf. Plut. 1141A, ch. 27; also *Archilochus.*

krousithyron (κρουσίθυρον; m. pr. krousíthiron);
See *thyrokopikon.*

krousta órgana (**κρουστά**; pl. of κρουστόν, neut.); also **krouomena (κρουό-μενα**), from κρούειν (krouein) = to strike. Instruments producing sounds by striking. So were generally called the stringed instruments.

Cf. *enchorda** organa. Nicomachus (Ench. ch. 2; ed. C.v.J. p. 240; Mb. pp. 5-6) uses the term clearly in the sense of percussion instruments, when he says "on the voice [sound] of the stringed, the wind and 'krousta' [percussion] instruments" («ἐπὶ τῆς τῶν ὀργάνων ἐντατῶν τε καὶ ἐμπνευστῶν καὶ κρουστῶν»). Percussion instruments were not in use for purely musical purposes. They were principally used at orgiastic cults and ceremonies, especially in honour of Cybele and Dionysus. Most of them were of foreign origin, mostly Asiatic.

Such instruments were the krembala*, the krotala*, the seistron*, the cymbals* and the tympanon*.

The adj. *kroustikós* (κρουστικὸς) was used in music in the sense "apt to produce a sound" (L.S.J. etc.: "able to sound the right note"); cf. Arist. Probl. (XIX, 10 «... κρουστικὰ δὲ μᾶλλον τὰ ὄργανα τοῦ στόματος» = ...

"but the instruments strike the note more effectively than the [human] mouth").

Ktesibius (Κτησίβιος; m. pr. Ktisívios); 3rd or 2nd cent. B.C. mechanician, born and lived in Alexandria.

Nothing is known about his life. In Athenaeus (IV, 174B and D, ch. 75) Alkeides says that he was a barber by profession, and that he lived during the time of [Ptolemaeus VII] Evergetes II (146-116 or 117 B.C.). Further in Athen. (ibid, 174E) it is said that, according to Tryphon's book about auloi and instruments, Ktesibius was a mechanician. As to his time, there have been different views; by some he is placed in the time of Ptolemaeus III-Evergetes I (246-222 B.C.), and others say that he flourished around 180 B.C.

Ktesibius is generally accredited with the invention of hydraulis*. He was a pioneer in the science of pneumatics, and wrote a book "On mechanics" («Ὑπομνήματα μηχανικά»), now lost. To his invention are also attributed the construction of a (hydraulic) water-clock and of various hydraulic machines.

L

Lamprocles (Λαμπροκλῆς; m. pr. Lamproclís); c. beginning of 5th cent. B. C. Athenian dithyrambic poet and musician. He belonged to the Athenian School, and was a disciple of Agathocles*.

Lamprocles became known through a Hymn to Athena ('Αθηνᾶ, Minerva) of which the beginning has survived.

According to the philosopher Lysis, 5th cent. B.C. (ap. Plut. De Mus. 1136D, ch. 16), Lamprocles was the first to establish that the Mixolydian harmonia as adopted by the tragedians was b-b (from paramese to hypate hypaton), and not the "Sapphic" Mixolydian (g-g) as almost all believed.

Cf. *Pythocleides*.

Some scholars believe that Lamprocles and Lamprus* are one and the same person (Gev. I, p. 50). In Athenaeus however two distinctly different persons are mentioned (cf. XI, 491C, ch. 80 for Lamprocles; I, 20F, ch. 37 and II, 44D, ch. 21 for Lamprus). Also ap. Plutarch (De Mus., as above, 1136D ch. 16; and for Lamprus 1142B, ch. 31).

Cf. Brgk Anth. Lyr. p. 272, PLG III pp 554-6 2 Frgs; Page PMG pp. 379-80 Frgs 735-6.

Lamprus (Λάμπρος; m. pr. Lámpros); b. ? d. ?

A musician mentioned by Aristoxenus (ap. Plut. 1142B, ch. 31) among celebrated lyric poets and musicians, together with Pindar, Dionysius* of

Thebes and Pratinas* («ποιηταὶ κρουμάτων ἀγαθοί»; "good (meritorious) composers of musical compositions"; cf. *krouma*).

Lamprus is mentioned also as a teacher of Sophocles (Athen. I, 20F, ch. 37) in dancing and music («ὀρχηστικὴν δεδιδαγμένος [Sophocles] καὶ μουσικὴν ἔτι παῖς ὢν παρὰ Λάμπρῳ»; "since Sophocles was a boy, he was taught dancing and music by Lamprus"). This however is questioned by some scholars (cf. H. Weil and Th. Rein. Plut. De la mus. p. 129, note 317). Lamprus is mentioned by Phrynichus (Th. Kock Comic. Att. Fr. vol. I, p. 388, fr. 69) as a delicate lament-poet and great sophist («νιγλάροις θρηνεῖν, ἐν οἷσι *Λάμπρος* ἐναπέθνησκεν ἄνθρωπος ὢν ὑδατοπότης, μινυρός, ὑπερσοφιστὴς» etc. "amid lamentations Lamprus died, having been a water-drinker, whining, a supersophist").

Lasus of Hermione (Λᾶσος ὁ Ἑρμιονεύς; m. pr. Lásos o Ermionéfs); b. c. 548-545 B.C. (according to Suidas during the 58th Olympiad) at Hermione (Ἑρμιόνη) of Achaïa in Peloponnesus. An important figure in the history of ancient Greek music, and a sophist of repute.

According to Diog. Laertius (book I, ch. I, § 42), Hermippus (Ἕρμιππος) in his work "On the sages" reckons seventeen including Lasus as one; Suidas, on the other hand, reports that some included him in the seven wise men in place of Periandrus. Suidas also says that Lacus was the first to write a book on music («Πρῶτος δὲ οὗτος περὶ μουσικῆς λόγον ἔγραψε»), now lost; its plan was preserved by Martianus Capella (book IX, 936 [317C], ed. A. Dick, 1969). He was a rival of Simonides and a teacher of Pindar.

Lasus is mentioned as one of the principal innovators in music, and exercised a considerable influence; among his successors are cited Eratocles*, Agenor* and Pythagoras of Zante*. He was credited by some grammarians with the creation of the Attic dithyramb; through Hipparchus, he succeeded in imposing the introduction of the dithyramb in musical contests. He enriched the instrumental (aulos) accompaniment of dithyrambs by adding ornamentations, with the use of more numerous and spaced notes (moving by leaps) (Plut. De Mus. 1141C, ch. 29 «πλείοσί τε φθόγγοις καὶ διερριμμένοις χρησάμενος»).

Lasus, as also some of Epigonus' School, held that sound had "breadth", a view criticized by Aristoxenus as erroneous (Harm. I, p. 3, 23 Mb).

He was interested in acoustics and held experiments with Hippasus of Metapontium; some even attribute to him the discovery of vibrations as the cause of sound (cf. *Archytas*). Preoccupied always with the refinement of tone quality, he composed poems in which he avoided the use of the letter

S as hard; such was a Hymn to Demeter which was "asigmos"* (without an *S* used in the words). Athenaeus preserved three verses of this Hymn in which indeed no *S* is used (XIV, 624 E-F, ch. 19):

«Δάματρα μέλπω Κόραν τε Κλυμένοι ἄλοχον,
μελιβόαν ὕμνον ἀναγνέων
Αἰολίδ᾽ ἀνὰ βαρύβρομον ἁρμονίαν»

"I celebrate Demeter and Kore (i. e. Persephone), wedded wife of Pluto, raising unto them a sweet-voiced hymn in the deep-toned Aeolian mode" (transl. by Ch. B. Gulick, vol. VI, pp. 367-9).

See PLG III pp. 376-7 4 Frgs; Page PMG pp. 364-6 Frgs 702-6.

leimma (λεῖμμα; m. pr. límma) from leipein (λείπειν) = to be wanting; hence the "remnant", the "remainder". a) In music a term by which the Pythagoreans denoted the minor semitone. The tone being divided into two unequal parts, the smaller was called *leimma*, and the major apotome*.

Plutarch "De animae procr. in Tim." (ch. 17, 1020 E-F): "The harmonists believe that the tone is divided into two intervals, each of which they call semitone, but the Pythagoreans disapproved the division into equal parts, and the parts being unequal they call the minor *leimma*, as it is smaller than the half". M. Psellus (Schol. in Plato's Timaeo; ap. Vincent "Notices" p. 318) «λεῖμμα, ὅπερ ἐστιν ἔλαττον τμῆμα τοῦ τόνου καὶ τὴν ἀποτομήν, ὅπερ ἐστι μεῖζον» ("*leimma*, which is the smaller part of the tone, and the *apotome* which is the larger").

Ptolemaeus (Harm. I, ch. 10; ed. I.D. p. 23, 2) defines the leimma as the interval by which the fourth exceeds the ditone, and as smaller than the semitone («ἣ ὑπερέχει τὸ διὰ τεσσάρων τοῦ διτόνου, καλουμένην δὲ λεῖμμα· ἔλαττον δὲ ἡμιτονίου»). Cf. Porphyr. Comment. (ed. I.D. p. 129, 23-24).

Pachymeres (Harm. ap. Vincent "Notices", p. 459) says that Aristoxenus and his School considered the leimma as a complete semitone («λαμβάνοντες τὸ λεῖμμα ὡς ὁλόκληρον ἡμιτόνιον, ἔλεγον καὶ τὸ διὰ πασῶν ἕξ τόνων»; "considering [i.e. Aristoxenus and his School] *the leimma* as a complete semitone, they said that the octave had six tones").

Cf. *apotome** and *hemitonion**.

b) leimma was also used for the shorter silence (rest) and was noted by the letter Λ (the first letter of the word Λεῖμμα); cf. *parasemantike**.

leon (λέων); lion. A kind of dance mentioned in Athen. (XIV, 629F, ch. 27) among comical or ludicrous dances, like igdis*, glaux* etc. Pollux (IV, 103) says that "*leon* is a kind of terrifying dance" («ὁ δὲ λέων ὀρχήσεως φοβερᾶς εἶδος»).

lepsis (λῆψις; m. pr. lípsis) from λαμβάνειν (lambanein = to take); one of the three parts of the melopoeia. Aristides (I, p. 29 Mb; R.P.W-I, p. 29); "The parts [of the melopoeia] are *lepsis**, mixis* and chresis; *lepsis* is that part by which the musician [composer] determines the region of the voice to be used in the system" («λῆψις μέν, δι' ἧς εὑρίσκειν τῷ μουσικῷ περιγίνεται ἀπὸ ποίου τόπου τῆς φωνῆς τὸ σύστημα ποιητέον»).

lepsis dia symphonias (λῆψις διὰ συμφωνίας; m. pr. lípsis diá simphonías); a method of determining, or tuning, intervals by a series of consonances. Aristoxenus (Harm. II, 55, 13ff. Mb) gives the following example: in order to find a certain discord below a given note, such as the ditone, one should take the Fourth above the given note, then descend a Fifth, then ascend a Fourth again, and finally descend another Fifth (transl.H. S. M., p. 206). See also Laloy, Lexique d'Aristoxène p. XXI, and H. Weil & Th. Rein. Plut. "De la musique" 1145C, note 397, p. 151.

lexis (λέξις); word, speech. In music it is often used in contradistinction to "krousis"* (κροῦσις; instrumental, string music) or to "ode" (tune, song).
Bell. Anon. (§ 68, p. 78) «Διπλοῦς ὁ χαρακτὴρ τῶν φθόγγων εἴληπται, ἐπειδὴ καὶ διπλῆν ἔχει τὴν χρῆσιν· ἐπὶ λέξεως γὰρ καὶ κρούσεως» ("The notation of the sounds [notes] is twofold, because it serves a double purpose; [to denote] *the text [words]* and the instrumental part").
Plato (Laws, 816D): «κατὰ λέξιν τε καὶ ᾠδὴν καὶ κατὰ ὄρχησιν» ("according *to words*, song and dancing").

Libys aulos (λίβυς αὐλός; m. pr. lívis aulós); Libyan aulos, so called because, according to Douris (ap. Athen. XIV, 618C, ch. 9), a Libyan first invented the auletic art and played on the aulos the Metroa* (in honour of Cybele); «Λίβυν δὲ τὸν αὐλὸν προσαγορεύουσιν οἱ ποιηταί, φησὶ Δοῦρις ...ἐπειδὴ Σειρίτης, ὃς δοκεῖ πρῶτος εὑρεῖν τὴν αὐλητικήν, Λίβυς ἦν τῶν νομάδων» ("And the poets call *the aulos Libyan*, says Douris, ... because Seirites who, it appears, first invented the auletic art, was a Libyan of the Numidian tribe". The Libyan aulos was probably a certain kind of aulos brought, according to tradition and as its name implies, from Libya.

lichanoeides (λιχανοειδής; m. pr. lichanoïdís); belonging to the property of the string lichanos; *lichanoeides topos* (λιχανοειδὴς τόπος), locus of the lichanos on the lyra or the kithara; or locus of the voice on the lichanos' place. Aristox. Harm. (I, p. 26, 18 Mb): «διάκενον δ' οὐδέν ἐστι τοῦ λιχανοειδοῦς τόπου» ("in the locus of the lichanos there is no empty space": transl. H.S.M. p. 184).
lichanoeides phthongos (λιχανοειδὴς φθόγγος); according to Bacchius (Isag.

§ 43; C.v.J. p. 302; Mb p. 11) "the highest note of the pycnon" («ὀξύτατον τοῦ πυκνοῦ»).

See also *parhypatoedes**.

lichanos (λιχανὸς and λίχανος); fore-finger. The string and the note produced by the string played by the fore-finger; Arist. Quint. (Mb p. 10; R.P.W-I, p. 8) "they were called *lichanoi* (pl.) from the homonymous finger which strikes the string that produces them" («λιχανοὶ προσηγορεύθησαν, ὁμωνύμως τῷ πλήττοντι δακτύλῳ τὴν ἠχοῦσαν αὐτὰς χορδὴν ἐπονομασθεῖσαι»). Lichanos was the third note from below of the heptachord and the octachord:

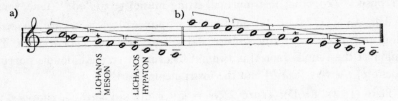

In both the Lesser (a) and the Greater Perfect (b) Systems there were two strings (or notes) with the name of lichanos: the lichanos hypaton (λιχανὸς ὑπατῶν) and the lichanos meson (λιχανὸς μέσων):

a)   b)

LICHANOS MESON

LICHANOS HYPATON

The lichanos was sometimes also called "diátonos" (διάτονος).

Cf. *paraphonia; hypermese; lichanoeides.*

ligyeches (λιγυηχής; m. pr. ligiichís) from *ligys* (λιγύς), clear, piercing, also melodious, sweet; and *echos* (ἦχος; sound); sweet- or clear-sounding. *ligyeches kithara* (λιγυηχὴς κιθάρα); clear-toned, or sweet-(melodiously-) sounding kithara.

ligythroos, ligythrous (λιγύθροος, λιγύθρους; m. pr. ligíthroos, -rous); clear-toned; sweet- or loudly-sounding. Same as ligyeches.

ligythroos pektis (λιγύθρους πηκτίς); clear-toned pektis; also loudly-sounding pektis.

Other adjs., formed from ligys and met with in music, were: ligymolpos, ligykrotos ligyphonos, ligyphthongos (having sonorous, strong or clear voice).

Limenius (Λιμένιος; m. pr. Liménios); Athenian composer of unknown date (probably 2nd cent. B.C.) to whom many scholars ascribe the composition of the Second Delphic Hymn to Apollo. He was the son of Thoïnos (Th. Reinach: La mus. gr., p. 183), but nothing else about his life is known.

186

linodia (λινῳδία); see *linos**, below.

linos (λίνος); a funeral song in memory of the unhappy death of the poet-musician Linus*; also called *linodia* (λινῳδία). The Linus song is first mentioned in Homer (see below).

Another expression for linos was *oetolinos* (οἰτόλινος; m. pr. itólinos) from οἶτος (oetos; fate, disaster, death) and linos. The linos was known in Egypt and was called *maneros**.

Cf. Herod. book II, ch. 79.

Hesiod says that the linos was sung by minstrels (aoedoi) and kitharodes "in banquets and dances"; Athen. also (XIV, 619C, ch. 10) says that according to Euripides (Herc. v. 348) "*linos* and aelinos* [are sung] not only in mourning but also at a happy event";

Cf. *aelinos*, also Hom. Il. XVIII, 570-571, and "Scholia Graeca in Homer Iliadem" by G. Dindorf (Oxford, 1875) vol. II, p. 177 and vol. IV, p. 200.

Linus (Λίνος; m. pr. Línos); mythical poet-musician (minstrel), son of Apollo. According to Heracl. (ap. Plut. 1132A, ch. 3) a contemporary of Amphion*, and a composer of laments. He was, by legend, credited with the invention of the trichord lyra, or with the addition of the 4th string to the trichord lyra he had from his father, Apollo. Diod. Sikel. (III, ch. 59, § 6) ascribes to Linus the addition of the lichanos* string; cf. *Marsyas*.

He gave his name to a kind of lament (linos, see above) owing to his regrettable death. There were many different legends about his death; according to one he was killed by Apollo because of his boast of being equal to the God in song and art. Another legend says that he was torn apart by dogs (Paus. I, ch. 43, § 7), while according to a third legend he was killed by Heracles (whom he taught music) because during a music lesson Linus scoffed at him for awkwardness in lyra playing. Pausanias (IX, ch. 29, § 6) records that his death provoked such sorrow that the mourning reached all lands, even barbarian ones, and he was lamented by a special song (*linos** and maneros*).

lityerses (λιτυέρσης; m. pr. litiérsis); song of the reapers; Athen. (XIV, 619A, ch. 10) «ἡ δὲ τῶν θεριστῶν ᾠδὴ λιτυέρσης καλεῖται» ("the song of the reapers is called lityerses"). As a proper name Lityerses and Lityersas (Λιτυέρσης, -σας) was the name of an illegitimate son of Midas, king of Phrygia, who, being an extraordinarily skilful reaper used to challenge the passers-by at reaping, and bound the heads of the defeated in the sheaves. He was killed, according to a legend, by Heracles.

Hes. "*Lityersas*; a kind of song; also, Lityersas was an illegitimate son of Midas and very musical" ("*Λιτυέρσας*, ᾠδῆς εἶδος· ἔτι δὲ ὁ Λιτυέρσας Μίδου νόθος υἱὸς ᾠδικώτατος»).

According to Pollux (IV, 54) Lityerses was a king of Phrygia (of Kelaenai in Phrygia).

Probably the song lityerses was named after him.

Locrios [Locrian] *harmonia,* also *Locristi,* and *Locrike* Harm. (Λόκριος ἁρμονία, λοκριστί, λοκρική); the octave-series better known as Aeolia, i.e.

a - g - f - e - d - c - b - a   (Diatonic genus)

Its introduction was ascribed to the Locrian lyric poet and musician Xenocritus* who lived in the 7th cent. B.C.

The Locrian harmonia derived its name from Locris, a district of ancient Greece between Thermopylae and lake Kopais, and it was probably a fairly local harmonia. It belonged to the group of Dorian harmoniai and was called by some writers "common" (κοινή).

Cf. Cleon. Isag. ch. 9 (C.v.J. p. 198; Mb p. 16); Bacch. Isag., § 77 (C.v.J. p. 309; Mb p. 19).

The Locrian harmonia, after having been used during the time of Simonides* and Pindar*, fell into disuse.

Cf. Athen. XIV, 625E, ch. 20.

From the time of Aristoxenus the term Hypodorios was generally used for this octave-series.

Cf. *Aeolios, Hypodorios* and *harmonia.*

logodes melos (λογῶδες μέλος); spoken "melody". A term used by Aristoxenus for the "melody" of speech; Harm. Elem. (I, p. 18, 12-15) «λέγεται γὰρ δὴ καὶ *λογῶδες* τι *μέλος,* τὸ συγκείμενον ἐκ τῶν προσῳδιῶν τῶν ἐν τοῖς ὀνόμασιν· φυσικὸν γὰρ τὸ ἐπιτείνειν καὶ ἀνιέναι ἐν τῷ διαλέγεσθαι» (= "for there is also a kind of *melody in speech* which depends upon the accents of words, as the voice in speaking rises and sinks by a natural law"; transl. H.S.M. p. 177).

lombroteron (λομβρότερον; m. pr. lomvróteron); a kind of indecent dance mentioned by Pollux (IV, 105): «*λομβρότερον* δέ, ἣν ὠρχοῦντο γυμνοὶ σὺν αἰσχρολογίᾳ» ("the *lombroteron,* which was danced by naked men with obscene language"). According to Dem. and LS, Gr., lombroteron is the comparative of lombros, and means "more indecent, more obscene".

(Cf. Dem. p. 4376, and LS, Gr., vol. III, p. 58).

Lycaon (Λυκάων; m. pr. Likáon); 6th to 5th cent. B.C. musician from Samos, to whom Boethius attributed the addition of the 8th string to the lyra, which by Suidas was attributed to Simonides and by Nicomachus to Pythagoras; cf. *lyra*. It may be possible that Lycaon as a disciple of Pythagoras in Samos knew and used the octachord lyra. No more details are known of his life.

Lydios [Lydian] *harmonia,* and **Lydisti** (λύδιος, λυδιστὶ ἀρμονία; m. pr. lidios, lidisti); the following octave-series (διὰ πασῶν, octachord) was generally accepted by most ancient theorists and writers as Lydian harmonia:

$$c - b - a - g - f - e - d - c \quad \text{(Diatonic genus).}$$
$$\tfrac{1}{2} \quad 1 \quad 1 \quad 1 \quad \tfrac{1}{2} \quad 1 \quad 1$$

Cf. Gaudent. Isag. (ch. 19, C.v.J. p. 347; Mb p. 20).

For others, including Aristides, it was the octave f-f. The Lydian harmonia and the Phrygian were among the non-Greek harmoniai, which came to Greece from Asia Minor; cf. Athen. XIV, 625E, ch. 21 ("the Phrygian and the Lydian harmoniai became known to the Greeks from the Phrygians and Lydians who emigrated with Pelops to Peloponnesus").

The Lydian harmonia was however known from remote times, as also the Dorian and the Phrygian. According to Aristoxenus (first book "On music", ap. Plut. De Mus. 1136C, ch. 15), Olympus* was the first to play on the aulos a funeral tune in the Lydian mode (Lydisti) on Python's death. Pindar says in Paeans (Plut. ibid) that the Lydian harmonia was first performed at Niobe's marriage; while, as Dionysius the Iambus* relates, Torebus* introduced it.

See *ethos.*

lyra (λύρα; m. pr. líra); the pre-eminent national instrument of ancient Greece; the most important and most widely known of all instruments. Associated with Apollo's cult, it was very respected. Owing to its simple mechanism, and its peculiar and characteristic tone-quality, which was noble, serene and virile, the lyra was used as the chief instrument for the education of youth. Not being complex, or particularly sonorous, it was not used at open-air performances or competitions but was associated with the intimate social life of Greece.

History and legend. According to a widely spread legend (cf. Hom. Hymn to Hermes v. 24ff; Apollod. Atheniensis Biblioteca, III, ch. 10, 2, pp. 139-140; etc.) Hermes, soon after his birth in a cave on mount Kyllene, got out of his cradle during the night, stole the oxen guarded by Apollo, and came back, pretending to be asleep. Seeing outside the cave a tortoise, he took off its body, fixed on the carapace strings of ox-gut, and thus made the first lyra (chelys). When Apollo discovered the theft and the thief, and complained to Zeus, Hermes in order to appease his brother offered the lyra to Apollo, who was enchanted by its sound. The lyra was known in Greece from remotest antiquity. Legendary musicians and epic singers, such as Orpheus, Thamyris, Demodocus and others used to accompany their songs with the lyra, the phorminx* or the kitharis*.

Nicomachus (Excerpta ex Nicom., ch. 1; C.v.J.p. 266; Mb p. 29) relates that Hermes, after having constructed the seven-stringed lyra, taught Orpheus

189

how to play on it.   Orpheus in his turn taught Thamyris and Linus; this last taught Amphion* of Thebes who by his seven-stringed lyra bruilt up the "heptapylos" walls of Thebes (with seven gates).   When Orpheus was killed by the Thracian women (the "Maenads") his lyra fell into the sea and was taken by the waves to Lesbos; there it was found by fishermen who brought it to Terpander*.   This chain of legends tends to establish the Thracian origin of the lyra.

Construction. The primitive lyra was based on the carapace of a tortoise which served as the sound-box (echeion*); hence the poetic name *chelys* of the old lyra (χέλυς from χελώνη = tortoise). In later times the sound-box was also made of wood but in similar shape. Over the concave side a vibrating membrane of oxhide was stretched.   On either side of the carapace two arms, made of horn of a wild goat, or wood, were fixed parallel to the sound-box; they were light and slightly curved, and were called *pecheis* (πήχεις; arms) or *horns* (κέρατα). These arms were joined, slightly under their upper end, to a cross-bar, made of box-wood and called zygon or *zygós* (ζυγόν; cross-bar, or joining-bar).   The strings (chordai, neurai; χορδαί, νευραί) made of gut or sinew (in older times of linen or hemp), were stretched by a knot on a little board (called *chordotónion** or *chordotónos**) on the lower part of the sound-box; they passed over a bridge (called *magas**, μαγὰς) which isolated the vibratory part of the strings, and were stretched along the instrument to the cross-bar on which they were fastened.   In older times the strings were tied by a thong of leather, but in classical times pegs were used made of wood, metal or ivory, which, fixed by a mechanism on the cross-bar, tightened the strings by rotary motion; these pegs, as well as the thongs, were called *kollaboi** and *kollopes** (κόλλαβοι, κόλλοπες).   All the strings had the same length, but differed in thickness and bulk, and each gave one sound.

The number of strings varied greatly during historial times but for a long period they were seven. According to some ancient writers the primitive lyra had four or even three strings.   Diod. Sikel. (Bibliot. Hist., book I, p. 10) writes that "Hermes invented the lyra and made it trichord in imitation of the three seasons of the year. Thus he established three sounds, a high, a low and a medium". Nicomachus (see above), on the other hand, says that Hermes from the very beginning made the lyra with seven strings. Lucian ("Dialogue of Apollo and Hephaestus") and others repeat this legend, as it appears in Homer's Hymn to Hermes (v. 51). It is certain beyond doubt that from Terpander's time (8th-7th cent. B.C.) the lyra was heptachord. Terpander was credited with this invention by many writers; a tradition kept alive until the 4th cent. B.C. closely connected Terpander with the heptachord lyra.   To Terpander was attributed also, by some historians, the addition of the octave; Terpander took off the "trite" and

190

added instead the "nete", i.e. the octave. Arist. Probl. (XIX; 32) clearly refers to it ("why is the octave called diapason instead of 'di'octo' [δι'ὀκτὼ] according to the number of the strings [notes] in the same way as we say dia-tessaron [for the fourth] and dia-pente [for the fifth]? is it because in ancient times the strings were seven? and then Terpander taking out the trite added the nete, and for this it was called 'dia pason' (through all, octave) and not di'octo, as they were seven in all").

An 8th string was added in the 6th cent. B.C.; this addition was attributed by some writers to Pythagoras. Nicomachus (Enchir. ch. 5; C.v.J. p. 244; Mb p. 9) says that Pythagoras first of all («πάμπρωτος»; the very first) added the 8th string between the mese and paramese thus forming a complete harmonia with two disjunct tetrachords (e-d-c-b-a-g-f-e). Boethius attributes the addition of the 8th string to Lycaon* of Samos, and Suidas to Simonides*.

The heptachord lyra remained in use for a very long period throughout classical times; most of the lyras on ancient vase-paintings are depicted with seven strings. If we take into consideration the fact that the lyra was closely connected with Apollo's cult, and that it was the national instrument par excellence for the education of youth, we can understand that the Greek people, including some of the most eminent poets and authors like Pindar, Plato and Aristotle, could not easily give way to innovations regarding such a sacred instrument. Side by side however with the use of the heptachord (and octachord) lyra, use was made of instruments with more strings. Already from the 5th cent. B.C. appeared lyras (and kitharas) with nine to twelve strings. The addition of the 9th string was attributed to Prophrastus* (or Theophrastus) of Pieria, of the 10th to Histiaeus* of Colophon, of the 11th to Timotheus (cf. Nicom. Exc. ex. Nicom. ch. 4; C.v.J. p. 274; Mb p. 35). Other sources attribute to Melanippides* and to Timotheus the addition of the 12th string (Pherecrates in "Cheiron" ap. Plut. De Mus. 1141D-1142A, ch. 30).

The mode of playing on the lyra and similar instruments has been the subject of various hypotheses, based mainly on the evidence of vase-paintings and of some rare literary sources. It is generally believed that the strings were plucked by the right hand, usually with a plectrum, though playing with bare fingers cannot be excluded. The left hand was used probably to deaden the strings; but judging from the position of the fingers of the left hand in many vase-paintings we are bound to accept that undoubtedly it was also used to play with bare fingers. This is supported by some literary evidence; Philostratus Minor says (Imag., 6, Orpheus; Leipzig, T., 1902) that while the right hand plays with the plectrum firmly held (see the text under *plectron*), "the left hand strikes the strings with straight fingers" («ἡ λαιὰ δὲ ὀρθοῖς πλήττει τοῖς δακτύλοις τοὺς μίτους»).

See also Philostrati Majoris Imagines, No. 10, Amphion. Cf. Gombosi: "Die Tonarten und Stimmungen der antiken Musik" (Kopenhagen, 1939, pp. 116-122); C. Sachs Hist. of Mus. Inst., pp. 132-3.

The lowest string (hypate) was placed at the end farthest from the executant, and the highest (nete) at the nearest (see *onomatothesia, hypate, nete*). The performer on the lyra was usually seated.

The tuning of the lyra (and of the kithara) is a question which has not been definitely clarified owing to insufficient ancient information. Curt Sachs offered a solution of the problem ("Die griechische Instrumentalnotenschrift, Zeitschrift für Musikwissenschaft", VI, 1924; pp. 289-301; Hist. of Mus. Instr. pp. 131-2) according to which "the customary tuning was pentatonic without halftones in EGABD (but not necessarily in this order). Additional strings duplicated these notes in the higher or lower octave instead of filling in the missing diatonic notes, F and C". The original trichordal (three-stringed) was E′ AE (nete, mese, hypate)

To these were later added the paramese (B), and then the paranete (D), and the lichanos (G):

When the two missing diatonic notes, F and C, and semitones and quartertones were needed, they were produced, according to Sachs, "by pressing and thus tightening the next lower string with one of the fingers".

This theory had a favourable reception by many scholars such as *H. Abert, W. Vetter, I. Düring, O. Gombosi* and *G. Reese,* and was subjected to a critical examination by Prof. *R. P. Winnington-Ingram* in his study "The Pentatonic tuning of the Greek lyre: a theory examined" ("Classical Quarterly", New Series, vol. VI, Nos 3-4, Oxford, 1956, pp. 169-186). See also *O. S. Gombosi :* op. cit. p. 166 ff; *G. Reese :* "Music in the Middle Ages", London, 1941, p. 25; *I. Düring :* "Studies in Musical Terminology in the 5th Century Literature", Eranos, vol. 43, 1945, p. 192; and the articles "Lyra" and "Musik" in Pauly-Wissowa (-Kroll) XIII, ii (XXVI), 1927, cols. 2479-2489 (esp. 2485) and XVI, i (XXXI), 1933, cols. 823-876 (esp. 851) by *H. Abert* and *W. Vetter* respectively. See also : *Samuel Baud-Bovy* "L'accord de la lyre antique et la musique populaire de la Grèce moderne", Revue de Musicologie, vol. LIII, 1; Paris, 1967, pp. 3-20.

For the playing the lyra the verb "kitharizein" was used (cf. kitharis); the verb "lyrizein" («λυρίζειν») is also met with but very rarely. The lyra was usually held aslant away from the performer; the player was usually seated with the instrument on his knees or between his arms, held by a leathern band (called telamon, τελαμών).

Generally speaking the lyra was used more by the amateurs while the kithara was left in the hands of the professionals.

According to many writers the Homeric phorminx* and kitharis* were kinds of lyra; this is refuted by others (C. Sachs ibid p. 130).

The maker of lyras was called *lyropoeos* (*λυροποιός*; m. pr. liropiós).

The player of the lyra was called *lyristes* (*λυριστής*; m. pr. liristís).

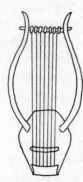

Fig. 3. Lyra

See PLATE VI

Bibliography (in addition to those mentioned in the article):

Th. Reinach: "Lyra" in DAGR; vol. VI, 1904, pp. 1437-1451.
Th. Reinach: La musique grecque; Paris 1926, pp. 117-121.
H. Abert: "Lyra" in Pauly's R.E., vol. XIII (XXVI) 1927, cols. 2479-2489.
A. Baines: "Lyre" in Grove, vol. V, 1954, p. 453 ff.
F. Zaminer: "Lyra" in Riemann Musik Lexikon, Sachteil, 1967, p. 536. For other bibliography see *enchorda.**

lyrodia, lyrodos (λυρῳδία, λυρῳδός; m. pr. lirodía, lirodós):

lyrodia (from lyra and ode, ᾠδή or ᾄδειν, to sing); singing to lyra accompaniment.

lyrodos; the musician who sang and accompanied himself on the lyra. Also as an adj.; Cf. Callistrati "Descriptiones" (Καλλιστράτου «Ἐκφράσεις»; T., Leipzig, 1902) ch. VII, § 4 «τὴν ἁρμονίαν τὴν λυρῳδόν».

The lyrodia was not widely propagated; it was confined to family and convivial circles. Contrary to the large scope of the kitharodia* and the extent and importance of the kitharodic nomoi, the songs of the lyrodia were more intimate in character, such as love-songs and drinking-songs (table-songs, "paroenia" etc.).

lyrogethes (λυρογηθής; m. pr. lirogithís); one who rejoices in playing the lyra. Another denomination used: *lyrothelges* (λυροθελγής; m. pr. lirothelgís), one who is delighted to play or to listen to the lyra.

lyrophoenix (λυροφοῖνιξ; m. pr. lirophínix); also *lyrophoenikion* (λυρο-φοινίκιον; m. pr. lirophiníkion); a kind of lyra or kithara of Phoenician origin.

It was probably the same as the *phorminx** and the *phoenikion** (φοινί-κιον); for some writers the lyrophoenix was a sambyke*; cf. Iobas, king of Mauritania and historian of the 1st cent. B.C. (ap. Athen. IV, 175D, ch. 77). Hes. «λυροφοῖνιξ· εἶδος κιθάρας» ("*lyrophoenix*; a kind of kithara"). Pollux (IV, 59) mentions only the lyrophoenikion. Herodotus says that the arms of the lyrophoenix were made of horn of the roe-deer; while Semus of Delos (ap. Athen. XIV, 637B, ch. 40) claims that its name was due to the fact that its arms were made from palm-tree-wood (phoenix = palm-tree).

Note: The word phoenikion is a dimin. of phoenix, and lyrophoenikion of lyrophoenix.

Lysandrus, Lysander, of Sicyon (Λύσανδρος ὁ Σικυώνιος; m. pr. Lí-sandros Sikiónios); ? 6th cent. B.C. musician and kitharist, from Sicyon.

Philochorus in the third book of his "History of Attica" (ap. Athen. XIV, 637F-638A, ch. 42; FHG I, p. 395, fr. 66) attributes to Lysandrus many innovations; "Lysandrus of Sicyon, he says, was the first kitharist to institute the art of solo kithara playing (the 'psilokitharistike'; introduced first, accord-ing to Menaechmus, by Aristonicus*) by tuning his strings high and augment-ing the volume of the tone; he also used the 'enaulos kitharisis*' (i.e. kithara playing to aulos accompaniment) which Epigonus' School first adopted. And by abolishing the simplicity prevailing among the kithara soloists, he was the first to play on the kithara richly chromatic compositions («χρώματά τε εὔ-χροα»), as also iambuses* and the magadis which is called syrigmos*".

See FHG I, p. 395.

lysiodos (λυσιῳδός; m. pr. lisiodós); a pantomime and singer who in a theatrical performance, dressed in male costume, imitated female characters.

Some writers confused the lysiodos with the magodos*, but Aristoxenus (ap. Athen. XIV, 620F, ch. 13) distinguishes them as follows: "the actor who imitated male and female characters is called magodós, while he who in male dress imitated female characters is called *lysiodos*".

Lysiodos as an Adj. signified that which was connected with the songs of the lysiodos; *lysiodoi auloi* (λυσιῳδοὶ αὐλοί) = auloi accompanying (or play-ing) these songs.

M

magadion (μαγάδιον);
See *magas*.

magadis (μάγαδις);

a) a stringed instrument widely known in ancient Greece.

Its form was triangular, the number of its strings twenty and it was played by both hands without the aid of plectrum; thus it belonged to the so-called "psaltika" instruments (played by bare fingers). Its main characteristic was that its strings were tuned in pairs, each one with its octave (ten double strings); this allowed playing in octaves which was termed "magadizein" («μαγαδίζειν»; cf. *antiphthongos*).

Its name was derived by some writers from magas, the bridge of stringed instruments; this would mean perhaps that the magas filled some particular role in the playing. The historian Douris derived the name magadis from a certain Magdis from Thrace (ap. Athen. XIV, 636F, ch. 40). Its tone quality, according to Telestes, who speaks of a five-stringed magadis, was horn-like (κερατόφωνος). The origin of the *magadis*, according to Anacreon, was Lydian («ἡ γὰρ μάγαδις ὄργανόν ἐστι ψαλτικόν, ὡς ᾿Ανακρέων φησὶ, Λυδῶν τε εὕρημα»; "for the magadis, as Anacreon says, is a "psaltikon" instrument, and an invention of the Lydians"). Pollux (IV, 61), on the other hand, says that according to Kantharus the magadis was an invention of the Thracians. What is certain is that it was an ancient instrument, mentioned already by the lyric poet Alcman in the 7th cent. B.C.; it was in current use in Lesbos at the time of Anacreon (6th cent. B.C.); cf. Euphorion ap. Athen. ibid, 635A ch. 36). The magadis was held in great honour especially by Anacreon, and to its accompaniment he used to sing his love-songs; Athenaeus (ibid) preserved the following verse by Anacreon; «ψάλλω δ᾽ εἴκοσι χορδαῖσι μάγαδιν ἔχων, ὦ Λεύκασπι»; "I play on a twenty-stringed magadis, O Leucaspis" (see *Anacreon* and *psallein*).

The *magadis* was one of the so-called polychord (many-stringed) instruments, such as pektis, sambyke and phoenix, condemned by Plato (Repub. III, 399D) and by Aristoxenus who called them "foreign instruments".

b) magadis was also a Lydian aulos ("Lydian magadis aulos" according to Ion of Chios). Anaxandrides (ap. Athen. IV, 182D, ch. 80) suggests that the magadis, also called "plagiomagadis" (cross-magadis) or palaeomagadis (old magadis), can produce a high and a low tone at the same time; this is repeated by Tryphon (ap. Athen. XIV, 634E, ch. 36).

Didymus and Hesychius speak of magadis as being a kitharisterios* aulos (accompanying the kithara); Hes. «μαγάδεις (pl.) αὐλοὶ κιθαριστήριοι· ὄργανον ψαλτικὸν» ("*magádeis* kitharisterioi auloi; also a psaltikon instrument"; see above a). These auloi would probably accompany also the stringed instrument magadis from which they derived their name; cf. Athen. ibid.

c) In Athenaeus (XIV, 638A, ch. 42) the word magadis is used also in the sense of syrigmos* ("harmonics"?).

Note: Much information regarding the magadis is to be found especially in Athen. XIV, 634C to 637A, between chapters 35 and 41. The discussion on magadis begins with the question of Aemilianus "what instrument is magadis, a kind of aulos or a kind of kithara?"

Bibliography:

Th. Reinach: DAGR, vol. III2 (VI) 1904, p. 1449, s.v. Lyra (Famille de la harpe, p. 1448 ff).

H. Abert: Pauly's RE, vol. XIII (XXVI) 1927, col. 2486, s.v. Lyra.

W. Vetter: "Magadis" in Pauly's RE, vol. XIV (XXVII) 1928, col. 288-291.

magas (μαγάς); the bridge of the lyra and the kithara; it was a narrow wooden board placed above the sound-box at a distance from the chordotonion*.

The magas was used to isolate the vibratory part of the strings, exactly as the modern bridge of stringed instruments.

Hes. «μαγάς· σανὶς τετράγωνος ὑπόκυφος δεχομένη τῆς κιθάρας τὰς νευρὰς καὶ ἀποτελοῦσα τὸν φθόγγον» ("*magas*, a wooden quadrangular board slightly curved which supports the strings and produces the note").

Its dimin. *magádion* (μαγάδιον) is also used; Lucian "Dialogues of Gods" (IV, 7, 4 "Dialogue of Apollo and Hephaestus [Vulcan]") «πήχεις γὰρ ἐναρμόσας καὶ μαγάδιον ὑποθεὶς» ("for [Hermes] having adopted [on the tortoise] arms and placed a *magadion* [a little bridge]...").

Hesychius on the word "magadion" writes "a charming kithara solo" («ὡραῖ- ον κιθάρισμα»); he evidently derives the word from the instrument magadis.

magodos, magodía (μαγῳδός, μαγῳδία);

magodos; a comic pantomimist who, accompanied by tambours (τύμπανα) and cymbals, imitated indecent and wicked characters, such as adulterers, procurers etc. Athen. (XIV, 621C, ch. 14) "the magodos, as he is called, has tambours (τύμπανα) and cymbals, and all his garments are feminine; he dances with indecent gestures, he does everything that is shameless, at one time acting the part of women as adulteresses or procuresses, at another, of a drunken man going to meet his sweetheart in a revel-rout".

magodia and *magode* (μαγῳδία, μαγῳδὴ) is the pantomimic performance of the magodos. The magodia took its name from the fact of using spells (charms) and exhibiting magical powers (Athen. ibid.).

makron (μακρόν); long. The name for the third of the seven parts of the *parábasis**. According to Pollux (IV, 112) "the *makron* is a short little melody in the parabasis sung without breathing [in one breath]" («τὸ δὲ ὀνομαζόμενον μακρὸν ἐπὶ τῇ παραβάσει, βραχὺ μελύδριόν ἐστιν ἀπνευστὶ ᾀδόμενον»).

maktrismos (μακτρισμός); a lustful dance danced by women with rotary motion of the belly. In Athenaeus (XIV, 629C, ch. 26) maktrismos is a later name of *apokinos**; in another paragraph however (629F) maktrismos and apokinos are mentioned separately in a list of ludicrous dances.

Pollux (IV, 101) uses the word *baktriasmos** for maktrismos.

malakos (μαλακός); soft. A term used in the Diatonic and the Chromatic genera to imply a certain "shade" in the formation of each genus. Opp. of tense (σύντονος). In the Soft Diatonic the tetrachord was composed (from low to high) of a semitone, 3/4 of tone and 5/4 of tone. In the Soft Chromatic the intervals used were (again from low to high) $\frac{1}{3}$ of tone, $\frac{1}{3}$ of tone and $1\frac{1}{2}$ tone plus $\frac{1}{3}$, i.e. in twelfths $\frac{4}{12} + \frac{4}{12} + \frac{22}{12}$.

The question of the Soft shade is discussed in some detail under *Diatonon* and *Chromatikon*.

As an Adj. the word *malakos* was used in the sense of music somewhat effeminate, or lacking in manly character.

Note: The vb malassein (μαλάσσειν, Attic μαλάττειν), to soften, in music signified to lower, to flatten, to relax; Plut. De Mus. 1145D, ch. 39 «μαλάττουσι γὰρ ἀεὶ τάς τε λιχανοὺς καὶ τὰς παρανήτας» = "because they always *flatten* (*lower*) the lichanoi and the paranetai".

maneros (μανερῶς); a funeral song in Egypt corresponding to *linos**. According to Pausanias (IX, ch. 29, § 6; cf. *Linus**) the origin of this lament or dirge was connected with the unhappy death of Linus. The name of the dirge came from *Maneros** (Μανερῶς), son of the first king of Egypt; Plut. "De Iside et Osiride" («Περὶ Ἴσιδος καὶ Ὀσίριδος», 357E, ch. 17) "... ὃν γὰρ ᾄδουσιν Αἰγύπτιοι παρὰ τὰ συμπόσια Μανερῶτα τοῦτον εἶναι..." ("for that which the Egyptians sing at banquets is the *maneros*"). Cf. *linos*, which was also sung not only at mourning but also at happy events.

manos, manotes (μανός, μανότης; m. pr. manós, manótis);

manos, loose, not dense, sparse; *manotes*, the quality or virtue of being manos; looseness, sparseness.

Manos oppos. of pycnos*, and manotes oppos. of pycnotes*. Ptolem. (Harm. I, ch. 3; Wall. III, p. 6; I. D. p. 7, 17) «Διὰ δὲ τὴν τῆς μανότητος ἢ πυκνότητος ... ποιότητα· καθ᾽ ἃς πάλιν ὁμωνύμως λέγομέν τινας ψόφους

197

πυκνοὺς ἢ χαύνους...» ("As to the quality of *looseness* or denseness ... according to which we again call some sounds homonymously dense or loose").

Cf. also Porph. Comment. (Wall. p. 225, I. D. p. 44,4).

Plato (Laws book VII, 812D) «καὶ δὴ καὶ πυκνότητα μανότητι καὶ τάχος βραδυτῆτι» etc. ("when there results a combination of denseness and *looseness* [of high and low notes], of rapidity and slowness" etc.).

See the beginning of that paragraph under *heterophonia*.

Marsyas (Μαρσύας; m. pr. Marsías); mythical shepherd and musician, son of Hyagnis*. He was one of the triad of Phrygian musicians, with Hyagnis and Olympus*, who introduced to Greece the aulos and the auletic art, and the Phrygian harmonia. According to a legend, preserved until classical times, Marsyas was even the inventor of the aulos; Plato called the aulos "Marsyas' instrument". According to another legend (Plut. "De Cohibenda ira", 456 B-D, chs. 6-7) Athena (Minerva) invented the aulos, but seeing in the reflection of the water that her face was deformed, she threw it away; the aulos fell in Phrygia and was found by Marsyas (cf. *aulos*). Pausanias (I, ch. 24, § 1) says that a statue of Athena shows the goddess striking Marsyas, the Silenus, for taking up the auloi that she wished to be thrown away; Paus. (X, ch. 30, § 9) also says that to Marsyas was attributed the invention of the *Metroa** (Μητρῷα), which the "Parion Chronikon"* attributes to Hyagnis.

The legend of the contest with Apollo is well-known (cf. Diod. Sikel. III, ch. 59, §§ 2-5); Marsyas and his aulos were defeated by Apollo and his kithara, Marsyas was hanged and had his skin stripped off by Apollo. This contest can be explained as a fight of the national art and tradition against foreign influence and intrusion; and Apollo, representing the national art, in fact its God protector, should win. But in spite of the "victory" foreign elements had to be accepted little by little and by selection, and to be assimilated into Greek art. The legend is completed however in a charming way: Apollo, repentant for what he did to Marsyas, destroyed "his kithara and the harmonia"; of this harmonia (Paus. ibid, § 6) the Muses found the mese (μέση), Linus the lichanos, Orpheus *and Thamyras* the hypate and parhypate respectively.

Another name for Marsyas was Masses (Μάσσης; Plut. De Mus. 1133F, ch. 7).

Melampous of Cephalonia (Μελάμπους ὁ Κεφαλλήν); 7th to 6th cent. B.C. kitharode from Cephalonia. He competed at the Pythian Games at Delphi in 586 B.C., and won the first prize for the kitharodike, while the victors for the aulodike and auletike were Echembrotus* and Sakadas* respectively (Paus. X, ch. 7, § 4).

Melanippides (Μελανιππίδης; m. pr. Melanippídis); b. c. 480 B.C.; d. c. 414 B.C. Composer of dithyrambs of repute from Melos (Μῆλος; hence Μήλιος, Melios). He was the grandson of another Melanippides, also a composer of dithyrambs ("Par. Chron." v. 47).

To Melanippides the younger are attributed, according to Suidas, many innovations in the melopoeia of the dithyrambs. Among his innovations the *anabole** was one of the most important; the dithyramb now became a free composition like the nomos, without strophes-antistrophes. As Aristotle says (Probl. XIX, 15) in the nomoi the tunes followed the action («καὶ τὰ μέλη τῇ μιμήσει ἠκολούθει») and "for the same reason the dithyrambs, having become imitative, no longer have antistrophes, as they did before".

To Melanippides was attributed also the addition of the 12th string. Generally speaking Melanippides was one of the prominent figures of a group of innovators in the 5th cent. B.C., who following the example of Lasus* of Hermione, did not employ the range of the pre-existing music (cf. Plut. De Mus. 1141C, ch. 30).

In Pherecrates' comedy "Cheiron" Music, personified as a woman, protests to Justice and accuses Melanippides as the origin of all her misfortunes, who started her maltreatment by introducing the 12th string.

Melanippides, however, is praised by others as an important innovator of the art; Aristodemus, the philosopher, asked by Socrates whom he admired most for their ability, replied 'For epic poetry I most admired Homer, while for the dithyramb Melanippides" (Xen. "Memorabilia", I, ch. 4, § 3: «Ἐπὶ μὲν τοίνυν ἐπῶν ποιήσει Ὅμηρον ἔγωγε μάλιστα τεθαύμακα, ἐπὶ δὲ διθυράμβῳ Μελανιππίδην...»).

Melanippides, at the invitation of Perdiccas II, king of Macedonia (454-412 B.C.), passed the last part of his life in his court, where he died (Suidas); perhaps around 414-413 B.C.

Of his works only a few verses survived, principally from the dithyrambs Danaides, Persephone and Marsyas;

Cf. Brgk PLG III, pp. 589-92, and Anth. Lyr. pp. 286-7, especially nos 1-3. Also Page PMG pp. 392-396, Frgs 757-766.

meleazein (μελεάζειν; m. pr. meleázin); to speak or read with a certain musical undulation of the voice. This term is used by Nicomachus in the Enchiridion (ch. 2; C.v.J. p. 239; Mb p. 4), and may be interpreted as meaning something between speaking and singing, like the "recitativo parlando". In this respect meleazein is distinctly different from the "logodes* melos" of Aristoxenus.

meligerys (μελίγηρυς; m. pr. melígiris) from meli (μέλι) honey, and gerys (γῆρυς), voice, sound; sweet-singing or sounding; very melodious.

Plut. "De Pythiae oraculis", 405F: «μελιγήρεας ὕμνους» (pl.); "*very melodious* hymns".

melisma (μέλισμα); melos, song.

melisma of lyra or kithara (μέλισμα λύρας or κιθάρας); a melody of lyra or kithara.

The dimin. *melismátion* (μελισμάτιον) is also met with; a little tune, a short melody.

Another word for melisma is *melismós* (song). But *melismos* (cf. M. Bryen. and Anon. Bell.; see under *kompismos-melismos*) was the repetition of the same note in vocal music.

The verb *melizein* («μελίζειν») was used in the sense: to sing, to perform a melos; LSJ "to make musical"; Sextus Empir. VI, 16 «ταύτην δὲ [ποιητικὴν] φαίνεται κοσμεῖν ἡ μουσικὴ μελίζουσα» ("and music appears to adorn it [i.e. the poetry] by making it melodious, musical"). Also in Med. *melizesthai* (μελίζεσθαι); Plato, the Comic (ap. Th. Kock. Comic. Att. Fr., vol. I, p. 620, Fr. 69);

See the text under *Karikon melos*.

melodema (μελῴδημα; m. pr. melódima); song, melody, melos. From melodein (μελῳδεῖν), to set to music, to sing, to perform a song.

melodós (μελῳδός); the singer, the performer of songs or mele. The word is often used in the sense of melopoeós = the composer, the lyric poet. Melodos as an adj. signified "musical", "melodious". Pollux (IV, 64) «Ἀριστοφάνης δέ, μελῳδὸς καὶ προσῳδὸς εἴρηκε» ("and Aristophanes said, 'melodos and prosodos' ";* cf. Kock Com. Att. Fr., vol. I, pp. 580 and 583, Frgs 818 and 844).

The expression «τὰ μελῳδούμενα» (pl. of «τὸ μελῳδούμενον» neut.) signified melodic; everything sung, and by extension everything performed in music.

melodia (μελῳδία); song, melody; also the act of singing. Plato Laws (935E); «ποιητῇ ... μελῳδίας». Aristox. (Harm. El. I, p. 27, 18-20 Mb): «Φαίνεται δὲ τοιαύτη τις φύσις εἶναι τοῦ συνεχοῦς ἐν τῇ μελῳδίᾳ οἷα καὶ ἐν τῇ λέξει περὶ τὴν γραμμάτων σύνθεσιν» ("It seems that continuity *in melody* corresponds in its nature to that [continuity] in speech [as it is observed] in the collocation of the letters").

In a more general sense melodia meant "music".

The term «μελῳδίας τάξις» (*melodic order*; the order of the sounds in the melody itself) is used by Aristoxenus (ibid, II, p. 38, 12-13 Mb).

melodikós (μελῳδικός); melodic; musical; *melodike kinesis* = musical motion of the voice (cf. *kinesis*).

200

melodos (μελῳδός);

See above, under *melodema*.

melographia (μελογραφία); (L.S.J.) song-writing; and *melopoeia* (Dem.). Also noting down a melos.

melographos (μελογράφος) = *melopoeos**; composer of songs.

Cf. *H. I. Marrou:* "Melographia" AC, 15, 1946; p. 289 ff.

melopoeein, vb (μελοποιεῖν; m. pr. melopiín); to compose mele (music); to set poems to music; to write lyric poems; to express through melody or song.

Plut. de Mus. (1134A, ch. 8) «ἐν ἀρχῇ γὰρ ἐλεγεῖα μεμελοποιημένα οἱ αὐλῳδοὶ ᾖδον· τοῦτο δὲ δηλοῖ ἡ τῶν Παναθηναίων γραφὴ ἡ περὶ τοῦ μουσικοῦ ἀγῶνος» ("at the beginning the aulodes used to sing elegeia set to music (to melos); as is shown in the Register (Record) of the Musical Contest, at the Panathenaean Games"). *Melopoeos* (μελοποιός); the composer of mele (of music); tune-maker; lyric poet.

melopoeia (μελοποιΐα; m. pr. melopiía); in a general sense, melodic composition.

Aristides (Mb p. 28; RPW-I, p. 28) defines melopoeia as "the faculty which creates the melody" («μελοποιΐα δέ ἐστι δύναμις κατασκευαστικὴ μέλους»).

According to Cleonides too (Isagoge; ch. 14, C.v.J. pp. 206-7; Mb p. 22) the purpose of melopoeia is to choose and use in a proper way the elements of the Harmonike* (the parts of the Harmonike are the seven following: the notes, the intervals, the genera, the systems, the tones, the modulation, the melopoeia itself). This can be attained in four ways: the *agoge** (ἀγωγή), the *ploke** (πλοκή), the *petteia** (πεττεία) and the *tone** (τονή), explained separately under their headings. The parts of the melopoeia are, according to Aristides (Ibid, p. 29 Mb and RPW-I), the three following:

1) the *lepsis** (λῆψις), "by which the composer ("the mousikos") chooses the region of the voice to be used in the system";

2) the *mixis** (μίξις; *mixing*) by which he adjusts and binds together the sounds, the regions of the voice, the genera of the melody, or the systems, and

3) the *chresis** (χρῆσις; *application*) which is the completion of the melody. Aristides (ibid, p. 30) defines three generic modes (styles) of the melopoeia: the dithyrambic, the nomic and the tragic («τρόποι δὲ μελοποιΐας γένει μὲν τρεῖς· διθυραμβικός, νομικός, τραγικός»). The various melopoeiai differ between themselves, always according to Aristides,

a) as *to genus* («γένει»), as Enharmonic, Chromatic, Diatonic;

b) as *to system* («συστήματι»), as hypatoeides, mesoeides, netoeides;

c) as *to tonos* («τόνῳ»), as Dorian, Phrygian;

d) as *to mode, style* («τρόπῳ»), as nomic, dithyrambic, tragic;

e) as *to ethos* («ἤθει»), "as we say, the systaltic, by which we express painful feelings, the diasta[l]tic [exalting] by which we incite to uplifting feelings, and the medium, by which we lead the soul to calmness".

Cf. Cleonides Ibid, ch. 13, C.V.J. p. 206; Mb. p. 21.

melos (μέλος); originally limb, member, part. In music song; tune; choral or lyric song; melody generally. In vocal music it was composed of three elements: the sounds (notes), the rhythm and the words.

Anon. Bell. (p. 46, § 29) calls *perfect melos* "that which is composed of words, melody and rhythm" («τέλειον δὲ μέλος ἐστὶ τὸ συγκείμενον ἔκ τε λέξεως καὶ μέλους καὶ ρυθμοῦ»). The use by Anon. of the word "melos" in the place of "phthongos" (or "harmonia") is characteristic, and shows the use of the term "melos" in the sense of alternation of sounds. Plato (Rep. III, 398D) defines the constituent parts or elements of melos as follows: "the melos has three elements, the words, the melody and the rhythm" («λόγος, ἁρμονία, ρυθμός»). Bacchius (Isag. § 78; C.v.J. p. 309, Mb p. 19) defines melos as "that which is composed of sounds (notes) and intervals and durations" («τὸ ἐκ φθόγγων καὶ διαστημάτων καὶ χρόνων συγκείμενον»). Thus, the *melos* (alternation of sounds and intervals together with times [durations] is also a synonym of melody in the general sense. This applies especially in instrumental music where there are no words; Sopatrus (ap. Athen. IV, 176A, ch. 78) says «καὶ τὸ μόναυλον μέλος ἤχησε» ("and he sounded *the tune* from a single-piped aulos").

Musical melos (mousikon melos; μουσικὸν μέλος) signified the vocal melos in contradistinction to "organikon melos" (instrumental melos).

See also *hermosmenon melos,* and *logodes melos.*

melourgein, v. (μελουργεῖν; m. pr. melourgín); to compose melos (music). Synonym of melopoeein*.

melourgema (μελούργημα; m. pr. meloúrgima); song, melody; Synonym of melodema*. Also *melourgia* (μελουργία), which is more modern.

melourgós (μελουργός); composer of mele; melopoeos*.

melpein vb. (μέλπειν; m. pr. mélpin); to sing; to praise with song and dance; to celebrate with song.

Hes. «μέλπει· ᾄδει, ὑμνεῖ» ("*melpei*; sings, praises with song"). Philochorus (ap. Athen. XIV, 628A, ch. 24) says that the ancients "when they

202

pour libations, are *celebrating* («μέλποντες») Dionysus with wine and drunkenness, but Apollo with quietness and order" («ὅταν σπένδωσι τὸν μὲν Διόνυσον ἐν οἴνῳ καὶ μέθῃ, τὸν δ᾽ Ἀπόλλωνα μεθ᾽ ἡσυχίας καὶ τάξεως μέλποντες»).

Med. *melpesthai* (μέλπεσθαι; m. pr. mélpesthe); to be entertained; to sing to the lyra or the kithara; Hom. Odys. IV, 17 «μετὰ δέ σφιν ἐμέλπετο θεῖος ἀοιδός, φορμίζων» ("and among them a divine minstrel was singing to the phorminx").

Melpodós (μελπῳδός); singer; he who praises by singing (Hes. «μελπῴδιοι»).

melydrion (μελύδριον; m. pr. melídrion); dim. of melos. A little tune, song, or ode.

menes (μῆνες; m. pr. mínes); a kind of dance mentioned by Pollux (IV, 104) as having taken its name from its inventor, a combatant or athlete (Men; Μήν); «ἐπώνυμον δ᾽ ἦν τοῦ εὑρόντος ἀθλητοῦ». The word is not found elsewhere.

meniambos (μηνίαμβος; m. pr. miníamvos), usually in plural, meniamboi; a kitharisterios* nomos (a solo for kithara to aulos accompaniment).

Pollux (IV, 83) «καὶ μηνίαμβοί τε καὶ παριαμβίδες, νόμοι κιθαριστήριοι, οἷς προσηύλουν» ("and the *meniamboi* and pariambides* [were] nomoi for kithara solo with aulos accompaniment").

Cf. *pariambides* and *enaulos kitharisis.*

mese (μέση; m. pr. mési); the middle or central note of the heptachord system; also the corresponding string of the lyra or of the kithara:

In the octachord system the mese was the first note of the second (lower) tetrachord, or the top note of the first tetrachord taken upwards;

The tetrachord beginning (downwards) with the mese (a - g - f - e) or leading upwards to the mese (e - f - g - a) was called tetrachord meson. The mese retained its name also in the Perfect Systems in which it was not always the central note.

In the "Harmonia of the Spheres"* mese was the one which corresponded to the Sun (Helios).

mesoeides (μεσοειδής; m. pr. mesoidís) topos, locus; the medium region of the voice; the region of the mese. Aristides (De Mus. p. 30 Mb & RPW-I) says that of the three generic modes (styles of the melopoeia) the dithyrambic is mesoeides;

> Cf. *melopoeia*.

mesokopos, aulos (μεσόκοπος, αὐλός); aulos of a medium size. Alkeides (ap. Athen. 176F, ch. 79) speaking to Ulpianus says that the Alexandrians know, among other kinds of aulos, the "middle-sized auloi" («ἔτι τε μεσοκόπους»).

Mesomedes (Μεσομήδης; m. pr. Mesomídis); 2nd cent. A. D. Cretan lyric poet and composer. He lived during the reign of Emperor Hadrianus (117-138 A.D.) who held him in friendly favour. Suidas in a short biographical note says that Mesomedes wrote an Encomium to Antinoos, and also various other mele.

Mesomedes' name has been mentioned by several scholars in connection with the composition of the three Hymns (to the Muse Calliope, to Helios and to Nemesis) published first in V. Galilei's "Dialogo della Musica antica e della moderna" (Florence, 1581, p. 97). To Mesomedes is unquestionably attributed the composition of the Hymn to Nemesis, and by some as probably also that of the Hymn to Helios. For some scholars he was the composer of all three; among them Th. Reinach who in his "Conférence sur la musique grecque et l'hymne à Apollon [i.e. to Helios]" (Paris, 1894) supports this view indirectly (p. 8): "Ces hymnes (all three) conservés par plusieurs manuscrits sont attribués à deux compositeurs, Denys, dont l'existence est aujourd'hui contestée, et Mesomède, qui jouissait d'une assez grande célébrité".

In his book "La mus. gr." pp. 196, 199, Reinach attributes only the last two to Mesomedes.

See the article *"Remains of Greek music"* (Nos 8-10) where the question of the authorship of the three Hymns is discussed in some detail.

Also *W. Vetter's* art. in Pauly's R. E. vol. 29, col. 1103.

> *Konstantin Horna*: Die Hymnen des Mesomedes (Wien u. Leipzig, 1928; Akad. der Wissenschaften in Wien, Band 207, Abh. 1; 8°, pp. 40).
> *Guido Martelotti*: Mesomede (Roma, 1929; Scuola di Filologia Classica dell' Università di Roma; 8°, pp. 47).

mesopycnoi, pl. (μεσόπυκνοι; m. pr. mesópicni); the middle notes of the pycnon*. The mesopycnoi were five, the two parhypatai (hypaton and meson), and the three tritai (diezeugmenon, synemmenon and hyperbolaeon). The mesopycnoi being in the middle of the pycnon are included in the "movable" (κινούμενοι) notes of the tetrachord.

Cf. Aristides De Mus. (Mb p. 12, RPW-I, p. 9); also *barypycnos**, *oxypycnos**, *hestotes** and *mesos**.

mesos (μέσος); middle, intermediate. *Mesoi* (pl., μέσοι) were the notes (or strings) found between the two extremes of a tetrachord or system.

The intermediary notes of the tetrachord were movable (κινούμενοι; i.e. changing);

Cf. *hestotes**.

metabole (μεταβολή; m. pr. metavolí); modulation. The sixth part of the *Harmonike**. Metabole was the change made during the course of a melody as to the genus, the system, the tonos, the ethos etc.

Cleonides (Isag. ch. 1; C.v.J. p. 180; Mb p. 2) gives the following definition: "*metabole* is the transposition from a similar to a dissimilar locus [region]" («μεταβολὴ δὲ ἐστιν ὁμοίου τινὸς εἰς ἀνόμοιον τόπον μετάθεσις»).

Arist. Quint. (De Mus. p. 24 Mb; p. 22 RPW-I) defines the metabole as "the change of the existing system and of the character of the voice" («ἀλλοίωσις τοῦ ὑποκειμένου συστήματος καὶ τοῦ τῆς φωνῆς χαρακτῆρος»).

Bacchius (Isag. §§ 50-57; C.v.J. pp. 304-305; Mb. pp. 13-14) enumerates seven species of metabole, and analyses them as follows:

1) *systematike* («συστηματική»), "when from the existing system the melody moves to another system, by establishing another mese";

2) *genike* («γενική»; as to genus), "when a change is made from one genus to another, as from Enharmonic to Chromatic";

3) *as to the mode* («κατὰ τρόπον»), "when a change is made from Lydian to Phrygian or to any of the others";

4) *as to the ethos* («κατὰ ἦθος»), "when it changes from humble (ethos) to majestic, or from quiet and thoughtful to stimulating";

5) *as to the rhythm* («κατὰ ρυθμόν»), "when from a choreios it changes to a dactyl or any other (i.e. foot)";

6) *as to the rhythmical progression*, agoge («κατὰ ρυθμοῦ ἀγωγήν»), "when the rhythm instead of beginning with arsis changes to thesis";

7) *as to position* [arrangement] *of the rhythmopoeia* («κατὰ ρυθμοποιίας θέσιν»), "when the whole rhythm goes by 'monopody' (by single feet) or by 'dipody' ('syzygy')".

Anon. Bell. (pp. 31-32, § 27) recognizes four kinds of metabole of tones, as to genus, ethos, region and rhythm. Cleonides (ibid C.v.J. pp. 204-6;

Mb pp. 20-21) also recognizes four ways of metabole but not exactly the same; as to genus, system, tonos and melopoeia. According to him the metabole as to the *system* is made when a change is made from a conjunction to disjunction or vice-versa (e.g. a change from the Lesser to the Greater Perfect System or vice-versa). As to *the tonos*, when from the Dorian tonos a change is made to the Phrygian or generally from any one of the thirteen tonoi a change is made to one of the rest. Metabole in *melopoeia* is made when from the diastaltic [ethos] it changes to the systaltic or hesychastic.

Modulation was unknown to primitive art; in the kitharodic nomoi no change was allowed. Plutarch (De Mus. 1133B-C, ch. 6) says that "the kitharodia of Terpander's style was completely simple until the time of Phrynis (5th cent. B.C.); for at that early time it was not permitted to compose the kitharodiai as nowadays, nor to change the harmoniai and the rhythms at pleasure. Because in each nomos they retained the proper diapason; for this reason they were called nomoi [laws]".

The tripartite nomos (cf. *trimeres or trimeles*) composed around the beginning or the middle of the 6th cent. B.C. by Sakadas* is an early example of modulation. From Lasus* of Hermione (b. c. 548 B.C.) onwards, modulation became little by little more frequent.

See: *W. Vetter*: Metabole; art. in Pauly's R. E., vol. 30, cols. 1313-1316.

metabolos (μετάβολος; m. pr. metávolos); modulating.

metabolon systema (μετάβολον σύστημα); modulating system as opposed to "haploun" (simple, non-modulating) system.

Cf. *haploun** and *metabole**.

metakatatropa (μετακατατροπά); the fourth part of the kitharodic nomos.

Cf. *kitharodikos** nomos.

metarcha (μεταρχά); the second part of the kitharodic nomos.

Cf. *kitharodikos** nomos.

Metellus of Agrigente (Μέτελλος ὁ Ἀκραγαντῖνος; m. pr. Métellos Akragantínos); a musician of the 5th cent. B.C. cited by Aristoxenus (ap. Plut. De Mus. 1136F, ch. 17) as one of Plato's teachers in music. His name is also mentioned in Plut. Praecepta Gerendae Reip. (Πολιτικὰ Παραγγέλματα) 806D. The names Μέγυλλος or Μέγιλλος or Μέταλλος appear in various editions of De Musica.

metharmoge (μεθαρμογή; m. pr. metharmogí); re-tuning; change of tuning. Ptolem. Harm. (II, ch. 8; ed. I. D. p. 58, 29): «ἐν ταῖς μεθαρμογαῖς (pl.), ὅταν τὸν τῷ διὰ πασῶν ὀξύτερον ἢ βαρύτερον θελήσωμεν μεταβαλεῖν» ("in *the changes of tuning*, i.e. when we want to substitute a higher or lower diapason"); cf. also II, ch. 11, ed. I. D. p. 65, 16 «ἐν ταῖς τῶν τόνων μεθαρμο-γαῖς» ("in the re-tunings of the tonoi").

metrike (μετρική; m. pr. metrikí); metrical science; the science of metre, to be distinguished from rhythmike, the scope of which is more general and larger.

Cf. *metron** and *rhythmopoeia**.

metroa, pl. (μητρῷα; m. pr. mitróa), so-called the songs sung in honour of the great goddess Cybele. These songs had a very old tradition leading far back into mythology; their origin was connected with the Phrygian nomoi invented by Hyagnis*, Marsyas* and Olympus*.

Plutarch (De Mus. 1141B, ch. 29) says that to Olympus (the elder) was attributed, among other things, the invention of the choreios (= metrical foot consisting of three short syllables) largely used in the metroa mele.

b) *metroon aulema*, (μητρῷον αὔλημα; neut. sing.); an aulos-solo in honour of Cybele. There have been different legends as to its invention. In "Parion Chronikon" (v. 10) it is said that Hyagnis first played on the aulos also "other nomoi of the Mother (Cybele) [Metroa]". Pausanias (X, ch. 30, § 9) says that "as it is believed the *Metroon aulema* was an invention of Mar-syas*" («ἐθέλουσι δὲ καὶ εὕρημα εἶναι τοῦ Μαρσύα τὸ Μητρῷον αὔλημα»). Douris (ap. Athen. XIV, 618C, ch. 9) reports that "a certain Seirites (Σειρίτης), a Libyan of the Numidian tribe, was the first to play *the metroa* on the aulos".

c) *Metroon* (Μητρῷον; m. pr. mitróon); the temple of Cybele. And *Metroa* (μητρῷα; in pl.); the mysteries; the celebration; the worship of Cybele. Cf. Plut. "De Pyth. Orac." 407C.

Note: The word «μητρῷος» (metroos) is derived from «μήτηρ» (meter; mother) and meant principally "of a mother", motherly.

metron (μέτρον); measure.

a) According to Aristides (De Mus., Mb p. 49; RPW-I p. 45) metron is a system of feet composed of dissimilar syllables in a symmetrical length. It differs from rhythm in being part, or the constituent parts, of the whole. He derives the word "metron" from the verb "meirein"; «μείρειν» (μείρομαι) which means, as he says, "to divide"; he considers nine metres as "simple", namely the dactylic, anapaestic, iambic, trochaic, choriambic, antispastic, two Ionian, and paeonic. Cf. *pous**. Metres having their last foot complete are called *acatalectic* (ἀκατάληκτα, or ὁλόκληρα, complete); those which have their last foot incomplete are called *catalectic* (καταληκικά). In the second case the missing syllable is replaced by a *leimma** (Λ; see *parasemantike**).

b) The term "metron" is also met in the meaning of a quantum, a measure of intervals taken as a unit; Aristox. Harm. (II, p. 50, 31 Mb) «τὸ δὲ λοιπὸν [τοῦ πυκνοῦ] δύο *μέτροις* μετρεῖται» ("while the pycnon's complement is expressed in terms of two *quanta*"; transl. H.S.M. p. 203).

c) In orchestics each step was called a "metron", a movement of the dancer made according to the rhythm of the music.

Bibl. *R. Westphal:* Scriptores Metrici Graeci (vol. I, Leipzig, 1866): Ἡφαιστίωνος: «Ἐγχειρίδιον περὶ μέτρων» pp. 3-77; Λογγίνου τοῦ Φιλοσόφου: «Προλεγόμενα εἰς τὸ τοῦ Ἡφαιστίωνος Ἐγχειρίδιον», pp. 81-94 and Schol. pp. 95-226.

Wilamowitz-Möllendorf, "Griechische Verskunst", Berlin 1921.

W. I. W. Koster, "Traité de métrique grecque", 3rd impression, Leyden 1962.

Paul Maas, "Greek Metre", transl. by Hugh Lloyd-Jones, Oxford, 1962.

Amy M. Dale, "The Lyric Metres of Greek Drama" 2, Cambridge 1968.

Midas (Μίδας); 6th to 5th cent. B.C. aulete of repute from Akragas. He competed and won the first prize in aulos-playing at the 24th and 25th Pythian Games; also at the Panathenaea. Pindar wrote for him his 12th Pythian Ode («Μίδᾳ αὐλητῇ Ἀκραγαντίνῳ»). There is a story that a rare accident befell his mouthpiece at a competition. It is said that, while playing, his mouthpiece slipped out and stuck on his palate. Midas continued to play in the manner of a syrinx. The public, surprised by the tone, was delighted, and Midas won the prize. Cf. A. R. Drachmann: Schol. Vet. in Pind. Carm., vol. II pp. 263-4.

miktos (μικτός); mixed.

a) *miktón systema*, neut; (mixed system); the system in which both the tetrachords of synemmenon and diezeugmenon are mixed. Aristox. Harm. (I, p. 17, 26 Mb): "every system of a certain compass becomes either conjunct or disjunct or *combines both of them*" («πᾶν γὰρ σύστημα, ἀπό τινος μεγέθους ἀρξάμενον, ἢ συνημμένον ἢ διεζευγμένον ἢ μικτὸν ἐξ ἀμφοτέρων γίγνεται»).

b) *miktón melos* (mixed melos); the melos in which two or three genera were mixed. It was also called "common" («κοινόν») to these genera; Aristox. Harm. (II, p. 44, 26 Mb) "every melos [tune, melody] should be either Diatonic or Chromatic or Enharmonic, or *mixed* of these [genera] or *common* to them" («πᾶν μέλος ἔσται, ἤτοι διάτονον, ἢ χρωματικὸν ἢ ἐναρμόνιον, ἢ μικτὸν ἐκ τούτων ἢ κοινὸν τούτων». Cf. Cleonides Isag. (ch. 6, C.v.J. p. 189; Mb p. 10).

mimaulos (μίμαυλος; m. pr. mímavlos); a mime accompanied on the aulos; cf. Athen. X, 452F («Κλέων ὁ μίμαυλος»). From mimos (mime) and aulos; *mimaulein*, vb (μιμαυλεῖν) "to be a mimaulos" (Hes. «εἰμὶ μίμαυλος»).

mimetike (μιμητική; m. pr. mimitikí); imitative; the art of imitating. According to Pollux (IV, 104) it was a kind of dancing in which the dancers imitated "those who were caught stealing".

208

Mimnermus (Μίμνερμος; m. pr. Mímnermos); b. c. 629 B.C. at Colophon or Smyrna in Asia Minor.   Elegiac poet and musician, known as a distinguished aulete.

According to the iambic poet Hipponax (ap. Plut. De Mus. 1133F, ch. 8) Mimnermus was the performer of the auletic nomos called Kradias*, a rather doubtful fact.

Mimnermus was surnamed Ligyastades (Λιγυαστάδης) for his "emmelés" (melodiousness) and sweetness (λιγύ).

He was a contemporary and close friend of the Athenian legislator Solon, one of the seven wise men of ancient Greece. Solon was the first to introduce the teaching of music into education in Athens at the beginning of the 6th cent. B.C.

Mimnermus was the creator of the erotic elegy, a charming singer of the joys of youth; his style became famous for its sweetness and melancholic character.

Cf. Brgk PLG II, pp. 25-33; Anth. Lyr., pp. 30-34.

minyrismos (μινυρισμός; m. pr. minirismós); singing (or crying) in an undertone. *minyrisma* (μινύρισμα; minírisma); whimpering; also quiet, sweet tune.   Sextus Emp. (VI, § 32) «νήπια γοῦν ἐμμελοῦς μινυρίσματος κατακούοντα κοιμίζεται» ("infants, certainly, are lulled to sleep by listening to a sweet, gentle tune"). *minyros* (μινυρός; minirós); complaining or lamenting (or singing) in an undertone (cf. *Lamprus**).

minyrizein vb (μινυρίζειν; m.pr. minirízin); to sing "sotto voce", in an undertone; to hum a song; also to sing in a plaintive way.

anaminyrizein (ἀναμινυρίζειν); to sing again in an undertone; Athen. (IV 176B, ch. 78) «τῷ τε ἡδεῖ μοναύλῳ τὰς ἡδίστας ἁρμονίας ἀναμινυρίζει» ("and to the sweet single-piped aulos he *hums again* the sweetest harmoniai").

mitos (μίτος); thread of the warp, also string of the lyra (LSJ, Dem.). Philostrati Minoris Imagines (Leipzig, T., 1902; 6, "Orpheus"): «ἡ λαιὰ δὲ ὀρθοῖς πλήττει τοῖς δακτύλοις τοὺς μίτους» ("while the left hand strikes *the strings* with straight fingers").

mixis (μίξις); mixing; one of the three parts of the melopoeia.
Cf. Aristides (De Mus., Mb p. 29; RPW-I p. 29) and *melopoeia**.

Mixolydios harmonia, or **Mixolydisti** (μιξολύδιος ἁρμονία or μιξολυδιστί; m. pr. mixolídios, mixolidistí); generally accepted as the b-b octave series (diapason, octachord)

$$b - a - g - f - e - d - c - b \quad \text{(in the Diatonic)}$$
$$1 \;\; 1 \;\; 1 \;\; \tfrac{1}{2} \;\; 1 \;\; 1 \;\; \tfrac{1}{2}$$

Plutarch (De Mus. 1136C-D, ch. 16) writes that "the Mixolydian thanks to its pathetic (emotional) character is suitable for tragedy". According to Aristoxenus (ap. Plut. ibid) Sappho was its inventor, and it was from her that the tragedians learned to use it, by combining it with the Doristi which expresses the majestic and the dignified.

Lamprocles* established that the Mixolydian as introduced by Pythocleides* and adopted by the tragedians was the b-b octave, while that of Sappho was the g-g octave.

molossike (μολοσσική; m. pr. molossikí); a kind of dance mentioned in Athen. (XIV, 629D, ch. 27) as one of the less animated and more varied, simpler dances.

molossos (μολοσσός); metrical foot consisting of three long syllables -' - - or - -' -. *Molossiambus* (μολοσσίαμβος), a foot consisting of a molossos and an iambus - - - υ -.

molpe (μολπή; m. pr. molpí) from melpein* = to sing, to praise with song; song, ode.   In Homeric language a song or ode often with dance; also a game with song («παίγνιον»).   Suidas «μολπή· ᾠδή· παρὰ Ὁμήρῳ δὲ τὸ παίγνιον» ("*molpe*; ode; and in Homer the game").

   Molpe (fig.) meant also "pleasant tone"; «μολπὴ σύριγγος» = molpe, i.e. pleasant tone, of syrinx.

   molpetis (μολπῆτις; molpítis); a woman singing and dancing at the same time.

   molpedon, adv. (μολπηδόν; molpidón); in the manner of a molpe; like a molpe.

   molpós (μολπός); Hes. "a singer, hymnode, poet" («ᾠδός, ὑμνῳδός, ποιητής»).   In pl. *molpoi* (μολποί; molpí) a group of singers; a guild of musicians at Miletus (LSJ), in Ionia (Dem.).   Also *molpikoi* (μολπικοί).

monaulia (μοναυλία; m. pr. monavlía); playing on the monaulos, and by extension a solo on any aulos.   Pollux (IV, 82) «γίγγλαρος ... μοναυλίᾳ πρόσφορος» ("ginglaros... suitable for *solo [aulos] playing*").

monaulion (μοναύλιον; m. pr. monávlion); dimin. of monaulos*; a kind of small aulos; a solo instrument (LSJ and Dem.).

   Poseidonius (ap. Athen. IV, 176C, ch. 78) «φωτίγγια καὶ μοναύλια (pl.), κώμων οὐ πολέμων ὄργανα» ("small photinges and *single-pipes*, implements of merry-making (revel), not of war").

   See *photinx**.

monaulon, neut. (μόναυλον; m. pr. mónavlon); a solo on the monaulos.

210

The word here is used as an adj., while the noun "monaulos" is the instrument. Sopatrus (ap. Athen. IV, 176A, ch. 78) «*μόναυλον μέλος*» ("solo from a single-piped aulos"). Cf. *melos**.

monaulos (μόναυλος; m. pr. mónavlos);

a) single aulos, a single-piped aulos. Iobas in his fourth book on the "History of the Theatre" (ap. Athen. IV, 175E, ch. 78) says that the Egyptians attributed the invention of the monaulos to Osiris. Pollux (IV, 75): "The monaulos is the invention of the Egyptians; it is recalled by Sophocles in Thamyris, and it even plays the nuptial song" («*Μόναυλος, εὔρημα μέν ἐστιν Αἰγυπτίων, μέμνηται δὲ αὐτοῦ Σοφοκλῆς ἐν Θάμυρι, αὐλεῖ δὲ μάλιστα τὸν γαμήλιον*»).

b) the player of a single aulos; Hedylus' Epigr. (ap. Athen. ibid) «*τοῦτο Θέων ὁ μόναυλος ὑπ᾽ ἠρίον ὁ γλυκὺς οἰκεῖ αὐλητὴς*» ("under this tomb rests Theon the sweet *player of the single-aulos*"). The monaulos was also called calamaules*.

See: *W. Vetter*: "Monaulos" in Pauly's R. E., vol. 31, cols. 74-75.
Th. Reinach: "Monaule" in DAGR, vol. IX, pp. 313-4; s.v. Tibia.

mone (μονή; m. pr. moní) from menein (μένειν), to stay; staying on one note (pitch); a certain persistence of the voice. Cleon. (Isag. § 14; C.v.J. p. 207; Mb p. 22): "tone (τονή) is the *mone* (staying on one degree) in more than one time at one utterance of the voice". Cf. Aristoxenus Harm. (Mb I, p. 12, 3: «[τάσις ἐστὶ] *μονή* τις καὶ στάσις τῆς φωνῆς»; "[tasis* is] a certain *persistence* and stationary position of the voice") and Aristides (Mb p. 8, RPW-I p. 6; same definition).

Bacchius (Isag. § 45; C.v.J. p. 302; Mb p. 12) defines that *mone* is made "when more words are sung on the same note" («ὅταν ἐπὶ τοῦ αὐτοῦ φθόγγου πλείονες λέξεις μελῳδῶνται»).

Cf. *petteia**.

mongas (μογγάς); a kind of passionate dance, mentioned in Athenaeus (XIV, 629D, ch. 27): «μανιώδεις δ᾽ εἰσὶν ὀρχήσεις κερνοφόρος καὶ *μογγὰς* καὶ θερμαστρὶς» ("passionate (or furious) dances are the kernophoros*, the *mongas* and the thermastris*").

monochordon (μονόχορδον); as its name implies, an instrument with one string. Some scholars place it in the lute family (Th. Rein. "La mus. gr.", p. 127), i.e. with a neck.

Generally speaking the monochord was used for the determination of the mathematical relations of musical sounds, i.e. it was a canon*, usually surnamed "the Pythagorean canon" because its invention was attributed to Pythagoras. Pollux (IV, 60) says that the monochord was an Arabic invention; in mythology it was Apollo's invention offered in the form of an arch to Diana (Censorinus).

Nicomachus (Enchir. ch. 4; C.v.J. p. 243, Mb p. 8) says that "the monochords are called by many people "phandouroi", while the Pythagoreans call them "canons";

Cf. *pandoura**.

Famous mathematicians, such as Archytas*, Eratosthenes* and Didymus* worked out the ratios on the monochord.

Cf. *canon** and *helicon**. See *S. Wantaloeben*: "Das Monochord", 1911.

monodia (μονῳδία); m. pr. monodía); solo singing, monody; also lament, threnody. Principally the song of one person but by ext. also a solo performance. Plato in Laws (VI, 764D-E) clearly gives the term a general meaning when he suggests that different judges should be set for the soloists (for those competing in "monody") "such as rhapsodes, kitharodes, auletes and all the like, and other judges for those competing in choral singing" («... μουσικῆς δὲ ἑτέρους μὲν τοὺς περὶ *μονῳδίαν* τε καὶ μιμητικήν, οἷον ραψῳδῶν καὶ κιθαρῳδῶν καὶ αὐλητῶν καὶ πάντων τῶν τοιούτων ἀθλοθέτας ἑτέρους πρέπον ἂν εἴη γίγνεσθαι, τῶν δὲ περὶ *χορῳδίαν* ἄλλους»).

monodion (μονῴδιον; m. pr. monódion); dim. of monodia.

morphasmos (μορφασμός); a kind of ludicrous dance in which the dancers imitated various animals. Pollux (IV, 103 "On kinds of dancing") says that "the *morphasmos* [was] an imitation of all sorts of animals" («ὁ δὲ *μορφασμὸς* παντοδαπῶν ζῴων μίμησις ἦν»).

In Athen. (XIV, 629F, ch. 27) *morphasmos* is included in a list of ludicrous (comic) dances.

mothon (μόθων);

a) a kind of indecent and licentious dance, with leaps of the feet kicking the breeches. Pollux (IV, 101) «ὁ δὲ *μόθων*, ὄρχημα φορτικὸν καὶ ναυτικὸν» ("and the *mothon* is an indecent and nautical dance").

b) a kind of aulos-melody. It is included in Tryphon's catalogue of auleseis (aulos-solos) in his second book of Denominations (ap. Athen. XIV, 618C, ch. 9).

Note: The word is met also in the plural: *móthones* (μόθωνες); Suid. "a kind of dance".

Mothon meant a man indecent, licentious, immoral and insolent; Suid: «ὁ φορτικὸς καὶ ἄτιμος καὶ εἶδος αἰσχρᾶς καὶ δουλοπρεποῦς ὀρχήσεως καὶ φορτικῆς» ("the indecent and dishonest man; also a kind of licentious, servile and indecent dance").

Mousa, Muse (Μοῦσα); deity of music, poetry, orchestics, drama and

212

generally protectress of arts and letters. In the Dorian dialect: *mósa* (μῶσα), as it was derived from the verb "mo" (μῶ), to ask for, to seek. Suid.: «Μοῦσα· ἡ γνῶσις· ἀπὸ τοῦ μῶ ζητῶ· ἐπειδὴ ἁπάσης παιδείας αὕτη τυγχάνει αἰτία» ("*Muse*; knowledge; from the verb mo, to ask for; as she is the cause of every culture"). Diod. Sikel. (IV, ch. 7, § 4) says that Mousai (pl.) were so called from «μυεῖν τοὺς ἀνθρώπους» ("to initiate the men": «τοῦτο δ᾽ ἐστὶν ἀπὸ τοῦ διδάσκειν τὰ καλὰ καὶ συμφέροντα καὶ ὑπὸ τῶν ἀπαιδεύτων ἀγνοούμενα» ("from teaching those things that are good and beneficial, and those which are not known to uneducated people").

In general use the word "mousa" is met also in the sense of music, song, or arts and culture in general.

mouseion (μουσεῖον; m. pr. mousíon) neut.; (Dem. and LSJ): temple or shrine of the Muses; home of music or poetry, generally a school of arts or letters (Athen. V, 187D «τὸ τῆς Ἑλλάδος μουσεῖον» [of Athens]). Metaphorically «ἀηδόνων μουσεῖα» (pl.) = *choir* of nightingales.

In pl. *Μουσεῖα* (*Mouseia*), festival of the Muses; usually in sing. *Μουσεῖον* as Temple (Athen. XIV, 629A, ch. 26: «᾽Αμφίων δὲ ὁ Θεσπιεὺς ἐν δευτέρῳ περὶ τοῦ ἐν Ἑλικῶνι Μουσείου ἄγεσθαί φησιν ἐν Ἑλικῶνι παίδων ὀρχήσεις μετὰ σπουδῆς» ("Amphion of Thespiai in his second book *On the Muses' Temple* on Helicon says that dances of boys are held in earnest [with zeal] on [mount] Helicon").

mouseios (μούσειος; m. pr. moúsios); adj., musical («μούσειος κέλαδος»; musical sound). Λίθος Μοισαῖος (Aeol. type); a monument of song (LSJ and Dem.).

mousike (μουσική; m. pr. mousikí).

The word «μουσικὴ» appears for the first time (in preserved texts so far) in the 5th cent. and in the following texts in chronological order:

a) *Pindar*, Olympian I, antistrophe A, vs 14-15 (PLG I, p. 15) «ἀγλαΐζεται δὲ καὶ μουσικᾶς ἐν ἀώτῳ» ("while he rejoiceth in the bloom *of music* [song]"); the first Olympian was written for Hieron of Syracuse (476 B.C.).

b) *Pindar*, Hymn (PLG I, p. 288; Fr. 9).

«... τοῦ θεοῦ ἄκουσε Κάδμος μουσικὰν (-ὴν) ὀρθὰν ἐπιδεικνυμένου» ("Kadmus heard the god (Apollo) displaying uplifting *music*");
Cf. Plut. De Pyth. orac., ch. 6, 397B.

c) *Herodotus*, Historiae (book VI, ch. 129) «οἱ μνηστῆρες ἔριν εἶχον ἀμφί τε μουσικῇ» ("the pretenders quarrelled about *music*");

d) *Thucydides*, Historiae (book III, ch. 104) «῞Οτι καὶ μουσικῆς ἀγὼν ἦν ...» ("That there took place a *music*-contest [in Delos] ....").

By "Mousike" ancient Greeks meant for a long period the whole of spiritual and intellectual faculties, and especially art (any art under the protection of the Muses), and more specifically lyric poetry, i.e. poetry with music. For those faculties concerned with the body they used the term «Γυμναστική» (Gymnastike). Plato (Rep. II, 376 D-E.) says: "that which is concerned with the body is Gymnastike, while that concerned with the soul is *Mousike*" («Ἔστι δέ που ἡ μὲν ἐπὶ σώματι γυμναστική, ἡ δ᾽ ἐπὶ ψυχῇ μουσική»).

The term "mousike" in the sense of music as we understand it now, as an independent art separated from poetry, was generally used in the 4th cent. B.C. Before this time no specific term for music was used; terms like "kroumata", "aulesis", "kitharisis" etc. are met with for instrumental music. Also instead of the term "mousikos"* (musician) we meet the terms "auletes" (αὐλητής), "kitharistes" (κιθαριστής) etc. During the 5th cent. B.C. the music evolved steadily as an independent art; the construction and the technique of both the aulos and the lyra-kithara were greatly improved (cf. *aulopoeia** and *lyra**). Important executants and innovators appeared in this century and the study of the theory of music had its scientific foundation.

The first to attempt a classification of the branches of musical education was probably Lasus of Hermione* in the 6th cent. B.C.; he divided music into three parts: the technical («ὑλικόν»), the "practical" («πρακτικὸν») and the "executive" («ἐξαγγελτικόν»), each of these three divided into three subdivisions (cf. Gev. I, pp. 69-70). Many others attempted a classification of all the branches of music, and a definition of music. Two of these definitions are as follows:

a) Aristides (De Mus. Mb 6; RPW-I p. 4): "Music is a science of melos and of all related to it" («Μουσικὴ ἐστὶν ἐπιστήμη μέλους καὶ τῶν περὶ μέλος συμβαινόντων»).

b) Anon. Bell. (§ 29, p. 46): "Music is a science, theoretical and practical, of the perfect [vocal] and of the instrumental melos" («Μουσικὴ ἐστιν ἐπιστήμη, θεωρητικὴ καὶ πρακτική, μέλους τελείου τε καὶ ὀργανικοῦ»). Alypius recognizes three principal sciences comprised in music: the Harmonike ('Αρμονική), the Rhythmike (Ρυθμικὴ) and the Metrike (Μετρική). (Isag. § 1; C.v.J. p. 367, Mb p. 1). The most comprehensive analysis so far has been that of Aristides (op. cit. Mb p. 8; RPW-I, p. 6).

According to this conception "music in its entirety" comprises two parts, a *theoretical* and a *practical*.

A) The *theoretical* part is divided into two sections; a) *the physical* (φυσικόν), and b) the *technical* (τεχνικόν). The physical contains 1) the *arithmetikon* (ἀριθμητικὸν and 2) the *physical*, while b) the technical is subdivided into 1) the *harmonikon* (ἁρμονικόν), 2) the *rhythmikon* (ρυθμικὸν) and 3) the *metrikon* (μετρικόν).

B) The *practical* part, called educational (παιδευτικὸν) also comprises two sections a) the *chrestikon* (χρηστικόν; the putting into order of the above elements, i.e. composition) and b) the *executive* (ἐξαγγελτικόν).

The *chrestikon* comprises 1) the *melopoeia*, 2) the *rhythmopoeia* and 3) the *poeesis* (ποίησις). The second section (called ἐξαγγελτικόν, executive) comprises 1) the *instrumental* (ὀργανικόν), 2) the *singing* (ᾠδικόν), and 3) the *dramatic acting* (ὑποκριτικόν).

As to the perception of music there were two principal schools of conception: a) the Pythagorean, and b) the Aristoxenean. According to the first, the perception and judgment of music should be made by the intellect, not by the sense of hearing (Plut. De Mus. 1144F, ch. 37 "Pythagoras the sage disapproved of the judgment of music by the senses [«διὰ τῆς αἰσθήσεως»]; the virtue of this art, he said, was to be perceived by the intellect [spirit]; he consequently did not judge it by the sense of hearing but by the proportional harmonia"; «τῇ ἀναλογικῇ ἁρμονίᾳ»).

Aristoxenus on the contrary (Harm. II, p. 33 Mb) supported a twofold scientific conception (or system); on one hand he relied on *the sense of hearing* as to the perception and judgment of pitch, intervals etc., and on the other hand on *the intellect* as to the discrimination of the functions of sounds («τῇ μὲν γὰρ ἀκοῇ κρίνομεν τὰ τῶν διαστημάτων μεγέθη, τῇ δὲ διανοίᾳ θεωροῦμεν τὰς τῶν φθόγγων δυνάμεις»).

General Bibliography

Fr. Aug. Gevaert: "Histoire et Théorie de la Musique de l'antiquité"; 2 vols, Ghent, 1875, 1881.
Ch. Ém. Ruelle: "Études sur l'ancienne musique grecque" (Rapports littéraires); 2 vols; Paris 1875, 1890.
Rud. Westphal: "Die Musik des griechischen Altertums"; Leipzig, 1883.
D. B. Monro: "The Modes of Ancient Greek Music"; Oxford, 1894.
H. Abert: "Die lehre vom Ethos in der griechischen Musik"; Leipzig, 1899.
L. Laloy: "Aristoxène de Tarente et la Musique de l'antiquité"; Paris, 1904.
H. Riemann: "Handbuch der Musikgeschichte"; Leipzig (1904) 1923, 3rd Ed.
Th. Reinach: "La musique grecque"; Paris, 1926.
W. Vetter: "Musik" in Pauly's R.E.; Stuttgart, 1933, vol. 31, cols. 823-876.
W. Vetter: "Antike Musik"; München, 1935.
R. P. Winnington-ingram: "Mode in Ancient Greek Music"; Cambridge, 1936.
O. Gombosi: "Tonarten und Stimmungen der antiken Musik"; Kopenhagen, 1939.
G. Reese: "Music in the Middle Ages"; New York 1940, pp. 11-51.
C. Sachs: "The History of Musical Instruments"; New York, 1940/London, 1942; pp. 128-150.
O. Tiby: "La musica in Grecia e a Roma"; Firenze, 1942.

C. Sachs: "The Rise of Music in the Ancient World, East and West"; New York, 1943, pp. 197-271, 277-284.

Th. G. Georgiades: "Der griechische Rhythmus, Musik, Reigen, Vers und Sprache"; Hamburg, 1949.

J. E. Mountford and R.P. Winnington-ingram: "Music", in Oxford Classical Dictionary, 1949; pp. 584-591.

M. Wegner: a) "Das Musikleben der Griechen"; Berlin, 1949.
    "   "   b) "Die Musikinstrumente des alten Orients"; Münster, 1950.

H. Ir. Marrou: "Histoire de l'éducation dans l'antiquité"; Paris, 1950 (2nd Ed.).

Fr. Behn: "Musikleben im Altertum und frühen Mittelalter"; Stuttgart, 1954.

R. P. Winnington-ingram: "Ancient Greek Music" in Grove's Dictionary of Music and Musicians; 5th Ed., London, 1954, vol. III, pp. 770-781.

W. Vetter: "Antike Musik" in "Die Musik in Geschichte und Gegenwart"; Kassel, 1956, vol. V, cols. 840-865.

M. Wegner: "Griechische Instrumente und Musikbräuche" in "Die Musik in Gesch. u. Gegenw."; Kassel, 1956, vol. V, cols. 865-881.

Ingemar Düring: "Greek Music: Its Fundamental Features and its Significance"; Journal of World History, 3 (1956), 302-29.

I. Henderson: "Ancient Greek Music" in "New Oxford History of Music"; London OUP, 1957, vol. I, pp. 336-403.

Th. G. Georgiades: "Musik und Rhythmus bei den Griechen"; Hamburg, 1958.

R. P. Winnington-ingram: "Ancient Greek Music - A Bibliography 1932-1957"; Lustrum, 1958, Band 3, pp. 5-57.

E. Pöhlmann: "Griechische Musikfragmente, ein weg zur altgriechischen Musik" (Erlanger Beiträge zur Sprach- und Künstwissenschaft; Band VIII); Nürnberg, 1960.

W. Vetter: "Mythos-Melos-Musica"; Leipzig 1961, (esp. pp. 431-500).

H. Koller: "Musik und Dichtung im alten Griechenland"; Bern/München, 1963.

Ed. A. Lippman: "Musical Thought in Ancient Greece"; N. York/London, 1964.

M. Wegner: "Musikgeschichte in bildern", Band II, "Musik des Altertums (Griechenland)"; Leipzig, 1966.

Th. G. Georgiades: "Griechische Musik" in Riemann Musik Lexikon, Sachteil; Mainz, 1967, pp. 351-354.

I. Henderson: "Greece", I-III, in Harvard Dictionary of Music; Cambridge, Mass., 1969, 2nd Ed., pp. 351-354.

Th. G. Georgiades: "Music" in "History of the Greek Nation" ("Mousike" in "Historia tou Hellenikou Ethnous"); Athens, 1972, vol. III, pp. 334-351.

Other more specific bibliography may be found in several other articles of this Dictionary.

mousikeuesthai; vb (μουσικεύεσθαι; m. pr. mousikévesthe); to sing; to cultivate a taste for music (LSJ); to cultivate one's talent, to study music (Dem.). Sext. Empir. ("Against Musicians", VI, § 29): «ὁ μουσικευσάμενος πλεῖον παρὰ τοὺς ἰδιώτας τέρπεται πρὸς μουσικῶν ἀκροαμάτων» ("the man cultivated in musical appreciation [or, he who has studied music] gets more pleasure from listening to musical performances than do ordinary people"); cf. also ibid, § 35.

mousikos (μουσικός), Dorian type mosikòs (μωσικός); principally the

216

master in the art of music.   The term "mousikos" in the modern sense of "musician" appears in current use as late as the 4th cent. B.C., when Music became a completely autonomous and independent art.   In older times such terms as "auletes" (αὐλητής), "kitharistes" («κιθαριστής»), aoedos (ἀοιδὸς) etc. were used according to the case.

Aristoxenus, who was the most eminent "mousikos" (musician) in this sense of ancient Greece, defines that the equipment of the "mousikos" is the possession of all that is embraced in the science of music (Harm. I. p. 2, 4-6 Mb).   And further (ibid, II, p. 32, 5-7) he explains that "the Harmonic science is a part of the musician's equipment which includes also the sciences of Rhythm (Ρυθμική), of Metre (Μετρική) and of Instruments ('Οργανική); «μέρος γὰρ ἐστιν ἡ ἁρμονικὴ πραγματεία τῆς τοῦ μουσικοῦ ἕξεως, καθάπερ ἦτε ρυθμικὴ καὶ ἡ μετρικὴ καὶ ἡ ὀργανική»).   Anon. Bell. (§ 12, p. 27) defines also that "musician is the man versed (skilled) in melodic composition and he who can with precision observe and appreciate everything which is right (fitting)"; («Μουσικὸς δ' ἐστιν ὁ ἔμπειρος τοῦ τελείου μέλους καὶ δυνάμενος ἐπ' ἀκριβείας τὸ πρέπειν τηρῆσαί τε καὶ κρῖναι»).   Cf. Plato Rep. III 398E and 402D.   Another category of "mousikos" was the executant (singer or instrumentalist), and the composer as well.   In old times the executant was also the composer and the poet.   Very rare was the case of a poet-composer-executant who was at the same time a master of the musical art as defined by Aristoxenus or Anonymous; such was the perhaps singular case of Lasus of Hermione* (6th cent. B.C.). Besides, the theory of music had its scientific beginnings later (cf. *mousike*).

b) The word "mousikos" is met with as an adj. and meant "musical". Thucyd. Hist. (III, ch. 104) «καὶ ἀγὼν ἐποιεῖτο αὐτόθι [ἐν Δήλῳ] καὶ γυμναστικὸς καὶ μουσικὸς» ("and there took place [in Delos] both a gymnastic and a *musical* contest").

«Τὰ μουσικὰ» (pl. of neut. «τὸ μουσικὸν») meant generally *music*; also pleasant, delightful tunes. Suidas: «Μουσικά· τερπνά. Τὰ δι' αὐλῶν καὶ κινύρας καὶ τὰ ὅμοια» ("*Mousika*; the pleasant [tunes]; those produced by auloi, kinyra and similar instruments").

Cf. *melos** (*mousikon melos*).

mousizein (μουσίζειν; m. pr. mousízin); to sing, or play music. Cf. Eurip. Cyclops, v. 489 «ἄχαριν κέλαδον μουσιζόμενος» ("performing a graceless [disagreeable] sound [noise]").

See v. 490 under *apodos**.

mousopoeos (μουσοποιός; m. pr. mousopiós); lyric poet;

mousopoeein, vb (μουσοποιεῖν; m. pr. mousopiín); to write lyric poetry;

to compose lyric songs; Dem.: to sing or praise by lyric poetry.

mousotechnes (μουσοτέχνης; m. pr. mousotéchnis); musician; mousour-gós*.

mousothetos (μουσόθετος); LSJ (Suppl.) set up by music.

mousotraphes (μουσοτραφής; m. pr. mousotraphís); cultivated by muses, in art and letters.

mousoumai (μουσοῦμαι; m. pr. mousoúme) vb; to be educated in the arts; to be set to music (as melopoeoumai). Sext. Emp. (VI, § 2) «μεμουσωμένον τι ἔργον» ("a *musical* work"). Dion. Hal. Demosthenes 40 «μέλη καὶ κρού-ματα δι' ᾠδῆς καὶ ὀργάνου μουσωθέντα» ("vocal tunes and instrumental pieces set to music through singing and playing").

mousourgema (μουσούργημα; m. pr. mousoúrgima); melos; a musical piece. From mousourgein, vb (μουσουργεῖν); to compose mele, mousopoeein*.

  mousourgia (μουσουργία); the art of writing lyric poetry or of composing mele.
    Cf. *melopoeia*.

mousourgos (μουσουργός); cultivating music (L.S.J.); musician. Very often fem., a music-girl; a singer or a psaltria (see *psaltis**). The word is met often in pl., mousourgoi (μουσουργοί); these were foreign women singing or playing on the aulos or on the kithara at banquets. Suidas: *"mousourgoi*; psaltriai; barbarian women ... Some of them play the aulos, while others play on a pentachord* or on a heptachord psalterion; and they sing to the instrumental playing". In Athenaeus (IV, 129A) it is said that they appeared naked; "auletrides and *mousourgoi* and players of sambyke from Rhodes, naked as I believe, though, as some people have said, they have gowns".

  Xen. Cyropaedia (IV, ch. 6, § 11) «καὶ μουσουργοὺς δὲ δύο τὰς κρατί-στας» ("and two of the most accomplished *music-girls* [they gave to Cyrus]").

Musaeus (Μουσαῖος; m. pr. Mouséos);
  a) mythical poet-musician and epic singer who lived in Attica; according to Aristoxenus (ap. FHG II, p. 23, Fr. 1) he came from Thrace or from Eleusis. He was, according to some legends, son of Eumolpus*, while Suidas says he was Eumolpus' father. Diogenes Laertius (Book, I, Prooemion, § 3), who holds that he was the son of Eumolpus, says that Musaeus "wrote a genealogy of Gods and maintained that all things proceed from unity to unity and are resolved again into unity. He died in Phalerum and this is his epitaph:

  Musaeus, to his sire Eumolpus dear,
  In Phalerean soil lies buried here".

  (Transl. by R.D. Hicks, Diog. Laert. "Lives of Eminent Philosophers", London, 1925; vol. I, p. 5).

218

Musaeus was placed as contemporary of Orpheus*, who is often mentioned as his pupil, or on the other hand as his teacher. Herodorus of Heracleia ('Ηρόδωρος 'Ηρακλειώτης; c. 400 B.C.), the mythographer, wrote "the story of Orpheus and Musaeus" (cf. Photius 80, 61A). To Musaeus were attributed poems of a sacred character, various hymns, even oracles.

2. Suidas mentions also another Musaeus of Thebes (Μουσαῖος Θηβαῖος), son of Thamyris*, who was a song-writer (μελοποιός), long before the Trojan wars. He composed songs (μέλη καὶ ᾅσματα).

myrmekia (μυρμηκιά; m. pr. mirmikiá); ant-hill. Metaph. throng of people (LSJ, Dem.). A similar expression "*myrmekos atrapoi*" («μύρμηκος ἀτραποί»; m. pr. mírmikos atrapí) = ant-tracks. The word "myrmekia" appears in Pherecrates' comedy "Cheiron" in connection with Timotheus; «ᾅδων ἐκτραπέλους μυρμηκιάς». The metaphor may be explained in relation to chromatic music. Cf. Ingemar Düring "Studies in musical terminology in 5th century literature"; Eranos 43, 1945, and E. K. Borthwick's article in Hermes 96, 1968, p. 69 ff. Also Timotheus*.

Myrtis (Μυρτίς; m. pr. Mirtís); 6th cent. B.C. poetess and composer from Anthedon of Boeotia.

According to Suidas she was teacher of Pindar and Corinna*. Plutarch (Quaest. Graec., § 40) calls her "poetess [composer] of mele" («Μυρτὶς ἡ 'Ανθηδονία, ποιήτρια μελῶν»).

Brgk PLG III, p. 542 one Frg.; Page PLG p. 371 Frg. 716.

N

nablas, masc. or **nabla** fem. (νάβλας, νάβλα; m. pr. návlas); a stringed instrument of the psalterion family. It had ten or twelve strings, and was played by the bare fingers, without a plectrum; it was of Phoenician origin and its tone was considered unpleasant. Sopater, the parodist (ap. Athen. IV, 175C, ch. 77; G. Kaibel Com. Gr. Fr. pp. 194-5, Fr. 16) says that "*náblas* is an invention of the Phoenicians" and "is [in tone] not melodious" («οὐκ εὐμελής»).

Hesychius considers the nabla to be an instrument like the psalterion or the kithara ("*nabla*, a kind of musical instrument, or a psalterion or a kithara").

Also Hes. "*nablas*; kitharistes [and] a kind of unpleasant musical instrument". The vb *nablizein* (ναβλίζειν; navlízin) = to play the nabla; *nablistes* (ναβλιστής), the player of the nabla.

nenia fem. (νηνία; m. pr. ninía); encomium of men, sometimes accompanied by aulos; a lament.

neniaton, neut. (**νηνίατον** m. pr. niníaton); a tune for aulos or song for maidens, of Phrygian origin. Pollux (IV, 79) «τὸ δὲ νηνίατον [αὐλητικὸν μέλος] ἔστι μὲν Φρύγιον, Ἱππῶναξ δ᾽ αὐτοῦ μνημονεύει» ("the *neniaton* [auletic tune] is of Phrygian origin, and is mentioned by Hipponax").

Note: neniaton is derived from nenis (νῆνις, νεᾶνις, neanis), maiden.

nete, neate (**νήτη, νεάτη**; m. pr. níti, neáti); the extreme note or string; the string nearest to the performer; in fact the highest. 1) In the heptachord scale it was the highest note of the tetrachord of synemmenon (d) and 2) in the octachord the highest note of the tetrachord of diezeugmenon (e); 3) in the Greater Perfect System there were two netai (νῆται), the nete hyperbolaeon (a) and the nete diezeugmenon.

Diatonic Genus

Note: nete (= lowest) was so called because it was sounded by the string which was placed nearest to the performer. Aristides (Mb. p. 11; RPW-I p. 8) «νήτη, τουτέστιν ἐσχάτη· νέατον γὰρ ἐκάλουν τὸ ἔσχατον οἱ παλαιοί»; ("*nete,* that is the extreme (the uttermost); because the ancients called the extreme néaton").

Cf. *onomatothesia*; EM p. 598, 7.

netoeides (**νητοειδής**; m. pr. nitoidís) of locus; region of the nete.

Of the three tropoi (styles) of melopoeia defined by Aristides (Mb. p. 30, RPW-I p. 30) the "nomikos" was netoeides.

neura (**νευρά**; m. pr. nevrá); bowstring, string. Synonym of *chorde** (*χορδή*). Cf. Pollux, IV, 62.

Hes. «μαγὰς ... δεχομένη τῆς κιθάρας τὰς νευρὰς (pl.)" ("magas [bridge] ... which receives [supports] *the strings* of the kithara").

The word "neuron" (νεῦρον; névron) sinew, is synecdochically used for string, cord of sinew.

nibatismos (**νιβατισμός**; m. pr. nivatismós); a kind of Phrygian dance mentioned in Athen. (XIV, 629D, ch. 27) without any other indication.

Hes. «εἶδος ὀρχήσεως βαρβαρικῆς» ("a kind of barbaric [foreign, non-Greek] dance").

Nicomachus [Nicomach] of Gerasa (Νικόμαχος ὁ Γερασηνός; m. pr. Ni-

220

cómachos Gerasinós); 2nd cent. A. D. Pythagorean mathematician and musical theorist, born at Gerasa in Syria (Γέρασα, hence his surname Γερασηνός).

He wrote a Manual or Enchiridion of Harmonike (Ἁρμονικῆς Ἐγχειρίδιον or also Ἁρμονικὸν Ἐγχειρίδιον) in which he describes and expounds the Pythagorean doctrines on music. The Greek text of this Enchiridion was first edited in Johannes Meursius "Auctores veteris musices antiquissimi" (Leyden, ap. Elzevir, 1616) together with Aristoxenus' Harmonic Elements and Alypius' Isagoge. Next edition of the Greek text with a Latin translation by Marc Meibom (Marcus Meibomius "Antiquae musicae auctores septem, Graece et Latine"; Amsterdam, 1652; vol. I, iii pp. 1-28), under the title «Νικομάχου Γερασηνοῦ Πυθαγορικοῦ Ἁρμονικῆς Ἐγχειρίδιον».

Third edition, including Meibom's Latin translation, in Meursius' complete works published by Lami (Florence, 1745; vol. VI, p. 123 ff). Carl von Jan included the Greek text of the Enchiridion in his "Musici scriptores graeci" (Leipzig, ap. Teubner, 1895; V, pp. 236-265, under the title «Νικομάχου Πυθαγορείου Γερασηνοῦ ἁρμονικὸν ἐγχειρίδιον ὑπαγορευθὲν ἐξ ὑπογύου [off-hand] κατὰ τὸ παλαιόν»).

In both Meibom's and Jan's editions there are certain excerpts that are considered to be book two of the Enchiridion (τοῦ αὐτοῦ Νικομάχου, Excerpta ex Nicomacho; Mb pp. 29-41, C.v.J. pp. 226-282).

Ch. Ém. Ruelle in his "Collection des auteurs grecs relatifs à la musique" (vol. II, Nicomaque de Gérase: "Manuel d'Harmonique", Paris, 1881; pp. 9-40) published a French translation, after Meibom's text, with an "Avertissement" (pp. 1-8) and commentary. Ruelle included in this edition (pp. 41-55) the translation of six fragments, the ensemble of which, according to him, constitute the supposed Second Book of the Enchiridion.

It seems that besides the Enchiridion Nicomachus wrote a book "On Music" («Περὶ μουσικῆς») in several volumes, now lost (cf. Eutocii Askalenitae in Archimedes libros: "De sphaera et cylindro"; Basle, 1544; ap. Ruelle's op. cit. p. 2). Ruelle suggests that some parts of this work have perhaps survived and are those considered to be the Second Book of the Enchiridion.

niglaros (**νίγλαρος**); otherwise "ginglaros*" (γίγγλαρος); a kind of small aulos of Egyptian origin by which the movements of the rowers were regulated (Dem.; LS in Gr.). Probably more correct: the sound, a kind of whistling, and in pl. trill, chirping, perhaps somewhat similar to the modern "fluttertonguing" or "flageolet-tones".

Aristoph. Acharnes, v. 554 «αὐλῶν κελευστῶν, νιγλάρων, συριγμάτων» ("of boatswains' auloi, of *whistlings*"). Pherecrates (ap. Plut. De Mus. ch. 30,

1142A) includes *niglaroi* among the evils that Timotheus caused to Music by his innovations; «ἐξαρμονίους, ὑπερβολαίους τ᾽ ἀνοσίους καὶ νιγλάρους» ("[sounds] out of tune, excessively high and impious; and *whistlings*").

niglareuein, vb (νιγλαρεύειν) to warble.

nomion (νόμιον); a pastoral song (from nome [νομή] = pasturing; nemein, vb [νέμειν] to pasture).

Clearchus in his First Book of Erotica (ap. Athen. XIV, 619C, ch. 11) relates that the lyric poetess Eriphanis (Ἠριφανίς), deceived in her love for Menalcas, created the *nómion* melos; after having composed (the melos) "she wandered about in the wilderness calling aloud and singing the so-called *nomion* melos in which there were the words "Tall oaks, oh Menalcas" ".

nomos (νόμος); in its general sense, law, custom, convention. In music *nomos* was the most important type of musical composition and performance.

It seems that the nomos evolved from a very old tradition according to which the laws were sung by the people so that they could be easily memorized and followed (cf. Arist. Probl. XIX, 28). Later on, religious and songs (odes, hymns) in general addressed to Gods were governed by laws. This led to the establishment of certain definite forms (types) of musical composition of a very disciplined and serious character, and of highly aesthetic and artistic demands. These types of composition were called "*nomoi*" (νόμοι, pl.) as it was strictly forbidden to deviate from their governing principles. Plutarch in De Mus. (1133C, ch. 6) says that «νόμοι γὰρ προσηγορεύθησαν, ἐπειδὴ οὐκ ἐξῆν παραβῆναι καθ᾽ ἕκαστον νενομισμένον εἶδος τῆς τάσεως» ("they were called *laws* [*nomoi*] because it was not permitted to deviate from the legitimate [established] diapason [pitch, tension, tuning]"). In Weil's and Reinach's Plut. (p. 29) «εἶδος τῆς τάσεως» is translated "type of scale" ("type d' échelle).

The principal categories of nomoi were three:

a) the *kitharodikos* nomos* (κιθαρῳδικὸς νόμος); the oldest type, a solo song with kithara accompaniment, invented by Terpander* in the 7th cent. B.C.;

b) the *aulodikos* nomos* (αὐλῳδικὸς νόμος), a solo song with aulos accompaniment invented by Polymnestus* in the 6th cent. B.C.; and

c) the *auletikos nomos* (αὐλητικὸς νόμος), a solo for aulos, of which the most important was the Pythikos* nomos (Πυθικὸς νόμος) established by Sakadas* at the Pythian Games in 586 B.C., and with which he won the first prize.

A fourth category, the *kitharistikos nomos* (κιθαριστικὸς νόμος), solo kithara (psile kitharisis), was a later type which followed principally the prototype (the auletikos nomos) of Sakadas. The "psile kitharisis" (solo kithara playing) was however known from the beginning of the 7th cent. (see *Aristonicus of Argos*), and was introduced at the Pythian Games in 558 B.C. (cf. *Agelaus of Tegea*).

The performance of the nomoi (in fact both composition of the nomos and performance) was very exacting and set up high professional standards at the contests, especially in the four National Games (Olympic, Pythian, Isthmian, Nemean) where the most eminent musicians—composers and executants—of the time used to take part. Some nomoi had a special surname derived from the divinity, the place or the musician with whom each one was connected; such were, besides the Pythian mentioned above, the Boeotian, the Terpandrean etc.

Proclus Chrestom., 13 «Ὁ μέντοι *ΝΟΜΟΣ*, γράφεται μὲν εἰς Ἀπόλλωνα, ἔχει δὲ καὶ τὴν ἐπωνυμίαν ἀπ' αὐτοῦ· *νόμιμος* γὰρ ὁ Ἀπόλλων ἐπεκλήθη» ("and certainly the *nomos* is composed in honour of Apollo, and from him it takes its name, because Apollo was called *nómimos* [customary]").

Cf. *Heinz Grieser*: "Nomos"; Heidelberg, 1937.

O

octachordon; neut. (ὀκτάχορδον); the system with eight strings or notes; a scale of eight notes. It was called, before Aristoxenus, "harmonia" (cf. Aristox. Harm. II, p. 36, 30 Mb, in *harmonia**). After Aristoxenus the term "harmonia" for the octachord was replaced by the term "dia pason*" (διὰ πασῶν).

The transformation of the heptachordon into the octachordon was completed in the 6th cent. B.C.; Nicomachus (Enchir. ch. 5, C.v.J. p. 244; Mb p. 9) claims that Pythagoras first of all («πάμπρωτος») added the 8th string between the mese and the paramese (a-b) thus forming a complete harmonia with two disjunct tetrachords (e - f - g - a - b - c - d - e); or e - d - c - b - a - g - f - e.

Cf. *lyra**.

octasemos (ὀκτάσημος; m. pr. octásimos) chronos (χρόνος, time); of eight time-units (of eight short [βραχεῖς] times); as in the dochmios υ--υ-.

ode (ᾠδή; m. pr. odí) from ἀείδειν, ᾄδειν = to sing (uncontracted form, ἀοιδή, ἀϊδί); a poem set to music; a song. It seems that in old times poems were also composed to fit already existing melodies.

Odai, pl. (ᾠδαί) were especially the short lyric poems with music (lyric poetry) of Alcaeus, Sappho and Anacreon, but also more extended compositions like the "Epinikia" of Pindar; the form of this class of odes was ternary (strophe, antistrophe, epode). Odes were generally almost all kinds of songs either of a joyful or of a lamenting character; also the songs sung at work (folk-songs as we would now say) etc.

Ode (ᾠδή) by extension was applied to the singing of the birds.

odikós (ᾠδικός), adj.; skilled in singing (Hes. «εὖ ᾄδων» = pleasingly [well] singing". By extension, musical; as a n., musician.

odeion (ᾠδεῖον; m. pr. odíon); an edifice where musical and other performances and contests took place. So was called such a building in Athens erected by Pericles ("The Odeion"). According to Hesychius odeion was "a place where, before the theatre was erected, the rhapsodes and the kitharodes competed" («τόπος ἐν ᾧ, πρὶν τὸ θέατρον κατασκευασθῇ, οἱ ῥαψῳδοὶ καὶ οἱ κιθαρῳδοὶ ἠγωνίζοντο»).

odontismos (ὀδοντισμός); a kind of aulesis used in the third part of the Pythian nomos, by which the aulete imitated the grinding of the Dragon's teeth.

    Cf. Pollux, IV, 84; also see under *Pythikos nomos** and *iambikon**.

odos (ᾠδός), contracted form of ἀοιδός (*aoedos**); singer. Heracl. Pont. "De Rebus Publicis" (ap. FHG, II, «Περὶ Πολιτειῶν» § 6) «Λακεδαιμόνιοι τὸν Λέσβιον ᾠδὸν [Τέρπανδρον] ἐτίμησαν» ("the Lacedaemons honoured the Lesbian *singer* [Terpander]"). Plato (Laws, VII, 812B) «τοὺς τοῦ Διονύσου ἑξηκοντούτας ᾠδοὺς» ("the sixty-year-old *singers* of Dionysus").

    Cf. also Clem. Alex. Protrepticus, ch. I, § 2.

oektos (οἶκτος; m. pr. íktos); lamentation, piteous wailing (LSJ). Plut. De Mus. (1136F, ch. 17) «τραγικοὶ οἶκτοι ποτε ἐπὶ τοῦ Δωρίου τρόπου ἐμελῳδήθησαν» ("and tragic *lamentations* were set to music in the Dorian mode").

oetolinos (οἰτόλινος; m. pr. itólinos); a mournful song in memory of the unhappy death of Linus*.

    Cf. *linos**.

Oetolinos (Οἰτόλινος) was also another name for the poet-musician Linus.

oklasma (ὄκλασμα); a kind of lively dance, of Persian origin, in which they used to squat. It was performed by women during the ceremony of Thesmophoria in honour of Demeter, the Thesmophoros. Pollux (IV, 100) «καὶ ὄκλασμα, οὕτω γὰρ ἐν θεσμοφοριαζούσαις ὀνομάζεται τὸ ὄρχημα τὸ περσικὸν καὶ σύντονον ...» ("and *oklasma*; so was called the very lively Persian dance danced by thesmophoriazousai [women taking part at the thesmophoria, which was a women's festival in honour of Demeter]").

Olen ('Ωλήν; m. pr. Olín); Mythico-historical epic poet and musician of the oldest antiquity whose name is connected with Apollo's worship.

According to Herodotus (Hist. IV, ch. 35) he came from Lykia (Λυκία, to the south of Asia Minor), sacred land of Apollo, and composed the first Hymns sung at the Delos sanctuary of Apollo («οὗτος δὲ ὁ Ὠλὴν καὶ τοὺς ἄλλους τοὺς παλαιοὺς ὕμνους ἐποίησε ἐκ Λυκίης ἐλθὼν τοὺς ἀειδομένους ἐν Δήλῳ»). Suidas and Hesychius call him Dymaeus (Δυμαῖος) or Hyperboreios (Ὑπερβόρειος; coming from the extreme North), or Lykios (from Lykia); Suidas prefers the epithet «Λύκιος» (Lykios) as he came from the town Xanthos (Ξάνθος) in Lykia.

Pausanias (X, ch. 5, § 8) says that "*Olen* became the first prophet of Apollo and the first epic poet". He is often mentioned by Pausanias (I, ch. 18 § 5; II, ch. 13 § 3; V, ch. 7 § 8; VIII, 21, 3; IX, 27, 2).

Some legends credit him with the invention of the hexameter, and the foundation of the Delphic Oracle.

oligochordía (ὀλιγοχορδία);

See *polychordia**

ololygmos (ὀλολυγμός; m. pr. ololigmós); a hymn or song of triumph. Aesch. Choephoroi, v. 387 «ἐφυμνῆσαι, .. πυκάεντ᾽ ὀλολυγμὸν» ("to sing a piercing *triumphant hymn* [song]").

olophyrmos (ὀλοφυρμός; m. pr. olophirmós); loud lamentation, also a song sung on occasions of grief and death; a dirge. Athen. (XIV, 619B, ch. 10) «ἡ δὲ ἐπὶ τοῖς θανάτοις καὶ λύπαις ᾠδὴ ὀλοφυρμὸς» ("and the song sung on occasions of death and grief [is called] *olophyrmos*").

Olympus (Ὄλυμπος; m. pr. Ólimpos); name of many musicians and poets of ancient Greece.

1) Mythico-historical musician from Phrygia, pupil of Marsyas, belonging to the triad (Hyagnis*, Marsyas* and Olympus*) of Phrygian music. He was credited by various legends with the invention (with the other two) of the auletic art and its introduction and dissemination in Greece.

2) A second Olympus, the younger, from Mysia in Asia Minor (called Mysós, Μυσός), often confused with the first, is placed in the 7th cent. B.C. Suidas places him in Midas' (son of Gordius) time; Midas, acc. Eusebius, lived between 738-696 (or 695) B.C., and, acc. J. Africanus, died in 676 B.C. According to Aristoxenus (ap. Plut. De Mus. 1134F, ch. 11) "he

was considered by the musicians as the inventor of the Enharmonic genus; before him all were Diatonic and Chromatic". He was also credited with the invention of the "harmatios*" nomos. Generally speaking Olympus was the first principal figure in the history of ancient Greek music, so that "the origin of the Greek and nomic muse is attributed to him" (Soterichus ap. Plut. op. cit. 1141B, ch. 29); he was the leader, the founder of Greek music.

To him many inventions were attributed; besides the "harmatios" nomos, Athena's* nomos, the "polykephalos" (many-headed) and the "threnetikoi" nomoi; also the double-aulos (attributed to Hyagnis and Marsyas as well). Olympus introduced to the Greeks instrumental music (kroumata*), and the Lydios harmonia (Clem. of Alexandria «Τὰ εὑρισκόμενα» p. 132); the invention of the Lydios* harmonia is also attributed to many other musicians.

omphalos (ὀμφαλός); the fifth and central section of the kitharodikos nomos*. Omphalos = navel.

onomasia or **onomatothesia** (ὀνομασία or ὀνοματοθεσία); nomenclature· In ancient Greek music use was made of names to designate the notes (M. Psellus, "Syntagma" p. 21a *prosegoriai, προσηγορίαι*; names). Originally these names were given to the strings of the lyra according to their position on the instrument; when the word «χορδὴ» (string) became by continual and practical use a synonym of sound (φθόγγος, phthongos), the names were indiscriminately used to designate both the strings and the corresponding notes.

From the 6th cent. B.C., when the heptachord lyra became octachord, the names were as follows:

Nete or Neate (νήτη, νεάτη; = lowest) the highest note
Paranete (παρανήτη; next to the Nete)
Trite (τρίτη; third)
Paramese (παραμέση; next to the Mese)
Mese (μέση; middle)
Lichanos (λιχανός; forefinger; the string played by the forefinger)
Parhypate (παρυπάτη; next to Hypate)
Hypate (ὑπάτη; highest); the lowest note.

The above nomenclature needs some explanation.

a) *Nete** (= lowest) is in fact the highest string; this is due to the position of the string Nete which was placed nearest to the performer; cf. Aristides (Mb p. 11; RPW-I p. 8) under *Nete**.

b) *Hypate** (= highest) is in fact the lowest because the corresponding string was placed at the other end, the farthest from the performer; cf. Aristides (Mb p. 11) under *Hypate**. Nicomachus (Enchir. ch. 3; C.v.J. p. 241; Mb p. 6) says that by analogy with the planet Saturn (Κρόνος) which is the highest and remotest from us the lowest sound in the diapason was called *Hypate,* because hypaton (ὕπατον) is the highest. In the same way by analogy with the Moon which is the lowest and nearest to the Earth the highest sound took the name *Nete* which signifies lowest. Some scholars argue that this contradictory phenomenon in these two terms (Hypate, Nete) is due only to the fact that, as Aristides says, the ancients used to call the first hypaton (highest) and the remotest néaton (lowest). C. Sachs (Hist. of Mus. Instr., p. 135) holds that "the nete or low string surprisingly designates the highest note in Greek music, not because it is the lowest when the lyre is held in its normal, inclined position, but because the Semitic Orient calls high sounds low, and low sounds high". Cf. Arist. Probl. XIX, 3; Plut. 'Platonicae quaestiones' (Πλατωνικὰ ζητήματα') IX, 2, 1008E.

c) All the above names were in the feminine gender because of the word «χορδή» (string), fem; it was actually an Adj. to the noun «χορδή», e.g. Νήτη χορδή (lowest-highest note).

In the Greater Perfect System the names were as follows with the added note (Proslambanomenos).

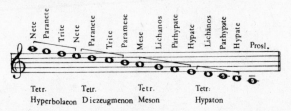

The notes of the tetrachord synemmenon in the Lesser Perfect System were named:

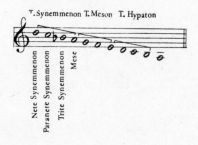

The names remained the same in all three genera for the corresponding notes and strings:

In the old system the Harmoniai ("octave-species"), being practically segments of the Greater Perfect System, retained the names of their respective notes according to their place (or function) in the Gr. P. S. Thus the Mixolydian (b-b) taken upwards began on the Hypate Hypaton, the Lydian (c-c) on the Parhypate Hypaton, and so on.

Ptolemaeus introduced the «κατὰ θέσιν» ("in respect to position") nomenclature. According to this principle the first note of every harmonia (octave-species) was named in respect to its position in the scale Hypate, the second Parhypate, the third Lichanos, the fourth Mese, and so on; on the other hand each note of the same harmonia was also named "after its function" («κατὰ δύναμιν») in the Greater Perfect System.   In the following example we have both denominations:

GREATER PERFECT SYSTEM

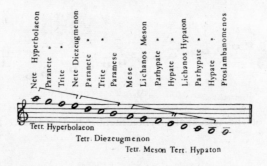

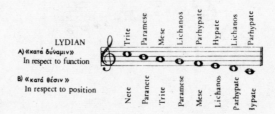

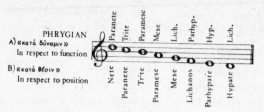

PHRYGIAN
A) «κατά δύναμιν»
In respect to function

B) «κατά θέσιν»
In respect to position

Note: Only in the Dorian do both nomenclatures coincide.

orchesis (ὄρχησις; m. pr. órchisis); dancing; dance.

orchestike (ὀρχηστική, τέχνη); the art of dancing.

Dancing was an art which the Greeks cultivated from very remote times. According to ancient tradition Rhea, the mother of the Olympic Gods, was the first to be enchanted by this art; she in turn taught the dance to her priests, the Kouretes (Κουρῆτες) in Crete and the Corybants (Κορύβαντες) in Phrygia. In Homeric times both song and dance were the indispensable embellishments of every religious ceremony, and of every national or social feast. Even in ancient mysteries, dance was a means of initiation; Lucian in his book "On dancing" («Περὶ ὀρχήσεως», § 15) says that no ancient ceremony could be found without dancing; and Orpheus and Musaeus, excellent dancers themselves, "have legislated that initiation should be made in the rhythm of dancing" («σὺν ῥυθμῷ ὀρχήσει μυεῖσθαι»). It was considered as an advantage for everybody, including those of the higher classes, to be initiated in the secrets of Terpsichore's art; the two sons of Alkinoos, king of Phaeacians, danced with admirable art at the feast given in honour of Ulysses (Odyss. IX, 370-380). Lucian (op. cit. § 25) cites the example of Socrates as one of the admirers of this art and its beneficial influence.

We can have an idea of the steps, movements, choreographic combinations and generally of the character of various dances from vase-paintings, bas-reliefs, frescoes, inscriptions, as well as from a few ancient writers who deal with the art of dancing and of various dances of their time. Mention may be made of the following: *Plato*: Laws, VII; *Xenophon*: Banquet II, IX («Συμπόσιον»; description of dances performed by professional dancers); *Plutarch*: "Sympos. problems" («Συμποσιακὰ προβλήματα» IX, 15; technical analysis of the three parts of dancing); *Lucian*: "On dancing" («Περὶ ὀρχήσεως»; detailed examination of the art of dancing and of its great moral and educational value, description of certain dances, etc.); *Libanius*; «Πρὸς Ἀριστείδην ὑπὲρ τῶν ὀρχηστῶν ἢ ὑπὲρ τῶν μίμων». Also Athenaeus "Deipnosophistai" XIV; Pollux: Onomastikon, IV, ch. 14 etc.

orchestes masc., *orchestris* fem. (ὀρχηστής, ὀρχηστρίς); dancer.

orchestodidascalos (ὀρχηστοδιδάσκαλος); master of dancing.

229

orchema (ὄρχημα); dance. *Iaptein orchemata* (ἰάπτειν ὀρχήματα) meant to get ready to begin the dance.

orcheseos schemata (ὀρχήσεως σχήματα); dance-figures. Many and various dance-figures are mentioned in Athen. op. cit. (XIV, 629F, ch. 27); also in Pollux, Hesychius and others.

The best known dances and dance-figures are examined in this encyclopaedia under special headings.

Bibliography:
1. *Maurice Emmanuel :* "Essai sur l'Orchestique Grecque", Paris 1895; pp. 329, with five Plates and 600 Figures.
2. *Louis Séchan :* "La danse grecque antique", Paris 1930; pp. 371 with 19 Plates and 71 Figures.
3. *Lillian B. Lawler :* "The dance in ancient Greece with sixty-two illustrations"; London 1964; pp. 160.
4. *Germaine Prudhommeau :* "La danse grecque antique"; Paris 1965; two vols, 4°, pp. 721 including 870 plates. First vol. Text; second vol. "Annexes et Planches".

orchestra (ὀρχήστρα; m. pr. orchístra); the circular or semi-circular space in ancient theatres which was found between the actual stage and the benches (ἑδώλια) of the spectators. In the orchestra the chorus stood, danced and sang. In the beginning the action also took place in the orchestra; but in classical times the actors stayed mostly on the stage, which was behind the orchestra on a higher level, while the chorus moved on to the orchestra. The aulete who accompanied the dancing and singing also stayed in the orchestra.

The orchestra was separated from the benches of the public, which also held a semi-circular space in front of and partly around the orchestra and the stage, by a low wall; in the middle of the orchestra the thymele (θυμέλη; altar of Dionysus) was placed.

organon (ὄργανον); gen. instrument; musical instrument, stringed or wind.

organike (ὀργανική); the science of instruments; the art of playing instruments; Aristox. (Harm. II, p. 32, 7-8 Mb): «καθάπερ ἥτε ῥυθμικὴ καὶ ἡ μετρικὴ καὶ ἡ ὀργανική» ("as the sciences of Rhythm, of Metre and of Instruments").

organikós (ὀργανικὸς) adj.; instrumental. *organike phone* (ὀργανικὴ φωνή); instrumental voice, sound. Aristox. (op. cit. I, p. 14, 4-5): «ἁπάσης γὰρ φωνῆς ὀργανικῆς τε καὶ ἀνθρωπικῆς ὡρισμένος ἐστί τις τόπος» ("for every *instrumental* and human voice there is a definite compass...").

Orpheus (Ὀρφεύς; m. pr. Orféfs); mythical poet and epic singer, the most famous of all mythical musicians of ancient Greece. He was of Thracian origin, son of Oeagrus (Οἴαγρος) and the Muse Calliope or Polymnia. He had his lyra directly from Apollo and by his divine singing he could charm the beasts and trees and, as Aeschylus and Euripides said, even the stones. Orpheus followed the Argonauts to Colchis encouraging them by his enchanting music.

To him is attributed the foundation of the Orphic mysteries. It is stated by some mythographers that he was king of the Macedonians or of Bistones (Βίστονες, a Thracian tribe). Apollodorus (Bibliotheca I, ch. 3, § 2, ap. FHG I, p. 106) says that Orpheus established the Dionysian mysteries («καὶ Ὀρφεὺς ὁ ἀσκήσας κιθαρῳδίαν, ὃς ᾄδων ἐκίνει λίθους τε καὶ δένδρα .. εὗρε δὲ Ὀρφεὺς καὶ τὰ Διονύσου μυστήρια»; "and Orpheus the kitharode, who by his singing moved stones and trees...; and he founded also the Dionysian mysteries").

A multitude of legends has been created around his life and death. According to the most propagated legend he was killed by the "Maenads" («μαινάδες»), Thracian women at the service of Dionysus, because he did not care to honour the God when Dionysus visited and conquered Thrace, or because he disdained their love.

His body was cut in pieces, and both his lyra and the pieces of his body were thrown into the sea. His lyra and his head were carried by the waves to Antissa on Lesbos, where his tomb was shown (see *Terpander*).

According to Diodorus Sikeliotes (III, ch. 59, § 6), to Orpheus was attributed the addition of the Hypate string to the lyra. Alexander in his Book on Phrygia (ap. Plut. De Mus. 1132F, ch. 5) says that Terpander* had as model Homer for the epic poems and Orpheus for the songs (μέλη, mele); and that Orpheus imitated nobody in his works, which bear no resemblance to those of the aulodic composers.

The legend of Orpheus and Eurydice is universally known; his ability to descend to Hades shows in a way the faith of the Greek people in the penetrating and irresistible power of music.

orsites (ὀρσίτης; m. pr. orsítis); a kind of Cretan war-dance mentioned in Athen. XIV, 629C, ch. 26 (see the text under *epikredios**). Some writers believe that both *orsites* and epikredios are different names for the same dance. Nothing is known about its character.

orthios (ὄρθιος); erect, upright. In music, high (as ὀξύς, oxys*). Eurip. Troades, v. 1266 «ὀρθίαν ... σάλπιγγος ἠχήν» ("high [penetrating] tone [or sound] of the trumpet, salpinx"). The same as *orthia phone*.

orthios nomos (ὄρθιος νόμος); a nomos high in pitch and uplifting [elevating] in character and feeling. Aristoph. Knights (Ἱππῆς), 1279. Herod. (1.24) relates the story of Arion singing this song in the dolphin story.

orthia melodia (ὀρθία μελῳδία); high-pitched melody.

orthios pous (ὄρθιος πούς); a foot consisting of two long and two short syllables - - υ υ. Bacchius (Isag. § 101; C.v.J. p. 315, Mb p. 25) calls *orthios* the foot composed "of an irrational arsis and a long thesis" υ | -.

oschophorika, mele (ὠσχοφορικά, or ὀσχοφορικὰ μέλη); songs sung during the ceremony called Oschophória ('Ωσχοφόρια).

Procl. Chrest., 28: "*Oschophorika* mele (songs) were sung among the Athenians; two young men in women's dress carrying vine-shoots full of grapes (which they called osche) led the festival".

The Oschophoria (from ὤσχη or ὠσχός; oschos, vine-shoot with grapes, and the vb φέρειν, pherein, to carry) was a part of the Athenian festival, called Skira, in honour of Athena (Minerva) in which boys at the age of puberty wearing women's dresses and carrying vine-shoots went in procession from the temple of Dionysus to that of Skirás Athena.

According to Proclus it was Theseus who first introduced this ceremony, after he had saved the youths from the Minotaur.

ostrakon (ὄστρακον); vessel of clay, or fragment of pottery; shell. Usually in pl. ostraka; krotala*.

vb. *krotein ostrakois* (κροτεῖν ὀστράκοις); to strike the ostraka, and "pros ostraka adein" or "adesthai", «πρὸς ὄστρακα ᾄδειν» or «ᾄδεσθαι» = to sing to ostraka [krotala] accompaniment, signified the oppos. of "to sing to kithara or to lyra", i.e. to sing or play ugly tunes; Phryn. Epitome (ed. de Borries; p. 79). Cf. Aristoph. Frogs v. 1305, where Aristophanes satirizes Euripides' muse as «ὀστράκοις κροτοῦσα» (as "singing" to shells' accompaniment).

oulos (οὖλος); a hymn to Demeter. The same as *ioulos*.

Also a dance performed with rapid and skilful movements.

oupingos (οὔπιγγος) ode; a hymn sung as a prayer to Oupis Artemis (Diana) at a child-birth. The surname Oupis (Οὖπις) was given to Diana as protectress of women ready to bring forth.

Pollux (I, 38) «ἰδίᾳ δὲ 'Αρτέμιδος ὕμνος οὔπιγγος» ("and especially a hymn to Diana, called *oupingos*").

Athen. (XIV, 619B, ch. 10) «οὔπιγγοι (pl.) δὲ αἱ εἰς "Αρτεμιν ᾠδαὶ» ("*oupingoi* [are] those odes to Artemis [Diana]").

oxybaphoi (ὀξύβαφοι; m. pr. oxívaphi); percussion instrument consisting of a series of small clay or shell-pots (or vessels) which when struck by a wooden stick produced different sounds. Suidas on the word Diocles* (Διοκλῆς) «... τοῦτον δέ φασιν εὑρεῖν καὶ τὴν ἐν τοῖς ὀξυβάφοις ἁρμονίαν, ἐν ὀστρακίνοις ἀγγείοις, ἅπερ ἔκρουεν ἐν ξυλυφίῳ» ("Diocles ...; it is said that he invented a harmonia [a series of notes] on the *oxybaphoi,* made of shells, by striking them with a small wooden stick"). Anon. Bell. (§ 17, p. 28) «οἱ ὀξύβαφοι, δι' ὧν κρούοντές τινες μελῳδοῦσι» ("the *oxybaphoi* by which some people produce, by striking, musical sounds").

oxyeches (ὀξυηχής; m. pr. oxiichís); having a piercing, sharp sound; high-pitched.

oxypycnos (ὀξύπυκνος; m. pr. oxípicnos); the highest note of the pycnon*. Altogether there were five oxypycnoi in the Greater Perfect System, namely, the two lichanoi (lichanos hypaton, and lichanos meson) and the three paranetai (paranete diezeugmenon, paran. synemmenon, and paran. hyperbolaeon). All these five oxypycnoi were movable (κινούμενοι, changing) notes of the tetrachord.

For more details see under *pycnon;* also under *barypycnoi, mesopycnoi* and *hestotes.*

oxys, oxytes (ὀξύς, ὀξύτης; m. pr. oxís, oxítis).

oxys; high-pitched, opp. *barys*.

oxytes; sharpness; also height of pitch, the result of *epitasis*. Aristox. (Harm. I, p. 10, 27 Mb): «ὀξύτης δὲ τὸ γενόμενον διὰ τῆς ἐπιτάσεως» ("height of pitch is the result of tension [produced by the stretching of the string]"). Oppos. *barytes*. According to Aristotle (Probl. XIX, 8) the "oxy" (high-pitched) was less important than the low.

In prosody oxeia, the acute accent.

oxytonos (ὀξύτονος; m. pr. oxítonos); sounding in a sharp and piercing tone; also the high-pitched tone. *Oxyphonos* (ὀξύφωνος; m. pr. oxíphonos); having a sharp-piercing voice; high-pitched voice. Synonym of oxytonos.

P

Pachymeres, Georgios (Παχυμέρης, Γεώργιος; m. pr. Pachyméris Geórgios); b. 1242; d. 1310 A.D. Byzantine writer, historian and theorist, born at Nikaea of Bithynia in Asia Minor. He studied in Constantinople and entered the ecclesiastical order, holding high offices. He died in Constantinople.

He was a biographer of Michael Palaeologus, and among his writings is included a book "On Music" («Περὶ ἁρμονικῆς ἤγουν περὶ Μουσικῆς»; "On Harmonic that is On Music"). It was published for the first time by A. J. H. Vincent in his "Notices" (Paris, 1847; pp. 401-552). In this important book, divided into 32 chapters, Pachymeres speaks in detail about ancient Greek music (Harmonike, Systems, Genera, Chroai, Ethos etc.).

Pachymeres is considered by Vincent as the link which unites the Greek Antiquity with modern times.

Other Bibliography:

Paul Tannery: Quadrivium de Georges Pachymère ou Σύνταγμα τῶν τεσσάρων μαθημάτων: ἀριθμητικῆς, μουσικῆς, γεωμετρίας καὶ ἀστρονομίας. Texte révisé et établi par le Rév. P. E. Stéphanou, pp. cii, 456. Città del Vaticano. 8o. Studi e testi, vol. 94.

Elpidios Stéphanou ; see above P. Tannery.

pachys (παχύς; m. pr. pachís); thick, bulky, stout. In music metaph. heavy (sound), rough, coarse. Oppos. fine, delicate. Ptolem. (Harm. I, ch. 3; Wallis III, p. 6) «παχεῖς ψόφοι» ("thick sounds").

pachytes (παχύτης; m. pr. pachítis); density of sound. Ptolem. ibid «διὰ τὴν τῆς παχύτητος ἢ λεπτότητος ποιότητα» ("for the quality of *thickness* or thinness").

paean (παιάν; m. pr. peán); choral song, hymn addressed at first to Apollo and Artemis, especially as thanksgiving for deliverance from evil (illness, famine etc.); later it was addressed to any other god. Paean was also a song of triumph after a victory at war, or at National Games. In general a solemn ode.

Proclus Chrest., 11 «ὁ δὲ *Παιάν*, ἔστιν εἶδος ᾠδῆς εἰς πάντας νῦν γραφόμενος θεούς· τὸ δὲ παλαιόν, ἰδίως ἀπενέμετο τῷ Ἀπόλλωνι καὶ τῇ Ἀρτέμιδι ἐπὶ καταπαύσει λοιμῶν καὶ νόσων ᾀδόμενος· καταχρηστικῶς δὲ καὶ τὰ προσῴδια τινὲς παιᾶνες λέγουσιν» ("the *Paean* is a kind of ode addressed now to all Gods; in old times it was addressed especially to Apollo and Artemis on deliverance from plagues and diseases; and by misuse some people also call the prosodia* paeans").

paeon (παίων; m. pr. péon); a metrical foot of one long and three short syllables; there were four forms of paeon: 1) the *paeonikos* - υ υ υ; 2) the *kouretikos* (κουρητικὸς) or *symbletos* (σύμβλητος) υ - υ υ; 3) the *didymaeos* (διδυμαῖος) or *Delphic* or *bromios*, υ υ - υ; and 4) the *Cretan* or *hyporchematic* υ υ υ -.

Aristides (De Mus. Mb p. 38; RPW-I p. 37) distinguishes in the paeonic genus two simple feet: the *paeon diagyios* (παίων διάγυιος) - υ -, and the *paeon epibatos* (ἐπιβατός) - - | - - - .

paeonic metre (παιωνικὸν μέτρον); a metre of paeons.

paedikos (παιδικός; m. pr. pedikós); of a boy.

paedikos choros (παιδικὸς χορός); chorus of boys. Plato Laws (book II, 664C): «ὁ Μουσῶν χορὸς ὁ παιδικὸς» ("the Muses' boys-chorus").

paedikoi auloi (pl.; παιδικοὶ αὐλοί); a class of auloi with a range of pitch lower than the parthenioi* and higher than the kitharisterioi, according to the classification of auloi by Aristoxenus (see *aulos**).

Pollux (IV, 81) «τοῖς δὲ παιδικοῖς [αὐλοῖς], παῖδες προσῇδον» ("to the *infantine* [auloi] accompaniment boys were singing").

palinodía (παλινῳδία); recantation. This was used first by Stesichorus* in an ode in which he revoked his former attacks against Heleni (Helen) of Troy.

Suid. "παλινῳδία, ἐναντία ᾠδή· ἢ τὸ τὰ ἐναντία εἰπεῖν τοῖς προτέροις» ("*palinode*, a contrary ode; or saying the opposite to those previously said").

pamphonos (πάμφωνος); producing all tones; full-toned or many-toned (LSJ); by extension, expressive.

Pind. 12th Pythian Ode, v. 32 «παρθένος αὐλῶν τεῦχε *πάμφωνον* μέλος» ("the maiden [goddess; Athena] invented *the many-toned* [or the expressive] music [melos] of the auloi").

pandoura, also **pandouris** and **pandouros** (**πανδούρα, πανδουρίς, πάν-δουρος**); a three-stringed instrument of the lute family, called by the ancients *"trichordon"** («*τρίχορδον*»). In Alexandrian times the name "pandoura" was used to signify also the whole family of similar instruments, struck by plectrum. "It had a long neck without pegs, a small body, frets and three strings" as C. Sachs says (Hist. of Mus. Instr. p. 137).

Pollux (IV, 60) «*τρίχορδον* δέ, ὅπερ Ἀσσύριοι *πανδοῦραν* ὠνόμαζον· ἐκείνων δ' ἦν καὶ τὸ εὕρημα» ("*the trichord* [three-stringed] which the Assyrians called *pandoura*; and it was their own invention").

According to Pythagoras (ap. Athen. IV, 183F-184A, ch. 82) "*the pandoura* was made by the troglodytes out of the white mangrove which grows in the sea". Nicomachus (Enchir. ch. 4; C.v.J. p. 243, Mb p. 8) says that the monochord* was called *phandouros* (φάνδουρος). Hesychius also uses the word "*pandouris*" for the instrument, and the term "*pándouros*" for the player of the instrument; «*πανδοῦρα* ἢ *πανδουρίς*, ὄργανον μουσικόν. Πάνδουρος δὲ ὁ μετα-χειριζόμενος τὸ ὄργανον» ("*pandoura* or *pandouris* a musical instrument. And *pándouros* [was] the player of the instrument").

pandourizein (πανδουρίζειν) vb, to play the pandoura.

pandouristes (πανδουριστής; m. pr. pandouristís); the pandoura-player.

pandourion (πανδούριον), dimin. of pandoura; ap. Hesychius. Photius (427, 26) says that "the *pandourion* is a Lydian instrument played without plectrum" («*πανδούριον*, ἤτοι Λύδιον ὄργανον χωρὶς πλήκτρου ψαλλό-μενον»). In Zonaras Lex. p. 1512 "*pandourion*, a kind of kithara" («*πανδού-ριον*... εἶδος μουσικόν· εἶδος κιθάρας»).

235

Pankrates (Παγκράτης; m. pr. Pangrátis); a composer of unknown date, perhaps of the 5th-4th cent. B.C., later than the time of Pindar and Simonides, whom he had as models (Plut. De Mus. ch. 20, 1137 F). He is mentioned (Plut. ibid) as one of those who followed the old tradition; he mostly avoided the chromatic genus, and by choice made use of it in only a few of his compositions («ἔν τισιν»).

Pappus of Alexandria (Πάππος ὁ ᾽Αλεξανδρινός; m. pr. Páppos Alexandrinós); c. end 3rd cent. A.D., mathematician, known also as a music theorist. He flourished in Alexandria (hence his surname). He wrote a great work on Mathematics («Συναγωγὴ») in eight books and Commentaries on the Elements of Euclid, Ptolemy's "Syntaxis Mathematica" and on works of other ancient mathematicians (Suid.).

To Pappus was once attributed the "Isagoge" published under the name of Euclid by Meibom and now ascribed to Cleonides*; his name as author was cited in many MSS of the Isagoge (Barberine II 86, 2nd copy, Rome; Naples No 260; Paris No 2460 2nd copy). To Pappus was also attributed, by some, the last part of Porphyry's Commentary on Ptolemaeus' Harmonika (after ch. 4 of Book I).

parabasis (παράβασις; m. pr. parávasis). A part of the ancient comedy in which the chorus came forward and addressed the public in the Poet's name (LSJ); through the parabasis the poet expressed his personal views on public affairs. Schol. Aristoph., Peace, 733 "it seems that the parabasis is said by the chorus but in the poet's name"; cf. Plut. Mor. 711F.

The parabasis was composed of seven parts, enumerated by Pollux (IV, 112) as follows; 1) kommation* (κομμάτιον), 2) parabasis (παράβασις), 3) makron* (μακρόν), 4) strophe* (στροφή), 5) epirrhema* (ἐπίρρημα), 6) antistrophos* (ἀντίστροφος), and 7) antepirrhema* (ἀντεπίρρημα). According to this enumeration parabasis was also the term for the second part which was composed in anapaestic metre.

parachordos (παράχορδος); unattuned, out of tune, discordant.

   parachordizein, vb (παραχορδίζειν); to play out of tune; to strike wrong notes.
   Cf. *paramousos**.

parachoregema (παραχορήγημα; m. pr. parachorígima); a small part (role) of a fourth actor in the Greek drama taken in certain cases. Pollux (IV, 110): "and if a fourth actor intervened to say something this was called *parachoregema*" («εἰ δέ τις τέταρτος ὑποκριτής τι παραφθέγξαιτο, τοῦτο παραχορήγημα ἐκαλεῖτο»).

236

2) the part of a secondary chorus retiring from the orchestra when no longer wanted; Aesch. Eum. 1032 (Dem.).

paradiazeuxis (παραδιάζευξις; m. pr. paradiázefxis); sub-disjunction. It is formed when between two tetrachords, placed one beside the other, there is a distance of one tone, i.e. between their first notes; cf. Bacchius (Isag. § 86; C.v.J. pp. 311-2, Mb p. 21); M. Bryen. (Harm., Sect. XI, Wallis III, p. 506). The paradiazeuxis is formed between the tetrachords of synemmenon and diezeugmenon:

parakataloge (παρακαταλογή; m. pr. parakatalogí); a kind of accompanied recitative; a declamation with an instrumental accompaniment, usually of aulos.

Its invention was attributed to Archilochus (Plut. De Mus. 1141A, ch. 28).

parakrousis (παράκρουσις); performance of a false note; wrongly struck note; false note.

paramese (παραμέση; m. pr. paramési); the note and string "by the side" of the mese (a) on the second above (b); it is at the distance of a tone from the mese; a-b. When the note above the mese (a) is a semitone apart, as in the heptachord or in the Lesser Perfect System, it is not called paramese but trite synemmenon;

See *onomatothesia*.

paramousos (παράμουσος); unattuned, out of tune, discordant. Synonym: *parachordos**. Eurip. Phoen., v. 791 «καὶ θανάτῳ κατέχει Βρομίου παρά-μουσος ἑορταῖς» ("and for death, *unattuned* to the feasts of Bacchus"). Bromios an epithet of Bacchus.

paranete (παρανήτη; m. pr. paraníti); the note and string "by the side" of nete, a second below. In both the Heptachord and the Lesser Perfect System paranete (synemmenon) was the note corresponding to c[1], below:

In the Greater Perfect System and the octachord paranetai were a) the

237

note corresponding to g^1 (hyperbolaeon) and b) the note corresponding to d^1 (diezeugmenon):

PARANETE HYPERBOLAEON PARANETE DIEZEUGMENON

The paranete keeps its name in all three genera independently of its distance from the nete, e.g):

1. Chromatic Genus. 2. Enharmonic Genus.

See *onomatothesia**.

paranienai, vb (παρανιέναι; m. pr. paraniéne); same as anienai (ἀνιέναι), cf. *anesis** (ἄνεσις). To relax, to slacken the strings (Dem. and LSJ). Plut. De Mus. (ch. 39, 1145D) «καὶ τῶν ἑστώτων τινὰς παρανιᾶσι φθόγγων» ("and they [even] flatten some of the immovable notes").

See also *prosanienai.*

paraphonia, paraphonoi phthongoi, pl. (**παραφωνία, παράφωνοι φθόγγοι**; m. pr. paraphonía, paráphoni phthóngi); according to Bacchius (Isag. § 61; C.v.J. p. 305, Mb p. 15) *paraphonia* is a concord; "when two dissimilar sounds played [at once] present no difference between themselves"; according to Gaudentius it is something between concord and discord. In his Isagoge (ch. 8, C.v.J. p. 338, Mb pp. 12-13) he says that "*paraphonoi* are those which are between concord and discord; when struck they give the impression of being concordant, as in the case of three tones from parhypate meson (f) to paramese (b) and in the case of two tones from lichanos (diatonos) meson (g) to paramese (b)". Thus for Gaudentius the tritone (f-b) and the ditone (major third, g-b) are paraphoniai (pl.). The term is used in Longinus (28.1) in the sense of "sweetening the *kyrios (principal) phthongos*".

Note: paraphonos from para- (beside) and phone = sounding beside.

paraplasmos (**παραπλασμός**); wax used to stop the finger-holes of the aulos. Hes. «ὁ ἐν ταῖς τῶν αὐλῶν τρύπαις ῥύπος» ("the sealing-wax of the finger-holes of the auloi").

parasemantike (**παρασημαντική**; m. pr. parasimantikí); musical notation. From the vb "parasemaenesthai" (παρασημαίνεσθαι) = to note or represent by signs the musical sounds, their duration, etc. Aristox. (Harm. II, p. 39, 6)

238

«τὸ *παρασημαίνεσθαι* τὰ μέλη» ("the marking of the mele by notation"); further (ibid) the term «παρασημαντικὴ» (parasemantike) is used in the sense of notation.

The term notation is also expressed by the words *semasia* (σημασία) and *stixis* (στίξις); Gaud. (Isag. ch. 20, C.v.J. p. 347, Mb p. 20) «ἐχρή-σαντο δὲ οἱ παλαιοὶ [ὀνόμασι] πρὸς τὴν *σημασίαν* τῶν ὀκτωκαίδεκα φθόγ-γων καὶ γράμμασι τοῖς καλουμένοις *σημείοις* μουσικοῖς» ("the ancients used names and letters, the so-called musical signs for the *notation* of the eighteen notes"). Anon. (Bell. § 68, p. 79) «καὶ ὅτι οὐ ῥητῷ παραλέλειπται ἡ *στίξις*» ("and that the [instrumental] *notation* is independent of the text").

The signs used for the musical notation were called σημεῖα (*semeia*); cf. Aristox. (op. cit. Mb pp. 40, 8 and 10); Anon. (Bell. § 2, p. 19) etc.

The Greeks had two systems of notation, one for instrumental and the other for vocal music. Thanks to Alypius' Isagoge (Εἰσαγωγὴ Μουσική; Musical Introduction or Isagoge) the Greek notation has been preserved; Alypius gives in it complete tables in all fifteen tonoi in all three genera. Of the two notations it is supposed that the instrumental was older; the vocal was based on the Ionian alphabet which was adopted in the 5th cent. B.C. [1]

Both notations were used. Aristides (De Mus., Mb p. 26, RPW-I p. 23) says that "by the lower signs we note the instrumental music as also the ritor-nelli of the wind instruments and the section for solos of stringed instruments (μεσαυλικὰ ἢ ψιλὰ κρούματα) which are found in odes; by the higher signs we note the vocal parts themselves (τὰς ᾠδάς)"; cf. Gaud. op. cit. ch. 21, and Anon. Bell. § 68, p. 79 («καὶ τὰ μὲν ἄνωθεν τῆς λέξεως ... τὰ δὲ τῆς κρούσεως κάτωθεν»; "and those signs placed above are for the words [vocal part] ... while those below are for the instrumental part").

In the instrumental notation the signs were used by triads, i.e. by three different positions of the same sign-letter, of which the first was the regular form (σημεῖον *ὀρθόν*, *upright* sign), the second was turned round (ἀπεστραμ-μένον) and the third *reversed* (ἀνεστραμμένον):

a) E (note C); b) Ǝ (note C♯); c) ɯ (C¼)

The principal signs used in the Diatonic genus are the following 17 (instru-mental notation):

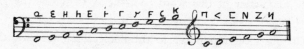

1. Mrs Denise Jourdan-Hemmerdinger in a statement to the "Académie des Inscrip-tions et Belles-Lettres" in Paris, on June 1st 1973, refers to "another ancient musical notation" she has discovered, without giving any other indication ("Comptes Rendus des Séances de l'année 1973, avril-juin"; Paris éd. Klincksieck, Nov. 1973, p. 292).

(the notes above A³ (17th), are noted by the same signs with a dash: K′ ⌐′ <′ etc).

The same notes (vocal notation) have the following signs (in the Diatonic genus); it will be noticed that these signs are more directly derived from the letters of the alphabet:

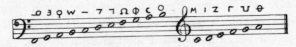

(the notes above A³ had the corresponding signs of the same notes with a dash, as in the instrumental notation).

The lowest of the 15 tonoi* (the Hypodorian) would appear in both notations (Diatonic genus) as follows (cf. Alypius, ch. 14 C.v.J. p. 382, Mb pp. 20-21):

The question of the Greek notation is not as simple as it may appear because of certain anomalies in the tables of Alypius, one being that different symbols are used for the same note in different tonoi.

The Greeks used also signs for the rhythmical notation. The first time-unit (chronos protos, χρόνος πρῶτος; as called by Aristoxenus) was noted by the sign υ. Of the long times there were, the ordinary long (called «μακρὰ δίχρονος»; or δίσημος; double) noted —; the three-time long («μακρὰ τρίχρονος» or τρίσημος; triple) noted ⌐; the four-time long («μακρὰ τετράχρονος» or τετράσημος; quadruple) noted ⊔; the five-time long («μακρὰ πεντάχρονος» or πεντάσημος) noted ⊔⊔ .

These rhythmical signs were placed above the signs of the vocal or the instrumental notation.

They also had signs to express the silences (rests; the χρόνοι κενοί = empty times). The shorter silence, which was called leimma* (Λεῖμμα) was noted by the first letter of this word (Λ); the Λ then was the χρόνος κενὸς βραχὺς (short empty time).

The other rests corresponding to the note-values were noted as follows:

1) long empty (rest) two-time (κενὸς μακρὸς δίχρονος) $\overline{\Lambda}$;

2) long empty three-time (κενὸς μακρὸς τρίχρονος) $\stackrel{\llcorner}{\Lambda}$;

3) „ „ four „ („ „ τετράχρονος) $\stackrel{\sqcup}{\Lambda}$;

4) „ „ five „ („ „ πεντάχρονος) $\stackrel{\sqcup\sqcup}{\Lambda}$·

240

Besides the signs indicating the silences, two other signs are given; *the stigme* (στιγμή; point) (.) used to indicate the thesis (Anon. Bell. §§ 3, 85, p. 21) and the *diastole** (διαστολή; pause) noted by two lines, like the double bar-line, with dots II: (Anon. § 11, p. 26). Cf. M. Bryen., Wallis III, p. 480.

Note: For a more complete study of the Greek notation the following among others may be consulted:

Alypius Isagoge (C.v.J. p. 366 ff; Mb p. 1 ff);

Aristides Quintilianus: De Musica (Mb Antiq. Mus. Auct. Sept., Gr. et Lat.; vol. II, Amsterdam 1652; *A. Jahn*, Berlin 1882; R. P. Winnington-Ingram, Leipzig, 1963).

R. Westphal: Harmonik und Melopoeie der Griechen; Leipzig, 1886.

F. A. Gevaert: "Histoire et Théorie de la Musique de l'Antiquité"; vol. I, pp. 393-418.

D.B. Monro; "The Modes of Ancient Greek Music", Oxford, 1894. § 27 pp. 67-77.

H. S. Macran: "The Harmonics of Aristoxenus"; Oxford, 1902. Introduction, pp. 45-61.

paraskenion (παρασκήνιον; m. pr. paraskínion); side-scene; the interpolation of a member of the chorus in the place of the fourth actor. Pollux (IV, 110) "indeed when instead of the fourth actor one of the dancers would sing, this is called side-scene [paraskenion]".

paraulos (πάραυλος; m. pr. páravlos); unattuned, out of tune, not in concord to the aulos; cacophonous.

paraula mele pl. (πάραυλα μέλη); unmelodious, cacophonous, discordant tunes.

par[h]elkysmos (παρελκυσμός; m.pr. parelkismós); prolongation of a sound. From *parhelkein* (παρέλκειν) vb, to draw aside; Pass. "to be brought in as an accompaniment", Philod. De Mus. p. 95 J.K. (LSJ). Cf. Anon. Bell. 68.

parhypate (παρυπάτη; m. pr. paripáti); the note and string next to (a second above) the hypate. There were two parhypatai: the parhypate hypaton and the parhypate meson. Cf. *onomatothesia.*

parypatoeides phthongos (παρυπατοειδής φθόγγος; m. pr. paripatoïdís); sounding like the parhypate, also the sound produced by the string parhypate. Bacchius (Isag. § 43, C.v.J. p. 302, Mb p. 11) *"parhypatoedes* is the middle [note] of the pycnon"; cf. Aristides (De Mus. Mb p. 12, RPW-I p. 9) «τῶν φερομένων οἱ μὲν παρυπατοειδεῖς, οἱ δὲ λιχανοειδεῖς» ("of the movable notes [of the tetrachords] others are *parhypatoeides* and others lichanoeides"). The hypate keeps its name in all three genera.

pariambis (παριαμβίς; m. pr. pariamvís); a solo for kithara to aulos accompaniment. Epicharmus, the comic poet from Sicily, in his "Periallos" (ap. Athen. IV, 183C, ch. 81) says "Semele dances, and a skilled kitharist plays pariambides to aulos accompaniment; and she rejoices as she listens to the sparkling sounds".

In a broader sense *pariambides* (pl.) were a kitharisterios nomos; Pollux (IV, 83) «καὶ παριαμβίδες νόμοι κιθαριστήριοι, οἷς καὶ προσηύλουν» ("and the *pariambides* were kitharisterioi nomoi to aulos accompaniment"). See also *meniambus* and *enaulos kitharisis*.

Another term for pariambis was *iambis* (ἰαμβίς; m. pr. iamvís), ap. Hesychius.

pariambos (παρίαμβος; m. pr. paríamvos); a stringed instrument of unknown form and character, mentioned by Pollux (IV, 59) among other stringed (krouómena) instruments.

Pariambus (παρίαμβος) was also the metrical foot consisting of two short syllables (υυ); otherwise called pyrrhichios (πυρρίχιος).

Parion Chroni[k]cón or **Marble** (Πάριον Χρονικὸν or Μάρμαρον); an extremely interesting Greek inscription written in Attic dialect by an unknown writer during the rule of Diodmetus (Διόδμητος) in Athens, in 264 or 263 B.C.

It is a chronological table of the most important historical events from the time of Kekrops (Κέκροψ), the mythical first king of Athens, down to the time of Diodmetus, as is stated at the beginning of the inscription («'Ἀπὸ Κέκροπος τοῦ πρώτου βασιλεύσαντος 'Ἀθηνῶν εἴως... 'Ἀθήνησιν δὲ Διογνήτου»). It contains, in chronological order, important facts concerning among others the history and evolution of literature, music and drama, the establishment of the National Games, poetical and musical contests with the names of victors, and the most prominent men of letters and music.

The Parion Chronicle was found in the 16th cent. A.D. on a mutilated column in the island of Paros (hence its name); it was bought in Smyrna by Earl of Arundel in 1627 and transported to London where it was placed first in the gardens of Henry Howard, a relative of Arundel. The column became known as the "Arundel Marble"; in 1667 it was offered to the University of Oxford where it was transferred.

It was first published in London by John Selden in 1628 ("Marmora Arundelliana"; Joannes Seldenus, in 4°). Since then it has been published several times: by Prideaux (Oxford, 1676), M. Maittaire (London, 1732), J. Baumgarten (with a German translation, 1747), Christian Wagner (1790), A. Boeckh (1843, in "Corpus Inscriptionum Graecorum", vol. II, p. 293 ff), C. Müller (in FHG 1853, vol. I, p. 535 ff), Johannes Flach (Tübingen, 1884), and perhaps the most interesting and complete by Felix Jacoby (Berlin, 1904) with Comments and a chronological Canon; this last edition (to which reference is often made in this encyclopaedia) includes the newly found fragments of the Chronicle by A. Wilhelm in 1897, as Part B.

The Column of the University of Oxford contains 93 verses covering the period from Kekrops to Callistratus (355/4 B.C.); the next fragments contain another 34 verses covering the period 336 B.C. (the time of Pythodelus, Πυθόδηλος), to 299/8 (the time of Euctemon, Εὐκτήμων).

Cf. F. Jacoby "Das Marmor Parium", Berlin, 1904 (I part pp. 3-20, II part pp. 20-24). The verses in both parts are not wholly preserved.

parodos (πάροδος); entry, passage, narrow pass etc.

a) Either of the two side-entries of the ancient theatre, leading to the orchestra*;

b) the first entrance of the chorus through the side-entries. Pollux (IV, 108) «καὶ ἡ μὲν εἴσοδος τοῦ χοροῦ πάροδος καλεῖται»; "and the first entrance of the chorus is called *párodos*");

c) synecdochically, the first choral song sung by the chorus during its entrance through the lateral passage; Arist. Poet. (1452B, ch. 12) «χορικοῦ δὲ πάροδος μὲν ἡ πρώτη λέξις ὅλη» ("*párodos* is the whole of the first choral song").

The second entrance of the chorus after the "metastasis" (exit) was called *epipárodos* (ἐπιπάροδος); so also was called the choral song sung during the second entrance.

Cf. Pollux (IV, 108). See *exodion*.

partheneia, and **parthenia** (παρθένεια, παρθένια; m. pr. parthénia); songs sung by a chorus of maidens in ceremonies in honour of various gods, and especially of Apollo or Artemis. The songs were often combined with dancing. Hence parthenia was also the dance. Many lyric poets, among others Alcman, Pindar and Simonides, wrote partheneia. Cf. Aristoph. Birds 919.

parthenios (παρθένιος) adj.; virginal, maidenly. *Parthenios aulos*; the highest in pitch-range aulos. To the class of the "virginal" auloi belonged the gingras*, the photinx* (φῶτιγξ) and the lamenting (querulous) aulos.

Pollux (IV, 81) says that "maidens used to dance to the parthenian auloi".

pathos (πάθος); in a general sense everything that one could suffer, experience or undergo; accident; incident; passion, emotion. In drama the feeling which is caused in the soul of the spectator by a theatrical performance (or a reading of a text). Longinus: "the pathos is very strong in tragic poetry". Aristides (Mb p. 63) on the other hand says that poetry *without melody* (δίχα μελῳδίας) does not cause pathos (emotion).

In music "pathos" was sometimes used to mean a modification in the melodic order; Aristoxen. (Harm. II, p. 38, 12 Mb) «πάθους τίνος συμβαίνοντος ἐν τῇ τῆς μελῳδίας τάξει» ("to what modification [πάθος] in the melodic order [the modulation owes its existence]").

pechys (πῆχυς; m. pr. píchis); forearm. In pl. *pecheis* (πήχεις; píchis); the two arms of the lyra and the kithara, which were fixed on the sound-box. Those of the lyra were usually made of wild goat horn, and in classical times also of wood; they were light and slightly curved; those of the kithara were wooden and more compact.

They were joined, slightly below their upper end, to a cross-bar (zygon*, ζυγόν).

The pecheis were also called "kérata" (κέρατα; horns).

Cf. Pollux (IV, 62).

peira (πεῖρα; m. pr. píra); attempt, test. The first part of the Pythikos* nomos, the introductory part.

pektis (πῆκτις and πηκτίς; m. pr. píktis or piktís); 1) widely known stringed instrument. It was closely associated with the mágadis*; like the magadis it was a large instrument with 20 strings tuned in pairs, each one with its octave. It belonged to the "psaltiká" instruments, which were played by bare fingers without a plectrum. According to Aristoxenus and Menaechmus (ap. Athen. XIV, 635E, ch. 37) "the pektis and the magadis were one and the same instrument". The pektis was of Lydian origin, and Sappho was considered the first to have used it.

Sopater, the parodist, (ap. G. Kaibel Com. Gr. Fr. p. 194, Fr. 11; and Athen. IV, 183B, ch. 81) says in his "Mystacus' Theteion" (Slavey): «πηκτὶς δὲ Μούσῃ γαυριῶσα βαρβάρῳ δίχορδος εἰς τὴν χεῖρα πῶς κατεστάθη;» ("and the *two-stringed pektis* which boasts of its barbaric muse, how has it been placed in thy hands?").

This information in the above fragment of Sopater, that the pektis was also "two-stringed" (dichord), is not confirmed by other sources; perhaps the meaning might be "double-stringed". The pektis however belonged, with the magadis and the sambyke, to the so-called polychord (many-stringed; πολύχορδα) instruments, condemned by Plato (Rep. III, 399D) and Aristoxenus (ap. Athen. IV, 182F, ch. 80, and FHG II, 286, Fr. 64), who called all these instruments "foreign" («ἔκφυλα»).

2) *Pektis* was also a kind of pastoral syrinx, similar to Pan-pipes. Hes. «πηκτίδες (pl.) καὶ σύριγγες ὄργανα μουσικὰ» ("*pektides* and syrinxes, musical instruments").

pelex (πήληξ; m. pr. pílix); a stringed instrument of the psalterion family mentioned by Pollux (IV, 61) «καὶ *πῆληξ* δὲ ού μόνον ὁ τῆς περικεφαλαίας λόφος, ἀλλὰ καὶ ὄργανόν τι ψαλτήριον» ("and *pelex* which is not only the tuft of a helmet but also a psalterion instrument"). Nothing else is known about it. Th. Reinach supposes that it may be a kind of harp (DAGR, III₂ (VI), p. 1451, s.v. Lyra).

pentachordon (πεντάχορδον; from pente, πέντε, five, and chorde); a five-stringed instrument mentioned by Pollux (IV, 60) who says that "it was of Scythian origin, was hung by leathern straps of ox-hide, and was played with a plectrum made of goat's hoof" («πεντάχορδον, Σκυθῶν μὲν τὸ εὕρημα, καθῆπτο δὲ ἱμάσιν ὠμοβοΐνοις· αἰγῶν δὲ χηλαὶ τὰ πλῆκτρα»).

Telestes (ap. Athen. XIV, 637A, ch. 40) speaks of a pentachord (five-stringed) magadis*.

Theon of Smyrna mentions *the pentachord* system together with the tetrachord and the octachord («τὰ λεγόμενα συστήματα, τετράχορδα καὶ πεντάχορδα καὶ ὀκτάχορδα»; p. 49, ed. Hiller).

pentasemos (πεντάσημος; m. pr. pentásimos) chronos, time; consisting of five time-units. See *chronos*.

pentekaedekachordon, systema (πεντεκαιδεκάχορδον, σύστημα; m. pr. pentekedekáchordon) from pente-kai-deka (fifteen) chordai; the system with fifteen notes, otherwise called "dis-diapason" (δὶς διαπασῶν) or Greater Perfect System (see *systema*).

It was introduced after Aristoxenus' time in the 3rd cent. B.C. and consisted of four tetrachords, conjunct by pairs with a disjunction in the middle (between the mese and the paramese), and of an added note at the lowest end (the proslambanómenos):

Prosl.

periadein, vb (περιᾴδειν; m. pr. periádin); to sing while walking about.

periodos (περίοδος); period; the ensemble of two or more parts, or sentences ("kolons"; κῶλα) of a melody.
See *kolon*.

peripheres (περιφερής; m. pr. periferís); revolving. In the case of *agoge* (ἀγωγὴ περιφερής; *agoge peripheres*) melodic progression ascending and descending in stepwise order.
See *agoge*.

245

periphora (περιφορά); circular motion. *Periphora* of intervals («περιφορὰ διαστημάτων»): recurrence of intervals. According to Aristoxenus (Harm. I, p. 6, 21-24) Eratocles "has attempted in the case of one System, in one genus, to enumerate the forms or species of the Octave, and to determine them mathematically by the periodic *recurrence* of the intervals" («τῇ περιφορᾷ τῶν διαστημάτων»; transl. by D.B. Monro "The Modes of Ancient Greek Music" p. 50). Thus Eratocles, by proceeding through the various arrangements which can be obtained by beginning each octave species successively with e, f, g etc., has arrived empirically at the enumeration of seven different figures (σχήματα). This method is criticized by Aristoxenus (op. cit. I, p. 6, 25 ff).

perispomenos (περισπώμενος), pres. part. Pass. of "perispao" («περισπάω»), to pronounce a vowel or word with the circumflex, LSJ; pronounced with the circumflex (pitch) accent. Perispomenos phthongos in prosody.

Cf. *barys*, oxys*, tonos**.

peristomion (περιστόμιον); see *phorbeia*.

Persikon, Persian dance (περσικόν, neut.); a kind of dance of Persian origin. Xen. Anabasis (VI, ch. 1, § 10): "Lastly [the Mysian] danced the Persian dance clashing the light shields together, crouching down and rising up again; and he was doing all these in rhythm, to aulos accompaniment" («τέλος δὲ [ὁ Μυσὸς] τὸ περσικὸν ὠρχεῖτο κρούων τὰς πέλτας καὶ ὤκλαζε καὶ ἐξανίστατο· καὶ ταῦτα πάντα ἐν ρυθμῷ ἐποίει πρὸς τὸν αὐλόν»). Aristoph. Thesmoph. 1175 «ἐπαναφύσα περσικὸν» ("play again on the aulos the Persian [dance-tune]").

petteia (πεττεία; m. pr. pettía); repetition of the same note. Cleon. Isag. (ch. 14, C.v.J. p. 207; Mb p. 22) "*petteia* is the striking of a note repeatedly" («πεττεία δὲ ἡ ἐφ' ἑνὸς τόνου πολλάκις γιγνομένη πλῆξις»).

Aristides (De Mus., Mb p. 29, RPW-I p. 29) speaks of *petteia* as of a procedure of melodic composition (one of the three kinds of *chresis**) by which "we know which notes to omit, and which ones to use. And from which one to start and on which to finish. This also becomes productive of ethos."

phallikon, melos (φαλλικόν, μέλος); song sung during the procession of the phallus in a ceremony in honour of Dionysus. Also the orchema (dance) performed at this ceremony. Pollux (IV, 100) "*phallikon* orchema (dance) in honour of Dionysus".

phandouros (φάνδουρος); see *pandoura*.

Phemius (Φήμιος; m. pr. Phímios); renowned epic singer (aoedos, ἀοιδὸς) from Ithaca often mentioned in Homer's Odyssey (XI, XVI). He lived in the palace of Ulysses, who during his absence at Troy entrusted Penelope to him; Phemius had accompanied her from Sparta. He sang of the nostalgia of the Greeks, their longing to return home from Troy. He had been forced however to entertain the "pretenders" at their banquets with his music, and risked being killed by Ulysses when on his return home he killed the pretenders.

Cf. Plut. De Mus. 1132B, ch. 3.

Pherecrateios, stichos (**φερεκράτειος**, στίχος; m. pr. pherecrátios, stíchos); also Pherecrateion metron, or simply Pherecrateion.

Pherecratean line, verse; so called after the name of the comic poet Pherecrates who made extensive use of it. The Pherecratean line was a logaoedic (mixed) tripody consisting of two trochees and one dactyl; there were two kinds depending on the place of the dactyl:

A_1 : $— \cup\cup \quad — \cup \quad — \overline{\cup}$ (acatalectic; ἀκατάληκτος)
A_2 : $— \cup\cup \quad — \cup \quad — \overline{\wedge}$ (catalectic ; καταληκτικὸς)
B_1 : $— \cup \quad — \cup\cup \quad — \cup$ (acatalectic)
B_2 : $— \cup \quad — \cup\cup \quad — \wedge$ (catalectic)

Cf. *Anacreon*.

Notes: 1. For acatalectic and catalectic metres, see under *metron*.
2. The sign $\wedge$ is for leimma (short empty time); see under *leimma* and *parasemantike*.

Pherecrates (**Φερεκράτης**; m. pr. Pherecrátis); c. 420 B.C., comic poet and musician. To him we owe a document on the evolution of music in the 5th cent. B.C. In his comedy "Cheiron" («Χείρων») he represents Music as a woman complaining to Justice of all the misfortunes she suffered from the innovations of Melanippides*, Kinesias*, Phrynis* and Timotheus*. This substantial part of the comedy (25 verses) has been preserved by Plutarch in 'De Musica" (1141D-F and 1142A, ch. 30).

Philammon (**Φιλάμμων**); mythical poet-musician, son of Apollo, father of Thamyris*. According to some legends he was the first to institute songs and dances at the Delphic sanctuary (Plut. De Mus. 1132D, ch. 3). Terpander, it is said, based his compositions on Philammon's nomoi.

philhelias ode, fem. (**φιληλιάς** ᾠδή; m. pr. phililiás) from philein (φιλεῖν) vb, to love, and helios (sun); an ode to Apollo (Helios, Sun-God). Athen. (XIV, 619B, ch. 10) "and the ode to Apollo [is called] philhelias, as Teléssilla testifies" («ἡ δὲ εἰς Ἀπόλλωνα ᾠδὴ [καλεῖται] φιληλιάς, ὡς Τελέσιλλα παρίστησι»).

Philodemus (Φιλόδημος; m. pr. Philódimos); 1st cent. B.C. poet and Epicurean philosopher from Gadara of Cale-Syria. He lived in Rome during the time of Cicero—and more precisely around 60 B.C.—who knew him and praised his erudition. Among his many writings a work "On Music" («Περὶ μουσικῆς») is included. The text of this work, severely mutilated, was found, with other papyri, at Herculaneum (Ercolano; Ἡράκλειον), SE of Naples, near Pompeii, in Italy; of the work a substantial part of the fourth book has been preserved. It was edited, with Latin translation, together with other works of Philodemus, in "Herculanensium voluminae quae supersunt" (Napoli, 1793; Tomus I, pp. 1-144) under the title: Philodemi De Musica, IV («Περὶ μουσικῆς», Δ΄); the text was published in columns with photos of the papyri, and further comments in Latin, pp. 145-163.

The fourth book was also edited in the "Varietà nei Volumi Ercolanesi" by Lorenzo Blanco (Naples, 1846); Greek text with a translation into Italian (vol. I, part I, pp. 1-665) and a Latin translation (vol. I, part II, pp. 79-136) and "commentarius" (pp. 143-221). A very careful edition of the Greek text was published by Johannes Kempe ("Philodemi: De Musica librorum quae extant", Leipzig, 1884, ap. Teubner). This edition, as its title suggests, contains, besides the fourth book (pp. 62-111), also fragments of the first and third books (pp. 1-20, 21-55 respectively), also fragments from other papyri (pp. 56-61).

Other bibliography: *D. A. van Krevelen*: "Philodemus de Muziek" (Amsterdam, 1939); *Otto Luschnat*: "Zum text von Philodemos schrift de musica" (Deutsche Akademie der Wissenschaften zu Berlin; Institut für hellenistische-römische Philosophie, Veröffentlichung No 1, 1953, pp. 5-36, with Tables of photos of the papyri); *Armando Plebe*: "Filodemo e la musica", Torino, 1957, pp. 22; *G. M. Rispoli*, article on Philodemus, book I in Ricerche sui papiri ercolanesi, ed. F. Sbordone, Naples 1969.

philodos (φιλῳδός; from philein, vb (φιλεῖν) to love, and ode); fond of songs; loving ode-singing and generally song-loving. Phryn. Epitome (ed. I. de Borries, p. 123) «ὁ φιλῶν ᾄδειν» ("he who loves singing").

Philolaus (Φιλόλαος; m. pr. Philólaos); 5th cent. B.C. philosopher from Tarentum, disciple of the Pythagoreans, contemporary of Socrates. In his "De Naturae" («Φυσικά»), a fragment of which has survived, he analyses and explains the Pythagorean doctrines on music. His commentary on the Pythagorean ratios was the occasion of Plato's Timaeus.

Nicomachus analyses the views of Philolaus, Pythagoras' successor, as he calls him (Enchir. ch. 9 «Μαρτυρία τῶν εἰρημένων ἀπὸ τοῦ Φιλολάου»; Mb pp. 16-18, C.v.J. pp. 252-254). A.E. Chaignet in his book "Pythagore et la philosophie Pythagoricienne" (2 vols, Paris, 1873) publishes the fragments of Philolaus and Archytas. He also analyses (vol. I, p. 225 ff) the Pythagorean

248

principles, as expressed by Philolaus, concerning the constitution of the Harmonia (a Syllabe*, 4th, plus a Dioxeion*, 5th), the division of tone into diesis ($\frac{13}{27}$) and apotome* ($\frac{14}{27}$), the comma, the schisma etc.

See also: *Walter Burkert*: "Wisheit und Wissenschaft, Studien zu Pythagoras, Philolaos und Platon"; Nürnberg, 1962, pp. XVI, 495. Especially pp. 365-378.

philomousos (φιλόμουσος; from philein, vb, to love, and muse); loving music or the Muses; loving the arts. Arion (ap. Brgk PLG III, p. 872) «φιλό-μουσοι δελφῖνες» ("*music-loving* dolphins").

philomousia (φιλομουσία); fondness, love of music and arts.

philomousein vb (φιλομουσεῖν); to love music and the arts (Muses) generally.

philorrhythmos (φιλόρρυθμος; m. pr. philórithmos); fond of rhythm. Cf. Plut. De Mus. ch. 21, 1138B.

philotechnos (φιλότεχνος); almost a synonym of philomousos. Loving the arts; *philotechnia* (φιλοτεχνία); love of the arts; ingenuity (LSJ).

Philoxenus (Φιλόξενος; m. pr. Philóxenos); composer of dithyrambs, b. c. 435 B.C., d. c. 380-379 B.C.; he was born at Kythera (Κύθηρα, hence his surname Κυθήριος, Kytherios) and died at Ephesus. His death is recorded in the "Parion Chronikon" (v. 69; as 380-379 B.C.).

Taken prisoner in 424-3 he was sold as a slave to a certain Agesylas and by him to the lyric poet Melanippides*, who emancipated him and taught him music. His name is often mentioned in Plutarch's De Musica, with that of Timotheus, as an important figure in the field of innovations of his time (1141C, ch. 30; 1142C, ch. 31). He became known as one of the leading composers of dithyrambs of his day. According to Suidas he wrote 24 dithyrambs praised by some for the originality of expression, melodic flavour and variation, and blamed by others for his very ornamental style and his daring innovations. The comic poet Antiphanes in his "Tritagonistes" (ap. Athen. XIV, 643D-E, ch. 50) highly praises him and adds that "he was a god among men, as he knew the real music" («Θεὸς ἐν ἀνθρώποις ἦν ἐκεῖνος, εἰδὼς τὴν ἀληθῶς μουσικήν»).

Philoxenus lived for some time at the court of the tyrant of Syracuse, Dionysius the Elder, with whom he developed friendly relations; but the friendship broke down owing to Philoxenus' sarcastic criticisms of the tyrant's dramatic works. The tyrant flung him into the quarries, where he wrote his "Cyclops" or "Polyphemus and Galatea" in which he satirizes the tyrant. According to a charming legend Philoxenus was taken from the quarry, and led before Dionysius he was asked if he still insisted on his opinion about the tyrant's dramas; Philoxenus replied "I prefer to go back to the quarry". At another attempt, he replied "pitiable" (οἰκτραί; in pl., i.e. the tyrant's dramas are pitiable), but Dionysius, interpreting the reply as meaning that his dramas provoked pity in the hearts of the public, liberated him.

Diogenes Laert. (IV, ch. 6, § 36) relates another anecdote of the eventful life of Philoxenus; once when he heard some brickmakers singing some of his melodies out of tune, he retaliated by trampling on the bricks and saying "As you spoil my works, so I spoil yours".

According to Plutarch (Vita Alexander, § 8) Ardalus sent to Alexander the Great, among other works, dithyrambs of Philoxenus to be performed at the marriage festivities at Sousa.

Philoxenus became legendary for his gluttony, of which he died; Machon (Μάχων), the comic poet, relates the story of his gluttony and death (ap. Athen. VIIIA, ch. 26).

Cf. Brgk PLG III, pp. 601-618 and Anth. Lyr. pp. 289-294. Also Page PMG, pp. 423-432, Frgs 814-35.

phlyax (φλύαξ; m. pr. phlíax), pl. *phlyakes* (φλύακες; m. pr. phlíakes); a kind of tragic burlesque initiated by the poet Rhinthon (Ρίνθων). It was formed of elements of folk comic, satirical and even indecent songs of the Dorians in Sicily and South Italy.

phoenix (φοῖνιξ; m. pr. phínix); a stringed instrument similar to magadis* and pektis*; it was a polychord (many-stringed) instrument and its strings were tuned in pairs, each one with its octave as in the other two instruments. Its origin was Phoenician, hence its name; but according to Semus, a poet from Delos, (ap. Athen. XIV, 637B, ch. 40) it was so called because its arms were made of Delian phoenix (= palm-tree).

Phoenikion (φοινίκιον; phiníkion) Dimin. of phoenix. Though the term would imply a small phoenix, the word phoenikion is always met as another name of the same instrument. Arist. Probl. (XIX, 14) "Why is it that the consonance of the octave passes unperceived and appears to be a unison on *the phoenikion* as well as in the human voice?"

phoetetes (φοιτητής; m. pr. phititís); pupil, disciple, student. According to Phrynichus (Epitome; ed. I. de Borries, p. 124) "phoetetai (pl.) are principally those who study (attend lessons) in grammar or music" («κυρίως δὲ λέγονται φοιτηταὶ οἱ γραμματικὴν ἢ μουσικὴν μανθάνοντες»).

phonaskía (φωνασκία); exercise of the voice. From the verb *phonaskein* (φωνασκεῖν; phone- [φωνή; voice] and askein [ἀσκεῖν; to exercise] = to train the voice. Cf. Theophr. Hist. Plant., book IX, ch. 10.

Phonaskós (φωνασκός) = voice trainer; teacher of singing, of voice training. The Greeks introduced and developed a method of solmisation. As basis of this method they had the tetrachord; for "the execution of melos, we have chosen among the letters of the alphabet those which are the most suitable" (Aristides, Mb p. 91). As such they chose four vowels (α, η, ω, ε) to which they prefixed "the best of the consonants" (the letter τ; t), in order to avoid the hiatus (χασμῳδία) which would occur by the exclusive use of vowels. The first (lowest) note of the tetrachord was called «τὰ» (ta), the second «τη» (te, m. pr. *ti*), the third «τω» (to) and the fourth «τε» (te)

If the highest note of the tetrachord was at the same time the first (lowest) of the next tetrachord, i.e. if there was a conjunction, then the fourth note took the syllable τα (ta) which was given to the first of the tetrachord. Thus the two conjunct tetrachords would have the following syllables:

Anon. Bell. (§ 77, pp. 80-81) defines as follows the syllables for the various degrees of the 15 tonoi:

"The proslambanomenoi of the 15 tropoi are called «τω» (to; it evidently should be «τε», te); the hypatai «τα» (ta), the parhypatai «τη» (te, ti), the lichanoi «τω» (to), the mesai «τε» (te), the paramesai «τα» (ta), the tritai «τη» (te, ti), the paranetai «τω» (to) and the netai «τε» (te)".

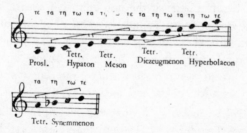

Notes: a) The mese synemmenon had «τα» (ta) as first note of the tetrachord, while the mese diezeugmenon as last note of the tetrachord had «τε» (te).

b) The same happens with the nete diezeugmenon (τα, ta), while the nete synemmenon and the nete hyperbolaeon both had τε (te).

In the case of the instrumental figures *prokrousis**, *prokrousmos** etc.,

251

the notes kept their corresponding syllables:

In the vocal figures *prolepsis**, *prolemmatismos** etc., and when there was a hyphen* the syllable was used without the consonant:

Vocal

In the *melismos**, the *kompismos** and the *teretismos** they used to intercalate an *n* (ν) or two *nn* (νν):

See Aristides (De Mus. Mb p. 91-94), Anonymous (Bell. § 77, pp. 80-81); also Gevaert I, pp. 418-423.

phone (**φωνή**; m. pr. phoní); principally the human voice or the sound of the human voice; also of animals. By extension the sound of any musical instrument. Aristotle ("De Anima" 420 B) says: *"the voice* is a certain sound of a living being; because none of the non-animated speaks, but by similarity (analogy) it is said «to speak» (to sound; φωνεῖν, phonein vb), as for instance aulos and lyra and all those which have duration, melody and expression" («ἡ δὲ φωνὴ ψόφος τις ἐστιν ἐμψύχων· τῶν γὰρ ἀψύχων οὐδὲν φωνεῖ, ἀλλὰ καθ᾽ ὁμοιότητα λέγεται φωνεῖν, οἶον αὐλὸς καὶ λύρα καὶ ὅσα ἄλλα τῶν ἀψύχων ἀπότασιν ἔχει καὶ μέλος καὶ διάλεκτον»).

Plato (Rep. 397A): «πάντων ὀργάνων φωνὰς (pl.)»; *"sounds* of all instruments". Eurip. Troades, v. 127 «συρίγγων φωναῖς» ("by *the sounds* of syrinxes").

Aristoxenus uses also the term *phone* (φωνὴ) in the sense of both the vocal and the instrumental sound; cf. Harm. I, p. 8, 16; p. 9, 10 etc. But he uses as well the term φωνὴ ὀργανικὴ (*instrumental voice*, sound) especially for the instrumental sound; cf. I, p. 14, 4-5 (see the text under *organon**).

The word phone is by extension used in the sense of phrase, song, melody;

252

cf. Plut. De Mus. ch. 33, 1143A. «πολυηχὴς φωνὴ ἀηδόνος» ("richly diverse *song* of nightingale").

phonarion (φωνάριον); dim. of phone. A little voice or cry.

phorbeia, fem. (**φορβειά**, ἡ; m. pr. phorviá); in general use a halter (Lat. capistrum). In music, the leather band which the auletai used to put around the mouth and the cheeks; it left an open hole in front of the mouth to allow blowing into the aulos, and it was tied behind the head. Hes. «φορβειά· ἡ αὐλητικὴ στομίς· λέγεται δὲ καὶ χιλωτήρ» ("*phorbeia*; the auletic mouthband; it is also called chilotir [nose-bag]"). Hesychius gives also another more specific explanation: "the leather band which is placed around the mouth of the aulete to protect his lip from being cleft" («τὸ περικείμενον τῷ στόματι τοῦ αὐλητοῦ δέρμα, ἵνα μὴ σχισθῇ τὸ χεῖλος αὐτοῦ»). The phorbeia is also called *peristomion* (περιστόμιον) and *epistomis** (ἐπιστομίς); Cf. EM p. 798, 32 «περιστόμιον· καπίστριον».

There have been different views about the real purpose of the phorbeia; the more generally accepted view is that the phorbeia's use was to strengthen blowing by concentration. Another view is that it was used to regulate the sound produced; Schol. Aristoph. "in order that by regulating the blowing the aulete could make the sound sweet [pleasant, melodious]"; Wasps, 581-2 «κἂν αὐλητής γε δίκην νικᾷ ταύτης ἡμῖν ἐπίχειρα ἐν φορβειᾷ τοῖς δικασταῖς ἔξοδον αὔλησ᾽ ἀπιοῦσιν» ("and if an aulete wins a suit he plays on the aulos, with the *mouthband* on, a marching-out tune for the judges as they depart").

See also *aulos** and PLATE I.

phorminx (**φόρμιγξ**); a variety of primitive lyra or kithara (Sachs claims that it was "unmistakably a kithara"; Hist. of Mus. Instr. p. 130). It was probably the most ancient stringed instrument in the hands of the epic-singers, the aoedoi*. It appears on ancient vase-paintings usually with four strings (it had three to five), though ancient writers speak also of seven-stringed "phorminxes"; Pind. Pyth. II, v. 70-71, heptaktypos*; Nem. V, v. 24, heptaglossos*, Strabo XIII, 2, 4, 618, heptatonos* (see under *tetragerys*). This is an indication that the word phorminx was often used as the more generic name of lyra; it was small, hollow, and was held in a slanting position like the lyra.

The phorminx was considered a sacred instrument, the instrument of Apollo; a number of epithets given to it by Homer and others show in what consideration the phorminx was held. It was called *perikalles* (περικαλλής; very beautiful); Hom. Il. I, 603-4 «οὐ μὲν φόρμιγγος περικαλλέος, ἣν ἔχ᾽ Ἀπόλλων Μουσάων θ᾽, αἳ ἄειδον ἀμειβόμεναι ὀπὶ καλῇ» ("nor of the beauteous lyre [phorminx], that Apollo held, nor yet of the Muses, that sang replying one to another with sweet voices"; transl. A. T. Murray, Il. vol. I, p. 49).

It was called *ligeia* (*λίγεια*; clear-toned, sweet-voiced), *golden, elephantodetos* (ivory-made, inlaid with ivory), *glaphyra* (*γλαφυρά*, hollow) etc. Iliad. IX, 186 «τὸν δ' εὗρον φρένα τερπνόμενον φόρμιγγι λιγείῃ» ("and they found him [Achilles] delighting his soul with a clear-toned lyre [sweet-voiced phorminx]". Also: XVIII, 569; Odyss. VIII, 67 («φόρμιγγα λίγειαν»; "sweet-voiced phorminx").

Hesiod I, 203 « ... χρυσείῃ φόρμιγγι» ("... by a golden phorminx"). Aristoph. Birds, 217-219 «ὁ χρυσοκόμας Φοῖβος ἀκούων τοῖς σοῖς ἐλέγοις ἀντιψάλλων ἐλεφαντόδετον φόρμιγγα» ("the golden-haired Phoebus (Apollo) listening to you, and accompanying thy elegies on his *ivory-made phorminx*"). Cf. *antipsalmos**.

Both the verbs *phormizein* (*φορμίζειν*; to play the phorminx) and *kitharizein* (*κιθαρίζειν*; see *kitharis**) are used for playing the phorminx or the kitharis; e.g. «φόρμιγγι κιθαρίζειν» (Hom. Il. XVIII 569-570 «τοῖσιν δ' ἐν μέσσοισι πάϊς φόρμιγγι λιγείῃ ἱμερόεν κιθάριζε»; "and in their midst a boy played charmingly a clear-toned phorminx"). Also Odys. I, 153-155 «κίθαριν ... φορμίζων» ("playing the kitharis").

phormiktes and *phormikter* (*φορμικτής, φορμικτήρ*; m. pr. phormiktís, -ír); phorminx player.

phormiktón melos (*φορμικτὸν μέλος*); song to phorminx accompaniment.

Bibliography:
   Ludwig Deubner: "Die viersaitige Leier" in Mitteilungen des deutschen Archäologischen Instituts, Athenische Abteilung; Band LIV, 1929, pp. 194-200.

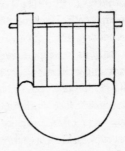

Fig. 4. Phorminx

photinx (**φῶτιγξ**); a "transverse" aulos made of lotus wood, of Egyptian origin.

It is said that it was Osiris' invention (Jubas ap. Athen. IV, 175E, ch. 78 «τὸν μόναυλον Ὀσίριδος εἶναι εὕρημα καθάπερ καὶ τὸν καλούμενον φώτιγγα πλαγίαυλον... ἐπιχωριάζει γὰρ καὶ ὁ φῶτιγξ αὐλὸς παρ' ἡμῖν»; "that the single-piped aulos was an invention of Osiris, as was also the cross-aulos called *photinx* ... which is customary in our country [Egypt]"). And further (ibid, 182D, ch. 80) there is a more precise passage on photinx: "and the so-called lotus-made auloi are called by the Alexandrians *photinges*. They are made of lotus wood which is grown in Libya".

Hesychius also says that *the photinx* is a transverse aulos («φῶτιγξ ... πλάγιος αὐλός»). See under *plagiaulos*.

Phrygios harmonia, or **Phrygisti** (**φρύγιος** ἁρμονία, **φρυγιστί**; m. pr. phrígios, phrigistí); generally accepted as Phrygian harmonia was the following octave-species (διὰ πασῶν, diapason, octachord):

$$d - c - b - a - g - f - e - d \qquad \text{(Diatonic genus)}$$
$$1 \quad \tfrac{1}{2} \quad 1 \quad 1 \quad 1 \quad \tfrac{1}{2} \quad 1$$

The Phrygian harmonia was, like the Lydian, of those harmoniai which were introduced to Greece from Asia Minor. As Athenaeus records (XIV, 625E, ch. 21) both the Phrygian and the Lydian harmoniai were made known to the Greeks by the barbarians, Phrygians and Lydians, who accompanied Pelops to Peloponnesus (Note: King Pelops, son of Tantalus, King of Lydia and Phrygia, came to Greece from Asia Minor with Lydians and Phrygians and colonized that part of Greece which was called after his name, Peloponnesus = island of Pelops).

The poet Telestes* of Selinous also says (ap. Athen. ibid, 626A) that "the Phrygian nomos in honour of the Mountain-Mother (Rhea) was performed on the aulos by Pelops' companions; and on high-pitched pektides they struck up a resounding Lydian hymn".

The Phrygian harmonia was quickly received and assimilated in all Greece, and became especially the harmonia of the dithyrambs. It was considered as inspiring enthusiasm and as such it was most suitable for music in honour of Dionysus. In fact it remained as the pre-eminently Dionysiac harmonia; its instrument was the aulos. Sophocles* is credited with the introduction of the Phrygian melopoeia into tragedy.

Cf. *ethos*.

Phrynichus (**Φρύνιχος**; m. pr. Phrínichos); 1) b. 510; d. 476 B.C. Athenian tragedian and musician.

Besides his contribution to the evolution of the classical drama, Phrynichus was a composer of charming and much admired melodies (cf. Arist. Probl. XIX, 31; Aristoph. Birds 749-751 «ἔνθεν ὥσπερ ἡ μέλιττα Φρύνιχος ἀμβροσίων μελέων ἀπεβόσκετο καρπὸν ἀεὶ φέρων γλυκεῖαν ᾠδάν» = "whence *Phrynichus*, like a bee, used to feed upon the fruit of ambrosian songs, ever bringing a sweet-strain"; transl. W. J. Hickie, Aristoph. vol. I, p. 341).

Phrynichus, like his contemporary Aeschylus, avoided the chromatic genus (Plut. De Mus. 1137E, ch. 20; "would it not be absurd to assert that Aeschylus and *Phrynichus* avoided the use of the chromatic genus out of ignorance?").

According to Aristocles (ap. Athen. I, 22A, ch. 39) "the old poets Thespis, Pratinas [Kratinus], Phrynichus, were called orchestai (ὀρχησταὶ) not only because they applied the orchesis of the chorus in their dramas, but also because besides their poetic works they taught dancing to those willing".

Cf. Brgk PLG III, p. 561; Aug. Nauck Trag. Gr. Fr., (suppl. Br. Snell, 1964) pp. 720-725.

2) Athenian comic poet of the 5th cent. B.C., contemporary of Aristophanes. Cf. Th. Kock Com. Att. Fr., vol. I, p. 370 ff.

Phrynis (Φρῦνις; m. pr. Phrínis); b.c. 475 B.C.; d.?

He was born in Mytilene (Μυτιλήνη, hence his surname Μυτιληναῖος, Mytilenaeus). According to Suidas he began his career as an aulode but soon he turned to the kithara, under the guidance of the reputed kitharist («εὐδόκι-μος κιθαριστὴς») Aristocleides («παραλαβὼν δὲ [Aristocleides] Φρῦνιν αὐλῳ-δοῦντα κιθαρίζειν ἐδίδαξεν»). In 446 B.C. he competed at the Panathenaea as a kitharode, winning the first prize.

Phrynis is regarded as the chief of the school of innovators of the 5th-4th cent. B.C. in Greece. He is credited with the development of the kitharodic nomos and its transformation into the "concert-aria"; he used an ornamented and modulating style in the melopoeia, and the nine-stringed kithara.

Once when he went to Sparta, the Ephor (Ἔφορος, Magistrate), before the performance, cut two strings of his nine-stringed instrument by which it exceeded the traditional seven, telling him that he would not be allowed to corrupt music. A similar incident happened later to Timotheus*. In his mature age his style became more reserved so that Music (in Pherecrates' comedy "Cheiron"; cf. Kinesias*, Melanippides*, Timotheus*) forgives him "for though he erred, he afterwards repented".

Though he was criticized by the comedians for his innovations, he was held by others in high esteem.

Aristotle in "Metaphysics" (I, 993B) writes "if Timotheus did not exist we would not have so many melodic compositions, and if Phrynis did not exist Timotheus would not exist either".

Nothing of his works survives.

phthongos (φθόγγος); sound, voice. In music a distinct sound with defi-nite pitch produced by the voice or any musical instrument; in pl. usually "notes" and "strings". Here are some definitions of phthongos:

Aristox. Harm. (I, p. 15, 15 Mb) "To put it briefly, *phthongos* is the incidence of the voice upon one pitch" («Συντόμως μὲν οὖν εἰπεῖν, φωνῆς πτῶσις ἐπὶ μίαν τάσιν φθόγγος ἐστί»).

Cleon. Isag. (ch. 1; C.v.J. p. 279, Mb p. 1) "*phthongos* is the musical incidence of a voice on one pitch" («φθόγγος μὲν οὖν ἐστι φωνῆς πτῶσις ἐμμελὴς ἐπὶ μίαν τάσιν»).

Bacchius (Isag. § 4; C.v.J. p. 292, Mb. p. 2) gives much the same definition by adding "a single pitch taken in the voice results in a musical *sound*" («μία γὰρ τάσις ἐν φωνῇ ληφθεῖσα ἐμμελῆ φθόγγον ἀποτελεῖ»).

Nicomachus in a more analytical way says (Enchir. ch. 11; C.v.J. p. 261, Mb p. 24) that "*phthongos* is an indivisible sound like a unit in hearing; as the more modern say, an incidence of a voice upon one simple pitch; and as some people say, a sound breadthless and continuous [without intermission]". («φθόγγος ἐστὶ φωνὴ ἄτομος, οἷον μονὰς κατ' ἀκοήν· ὡς δὲ οἱ νεώτεροι, ἐπίπτωσις φωνῆς ἐπὶ μίαν τάσιν καὶ ἁπλῆν· ὡς δ' ἔνιοι, ἦχος ἀπλατὴς κατὰ τόπον ἀδιάστατος»). Aristides (De Mus. Mb. pp. 12-13, RPW-I p. 10) distinguishes five differences between the musical sounds («διαφοραὶ φθόγγων»), as to the pitch («κατὰ τὴν τάσιν»), as to the interval (participation in one or more intervals; «κατὰ διαστήματος μετοχήν»), as to the system (as to participation in one or two systems; «κατὰ συστήματος μετοχήν»), as to the locus of the voice («κατὰ τὸν τῆς φωνῆς τόπον») and as to the ethos («κατὰ ἦθος»; the ethos varies according to the pitch of the sounds).

physallis (φυσαλλίς; m. pr. phisallís); a kind of aulos. Aristoph. Lysistr. 1245-6 «λαβὲ δῆτα τὰς φυσσαλλίδας (pl.) πρὸς τῶν Θεῶν, ὡς ἥδομαί γ' ὑμᾶς ὁρῶν ὀρχουμένους« ("take, then, *the pipes*, by the Gods, for I am pleased to see you dancing"; transl. W. J. Hickie, Aristoph., vol. II, p. 46). Schol. Aristoph. «λαβὲ δῆτα τὰς φυσαλλίδας» «τοὺς αὐλούς, ἀπὸ τοῦ φυσᾶν» ("take, then, the physallides", "the auloi [pipes] from the vb *physan* [to blow]").

pinakis, pl. pinakídes (πινακίς, pl. πινακίδες); a kind of dance accompanied by aulos.

Athen. (XIV, 629F, ch. 7) "they danced to the aulos the boatswain's dance and the so-called *pinakis* [platter-dance]". Pollux (IV, 103) «τὰς δὲ πινακίδας ὠρχοῦντο οὐκ οἶδα εἴτ' ἐπὶ πινάκων, εἴτε πίνακας φέροντες» ("they danced *the pinakides* [platter-dances], but I don't know whether on plates or carrying plates").

Note: pinakis (πινακίς); a small plate or platter, made of various materials covered with wax and used as a board to keep notes, accounts etc.

Pindarus, Pindar (Πίνδαρος; m. pr. Píndaros); b. c. 522 B.C.; d. c. 446 B.C.; he was born at Cynos Cephalai (Κυνὸς Κεφαλαί) near Thebes in Boeotia and died in Argos. This most celebrated of all lyric poets of ancient Greece studied music with Lasus* of Hermione, a prominent musician of the 6th century. Pindar's father, Daïphantus (Δαΐφαντος) was a practising musician, as was also his uncle Skopelinus (Σκοπελῖνος), from whom he received his first lessons in music and the auletic art.

Pindar composed hymns, paeans, dithyrambs, prosodia, parthenia, hypor-chemata, engomia, threni, and above all epinikoi (odes or hymns; Olympic, Pythian, Nemean, Isthmian hymns). As a musician Pindar remained a conser-vative, faithful to the tradition (cf. Plut. De Mus. 1134D, ch. 9; 1136F, ch. 17; 1137F, ch. 20; 1142B, ch. 31); he showed no interest in the innovations of his time. His simple and reserved classical style had a general appeal for all the Greeks.

Of Pindar's music nothing survives. The authenticity of a melodic frag-ment, pretending to be the opening lines of his First Pythian Ode, published by the Jesuit Athanassius Kircher in his "Musurgia Universalis" (Rome, 1650; vol. I, pp. 541-2) has been seriously disputed; see under *"Remains of Greek Music"** where this question is discussed.

Cf. among others, A. B. Drachmann: Scholia Vetera in Pindar's Carmina (Lipsiae, 1903); Brgk PLG part I (Olympic I-XIV, pp. 15-96; Pythians I-XII, pp. 101-184; Nemeans I-XI, pp. 186-242; Isthmians I-VIII, pp. 243-279) and various Fragments (Hymns, Paeans Prosodia, Parthenia, Hyporchemata, Enkomia, Threni, and Fragmenta Incerta, pp. 285-382).

plagia glossa (πλαγία γλῶσσα); see *synkrotetikai glottai.*

plagiaulos (πλαγίαυλος; m. pr. plagíavlos); transverse aulos.

It was held like the modern cross-flute but it had a reed inserted laterally at about the place where the modern flute has its hole. According to Pollux (IV, 74) the plagiaulos was of Libyan origin, and was made of lotus wood; «αὐλῶν δὲ εἴδη, πλάγιος, λώτινος, Λιβύων τὸ εὕρημα, πλαγίαυλον δὲ αὐτὸν Λίβυες καλοῦσιν» ("species of auloi are the oblique, lotus-made, invention of the Libyans, called by them plagiaulos").

Cf. *photinx*; *Th. Reinach*: "Plagiaule" in DAGR: vol. IX, 1919, p. 314; s.v. Tibia.

plasma (πλάσμα) from vb plassein (or plattein; πλάσσειν, πλάττειν) to mould, to form; in music, affected execution (LSJ; Dem.). Theophr. Hist. Plant. IV, ch. XI, 5 «τοῦτο δὲ ἀναγκαῖον τοῖς μετὰ πλάσματος αὐλοῦσι» ("this is necessary to those who play (the aulos) in an affected way" (with ornaments, trills etc.).

Opp. aplástos, adv. (ἀπλάστως) = naturally, without disguise (LSJ; Dem.).

plastinx (πλάστιγξ); part of aulos or syrinx. Hes. «μέρος τι τοῦ αὐλοῦ καὶ σύριγγος τὸ ζύγωμα».

Platon, Plato (Πλάτων; m. pr. Pláton); b. c. 429 or 427 B.C.; d. 347 B.C.

Plato's principal master was Socrates with whom he stayed for over eight years. After the death of Socrates (399) he travelled extensively, and in 387 he founded his School, the Academy (Ἀκαδημία).

The great philosopher studied music with Dracon* the Athenian and Metellus* of Agrigente (Plut. De Mus. 1136F, ch. 17); but he was greatly influenced by Damon's views on the ethical value of music and preserved for him a deep respect (Rep. IV, 424C). As a writer on music Plato was a Pythagorean; he recognized the Pythagorean (Diatonic) harmonia as formed by consonances, and much admired the Pythagorean definition of musical intervals by numerical ratios. He considered the Dorian harmonia as Hellenic par excellence in character and in virtuous quality (conceding the use of the Phrygian for the young warriors).

Generally speaking Plato was a musical purist, conservative and intransigent in his beliefs; for him beauty in music is expressed by simplicity, clarity, the preservation of the good tradition by orthodox means. He deeply and firmly believed that music is a divine art, has a lofty purpose, and is therefore a most suitable and efficacious means of education. In Phaedon (XXXVI, 85E) he says that "the harmonia is something invisible and immaterial, and something most beautiful and divine in the well-tuned lyra" («ἡ μὲν ἁρμονία ἀόρατόν τι καὶ ἀσώματον καὶ πάγκαλόν τι καὶ θεῖόν ἐστι ἐν τῇ ἡρμοσμένῃ λύρᾳ»).

A detailed account of his views is found in the Laws, esp. Book II; the following passage summarizes in a few words his view on the preservation of the tradition: "It never was and still is not permitted to any arist, painter or other, or to anybody regarding music to innovate or to pass over the laws of the country" (656D).

Plato also professes the ethical value of music and discusses the ethical importance of certain harmoniai and rhythms in the "Republic" (III, 398B-400C; cf. *ethos** and *harmonia**). He is against the confused mixture of the genera, the use of polychord and polyharmonic instruments, and of everything affected, excessively refined and unreasonably complicated. He advises against the use of "heterophonia"* in the education of boys.

Important parts of his philosophical conception of music can be found in his "Timaeus". But references to music are found also in "Protagoras" (e.g. 326A), in "Laches" (XIV, espec. 188D), in Phaedon (IV, 60E; XXXVI, 85E), Criton (50D), Alcibiades I (106E) etc.

Bibliography:

W. *Vetter*: "Die Musik im platonischen Staate"; Neue Jahrbücher für Wissenschaft und Jugenbildung 11, 1935, pp. 306-320.

Pierre *Maxime Schuhl*: "Platon et la musique de son temps"; Revue Internationale de Philosophie, No. 32, Bruxelles 1955, Fasc. 2, pp. 276-287.

Evanghélos *Moutsopoulos*: "La musique dans l'oeuvre de PLATON", Paris, 1959 (pp. 398 & 38, 8°).

Lukas *Richter*: "Zur Wissenschaftslehre von der Musik bei Platon und Aristoteles"; Berlin, 1961 (pp. XI & 202).   See also *Pythagoras.**

platos (πλάτος); breadth.   A term used by Lasus and some of the School of Epigonus; they thought that sound had a certain "quality" or breadth. This view is criticized by Aristoxenus (Harm. Elem. p. 3, 23-24 mb).   Cf. *aplates**.

plectron (πλῆκτρον); m. pr. plíctron); an implement (plectrum) by which the strings were struck; it was made of hard wood, or ivory, or horn, or metal, and as it often appears on vase-paintings was long and bulky.   Plato Laws (VII, 795A): «ἐν κερατίνοις πλήκτροις» ("by horn-made plectrums"). According to one tradition (Suid.) its invention was attributed to Sappho but its use was, it seems, known long before Sappho's time.   Apollodorus (III, ch. 10, § 2) attributes its invention to Hermes («καὶ ἐργασάμενος λύραν εὗρε καὶ πλῆκτρον»; "and [Hermes] having made the lyra, found also the plectrum"); cf. Homer Hymn to Hermes, v. 53; Pind. Nem. V under *heptaglossos**).   According to an old tradition Linus was killed by his pupil Heracles, who, being offended by his teacher's scoffing at his awkwardness, beat him to death with the kithara or the plectrum.   The plectrum, as shown on vasepaintings, was firmly held by the right hand; cf. also Philostrati Minoris Imagines, (Leipzig, T., 1902), Imag. 6 "Orpheus" «ἡ μὲν δεξιὰ ξυνέχουσα ἀπρὶξ τὸ πλῆκτρον ...».

It was attached by a ribbon to the lower part of the lyra or the kithara. Playing by the plectrum was called "plessein" (πλήσσειν) vb, to strike; use was also made of "krekein"* («κρέκειν») and "krouein" (κρούειν, to strike).

The maker of plectrums was called *plectropoeos* (πληκτροποιός).

See Plates III and IV.

ploke (πλοκή; m. pr. plokí); proceeding of the melody by skips.

Aristides (De Mus. Mb p. 19; RPW-I p. 16): «*πλοκὴ* δέ, ὅτε διὰ τῶν καθ᾿ ὑπέρτασιν λαμβανομένων» ("*ploke* then, when the melody proceeds by leaps"; cf. ibid, p. 29).

In Cleon. Isag. (ch. 14; C.v.J. p. 207, Mb p. 22) *ploke* is defined as the alternate use of ascending and descending skips:

The tunes (mele) formed principally by skips were called "mele keklas-ména"* («μέλη κεκλασμένα»).

Plutarchus, Plutarch (Πλούταρχος; m. pr. Ploútarchos); b. c. 46-48 A. D.; d. probably after 120 A. D. Suidas says that he lived before and during the time of Emperor (Marcus Ulpius) Trajanus (98-117 A.D.). Philosopher, biographer and historian, born at Chaeroneia (Χαιρώνεια) in Boeotia. His works are divided into two great groups, "The Parallel Lives" («Βίοι Παράλληλοι») and the "Moralia" («Ἠθικά»), in which there are frequent references to music. But there are especially two extensive studies on music, the "De procreatione in Timaeo" («Περὶ τῆς ἐν Τιμαίῳ Ψυχογονίας»), which is a commentary on Plato's musical theories in "Timaeus", and the dialogue "On Music" («Περὶ μουσικῆς»; "De Musica"); the latter is a treatise containing much information regarding principally the history but also the theory of ancient Greek music, derived from various older sources, Glaucus, Heraclides Ponticus, Aristoxenus, Plato, Aristotle and others. The fact that this Dialogue is mostly based on older authorities and sources, many of which are now lost, makes the book a valuable work of reference on many aspects and in particular on history of ancient Greek music.

The authenticity of the book is questioned by many scholars (Amyot, Benseler, Fuhr, Weissenberger, Lasserre), while some (Burette, Reinach) are inclined to regard it as a genuine work; this divergence of opinions does not alter its musical importance.

Many editions of the Dialogue have been published; the principal are the following:

1) *J. H. Bromby*: Plutarch's "On Music"; Greek text with an English translation (Chiswick, 1822);

2) *Rudolf Westphal*: "Plutarch über die Musik" with a German translation (Breslau, 1866);

3) *Henri Weil* et *Th. Reinach*: Plutarque: De la musique (édition critique et explicative; Paris, 1900); with a French translation;

4) *K. Ziegler*: Plutarchos, Moralia VI, 3 (Leipzig, 1953);

5) *François Lasserre*: "Plutarque de la Musique" (Olten et Lausanne, 1954) with an extended study on musical education in ancient Greece (pp. 13-95), prolegomena (pp. 99-104), the MS tradition (pp. 105-109), the Greek text (pp. 111-132), French translation (pp. 133-151) and Commentary (pp. 152-180).

Note: P. J. Burette published a number of studies on Plutarch's Dialogue in the "Mémoires de Littérature":

1) April, 1728 "Examen du traité de Plutarque";

2) May, 1729 "Observations touchant l'histoire littéraire du dialogue de Plutarque sur la musique";

3) March, 1730 "Analyse du dialogue de Plutarque sur la musique".

pneuma (πνεῦμα; m. pr. pnévma); the breath by which the player of the aulos or other wind instrument could produce or modify the pitch. Aristox. (Harm. p. 42, 13 Mb) «τῷ πνεύματι ἐπιτείνοντες καὶ ἀνιέντες» ("raising or lowering the pitch by regulating [the pressure of] *the breath*").

Pollux (IV, 69) says that "an aulete would be praised for the length (duration), the intensity and the power of his breath".

The vb *pneein* (πνέειν) signified, in the case of the player, to blow [or play by blowing] into the instrument, and in the case of the instrument itself, to produce a sound by blowing.

pneusis (πνεῦσις; m. pr. pnéfsis); breathing, blowing.

pnoe (πνοή; m. pr. pno·í·); breath of a wind instrument (LSJ). «αὐλοῦ τε σύριγγος πνοή» = "*breath* of an aulos or syrinx".

podikra (ποδίκρα); a kind of Laconic dance, mentioned by Hesychius with no indication of its character («ὄρχησις πρὸς πόδα γινομένη, Λάκωνες»).

podismos (ποδισμός); a kind of dance mentioned by Pollux (IV, 99) in the chapter "On kinds of dancing" without any indication of its character.

podopsophos (ποδοψόφος); a man who produced a noise (percussion sound) by beating his foot. In theatrical performances a musician was so called who had a metallic plate fastened under his sandal, by which he kept the time for the group of auletes; he was in some sort a primitive conductor.

Philostratus Minor writes in *Imag*. 6 ("Orpheus"; Leipzig, T., 1902) that of the two feet the left one supports the kithara while the right one begins to beat the rhythm by clapping on the ground with the sandal («ὁ δεξιὸς δὲ ἀναβάλλεται τὸν ρυθμὸν ἐπικροτῶν τοὔδαφος τῷ πεδίλῳ»).

poeema (ποίημα; m. pr. píima); see *poeesis*, below.

poeesis (ποίησις; m. pr. píisis); the word had a wide scope of significations in the ancient Greek language. It was used to mean, especially in old times, the creation or construction of almost everything (Thucyd. III, 2 «ποίησις νεῶν» = construction of ships).

Its specific signification in the sense of "creation of works of art" (e.g. poeesis epon, melon [composition of epi, mele] etc.) was attributed to Simonides*.

Plato (Sympos. 205B) gives the following interpretation of the term "poeesis": "*Poeesis* is something very wide; when something from non-existence

262

proceeds to being, the cause is wholly *creation* (ποίησις), so that all works made under the guidance of arts are creations (poeeseis) and their *creators* are *poeetai*".

In ancient texts we often meet with the term *poeetes* (ποιητὴς) for the composer of music, and *poeema* (ποίημα) for a poem but also for a musical composition. Plut. De Mus. 1137B, ch. 18: «μαρτυρεῖ γοῦν τὰ Ὀλύμπου τε καὶ Τερπάνδρου *ποιήματα* καὶ τῶν τούτοις ὁμοιοτρόπων πάντων»; "witness of that are the *compositions* of Olympus and Terpander and of all their colleagues". Dio Chrys. ("On reigning I", § 10; «οὐκ ᾠδοί τινες, οὐδὲ *ποιηταὶ μελῶν*»; "not singers, nor composers of mele").

Poetike (ποιητικὴ) was also the art of composing.

The relation of poetry and music, of poet and composer of music was so deep, in fact inseparable, that for centuries (until the time of Aristoxenus in the 4th cent. B.C.) the poet was at the same time a composer of mele, and in older times also an executant of music. When they used the term "melos" they meant "poetry and melody". The "lyric poetry" (λυρικὴ ποίησις; a term which appears after classical times) was in fact verses sung, principally to lyra (hence the Adj. "lyric") but also to other instruments' accompaniment.

Chorike poeesis (χορικὴ ποίησις) from chorus (χορός, dance); the songs sung by the chorus with instrumental accompaniment. It originated from the ancient orchesis, and was developed after the epic poetry. Usually the choral poetry was combined with dancing, and it may be said that it represented the triple combination of poetry, music and orchesis. The choral poetry began to flourish in the 7th cent. B.C. with the establishment of the gymnopaediai in Sparta, one of its masters being Thaletas. Other masters of the chorike poeesis, which flourished especially in the Dorian cities, were Xenocritus*, Xenodamus*, Alcman*, Stesichorus*.

In classical times choral lyricism finds its finest flourish with such great lyric poets as Simonides*, Bacchylides* and the supreme master, Pindar*.

The principal species of "choral poetry" were the dithyramb, the paean, and the hymn; also the hyporchema, the encomium, the epinikos etc.

Cf. *choral* [chorikon] *melos*, under *chorikos**.

poeetes (ποιητής; m. pr. piitís); *poeetike* (ποιητική; m. pr. piitikí); the art of the poeetes, the art of composing. See *poeesis*, above.

poekilos (ποικίλος; m. pr. pikílos); varied, diversified; ποικίλος ὕμνος = a song of changeful strain or full of diverse art (LSJ).

poekilia (ποικιλία; m. pr. pikilía); variety, ornamentation (LSJ) «πολυχορδία καὶ *ποικιλία*» (Plut. De Mus. ch. 18, 1137B)= "multiplicity of strings (notes) and *variety*".

poephygma (ποίφυγμα; m. pr. píphigma); after Hes. a dance-figure («σχῆμα ὀρχηστικόν»). General meaning hissing, blowing (Dem., LSJ).

polemikón (πολεμικὸν) melos; 1) a kind of aulesis (aulos-solo) of a war-like character. The polemikon (= of war) is included in Tryphon's catalogue of Denominations of auleseis (ap. Athen. XIV, 618C, ch. 9). The full catalogue of auleseis (pl.) may be seen under *aulesis**.

2. Polemikon was also used in the sense of a trumpet-call; Xen. Anab. IV, ch. 3 § 29 «ἐπειδὰν ... ὁ σαλπικτὴς σημήνῃ τὸ *πολεμικὸν*» ("whenever ... the trumpeter plays the *war-call*").

pollaploun systema (πολλαπλοῦν σύστημα); multiple system. Also *pollaplásion*. See under *haploun** and *systema**.

polychordia, oligochordia (πολυχορδία, ὀλιγοχορδία);

a) *polychordia* (m. pr. polichordía); the use of many strings, the fact of being "polychordos"* (many-stringed).

b) *oligochordia*; the use of a few strings; the fact of being "oligochordos".

Both these terms were used in contradistinction to each other. The "oligochordia" and simplicity were connected with the good old tradition and purity of style. The "polychordia" was connected with the innovations of Melanippides*, Phrynis*, Timotheus* and others, with the abandonment of tradition and the adoption of a new style richer in diversity. Plato was perhaps the chief defender of the first and condemned the use of "polychord" and "polyharmonic" instruments.

Cf. Plut. De Mus. 1135D, ch. 12, and 1137A, ch. 18.

polychordon, organon, neut. (πολύχορδον, ὄργανον; m. pr. políchordon); having many strings, a many-stringed instrument. The term is used also in the sense of producing many sounds, as *polyphone* (πολύφωνος); «πολύχορδος αὐλός», many-toned aulos. See *chorde**.

To the category of polychord (many-stringed) instruments belonged those of the psalterion family, namely the magadis, pektis, phoenix or phoenikion, sambyke and others.

Cf. Plato Rep. III, 399D; also *enchorda**.

Polydeukes Iulius, Pollux (Πολυδεύκης Ἰούλιος; m. pr. Polidéfkis Ioúlios); grammarian and lexicographer of the 2nd cent. A.D. generally known as Pollux. Born at Naucratis (Ναύκρατις) in Egypt he studied under the orator Adrianus, pupil of the sophist Herodes Atticus, in Athens, where he lived until his death at the age of 58. After exercising the profession of sophist and of teacher of oratory he was appointed in 178 A.D. to the chair of oratory by the

Emperor Commodus (161-191). His most important work was his "Onomastikon" (Ὀνομαστικόν), a Lexicon consisting of ten books and containing knowledge on every aspect of life; the words (of the Attic dialect) are classified not alphabetically but in chapters of various categories and classes. In the Fourth Book there is most valuable information regarding music; this makes the "Onomastikon" an important source of information on ancient Greek music, as also on orchesis and theatre; frequent reference to the "Onomastikon" is made in the present encyclopaedia.

It seems that the existing Lexicon is an abridged edition of a larger work; the abridged form was preserved through the Archbishop of Caesarea Arethas (Ἀρέθας; 850-935 AD), who held a copy. Several editions have been published; among others: first by A. P. Manutius (Venice, 1502); 2) by R. Gualther—W. Seber (Frankfurt, 1608); 3) by Gulielmus Dindorfius (Leipzig, 1824); 4) by I. Bekker (Berlin, 1846); 5) by E. Bethe (Leipzig, T., Lexicographi Graeci, vol. IX, 1900).

Note: The following chapters from the Fourth Book dealing principally with music will give an idea of the contents and the form of the Onomastikon:

ch. VII. About national songs (Περὶ ᾀσμάτων ἐθνικῶν).

About Music and names appropriate to it (Περὶ μουσικῆς καὶ τῶν προσφόρων αὐτῇ ὀνομάτων).

ch. VIII. About musical instruments and musicians and all concerning them (Περὶ μουσικῶν ὀργάνων καὶ μουσικῶν καὶ τῶν περὶ αὐτά).

ch. IX. a) About stringed instruments (Περὶ κρουομένων ὀργάνων);

    b) About instruments found among nations (Περὶ ὀργάνων εὑρεθέντων ἔθνεσιν);

    c) About parts of the stringed instruments (Περὶ μερῶν τῶν κρουομένων ὀργάνων);

    d) About harmonias and nomoi (Περὶ ἁρμονιῶν καὶ νόμων);

    e) About wind instruments (Περὶ ἐμπνευστῶν ὀργάνων);

    f) About the aulos-maker and his material (Περὶ αὐλοποιοῦ καὶ τῆς ὕλης αὐτοῦ);

ch. X. a) Kinds of instruments (Εἴδη ὀργάνων);

    b) About auletic harmonias, melodies and nomoi of Olympus and the others (Περὶ ἁρμονιῶν αὐλητικῶν, μελῶν καὶ νόμων Ὀλύμπου καὶ λοιπῶν);

    c) About their difference (Περὶ διαφορᾶς αὐτῶν);

    d) About aulemata and lessons (Περὶ αὐλημάτων καὶ μαθημάτων);

e) About the five Pythian contests (Περὶ τῶν πέντε Πυθικῶν ἀγώνων);

ch. XI. About the salpinx (Περὶ σάλπιγγος);

ch. XIII. About orchestes and orchesis (Περὶ ὀρχηστοῦ καὶ ὀρχήσεως);

ch. XIV. About kinds of orchesis (Περὶ εἰδῶν ὀρχήσεως);

ch. XV. About the chorus, choreutai and the like (Περὶ χοροῦ, χορευτῶν καὶ τῶν τοιούτων);

ch. XVI. On choral songs (Περὶ χορικῶν ᾀσμάτων);

ch. XVII. On theatrical actors and acting (Περὶ ὑποκριτῶν καὶ ὑποκρίσεως).

Polyeidus or **Polyidus** (**Πολύειδος** or **Πολύϊδος**; m. pr. Políidos); b. c. 440 or 430 B.C.; d. 4th cent. B.C.; composer of dithyrambs, born at Selymbria in Thrace (Σηλυμβρία, hence Σηλυμβριανός, Selymbrianos).

According to Diodorus Sikeliotes (XIV, ch. 46, § 6) Polyidus was one of the celebrated (ἐπισημότατοι) composers of dithyrambs of the time, together with Philoxenus, Timotheus and Telestes; Diodorus adds that Polyidus was also a painter («Πολύειδος, ὃς καὶ ζωγραφικῆς καὶ μουσικῆς εἶχεν ἐμπειρίαν»).

He competed and won in Athens as a composer of dithyrambs ("Par. Chron." I, v. 68; Athen. VIII, 352 B). In Plutarch (1138B, ch. 21) his works are called patchwork pieces («καττύματα» = pieces of hard leather put under the sandals).

Very few fragments of his poetry survive: Brgk PLG III, p. 632; FHG II, p. 781; Page PMG p. 441, frg. 837.

polyharmonion, organon (**πολυαρμόνιον**; m. pr. poliarmónion); an instrument capable of producing many and various harmonias; upon which many harmonias could be played. This term was used by Plato in the "Republic" (399D) together with "polychorda" («πολυαρμόνια καὶ πολύχορδα»).

polykephalos, nomos (**πολυκέφαλος**, νόμος); "many-headed" nomos, an auletic nomos in honour of Apollo attributed to Olympus.

Plut. De Mus. (1133D, ch. 7): "it is said that the aforesaid Olympus, the Phrygian aulete, invented an auletic nomos in honour of Apollo, called *many-headed*" («λέγεται γὰρ τὸν προειρημένον Ὄλυμπον, αὐλητὴν ὄντα ἐκ Φρυγίας, ποιῆσαι νόμον καλούμενον πολυκέφαλον»). Some writers attributed the polykephalos nomos to Olympus' pupil Krates*; Pratinas attributed this nomos to Olympus the younger (Plut. op. cit. 1133E, ch. 7), while according to one tradition it was attributed to Athena. It was called polykephalos (many-headed) because the melody imitated the whistlings of the many

266

serpents on the heads or the Gorgons who were lamenting the beheading of their sister Medusa by Perseus. Cf. Pindar 12th Pythian Ode, and A. B. Drachmann "Scholia Vetera in Pindari Carmina" (Leipzig, 1910, vol. II p. 265): «ὠνόμασαν κεφαλᾶν πολλᾶν νόμον» ("and called it the *many-headed* nomos»).

See *auletike**.

Polymnestus or **Polymnastus** (Πολύμνη[α]στος; m. pr. Polímni[a]stos); 7th to 6th cent. B.C., poet and musician from Colophon (Κολοφῶν) of Ionia in Asia Minor.

To Polymnestus were attributed the invention of the Ionian (later Hypolydian) harmonia, and of the use of a much wider eklysis* and ekbole* (Plut. De Mus. 1141B, ch. 29).

Polymnestus was a successor of Clonas*, the initiator of the aulodic nomos, and composed songs, generally of an indecent character, to aulos accompaniment; hence, from his name all indecent and lascivious songs were called "Polymnesteia" («πολυμνήστεια»), and the expression "to compose Polymnesteia" («πολυμνήστεια ποιεῖν») was used in the sense "to compose indecent songs"; cf. Aristoph. Hipp. (Knights) v. 1287 «πολυμνήστεια ποιῶν» ("[the brother of Arignotus] composing Polymnestean [indecent] songs or poems").

See also Brgk PLG III, p. 13 one fragment.

polyphonos (πολύφωνος; m. pr. políphonos); having many voices (sounds); many-toned.   Same as polyphthongos.

polyphonia (πολυφωνία; m. pr. poliphonía); multiplicity of voices (sounds); variety of tones (LSJ).

polyphthongos (πολύφθογγος; m. pr. políphthongos);

1) Adj; of having or producing many sounds; many-toned. *Polyphthongos aulos* (πολύφθογγος αὐλὸς) many-toned aulos (Pollux IV, 67). "polyphthonga psalteria" («πολύφθογγα ψαλτήρια») = psalteria producing many notes ("many-toned" psalteria; ap. Plut. 827A).   Cf. *polychordos**.

2) Neut. subst.; a many-stringed instrument of the harp family played by bare fingers. It is mentioned by Aristides (De Mus. Mb p. 101, RPW-I p. 85) as an instrument which, compared as to ethos or character with other instruments "partakes, according to Aristides, more of femininity" («τὸ δὲ πολύφθογγον πλέον μετέχον θηλύτητος»).

polytropos (πολύτροπος; m. pr. polítropos); manifold; with many modulations; often in the sense of *poekilos**.

Cf. Plut. De Mus. ch. 18, 1137B.

poppysma, poppysmos (πόππυσμα, ποππυσμός; m. pr. póppisma, pop-

267

pismós); smacking of lips, clucking (LSJ);

See *syrigmos**.

Porphyrius, Porphyry (Πορφύριος; m. pr. Porphírios); b. 232 or 233 A.D. at Tyros (Τύρος, hence Τύριος, Tyrius) in Syria; d. 304 or 305 A.D. in Rome(?). His original name was Malchus (Μάλχος; in Arab Malik = king) and was changed by his teacher Gaius Cassius Longinus to Porphyrius (Πορφύριος; πορφύρα = purple; dressed or robed in purple; figur. regal). He was a pupil of the Neoplatonic philosopher Longinus, and was himself one of the last representatives of the Alexandrian Neoplatonic School. He passed some time in Sicily and in Rome, and wrote several philosophical, historical, mathematical and other works.

His contribution to the study of music is his important Commentary on Ptolemaeus' Harmonika published by Iohannes Wallis, with a Latin translation, in the third volume of his "Opera Mathematica" (Oxford, 1699; "Porphyrii Commentarius", pp. 189-355); and by Ingemar Düring with a German translation ("Porphyrios Kommentar zur Harmonielehre des Ptolemaios"; Göteborg, 1932).

Porphyrius is considered by some scholars as the author of only the first four chapters of Book I, the remainder being ascribed to Pappus* of Alexandria.

pous (πούς); foot; the main rhythmical unit consisting of two or more syllables or "times" (χρόνοι). The syllables or "times" (chronos*) can be interlaced, according to Bacchius (§ 96; C.v.J. p. 314. Mb p. 23), in four ways, 1) short to short (υ υ), 2) long to long (- -), 3) long to short (- υ) and 4) irrational to long («ἄλογος μακρῷ» (υ | -). Two such syllables constitute a disyllabic foot; disyllabic feet were the iambos* (υ-); the dibrachys (δίβραχυς; with two short syllables, υ υ) also called hegemon (ἡγεμών) or pyrrhichios; the spondee* (- -); the trochee* (- υ) also called choreios. Trisyllabic feet were the anapaest* (υ υ -); the dactyl (- υ υ); the amphibrachys, also called Cretan (- υ -). Tetrasyllabic feet were the paeon* (with its various species, - υυυ, υ - υυ, υυ-υ, υυυ -); the baccheios* (- υυ -); the Ionikos - - υυ).

In all the above cases the feet are composed of simple times (chronos* disemos, trisemos, tetrasemos).

Bacchius and Aristides call the feet "rhythms" (ρυθμοί); Bacchius (§ 100) enumerates ten, of which six are simple (hegemon, iambus, choreios, anapaest, orthios [of irrational arsis and long thesis, υ | -] and spondee), and four are compound (paean [paeon], baccheius, dochmios* [composed of an iambus, an anapaest and a paeon] and enoplios [composed of iambus and hegemon and choreios and iambus].

The feet, according to the length of the interlaced syllables, may constitute a binary or ternary rhythm. Aristides (De Mus., Mb p. 36ff, RPW-I p. 35ff) distinguishes simple and compound rhythms; 1) the simple binary (dactylic genus), which are, a) the hegemon or prokeleusmatikos (υ υ); b) the prokeleusmatikos double (προκελευσματικὸς διπλοῦς, υ υ υ υ); c) the dactyl or anapaest a majore (ἀπὸ μείζονος; - υ υ); d) the anapaest a minore (ἀπὸ ἐλάσσονος; υυ -); e) the spondee simple (- -) and f) the spondee major (σπονδεῖος μείζων or διπλοῦς; υ υ υ υ | υ υ υ υ). 2) The simple ternary rhythms a) the iambus (υ -); b) the trochee (- υ); c) the orthios (irrational, υ | -) and d) the trochee semantic (τροχαῖος σημαντός; - | υ or the opposite of the orthios). 3) The simple quinary: a) the paeon diagyios (- υ -) and b) the paeon epibatos (- | - - - -).

The compound rhythms are: a) those composed of a syzygy (συζυγία) of two simple binary rhythms; b) those composed of a syzygy of two simple ternary rhythms and c) those composed of a syzygy of two simple rhythms of different genus. For more details one has to consult Aristides chs. XIV-XVIII, Mb pp. 34-42, R.P.W-I. pp. 33-39.

Bibliography: see under *rhythmos*.

Pratinas of Phlious (**Πρατίνας** ὁ Φλιάσιος); 6th to 5th cent. B.C. dramatic and lyric poet, born at Phlious (Φλιοῦς, hence Phliásios) in Peloponnesus. He was a contemporary of Aeschylus and Choerilus, against both of whom he competed at the 70th Olympiad (499-496 B.C.).

According to Suidas he wrote 50 dramatic works including 32 satirical ones («Σάτυροι»), a theatrical innovation of his. He won once at the contests, Suidas records.

Pratinas composed also hyporchemata, all lost except one consisting of 20 verses preserved by Athenaeus in the Deipnosophists (XIV, 617 C-F, ch. 8).

Cf. Brgk PLG III, pp. 557-560, and Anth. Lyr. pp. 273-274; Fr. Lasserre "Plutarque de la Musique" (Olten et Lausanne, 1954; ch. V "Les débuts de l'éthique musicale", Pratinas pp. 45-47). Also Page PMG pp. 367-9, frgs 708-713.

proanabole (**προαναβολή**; m. pr. proanavolí), poet. proambole (προαμβολή); a short introductory melos leading to the prooemion (προοίμιον; the main introduction) of the principal ode. What comes before the anabole* (prelude).

proanakrousma (**προανάκρουσμα**); an instrumental prelude, usually short, before the principal ode or piece. Also *proanákrousis* (προανάκρουσις).

Cf. proaulema*, *prooemion*.

proasma (**πρόασμα**); a short introductory song before the principal ode or hymn. It was also called prooemion*. From pro- (before) and asma (song).

269

proaulema (προαύλημα; m. pr. proávlima); a short prelude on the aulos played by the aulete before the beginning of the aulodia*. From pro- (before) and aulema (aulos-solo). The vb proaulein (προαυλεῖν), to play a prelude on the aulos.

proaulia, fem. and **proaulion**, neut. (προαυλία, προαύλιον; m. pr. proavlía, proávlion); prelude on the aulos. Synonyms of proaulema.

Cf. Pollux IV, 53.

Proclus (Πρόκλος; m. pr. Próclos); b. c. 400-412; d. 485 A.D. Neoplatonic philosopher and mathematician. His numerous works include commentaries on Euclid's First Book of Elements (Στοιχεῖα) and on Ptolemy; also Commentaries (Ὑπομνήματα) on Plato's Timaeus, Republic etc., in which he gives information regarding Plato's musical conceptions. In his "Chrestomatheia" (Χρηστομάθεια) we find information concerning various kinds of composition, such as the prosodion, dithyramb, nomos, scolion, partheneia, tripodikon, oschophorika etc. It has been edited by *Th. Gaisford* (Leipzig, 1832); cf. also *R. Westphal*: "Scriptores Metrici Graeci" (Leipzig, 1866; «ἐκ τῆς Πρόκλου Χρηστομαθείας Β»); vol. I, p. 242 ff.

prokeleusmatikos (προκελευσματικός; m. pr. prokelefsmatikós); metrical foot, simple υυ, double υυυυ. See under *pous**.

prokrouma (πρόκρουμα) from pro- (before) and krouma* (instrumental sound or piece); an instrumental prelude. Synonym of *proanakrousma**.

prokrousis-prolepsis (πρόκρουσις, πρόληψις; m. pr. prókrousis, prólipsis); *prokrousis* was a term signifying the proceeding from a lower note to a higher one in instrumental melody; the equivalent in vocal melody was called *prolepsis*.

The prokrousis and the prolepsis could be made either directly (ἀμέσως), i. e. by step (ex. a, below), or indirectly (ἐμμέσως), i.e. by a leap of a 3rd, 4th or 5th (ex. b).

When the notes were tied it was called "hyphen from inside" («ὑφ' ἕν ἔσωθεν»; cf. *ekkrousis-eklepsis**) ex. c.

Cf. Anon. Bell (§§ 5 & 86 p. 22, and §§ 6 & 88, p. 24); Man. Bryen. Sect. III (ed. J. Wallis III; p. 479). A. J. H. Vincent (Notices, p. 53) prefers the term πρόσ-κρουσις (*proskrousis*) and πρόσ-ληψις (*proslepsis*) which are also met with.

The prokrousis and the prolepsis were schemata of the melos.

See also *ekkrousis-eklepsis**, *prokrousmós-prolemmatismos**, *ekkrousmos-eklemmatismos**, *kompismos-melismos**, *teretismos** and *diastole**.

prokrousmos-prolemmatismos (προκρουσμός, προλημματισμός; m. pr. prokrousmós, prolimmatismós); both were schemata of the melos; the first was the intercalation of a higher note between two enunciations of the same note in instrumental melody, and the second (prolemmatismos) the equivalent in vocal melody (in «μουσικὸν μέλος»).

This was done either directly (i.e. by step, ex. a) or indirectly (i.e. by a leap of a 3rd, 4th and 5th; ex. b). Compare with the previous entry: prokrousis-prolepsis.

Cf. Man. Bryen. (ap. Wallis, III; p. 480); Anon. Bell. p. 24.
For other schemata see under the *prokrousis-prolepsis**.

A. J. H. Vincent (Notices, p. 53) prefers the terms *pros-krousmos* and *pros-lemmatismos*.

pronomion (προνόμιον); a prelude, vocal or instrumental, sung or played before the performance of the nomos.

It was somewhat similar to the prooemion, the proasma, the proaulema and the proaulion.

Pronomus (Πρόνομος; m. pr. Prónomos); 5th cent. B.C. aulete of repute from Thebes. He was the first to play all the harmonias on the same aulos. Before him the auletes (αὐληταί, auletai) used in the public contests different auloi for every harmonia (cf. Athen. XIV, 631E; ch. 31).

Pausanias (IX, ch. 12, §5) says that a statue in his honour was erected in Thebes for the highly artistic entertainment he offered to the public; "it is said also that when he played he gave the audience great delight by the expression of his face and by the movements of his whole body" («λέγεται δὲ ὡς καὶ τοῦ προσώπου τῷ σχήματι καὶ τῇ τοῦ παντὸς κινήσει σώματος περισσῶς δή τι ἔτερπε τὰ θέατρα»).

Duris in his work on Euripides and Sophocles (ap. Athen. IV, 184D, ch. 84) says that "Alcibiades learned the art of aulos-playing from no ordinary master but from Pronomus, who acquired very great reputation" («τοῦ μεγίστην ἐσχηκότος δόξαν»).

Pronomus' name is associated with a famous crater (National Museum of

271

Naples), known as "Pronomus' vase" («Προνόμου ἀγγεῖον»). On this beautiful vase, of probably the beginning of the 4th cent. B.C., Pronomus is presented on the lower part playing his aulos by the side of king Laomedon.

See PLATE VII

Note: Together with Pronomus the name of Diodorus may be cited, as one of the auletai innovators of the Theban school. *Diodorus (Διόδωρος;* m. pr. Diodoros), probably a contemporary of Pronomus, is mentioned by Pollux (IV, 80) as having augmented the number of the aulos-holes («καὶ τέως μέν, τέτταρα τρυπήματα εἶχεν ὁ αὐλός, πολύτρητον δ' αὐτὸν ἐποίησε Διόδωρος ὁ Θηβαῖος, πλαγίας ἀνοίξας τῷ πνεύματι τὰς ὁδούς» = "and until that time the aulos had four holes, and Diodorus the Theban made it 'polytretos' [with many holes] by opening oblique ways for the breath").

proodós (προῳδός); prelude; a short melos performed before the main ode. From pro- (before) and ode.

Cf. *proasma*, prooemion*,* etc.

prooemion (προοίμιον; m. pr. pro·í·mion); an introductory melody to the principal ode; a short lyric song sung as an introduction to a more extended and more important ode or hymn; also an instrumental prelude by which the kitharode began his performance (the kitharodia; cf. *kitharodos**).

In epic poetry it signified a prologue.

Hes. "*Prooemion* [is] a prologue, a beginning of every talk (story, speech, statement)" («*Προοίμιον·* πρόλογος, ἀρχὴ παντὸς λόγου»).

Cf. *proasma*, proanakrousma*, proaulema*, proaulion*.*

Prophrastus of Pieria (Πρόφραστος ὁ Πιερίτης; m. pr. Próphrastos Pierítis); c. middle of 5th cent. B.C. musician.

He was accredited with the daring innovation of adding the 9th string to the lyra (Excerpta ex Nicom.; ch. 4, C.v.J. p. 274; «Πρόφραστός τε ὁ Πιερίτης τὴν ἐνάτην χορδὴν προσκαθῆψε» = "and Prophrastus of Pieria added the 9th string").

Note: In Meibom's Excerpta ex Nicom., p. 35, the name was corrected to Theophrastus (Θεόφραστος).

propoda mele (πρόποδα μέλη); songs sung before the procession; preceding the actual procession (Dem. and LSJ s.v. πρόπους, "propous").

prosanienai, vb (προσανιέναι; m. pr. prosaniéne); to lower the pitch of besides (LSJ, Dem.). Plut. De Mus. (ch. 39, 1145D): «ἀλόγῳ τινὶ διαστήματι προσανιέντες αὐτοῖς τάς τε τρίτας καὶ τὰς παρανήτας» ("*lowering moreover* the tritai and the paranetai by an incommensurable interval").

prosaulein, vb (προσαυλεῖν; m. pr. prosavlín); to accompany by the aulos;

to sing to aulos accompaniment. It seems that the verb was used only in the sense of accompanying in unison.

prosaulema (προσαύλημα; m. pr. prosávlima); a tune or melody played on the aulos to accompany (in unison) a song.

See *prosaulein*, above.

prosaulesis (προσαύλησις; m. pr. prosávlisis); an accompaniment on the aulos (in unison with the main song). Pollux (IV, 83) «οἱ δέ, τὴν συναυλίαν εἶδος *προσαυλήσεως* οἴονται, ὡς τὴν αὐλῳδίαν» ("and others believe that the synaulia* is a kind of *prosaulesis* like the aulodia*"; i.e. as in the aulodia the aulos accompanies the song).

See *prosaulein*.

proschordos (πρόσχορδος); attuned to a stringed instrument; in harmony (probably in unison) with a stringed instrument;

proschorda (neut., pl.) ásmata (*πρόσχορδα ᾄσματα*); melodies attuned (or sung in unison) to a stringed instrument; cf. Pollux, IV, 63. Also *proschórdasma* (προσχόρδασμα).

proschorda krouein (vb; «*πρόσχορδα κρούειν*») was an expression used most probably in the sense of doubling the vocal part on the instrument; this should be distinguished from "krouein (or krousis) hypo ten oden" («κροῦσις ὑπὸ τὴν ᾠδήν»); Plut. De Mus. (1141B, ch. 28): «οἴονται δὲ καὶ τὴν *κροῦσιν* τὴν *ὑπὸ τὴν ᾠδὴν* τοῦτον (i.e. Κρέξον) πρῶτον εὑρεῖν, τοὺς δ᾽ ἀρχαίους πάντας *πρόσχορδα κρούειν*» ("they believe that he [i.e. Krexus] was the first to invent the accompaniment of the song on the stringed instrument with different notes, while the ancients used to double the song in unison").

proschoros (πρόσχορος); member of a chorus, esp. partner in the chorus. Pollux (IV, 106) «*πρόσχορον* δὲ καὶ *συγχορεύτριαν* εἴρηκε τὴν χορεύουσαν Ἀριστοφάνης».

Cf. Th. Kock Com. Att. Fr. vol. I, p. 582, Fr. 843; also Bothe PSGF, II, p. 192. See *synchoros*.

proslambanomenos (προσλαμβανόμενος; m. pr. proslamvanómenos); added note. So was called the added note below the lowest tetrachord (tetrachord of hypaton) of both the Lesser and the Greater Perfect Systems. By the addition of the proslambanómenos the Mese remained the real central note in the Greater Perfect System, as also in the Ametabolon (see under *systema**).

prosmelodein, vb (προσμελῳδεῖν; m. pr. prosmelodín); to sing songs to or besides (LSJ); to accompany by a melody (Dem.).

prosodia (προσῳδία); a) a song sung to instrumental accompaniment. Pollux (IV, 64) «καὶ γὰρ Πλάτων ... τὰς πρὸς κιθάραν ᾠδὰς προσῳδίας ἀρέσκει καλεῖν» ("and Plato ... prefers (likes) to call *prosodias* the odes to kithara accompaniment"). Hes. «προσῳδία μετ᾽ ὀργάνου ᾠδὴ» ("*prosodia*; an ode with instrument[al accompaniment]"). Cf. Etym. M. p. 690.

b) *Prosodia* (often in pl., prosodiai, προσῳδίαι); the particular accent on the words in speech; the variation in pitch of the speaking voice (LSJ). Aristox. (Harm. I, p. 18, 14 Mb) «λέγεται γὰρ καὶ λογῶδές τι μέλος, τὸ συγκείμενον ἐκ τῶν προσῳδιῶν τῶν ἐν τοῖς ὀνόμασιν» ("for there is also a kind of melody in speech which depends upon the *accents* of the words" (or "the variation in pitch of the words").

Cf. *logodes melos*.

prosodion (προσόδιον) melos; a song of a pompous and solemn character sung by chorus to aulos accompaniment with rhythmical movements, during a festal procession, and especially on approaching the temple or the altar.

Procl. Chrest., 10 "and it was called *prosodion* because [it is sung while] they approach the altars or the temples; and on approaching it was sung to aulos accompaniment; the principal hymn was sung to the kithara while standing" («ἐλέγετο δὲ προσόδιον ἐπειδὰν προσίασι τοῖς βωμοῖς ἢ ναοῖς· καὶ ἐν τῷ προσιέναι, ᾔδετο πρὸς αὐλόν· ὁ δὲ κυρίως ὕμνος πρὸς κιθάραν ᾔδετο ἑστώτων»); in Proclus (ed. Th. Gaisford, Leipzig 1832) evidently by mistake it is written προσῴδιον, instead of προσόδιον.

Hes. «προσόδιον· ᾠδὴ ὕμνον θεοῦ περιέχουσα» ("*prosodion*; an ode containing a praise to God"); cf. Athen. VI, 253B, ch. 62 «παιᾶνας καὶ προσόδια ᾄδοντες» ("singing paeans and *prosodia*").

According to Heracleides (ap. Plut. De Mus. 1132C, ch. 3) the *prosódia* (pl.) were introduced by Clonas* of Tegea. Prosodia were composed by Bacchylides*, Pindar* and others.

prosodos (πρόσοδος) fem.; among other meanings, a festival procession to the temple with music. Aristoph. Clouds, v. 307 «πρόσοδοι (pl.) μακάρων ἱερώταται» ("most sacred *processions* in honour of blessed gods"). Cf. *prosodion**.

prosodos (προσ-ῳδός) masc.; sounding in concord with the ode, or singing in concord.

Pollux (IV, 58) «προσῳδὰ (neut. pl.) ὄργανα» ("instruments played in concord with the ode [song]" or "accompanying in concord [in unison, probably] the vocal melody").

Cf. *proschordos**.

Plut. De Virtute morali («Περὶ ἠθικῆς ἀρετῆς»; 443A, ch. 4): «ψαλτήρια, διεξιὼν καὶ λύρας καὶ πηκτίδας καὶ αὐλοὺς καὶ ὅσα μουσικῆς *προσῳδὰ* καὶ *προσήγορα*» ("recounting psalteria, lyras, pektides and auloi, and all *concordant* and consonant instruments").

See *prosodia*.

prosthesis (πρόσθεσις); a silence (rest) equal to two short times (time-units); Aristides De Mus. (Mb p. 41; RPW-I p. 39): «*πρόσθεσις δὲ χρόνος κενὸς μακρὸς ἐλαχίστου διπλασίων*» ("*prosthesis* is a long empty time [silence, rest] equal to the double of the short time, [time-unit"]).

See under *parasemantike* the notation of the silences; also under *chronos*.

prylis (πρύλις; m. pr. prílis) fem.; a kind of war-dance; a Cretan pyrrhiche; it was danced in armour.

Callimachus Hymn to Zeus, v. 51 «Κούρητές σε περὶ *πρύλιν* ὠρχήσαντο» ("the Kouretes danced the war-dance around thee").

According to some sources the pyrrhiche was called *prylis* by the Cypriots (Aristotle Fr. 519 ap. A. B. Drachmann Schol. Pind. Carm., vol. II p. 52; FHG II, p. 166, Fr. 205, and p. 182 Fr. 257a).

psallein, vb (ψάλλειν; m. pr. psállin); a) in a general sense, to touch, to draw with the fingers (Aesch. Pers. 1062 «ψάλλ' ἔθειραν»; "tear your hair"); to draw and leave to sound (Eurip. Bacch. vs 783-4 «... καὶ τόξων χερὶ ψάλλουσι νευράς»; "they pluck by the hand the bowstrings").

In music the term "psallein" signified to play a stringed instrument by bare fingers without a plectrum; Athen. (IV, 183D, ch. 81) «Ἐπίγονος ... κατὰ χεῖρα δίχα πλήκτρου ἔψαλλε» ("Epigonus *played* ... on the strings *with bare hand* without plectrum").

The stringed instruments played directly by the fingers (without a plectrum) were called *psaltiká* and *epipsallómena* (cf. *enchorda**). The string itself when played in this way was called *psallomene* (ψαλλομένη; drawn by the fingers).

b) The term "psallein" in later times was used in the sense, to sing to a kithara accompaniment.

Note: From the vb "psallein" were derived various terms, *psalmos**, *psalter* or *psaltes**, *psaltinx**, *psalterion**; also *antipsalmos**, *epipsalmos** etc.

psalmodia (ψαλμῳδία); see next entry, *psalmos*.

psalmos (ψαλμός); putting into vibration a string (of a stringed instrument) directly by the fingers; also the sound produced in this way.

In later times, a song sung to a stringed instrument. Hence, *psalmodia* (ψαλμῳδία); the singing to a kithara accompaniment.

psalter, psaltes, masc. (ψαλτήρ, ψάλτης; m. pr. psaltír, psáltis); the kitharist who played with the fingers (without the aid of a plectrum); Cf. Hesychius.

The fem. *psáltria*; Sext. Empir. (Against the musicians, VI, § 1): «τὰς δὲ ψαλτρίας μουσικάς» ("[we describe] the female *kitharists* as musicians").

psalterion ψαλτήριον; m. pr. psaltírion); a generic term for stringed instruments played directly by the fingers without the aid of a plectrum. In this category belonged the *Epigoneion**, the *magadis**, the *pektis**, the *simikion**, the *sambyke**, the *nabla** and the *trigonon** (harp).

But the word "psalterion" is very often met in the sense of a specific instrument. Pollux (IV, 59) "... χέλυς, ψαλτήριον, τρίγωνα ...» etc. (" ... chelys, *psalterion*, trigona" etc.);

Athen. (IV. 183C, ch. 81) «τὸ δὲ ψαλτήριον, ὥς φησιν Ἰόβας, Ἀλέξανδρος ὁ Κυθήριος συνεπλήρωσε χορδαῖς» ("the *psalterion*, as Iobas [Jubas] says, was perfected by Alexander of Cythera with the addition of more strings").

It seems that the above instruments of the psalterion family, especially those with a great number of strings, did not differ substantially; Apollodorus (ap. Athen. XIV, 636F, ch. 40) says that "what we now call a *psalterion* is the magadis" («ὁ νῦν, φησὶν [Ἀπολλόδωρος], ἡμεῖς λέγομεν ψαλτήριον, τοῦτ' εἶναι μάγαδιν»).

psaltinx (ψάλτιγξ); a kind of kithara.

Hesychius and Suidas «ψάλτιγξ· κιθάρα» ("*psaltinx*; kithara").

Psellus, Michael (Ψελλός, Μιχαήλ; m. pr. Psellós Michaíl); b. Nicomedia 1018; d. Constantinople 1079 A.D. Byzantine author, philosopher, theoretician, and one of the most erudite men of Byzantium. He entered the monastic order (his social name was Constantine), and had been professor of philosophy at the Academy in Constantinople; he became a Secretary of State and first minister under Emperor Michael VII. In spite of his many political occupations, he wrote on various theological, philosophical, medical, mathematical and other subjects. Among his philosophical works an important place is held by his commentary on Plato's Psychogony (after Timaeo; Ὑπόμνημα εἰς τὴν τοῦ Πλάτωνος Ψυχογονίαν) published by A. J. H. Vincent in his "Notices sur divers manuscrits grecs relatifs à la musique" p. 316ff. Others of Psellus' writings on music include his treatise on the Four Mathematical Sciences, Arithmetic, Music, Geometry and Astronomy (Τοῦ σοφωτάτου Ψελλοῦ, σύνταγμα εὐσύνοπτον εἰς τὰς τέσσαρας μαθηματικὰς ἐπιστήμας, Ἀριθμητικήν, Μουσικήν, Γεωμετρίαν καὶ Ἀστρονομίαν»; Greek Text, published in Venice 1532; another ed., Paris, 1545). The part on music is entitled «Μουσικῆς Σύνοψις ἠκριβωμένη» ("An exact epitome of music") pp. 20-27 of the Paris edition. A Latin translation was published in 1557, ap. Gulielmum Cauellat.

Psellus' work is one of the links uniting the ancient Greek musical tradition with modern times.

psilos, psile, psilon Adj. (ψιλ-ός, -ή, -όν; m. pr. psilós. masc., psilí fem., psilón neut.); in a general way, bare, smooth, hairless, and figur. naked.

In poetry: ψιλὴ ποίησις (*psile poeesis*), poetry without melos or generally without music (or, according to Vincent, without musical accompaniment).

ψιλὸς λόγος (*psilós lógos*); prose; not in verse.

ψιλαὶ λέξεις (*psilai lexeis*) pl.; spoken words, not sung.

In music it was used in a similar way:

ψιλὴ αὔλησις (*psile aulesis*); solo aulos playing.

ψιλὸς αὐλητὴς (*psilos auletes*); solo-playing aulete; aulos-soloist.

ψιλὴ κιθάρισις (*psile kitharisis*); solo kithara playing.

ψιλὸν μέλος (*psilon melos*); an instrumental melody without words.

ψιλὸν μέρος (*psilon meros*; part); a solo.

ψιλὸν ὄργανον (*psilon organon*; instrument); the human voice; Anon. Bell. (§ 17, p. 28) «ψιλὰ (pl.) δέ, ὄργανον μὲν κύριον τὸ τοῦ ἀνθρώπου, δι' οὗ μελῳδοῦμεν» ("*psila*; principal instrument [is] that of the human voice by which we sing").

ψιλὴ ὄρχησις (*psile orchesis*); dancing without musical accompaniment.

ψιλὴ φωνὴ (*psile phone*); the simple sound of the human voice in contradistinction to the singing tone.

κρούειν τὰς χορδὰς ψιλαῖς χερσίν; to strike the strings with *bare hands* (without a plectrum).

ψιλοκιθαριστικὴ (*psilokitharistike*); the art of solo kithara playing (without singing).

ψιλοκιθαριστὴς (*psilokitharistes*); solo kitharist; kithara-soloist.

Plato (Laws, II, 669E) criticized the psile kitharisis and the psile aulesis, the separation, as he says, of the rhythm and the melody from the words; "it is impossible to understand what the rhythm and the harmonia want to express without words". See under *amousia**.

Note: A.J.H. Vincent published an interesting study on the word "ψιλός" ("Sur le mot ψιλός") in his "Notices"; vol. XVI. part II, Note D, pp. 112-118; Paris 1847. Much material of the above entry is based on this study.

psithyra (ψιθύρα; m. pr. psithíra); a percussion instrument of quadrangular form and of Libyan origin.

Pollux (IV, 60) "the *psithyra* [was] of Libyan invention and chiefly of the troglodytes; its form was quadrangular. Some people believe that the psithyra is the same as the instrument called *askaros**".

psophos (ψόφος); noise, inarticulate sound; mere sound. Sometimes it is met with the meaning of instrumental (musical) sound; Eurip. Cycl., 443 «ἥδιον ψόφον κιθάρας» ("sweeter *tone* of the kithara"). Often in Ptolemaeus and Porphyrius too. Cf. Arist. Propl. XI, 6 «ὁ δὲ ψόφος ἀήρ ἐστιν ὠθούμενος ὑπὸ ἀέρος» ("*sound* is air pressed by air").

ptaesma (πταῖσμα; m. pr. ptésma); see *epiptaesma*.

pteron (πτερόν); a wind instrument. It is found in Anon. Bell. (§ 17, p. 28) and Vincent ("Notices" p. 8) and in Agiopolites (ap. Vincent op. cit. p. 264). Anon. Bell. «ἔμπνευστὰ δὲ αὐλοί τε καὶ ὑδραύλεις καὶ πτερὰ» ("and wind instruments [are] the auloi, the hydrauleis and the *ptera*").

Agiopolites (III Fragm.): «ἔστι δὲ τὰ πέντε ὄργανα τάδε; σάλπιγξ, αὐλός, φωνή, κιθάρα, πτερὸν» ("the five instruments are the following, the salpinx [trumpet], the aulos, the human voice, the kithara and *the pterón*").

Note: The word pteron (πτερὸν) signifies principally, feather, wing.

ptistikon, ptismos (πτιστικόν, πτισμός);

a) a folk-song of women at winnowing; Phryn. Comastae (ap. Kock Com. Att. Fr. vol. I, p. 374, Fr. 14): «ἐγὼ δὲ νῦν δὴ τερετιῶ τι πτιστικόν» ("and I will sing [chirp] to us a *winnowing song*"). Cf. Pollux, IV, 55.

Aristoph. (ap. Athen. XIV, 619A, ch. 10) «καὶ τῶν πτισσουσῶν ἄλλη τις [ᾠδὴ]» ("and another [song], that of the women *winnowing*"). Cf. Bothe PSGF, II, p. 102, Fr. 28.

b) *ptismós* (= winnowing); melody played on the aulos with the song ptistikon.

Cf. Nicophon Cheirogastores, 17 (ap. Pollux, IV, 56).

Ptolemaeus Claudius, Ptolemy (Πτολεμαῖος Κλαύδιος; m. pr. Ptoleméos). Great geographer, astronomer, mathematician and musical theorist, born c. 108 A.D. (some give 85) at Pelusium (Πηλούσιον) in Egypt, and died between 163-168 A.D. at Canopus (Κάνωβος), near Alexandria. Suidas says that he lived during the reign of the Emperor Marcus Aurelius (161-180 A.D.; «γεγονὼς ἐπὶ τῶν χρόνων Μάρκου τοῦ βασιλέως»). He lived in Canopus and Alexandria where he had his studios.

Besides his numerous and important books on Astronomy, of which he is

278

one of the main founders, on Geography and Mathematics, Ptolemaeus wrote a most important scientific work on Music, the "Harmonika" in three books («Ἀρμονικῶν» βιβλία τρία).

This work constitutes a valuable appreciation, explanation and expansion of the Pythagorean doctrines on music. Gevaert (I, p. 12) places Ptolemaeus and his Harmonika on the same level of importance with Aristoxenus and his Harmonic Elements. They represent, for him, the two great schools of musical science in ancient times: the Pythagorean and the Aristoxenean.

The Harmonika of Ptolemaeus were first translated from the Greek into Arabic in the 9th cent. A.D. A Latin translation was published by Ant. Gogavinus, together with Aristoxenus' Elements (cf. "Ptolemaei Harmonicorum"; Venice, 1562, pp. 51-150).

A careful edition with Greek and Latin texts was included by John (Iohannes) Wallis in his "Opera Mathematica" (3 vols, Oxford, 1699). The third volume of this work contains:

a) *Ptolemaeus'* Harmonika, three books (pp. 1-152);

b) *Porphyrius'* Commentary on Ptol. Harmonika (Πορφυρίου «Εἰς τὰ Ἀρμονικὰ Πτολεμαίου Ὑπόμνημα»; pp. 189-355);

c) *Manuel Bryennius'* Harmonika (pp. 359-508); and also, works by Archimedes and Aristarchus of Samos. The best and most careful edition so far of the Greek text was published by Ingemar Düring ("Die Harmonielehre des Klaudios Ptolemaios", Göteborg, 1930; pp. CVI & 147; the Text pp. 1-121). A German translation by I. Düring followed ("Ptolemaios und Porphyrios über die Musik" (Göteborg, 1934) with valuable notes.

A. J. H. Vincent in his "Notices" includes some fragments («Πτολεμαίου Μουσικά»; pp. 252-255); also C.v. Jan in Musici Script. Gr. (pp. 411-421) publishes «Πτολεμαίου μουσικά» ("Excerpta Neapolitana").

Cf. R. P. Winnington-Ingram "Mode in ancient Greek music" (Cambridge, 1936; "The evidence of Ptolemy" pp. 62-71); M.I. Henderson in the New Oxford History of Music (1957; pp. 355-358) etc.

ptosis (πτῶσις); the incidence of the voice on a certain degree. Aristox. (Harm. I, p. 15 Mb): «φωνῆς πτῶσις ἐπὶ μίαν τάσιν ὁ φθόγγος ἐστὶ» ("the sound [note] is the *incidence* of the voice upon a pitch".

See *phthongos**.

pycnon (πυκνόν; m. pr. picnón); dense, compact, thick. In music, the sum of the two small intervals of a tetrachord when it is less than the remainder of the tetrachord. This happens in the Enharmonic (ex. a) and the Chromatic (ex. b) genera.

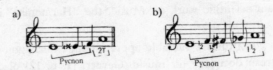

a) b)

Pycnon Pycnon

In the first ex. above (a) the sum of the two small intervals (e - e¼ - f) is a semitone while the remainder of the tetrachord (f - a) is a ditone. In the second ex. (b) the ensemble of the two small intervals (e - f - f♯) is one tone while the remainder is one tone and a half. In the Diatonic genus there is no pycnon because in the Tense (σύντονον) Diatonon the sum of the two first intervals (e - f - g, 1½t.) is on the whole larger than the remainder (g-a, 1 tone;), and in the Soft Diatonon the sum of the two small intervals is in size equal to the remainder ($\frac{6}{12} + \frac{9}{12}$; $\frac{15}{12}$; see *Diatonon**).

The notes which are placed on the lower part of the pycnon are called *barypycnoi** (βαρύπυκνοι), those in the middle of the pycnon *mesopycnoi** (μεσόπυκνοι), and those at the extreme top *oxypycnoi** (ὀξύπυκνοι).

Those notes of the tetrachord which do not enter into any relation with the pycnon are called *apycnoi* (ἄπυκνοι); these are the three following: 1) the proslambanomenos, 2) the nete synemmenon and 3) the nete hyperbolaeon. Cf. Arist. Quint. De Mus. (Mb p. 12, RPW-I p. 9); Cleon-Isag. (ch. 4; C.v.J. p. 186; Mb p. 7); Bacch. Isag. (§§ 27, 32-34, C.v.J. pp. 299-300, Mb pp. 8-9); Alyp. Isag. (ch. 4, C.v.J. p. 368, Mb p. 2); Anon. (Bell. § 56, p. 62); Pachym. (ap. Vincent "Notices" p. 391).

pycnon (adj.) *diastema* (interval); a very small interval. Aristides Quint. (op. cit., Mb p. 14, RPW-I p. 11): «πυκνὰ [διαστήματα] μὲν τὰ ἐλάχιστα, ὡς αἱ διέσεις, ἀραιὰ δέ, τὰ μέγιστα, ὡς τὸ διὰ τεσσάρων» ("*pycna* [intervals] are the smallest ones, such as the dieseis; *araea* (not pycna, not dense, loose) are the largest, like the fourth").

pycnotes (πυκνότης; m. pr. picnótis); the quality of being pycnos; opp. *manotes**. Cf. Ptolem. I, ch. 3; ed. Wallis III, p. 6; I.D. p. 7, 17.

Pylades (Πυλάδης; m. pr. Piládis); 1st cent. B.C. to 1st cent. A.D., famous mime from Kilikia in Asia Minor. He introduced in Rome during the reign of Emperor Augustus a kind of pantomimic art in the Roman Theatre (see *Bathyllus**). There were also other mimes with the same name.

pyrrhiche (πυρρίχη; m. pr. pirríchi); the most important kind (or class) of war-dance. The pyrrhiche was a majestic, quick, brilliant and impressive dance; it was danced either by one person, or by one or more pairs of dancers, who carrying arms (shield and spear or sword) imitated the movements of

280

warriors both in attack and in defence. It was danced especially in the Doric states, and above all in Laconia. In Sparta it was performed by youths at the ceremony of Dioscuri (Castor and Pollux). In the 6th cent. B.C. it was introduced in Athens where it was danced during the celebrations of Panathenaea, with the participation of boys, youths and men.

In later times the pyrrhiche degenerated into a dance of the symposia; Xenophon (Anab. VI, ch. 1 § 12) says that during a symposium an "orchestris" (dancing-girl) bearing a light shield danced the pyrrhiche lightly. At the time of Athenaeus (2nd-3rd cent. A.D.) the pyrrhiche still survived in Laconia, but as preparatory exercise (προγύμνασμα) to war; "all males in Sparta learn to dance the pyrrhiche from the age of five. The pyrrhiche in Athens being of a Dionysian character is milder than the old kind, because the dancers now carry 'thyrsoi' (wands with leaves of ivy and vine upon them) instead of spears, and fennel and torches" (XIV, 631A, ch. 29).

The derivation of the name pyrrhiche (πυρρίχη) has not been clarified. According to Aristoxenus (ap. Athen. 630D) the pyrrhiche took its name from a Laconian (or Cretan; Pollux IV, 99) hero or dancer called Pyrrhichus; Athenaeus adds that during his time the name Pyrrhichus was still met with in Laconia. Other writers state that it was derived from Pyrrhus, another name of Neoptolemus son of the Homeric hero Achilles, who, according to a tradition, was the first to dance it after the victory over Eurypylos. Another hypothesis was that the name was derived from the word «πυρὰ» (funeral-pyre) because Achilles danced it first in Troy around the pyre on which the dead body of his friend Patroclus was cremated (cf. A. B. Drachmann Schol. in Pind. Carm., vol. II, p. 52 (Note); Aristotle Fr. 519).

Proclus (in Chrest.) says that "some attribute the invention of the pyrrhiche to the Kouretes; some to Pyrrhus son of Achilles".

The pyrrhiche having an important educative character, special attention was given to the songs accompanying the dance, Athen. (ibid) «τακτέον δ' ἐπὶ τῆς πυρρίχης τὰ κάλλιστα μέλη καὶ τοὺς ὀρθίους ρυθμοὺς» ("use should be made in the pyrrhiche of the best [loveliest, most beautiful] melodies and up-lifting rhythms").

The pyrrhiche was accompanied by songs sung either by the dancers themselves or more usually by other people.

See: hyporchema*, cheironomia*, telesias*.

pyrrhichizein, vb (πυρριχίζειν); to dance the pyrrhiche.

2) pyrrhichios (πυρρίχιος; m. pr. pirríchios); pyrrhic dance; the dance of pyrrhiche. Also a metrical foot consisting of two short syllables, υ υ; otherwise dibrachys or hegemon.

See pous* (foot).

Pythagoras (Πυθαγόρας; m. pr. Pithagóras); 6th-5th cent. B.C.; he lived between 530 and 497 B.C.; born and died at Megapontium (Μεγαπόντιον), in Samos.

Great philosopher, mathematician and musical theorist. He visited many countries and then settled in Croton, South Italy, where he founded his School.

Pythagoras was the first to propound the scientific basis of music; his philosophical conception of the world was based on the belief that everything should be seen and explained by numbers. In music, he discovered the numerical ratios of the first consonances: a) the 8ve, 2:1 (dia pason, διὰ πασῶν), b) the 5th, 3:2 (dia pente, διὰ πέντε; called by the Pythagoreans dioxeia* or di' oxeion, διοξεῖα, δι' ὀξειῶν) and c) the 4th, 4:3 (dia tessaron, διὰ τεσσάρων; called by the Pythagoreans syllaba or syllabe, συλλαβὰ or -ή); also d) the major tone, 9:8 (μείζων τόνος) which is the difference between the 4th and the 5th. Nicomachus in the Enchiridion (ch. 6, «Πῶς οἱ ἀριθμητικοὶ τῶν φθόγγων λόγοι ηὑρέθησαν»; C.v.J. pp. 245-248; Mb pp. 10-13) describes in detail how Pythagoras arrived at the discovery of these ratios. To Pythagoras is also attributed the classification of the seven harmonias, and to his School the doctrine of the "Harmonia of the spheres"*.

Nicomachus (ibid, ch. 5) and other writers attribute to him the addition of the 8th string, between the mese and the paramese; Cf. *lyra**.

Many of Pythagoras' theories are still valid today.

Select Bibliography :
Armand Delatte : "Études sur la littérature pythagoricienne"; Paris, 1915 (pp. 314; 8°).
W. Burkert : "Weisheit und Wissenschaft Studien zu Pythagoras, Philolaos und Platon"; Nürnberg, 1962 (pp. XVI & 495; 8°).

Pythagoras, of Zante (Πυθαγόρας ὁ Ζακύνθιος; m. pr. Pithagóras Zakínthios); c. middle of 5th cent. B.C. Theoretician and musician to whom the grammarian Artemon (Ἀρτέμων, 2nd to 1st cent. B.C.) attributed the invention of the ingenious instrument *tripous** (tripod; cf. Athen. XIV, 637C, ch. 41).

He was considered as one of the founders of the Greek harmonike, but nothing of his writings survives. The theoretical views of his School are criticized by Aristoxenus in his Harm. Elements (II, p. 36, 35 Mb).

pythaules (πυθαύλης; m. pr. pithávlis); the aulete who played the Pythikos nomos*; also an aulete who competed at the Pythian Games. Among the most famous pythaulai known were Sakadas* and Pythocritus*.

Pythermus (Πύθερμος; m. pr. Píthermos); c. 6th cent. B.C. poet-musician. He was born in Teos (Τέως), an Ionian town on the Erythraean peninsula,

282

in Asia Minor, hence his surname Teios (Τήϊος).

He was considered as the inventor of the Ionios* or Iasti harmonia which is ascribed also to Polymnestus*. Pythermus composed scolia (convivial) songs. Heracl. Pont. (ap. Athen. XIV, 625 C-D, ch. 20) believes that Pythermus made the style of his songs to fit the character of the Ionians, and assumes that he did not compose in the Iasti harmonia but in a curious harmonic form.

pythikon (πυθικόν; m. pr. pithikón); a stringed instrument called also *dactylikon*: cf. Pollux (IV, 66); see the text under *dactylikon*. The word in the text of Pollux may be explained as an epithet.

Pythikos aulos (πυθικὸς αὐλός; m. pr. pithikós avlós); so was called the aulos on which the Pythikos nomos was performed. It was also played with the singing of paeans; Pollux (IV, 81) «πρὸς παιᾶνας δὲ (ἥρμοττον) οἱ πυθικοὶ (αὐλοί)· τελείους δ᾽ αὐτοὺς ὠνόμαζον· ηὔλουν δὲ τὸ ἄχορον αὔλημα» (*"the Pythian* auloi suited the paeans; they were also called perfect, and the achoron* Pythian solo was played on them"*).

The tone of the Pythian aulos was considered virile owing to its low register. *Pythikos auletes* or *kitharistes* (πυθικὸς αὐλητὴς or κιθαριστής); an aulete or kitharist competing at the Pythian Games (with the Pythikos nomos).

Pythikos nomos (πυθικὸς νόμος; m. pr. pithikós nómos); the most important auletic nomos, invented by Sakadas*, the chief aulete-composer of his time. When the auletike was introduced for the first time in 586 B.C. in the programme of the Pythian Games, Sakadas competed and won the first prize with his Pythikos nomos.

The Pythic nomos was the first known kind of programme music, and its aim was to describe the combat of Apollo with the monster Python (Πύθων). It was composed of five parts which, according to Pollux (IV, 84), were the following:

a) πεῖρα (*peira*; test, introduction), in which the God "examines the ground if it is suitable for the combat" («διορᾷ τὸν τόπον εἰ ἄξιός ἐστιν τοῦ ἀγῶνος»);

b) κατακελευσμὸς (*katakeleusmós*; provocation), in which "he challenges the dragon" («προκαλεῖται τὸν δράκοντα»);

c) ἰαμβικὸν (*iambikon*); in which "the combat is going on, and imitation is made of the trumpet-calls and the grinding of the dragon's teeth" (odontismos*);

d) σπονδεῖον (*spondeion*), in which the victory of the God is declared («δηλοῖ τὴν νίκην τοῦ θεοῦ»); and

e) καταχόρευσις (*katachoreusis*; victorious dancing), in which "the God celebrates his victory by dancing" («ὁ θεὸς τὰ ἐπινίκια χορεύει»).

283

The auletic Pythic nomos was imitated by kitharists who introduced a kitharistic nomos on the same lines. Strabo (IX, 3, 10, 421-2) speaks of such a kitharisterios Pythic nomos divided into the following five parts: a) *ἀνά-κρουσις* or *ἄγκρουσις* (*anakrousis** or *ankrousis*); introduction, prooemion; b) *ἄμπειρα* (*ampeira*); beginning of the combat; c) *κατακελευσμὸς* (*katake-leusmos**; cf. above b); description of the combat; d) *ἴαμβοι καὶ δάκτυλοι* (*iamboi** and *dactyloi*); triumphant hymn on God's victory; and e) *σύριγγες* (*syrinxes*); description of the hissings of the expiring dragon.

Pythocleides (Πυθοκλείδης; m. pr. Pithoclídis); b. c. 535; d. c. 472 B.C. Aulete and sophist born at Keos (Κέως, hence his surname Keios, Κεῖος). He was teacher of Agathocles* and Pericles, and founder of an important Athenian musical school. Pythocleides is mentioned by Plato in "Protagoras" (VIII, 316E) among those sophists who, like Agathocles and many others, "out of fear for other people's envy used music as pretence and screen"; see the Greek text under Agathocles.

Pythocleides introduced the Mixolydian into tragic drama by transform-ing the Sapphic Mixolydian (g-g) into the "tragic" Mixolydian (b-b).

Cf. *Mixolydios** *harmonia*.

Pythocritus (Πυθόκριτος; m. pr. Pithócritos); 6th cent. B.C. Sicyonian aulete of repute. Pausanias (VI, ch. 14, § 10) records that at the Pythian Games, after Sakadas' victories, Pythocritus won six times consecutively the first prize for the auletike. He also played the aulos six times at the Olympic Games during the contest of the pentathlon; cf. *endrome**.

In honour of Pythocritus a monument (στήλη) was erected at Olympia with the following inscription:

> "This is the monument of the aulete
> Pythocritus, son of Callinicus"

(«Πυθοκρίτου τοῦ Καλλινίκου μνᾶμα ταὐλητᾶ [τὸ] δε»).

Q

Quintilianus, Aristides (Κοϊντιλιανός, Ἀριστείδης);
See *Aristides Quintilianus*.

R

rapaules, and **rappaules**; also **rapataules** (ραπ[π]αύλης, ραπαταύλης; m. pr. rapávlis, rapatávlis); an aulete playing on a stalk-made aulos. The word rapa (ράπα) and rapate (ραπάτη) signified stalk, reed.

284

Amerias of Macedonia in his Dictionary (Γλῶσσαι; ap. Athen. IV, 176 D-E, ch. 78) says that "as we nowadays call calamaulai those who play on a reed-made aulos, so they used to call *rappaulai* those playing on a stalk-made aulos" («ὥσπερ οὖν τοὺς τῷ καλάμῳ αὐλοῦντας καλαμαύλας λέγουσι νῦν, οὕτω καὶ *ραπαύλας*, ὥς φησιν Ἀμερίας ὁ Μακεδὼν ἐν ταῖς Γλώσσαις, τοὺς τῇ καλάμῃ αὐλοῦντας»).

Notes: a) κάλαμος (calamus) = reed; by extension reed-aulos.

καλάμη, fem. (calame) = stalk; reed.

b) In Eust. Comment. ad Hom. p. 1157, 39 the word rapaules appears as *raptaules* (ραπταύλης).

Remains of Greek Music (Λείψανα Ἑλληνικῆς Μουσικῆς).

The remains of ancient Greek Music are a few vocal or instrumental melodies discovered, mostly, in a mutilated and fragmentary state. Except the Two Delphic Hymns (Nos 3 and 4, below), the Epitaph of Seikilos (no. 5) and the Three Hymns (Nos 8, 9 and 10), they are very short fragments. Thus, unlike the important corpus of surviving theoretical works and other sources of information regarding the theoretical side of Greek music, the relics of ancient Greek Music constitute a small and limited corpus of melody which can give us but a very faint idea of Greek music in its practical manifestations.

In chronological order the extant melodies are the following. In the first place would come a melody published by the Jesuit *Athanasius Kircher* in his "Musurgia Universalis" (Rome, 1650; vol. I, pp. 541-542, in Greek and modern notation), and alleged to be the beginning of Pindar's First Pythian Ode; but its authenticity has been seriously disputed. Kircher pretended to have copied it from a MS found in the Library of a Convent near Messina; the MS however has never been found, and the melody is now regarded by most scholars as a forgery. It has been published as a genuine work by P. J. Burette (in "Dissertation sur la Mélopée de l'Ancienne Musique"; fasc. 12, Nov. 1720, pp. 205-6), by Gevaert (1875; I, p. 142) and others.

In his valuable Bibliography (1932-1957) of Ancient Greek Music, published in "Lustrum" (Göttingen, 1958/3, pp. 5-57), Prof. R. P. Winnington-Ingram gives an interesting list with a brief account (pp. 11-12) of the principal contributions to the controversy raised by this problem, which appeared in various magazines between 1932 and 1940.

1. A fragment from the first stasimon (vs 338ff) of Euripides "Orestes" composed c. 408 B.C.; it is mutilated and very fragmentary (33 notes, in six lines none of which is complete). It was found in 1892 on a Rainer papyrus (published in "Pap. Erzherzog Rainer"; Wien, 1894; 4°, p. 126, No. 531 photo-

copy) and it was first transcribed by Dr. Carl Wessely (Mittellungen aus der Sammlung "Der Pap. Erzh. Rainer", vol. V; Wien, 1892).

It has been also published in D. B. Monro "The Modes of Ancient Greek Music" (p. 92, in Wessely's transcription, with a restoration proposed by Dr. Otto Crusius, pp. 130-131) and in C. v. Jan "Mus. Script. Gr.", 1895, pp. 430-431 and Suppl. pp. 6-7. The papyrus is dated by Dr. Wessely to the first cent. A.D., while others place it earlier; E. G. Turner in the J.H.S. 76, 1956, 95f. dates it to around 200 B.C.

2. A fragment found on a papyrus among a number of Zenon papyri in 1931 in the Museum of Cairo (No. 59533), dating from c. 250 B.C.; it is known as the Cairo Fragment. It was first published by J. F. Mountford in "The Journal of Hellenic Studies" (vol. LI, 1931; pp. 91-100, "A New Fragment of Greek Music in Cairo"; Mountford gives two renderings of the fragment a) Diatonic and Chromatic; b) Diatonic and Enharmonic, p. 99).

See a commentary by Henri-Irénée Marrou in the "Revue de Philologie, de Littérature et d'Histoire anciennes", vol. XIII, 1939, pp. 308-320.

3 and 4. Two Hymns to Apollo, called the Delphic Hymns. They were engraved on stone in the Athenian Treasury at Delphi and discovered by the French Archaeological School at Athens in 1893. They are two Paeans dated from the 2nd cent. B.C. (Th. Reinach dates them, c. 138 B.C. and c. 128 B.C.).

They were first transcribed in modern staff notation by Théodore Reinach, and published with commentaries by Henri Weil (on the text) and Th. Reinach (on the music) in the "Bulletin de Correspondance hellénique" (the first 1893, XVII, pp. 569-610; the second, 1894, XVIII, p. 345ff). Definitive edition by Reinach in "Fouilles de Delphes" III, 2 (1912). Cf. C.v.J. op. cit. pp. 435-449, and in particular, Suppl. (Nos 2 and 3) pp. 12-33. They represent the most extensive specimens of ancient Greek music discovered so far; the composer of the First is unknown, while the Second is ascribed to the Athenian composer Limenius.

The columns are exhibited at the Delphi Museum.

5. Epitaph of Seikilos, dating from the 2nd cent. B.C. or 1st cent. A.D.; it was discovered by W.M. Ramsay in 1883 engraved on a tomb-stone, "a small round marble column belonging to Mr. Purser brought from Aidin" ("Bulletin de Correspondance hellénique", VIII, 1883, p. 277, No. 21). Aidin is placed near the ancient town Tralleis (Τράλλεις) of Asia Minor, hence the Epitaph is also known as the Tralle[i]s or Aidin Inscription.

The little funeral column was exhibited until 1922 in the collection of Young, in Boudja, near Smyrna, where A. Laumonier, a member of the French School at Athens, was able to photograph it for the first time; he published it in the "Bull. de Corr. Hell.", XLVIII, 50. It disappeared after the burning of Smyrna, 13 Sept. 1923 (cf. Th. Reinach, "La mus. gr." pp. 191-2; Émile Martin "Trois documents de mus. grecque", Paris 1953, p. 49 and photo of the column facing page 49).

The inscription consists of two parts, the second being the Epitaph with music; Ramsay however "did not understand, as he writes, the meaning of the small letters placed above the lines of the second part". *Dr. Carl Wessely* was the first to discover that these "letters" were actually musical notes; he transcribed the music into modern notation and published both, the inscription and his transcription, with a commentary in "Antike Reste griechischer Musik" (1891, pp. 17-26; music pp. 21-24). He discussed it later with Ch. Ém. Ruelle in the "Revue des Études grecques" (V, 1892, pp. 265-280). The Epitaph has been published several times; mention may be made of the following: D. B. Monro op. cit. pp. 89-90 (Wessely's transcription) with an important correction at the end of the last word ($\dot{\alpha}\pi\alpha\iota$-$\tau\varepsilon\tilde{\iota}$ a-f$\sharp$-e) proposed by J. A. R. Munro (ibid, p. 145); C.v.J. op. cit. pp. 452-3, and Suppl. No. 4 "Sicili epitaphium" p. 38 (in the Suppl. the end is corrected [three notes, a - f$\sharp$ - e, instead of a - f$\sharp$] as in Monro's above; Th. Reinach: op. cit. pp. 191-2.

The poetic text is a little encomium of good living, a sort of scolion*. The melody, consisting of 37 notes in all, and of a compass of an octave, is in itself complete and has a distinct charm. As Reinach says "it is the most complete and legible specimen of the ancient notation which has reached us".

6. a) a little fragment (four lines) of a paean on Ajax's suicide;

b & c) two little fragments of instrumental melody (three lines each); d) another fragment of a paean (twelve lines); e) half a line of a lyric song. All the above (a-e) were found on a papyrus (Berlin Museum No. 6870) and date from the middle of the 2nd cent. A.D. (c. 160).

First edition by W. Schubart in 1918 ("Ein griechischer Papyrus mit noten" in "Sitzungberichte der Königlich Preussischer Akademie der Wissenschaften", XXXVI, pp. 763-8).

7. Four little instrumental melodies by an unknown composer published in Anon. Bell. (§§ 98, 99, 101, 104; pp. 95, 96, 98). They were published with slight differences by Vincent in "Notices" (1847; pp. 60-64). Also by R. Westphal in the Supplement to the 1st vol. of his "Metrik der Griechen" (1867; pp. 50-54) and in "Die Musik des griechischen Alterthums" (1883; pp. 337, 339-341); and by Fr. Aug. Gevaert (op. cit. I, pp. 141, 154).

Two more little fragments also published by Bellermann (§§ 97, 100; pp. 94, 96), by Gevaert (p. 146) and Westphal (op. cit., p. 338) may be considered as fragments of instrumental exercises.

8. Hymn to the Muse (Calliope);
9. Hymn to Helios (Sun);
10. Hymn to Nemesis;

These three Hymns (8-10) were first published in their Greek notation by Vincenzo Galilei in Florence, in 1581 ("Dialogo di Vincentio Galilei Nobile Fiorentino "Della musica antica e della moderna"; in Fiorenza, MDLXXXI; p. 97). Their composition is placed in the 2nd cent. A.D., and probably during the reign of Emperor Hadrian (117-138 A.D.); their authorship has been the object of various speculations and hypotheses. In Galilei's "Dialogo" the first Hymn has in Greek the heading «Διονυσίου· εἰς Μοῦσαν. Ἴαμβος βακχεῖος; the second and third have no name of composer. Burette (op. cit., pp. 183ff) discusses in detail the whole question of the Hymns and their authorship. On the MS of the three Hymns he discovered at the end of an edition of Greek poetry by Aratus (Oxford, 1672), the name of Dionysius appears as the author of all three; heading of the first: «Διονυσίου εἰς Μοῦσαν. Ἴαμβος βακχεῖος» ("Dionysius [Hymn] to the Muse. Iambus Baccheius", of the second: «Ὕμνος εἰς Ἀπόλλωνα τοῦ αὐτοῦ» ("Hymn to Apollo *of the same* [composer]"; and of the third «Ὕμνος εἰς Νέμεσιν τοῦ αὐτοῦ» ("Hymn to Nemesis, *of the same*"). Cf. also Fr. Bell. "Die Hymnen des Dion. u. Mesom." (1840; pp. 11-14). The Hymn to Nemesis was attributed by the Greek writer John of Philadelphia (Ἰωάννης Φιλαδελφεὺς) of Justinian's time, to the Greek poet Mesodmes (Μεσόδμης); this name was believed to be a wrong spelling of Mesomedes' name. Cf. *John Anthony Cramer*: "Anecdota graeca e codd. manuscriptis Bibliothecae Regiae Parisiensis" (vol. I, Paris 1839 p. 406). The problem of the authorship remains still unsolved; some scholars are inclined to attribute all three to Mesomedes: C.v.Jan op. cit. p. 460; in the Suppl. he ascribes Nos. 9 and 10 to Mesomedes; C. Sachs: "The Rise of Music in the Ancient World", p. 198: "probably all three were composed in the second century A.D. by Mesomedes (or the Hymn to the Muse perhaps by Dionysios)". Th. Reinach in "Conférence sur la mus. gr. et l'hymne à Apollon" p. 8, indirectly attributes them to Mesomedes "who enjoyed a great reputation" while Dionysius' "existence is now contested". In "La mus. Gr." pp. 196, 199, he definitely attributes the two last [Nos. 9 and 10] to Mesomedes. Others ascribe the two first (8,9) to Dionysius and the third to Mesomedes (Fr. Snedorf "De Hymnis Veterum Graecorum", Leipzig 1786, pp. 65-72; Snedorf publishes only the text; Monro op. cit. p. 87).

The most generally accepted view now is that the Hymn to Nemesis is by Mesomedes, and perhaps also the Hymn to the Sun (Helios). As to the Hymn to the Muse, which may be two separate pieces (a suggestion by Wilamowitz, "Timotheus Perser" p. 97; cf. Th. Reinach "Deux préludes citharodiques"), its composer is believed unknown (or a certain Dionysius, or even Dionysius the younger of Halicarnassos called "the musician"; cf. Westphal "Die Musik des gr. Alterth.", p. 327; Gev. I, p. 445 etc.).

A new point of view is put forward lately by Isobel Henderson ("The New Oxford History of Music", I, 1957, pp. 372-3) that the Hymns ascribed to Mesomedes may be regarded as Byzantine reconstructions ("The probability, then, perhaps seems to favour an erudite Byzantine reconstruction", p. 373).

All three have been published several times: by: *Burette* (op. cit. 1720 p. 169ff); *Fr. Bellermann* (op. cit. 1840 pp. 11-14); *R. Westphal* ("Metrik" suppl. 1867, pp. 50-54; "Die Mus. des gr. Alterth. "1883 pp. 327-336); *Gevaert* (I, pp. 445-449); *C.v.Jan* (op. cit. pp. 460-473 and Suppl. pp. 44-59; *Th. Reinach* ("La mus. gr. "pp. 194-201).

11. A fragment of a Christian Hymn in Greek notation dating from the 3rd cent. A.D. discovered by A. S. Hunt in 1918 on a papyrus at Oxyrhynchus in Egypt; it was published in the 15th vol. of "The Oxyrhynchus Papyri" (1922), and trancribed into modern notation by H. Stuart Jones. Several other transcriptions and studies have been published by various scholars: *Th. Reinach*, in Revue Musicale, 1922; *H. Abert*, in Zeitschrift für Musikwissenschaft, IV, 1922; *R. Wagner* in "Philologus" LXXIX, 1923; and *Egon Wellesz* in his "History of Byzantine Music and Hymnography", 1949, pp. 125-129.

12. "Fragments of an unknown Greek tragic text with musical notation"; cf. "Symbolae Osloenses" Fasc. XXXI; Oslo, 1955, pp. 1-87. This papyrus (P. Osl. Inv. No. 1413) belonged to a collection of Greek papyri purchased in Berlin, 1933, from Prof. Carl Schmidt. The publication contains Notes: I. on the Text (pp. 1-29) by S. Eitrem and Lev Amundsen, and II. on the Music (pp. 29-71) by R. P. Winnington-Ingram, who gives also a transcription of the Fragments A and B into modern notation on pp. 62-63. The date of composition is uncertain.

13. "Monody with Musical Notation"; "The Oxyrhynchus Papyri" Part XXV, London, 1959; Inv. No. 2436, pp. 113-122.

The publication contains Notes, I. On the Text by E. G. Turner (pp. 113-115) and II. On the Music, by R. P. Winnington-Ingram (pp. 116-121). The Monody, quite fragmentary, is published as transcribed by R. P. W.-Ingram into modern notation on p. 122, and is by him placed "later than the 2nd cent. B.C., but earlier than the 2nd cent. A.D.".

14. An Oxyrhynchus Papyrus, Mich. Un. Pap., Inv. No. 2958. It has been published by O. M. Pearl and R. P. Winnington-Ingram, under the title "A Michigan Papyrus with Musical Notation", in "Journal of Egyptian Archaeology" 51 (1965) pp. 179-195. The article includes a photograph and a transcription into modern staff notation.

15. A small fragment from Euripides' Iphigenia in Aulis discovered in December 1972 by Mrs Denise Jourdan-Hemmerdinger on a papyrus of the University of Leyden (Inv. No 510). Announcing her discovery Mrs. Jourdan-Hemmerdinger in a Communication to the "Académie des Inscriptions et Belles-Lettres" in Paris on June 1st 1973, claims that this musical fragment is probably older than the Zenon papyrus dated from c. 250 B.C. (see above No. 2), and consequently the oldest specimen of ancient Greek music discovered so far. The papyrus is very mutilated and contains "the remains of 16 lines, text and music, of which, as she says, only 8 can be restored"; she was able to read vs 784-792 of the Iphigenia. Most of the musical signs belong to the vocal notation while 2-3 to the instrumental.

Her Communication is published in the "Comptes Rendus des Séances de l'année 1973, avril-juin" of the Académie (Paris, Ed. Klincksieck, Nov. 1973, pp. 292-299), together with a photo of the papyrus (p. 295) and a provisional transcription (p. 294).

Besides those mentioned above, see also:

> H. *Hunger u. E. Pöhlmann :* "Neue griech. Musikfragmente...", Wiener Studien, LXXV, 1962.
>
> E. *K. Borthwick :* "The Oxyrhynchus Mus. Monody...", American Journal of Philology, LXXXIV, 1963.
>
> *Ebert Pöhlmann :* "Denkmäler altgriechischen Musik", Nuremberg 1971.

rhapsodos (ραψῳδός; m. pr. rapsodós) from rhaptein (ράπτειν), to stitch together, to compile, and aoede, ode (ᾠδή); a reciter of epic poems, especially of Homeric poems. He used to rove from one place to another carrying a stick of laurel and reciting at popular gatherings. The rhapsodes were also called Homeristai (Ὁμηρισταί; Athen. XIV, 620B, ch. 12).

The rhapsode must not be confused with the ancient "aoedos"* (ἀοιδός). While the aoedos was himself the poet, composer and singer, the rhapsodos was a compiler of epic poems of other poets, a reciter not a singer; and while the aoedos accompanied himself on the phorminx, the rhapsodos never used an instrument. The aoedos was a poet-musician of the remotest antiquity; the rhapsodos appeared in more recent times, in the 7th cent. B.C.

rheton - alogon (ρητὸν - ἄλογον; m. pr. ritón, álogon);

a) *rheton diastema* (ρητὸν διάστημα); rational interval. According to Aristoxenus an interval is rational in respect to melody, i.e. 1) that which can be sung, or 2) that which can be evaluated by the ear («γνώριμον κατὰ μέγεθος, ἤτοι ὡς τά τε σύμφωνα καὶ ὁ τόνος ἢ ὡς τὰ τούτοις σύμμετρα»; "that [interval] the size of which is known (recognizable), as the concords and the tone, or as the intervals commensurate with these").

This view is basically different from that of the Pythagoreans for whom the

290

intervals are measured by ratios (numerical relations).

b) *alogon* (irrational) is, according to Aristoxenus, the interval which cannot be sung or is not readily recognizable by the ear.

c) The terms rhetos-alogos (masc.) are used in an analogous sense in Rhythm; pous rhetos, pous alogos (ποῦς ῥητός, ποῦς ἄλογος); rational foot, irrational foot.

The irrationality was called *alogia* (ἀλογία).

See *chronos*.

rhythmike (ρυθμική; m. pr. rithmikí); the science of rhythm. To be distinguished from metrike*, the scope of which is more limited.

See *rhythmopoeia*.

rhythmoeides (ρυθμοειδής; m. pr. rithmoïdís); time not completely rhythmical. In pl. times (or durations) not having between themselves exact rhythmical relations. Ptolem. Musica (C.v.J. Excerpta Neapolitana § 12, p. 414): "*rhythmoeideis* [pl.] are those times [χρόνοι] which do not keep good rhythmical order [between themselves] exactly (too much) but they seem (appear) as having some kind of rhythm".

Cf. Aristides De Mus. (Mb p. 33; RPW-I p. 33).

See *eurhythmos**

rhythmographia (ρυθμογραφία; m. pr. rithmographía); noting down of rhythm (LSJ, Dem.); composition of rhythmical figures (Gev. II, p. 584).

rhythmographos; writing on rhythms (LSJ); he who treats of rhythms (Dem.).

rhythmopoeia (ρυθμοποιΐα; m. pr. rithmopiía); the science of "realizing" the rhythm. Aristides (De Mus. Mb p. 42, RPW-I p. 40) "*rhythmopoeia* is a faculty creative of rhythm" («ρυθμοποιΐα δέ ἐστι δύναμις ποιητική ρυθμοῦ»).

The rhythmopoeia is subdivided, according to Aristides (ibid, Mb p. 43, RPW-I p. 40), like the melopoeia, into "the *lepsis* (λῆψις; choice) by which we learn what species of rhythm must be chosen, the *chresis* (χρῆσις; application) by which we adjust the arseis (upbeats) and the theseis (downbeats), and the *mixis* (μίξις; mixing) which teaches us how to interlace properly the rhythms".

The purpose of the rhythmopoeia is the adjustment of the words, of mele and of movements into rhythmical forms. In a general way the rhythmopoeia is concerned with the realization of the abstract rhythm into concrete rhythmical forms, i.e. it is the rhythmical composition, while the rhythmike* is the science which deals with the technical aspects of rhythm.

rhythmos (ρυθμός; m. pr. rithmós); in Ionian rhysmos (ρυσμός); the word appears first in Archilochus (Th. Brgk PLG, II, p. 401, Frg. 66 [31];

also E. Diehl Anth. Lyr. Gr. p. 231, Frg 67a): «γίγνωσκε δι' οἷος ῥυσμὸς ἀνθρώπους ἔχει» ("learn that a disposition [state] masters the men" or "keeps the men prisoners").

As it is clear from the above fragment of Archilochus the word "rhythmos" did not have at the beginning a "musical" meaning. It is especially in the 4th cent. B.C. that it was conceived and used as a musical term. Aristoxenus was the first to study in a systematic way the phenomenon of musical rhythm.

There have been various definitions of the term "rhythmos" by different ancient writers and theorists. Plato (in Laws, II, 665A) defines: «τῇ δὴ τῆς κινήσεως τάξει ῥυθμὸς ὄνομα εἴη» ("and that the order of motion is called *rhythmos*"). Aristides (De Mus. Mb p. 31; RPW-I p. 31) defines the rhythm as "a system of times lying together in a certain order" («ῥυθμὸς τοίνυν ἐστὶ σύστημα ἐκ χρόνων κατά τινα τάξιν συγκειμένων»). Bacchius (Isag. § 93, C.v.J. p. 313, Mb p. 22) defines the rhythm as "measuring of time made with some motion" («χρόνου καταμέτρησις μετὰ κινήσεως γινομένη ποιᾶς τινος»). He also gives definitions by other writers. Aristoxenus' conception is based on the idea that the rhythm exists by itself independently of any realisation, and flows into an abstract duration, (cf. L. Laloy Lex. d' Aristox. p. XXXI); "the rhythm never mingles with the rhythmical matter but it gives a certain order to the 'rhythmizomenon' (ρυθμιζόμενον; the material which is being regulated) in making the times to succeed in this or that way. The rhythm and the form resemble each other as both have no proper reality. In fact, the form could not exist in the absence of a matter which would receive it; similarly the rhythm, in the absence of an element which is susceptible of being measured and of dividing the time, could not exist either; because the time cannot be divided by itself, there must be something else to divide it. It is therefore necessary that the rhythmical matter be divisible in conceivable parts by which the division of the time could be realized" (Aristox. Rhythm, Feussner, ch. 2).

The materials of the rhythm are "the words, the melos and the motion of the body".

Aristides (ibid) says that the rhythm can be perceived by three senses: a) the sense of sight («ὄψει»), as in the dancing; b) the sense of hearing («ἀκοῇ»), as in the melos; and c) the sense of touch («ἀφῇ»), as with the pulses of the arteries. But in music the rhythm is perceived only by two senses, those of sight and of hearing.

The vb *rhythmizein* (ρυθμίζειν; m. pr. rithmízin), to regulate, to bring into a regulated (measured) time, to bring into rhythm.

"Ta *rhythmizomena*", neut. pl. («τὰ ρυθμιζόμενα»; m. pr. tá rithmizó-mena) = the elements of rhythm (syllables, notes and gestures).

Bibliography: Rudolf Westphal: a) "System des antiken Rhythmik"; Leipzig, 1865.

b) "Metrik der Griechen"; Leipzig, 1867-8 (2 vols).

c) "Aristoxenos von Tarent. Melik und Rhythmik des classischen Hellenentums"; Leipzig, 1883-1893, (2 vols).

Carlo del Grande: "L'espressione musicale dei poeti greci"; Napoli, 1932.

Thras. G. Georgiades: "Der griechische Rhythmus, Musik, Reigen, Vers und Sprache"; Hamburg, 1949.

Thras. G. Georgiades: "Musik und Rhythmus bei der Griechen". Hamburg, 1958.

Émile Martin: "Essai sur les rythmes de la chanson grecque antique"; Paris, 1953. Also *Gev.* II, 1-240; *Th. Reinach:* La mus. gr., pp. 72-116.

rombos, or **rhymbos** (ρόμβος, ρύμβος; m. pr. rómvos, rímvos);

a) the percussive sound produced by the clapping of the krotala or by beating the tympanum (drum, tambour). Pind. Dithyr. II (for Thebes) v. 9 «*ρόμβοι* τυπάνων» ("thunders of drums").

b) a small wooden stick fastened to a string which was whirled around; when it was turned slowly it produced a low sound, and when it was whirled very quickly it gave a piercing sound. The rombos was used by Corybants in their ceremonies. Hes. «*ρόμβος*, ψόφος, στρόφος, ἦχος, δῖνος, κῶνος, ξυλήριον οὗ ἐξῆπτον σχοινίον καὶ ἐν ταῖς τελεταῖς δονεῖται» ("*rombos* [is] a percussive sound, a cord, sound, whirling, a little wooden stick with a string which is whirled round in the ceremonies"). Archytas I «καὶ *τοῖς ρύμβοις* τοῖς ἐν ταῖς τελεταῖς κινουμένοις, τὸ αὐτὸ συμβαίνει· ἥσυχα μὲν κινούμενοι βαρὺν ἀφίεντι ἦχον, ἰσχυρῶς δὲ ὀξύν» ("and the same happens with *the romboi* which are moved [whirled] in the ceremonies; when they are whirled quietly they produce a low tone, and when vigorously [quickly] a high sound").

c) The same as *roptron**; EM "*rombos*; roptron, tympanum (drum, tambour)".

roptron (ρόπτρον); a tambourine in the modern sense, i.e. a small and light drum consisting of a wooden hoop with a piece of parchment stretched over it, and small pieces of metal fastened around it. It was used by the Corybants in their ceremonies. Plut. Krassus (ch. 23, § 7, 557E). «Πάρθοι γὰρ οὐ κέρασιν οὐδὲ σάλπιγξιν ἐποτρύνουσιν ἑαυτοὺς εἰς μάχην, ἀλλὰ *ρόπτρα* βυρσοπαγῆ καὶ κοῖλα περιτείναντες ἠχείοις χαλκοῖς ἅμα πολλαχόθεν ἐπιδουποῦσι» ("For the Parthians do not incite themselves to battle with horns or trumpets, but [they use] hollow *tambourines* made of hides around which metallic krotala (jingles) are fastened, and they beat them all together from many sides").

S

Sakadas (Σακάδας); 7th-6th cent. B.C. celebrated composer and aulete from Argos (Ἄργος, hence his surname Ἀργεῖος, Argeius). At the beginning of his career he was an aulode and composed elegies (cf. Plut. De Mus. 1134C, ch. 9) but he turned later to the auletic art.

When in 586 B.C. the aulos was accepted for the first time at the Pythian Games, Sakadas competed and won the first prize for the auletic; the first prize for the aulodic went to Echembrotus* and that for the kithara-playing to Melampus*. He was also victorious, again for the auletic, at the following two Pythians in 584 and 582 B.C. (cf. Pausanias X, ch. 7, § 4; Plut. ibid, ch. 8). His tomb was still shown in Pausanias' time (cf. Paus. II, ch. 22, § 9).

The glory for Sakadas was that he initiated in the Pythian Games the so-called Pythikos* (or Pythian) nomos, by which he described the combat of Apollo with Python, and with which he competed and won. To Sakakas was also attributed the introduction of the *trimeres** (*tripartite*) or *trimeles** nomos, according to which each one of its three parts was composed and sung alternately in the Dorian, the Phrygian and the Lydian harmonias (cf. Plut. ibid).

Sakadas is placed between the archaic and the classical periods of ancient Greek music.

See Brgk PLG III, p. 203 a fragment «Ἰλίου πέρσις» ("the sacking of Ilion"). Also *H. Albert*: Sakadas in Pauly's R.E. vol. 45, cols. 1768-9.

salpinx (σάλπιγξ); trumpet. It was made either of brass (the straight one) or of horn (the curved one). Both had mouth-pieces. The horn trumpet was called *kéras* (κέρας; horn).

The salpinx was not used for purely musical purposes by the Greeks. It was usually used either for military calls or by heralds to call the attention of the people; sometimes also for ceremonial purposes, and in such a case it was called "the sacred trumpet" («σάλπιγξ ἡ ἱερά»).

It was of Etruscan origin; Athen. (IV, 184A, ch. 82): «Τυρρηνῶν δ' ἐστὶν εὕρημα κέρατά τε καὶ σάλπιγγες» ("and both the horns and the trumpets were invented by the Etruscans"). Pollux (IV, 75) «καὶ κέρατι μὲν αὐλεῖν Τυρρηνοὶ νομίζουσι» ("and the Etruscans customarily play the horn"). The use of the vb "aulein" (αὐλεῖν) in the sense of playing the horn or trumpet is characteristic. A Greek trumpet made in thirteen sections of ivory fitting into one another is found at the Museum of Fine Arts in Boston (C. Sachs: Hist. of Mus. Instr. p. 145). The adj. «Τυρρηνικὸς» (Etruscan, Tyrrhenean) meant metaphorically "aloud"; «τυρρηνικὴ σάλπιγξ» ("Tyrrhenean trumpet"), a sonorous, loudly-sounding trumpet.

See *bycane**.

salpinktes and *salpistes* (σαλπιγκτής, σαλπιστής; m. pr. salpingtís; salpistís); the player of salpinx, trumpeter. Also in Attic dialect *salpiktes* (σαλπικτής).

Cf. Moeris: Lex. Atticum, p. 354.

Bibliography:

C. *Sachs:* Hist. of Mus. Instr. (N. York, 1940); Trumpets, pp. 145-148.
M. *Wegner:* Das Musikleben der Griechen (Berlin, 1949); pp. 60-61.

sambyke (σαμβύκη; m. pr. samvíki); also **sambyx** (σάμβυξ); a big stringed instrument of over one metre of size. Its form was triangular, and according to Athenaeus (XIV, 634 A, ch. 34) it was similar to that of a siege-engine with the same name. Andreas of Panormus (ap. Athen. ibid) says "that it was called *sambyke* because when raised aloft, its appearance as a united whole becomes that of a ship and a ladder, and the appearance of the musical sambyke is somewhat similar" (transl. by Ch. B. Gulick, vol. VI, p. 421). Thus the sambyke as described above, had a ship-formed body in a horizontal position with an upright string-holder upon it (cf. C. Sachs p. 84).

The sambyke had a great number of strings, tuned probably in pairs and in 8ves as the magadis, and was played without a plectrum. There were, it seems, sambykai with few strings (four). It became known to Greece from Syria or Egypt.

According to Suidas and the historian Neanthes of Kizycus (ap. Athen. IV, 175 D-E, ch. 77) the sambyke was invented by the poet Ibycus* (6th cent. B.C.), or it was reformed by him (Strabo, 637B, 40); Skamon (ap. Athen. XIV, 637B, ch. 40) says that the sambyke was first played by Sibylla and its name was taken from its inventor's name Sambyx (Σάμβυξ). Clem. of Alexandria «Τὰ εὑρισκόμενα»; ed. 1592, p. 132) holds that the sambyke was invented by the Troglodytes. According to Iobas (Fourth Book of Theatrical History, ap. Athen. IV, 175D, ch. 77) the sambyke was identical with the lyrophoenix*, while Euphorion, the poet, says that the sambyke was an old magadis remodelled. (cf. *magadis**).

Arist. Quint. considers the character of the sambyke as effeminate owing to its short strings and piercing tone (Mb p. 101, RPW-I p. 85: «τὴν δὲ σαμβύκην πρὸς θηλύτητα ἀγεννῆ τε οὖσαν καὶ μετὰ πολλῆς ὀξύτητος διὰ τὴν μικρότητα τῶν χορδῶν εἰς ἔκλυσιν περιάγουσαν»). The player of sambyke was called *sambykistes* (σαμβυκιστὴς masc.) and the woman executant *sambykistria* (σαμβυκίστρια). The sambyke, as also the magadis, the phoenix, the pektis and others, was condemned by Plato (Rep. III, 399D) and Aristoxenus who called all these "foreign instruments" («ἔκφυλα ὄργανα»).

Bibliography:

Th. *Reinach:* DAGR, vol. VI (1904), p. 1449 s.v. Lyra, ("Famille de la harpe", p. 1448 ff).

Maux: "Sambuca" in Pauly's R.E. (1920), 2 Reihe 1, cols. 2124-2125.

W. Vetter: Pauly's R.E., vol. XIV (XXVII) 1928, col. 290, s.v. Magadis.

Sappho (Σαπφώ); b. c. 630; d. c. 570 B.C. Her name in the Aeolian dialect was Psappha or Psappho. She was born at Eresós (Ἐρεσὸς) of Lesbos and lived in the town of Mytilene. She was forced to leave the island for some time and lived in exile in Syracuse; "Parion Chronicon" (v. 36) places her going to Sicily around 603-2 «ἀφ' οὗ Σαπφὼ ἐκ Μυτιλήνης εἰς Σικελίαν ἔπλευσε, φυγοῦσα ... ἄρχοντος Ἀθήνησιν μὲν Κριτίου τοῦ προτέρου» (603-2); she returned home around 590.

The greatest lyric poetess of ancient Greece who was called "the Tenth Muse" or "the Mortal Muse", or "the Feminine Homer", besides her poetical work was also famous as a musician, both poetry and music being indissolubly integrated in her nature. She was accredited, according to Aristoxenus (ap. Plut. De Mus. 1136C-D, ch. 16), with the invention of the Mixolydian harmonia (cf. Pythocleides*); and Suidas says that she was the first to use the plectrum* in kithara playing. She composed hymns, epithalamia, epigrams etc.

Her death is connected with various legends; according to the most widely spread Sappho, disappointed in her unlucky love for a beautiful young man, Pháon (Φάων), committed suicide by throwing herself into the sea near cape Leucata in the island of Leucadia. But it is said that her tomb was shown in Mytilene.

See Brgk PLG III, pp. 83-140 and Anth. Lyr., pp. 193-208. *Edgar Lobel:* The Fragments of the lyrical poems of Sappho (Σαπφοῦς Μέλη); Oxford 1925; *E. Lobel and D. L. Page:* Poetarum Lesbiorum Fragmenta, Oxford 1955; *D. L. Page:* Sappho and Alcaeus, Oxford 1959.

schema (σχῆμα; m. pr. schíma); form, figure.

In the theatre, the character, part or role expressed by an actor. In orchesis, a figure of the dance; in pl. schemata (σχήματα) the cheironomiai*, the pantomimic movements of the hands during the performance. In music, it is met with the meaning of a melodic figure; it was the form of a system (e.g. tetrachord) as to the arrangement of its intervals or parts. Thus, the schema of a Dorian tetrachord differs from that of a Phrygian tetrachord. In rhythmopoeia, the form of a metre (iambic, anapaestic). For various melodic schemata see under *prokrousis-prolepsis*.* Cf. Anon. Bell. §§ 2, 4 ff, and Man. Bryen. Harm. Sect. III.

schisma (σχίσμα); a) according to some theorists, the difference between the Pythagorean comma and the comma of Didymus (cf. *comma**), or the difference between five octaves and eight perfect fifths and a true major third.

b) a figure of dancing.

Note: schisma (σχίσμα); division. From schizein (σχίζειν), to divide, to separate.

schistas helkein (σχιστὰς ἕλκειν); to dance, to perform a certain figure of a dance danced by women with bold movements of the legs. Pollux (IV, 104) "and there was also the *schistas helkein*, a form of choral dancing [in which] one should leap and cross the legs" («ἦν δὲ καὶ τὸ *σχιστὰς ἕλκειν*, σχῆμα ὀρχήσεως χορικῆς, ἔδει δὲ πηδῶντα καὶ ἐπαλλάττειν τὰ σκέλη»).

Cf. *schisma*.

schoenion, nomos (σχοινίων, νόμος; m. pr. schiníon nomos); an aulodic nomos the invention of which was ascribed to Clonas* (cf. Pollux, IV, 79); and Plut. De Mus. 1133A, ch. 5). Some others attribute its invention to Sakadas.

The schoenion was considered an effeminate nomos.

Note: In Pollux the schoenion is wrongly called auletic nomos instead of aulodic; cf. Plut. above.

schoenotenes (σχοινοτενής; m. pr. schinotenís); stretched out, prolix (LSJ). "Schoenotene asmata" («σχοινοτενῆ ᾄσματα») songs exceeding a certain length.

scolion (σκόλιον) melos, neut., from scoliós = crooked, curved, not straight; a song to lyra accompaniment sung towards the end of a banquet in an uneven (irregular) order; usually one of the more skilful table-companions initiated the singing, holding at the same time in his hand a myrtle-branch, which he passed on, when he finished his singing, to another table-companion, but not the one sitting next to him, and so on in a crooked order (cf. Athen. XV, 694 A-B).

FHG II, p. 248, Fr. 43 (Dicaearchi Messenii; Δικαιάρχου ἐκ Μεσσήνης): «τὸ δὲ ὑπὸ τῶν συνετωτάτων, ὡς ἔτυχεν τῇ τάξει, ὃ δὴ καλεῖσθαι διὰ τὴν τάξιν *σκολιὸν*» ("and [thirdly] that which was sung by the wisest as they were seated by chance, and which is called *scolion* owing to the [crooked] order they kept"). And (ibid, Fr. 44): Schol. Aristoph. Nub. 1364 «Δικαίαρχος ἐν τῷ Περὶ μουσικῶν ἀγώνων... οἶτε γὰρ ᾄδοντες ἐν τοῖς συμποσίοις ἐκ παλαιᾶς τινος παραδόσεως κλῶνα δάφνης ἢ μυρρίνης λαβόντες ᾄδουσι» ("Dicaearchus in his work About the musical contests says ... at the banquets, after an old tradition, they used to take a laurel- or myrtle-branch and then proceeded to sing").

Procl. Chrest., 19 "the scolion melos was sung at banquets (carousals); hence it is sometimes called also a drinking song" («τὸ δὲ Σκόλιον μέλος ᾔδετο παρὰ τοὺς πότους· διὸ καὶ παροίνιον ἐσθ' ὅτε καλοῦσιν»). According to Pindar (ap. Plut. De Mus. 1140F, ch. 28) the scolia mele (pl.) were invented by Terpander.

See: *D. L. Page*: "Poetae Melici Graeci" (Oxford 1962) Carmina Convivialia, pp. 471-482, Frgs 884-917.

Seikilos (Σείκιλος; m. pr. Síkilos); lyric poet and musician of Roman times. His name became known thanks to a Funeral Inscription found near Tralles in Asia Minor; the Epitaph is discussed in some detail under the heading *Remains of Greek Music* (No 5).

It is a votive offering [of Seikilos in memory of a female relative or perhaps his wife (?) Euterpe]. The poetic text of the inscription is in two parts; the first, without music, is the dedication: «Εἰκὼν ἡ λίθος εἰμί, τίθησί με Σείκιλος ἔνθα μνήμης ἀθανάτου, σῆμα πολυχρόνιον» ("Image I am, this stone; Seikilos dedicates me in immortal memory, a monument for a long time"). The second part, the actual Epitaph with music, is a little encomium of good living: «Ὅσον ζῆς φαίνου,   "As long as you live, appear (be bright),
μηδὲν ὅλως σὺ λυποῦ,   Do not regret at all,
πρὸς ὀλίγον ἐστὶ τὸ ζῆν,   Short is the life,
τὸ τέλος ὁ χρόνος ἀπαιτεῖ».   Time leads to (demands) the end".

The Epitaph concludes with the words Σείκιλος-Εὐτέρ[πη] (Seikilos-Euterpe) or perhaps (?) «Εὐτέρ[πη]» ("to Euterpe").

seistron (σεῖστρον; m. pr. sístron) from seio (σείω), to shake; a small percussion instrument; sistrum; its form was of a spur or of a horse-shoe with a handle and a number (up to seven) loose cross-bars, or little bells. It was in metal, and when shaken it produced a piercing sound of indefinite pitch. It came from Egypt where it was used in ceremonies in honour of Isis (cf. Plut. Moral. 376 C).

The seistron was also a toy by which "the wet-nurses lulled to sleep by entertaining those of the children who did not easily fall asleep" (Pollux IV, 127). See also *katabaukalesis**, and *xylophonon**.

semasia (σημασία; m. pr. simasía); a term for notation. Cf. Gaud. Isag. (§ 20; C.v.J. p. 347, Mb p. 20).

See under *parasemantike*.

semeion (σημεῖον; m. pr. simíon); sign. In music sign of notation; musical sign. See *parasemantike**.

b) the shortest time in ancient metrics; the time-unit; the short syllable (βραχεῖα συλλαβή).

sigmos (σιγμός); hissing (LSJ). See *syrigmos**.

síkinnis (σίκιννις); a dance of the satirical drama danced with quick, lively and violent movements and leaps, and with much tumult. Pollux (IV, 100) considers sikinnis as one of the three principal kinds of dances, the other two being the *emmeleia** and the *kordax** («Εἴδη δὲ ὀρχημάτων, ἐμμέλεια, τραγική, κόρδακες, κωμική, σίκιννις, σατυρική»).

Athenaeus says (XIV, 630B, ch. 28) that some people believe that it was invented by a barbarian or Cretan called Sikinnus; that Skamon holds that its name was derived from the verb "seiesthai" (σείεσθαι; to shake oneself), and that Thersippus was the first to dance it. Others believed that it was danced by Satyrs and that its name came from the extremely quick movements of the dance.

Lucian ("On dancing", § 22) holds that the sikinnis was invented either by Sikinnus "or by Sikinnis, a nymph of Cybele, though from the beginning it was danced in honour of Savazios" («ἢ ἐκ Σικίννιδος, νύμφης τῆς Κυβέλης, καίπερ ἐξ ἀρχῆς ἐχορεύετο πρὸς τιμὴν τοῦ Σαβαζίου»). Savazius or Sevazius was a Phrygian deity whose mysteries resembled the ceremonies of Bacchus.

sikinnotyrbe (σικιννοτύρβη; m. pr. sikinnotírvi); a kind of aulesis played at the dancing of the sikinnis*.

It was one of the kinds of auleseis (solos for aulos) included in Tryphon's catalogue of Denominations (ap. Athen. XIV, 618C, ch. 9).

See the full catalogue under *aulesis**.

simai (σίμαι; m. pr. síme) pl.; the ends of the lyra or the kithara. Hes. «τῆς κιθάρας τὰ ἄκρα»; also «τὰ ἄκρα τῆς λύρας» ("the ends of the kithara" and "of the lyra").

sime (σιμή m. pr. simí); one of the figures of the tragic orchesis, mentioned by Pollux (IV, 104) «καὶ μὴν τραγικῆς ὀρχήσεως τὰ σχήματα σίμη ...» ("and the figures of the tragic dancing are *sime* ..." etc.).

Cf. also Athen. XIV, 630A, ch. 27: "a dance-figure called «χεὶρ σιμή»" ("hand-slanting").

simikion (σιμίκιον); a stringed instrument with 35 strings, like the Epigoneion*, of the psalterion family, i.e. of those played directly by the fingers without the aid of a plectrum; cf. Pollux, IV, 59. Nothing definite regarding its character, its range and its form is known. Some scholars suppose that it was played like a board-zither, placed and played horizontally (Th. Reinach: La mus. gr., p. 126; C. Sachs: Hist. of Mus. Instr., p. 137).

This view, however, is not supported by the existing ancient sources.
See also *Epigoneion**.

simodia (σιμῳδία); a kind of indecent song; the singing of such songs. It took its name from a certain Simus, a poet of such songs from Magnesia.

simodós (σιμῳδός); singer of indecent songs.

Some writers identify the simodos with the hilarodos, who was a serious artist; cf. Athen. XIV, 621B, ch. 14; see *hilarodos**. Athen. (ibid. 620D, ch. 13) says "and the so-called hilarodoi whom some people call now *simodoi*" («καὶ οἱ καλούμενοι δὲ ἱλαρῳδοί, οὓς νῦν τινες σιμῳδοὺς καλοῦσιν»).

Simonides (Σιμωνίδης; m. pr. Simonídis); b. c. 556; d. 468-7 B.C. Lyric poet and composer, born at Iulis (Ἰουλὶς) on the island of Kea or Kos (Κέα, Κῶς; hence surnamed Κεῖος, Keius); he lived most of his life in Athens, but passed his last years in Syracuse (and Agrigente) where he died at the age of 88 (Par. Chronicon v. 57: «καὶ Σιμωνίδης ὁ ποιητὴς ἐτελεύτησεν βιοὺς ἔτη 88»).

One of the foremost lyric poets of ancient Greece, second only to Pindar; Simonides was also a prolific composer of hymns, hyporchemata, encomiums, paeans, elegies, parthenia, threnoi and epigrams. He invented the epinikos, and introduced the threnos* into choral song. Suidas attributes to him the addition of the 8th string of the lyra which Nicomachus ascribes to Pythagoras* and Boethius to Lycaon* of Samos.

During his long life he was greatly honoured, and won more than 55 prizes in contests.

See Brgk PLG III, pp. 382-535, 250 Frgs, and Anth. Lyr. pp. 233-267, the text of surviving enkomia, epinikoi, hyporchemata, threnoi, elegies, epigrams. Also Page PMG Frgs 506-653, pp. 237-323.

siphniazein (σιφνιάζειν; m. pr. siphniázin) vb; to use or perform pretentious (or over-elaborate) melodies.

This expression was derived from Philoxenus' island of Siphnos. Cf. Pollux, IV, 65; see the text under *chiazein**.

skazon (σκάζων); see *choliambus**.

skenikos (σκηνικός; m. pr. skinikós) from σκηνὴ (skene) stage; of the stage, theatrical (Dem.; LSJ). Σκηνικὴ μουσικὴ (Plut. De Mus. ch. 31, 1142C) = theatrical music.

skindapsos (σκινδαψός); see *kindapsos*.

skolion (σκόλιον).

See *scolion*.

skops (σκώψ), also **skopías** (σκωπίας); a kind of dance in which the dancers used to twist the neck imitating the owl. Pollux (IV, 103): "and there was also a kind of dance called *skops*, and *skopias*, with a twisting motion of the neck in imitation of the bird [owl] as taken by surprise" («ἦν δέ τις καὶ σκώψ, τὸ δ' αὐτὸ σκωπίας, εἶδος ὀρχήσεως ἔχον τινὰ τοῦ τραχήλου περιφορὰν κατὰ τὴν τοῦ ὄρνιθος μίμησιν, ὃς ὑπ' ἐκπλήξεως τὴν ὄρχησιν ἁλίσκεται»).

In Athen. (XIV, 629F, ch. 27) *skops* and *skopeuma* (σκώπευμα) are included among the dance-figures.   See *glaux**.

skytalion (σκυτάλιον; m. pr. skitálion); a small stick (dimin. of skytalon = stick).   Term for a very small aulos.   Pollux (IV, 82) «καὶ σκυτάλια (pl.), μικρῶν αὐλίσκων ὀνόματα» ("and *skytalia*, names of very small auloi").

The elymos* aulos was surnamed *skytalias* (σκυταλίας) because it resembled the "skytale" in thickness; Athen. (IV, 177A, ch. 79) «ὀνομάζεσθαι δὲ καὶ σκυταλίας κατ᾽ ἐμφέρειαν τοῦ πάχους» ("they [i.e. the elymoi auloi] were called *skytaliai* for their likeness in thickness [to the staff]").

Skytale (σκυτάλη) was a wooden stick (staff) used by Spartans as a means of carrying special or secret dispatches.

sobas, fem. (σοβάς; m. pr. sovás); a kind of humorous or comic dance; cf. Athen. XIV, 629F, ch. 27.

Sophocles (Σοφοκλῆς; m. pr. Sophoclís); b. Colonus, Athens, 496 B.C.; d. Athens, 406 B.C.

Sophocles studied music and dancing with the well-known Athenian musician Lamprus* (cf. Athen. I, 20F, ch. 37: «ὀρχηστικὴν δεδιδαγμένος καὶ μουσικὴν ἔτι παῖς ὢν παρὰ Λάμπρῳ»; "since [Sophocles] was a boy, he was taught dancing and music by Lamprus").   This is questioned by some scholars (cf. H. Weil et Th. Reinach Plut. de la Mus., p. 129, note 317).   It is known from ancient sources that he was a fine singer and dancer, and a skilful kitharist; he used to sing and accompany himself on the kithara. In 480 B.C., when a youth of about 16, he was chosen for his beauty and excellence in music to lead the choral procession at the celebrations for the victory at Salamis.

According to Suidas he wrote 123 plays, of which 18 were satirical, and was crowned 24 times at dramatic contests winning first or second prizes, never a third.   Sophocles led the dramatic art to perfection by his supreme technique of the organic structure of the drama and the masterly handling of the dramatic situations and conflicts, by the characterization of the personages, by the beauty and dignity of the tragic style, and his unfailing sense and command of form and equilibrium.   It may indeed be said that his work represents the classical period of the ancient tragedy.

Of his plays seven survive complete: Ajax, Trachiniae, Electra, Antigone, Oedipus Tyrannus, Philoctetes and Oedipus at Colonus; also a fairly substantial part (417 verses) of his satirical play Ichneutae (Trackers).   Fragments of several of his plays have been preserved (see below).   Of his music nothing unfortunately survives.   But from ancient sources we know that he was highly praised for the sweetness and suavity of his "mele" and the lyrical beauty and perfection of the structure of his choruses.   Aristophanes is particularly laudatory, in contrast to Euripides against whom he shows a continued scornful disposition; in the following two well-known verses he warmly praises Sophocles' sweetness:

«ὁ δ᾽ αὖ Σοφοκλέους τοῦ μέλιτι κεχρι(σ)μένου
ὥσπερ καδίσκου περιέλειχε τὸ στόμα».

"He used to lick the lips of Sophocles
Smear'd o'er with sweetness like a honey-jar"

(cf. Th. Kock Com. Att. Fr., No. 581; transl. by J. D. Denniston, quoted by C. M. Bowra in his "Sophoclean Tragedy", OUP, 1944; p. 357). Dio Chrysostomus quoting these verses remarks that Sophocles' mele had "admirable flavour (delight) and grandeur" («ἡδονὴν δὲ θαυμαστὴν καὶ μεγαλοπρέπειαν».). Suidas also says that Sophocles was called "Bee for the sweetness" («Μέλιτα διὰ τὸ γλυκύ»). He was credited with the introduction of the Phrygian melopoeia and dithyrambic tropos into tragedy.

Sophocles composed also Elegeia, a Paean to Asclepius and, according to a tradition, an Ode in honour of his friend Herodotus, the historian.

Cf. Brgk Anth. Lyr. p. 125, three elegiac fragments and 2 1/2 verses of a paean. Also Aug. Nauck T.G.F., pp. 131-360. Also O. Schroeder, Sophocles, Cantica, 2nd ed., 1923. The following may be consulted with regard to his rhythmopoeia and music:

    J. H. Heinrich Schmidt: "Die antike Compositionlehre", Leipzig, 1869; especially pp. I-CLXXXIII.

    F. A. Gevaert: "Histoire et Théorie de la Musique de l'antiquité"; Ghent, vol. II, 1881, pp. 531-538.

    Evanghélos Moutsopoulos: "Sophocle et la philosophie de la Musique" in "Annales de la Faculté des Lettres et Sciences Humaines d'Aix", vol. XXXIII, 1960, pp. 107-138.

spadix (σπάδιξ); a stringed instrument like the lyra. Nicomachus (Enchir. ch. 4; C.v.J. p. 243, Mb p. 8) mentions the spadix among the stringed instruments (entata; ἐντατά), the kithara and the lyra («καὶ τὰ ὅμοια τοῖς ἐντατοῖς, κιθάρᾳ, λύρᾳ, σπάδικι, τοῖς παραπλησίοις»; "and those similar to the stringed instruments, the kithara, the lyra, the *spadix* and the like"). Pollux (IV, 59) also mentions the *spadix* among the "krouómena" (stringed) instruments.

According to Marcus Fabius Quintilianus (1st cent. A.D; "Institutionis Oratoriae", book I, ch. X, § 31) the *spadix* had an effeminate character: "psalteria and *spadixes* (pl.) which are unsuitable even for the use of a maiden").

Note: spadix = a branch of palm-tree with the fruit on it.

Spendon (Σπένδων); ? 7th cent. B.C., poet-composer of Laconia cited by Plutarch (Vita Lycurgi, § 28) together with Terpander and Alcman; it is said, writes Plutarch, that those who were taken prisoners (during the Thebans' campaign) in Laconia when asked to sing the songs of Terpander, of Alcman and *Spendon* of Laconia refused to obey their masters.

sphragis (σφραγίς); name for the sixth part of the kitharodic nomos.

spondaules (σπονδαύλης; m. pr. spondávlis); the aulete who played the so-called "spondaulion* melos" during the performance of the official libations and oaths.

Spondaulein (σπονδαυλεῖν) vb = to play the aulos at a libation. *Sponde* (σπονδή); libation.

spondaulion melos (σπονδαύλιον μέλος; m. pr. spondávlion); a melody for aulos played during the performance of the official libations and oaths. Also *spondeiakon* melos.

spondeiakos, aulos (σπονδειακὸς αὐλός; m. pr. spondiakós avlós); 1) the aulos used by the spondaules* at libations; it joined in the singing of hymns.

Pollux (IV, 81) «ἥρμοττον δὲ πρὸς ὕμνοις μὲν οἱ σπονδειακοὶ [αὐλοὶ]» (pl.) ("the spondiac [auloi] were adopted for the hymns").

2) *spondeiakos* or *spondeiazon tropos* (σπονδειακὸς or σπονδειάζων τρόπος); spondiac style or scale. The scale in which use was made of the spondeiasmos*.

spondeiasmos (σπονδειασμός; m. pr. spondiasmós); the raising by three dieseis; oppos. eklysis* (ἔκλυσις). Aristides (De Mus., Mb p. 28, RPW-I p. 28) "and *spondeiasmos* [was] the raising by the same interval" (i.e. by three dieseis, as the *eklysis* was the lowering by three dieseis). Cf. eklysis*; and Plut. De Mus. 1135A, ch. 11. The spondeiasmos was used in the spondeion*.

spondeiazon tropos (σπονδειάζων τρόπος m. pr. spondiazon tropos); see *spondeiakos*.

spondeion (σπονδεῖον; m. pr. spondíon); primarily a vessel from which the libation was poured. In music:

a) a song sung or an instrumental melody played in front of the altar at the libation.

Cf. Pollux, IV, 79. According to Menaechmus (ap. Athen. XIV, 638A, ch. 42) Dion of Chios was the first to play the *spondeion melos* on the kithara. Cf. Sextus Empir. VI, § 8 under the heading *epaulein*. *Spondeion aulema* (σπονδεῖον αὔλημα); when played on the aulos.

b) So was called the fourth section of the Pythikos* nomos. In that section the victory of Apollo over the Python was declared. Cf. Pollux, IV, 84.

spondeios, spondee (σπονδεῖος); the well-known metrical foot; spondee simple - -, and spondee major (μείζων or διπλοῦς, double) υ υ υ υ | υ υ υ υ.
See *pous**.

stasimon (στάσιμον) melos; the choral song sung by the chorus of the ancient drama after the parodos*, when the chorus had already occupied its place on the orchestra. It was sung in a standing, stationary position, hence its name "stasimon" (= stationary).

The word "stasimon" was often used as a noun (neut.) signifying the same thing.

The adj. stasimos (masc.) signified steady; and figur. calm, majestic, grave. See under *ethos**.

stasis (στάσις); in music, a stationary position of the voice. Bacch. Isag. (§ 45; C.v.J. p. 303, Mb p. 12) «*Στάσις ἐστὶν ὕπαρξις ἐμμελοῦς φθόγγου*» ("*stasis* is the existence [presence] of a musical sound"). Cf. Aristox. Harm. (I, p. 12, 2 Mb).

Stesichorus (**Στησίχορος**, m. pr. Stisíchoros); b. c. 632; d. c. 556 B.C. According to Suidas he was born in the 37th Olympiad (632 B.C.) at Himera in Sicily (Ἱμέρα; hence, Ἱμεραῖος, Himeraeus) and died in the 57th Olympiad (556 B.C.) at Catane. Lyric poet and kitharode credited with the invention of the choral form: strophe-antistrophe-epodos, generally called the "Stesichorus triad". His original name was Teisias or Tisias (Τ[ε]ισίας) but he was named Stesichorus because he first set up (ἔστηκε) the chorus (Suid. «ὅτι πρῶτος κιθαρῳδίᾳ χορὸν ἔστηκε»; "as he first set up the chorus in the kitharody"), i.e. to stand and sing the epodos (standing) after the strophe and the antistrophe. Suidas also says in Stesichorus' biographical note that "having blamed Heleni of Troy he lost his sight, and then, after a dream, he retracted and wrote an encomium for her, and recovered sight (see *palinodia**).

Cf. Brgk PLG III, pp. 205-234 and Anth. Lyr. pp. 208-213; Helen's palinodia A, B, p. 210. Also Page PMG Frgs 178-281, pp. 94-141.

Note: Stesichorus is mentioned in the "Par. Chron."* (v.50) as having arrived in Greece in 485/4 B.C. («ἀφ' οὗ Αἰσχύλος ὁ ποιητὴς τραγῳδίᾳ πρῶτον ἐνίκησε, καὶ Εὐριπίδης ὁ ποιητὴς ἐγένετο καὶ Στησίχορος ὁ ποιητὴς εἰς τὴν Ἑλλάδα ἀφίκετο»). This led to some confusion as to his time; it is supposed that there were several poets with the same name (Wilamowitz), and that the one mentioned in the "Par. Chron." was the third. In v. 73 of the "Par. Chron." another "Stesichorus Himeraeus, the second, won in Athens" (around 370-369 B.C.).

stigme (στιγμή; m. pr. stigmi); a point (.) used to indicate the thesis. Cf. Anon. Bell. § 3; see also under *parasemantike**.

stixis (στίξις); a term for notation. Cf. Anon. (Bell. § 68, p. 79). See also under *parasemantike*.

stoecheion (**στοιχεῖον**; m. pr. stichíon); element; a simple sound of speech, as the first component of the syllable (LSJ). In pl. "stoecheia" = elements; ἁρμονικὰ στοιχεῖα = harmonic elements. Atistoxenus' treatise on the Harmonike is generally known as «Ἁρμονικῶν στοιχείων βιβλία τρία» ("Three books of Harmonic Elements" or "Harmonic Elements in three books").

b) *stoecheia* was a kind of ludicrous dance included in a list of humorous or comic dances («γελοῖαι ὀρχήσεις») mentioned in Athen. XIV, 629F, ch. 27.

Stratonicus (Στρατόνικος; m. pr. Stratónicos); c. 4th cent. B.C. Athenian poet and kitharode of the time of Philip and Alexander the Great.

To him was attributed, by the philosopher Phaenias, the introduction of the diagram* and the polychordia; FHG II, 298, and Athen. VIII, 352C, ch. 46: «Φαινίας δ᾽ ὁ περιπατητικὸς ἐν δευτέρῳ περὶ ποιητῶν «Στρατόνικος, φησίν, ὁ Ἀθηναῖος δοκεῖ *τὴν πολυχορδίαν* εἰς τὴν ψιλὴν κιθάρισιν πρῶτος εἰσενεγκεῖν καὶ πρῶτος τῶν ἁρμονικῶν ἔλαβε καὶ *διάγραμμα* συνεστήσατο» ("Phaenias the peripatetic [philosopher] in the Second Book 'On Poets' says 'it seems that *Stratonicus* the Athenian was the first to introduce the *polychordia** in the psile kitharisis* [solo kithara playing] and first of the harmonists to initiate the *diagram*'").

He was sentenced to death by Nicocles, king of Paphos in Cyprus, because he satirized him.

See Athen. VIII, 352C, ch. 46.

strobilos (στρόβιλος; m. pr. stróvilos); a kind of whirling dance similar to *ballismos**; cf. Pollux, IV, 101 and Athen. 630A, ch. 27.

Phryn. Epitome (I. de Borries, p. 110): «στρόβιλος ... καὶ μεταφορικῶς κέχρηται ἐπὶ ᾠδῆς κιθαρῳδικῶς πολὺν ἐχούσης τὸν τάραχον» ("*strobilos* ... metaphorically in a kitharodic song having much agitation").

Some scholars give to the word στρόβιλος, as it is used in Pherecr. "Cheiron", the meaning of a kind of staff which, inserted under the strings and turned, could modify the tuning of one or more strings.

Cf. 1. D. "Studies in Musical Terminology in 5th Century Literature" in Eranos, vol. 43, 1945, p. 187; K. Schlesinger "The Greek Aulos" p. 145.

strombos (στρόμβος; m. pr. strómvos); a spiral shell used as a trumpet; a conch (LSJ). Sext. Empir. ("Against the musicians", VI, § 24): «καὶ στρόμβοις τινὲς τῶν βαρβάρων βουκινίζοντες» ("and some barbarians blow the trumpet with *conches*"; transl. R. G. Bury, vol. IV, p. 385).

strophe (στροφή; m. pr. strophí);

a) The turning of the chorus in the ancient drama from left to right on the orchestra; the turning to the other side was called antistrophe (ἀντιστροφή). The ode sung during the turning was also called strophe, and the contrary antistrophe*.

b) Twist or turn (LSJ).

c) The first part of a lyric triad or triptych, of which the other two parts were the antistrophe and the epodos*.

d) The fourth part of the comic *parabasis**; cf. Pollux, IV, 112.

Suidas (Σουῖδας); Byzantine lexicographer who lived probably in the 10th cent. A.D., around 960-970.

He is known from the Lexicon bearing his name (in Greek «Σουῖδα Λεξικὸν» or simply «Σουῖδας» or «Σούδα»; "Suidas" or "Suidae Lexicon"). The Lexicon is a dictionary of ancient Greece, written in a peculiar alphabetical order (according to the pronunciation of the diphthongs and the vowels: α, β, γ, δ, αι, ε, ζ, ει, η, ι, θ, κ, λ, μ, ν, ξ, ο, ω, π, ρ, c, τ, οι, υ, φ, χ, ψ); it contains a great number of entries, 12,000 words, names, expressions etc., including 900 biographical notes, compiled, without particular critical attention, from other similar previous works. It is a valuable work of reference especially as regards the life and history of ancient Greece, with information on biographies which he preserved from older sources now lost. Among this material we find ample information concerning the life and works of ancient poets and musicians, musical instruments, terms and expressions.

In a note after the title it is stated that the "Present book 'Suidas' was written by the wise men, Eudemus the orator, Helladius, Eugenius, Zosimus" etc. («Τὸ παρὸν βιβλίον Σουῖδα [or Σούδα]· οἱ δὲ συνταξάμενοι τοῦτο, ἄνδρες σοφοί· Εὔδημος ῥήτωρ, Ἑλλάδιος ἐπὶ Θεοδοσίου τοῦ νέου· Εὐγένιος Αὐγουστοπόλεως τῆς ἐν Φρυγίᾳ, Ζώσιμος Γαζαῖος, Καικίλιος Σικελιώτης, Λογγῖνος ὁ Κάσσιος etc.).

After each name the special subject of each is noted. From all these writers (much older than his time), and from others, such as Pausanias, Dionysius and Hesychius, Suidas drew material for his Lexicon.

Many editions of Suidas have been made; mention may be made of the following:

1) Demetrius Chalcondyles (Milan, 1499);
2) Aemilius Portus, Greek and Latin text; Coloniae and Allobrogum, 1619 (Geneva, 1630, 2 vols);
3) L. Kusterus (Paris, 1700);
4) Th. Gaisford (with Latin translation; Oxford, 1834; 3 vols);
5) G. Bernhardy (1834);
6) I. Bekker (Berlin, 1854) epitome;
7) Ada Adler (Leipzig, ap. Teubner, 1928-1935, 5 vols with Addenda, corrigenda and indices). This is the edition we have used as reference in this encyclopaedia.

Note: Some scholars now believe that no lexicographer with the name of Suidas existed; it is suggested that the Lexicon was compiled by an unknown writer, and that the name Suidas was derived from the title Suda (Σούδα) of the compilation.

sybene (**συβήνη**, m. pr. sivíni); aulos-case; the case in which the aulos was kept. Hes. «αὐλοθήκη» ("aulos-case").

Also *aulodoke**.

sybotikon, melos (**συβωτικόν**, μέλος; m. pr. sivotikón); a pastoral song; folk-song of the swineherds. Plato the Comic (ap. Kock Com. Att. Fr., vol. I, p. 659, Fr. 211 and Note).

συβώτης (*sybotes*) = swineherd.

Cf. Pollux IV, 56.

syllabe and **syllaba** (**συλλαβή, συλλαβά**; m. pr. sillaví, sillavá); the interval of the perfect fourth, so called by the Pythagoreans; generally known as dia tessaron (διὰ τεσσάρων).

The word syllabe is derived from the verb "syllambanein" («συλλαμβά-νειν» = to take together, to combine, to put together); hence syllabe (in music) is a union or combination of notes. The term was used to mean the interval of the fourth as it was the first consonance; Nicom. Enchir. (ch. 9, C.v.J. p. 252, Mb p. 16) «συλλαβὰν δὲ τὴν διὰ τεσσάρων (πρώτη γὰρ σύλληψις φθόγ-γων συμφώνων)»; "[the most ancients called] *syllaba* the fourth, as it is the first combination of concordant sounds".

syllepsis (**σύλληψις**; m. pr. síllipsis); in music, combination of sounds; the taking together of sounds.

Cf. Nicom. Echir. 9; see above, *syllabe**.

symmetria, symmetros (**συμμετρία, σύμμετρος**; m. pr. simmetría, sím-metros);

a) *symmetria*; symmetry, due proportion, the quality of being symmetros; harmony in a general sense.

b) *symmetros*; commensurable, symmetric.

«σύμμετρα διαστήματα» ("symmetrical, commensurable intervals"). Pto-lem. Harm. (I, ch. 10; I.D. p. 24, 29): «ταῖς δὲ αἰσθήσεσιν εὐληπτότερα τὰ συμμετρότερα» ("the more *commensurable* [intervals] are the more intelli-gible to the senses").

symphonia, symphonos (**συμφωνία, σύμφωνος**; m. pr. simphonía, sím-phonos);

a) *symphonia*; concord. *symphonos*; concordant.

The concords recognized by the Greeks were the perfect fourth (dia tessa-ron), the perfect fifth (dia pente), the octave (dia pason), the double octave, the fourth and fifth compound with the octave (dis diatessaron, dis diapente; i.e. perfect eleventh and twelfth) and with the double-octave (tris dia tessaron, tris dia pente). The Pythagoreans considered as concords those intervals expressed by the simplest ratios, namely the octave (2:1), the fifth (3:2), the fourth (4:3), the twelfth (octave and fifth, 3:1), the double-octave (4:1) and the eleventh (octave and fourth, 8:3).

Ptolemaeus distinguishes the *homophones** (unison, octave, double-octave) from the other concordant sounds ("symphonoi"; the fifth and the fourth, simple and compound with the octave); in the first place he puts the "homophones", and after them the "symphonoi", which are the nearest to the "homophones" (Ptolem. Harm. book I, ch. 7; ed. Wallis, III, p. 16; I. D. p. 15; also Porphyr. Comment. in Wallis III, p. 292, I. D. p. 118).

Cleonides (Isag. ch. 5; C.v.J. pp. 187-8, Mb p. 8) defines the "symphonia" (concord) as "the blending of two sounds of which one is higher and the other lower" («ἔστι δὲ συμφωνία μὲν κρᾶσις δύο φθόγγων ὀξυτέρου καὶ βαρυτέρου»).

Porphyrius (Comment.; Wallis, p. 270; I.D. p. 96) quotes Aelianus' definition (from his "Timaeo"): "Concord is the coincidence and blending («ἐπὶ τὸ αὐτὸ πτῶσις καὶ κρᾶσις») of two notes different as to acuteness and depth"; i.e. different in pitch. He adds that Ptolemaeus admitted six concords (see above), while other theorists (like Aristoxenus, Dionysius and Eratosthenes) admitted eight. Gaudentius also admitted six.

Nicomachus (Enchir. ch. 12; C.v.J. p. 262, Mb p. 25) says that concordant systems (system = a combination of two or more intervals) are those in which the constituent notes when played at the same time («ἅμα κρουσθέντες») are blended with one another in such a way as to produce the effect of a single voice («ἑνοειδῆ φωνήν», as single), as if it were one voice".

See also Aristides de Mus. (Mb p. 12, RPW-I p. 10) and Gaudentius Isag. (ch. 8; C.v.J. p. 337; Mb p. 11).

Aristotle (Probl. XIX, 38) defines that "the reason that we enjoy concord is that it is a blending of opposites which have a relation to each other"; and in Probl. XIX, 35, he says that the octave is the most beautiful concord.

The "symphoniai" (concords) were divided into simple and compound. Simple were, according to ancient writers («οἱ παλαιοί»), the fourth and the fifth. Compound were all the rest, as composed from simple concords. According to Porphyrius (ibid) Thrasyllus included the octave in the simple ones.

b) The term "symphonia" is also met with in the sense of an ensemble of instruments; also of a percussion instrument (a kind of small tambourine). Polybius (ap. Athen. XIV, 615D, ch. 4): «ὀρχησταὶ δύο εἰσήγοντο μετὰ συμφωνίας εἰς τὴν ὀρχήστραν» ("two dancers entered the orchestra [stage] with castanets", as transl. by Gulick, VI, p. 315; or perhaps "with tambourines"). Cf. Polyb. ap. Athen. 439 A-D.

symploke (συμπλοκή; m. pr. simplokí);

a) interlacing of various notes; combination or twining of one note with another. Cf. Ptolem. Harm., II, ch. 12 (Wallis III, p. 85; I.D. p. 67, 7; Excerpta ex-Nicomacho ch. 6, C.V.J. p. 277; Mb p. 37).

b) the twining or combination of times (chronoi) in rhythm; Bacch. Isag. (§ 96; C.v.J. p. 314; Mb p. 23): "The combinations of times made in rhythm are four. A short time with a short one, a long with a long, a long with a short, an irrational with a long".

synagein (συνάγειν; m. pr. sinágin) vb; in the case of an interval, to reduce its size. Aristox. Harm. (I, p. 14, 9-10 Mb): «τὴν τοῦ βαρέος τε καὶ ὀξέος διάστασιν ... συνάγειν»» ("*to reduce* the distance [interval] between the low and the high"). The same applies in the case of durations.

synagoge (συναγωγή); contraction.

syn(h)aphe (συναφή; m. pr. sinaphí); conjunction, especially of two tetrachords. When between two contiguous tetrachords there is a common note, i. e. when the highest note of the lower tetrachord is at the same time the first note of the higher tetrachord. There are three conjunctions, namely 1) that which joins the tetrachord hypaton with the tetrachord of meson; 2) that which joins the tetrachord meson with that of the synemmenon, and 3) that which joins the tetrachord of diezeugmenon with that of hyperbolaeon:

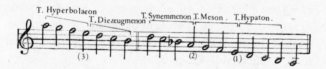

The first conjunction (1) was called *lowest* (βαρυτάτη; barytate), the second (2) *middle* (μέση; mese), and the third (3) *highest* (ὀξυτάτη; oxytate).

Cf. Bacch. Isag. (§ 81; C.v.J. p. 310, Mb p. 20); Man. Bryen. (ed. Wallis, III, p. 504).

The common note of the two tetrachords at the conjuction was called "*synhápton* phthongos" («συνάπτων φθόγγος»; masc.), joining together; conjoining note.

synaulia (συναυλία; m. pr. sinavlía), from "syn" (σύν), with, and aulos; in principle the simultaneous performance by auletai (aulos-players); "concerted" music. Pollux (IV, 83) «ʼΑθήνησι δὲ καὶ συναυλία τις ἐκαλεῖτο συμφωνία τις αὐλητῶν, ἐν Παναθηναίοις συναυλούντων» ("in Athens 'synaulia' was a concerted performance [concord] of auletai playing together at the Panathenaea").

Semus of Delos in his Fifth Book of History of Delos (ap. Athen. XIV, 618A, ch. 9) defines the synaulia as "a kind of concerted contest of aulos and rhythm without words added by the performer".

But the term was generally used to signify: a) a duet of auloi; i.e. the simultaneous performance by two auletai. The performance on a double-aulos was not considered a synaulia;

b) a duet of kithara and aulos, or a performance of two instrumentalists of whom one was always an aulete. A variety of this second was the "enaulos kitharisis"* (solo kithara to aulos accompaniment).

In the case of the second category, the stringed instrument, usually a kithara, played the principal part while the aulos accompanied (perhaps with an embellishing line).

See *heterophonia*.

It seems that the synaulia in its first form was of very old origin, and, according to tradition, was invented by Olympus. The synaulia as a solo-kithara to aulos accompaniment was first introduced by the School of Epigonus;

See under *enaulos kitharisis*.

The word *synaulos* (σύναυλος) signified, being in concord with aulos; but also in concord with the voice or with an instrument. The verb *synaulein* (συναυλεῖν); to play together (in concord) with aulos; also to accompany by the aulos. Athen. (XIV, 617, ch. 8): «Πρατίνας δὲ ὁ Φλιάσιος ... ἀγανακτήσας ἐπὶ τῷ τοὺς αὐλητὰς μὴ συναυλεῖν τοῖς χοροῖς, καθάπερ ἦν πάτριον» ("but Pratinas of Phlious ... became indignant at the way in which the aulos-players failed to accompany the choruses in the traditional manner"; transl. by Ch. B. Gulick, vol. VI, p. 325).

See *prosaulema*-*prosaulesis*.

synchordia (συγχορδία; m. pr. sinchordía); strings in concord or rather a group of notes (strings). L. Laloy believes that synchordia signified "an ensemble of contiguous notes taken at random in the scale" (Aristoxène de Tarente, Lexique p. XXXII). Cf. Aristox. Harm. (I, p. 22, 13 Mb) «τῶν δὲ συγχορδιῶν πλειόνων τ᾽ οὐσῶν τῶν τὴν εἰρημένην τάξιν τοῦ διὰ τεσσάρων κατεχουσῶν» ("further, while there are several *groups of notes* which fill this scheme of the Fourth"; transl. H.S.M. p. 180).

Sophocles in "Mysians" (ap. Athen. IV, 183E, ch. 82): «Λυδῆς ἐφυμνεῖ πηκτίδος συγχορδία» ("the [?] harmony [concord] of the Lydian pektis resounds").

310

synchoreia (συγχορεία; m. pr. sinchoría); according to Hes. "synchordia, synodia"* (συγχορδία, συνῳδία), singing together.

synchoreutes (συγχορευτής; m. pr. sinchoreftís); dancing with others (Dem.), companion in the dance (LSJ). Fem. *synchoreutria* (συγχορεύτρια). The vb synchoreuein (συγχορεύειν), to dance with others; to be partner in the dance.

synchoros (σύγχορος; m. pr. sínchoros); partner in a chorus (Dem., LSJ). Cf. *synchoreutes**.

syneches (συνεχής; m. pr. sinechís); continuous, successive, without interruption; *synecheis phthongoi* (συνεχεῖς φθόγγοι); successive notes.

    Aristox. Harm. (II, p. 53, 33 Mb) «ἡ νήτη, ἡ παρανήτη καὶ οἱ τούτοις συνεχεῖς» ("the nete, the paranete and those that follow in succession"). Cf. *hexes**.

    syneches kinesis (συνεχὴς κίνησις); continuous motion of the voice, as in speech, in contradistinction to the "diastematike kinesis" = melodic motion. Cf. *kinesis**. *synecheia* (συνέχεια); continuity. Cf. Aristox. op. cit. I, p. 27, 15ff.

synechesis (συνήχησις; m. pr. siníchisis); sounding together.

    See *heterophonia, paraphonia, symphonia*.

synemmenos (συνημμένος; m. pr. sinimménos) from *synhaptesthai* pass. vb (συνάπτεσθαι) = to be joined together; conjunct.

    Synemmena tetrachorda (συνημμένα τετράχορδα); two conjunct tetrachords.

    See *systema*; also *tetrachord*.

synermosmenos (συνηρμοσμένος; m. pr. sinirmosménos); attuned to. From "synharmozesthai" pass. vb (συναρμόζεσθαι): to be attuned to.

    Xenoph. Banquet (ch. III, § 1): «Ἐκ δὲ τούτου συνηρμοσμένη τῇ λύρᾳ πρὸς τὸν αὐλὸν ἐκιθάρισεν ὁ παῖς καὶ ᾖσεν» ("After that the boy *having attuned* his lyra to the aulos played and sang").

synkrotetikai glottai, pl. (συγκροτητικαὶ γλῶτται; m.pr. syngrotitiké glótte); an expression used by Porphyrius in Comment., (I.D. p. 71) and signifying most probably "double-reed" (figur. welded reeds, united into one body).

    In this passage Porphyrius differentiates between the "plagiai glossai", probably the single-reeds as they are placed sideways (plagiai), and the "synkrotetikai". In the first case, he says, "the tone produced is softer but not equally brilliant", while with the "synkrotetikai" (double-reed), "the tone is harsher and more brilliant".

synkrousis (σύγκρουσις; m. pr. síngrousis); rapid alternation of two notes (LSJ); sort of trill.

Cf. Ptolem. II, ch. 12; ed. Wallis III, p. 85; I. D. p. 67, 7
See *syrigmos*.

synodia, synodos (συνῳδία, συνῳδός; m. pr. sinodía, sinodós);

a) singing, and, by extension, sounding together. Metaph. harmonious (in concord) singing. Pollux (IV, 106).

b) *synodos*, and *synaoedos* (συνῳδός, συναοιδός); the singer singing in concord (in unison) with others. By extension, the player who plays in unison with the voice or with another instrument. Opposite of *diaeidein** (b).

See *synchoreia*.

syntagma (σύνταγμα; m. pr. síntagma); in music, harmonia, scale, system. Aristotle Polit. (book IV, ch. 3, § 4, 1290A; C.v.J. "De artis usu" pp. 22-23): «ὁμοίως δ' ἔχει καὶ περὶ τὰς ἁρμονίας, ὥς φασί τινες, καὶ γὰρ ἐκεῖ τίθενται εἴδη δύο, τὴν δωριστὶ καὶ τὴν φρυγιστί, τὰ δ' ἄλλα συντάγματα (pl.) τὰ μὲν δώρια, τὰ δὲ φρύγια καλοῦσιν» ("it is the same with the *harmonias*, as they say; there too they posit two kinds, the Dorian and the Phrygian, and as to all other *scales* (or *systems*) they class them as either Dorian or Phrygian").

synthesis (σύνθεσις; m. pr. sínthesis); old Att. ξύνθεσις (xynthesis).

a) composition; Plut. De Mus. (1143D, ch. 33) «τὴν τοῦ παίωνος ξύνθεσιν»; ("the composition of the paeon").

b) collocation or combination of simple intervals; Aristox. Harm. (I, p. 5,5) «περὶ συνθέσεως ἔχειν τι λέγειν τῆς τῶν ἀσυνθέτων διαστημάτων» ("to make some remarks *on the collocation* of the simple intervals"); see also p. 27, 20 "the collocation of letters" («τὴν τῶν γραμμάτων σύνθεσιν»).

The synthesis is called "emmeles" *(ἐμμελής; melodious) when it refers to the laws of melos; cf. Aristox. op. cit. p. 54, 1ff. Aristoxenus uses also the term «φυσικὴ σύνθεσις» (*natural collocation*), as it observes the natural laws of melos (ibid, p. 27).

In Psellus § 3 "collocation of durations".

c) a melodic figure which is formed by an ascending tetrachord sung alternately by contiguous notes and a leap (a, below), then repeated in contrary motion (b); *the synthesis* should proceed by stepwise order (c):

Cf. Anon. Bell. § 80, p. 84.

The inverse of the synthesis was called *analysis**.

synthetos (σύνθετος; m. pr. sínthetos); compound.

syntheton diastema (σύνθετον διάστημα); an interval comprised of non-contiguous notes. Oppos. *asynthetos**.

Cleon. Isag. (ch. 5; C.v.J. p. 188, Mb p. 9) «σύνθετα (pl.) δὲ τὰ ὑπὸ τῶν μὴ ἑξῆς [περιεχόμενα], οἷον μέσης καὶ παρυπάτης, μέσης καὶ νήτης» etc ("and *compound* [intervals] are those comprised by non-contiguous notes, such as mese and parhypate [a-f], mese and nete [a-d¹]" etc.).

Many intervals could be compound in one genus, and simple in another; i.e. they were *common* (κοινὰ) to both the compound (σύνθετα) and non-compound (ἀσύνθετα). The semitone (e-f) is compound in the Enharmonic genus and non-compound in the Diatonic and the Chromatic; in the first case it is compound because between its notes there is another note at a distance of a quarter-tone from each. In the second it is non-compound (i.e. simple) as both its notes are contiguous in the respective genus: a) Enharmonic: e - e¼ - f - a; b) Diatonic e - f - g - a; c) Chromatic e - f - f♯ - a

Compound   Simple   Simple

On the contrary the ditone (f - a) is simple in the Enharmonic genus, and compound in the other two genera: a) Enharmonic: e - e¼ - f - a;

b) Diatonic: e - f - g - a; c) Chromatic: e - f - f♯ - a.   Simple
       Compound   Compound

This view of the compound and non-compound intervals is amply explained by Aristoxenus (Harm. III, p. 60, 10 to p. 61, 5).

syntonos (σύντονος; m. pr. síntonos); tense, high-pitched, sharp.

a) a shade in the formation of the Diatonic genus, according to which the order of the intervals in the tetrachord was: semitone-tone-tone; see *Diatonon genus*. The term "syntonos" was sometimes used in the Chromatic genus instead of the term "toniaeon". The order of intervals in the tense chromatic was: semitone-semitone-one-and-a-half tones; see *Chromatikon genus*.

b) The term "syntonos" is also met with as the opposite of aneimenos, chalaros (loose), in the case of harmoniai; e.g. *syntonos* harmonia = tense, not loose harmonia.
Cf. *chalaros**.

syrigma (σύριγμα; m. pr. sírigma); see below, *syrigmos**.

syrigmos (συριγμός; m. pr. sirigmós); whistling, hissing. Gevaert (II, p. 268) suggests that both *syrigmos* and *syrma* (see below) signified an effect similar to the harmonics (of the harp); see *dialepsis*.

Ptolemaeus (Harm. II, ch. 12; Wallis III, p. 85, I.D. p. 67,7) uses the word *syrma* (σύρμα; from syrein [σύρειν] to pull, to draw) perhaps in a similar meaning; «καταπλοκῆς, σύρματος» etc.

Lysander of Sicyon, according to Philochorus (ap. Athen. XIV, 638A, ch. 42) was the first to introduce the *syrigmos*, among other innovations; he calls it also magadis («καὶ μάγαδιν, τὸν καλούμενον συριγμόν»).

Nicomachus (Excerpta, ch. 6; C.v.J., p. 277; Mb p. 37) uses for piercing, unpleasant and cacophonus sounds the words σιγμὸς (*sigmós*, hissing) and ποππυσμὸς (*poppysmos*; clucking). The word *syrigma* (σύριγμα) is also met with in the sense of hissing, or piercing sound of a pipe. Pollux (IV, 83): «μέλη αὐλημάτων, κρούματα, συρίγματα» ("melodies of aulos-solos, kroumata, *syrigmata*" etc.). Non. Dion. XL, 232 «ὦν ἀπὸ μυρομένων σκολιὸν σύριγμα κομάων θρῆνον» ("from the lamentations of their curling and *hissing* hairs").

syringion (συρίγγιον; m. pr. siríngion); dimin. of *syrinx**; a little syrinx, a small pipe.

syrinx (σῦριγξ; m. pr. sírinx); Pan's pipe, shepherd's pipe. The sound is produced by direct blowing into the hole, open at the upper end, without the intercalation of a reed. "Syrizein" or "syrittein" vb («συρίζειν» or «συρίττειν»), to play the syrinx; also to produce or make a whistling sound. The name of syrinx appears in the Iliad and the Hymn to Hermes v. 512; Il. X, 13 «αὐλῶν συρίγγων τ' ἐνοπὴν» (Agamemnon looking at the Trojan plain marvelled at the many fires that burned before Ilion "and at the sound [voice] of the auloi and the *syrinxes*"). Also, in XVIII, 526.

Generally speaking the term "syrinx" was also often used to mean the wind instruments without reed, while for the reed-blown they used the term "aulos".

There were two species of syrinx, the *monocalamus* (*single-caned*) and the *polycalamus* (*many-caned*); Agiopolites (ap. Vincent "Notices" p. 263): «Σύριγγος εἴδη δύο· τὸ μὲν ἐστι μονοκάλαμον, τὸ δὲ πολυκάλαμον, ὅ φασιν εὕρημα Πανός» ("There are two species of syrinx; the single-caned, and the many-caned, which is the invention, as they say, of Pan"). In both cases the syrinx was usually made of cane.

The monocalamus' tone was light, sweet and a trifle whistling, and its range rather limited to the high register, in comparison to the aulos which was often denominated «βαρύφθογγος» (deep-toned). The instrument was vertical and had a number of holes. The polycalamus (many-caned) was the well-known Pan-syrinx or Pan-pipes. The pipes were usually seven, with different size but forming a horizontal line at the upper end, without finger-holes, and interconnected (bound) by wax. Pollux (IV, 69): "on the syrinx the sound is produced by blowing; it is an ensemble of pipes bound by linen and wax; ...many pipes gradually decreasing in length".

Pollux (VIII, 72) speaks also of a five-caned syrinx (πέντε-σύριγγος, πεντασύριγγος); Agiopolites (op. cit. p. 260) speaks of ten pipes ("Attis, having made a ten-piped instrument, called it pastoral syrinx").

The Pan-pipes was a pastoral instrument used by shepherds (Pan was the pastoral god, protector of woods, flocks and shepherds) but never for art purposes; cf. Iliad XVIII, 526 «νομῆες τερπόμενοι σύριγξι».

In the case of equal-sized pipes they used to fill a part of each pipe with wax, thus gradually diminishing the vibrating column of air.

According to Diodorus Sikel. (III, ch. 58, § 2) Cybele invented the many-caned syrinx («πολυκάλαμον σύριγγα πρώτην [Κυβέλην] ἐπινοῆσαι»), while Pollux (IV, 77) says that it was of Celtic origin («ἡ δὲ ἐκ καλάμων σῦριγξ Κελτοῖς προσήκει καὶ τοῖς ἐν ὠκεανῷ νησιώταις»; "the many-caned syrinx belongs to the Celts and the islanders in the ocean"). The legend of the invention of the polycalamus syrinx by Pan is well-known. Pan fell in love with an Arcadian Nymph, named Syrinx, daughter of the river Ladon (Λάδων), who frightened at the god's love and pursuit prayed to Jupiter (Zeus) to save her; at the moment Pan reached her she was transformed into a calamus (reed); furious at the disappointment Pan cut the reed in pieces. But he soon understood that he was cutting in pieces the body of the Nymph, and repenting he began crying and kissing the pieces of cane, when he heard sounds coming from them. He was then led to make the syrinx.

Euphorion, the epic poet, in his Book about the musicians (ap. Athen. IV, 184A, ch. 82) says that the single-caned syrinx was invented by Hermes, and the many-caned by Seilenos, while the wax-bound by Marsyas («τὴν μὲν μονοκάλαμον σύριγγα Ἑρμῆν εὑρεῖν, τὴν δὲ πολυκάλαμον Σειληνόν, Μαρσύαν δὲ τὴν κηρόδετον»). Others (ap. Athen. ibid) attribute the invention of the single-caned to Seuthes (Σεύθης) and Ronakes (Ρωνάκης) of the Thracian tribe of Maedoi (Μαιδοί).

In a general way it may be said that the polycalamus (many-caned) syrinx was the principal precursor of hydraulis*.

The syrinx was also connected with charm and spell; Plut. De Sollertia animalium, 961E, ch. 3: «κηλοῦνται μὲν γὰρ ἔλαφοι καὶ ἵπποι σύριγξι καὶ αὐλοῖς» ("deer and horses are charmed by syrinxes and auloi").

Syrinx was also the mouthpiece of the single-reed aulos (cf. K. Schlesinger: The Greek Aulos, p. 54). According to A. A. Howard's theory (cf. Macran, Aristoxenus, p. 243) syrinx was a hole near the mouthpiece which acted like the "speaker" of the clarinet, and when open enabled the production of harmonics (see Aristox. Harm. I, p. 21, 1 Mb; Plut. Non posse suaviter, 1096A and De Mus. 1138A, ch. 21). For «κατασπᾶν» and «ἀνασπᾶν τὴν σύριγγα» ("kataspan and anaspan ten syringa") see Macran op. cit. pp. 243-244 on Howard's theory, and K. Schlesinger op. cit. p. 54ff; also among others H. Weil et Th. Reinach: Plutarque De la Musique, Note 196, pp. 82-83.

The word syrinx was also used in the meaning of whistle, hiss (LSJ).

Bibliography:
 Th. Reinach: "Syrinx" in DAGR, vol. VIII (1908), pp. 1596-1600.
 H. Abert: "Syrinx" in Pauly's RE, 2 Reihe IV, col. 1779.
 C. Sachs: "Pan-pipes" in Hist. of Mus. Instr. (1940), pp. 142-143.
 M. Wegner: Das Musikleben der Griechen (1949), pp. 58-60.

syrinxes (σύριγγες; m. pr. síringes) pl. of syrinx.

So was called the fifth part, after Strabo (IX, 421), of the kitharistic Pythian nomos.

See *Pythikos* nomos,* and *syrinx*,* above.

syrma (σύρμα; m. pr. sírma);

See syrigmos*.

syrtos (συρτός; m. pr. sirtós) or *syrtes* (σύρτης); a kind of dance, mentioned in the Inscription of Epaminondas dating from the middle of the 1st cent. A.D. and found in Boeotia; it runs as follows: «τὰς δὲ πατρίους πομπὰς μεγάλας καὶ τὴν τῶν συρτῶν πάτριον ὄρχησιν θεοσεβῶς ἐπετέλεσεν» ("he piously fulfilled the great national processions and the national dancing of *syrtos*").

systasis (σύστασις; m. pr. sístasis); constitution, composition.

systasis of melos (σύστασις τοῦ μέλους); constitution of the melody. Cf. Aristox. Harm. (I, p. 15, 7) «ἡ τοῦ μέλους σύστασις» ("*the constitution* of the melody").

systema (σύστημα; m. pr. sístima); a union of two or more intervals. This definition of the "systema" is given by several ancient theorists.

Aristoxenus (in Harm., I p. 16, 1) defines: «τὸ δὲ σύστημα σύνθετόν τι νοητέον ἐκ πλειόνων ἢ ἑνὸς διαστημάτων» ("the *systema* is to be conceived as a compound of more than one interval"). Same definition by Cleonides (Isag. ch. 1, C.v.J. p. 180, Mb p. 1); and Nicomachus (Enchir. ch. 4, C.v.J. p. 243, Mb p. 8 and ch. 12, C.v.J. p. 261, Mb p. 25). Bacchius (Isag. § 5, C.v.J. p. 292 Mb p. 2) defines: "*systema* is that which is sung [performed] through more than two notes". Cf. also Anon. Bell. § 23, p. 30.

According to the above definitions of the theorists a union of three notes

316

(trichord, τρίχορδον), of four (tetrachord) etc. would be considered as a system.

The first well-organized system, afterwards used as the foundation of the Perfect Systems, was the tetrachord. By the conjunction of two contiguous tetrachords the heptachord system was created: e.g. e - f - g - a - b♭ - c - d. The heptachord was attributed to Terpander. The next step was the creation of the octachord (6th cent. B.C.) by the intercalation of a disjunction between the two contiguous tetrachords: e - f - g - a - b - c - d - e.

The addition of the eighth string was ascribed to Pythagoras (see under *lyra** and *octachordon**).

The subsequent addition of more strings had as consequence the use of other systems.

The heptachord system was the principal system of classical times, while the octachord was the first complete system.

The systems, according to the Aristoxenean theory, differed in seven ways, 1) as to the size (μέγεθος); 2) as to the genus; 3) as to concord or discord (in the heptachord the two ends form a 7th, i.e. a discord, while in the octachord they form an 8ve, i.e. a concord); 4) as to rational or irrational (ρητοῦ ἢ ἀλόγου; see under reton-alogon); 5) as to continuous or non-continuous («συνεχοῦς ἢ ἑξῆς καὶ ὑπερβατοῦ»); 6) as to conjunct and disjunct; and 7) as to immutable and mutable («ἀμεταβόλου καὶ ἐμμεταβόλου»); cf. Cleon. Isag. ch. 8, C.v.J. p. 193ff, Mb p. 12ff; Aristox. Harm. I, pp. 17-18.

In the time of Ptolemaeus the octachord was considered the first real system, while the tetrachord was a constituent part of it. Ptolemaeus (II, ch. 4; ed. Wallis, III, p. 56; I.D. p. 50, 12ff) contends that *"system* is simply the extent (magnitude) which is composed of concords, in the same way as concord is the extent which is composed of emmeleiai*; the system is therefore like a concord of concords" («Σύστημα μὲν ἁπλῶς καλεῖται τὸ συγκεί-μενον μέγεθος ἐκ συμφωνιῶν· καθάπερ συμφωνία, τὸ συγκείμενον μέγεθος ἐξ ἐμμελειῶν καὶ ἔστιν ὥσπερ συμφωνία συμφωνιῶν τὸ σύστημα»). "And *perfect system* is that which contains all the concords with all their species" («Τέλειον δὲ σύστημα λέγεται τὸ περιέχον πάσας τὰς συμφωνίας μετὰ τῶν καθ᾽ ἑκάστην εἰδῶν»). Porphyrius (Comment.; Wallis III, p. 339; I.D. pp. 162-3) commenting on the above explains that the constituent concords of a system are the fourth and the fifth (the dia tessaron and the dia pente); the dia pason (octachord) is therefore the first complete system to be formed. And "perfect system" is that which "is wanting in nothing" («τὸ λεῖπον ἐν μηδενί»), i.e. the dis diapason.

After the octachord system the so-called Perfect Systems came into use because they comprised "all the partial systems of the 4th, 5th and 8ve" (Ptol. II, ch. 4), namely 1) the Lesser Perfect System, 2) the Greater Perfect System, and 3) the Immutable System.

1) The *Lesser Perfect System* (Σύστημα τέλειον ἔλαττον), also called «Διὰ πασῶν καὶ διὰ τεσσάρων» (System of one octave and a fourth) consisted of three conjunct tetrachords and the Proslambanomenos* (added). For this reason it was also known as the System of Synemmenon («Σύστημα συνημμένων»); it was also called *metabolon* or *metabolikon* (μετάβολον or μεταβολικόν; *mutable*) because it allows a metabole* of tone (Ptolem. II, ch. 6).

Proslamb

2) The *Greater Perfect System* (Σύστημα τέλειον μεῖζον), known also as the Disjunct System, owing to the disjunction between the mese and the paramese, consisted of four tetrachords conjunct by pairs with a disjunction in the middle:

Prosl

This system was a completion of another system the so-called *Dodecachordon* (δωδεκάχορδον; with twelve strings or notes), or the "Diapason and dia pente System" («Σύστημα διὰ πασῶν καὶ διὰ πέντε»):

This system consisted of three tetrachords of which the two lower were conjunct, with a disjunction between the second and the third (taken upwards). For a *Hendecachordon** system see under a special heading.

3) By the union of the two Perfect Systems, the L.P.S. and the G.P.S. (1 and 2 above), the so-called *Perfect Immutable System* was formed («Σύστημα τέλειον ἀμετάβολον»):

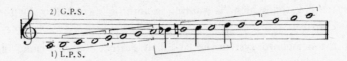

318

The three Perfect Systems are given above in the Diatonic genus but they should be conceived also in the Chromatic and the Enharmonic genera:

A) Chromatic

B) Enharmonic

See also *haploun**, *diploun** and *pollaploun**.

Notes: 1. The notation of these systems as given above is symbolic as to the pitch; it is expressive only of the inner disposition of their intervals. The systems should be conceived independently of any definite pitch, though, of course, a system could be placed on a specific pitch (see under Tonos).

2. The question of the existence of other "systems" or scales before the heptachord has been the object of studies and researches, and, in certain cases, of conjecture and speculation. It is generally accepted by most modern scholars and theorists that there is evidence in ancient writers (Plato, Aristides, Nicomachus, Plutarchus) of the use, especially in pre-classical times, of "defective" scales or scales with a smaller number of notes than that of the heptachord. Some of these scholars, based on the theory of the evolution of scales within the cycle of Fifths, suggested that the clue to the first primitive scale of ancient Greece is found in the instrument *Dichordon**; its two strings were probably tuned at a perfect Fourth (C-F or D-G; otherwise a perfect Fifth: F-C or G-D). New steps in the evolution of scales were reached, according to this theory supported by Ethnomusicology, by progressive additions of a third string-note (trichord lyra; F-C-G, or G-D-A; scale C-F-G, or D-G-A etc.) and a fourth one (tetrachord lyra, F-C-G-D, or G-D-A-E or D-A-E-B; scales, taken upwards, C-D-F-G, or D-E-G-A or D-E-A-B; but also trichord scales D-G-A-D or E-A-B-E). A very important stage was reached eventually by the addition of a fifth note (F-C-G-D-A or G-D-A-E-B; scales C-D-F-G-A, D-E-G-A-B etc), i.e. the "unhemitonic" or tonal pentatonic. In fact the pentatonic is a universally accepted stage in the evolution of scales, and of the music of mankind, and this fact is corroborated by contemporary ethnomusicological researches. It is supported that the pentatonic was in use in pre-classical times, and that old pentatonic tunes of libation were still performed until the time of Aristoxenus (4th cent. B.C.). The theory of a possible use of a hexatonic scale has also been put forward *(J. Chailley: "L'hexatonique grec d'après Nicomaque";* see bibliography below). This hypothesis is in accordance with the theory of the evolution of scales within the cycle of Fifths, as set out above. Jacques Chailley, based on certain passages of Nicomachus, supports the existence of such a scale, derived from six perfect Fifths (F-C-G-D-A-E; scale: E-F-G-A-C-D-E, or taken downwards E-D-C-A-G-F-E, without B and tritone). We do not intend to refer here to the "defective" scales of Plato-Aristides or the Spondeiazon tropos (mentioned elsewhere); entering into more detailed account of these theories and scales would be out of the scope of this book. We give however a *select bibliography* for those more interested in the matter:

L. *Laloy*: "Anciennes gammes enharmoniques" I & II, Revue de Philologie,

319

Paris, (1899) vol. XXIII, p. 238 ff and vol. XXIV (1900), pp. 31-43.

J. F. Mountford: 1) "Greek Music and its Relation to Modern Times"; JHS, vol. XL (1920), pp. 13-42.

2) "The Musical Scales of Plato's Republic"; Classical Quarterly, vol. XVIII (1923), pp. 125-136.

C. Sachs: 1) "Die griechische Instrumentalnotenschrift"; Zeitschrift für Musikwissenschaft, VI (1924), pp. 289-301.

2) The History of Musical Instruments; N. York (1940), pp. 131-2.

Th. Reinach: "La musique grecque"; Paris 1926, p. 16 ff.

J. Yasser: "A Theory of Evolving Tonality"; N. York, 1932, p. 40 ff. and p. 140 ff.

R. P. Winnington-Ingram: 1) "Mode in Ancient Greek Music"; Cambridge, 1936; "The evidence of early scales" pp. 21-30.

2) "The pentatonic tuning of the Greek lyre: a theory examined"; Classical Quarterly, New Series vol. VI, Nos 3-4, Oxford (1956), pp. 169-186.

O. Gombosi: "Tonarten und Stimmungen der antiken Musik"; Kopenhagen, 1939.

Fr. Lasserre: Plutarque De la musique; Olten et Lausanne, 1954, p. 152 ff.

J. Chailley: "L'hexatonique grec d'après Nicomaque"; Revue des Études grecques, vol. LXIX, Paris (1956), pp. 73-100.

S. Baud-Bovy: "L'accord de la lyre antique et la musique populaire de la Grèce moderne"; Revue de Musicologie, vol. LIII, Paris (1967), pp. 3-20.

See also under *harmonia**.

Systema in metrics was a series of two or more periods joined together in a rhythmic (or melodic) unity.

syzygia (συζυγία; m. pr. sizigía); syzygy, coupling, conjunction in pairs (L.S.J.) *kata syzygian* (κατὰ συζυγίαν), = in pair. Aristides (Mb p. 36, RPW-I p. 35) «κατὰ συζυγίαν μὲν οὖν ἐστι δύο ποδῶν ἁπλῶν καὶ ἀνομοίων σύνθεσις» ("conjunction *in pair* [or compound rhythms] is the union of two simple and unequal feet").

T

tasis (τάσις) from "teinein" (τείνειν), to stretch; tension of a string, hence pitch, a note.

Aristoxenus (Harm. I, p. 12, 2-3) says that by "tasis" we mean "a certain persistence or stationary position of the voice" («μονή τις καὶ στάσις τῆς φωνῆς»).

Aristides (Mb p. 9, RPW-I, p. 7) defines that "every simple motion [position] of the voice is tasis"; and "that of the melodic voice is called phthongos (note, tone)". In Anon. (Bell. § 21, p. 29) *tasis* is also defined as "a stationary position and stillness of the voice" («στάσις καὶ ἐνηρέμησις τῆς φωνῆς») and in p. 51 (§ 39) the same definition as that by Aristoxenus (above) is given.

Cleonides (Isag. ch. 2, C.v.J. p. 181, Mb p. 2) says that *"the taseis* (pl.) are called also phthongoi (notes); taseis from the stretching, while phthongoi [are so-called] because they are produced by voice" («καλοῦνται δὲ αἱ τάσεις καὶ φθόγγοι· τάσεις μὲν παρὰ τὸ τετάσθαι, φθόγγοι ἐπεὶ ὑπὸ φωνῆς ἐνεργοῦνται»).

taxis (**τάξις**); order, arrangement, disposition.

«Ἡ τῆς μελῳδίας τάξις» = the melodic order; the disposition of notes or intervals in a melody; cf. Aristox. Harm. I, p. 2, 16; II p. 38, 13 Mb. «Ἡ τοῦ ἡρμοσμένου [μέλους] τάξις» = the order pertaining to the hermosmenon* melos; cf. Aristox. op. cit. II, p. 42, 9; Cleon. Isag. ch. 1, C.v.J. p. 179, Mb p. 1. «Ἡ τῆς τῶν ἀσυνθέτων διαστημάτων τάξεως ἀλλοίωσις» ("the change [or variation] *in the disposition* of the simple intervals"; Aristox. II, p. 40, 4).

In rhythmopoeia, the disposition of durations.

technitai Dionysou (**τεχνῖται Διονύσου**; m. pr. techníte Dionísou); artists of Dionysus, very often called "the artists concerned with Dionysus" («οἱ περὶ τὸν Διόνυσον τεχνῖται») or "Dionysiakoi technitai" («Διονυσιακοὶ τεχνῖται») or even simply "the technitai" («οἱ τεχνῖται»). The *technitai* (pl. of technites, τεχνίτης = princ. craftsman, but also artist) were at first and for a long time only theatrical artists, actors and musicians (auletes, choral-singers, choral-dancers).[1] They were mockingly nicknamed *Διονυσοκόλακες* ("flatterers of Dionysus"); Arist. Rhet. (book III, ch. 2, 1405A, 23-24): "and some call them *Dionysokolakes* (*flatterers of Dionysus*), while they [call] themselves *artists*" («καὶ οἱ (or ὁ) μὲν διονυσοκόλακας, αὐτοὶ δὲ αὑτοὺς τεχνίτας καλοῦσι»).[2]

---

1. "Dionysiakoi auletai", "Dionysiakoi odoi" (ᾠδοί). Polybius (Historiae, IV, 20, § 8) speaking on the musical education of youth among the Arcadians says that their boys from infancy become accustomed to sing Hymns and Paeans («οἱ παῖδες ἐκ νηπίων ᾄδειν ἐθίζονται»).... (§ 9) "and after that, learning the nomoi of Philoxenus and Timotheus, they dance with ambitious eagerness every year in the theatres *to the Dionysiakoi auletai*" («πολλῇ φιλοτιμίᾳ χορεύουσι κατ' ἐνιαυτὸν τοῖς Διονυσιακοῖς αὐληταῖς ἐν τοῖς θεάτροις»), For *Dionysiakoi odoi* see Plato Laws VII, 812B, and *odos**.

2. The nickname *διονυσοκόλακες* is interpreted by some as referring here to the flatterers of Dionysius II, tyrant of Syracuse (367-345 B.C.), but as Ruelle remarks the use by Aristotle of the present tense «καλοῦσι» (they call) gives us to believe that he speaks exclusively of *the artists of Dionysus* (cf. *Ch. Ém. Ruelle* = "Aristote, Poétique et Rhétotique", Paris, 1882, p. 297, note 1). Theophrastus (ap. Athen. X, ch. 47, 435E) clearly refers to the tyrant's flatterers when he says "wherefore they were called *Dionysiokolakes* («διὸ κληθῆναι Διονυσιοκόλακας») which is more precise. In the same way Chares (ap. Athen. XII, 538F) calls Alexander's flatterers "Alexandrokolakes" («οἱ πρότερον καλούμενοι Διονυσοκόλακες Ἀλεξανδροκόλακες ἐκλήθησαν ...» "those who before were called Dionysokolakes were [now] called Alexander's flatterers...").

Reference to *the artists of Dionysus* is made by many ancient authorities: Demosthenes ("On the False Embassy", «Περὶ Παραπρεσβείας» II, § 192, 401) calls them simply *the artists* ("the technitai"):

"When Philip [of Macedonia] conquered Olynthus, he organized a feast in honour of Olympian Zeus, and at this sacrifice and feast he assembled *all the artists* («πάντας τοὺς τεχνίτας») ... entertained them at dinner and crowned the victors").

Plutarch ("Life of Aratus", § 53) says that at the funeral procession of Aratus:

"songs were sung by *the artists of Dionysus*" («μέλη δὲ ᾖδετο πρὸς κιθάραν ὑπὸ τῶν περὶ τὸν Διόνυσον τεχνιτῶν»). Also in "De Inimicorum utilate", § 3 "Nay more, we see *the artists around Dionysus* ..." («καὶ μὴν ὁρῶμεν τοὺς περὶ τὸν Διόνυσον τεχνίτας» ...).

See also Polybius Historiae (ed. Th. Buettner-Wobst, T., Leipzig 1893) vol. III, XVI, 21,8; Athen. V, ch. 49, 212D; IX, ch. 72, 407B etc.

As *Dionysus-flatterers*, Theopompus (ap. Athen. VI, ch. 65, 254B; FHG I, 328) "the most hostile" said that

"Athens is full of Dionysus-flatterers and seamen and thieves" («ὁ δυσμενέστατος Θεόπομπος ὁ φήσας σὺν ἄλλοις πλήρεις εἶναι τὰς Ἀθήνας Διονυσοκολάκων καὶ ναυτῶν καὶ λωποδυτῶν»).

The artists of Dionysus, in their heyday, were treated as privileged persons; protected and favoured by kings and tyrants they were acquitted of military service, enjoyed personal inviolability and were often entrusted with diplomatic missions. Their flourishing coincides with the decadence of the classical art; the gradual weakening of the basic, ethico-religious, principles of the classical ideal encouraged the development of the professional spirit and of the virtuoso-artist. As Gevaert appropriately writes (II, p. 581) "from the moment that the theatrical and musical performances, instead of [being] religious ceremonies, celebrated at great intervals, became a purpose of daily pleasure for the crowd, the practice of the art, which formerly was a religion, was naturally converted to a trade".

The conception of the artistic ideal has fundamentally been changed; new principles of art and the mission of the artist began to be broadly propagated. The "modern" spirit as regards music prevailing in the 3rd cent. B.C. and onward had as the main object of musical education the formation of skilled artists, technically well-equipped, conscious of their "metier" and their social-professional rights.

The artists of Dionysus, principal representatives of the new spirit, were organized in guilds called «κοινὰ» or «σύνοδοι τῶν περὶ τὸν Διόνυσον τεχνιτῶν» at the beginning of the 3rd cent. B.C.; these guilds spread little by little all over Greece. The most famous of them was "The Guild of the Dionysiac artists of Ionia and Hellespont" («Κοινὸν τῶν περὶ τὸν Διόνυσον τεχνιτῶν ἐπ' Ἰωνίας καὶ Ἑλλησπόντου»), the centre of which was the city of Teos

(Τέως) on the Ionian coast of Asia Minor. In 150 B.C. owing to political quarrels between the artists and the people of Teos, they were forced to move to Ephesus, from which they were led by Attalus to Myonnesus; finally they settled at Levedos (Λέβεδος) on an islet near the same coast of Asia Minor. Strabo (XIV, ch. 1, § 29) refers to the guild at Levedos (with a short account of its history) still existing towards the end of the 1st cent. B.C..

Members of the guilds were artists of all sorts: kitharists, kitharodes, auletes, aulodes, singers, composers ("melographoi"), actors, even poets. Head of the guild was the "priest" («ἱερεὺς») of Dionysus elected every year by the Assembly (cf. Athen. V, ch. 27, 198C); besides the priest there were several other officers, all elected democratically. There was also the temple («τέμενος») where sacrifices were regularly performed with libations and music (cf. Athen. V, ch. 49, 212E). To the guild a kind of school of music and drama was annexed; thanks to an Inscription found at Teos (cf. Corpus Inscriptionum Graecorum; ed. Aug. Boeckh, Berlin 1843; vol. II, No. 3088, pp. 674-675) we can read the names of successful students (or victorious contestants) and the courses, registered on two columns. The names are rather mutilated but on the second column including names of adolescent students or contestants («Νεωτέρας ἡλικίας») we read the following musical courses:

v. 6 ψαλμοῦ (*psalmos**; playing with bare fingers on stringed instruments);

v. 7 κιθαρισμοῦ (*kitharismos*; kitharisis**, kithara playing);

v. 8 κιθαρῳδίας (*kitharodia**; singing with kithara accompaniment);

v. 9 ρυθμογραφίας (*rhythmographia**; noting of rhythms, rhythmical composition);

v. 12 μελογραφίας (*melographia**; melodic composition).

In vs. 10 and 11 reference is made of comedy and tragedy respectively.[1]

Bibliography:

Otto Lüders: "Die Dionysischen künstler"; Berlin, 1873; 8°, pp. 200 (supplement, pp. 149-200); a notable and well-documented contribution to the subject. See also *Gev.* II, pp. 578-588 and *P.Foucart* "Dionysiaci artifices" in DAGR, vol. II (1892), pp. 246-249.

SirArthur W. Pickard-Cambridge: "The Dramatic Festivals of Athens", 2nd ed. revised by John Gould and D. M. Lewis; Oxford, 1968, ch. VII "The artists of Dionysus" pp. 279-321. For more bibliography see p. 336 of this last book.

1. From other inscriptions and some literary sources we have information regarding the activities or the existence of guilds established in other centres: 1) *Athens* (Corp. Inscr. Att., II, 551, 552); 2) *Isthmus and Nemea* («τῶν ἐν Ἰσθμῷ καὶ Νεμέᾳ τεχνιτῶν»; Corp. Inscr. Gr. Nos 1689, 3068, this last very extensive and informative [pp. 660-665 of vol. II], 3) *Cyprus* (Corp. Inscr. Gr. II pp. 458-9, Nos 2619, 2620, discovered at Famagusta near Salamis and at the ruins of ancient Paphos respectively); 4) *Thebes*; 5) *Chios*; 6) *Alexandria*; 7) *Ptolemais*; 8) *S. Italy* etc.

telamon (τελαμών); leather band or strap by which the lyra or the kithara was hung from the performer's breast; by holding the instrument the telamon could help the player to use both hands freely. The instrument was usually placed on the knees when the player was seated or was held from the breast when he was standing.

In the case of the lyra, the instrument was held aslant forwards, while in the case of the kithara, which was a much heavier instrument, it was held in an upright position, even somewhat inclined towards the executant.

See *lyra** and *kithara**.

teleios, hyperteleios aulos (τέλειος, ὑπερτέλειος αὐλός; m. pr. télios, ipertélios avlós); perfect and superperfect aulos. They constituted the last two classes, the fourth and fifth respectively, in the Aristoxenean classification of auloi; see *aulos**. Both classes are collectively called «ἀνδρεῖοι» (andreioi; manly). This surname was given to them in contradistinction to the "parthenioi"* (παρθένιοι; virginal) and to the "paedikoi"* (παιδικοί; of boys, infantile), and comprised all varieties of auloi used by men; especially those in use by professional musicians and in contests at the Pythian and other National Games; such were the Pythikos* aulos, the elymos*, the spondeiakos* and others.

b) *teleios* = perfect. Σύστημα τέλειον = Perfect System.

See *systema**.

Telephanes (Τηλεφάνης; m. pr. Tilephánis); famous aulete of the 4th cent. B.C., from Megara, surnamed Megarites or Megarikos (Μεγαρικός). He flourished during the time of Alexander the Great. According to Pausanias (I, ch. 44, § 6) however, on his tomb, which was erected by Cleopatra, daughter of Philip of Amyntas, on the way from Megara to Corinth, he is cited as Samios (from the island of Samos; «ἰοῦσι δὲ ἐκ Μεγάρων ἐς Κόρινθον ἄλλοι τέ εἰσι τάφοι καὶ αὐλητοῦ Σαμίου Τηλεφάνους» "on the way from Megara to Corinth there are other tombs too, and that of the aulete from Samos Telephanes").

According to Plutarch (De Mus. 1138A, ch. 21) "Telephanes objected to the use of the "syrinxes" on the aulos to such a degree that he never allowed the aulos-makers to adopt one on his instrument, and even abstained from competing at the Pythian Games for this reason".

Note: "syrinx" in the case above should be understood as the mouthpiece of the single reed aulos, or "speaker" of the aulos. For more details see under *syrinx**. See also for Telephanes: Dinse: De Antigen. Theb. p. 44.

Telesias (Τελεσίας); 4th cent. B.C. musician from Thebes, contemporary of Aristoxenus. He is cited by Aristoxenus (ap. Plut. De Mus. 1142B-C, ch.

324

31; FHG II, pp. 287-8, Fr. 73) as a typical example of the influence exercised (for good or bad) by education. "Telesias was educated in the most beautiful music («τραφῆναι τῇ καλλίστῃ μουσικῇ») and learned the compositions of Pindar, Dionysius of Thebes, Lamprus, Pratinas and other lyric poets, who were good composers of music. He became a fine aulete and in all respects he acquired a solid musical education. At a later age he turned to the music of such innovators as Philoxenus and Timotheus, but his attempts to compose in both styles, that of Pindar and that of Philoxenus, failed completely in the Philoxenean style; the cause being that he was brought up from boyhood with the best education."

telesias (τελεσιάς); a kind of armed-dance, or war-dance, named after the name of a certain Telesias who invented it. According to Hippagoras (ap. Athen. XIV, 630A, ch. 27) *"telesias* is a war-dance so-called from a certain Telesias who danced it in armour for the first time".

Pollux (IV, 100) cites *"telesias* and pyrrhiche as war-dances, named after two Cretan dancers, Pyrrhichus and Telesias" («ἐνόπλιοι ὀρχήσεις πυρρίχη τε καὶ τελεσιάς, ἐπώνυμοι δύο Κρητῶν ὀρχηστῶν, Πυρρίχου τε καὶ Τελεσίου»).

Telesilla (Τελέσιλλα; m. pr. Telésilla); 3rd cent. B.C. lyric poetess from Argos. She composed partheneia and other lyric songs. During Argos' siege by the King of Sparta, Kleomenes, Telesilla contributed to the deliverance of the city by actively trying to keep up the morale of the women of Argos.

See Page PMG Frgs 717-726, pp. 372-374.; Brgk PLG III pp. 380-1 9 Frgs.

Telestes (Τελέστης; m. pr. Teléstis); b. c. 420; d. c. 345 B.C., composer of dithyrambs from Selinous in Sicily (Σελινοῦς, hence Σελινούντιος, Selinountius). According to Diodorus Sikeliotes (XIV, ch. 46, § 6) he was one of a group of contemporary celebrated composers of dithyrambs, such as Philoxenus* of Kythera, Timotheus* of Miletos, and Polyeidus («Ἤκμασαν δὲ κατὰ τοῦτον τὸν ἐνιαυτὸν οἱ δαισημότατοι διθυραμβοποιοί, Φιλόξενος Κυθήριος, Τιμόθεος Μιλήσιος, Τελέστης Σελινούντιος, Πολύειδος»...).

In 402-1 B.C., still very young, he competed in Athens for the dithyramb and won a prize ("Par. Chron." v. 65).

To Telestes was attributed a change in the rhythmical structure of the dithyramb; for these changes and the mixing in the same work of different harmonias and genera, he is blamed by, among others, Dionysius of Halicarnassos.

He died in Sicyon where the tyrant Aristratus erected a monument in his honour. Dithyrambs by Telestes and Philoxenus, together with works by the three great tragedians, were invited for the festivities held at Susa on the occasion of Alexander's marriage; they were sent by Harpalus; cf. Plut. "De Vita Alexander", § 8.

Among his works are cited Argo (Ἀργὼ) and Asclepius, of which some fragments survive.

See Brgk PLG III, pp. 627-31, and Anth. Lyr. pp. 298-9.

teleute (τελευτή; m. pr. teleftí); end, extremity.
The final note of a tetrachord, taken in a downward motion.
Oppos. *arche*.

tenella (τήνελλα; m. pr. tínella); (LSJ and Dem.), a word formed by Archilochus to imitate the twang of a lyra- (or kithara-) string (PLG II, Fr. 119); he began a triumphant hymn to Heracles with the words «τήνελλα, ὦ καλλίνικε χαῖρε». Later the words «τήνελλα καλλίνικε» became a common mode of saluting victors in the games. See also *blityri*, *threttanello*, *torelle*.

teretisma, and **teretismos** (τερέτισμα, τερετισμὸς) from vb teretizein (τερετίζειν), to warble like the swallow or the cricket; a sort of trill; an imitation of the warbling of the swallow or the cricket in singing or playing on the kithara.

Anon. Bell. (§ 10, p. 26) and Man. Bryennius (ed. Wallis, III, p. 480) define teretismos as a mixture of kompismos* and melismos*. Hes. «τερετίσματα (pl.)· ᾠδαὶ ἀπατηλαί, τὰ τῆς κιθάρας κρούματα καὶ τὰ τῶν τεττίγων ᾄσματα» and also «τερετίζοντα· λαλοῦντα ἐκ μεταφορᾶς τῆς χελιδόνος» ("*teretismata*; deceptive songs, pieces (sounds) of kithara and the songs of the crickets", and also "*teretizonta* [*warbling*]; by metaphor from the swallow").

According to A.J.H. Vincent (Notices, p. 53) teretismos would be something like the following in which are mixed the kompismos and melismos (as he interprets the kompismos; see under *kompismos*):

Terpandrus, Terpander (Τέρπανδρος; m. pr. Térpandros); b. c. 710 B.C.; d. 7th cent. B.C. He was born at Antissa (Ἄντισσα) in Lesbos, the son of Derdenis (Δέρδενις; hence surnamed Δερδένεος in "Par. Chron." v. 34, or generally Antissaeus, Ἀντισσαῖος). According to a legend, when Orpheus* was killed by the Thracian Maenads his lyra was thrown in the sea, and reached Antissa in Lesbos; there some fishermen found it and brought it to Terpander

(Excerpta ex-Nicom., ch. 1; C.v.J. p. 266, Mb p. 29).

He went to Sparta where he was the first to win at the Carnean musical contests in 676 and 673 (Athen. XIV, 635E, ch. 37). He competed also and won four times successively at the Pythian Games; in the kitharodic art he was unrivalled (Plut. De Mus. 1132E; ch. 4). He passed most of his life in Sparta where he exercised a conciliatory role in civil quarrels, and established the name of the musician par excellence, the founder of its musical life. The Spartans used to place any prominent musician "after the Lesbian aoedos" («μετὰ Λέσβιον ἀοιδόν»; FHG II, p. 130 [Aristotelis Fragmenta] Fr. 87). Also Heracl. Pont. (De Rebus Publicis, «Περὶ Πολιτειῶν» II, Λακεδαιμονίων 6; ap. FHG II, p. 210) «Λακεδαιμόνιοι τὸν Λέσβιον ᾠδὸν (Terpandrum) ἐτίμησαν· τούτου γὰρ ἀκούειν ὁ θεὸς χρησμῳδουμένοις ἐκέλευεν» ("The Lacedaemons honoured the Lesbian epic singer [Terpander]; the God ordered them, when they asked for an oracle, to listen to him [to give ear to what he says]").

Among the inventions and innovations ascribed to Terpander the principal are the following:

1) the extension of the heptachord to the octachord by omitting the trite in the Dorian harmonia (6th degree from below, c), and adding the nete (octave, e); cf. Aristotle Probl. IX, 32; Plut. 1140F, ch. 28. See lyra*.

2) the establishment and the naming of the kitharodikoi nomoi ("Par. Chron." v. 34; Plut. 1132C, D, chs 3 and 4); one of these nomoi bears his name (Terpandreios; Τερπάνδρειος);

3) the transformation of the singing recitation of the epic singers (aoedoi) to real melody;

4) the introduction of the kitharodic prooemia* (preludes) into epic songs (Plut. 1132D, ch. 4);

5) the invention of barbitos*.

Gevaert (I, p. 182) supports that Terpander established the definitive basis of Greek music and deserves the title of its Founder.

See Brgk PLG III, pp. 7-12 and Anth. Lyr. p. 165, some fragments.

tetartemorion (τεταρτημόριον; m. pr. tetartimórion); quarter-tone. By some theorists it was considered as equal to a diesis.

According to Aristoxenus who claims that the Enharmonic, containing exact quarter-tones, was the only normal genus, the quarter-tone is equal to the minima enharmonic diesis; Harm. II, p. 46, 7: «καὶ τὸ τέταρτον [τοῦ τόνου] ὃ καλεῖται δίεσις ἐναρμόνιος ἐλαχίστη» ("and the quarter-tone which is called minima [smallest] enharmonic diesis"), Nicomachus (Enchir. ch.

12; C.V.J. p. 262, Mb p. 26) also considered the quarter-tone equal to the enharmonic diesis.

See under *diesis**.

tetrachordon (τετράχορδον); tetrachord, the ensemble of four contiguous strings or notes, forming a perfect fourth. Bacch. Isag. (§ 26; C.v.J. p. 298, Mb p. 7) "*tetrachord* is an order of notes sung contiguously (ἐξῆς μελῳδουμένων) of which the ends make the concord of a fourth". The tetrachord was the first system of prehistoric Greece; with the development of music in the historic era it became the basis of the formation of the heptachord and octachord scales, and later of the Perfect Systems.

There were three genera of the tetrachord: the Diatonic, the Chromatic and the Enharmonic. In the Diatonic use was made of tones (and semitone):

In the Chromatic use was made of the interval of one tone and a half, and in the Enharmonic of quarter-tones:

The extreme notes of the tetrachord were called *hestotes* (*immovable*) and the inner ones, which changed according to the genus, were called *kinoumenoi* (*movable*).

See under *hestotes**; also under *genus**, *Diatonon**, *Chromatikon**, *Enharmonion**.

Two tetrachords placed contiguously form either a heptachord when they are conjunct, or an octachord when they are disjunct. In the first case the tetrachords are called *synemmena* (conjunct), in the second *diezeugmena* (disjunct).

See *diazeuxis**, *synemmenos** and *systema**.

tetragerys (τετράγηρυς; m. pr. tetrágiris having four sounds, tetraphone, four-toned.

Strabo (XIII, 2, 4; ch. 618; on Terpander): «σοὶ δ' ἡμεῖς τετράγηρυν

328

ἀποστρέψαντες ἀοιδὴν ἑπτατόνῳ φόρμιγγι νέους κελαδήσομεν ὕμνους» ("to you, having abandoned the *four-toned* song, let us sing aloud new hymns to the seven-toned phorminx").

Note: gerys (γῆρυς) = voice, speech, sound.   The vb geryein (γηρύειν) = to sing.

tetragonos (τετράγωνος); tetrangular, square.   *Tetragonos chorus*; chorus drawn up in square; Timaeo (ap. FHG I, p. 201 Fr. 44 and Athen. V, 181C, ch. 28); «Οἱ δὲ Λακωνισταὶ λεγόμενοι ἐν τετραγώνοις χοροῖς ᾖδον» ("The so-called Laconistai sang in square figure").

tetrakomos (τετράκωμος);   a kind of war-dance; also a victorious song and dance in honour of Heracles (Hercules).

Pollux (IV, 100; "On kinds of dancing"); «καὶ τετράκωμος, Ἡρακλέους ἱερὰ καὶ πολεμικὴ [ὄρχησις]» ("and the *tetrákomos*, a war and sacred dance, in honour of Heracles"); cf. also Pollux, IV, 105.   Hes. «τετράκωμος, μέλος τι σὺν ὀρχήσει πεποιημένον εἰς Ἡρακλέα ἐπινίκιον» ("*tetrakomos*, a victo-rious song with dance in honour of Heracles").

b) also a kind of aulesis, included in Tryphon's catalogue of auleseis (ap. Athen. XIV, 618C, ch. 9).   See the full catalogue under *aulesis**.

tetraktys (τετρακτύς; m. pr. tetraktís); the total of the first four numbers, $1 + 2 + 3 + 4 = 10$.

Sext. Empir. (IV, § 3; "Against the Arithmeticians"): «τετρακτὺς δὲ προσηγορεύετο παρ' αὐτοῖς [τοῖς Πυθαγορικοῖς] ὁ ἐκ τῶν πρώτων τεσσάρων ἀριθμῶν συγκείμενος δέκα ἀριθμός· ἓν γὰρ καὶ δύο καὶ τρία καὶ τέσσερα δέκα γίνεται· ὃς ἐστι τελειότατος ἀριθμός» ("and *tetraktys* was called [by the Pythagoreans] the number ten which is composed of the four first numbers; for one and two and three and four make up ten, and this is the most perfect number").

The tetraktys was considered by the Pythagoreans as sacred and as "the source of the everlasting nature"; hence, the tetraktys was the basis of their most solemn oath «ναί, μὰ τὸν ἁμετέρᾳ ψυχᾷ παραδόντα τετρακτὺν παγὰν ἀεννάου φύσεως ριζώματ' ἔχουσαν» ("Yes, I swear on Him who conveyed to our soul the *tetraktys*, source of the everlasting nature").

In music, the tetraktys was considered of particular significance as it contained all the concords; Theon of Smyrna (ch. 37, pp. 146-7) writes "in these numbers [i.e. 1, 2, 3, 4] are included the dia tessaron in the ratio 4:3 (epi-tritos), the dia pente in the hemiolic ratio (3:2), the dia pason in the double (2:1), and the dis dia pason in the fourfold (4:1); all of which complete the immutable system [diagram]".

Select Bibliography:

Jean Dupuis: Θέωνος Σμυρναίου «Περὶ τετρακτύος καὶ δεκάδος» with French translation ("Du quartenaire et de la décade") in his edition of "Théon de Smyrne, 'Exposition des connaissances mathématiques utiles pour la lecture de Platon'" (Paris, 1892) pp. 152-175. See under Theon of Smyrna.

Armand Delatte: "La tetractys pythagoricienne"; art. in his "Études sur la littérature pythagoricienne" (Paris, 1915), pp. 249-268. See under *Pythagoras*.

Paul Kucharski: "Étude sur la doctrine pythagoricienne de la tétrade". Paris, ed. "Les Belles Lettres" 1952, pp. 85. 8°.

tetraoedios (τετραοίδιος; m. pr. tetra·í·dios); a kitharodic nomos ascribed to Terpander. It was probably a nomos with four strophes or melodic sections different in rhythm; something perhaps analogous to the trimeres* (tripartite) aulodic nomos.

Cf. Plut. De Mus. 1132D, ch. 4; Strabo XIII, 618.

tetrasemos (τετράσημος; m. pr. tetrásimos) chronos (time); the time which consists of four first (short) times, i.e. of four time-units.

See *chronos*.

Thaletas (Θαλήτας; m. pr. Thalítas); 7th cent. B.C. aoedos and musician, born at Gortys (Γόρτυς) of Crete; his birthplace was a well-known town to the NW of Knossos mentioned by Homer (Il. II, 646; Odyss. III, 294).

Thaletas was regarded as one of the principal figures of the second School of music in Sparta (the first being established by Terpander), and was accredited with the initiation in Sparta of the gymnopaediai*, together with Xenocritus*, Xenodamus*, Polymnestus* and Sakadas*. He was also considered as a leading composer of paeans and hyporchemata (Plut. De Mus. 1134B-E, chs 9-10).

According to a legend, Thaletas, invited to Sparta (around 665 B.C.) at the direction of the Oracle of Delphi, saved the city from a plague by his music (Pratinas ap. Plut. 1146C, ch. 42). It is said that Thaletas became a friend of Lycurgus, the great legislator of Sparta; but the time of Lycurgus is rather uncertain.

Thamyris and **Thamyras** (Θάμυρις; and Θαμύρας; m. pr. Thámiris, Thamíras); mythical epic singer from Thrace, mentioned by Homer. He was the son of Philammon* and the nymph Agriope or Argiope (᾿Αργιόπη), or, according to Suidas, Arsinoe (᾿Αρσινόη). He was the eighth epic poet before Homer (Suid.), and lived at the court of Eurytus (Εὔρυτος) king of Oechalia (Οἰχαλία).

Heracl. Pont. (ap. Plut. 1132A-B, ch. 3) records that Thamyris excelled among all in beauty and melodiousness of song; and that he composed the story of the war of the Titans and Gods. Beaten at a musical contest against the Muses, he was blinded by them and deprived of kitharody (cf. Apollodorus Bibliotheca, I, ch. 3 § 2 ap. FHG I, p. 106).

According to Diodorus Sikeliotes (book III, ch. 59, § 6) Thamyris was credited with the addition of the string parhypate, and by others with the invention of the Dorian harmonia (Clem. of Alexandria: «Τὰ εὑρισκόμενα» p. 132).

Theon of Smyrna (Θέων ὁ Σμυρναῖος; m. pr. Théon Smirnéos); 2nd cent. A.D. Platonic philosopher and mathematician. He was born and lived in Smyrna (hence his surname) during the reign of Hadrian. He is the author of a work dealing with the mathematical sciences (Arithmetic, Geometry, Stereometry, Astronomy and Music). It was first edited with the Greek text and Latin translation by *Ism. Bullialdus* (I. Bouillaud; Paris 1644) under the title "Theoni Smyrnei, Platonici 'Mathematica' " (Θέωνος Σμυρναίου, Πλατωνικοῦ «Τῶν κατὰ μαθηματικὴν χρησίμων εἰς τὴν τοῦ Πλάτωνος ἀνάγνωσιν». In the second book he writes "On Music" («Περὶ μουσικῆς»; pp. 73-188) giving valuable information and appreciation of ancient Greek music, especially of the Pythagorean School. Other edition by *Ed. Hiller*, Leipzig, 1878, T.

An important edition with a French translation was published by *Jean Dupuis*; Paris 1892 (Librairie Hachette), 8°, pp. XXVIII, 404; «Θέωνος Σμυρναίου, Πλατωνικοῦ τῶν κατὰ μαθηματικὴν χρησίμων εἰς τὴν Πλάτωνος ἀνάγνωσιν»; Théon de Smyrne, philosophe platonicien, "Exposition des connaissances mathématiques utiles pour la lecture de Platon", traduite pour la première fois du grec au français. The book "On Music" («Τὰ περὶ Μουσικῆς») is published on pp. 80-151 (Greek text pp. 80-150, and French translation pp. 81-151).

Theophrastus (Θεόφραστος; m. pr. Theóphrastos). b. 372 B.C., d. 237 B.C. Philosopher from Eresus of Lesbos; he studied at the Academy of Plato where he met Aristotle with whom he developed a friendship. He later joined Aristotle in the Lyceum and eventually became his successor (cf. Aristoxenus*). He was a prolific writer and among his many books there are also writings on music of which some fragmentary references survive.

thereios (θήρειος; m. pr. thírios) aulos; a kind of aulos used by the Thebans and made of a fawn's limb; according to Pollux the exterior was made of metal.

Pollux (IV, 75) «θήρ[ε]ιος αὐλός· Θηβαῖοι μὲν αὐτὸν ἐκ νεβροῦ κώλων εἰργάσαντο· χαλκήλατος δ᾽ ἦν τὴν ἔξωθεν ὄψιν» (*"thereios* aulos; the Thebans made it from fawn's limbs, and it was forged out of brass in its outer appearance").

therepodos (θηρεπῳδός; m. pr. thirepodós); charmer of wild beasts, by singing "epodes". See *epodos**.

Cf. Suidas s.v. «σοφός».

thermastris (θερμαστρίς); a kind of violent hopping dance in which the dancers used to leap in the air and cross the feet in the form of scissors.

Hes. «θερμαστρίς· ὄρχησις ἔντονος καὶ διάπυρος τάχους ἔνεκα» ("*thermastris*; a violent and fiery dance, owing to its speed"). Pollux (IV, 102) «θερμαστρίδες (pl.) ἔντονα ὀρχήματα ... ἡ δὲ θερμαστρὶς πηδητικὸν» ("the *thermastrides* [are] violent dances ... the *thermastris* is a hopping [dance]").

In Athenaeus (XIV, 629D, ch. 27) the thermastris is included among the "passionate" («μανιώδεις»; crazy) dances.

Note : The word *thermaustris* (θερμαυστρὶς) for thermastris is also met. The verb "thermastrizein" and "thermaustrizein" (θερμαστρίζειν, and θερμαυστρίζειν) signified, to dance the thermastris. Cf. Luc. "On dancing" (Περὶ ὀρχήσεως), §34.

thesis (θέσις).

See *arsis-thesis** ; also *dynamis**.

thixis (θίξις); "touching" of strings of lyra.

Cf. Plut. Moral. 802F.

Thrasyllus of **Phlious** (**Θράσυλλος** ὁ **Φλιάσιος**; m. pr. Thrásillos Phliásios); composer of unknown date. He is mentioned in Plut. De Mus. (1137F, ch. 21) together with Tyrtaeus* of Mantineia and Andreas of Corinth* as examples of composers keeping the ancient tradition, and avoiding the Chromatic genus, the modulations, the use of many strings and other innovations in rhythmopoeia, melopoeia and interpretation.

threnetikos, aulos (**θρηνητικός**, αὐλός; m. pr. thrinitikós); a kind of aulos used at funeral ceremonies, expressing strong lamentation (see *Karikon** melos). This aulos belonged to the «ἀνδρεῖοι» (manly) auloi; its length was considerable and its tone baritonal (βαρύφθογγος) and expressive. Aristotle called it *aeazon* aulos (αἰάζων), lamenting; aeazein, vb (αἰάζειν) == to wail.

Pollux (IV, 75) says that "the Phrygians invented a lamenting (threnetikos) aulos, which was used by the Karians who had it from them".

Threneterios (θρηνητήριος; m. pr. thrinitírios); an Adj. synonym of threnetikos.

threnos (θρῆνος; m. pr. thrínos); song expressing a strong lamentation. Also *threnodema* and *threnodia* (θρηνῴδημα, θρηνῳδία).

The threnos should be distinguished from the epikedeion*, in that it is sung without any limitation as to time or occasion, while the epikedeion is sung at the funeral with the dead body lying exposed. Procl. Chrest. 25

«Διαφέρει δὲ τοῦ ἐπικηδείου ὁ θρῆνος· ὅτι τὸ μὲν ἐπικήδειον παρ' αὐτὸ τὸ κῆδος, ἔτι τοῦ σώματος προκειμένου λέγεται· ὁ δὲ θρῆνος οὐ περιγράφεται χρόνῳ» ("the *threnos* differs from the epikedeion, because the epikedeion is said [sung] at the funeral with the body still lying exposed, while the threnos is not limited as to time").

There were professional mourners who were paid to sing the dirges; in Homer "leaders of the dirges" («θρήνων ἔξαρχοι») are mentioned. In Iliad, XXIV, 720-722 we read

...Παρὰ δ' εἶσαν ἀοιδοὺς
θρήνων ἐξάρχους, οἵ τε στονόεσσαν
ἀοιδήν, οἱ μὲν ἄρ' ἐθρήνεον, ἐπὶ δὲ
στενάχοντο γυναῖκες»

("and by his [Hector's] side set singers, *leaders of the dirge*, who led the song of lamentation; they chanted the dirge and thereat the women made lament"; transl. A. T. Murray, vol. II, v. 617).

Threnodia (θρηνῳδία); an ode, a song of a lamenting character, a threnody. Plut. Quaest. conviv. (book III, 8, § 2): «ὥσπερ [γὰρ] ἡ θρηνῳδία καὶ ὁ ἐπικήδειος αὐλὸς» ("for like the *threnody*, [so] also the funeral aulos"). Also *threnodema* (θρηνῴδημα).

Threnodos (θρηνῳδός; m. pr. thrinodós); singer of lament, of dirge. Also *threneter* (θρηνητήρ).

See *epikedeion*.

threttanelo (θρεττανελό; m. pr. threttaneló); LSJ, sound imitative of the kithara. Aristoph. Plutus 290 «καὶ μὴν ἐγὼ βουλήσομαι θρεττανελὸ τὸν Κύκλωπα».

Cf. *blityri**, *tenella**, *torelle**.

thyrokopikon, melos **(θυροκοπικὸν** μέλος; m. pr. thirokopikón); a song sung to aulos with dance, performed before the door of one's sweetheart. Also an aulesis (solo for aulos). Another term is *krousithyron* (κρουσίθυρον), also a kind of serenade. The Alexandrian lexicographer Tryphon (ap. Athen. XIV, 618C, ch. 9) includes both the thyrokopikon and the krousithyron in his catalogue of kinds of auleseis. See the full catalogue of auleseis under *aulesis**.

The vb *thyrokopein* (θυροκοπεῖν), to knock at the door; in Phryn. Epitome (ed. I. de Borries; p. 74) «θυροκοπεῖν· ἐπικωμάζειν» ("*thyrokopein*; to rush on or in with revellers"; LSJ).

krousithyron is derived from krousis (krouein, vb) and thyra (θύρα, door) = knocking at the door.

Timotheus of Miletos (Τιμόθεος ὁ Μιλήσιος; m. pr. Timótheos Milísios); b. c. 450; d. c. 360 B.C. Famous musician, composer of dithyrambs and kitharode from the island of Miletos. He was one of the principal innovators in the history of ancient Greek music, the most daring of his time. He was credited with: 1) the addition of the 11th string (cf. Excerpta ex-Nicomacho, ch. 4; C.v.J. p. 274, Mb p. 35), and perhaps also of the 12th string (Pherecrates, ap. Plut. De Mus. 1142A, ch. 30); 2) the replacement of the Enharmonic genus by the Chromatic; 3) the development of the vocal solo; 4) the new kitharodic style.

Timotheus studied music in Athens under Phrynis*, and at the beginning of his career he unsuccessfully took part at the Athens musical contests; encouraged by Euripides he competed again in 420 B.C. this time beating his own master, Phrynis. He celebrated his victory over his master by a song of which some verses survive.

His innovations provoked controversial disputes during his life and after his death. Pherecrates in his comedy "Cheiron" («Χείρων») represents Music as a woman complaining and protesting to Justice against her maltreatment by the innovators Kinesias*, Melanippides*, Phrynis* and above all Timotheus, from whom "the gravest miseries come"; "this red-haired man from Miletos, she says, surpassed all by singing perverse [strange] multitude of notes" («ᾄδων ἐκτραπέλους μυρμηκιάς»). Cf. Plut. De Mus. 1141F to 1142A, ch. 30, and *myrmekia**.

When Timotheus competed at the Carnean in Sparta one of the Ephors (Ἔφορος; magistrate, overseer) cut with a knife the strings of his instrument which exceeded the classical seven; and later a Spartan court condemned him to exile. In spite of the Spartans' conservatism, his reputation as one of the greatest artists of his time extended all over Greece. Aristotle praises him in the "Metaphysica" (I, 993 B) in these words: "if Timotheus did not exist we would not have so many melodic compositions" («πολλὴν μελοποιΐαν»); see the Greek text under *Phrynis*; cf. Sachs Hist. of Mus. Instr. p. 131. Very few fragments of Timotheus' poetry have survived, from "Cyclops", "Niobe", Hymn to Diana, and especially from his famous nomos "Persai" (Πέρσαι; about 253 verses) found in 1902 on a papyrus at Abusir in Egypt.

The following surviving verses of one of his songs express in a few words his artistic "credo":

> "I do not sing the old (antiquated),
> the new is much superior.
> To-day reigns the young Zeus,
> before [him] Kronus was the master.
> Away the old Muse [Let the old Muse go away]

(«Οὐκ ἀείδω τὰ παλαιὰ

κοινὰ γὰρ μάλα κρείσσω·

νέος ὁ Ζεὺς βασιλεύει,

τὸ πάλαι δ' ἦν Κρόνος ἄρχων.

Ἀπίτω Μοῦσα παλαιά»); PLG III, Fr. 12, p. 624.

Timotheus died in Athens at the age of 90; "Par. Chron." says 88 (v. 76).

See Brgk PLG III, pp. 619-626 and Anth. Lyr. pp. 295-7; Also Page PMG Frgs 777-804, pp. 399-418.

tityrinos, aulos (τιτύρινος, αὐλός; m. pr. titírinos); a shepherd's aulos made of cane (reed), and known among the Dorians of Italy. Athen. (IV, 182D, ch. 80 «ὁ δὲ καλάμινος αὐλὸς τιτύρινος καλεῖται παρὰ τοῖς ἐν Ἰταλίᾳ Δωριεῦσιν, ὡς Ἀρτεμίδωρος ἱστορεῖ ὁ Ἀριστοφάνειος» ("the reed-made aulos is called 'tityrinos' among the Dorians in Italy, as Artemidorus, the disciple of Aristophanes, records").

Cf. Athen. IV, 176C, ch. 78.

tityros (τίτυρος; m. pr. títiros); cane, reed; also aulos. Probably, a shepherd's aulos.

See *tityrinos,* above. Tityros is the Dorian name for Satyr.

tome (τομή; m. pr. tomí) from temnein, vb (τέμνειν), to cut, to divide; division made in a locus.

Aristox. Harm. (I, p. 48, 9) «ὁ τοῦ λιχανοῦ τόπος εἰς ἀπείρους τέμνεται τομὰς» ("the locus of the lichanos can be divided in infinite *divisions*"; "is infinitely divisible" translates H. S. Macran, p. 201).

b) *tome*; caesura; Aristides De Mus. Mb pp. 51-52, RPW-I, p. 47.

tone (τονή; m. pr. toní); prolongation of a note; the stay for a length of time on one note. Cleonides (Isag. ch. 14; C.v.J. p. 207, Mb p. 22): «τονὴ δὲ ἡ ἐπὶ πλείονα χρόνον μονὴ κατὰ μίαν γινομένη προφορὰν τῆς φωνῆς» ("*tone* is the stay for a longer time on one utterance of the voice").

See *agoge, petteia, ploke.*

tonos (τόνος);

The term tonos had various, and sometimes confusing, meanings in ancient Greek music.

Most writers agree on the following three significations:

a) as *tasis* (τάσις; tension, pitch); as "when we say that an executant uses a high or low tone" (Porphyr. Comment., Wallis, III, p. 258; I.D. p. 82,7); also pitch or accent of a word or syllable.

b) as *interval*, i.e. the interval by which the fifth exceeds the fourth; otherwise the major second, or as we say now "tone";

c) as *key*; as "locus of the voice", as we say Dorian tonos, Phrygian tonos etc. Cleonides (Isag. ch. 12; C.v.J. p. 202, Mb p. 19) gives a fourth signification, that of "phthongos" (sound, tone), as we say "seven-toned phorminx" («ἑπτά-τονος φόρμιγξ»).

The terms *tonos*, *tropos* and *harmonia* appear in ancient texts, not always clearly distinguished between themselves; (cf. *tropos**).

Tonos is often taken for harmonia; Aristoxenus (Harm. II, Mb p. 37, 9-10) gives the following rule for tonos "The fifth part [of the Harmonike] deals with *the tonoi* being placed on which the systems are sung" («Πέμπτον δ' ἐστὶ τῶν μερῶν [τῆς ἁρμονικῆς πραγματείας] τὸ περὶ τοὺς τόνους ἐφ' ὧν τιθέμενα τὰ συστήματα μελῳδεῖται»). Thus, tonos is *the key* on which a harmonia can be placed or reproduced. The necessity to meet the vocal difficulties, especially in choral unison performances, was probably the main cause for which the Greeks from the 4th cent. B.C. had recourse to transportations of the harmoniai. So, the keys as transposition types, were introduced and were called *tonoi*. They were named by analogy with the denomination of the harmoniai, Dorian, Phrygian, Lydian etc., but this denomination should be understood as distinctly different from that of the harmoniai. By harmonia is meant the different disposition of the intervals inside the octave (dia pason), independently of any definite pitch, and in this sense it was analogous to our modern "mode". By tonos, the key on which a harmonia is placed and performed; as we say, g major or d major, or e minor etc.

The tonoi did not differ between themselves as to the inner disposition of the intervals; the only difference between them was in the pitch. Actually the tonoi were transpositions of the Immutable System. Aristoxenus established a system of 13 tonoi, disposed at a distance of a semitone from one another; the mese of the lower tonos was at a distance of an octave from the mese of the higher tonos (f- f). The 13 tonoi of Aristoxenus were as follows (Diatonic Genus):

1. TONOS. Hypermixolydian. (ΥΠΕΡΜΙΞΟΛΥΔΙΟΣ)

2. T. Higher Mixolydian. (ΜΙΞΟΛΥΔΙΟΣ ὀξύτερος)

3. T. Mixolydian. (ΜΙΞΟΛΥΔΙΟΣ)

4. T. Lydian. (ΛΥΔΙΟΣ)

336

5. T.	Lydian Lower	(ΛΥΔΙΟΣ βαρύτερος)
6. T.	Phrygian.	(ΦΡΥΓΙΟΣ)
7. T.	Lower Phrygian.	(ΦΡΥΓΙΟΣ βαρύτερος)
8. T.	Dorian.	(ΔΩΡΙΟΣ)
9. T.	Hypolydian.	(ΥΠΟΛΥΔΙΟΣ)
10. T.	Lower Hypolydian.	(ΥΠΟΛΥΔΙΟΣ βαρύτερος)
11. T.	Hypophrygian.	(ΥΠΟΦΡΥΓΙΟΣ)
12. T.	Lower Hypophrygian.	(ΥΠΟΦΡΥΓΙΟΣ βαρύτερος)
13. T.	Hypodorian.	(ΥΠΟΔΩΡΙΟΣ)

To these 13 tonoi two more were added above the first (Hypermixolydian) with as Proslambanomenos and Mese, f♯ and g. The neo-Aristoxenean system did not retain the same nomenclature; only six of the seven principal tonoi retained their names, while all the rest were given new names taken from the ancient names of harmoniai. The complete system of 15 "tonoi" with the new nomenclature were as follows (from high to low):

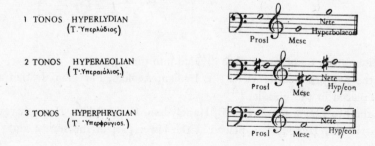

1 TONOS   HYPERLYDIAN
(Τ.Ὑπερλύδιος)

2 TONOS   HYPERAEOLIAN
(Τ.Ὑπεραιόλιος.)

3 TONOS   HYPERPHRYGIAN
(Τ. Ὑπερφρύγιος.)

337

4 TONOS   HYPERIASTIAN or HYPERIONIAN
(T. Ὑπεριάστιος or Ὑπεριώνιος.)

5 TONOS HYPERDORIAN; OLD MIXOLYDIAN
T. Ὑπερδώριος ; Παλαιός Μιξολύδιος.)

6 TONOS LYDIAN
(T. Λύδιος.)

7 TONOS AEOLIAN
(T. Αἰόλιος.)

8 TONOS PHRYGIAN
(T. Φρύγιος.)

9 TONOS IASTIAN or IONIAN
(T. Ἰάστιος or Ἰώνιος.)

10 TONOS DORIAN
(T. Δώριος.)

11 TONOS HYPOLYDIAN
(T. Ὑπολύδιος.)

12 TONOS HYPOAEOLIAN
(T. Ὑποαιόλιος.)

13 TONOS   HYPOPHRYGIAN
(T. Ὑποφρύγιος.)

14 TONOS HYPOIASTIAN or HYPOIONIAN
(T. Ὑποϊάστιος or Ὑποϊώνιος.)

15 TONOS   HYPODORIAN
(T. Ὑποδώριος.)

These fifteen tonoi (keys) were divided into three groups:

a) the five principal tonoi (6-10), Lydian, Aeolian, Phrygian, Iastian and Dorian, placed in the middle;

b) the five Lower tonoi (11-15), Hypolydian, Hypoaeolian, Hypophrygian, Hypoiastian and Hypodorian, placed at the lower part of the series; and

338

c) the five Higher tonoi (1-5), Hyperlydian, Hyperaeolian, Hyperphrygian, Hyperiastian and Hyperdorian, placed at the higher part of the series.

The above table of the fifteen tonoi should be seen for each in all three genera, e.g.:

In the same way all the other tonoi can be taken in the three genera. Of these fifteen tonoi Ptolemaeus recognized only the seven principal as seven were the octave-species (harmoniai). He derived them by starting from the Mixolydian (b) and proceeding by fifths (below) in the following order: Mixolydian, Dorian, Hypodorian, Phrygian, Hypophrygian, Lydian and Hypolydian, or placed in order of pitch: Mixolydian, Lydian, Phrygian, Dorian, Hypolydian, Hypophrygian and Hypodorian (from high to low). This series of tonoi is the inverse of the series of harmoniai. If now the seven harmoniai are placed on each one of the seven tonoi, there will be 49 different "scales". Actually the seven harmoniai are placed in the same range of pitch (the octave corresponding to f - f, as being within the vocal possibilities of most voices, was considered as the most suitable).

See under *onomasia, onomatothesia (nomenclature)* Ptolemaeus' theory on the "kata thesin" («κατὰ θέσιν»; "in respect to position") and the "kata dynamin" («κατὰ δύναμιν»; "in respect to function") nomenclature.

For Bibliography, see under *harmonia*.

topos (**τόπος**); locus, a position of the compass of the voice. Aristox. Harm. (I, p. 10, 24-26) «ἡ μὲν οὖν ἐπίτασίς ἐστι κίνησις τῆς φωνῆς συνεχὴς ἐκ βαρυτέρου τόπου εἰς ὀξύτερον, ἡ δ᾽ ἄνεσις ἐξ ὀξυτέρου τόπου εἰς βαρύτερον» ("tension is the continuous transition of the voice from a lower *position* to a higher, and relaxation that from a higher *position* to a lower"; transl. H.S.M. p. 172).

"Topos" of the voice: locus, region of the voice; Aristox. ibid (I, p. 7, 18) «περὶ τοῦ τῆς φωνῆς τόπου καθόλου» ("about *the region* of the voice in general").

Bacchius (Isag. § 44; C.v.J. p. 302, Mb p. 11) defines three "regions of the voice; high, medium, and low".

Anonymous (Bell. § 63, pp. 76-77) defines four: hypatoeides*, mesoeides*, netoeides* and hyperbolaeoeides*.

Torebus (**Τόρηβος**; m. pr. Tórivos); mythical musician, son of Atys, Head of the Lydians, and brother of Lydus (Λυδός), mythical king of the Lydians. He is known also as Tyrrenus (Τυρρηνός); he went from Lydia to Italy and gave his name to the people and the land of the Tyrrenians (Τυρρηνοί, Τόρηβοι; Etruscans); cf. Dionysius of Halic. "Roman Archaeology" (Book I, ch. 28, 2); and Strabo V, 215. According to Dionysius Iambus (ap. Plut. De Mus. 1136C, ch. 15) he invented the Lydian harmonia which Pindar ascribed to Anthippus*; by one legend the addition of the 5th string was also attributed to Torebus.

torelle (**τορέλλη**; m. pr. torelli); a Thracian threnetic exclamation accompanied by aulos (Hes.).

Cf. *blityri*, *tenella*, *threttanelo*.

toreuein oden, vb (**τορεύειν ᾠδήν**; m. pr. torévin odín); to sing with strong, sonorous, loud voice. In the case of style it might signify to enrich.

Aristoph. Thesmoph. v. 986 «τόρευε πᾶσαν ᾠδὴν» ("*raise* a *loftier music* now"; transl. by B.B. Rogers; Aristoph., vol. III, p. 219). LSJ: "sing a piercing strain".

trema, neut. (**τρῆμα**; m. pr. tríma); perforation, hole. Hence, tremata (pl.) the finger-holes of the aulos.

Other words also used for the finger-hole were *trypema*, neut. (τρύπημα; pl. trypemata), *tryme*, fem. (τρύμη; pl. trymai), and *diatome** (διατομή) fem.

The maker of the finger-holes was called *aulotrypes* (αὐλοτρύπης). See *aulos*.

340

trichordon (τρίχορδον); a three-stringed instrument, called also *pandoura*. It was perhaps the only instrument with a neck (lute family) used by the Greeks. See more details under *pandoura*.

PLATE VIII. A muse playing the trichordon. The mode of playing is distinctly displayed; the Muse "stops" the strings by the left hand and plucks them by the fingers of the right hand. This sculpture belongs to a group of three figures, two of which are Muses with a trichordon, discovered at Mantineia in Peloponnesus (Mantineia-Base) by the French archaeologist Gustave Fougères in 1887.

Bibliography :

Th. Reinach : a) "La guitare dans l'art grec" in "Revue des Études grecques", vol. VIII, Paris 1895, pp. 371-378.

b) "Famille du luth" in DAGR, vol. VI (1904), pp. 1450-1451, s.v. Lyra.

c) "La musique grecque" (1926), p. 127.

C. Sachs : "The Lute", Hist. of Mus. Instr. (1940), pp. 136-7.

M. Wegner : "Das Musikleben der Griechen" (1949), pp. 51-2.

H. R. Higgins and R. P. Winnington-Ingram : "Lute-players in Greek Art"; JHS, vol. 85, 1965, pp. 62-71.

H.R.H. is responsible for archaeological details; RPW-I is responsible for the literary and musical discussions in the article. An important contribution to the study of the "lute" in Greek art, well-documented, with a very useful bibliography (Note 1, p. 62), Notes and Plates at the end.

2. *trichordon systema* (τρίχορδον σύστημα); a system with three strings or notes. The use of such a system extends to the mythological times; according to certain traditions it was introduced either by Apollo, or Hermes, or even by Hyagnis. See under *lyra*.

tri[h]emitonion (τριημιτόνιον; triimitónion); the interval of one tone and a half. The interval between the lichanos and the mese (f♯ - a) or between the lichanos hypaton and hypate meson (c♯ or d♭ - e) in the Chromatic genus.

Also called *triemitonon* (τριημίτονον).

trieraules (τριηραύλης; m. pr. triirávlis); aulete regulating the movements of the rowers by his playing; cf. Pollux, IV, 71.

From *trieres* (τριήρης; *trireme*) and aulos.

trigonon (τρίγωνον) or **trigonos** (τρίγωνος); a stringed instrument of a triangular form, as its name indicates. It was actually a harp with strings of different length and played by the fingers, without the aid of a plectrum. The exact number of its strings is not known, but it belonged to those called "poly-chord" (many-stringed) instruments, which were condemned by Plato (Rep. III, 399D) and Aristoxenus (ap. Athen. IV, 182F, ch. 80).

Hesychius defines the trigonon : "a kind of psalterion" («τρίγωνον· εἶδος ὀργάνου ψαλτηρίου»).

The trigonon was considered as one of the ancient intruments, like the barbitos*, the magadis* and the sambyke* (cf. Athen. ibid). The origin of the trigonon was Phrygian, or Egyptian, or Syrian (Iobas ap. Athen., IV, 175D claims that "the trigonon was an invention of the Syrians").

It was usually played by women; Plato, the Comic (ap. Th. Kock Comic. Att. Fr.; vol. I, p. 620, Fr. 69, vs 13-14): «κἄλλην [κορίσκην] τρίγωνον εἶδον ἔχουσαν, εἶτ᾽ ᾖδεν πρὸς αὐτὸ μέλος Ἰωνικόν τι» ("and I saw another [little girl] holding a *trigonon* [harp], and then she sang to its accompaniment a certain Ionian tune").

See verses 12-13 of the same fragment under *"Karikon melos"*.

It became obsolete from the 2nd cent. B.C. (cf. Athen. XIV, 636F, ch. 40).

In the National Archaeological Museum of Athens there is an extraordinarily interesting figure of a harpist or player of the trigonon, known as the "Harpist of Keros" («Ἁρπιστὴς τῆς Κέρου»). It is made of Parian marble and is dated by some from the Bronze Age. Keros is a small island of the Cyclades group, near Theros (Θῆρος). See PLATE IX

Bibliography:

H. Abert: Pauly's RE, Stuttgart 1927, vol. XIII (XXVI), col. 2486; s.v. Lyra.
Reinhard Herbig: "Griechische Harfen" in "Mitteilung des deutschen Archäologischen Instituts, Athenische Abteilung; Band LIV, 1929, pp. 164-193.
W. Vetter: "Trigonon" in Pauly's RE, 1939, vol. 2 XIII, col. 142.
C. Sachs: "The Harp", Hist. of Mus. Instr. (1940), pp. 135-6.
M. Wegner: "Harfen" in "Das Musikleben der Griechen" (1949), pp. 47-51.

trimeles, and **trimeres**, nomos (**τριμελής**, and **τριμερὴς** νόμος; m. pr. trimelís, trimerís nómos); an aulodic nomos ascribed to Sakadas*, according to which each one of its three parts was composed and sung in a different harmonia; alternately in the Dorian, the Phrygian and the Lydian. For this reason it was called trimeres (tripartite) as consisting of three different parts, and trimeles, as consisting of three mele in different harmonias. Plut. De Mus. (1134 A-B, ch. 8) «τόνων γὰρ τριῶν ὄντων κατὰ Πολύμνηστον καὶ Σακάδαν, τοῦ τε Δωρίου, καὶ Φρυγίου καὶ Λυδίου, ἐν ἑκάστῳ τῶν εἰρημένων τόνων στροφὴν ποιήσαντα φασι τὸν Σακάδαν διδάξαι ἄδειν τὸν χορὸν Δωριστὶ μὲν τὴν πρώτην, Φρυγιστὶ δὲ τὴν δευτέραν, Λυδιστὶ δὲ τὴν τρίτην· καλεῖσθαι δὲ *τριμερῆ* τὸν νόμον τοῦτον διὰ τὴν μεταβολὴν» ("the tones [harmoniai] being three at the time of Polymnestus and Sakadas, i.e. the Dorian, the Phrygian and the Lydian, it is said that Sakadas composed three strophes in the three aforesaid tones and instructed the chorus to sing the first [strophe] in the Dorian, the second in the Phrygian and the third in the Lydian; and this nomos was called *trimeres* (tripartite) because of the change [modulation]"). Plut. (ibid) adds that in a Record in Sicyon about poets "it is written that

Clonas was the inventor of the tripartite nomos").

tripodiphorikon (τριποδιφορικòν) melos; a song sung especially in Boeotia while carrying the "tripous" (three-footed, tripod) given as a prize or dedicated to a god.

Procl. Chrest., 27 «τò δὲ τριποδιφορικὸν μέλος, τρίποδος προηγουμέ-νου παρὰ τοῖς Βοιωτοῖς ᾔδετο» ("*the tripodiphorikon* melos was sung among the Boeotians while carrying the tripod").

tripous (τρίπους); tripod; a rare three-legged stringed instrument invented by Pythagoras of Zante*, a musician of the 5th cent. B.C. It was an ingenious invention, much admired for some time but shortlived; it fell into oblivion after the death of its inventor. Artemon (ap. Athen. XIV, 637B, ch. 41) gives an interesting description of this instrument. The "tripous" was a three-legged instrument, similar in form to the Delphic tripod from which it took its name. Its basis was revolving, and between each two feet a whole kithara with strings, arms and string-holder was constructed; thus, in fact the "tripous" was a triple-kithara, consisting of three different kitharas tuned in the Dorian, the Phrygian and the Lydian harmonias respectively. The executant could revolve the base at will so as to play in the harmonia he wished.

trisemos (τρίσημος; m. pr. trísimos) chronos (time); the time which consists of three first (short) times, i.e. of three time-units.

See *chronos*.

trite (τρίτη; m. pr. tríti) fem., third; the string or note which was third from the nete. In the Lesser Perfect System there was only one "trite", that of synemmenon (b♭); in the Greater Perfect System there were two: the trite diezeugmenon (c) and the trite hyperbolaeon (f). In the Perfect Immutable System, all three were included.

tritemorion (τριτημόριον; m. pr. tritimórion); one third of the tone. Cf., Aristoxenus Harm. I, p. 25, 17 Mb.

See *diesis* and *Chromatikon genus*.

trochaeos (τροχαῖος; m. pr. trochéos); trochee. A metrical foot consisting of two syllables, a long and a short - υ.

Trochaic metre (τροχαϊκòν μέτρον); composed of trochaic feet; cf. Aristides De Mus. Mb p. 50; RPW-I, p. 45.

2) *Trochaeos* was also one of the kitharodic nomoi invented by Terpander; cf. Plut. De Mus. 1132D, ch. 4.

This nomos would be probably based on trochaic time.

LSJ: «οἱ σαλπικταὶ τροχαῖόν τι συμβοήσαντες» = "the trumpeters playing a brisk march".

tropos (τρόπος); mode, way, style. There has been a rather confusing use of this term in ancient texts; it often appears as a synonym of *tonos*. Aristides (Mb. p. 136) says «τρόποι, οὓς καὶ τόνους ἐκαλέσαμεν» ("*tropoi*, which we also called *tonoi*"). Alypius (Isag. § 3; C.v.J. p. 367, Mb p. 2) writes in a similar way «εἰς τοὺς λεγομένους τρόπους τε καὶ τόνους, ὄντας πεντεκαίδεκα τὸν ἀριθμὸν» ("to the so-called *tropoi* and *tonoi* which are fifteen").

In Plutarch *tonos*, *tropos* and *harmonia* often appear as synonyms; in "An seni resp. gerenda sit", ch. 18, 793A: «πολλῶν τόνων καὶ τρόπων ὑποκειμένων φωνῆς, οὓς ἁρμονίας οἱ μουσικοὶ καλοῦσι» (="since there exist many *tonoi* and *tropoi* of the voice, which the musicians call *harmoniai*"). Also in "De E apud Delphos", ch. 10, 389E: «καὶ πέντε τοὺς πρώτους εἴτε τόνους ἢ τρόπους εἴθ᾽ ἁρμονίας χρὴ καλεῖν» ("and the first five *tonoi* or *tropoi* or *harmoniai*, whatever one must call them").

Porphyrius (Comment.; Wallis III, p. 258; I.D. p. 82, 5-6) speaking on the various meanings of "tonos" says that "tonos is also the locus which according to Aristoxenus is capable of receiving a perfect system, as the Dorian, the Phrygian and the other similar *tropoi*" («ὁ δώριος καὶ ὁ φρύγιος καὶ οἱ παραπλήσιοι τρόποι»). Very often the term tropos is met with in the meaning of *style of composition*; Aristoxenus Harm. II, p. 40, 21 Mb «οὔτε τοὺς τῶν μελοποιϊῶν τρόπους» ("nor *the styles* of the melodic compositions"). Aristides also (op. cit., Mb p. 30, RPW-I, p. 30) «τρόποι μελοποιΐας» ("the *modes* [or *styles*] of melodic composition").

See also under *genus*.

trygodopoeomousike (τρυγῳδοποιομουσική; m. pr. trigodopiomousikí); the art of comedy (LSJ);

Cf. Th. Kock Comic. Att. Fr. vol. I, p. 480, Fr. 333, Aristoph. Thesmoph. II; Bothe: PSGF, II, p. 100.

Trygodos (τρυγῳδός), must-singer, comic singer.

See *komos* (κῶμος).

tymbaules (τυμβαύλης; m. pr. timvávlis); aulete who played at a funeral; at the procession and/or over the grave. Dio Chrys. 2,251 «τὸ καλεῖσθαι αὐλητὰς τοὺς τυμβαύλας».

tympanon, and **typanon** (τύμπανον, τύπανον; m. pr. tímpanon); percussion instrument in use especially at the rites of Cybele and Dionysus. It was made of a cylindrical box with skin membranes stretched on both sides; it was played by the hand, and usually by women.

Hes. «τύμπανα (pl.) τὰ δερμάτινα ρακτήρια κόσκινα, τὰ ἐν Βάκχαις κρουόμενα» ("*drums* [tambours], the leathern clamorous sieves, played [struck] at Bacchic orgies"). Pind. Dithyr. II, v. 9 «ρόμβοι τυπάνων» ("thunder of drums"); cf. *rombos**.

The tympanon was a kind of tambour, hand-drum, without jingles.
Cf. C. Sachs Hist. of Mus. Instr. p. 148.

See PLATE X

Bibliography:

    Ch. Avezou: "Tympanum" I, in DAGR, vol. IX (1919), pp. 559-560.
    C. Sachs: Hist. of Mus. Instr. (1940), pp. 148-9 (Tympanon).
    M. Wegner: "Tympanon"; Das Musikleben der Griechen (1949), pp. 64-66.

tyrbasia (τυρβασία; m. pr. tirvasía); a kind of Bacchic dance danced at a festival in honour of Dionysus; it was of a very lively and noisy character. Pollux (IV, 104) «τυρβασίαν δ᾽ ἐκάλουν τὸ ὄρχημα τὸ διθυραμβικὸν» ("they called *tyrbasia* a dithyrambic dance"). Hes. «τυρβασία· χορῶν ἀγωγή τις διθυραμβικῶν» ("*tyrbasia*; a certain course of dithyrambic dances").

Tyrbe (τύρβη; m. pr. tírvi); a clamorous Bacchic festival; Paus. (II, ch. 24, § 6 in Corinthiaka) «τῷ Διονύσῳ δὲ καὶ ἑορτὴν ἄγουσι [᾽Αργεῖοι] καλουμένην Τύρβην» ("they [i.e. the Argives] have also a festival in honour of Dionysus called *Tyrbe*"). *Tyrbe* was also the name of the dance itself performed at the festival. Tyrbasia and tyrbe may probably be the same thing.

Note: The word "tyrbe" meant clamour, tumult.

Tyrrhenos aulos (Τυρρηνὸς αὐλός; m. pr. Tirrinós avlós); Tyrrhenian, Etruscan aulos. Also *Tyrrhenikos* (Τυρρηνικὸς) and *Tyrsenos* (Τυρσηνός). According to Pollux (IV, 70) the Tyrrhenian aulos resembled an inverted syrinx; it was made of brass, and was open at the lower end. Its tone was sharp.

Tyrrhenike salpinx; Tyrrhenian trumpet.

Tyrtaeus (Τυρταῖος; m. pr. Tirtéos);

1) 7th cent. B.C. elegiac poet and musician, son of Archembrotus (᾽Αρχέμβροτος), born at Athens, or, according to some sources, in the town Aphidna (῎Αφιδνα) in Laconia. Suidas calls him Lacon or Milesios (Λάκων, ἢ Μιλήσιος); he says that he was contemporary with the seven wise men (sages) or even older, and that he flourished at the 35th Olympiad (around 640 B.C.).

After a Delphic oracle he was sent to Sparta in the second Messenian war (685-667 B.C.), and by his embateria and war-songs he inspired such enthusiasm to the Spartans that they beat the Messenians. When the war came to a successful end, Tyrtaeus became a citizen of Sparta. He was greatly admired and honoured by the Spartans; it was decided that his elegies and war-songs be sung by the Spartans on the eve of each campaign.

Some of his poems survive, namely "Eunomia" («Εὐνομία»), "Hypothekai" («Ὑποθῆκαι»; Counsels) and "Embateria" ("Marching songs"); see Brgk Anth. Lyr. pp. 24-29 a number of Elegies (13) in rather extended fragments; also PLG II, pp. 8-22 Eunomia, Hypothekai, Embateria.

2) *Tyrtaeus of Mantineia* (Τυρταῖος ὁ ἐκ Μαντινείας); composer of unknown date. He is mentioned in Plut. De Mus. (1137F, ch. 21), together with Andreas of Corinth and Thrasyllus of Phlious as examples of composers keeping the ancient tradition, and by preference avoiding the Chromatic genus, the modulations and other innovations in rhythmopoeia, melopoeia and interpretation.

X

Xanthus (Ξάνθος; m. pr. Xánthos); 7th cent. B.C. lyric-poet (μελοποιός). He is cited as a composer anterior to Stesichorus* who was influenced by him and imitated his subjects.

Among his works an Oresteia (Ὀρέστεια) is reported; Athen. XII, 513A, ch. 6: «Ξάνθος δ' ὁ μελοποιός, πρεσβύτερος δὲ Στησιχόρου» ("*Xanthus*, the lyric poet, older than Stesichorus").

Xenocritus (Ξενόκριτος; m. pr. Xenócritos); 7th cent. B.C. musician from Locroi (Λοκροὶ) in Italy. He was considered as the inventor of the Locrian harmonia, and belonged to the second School of music of Sparta (the first being established by Terpander). He was credited, together with Thaletas*, Xenodamus*, Polymnestus*, and Sakadas*, with the introduction to Sparta of the gymnopaediai (Plut. De Mus. 1134B-C, ch. 9). The subjects of his songs were of a heroic character and they were called by some people dithyrambs (Plut. ibid).

Xenodamus (Ξενόδαμος; m. pr. Xenódamos); 7th cent. B.C. musician from Kythera (Κύθηρα). He was one of the prominent members of the second School of music in Sparta, and was credited, together with Thaletas*, Polymnestus*, Sakadas* and Xenocritus*, with the introduction to Sparta of the gymnopaediai. He composed hyporchemata, one of which still existed at the time of Plutarch; cf. Plut. 1134B-C, ch. 9.

xiphismos (ξιφισμός); sword-dance.

Pollux (IV, 100) «ἐκαλεῖτο δέ τι καὶ *ξιφισμὸς*» ("and a certain kind of

346

dance was called *xiphismos*").

Hesychius and Athenaeus consider the xiphismos as a dance-figure; Hes. «σχῆμα ὀρχηστικὸν τῆς λεγομένης ἐμμελείας ὀρχήσεως» ("a dance-figure of the so-called emmeleia orchesis"). Cf. Athen. XIV, 629F, ch. 27.

The vb *xiphizein* («ξιφίζειν») meant to dance the sword-dance; Hes. «ξιφίζειν· ἀνατείνειν τὴν χεῖρα καὶ ὀρχεῖσθαι» ("*xiphizein*; to lift up the hand and dance").

xylophonon (ξυλόφωνον; m. pr. xilóphonon) from xylon (ξύλον, wood) and phone* (φωνή, voice, sound). The word "xylophonon" was unknown in ancient Greece, and the use of such an instrument by the Greeks is not certain. An instrument, of unknown name, in the form of a small ladder, is depicted on various S. Italian (mostly Apulian) vases (Fig. 5 below). Its shape led to the conjecture that it might be a xylophone, or a kind of sistrum (seistron*).

Bibliography:

Max Wegner: "Das Musikleben der Griechen"; Berlin 1949, pp. 66-67 and 229 (and Plate 24).

R. P. Winnington-Ingram: "Apulian sistrum" in "Ancient Greek Music: A Bibliography 1932-1957" in Lustrum, 1958, Band 3, p. 19.

N. Plaoutine et J. Roger: Corpus Vasorum Antiquorum, France 16, (Paris, Musée Rodin), 1945, pl. 35/3; ap. R.P.W-I here above.

Riemann Musik Lexikon, Sachteil; Mainz 1967, p. 1069.

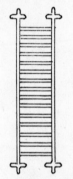

Fig. 5. Xylophonon

Z

zygos, masc. (ζυγός; m. pr. zigós), also **zygon**, neut.; the cross-bar of the phorminx, the lyra and the kithara, on which the strings were fastened. It was made of box-wood, and its form was approximately cylindrical.

See *lyra*.

347

ALPHABETICAL INDEX OF ENTRIES IN GREEK

A

Ἀγαθοκλῆς (Agathocles)
Ἀγάθων (Agathon)
Ἀγαθώνειος αὔλησις (Agathoneios aulesis)
ἀγγελική (angelike)
Ἀγέλαος (Agelaus)
ἀγέχορος (agechoros)
Ἀγήνωρ (Agenor)
ἀγκῶνες (ankones)
ἀγωγή (agoge)
ἀγωνιστής (agonistes)
ᾄδειν (adein)
ἀδώνια, ἀδωνίδια (Adonia, Adonidia)
ἀηδών (aedon)
Ἀθηνᾶ (Athena)
Ἀθήναιος (Athenaeus)
ἀθλοθέτης (athlothetes)
αἴλινος (aelinos)
αἰολία, -ική ἁρμονία (Aeolia, -ike harmonia)
αἰόλιος νόμος (Aeolios nomos)
αἰολίς (Aeolis)
αἰολόμολπος (aeolomolpos)
αἰολόφωνος (aeolophonos)
Αἰσχύλος (Aeschylus)
αἰώρα (aeora)
ἀκαριαῖος (akariaeos)
ἀκίνητοι, φθόγγοι (akinetoi, phthongoi)
ἀκλινεῖς (aklineis)
ἀκοή (akoe)
ἄκουσμα (akousma)

ἀκρόαμα (akroama)
ἀκρόασις (akroasis)
ἀκροατήριον (akroaterion)
ἀκροατής (akroates)
ἄκρος (akros)
ἀκρότητος (akrotetos)
ἀλητήρ (aleter)
ἀλῆτις (aletis)
Ἀλκαῖος (Alkaeus, or Alcaeus)
Ἀλκείδης (Alkeides)
Ἀλκμάν (Alkman, or Alcman)
ἄλογος, ἀλογία (alogos, alogia)
Ἀλύπιος (Alypius)
ἄλυρος (alyros)
ἀλώπηξ (alopex)
ἀμελῴδητος (amelodetos)
ἀμετάβολος (ametabolos)
Ἀμοιβεύς (Amoebeus)
ἄμουσος (amousos)
ἄμπειρα (ampeira)
Ἀμφίων (Amphion)
ἀνάβασις (anabasis)
ἀναβολή (anabole)
ἀναγωγή (anagoge)
ἀνάδοσις (anadosis)
ἀναδρομή (anadrome)
ἀνάκλασις (anaklasis)
ἀνάκλησις (anaklesis)
ἀνακρεόντειον μέτρον (Anacreonteion metron)
Ἀνακρέων (Anacreon)
ἀνάκρουσις (anakrousis)
ἀνάλυσις (analysis)
ἀναμέλπειν (anamelpein)

349

ἀναμινυρίζειν (anaminyrizein)
ἀνάπαιστος (anapaestos)
ἀναπάλη (anapale)
ἀνάπειρα (anapeira)
ἀναπλοκή (anaploke)
ἀνάρμοστος (anarmostos)
ἀνάτρητος τρόπος (anatretos tropos)
ἄναυλος (anaulos)
ἀναφύσησις (anaphysesis)
Ἀνδρέας ὁ Κορίνθιος (Andreas of Corinth)
ἀνειμένος (aneimenos)
ἄνεσις (anesis)
ἀνήκοος (anekoos)
ἄνθεμα (anthema)
Ἄνθης (Anthes)
Ἄνθιππος (Anthippus)
ἀνισότονοι (anisotonoi)
ἄνομος (anomos)
ἀνταπόδοσις (antapodosis)
ἀντεπίρρημα (antepirrhema)
ἀντήχημα (antechema)
Ἀντιγενίδης (Antigenides)
ἀντίμολπος (antimolpos)
ἀντίσπαστος (antispastos)
ἀντιστροφή (antistrophe)
ἀντίστροφος (antistrophos)
ἀντίφθογγος (antiphthongos)
ἀντίφωνον (antiphonon)
ἀντίχορδος (antichordos)
ἀντίψαλμος (antipsalmos)
ἄντυξ (antyx)
ἀοιδή (aoede)
ἀοίδιμος (aoedimos)
ἀοιδός (aoedos)
ἀπᾴδειν (apadein)
ἀπήχημα (apechema)
ἀπλάστως (aplastos)
ἀπλατής (aplates)

ἁπλοῦν (haploun)
ἀπόθετος νόμος (apothetos nomos)
ἀπόκινος (apokinos)
ἀπολελυμένα ᾄσματα (apolelymena asmata)
ἀπόμουσος (apomousos)
ἀπόσεισις (aposeisis)
ἀποστολικά (apostolika)
ἀπόστροφος (apostrophos)
ἀποτομή (apotome)
ἀπόχορδος (apochordos)
ἀπόψαλμα (apopsalma)
ἄπυκνον (apycnon)
ἀπῳδός (apodos)
Ἀργᾶς (Argas)
Ἄρδαλος (Ardalus)
Ἀριστείδης Κο[υ]ϊντιλιανὸς (Arist[e]ides Quintilianus)
Ἀριστόνικος (Aristonicus)
Ἀριστόξενος (Aristoxenus)
Ἀριστοτέλης (Aristoteles)
Ἀριστοφάνης (Aristophanes)
Ἀρίστων (Ariston)
Ἀρίων (Arion)
ἁρμάτειος νόμος (harmateios nomos)
ἁρμογή (harmoge)
ἁρμονία (harmonia)
ἁρμονία τῶν σφαιρῶν (harmonia of the spheres)
ἁρμονική (harmonike)
ἅρμοσις (harmosis)
ἅρπα (harp)
ἁρπαλύκη (harpalyke)
ἄρρυθμος (arrhythmos)
ἄρσις, θέσις (arsis, thesis)
ἀρχή (arche)
Ἀρχίλοχος (Archilochus)
Ἀρχύτας (Archytas)
ἄσιγμος (asigmos)

ἄσκαρος (askaros)
ἀσκαύλης (askaules)
ἀσκληπιάδειος στίχος (Asklepiadeios stichos)
ἆσμα (asma)
ἀσματοκάμπτης (asmatokamptes)
ἀσύμμετρος (asymmetros)
ἀσύμφωνος (asymphonos)
ἀσύνθετος (asynthetos)
Ἄττις (Attis)
αὐδὴ (aude)
αὔλημα, αὔλησις (aulema, aulesis)
αὐλητὴρ (auleter)
αὐλητής, αὐλητικὴ (auletes, auletike)
αὐλοβόας (auloboas)
αὐλοδόκη, αὐλοθήκη (aulodoke, aulotheke)
αὐλοποιὸς (aulopoeos)
αὐλὸς (aulos)
αὐλοτρύπης (aulotrypes)
αὐλῳδία, αὐλῳδικοὶ νόμοι (aulodia, aulodikoi nomoi)
αὐλῳδὸς (aulodos)
αὐτοκάβδαλος (autokabdalos)
ἀφόρμικτος (aphormiktos)
ἄφωνος (aphonos)
ἄχορδος (achordos)
ἀχόρευτος (achoreutos)
ἄχορος (achoros)

B

Βάθυλλος (Bathyllus)
βακτριασμὸς (baktriasmos)
βακύλιον, βαβούλιον (bakylion, baboulion)
βακχεῖος (baccheios)

Βακχεῖος ὁ Γέρων (Bacchius the Old)
Βακχυλίδης (Bacchylides)
βαλανέων ᾠδὴ (balaneon ode)
βαλλισμὸς (ballismos)
βάρβιτος (barbitos)
βαρυαχὴς (baryaches)
βαρύλλικα (baryllika)
βαρύπυκνος (barypycnos)
βαρύς, βαρύτης (barys, barytes)
βαρύχορδος (barychordos)
βάρωμος (baromos)
βάσις (basis)
βάταλον (batalon)
βατὴρ (bater)
βατραχίσκοι (batrachiskoi)
βαυκάλημα (baukalema)
βαυκισμὸς (baukismos)
βηχία (bechia)
βίβασις (bibasis)
βλίτυρι (blityri)
Βοιώτιος νόμος (Boeotios nomos)
βόμβος (bombos)
βομβυκίας (bombykias)
βόμβυξ (bombyx)
βουκολιασμὸς (boucoliasmos)
βραχὺς (brachys)
βρόμος (bromos)
βρυαλλίχα (bryallicha)
Βρυέννιος, Μανουὴλ (Bryennius, Manouel)
βυκάνη (bycane)
βυκάνημα (bycanema)
βώριμος (borimos)

Γ

γαμήλιον (gamelion)
Γαυδέντιος (Gaudentius)
γένος (genus)

351

γέρανος (geranos)
γεωργικά (georgika)
γίγγλαρος (ginglaros)
γίγγρας (gingras)
Γλαῦκος ὁ Ρηγῖνος (Glaucus of Rhegium)
γλαύξ (glaux)
γλυκώνειον μέτρον (Glyconeion metron)
γλωττίς (glottis)
γλωττοκομεῖον (glottokomeion)
γνωμολογικά (gnomologika)
γρόνθων (gronthon)
γυμνοπαιδία, -αι (gymnopaedia, -ai)
γυμνοπαιδική (gymnopaedike)
γύπωνες (gypones)

Δ

δακτυλικός (dactylikos)
δάκτυλος (dactylos)
Δάμων (Damon)
δαφνηφορικά (daphnephorika)
δεικηλιστική (deikelistike)
δενδρυάζουσα (dendryazousa)
δημήτρουλος (demetroulos)
Δημόδοκος (Demodocus)
Διαγόρας (Diagoras)
διάγραμμα (diagramma)
διάγυιος (diagyios)
διαείδειν (diaoedein)
διάζευξις (diazeuxis)
διακτηρία (diakteria)
διάλεκτος (dialectos)
διάληψις (dialepsis)
διὰ πασῶν (dia pason)
διὰ πέντε (dia pente)
διάστασις (diastasis)
διάστημα (diastema)

διαστηματικὴ κίνησις (diastematike kinesis)
διαστολή (diastole)
διάσχισμα (diaschisma)
διὰ τεσσάρων (dia tessaron)
διατομή (diatome)
διάτονον (diatonon)
διάτορος, διατορία (diatoros, diatoria)
διαυλία (diaulia)
διαύλιον (diaulion)
δίαυλος (diaulos)
διαφωνία (diaphonia)
διάψαλμα, διαψηλάφημα (diapsalma, diapselaphema)
Δίδυμος (Didymus)
δίεσις (diesis)
δίζυγοι αὐλοὶ (dizygoi auloi)
διθύραμβος (dithyrambos)
Δικταῖος Ὕμνος (Diktaeos Hymnos)
Διόδωρος (Diodorus)
Διοκλῆς (Diocles)
Διονύσιος (Dionysius)
Διονυσόδοτος (Dionysodotus)
Διονυσόδωρος (Dionysodorus)
διοξεῖα (dioxeia)
διπλοῦν, σύστημα (diploun, systema)
διποδία (dipodia)
δίσημος (disemos)
δίσκος (discos)
διστιχία (distichia)
δίτονον (ditonon)
δίχορδος (dichordos)
διχορία (dichoria)
διωρισμένοι, φθόγγοι (diorismenoi, phthongoi)
δόναξ (donax)
δόχμιος (dochmios)

Δράκων (Dracon)
δύναμις (dynamis)
δυσαυλία (dysaulia)
δύσαυλος (dysaulos)
δυσηχής (dyseches)
δωδεκατημόριον (dodecate-
    morion)
δωδεκάχορδον (dodecachordon)
δώριος άρμονία (Dorios harmonia)
Δωρίων (Dorion)

E

ἐγκεραύλης (enkeraules)
ἐγκώμιον (enkomion)
ἔγχορδα (enchorda)
εἴδη συνθέσεως (composition
    types)
εἶδος (eidos)
εἰρεσία (eiresia)
εἰρεσιώνη (eiresione)
ἑκατερὶς (hekateris)
ἐκβολὴ (ekbole)
ἔκκρουσις, ἔκληψις (ekkrousis,
    eklepsis)
ἐκκρουσμός, ἐκλημματισμὸς (ek-
    krousmos, eklemmatismos)
ἐκλάκτισμα (eklaktisma)
ἐκλελυμένα, μέλη (eklelymena,
    mele)
ἔκλυσις (eklysis)
ἐκμελὴς (ekmeles)
ἐκπύρωσις (ekpyrosis)
ἔκρυθμος (ekrhythmos)
ἐκτημόριον (hektemorion)
ἔκτονος (ektonos)
ἔκχορδος (ekchordos)
ἐλεγεία (elegeia)
ἔλεγος (elegos)
ἑλικὼν (helicon)

ἔλυμος (elymos)
ἐμβατήριον μέλος (embaterion
    melos)
ἐμβατήριος αὐλὸς (embaterios
    aulos)
ἐμβόλιμον (embolimon)
ἐμμέλεια (emmeleia)
ἐμμελὴς (emmeles)
ἔμμετρος (emmetros)
ἐμπνεόμενα (empneomena)
ἐμπνευστὰ (empneusta)
ἐμφυσώμενα (emphysomena)
ἐναρμόνιον γένος (Enharmonion
    genos)
ἐναρμόνιος (enharmonios)
ἐνάρμοσις (enharmosis)
ἔναυλος κιθάρισις (enaulos kitha-
    risis)
ἑνδεκακρούματος (hendekakrou-
    matos)
ἑνδεκάχορδον (hendekachordon)
ἐνδρομὴ (endrome)
ἐνεργμὸς (energmos)
ἔνερξις (enerxis)
ἔνηχος (enechos)
ἐννεάφθογγον (enneaphthongon)
ἐννεάχορδον (enneachordon)
ἐνόπλιος (enoplios)
ἔνρυθμος (enrhythmos)
ἔντασις (entasis)
ἐντατὸν (entaton)
ἔνῳδος (enodos)
ἐξαρμόνιος (exharmonios)
ἔξαρχος (exarchos)
ἑξάσημος (hexasemos)
ἑξάτονος (hexatonos)
ἔξαυλος (exaulos)
ἑξάχορδον (hexachordon)
Ἐξηκεστίδης (Exekestides)
ἑξῆς (hexes)

ἐξόδιον (exodion)

ἐπαγκωνισμὸς (epankonismos)

ἐπᾴδειν (epadein)

ἐπαυλεῖν (epaulein)

ἐπεισόδιον (epeisodion)

ἐπιβήματα (epibemata)

ἐπιγόνειον (Epigoneion)

Ἐπίγονος (Epigonus)

ἐπιθαλάμιον (epithalamion)

ἐπικήδειον (epikedeion)

ἐπικρήδιος (epikredios)

ἐπιλήνιος (epilenios)

ἐπίλογος (epilogos)

ἐπιμελῴδημα (epimelodema)

ἐπινίκιον (epinikion)

ἐπιπάροδος (epiparodos)

ἐπιπνεόμενα (epipneomena)

ἐπιπόρπημα (epiporpema)

ἐπίπταισμα (epiptaesma)

ἐπίρρημα (epirrhema)

ἐπισπονδορχησταὶ (epispondor-
    chestai)

ἐπιστομὶς (epistomis)

ἐπισυναφὴ (episynaphe)

ἐπίτασις (epitasis)

ἐπιτόνιον (epitonion)

ἐπίτριτος (epitritos)

ἐπιτύμβιος νόμος (epitymbios no-
    mos)

ἐπίφαλλος (epiphallos)

ἐπιψαλμὸς (epipsalmos)

ἐπόγδοος (epogdoos)

ἑπτάγλωσσος (heptaglossos)

ἑπτάγωνον (heptagonon)

ἑπτάκτυπος (heptaktypos)

ἑπτάσημος (heptasemos)

ἑπτάτονος (heptatonos)

ἑπτάφθογγος (heptaphthongos)

ἑπτάφωνος (heptaphonos)

ἑπτάχορδον (heptachordon)

ἐπῳδὴ (epode)

ἐπῳδὸς (epodos)

Ἐρατοκλῆς (Eratocles)

Ἐρατοσθένης (Eratosthenes)

ἐριβρεμέτης (eribremetes)

ἐρίγηρυς (erigerys)

ἑστῶτες, κινούμενοι (hestotes,
    kinoumenoi)

ἑτεροφωνία (heterophonia)

εὐάρμοστος (euharmostos)

εὔγηρυς (eugerys)

εὐεπὴς (euepes)

εὐηχὴς (eueches)

εὐθὺς (euthys)

Εὔιος (Euius)

Εὐκλείδης (Eucleides)

εὐκτικὰ (euktika)

εὔλυρος (eulyros)

εὐμελὴς (eumeles)

εὔμετρος (eumetros)

εὔμολπος (eumolpos)

Εὔμολπος (Eumolpus)

εὔμουσος (eumousos)

Εὐνίδης (Eunides)

Εὔνομος (Eunomus)

Εὐριπίδης (Euripides)

εὔρυθμος (eurhythmos)

εὔτονος (eutonos)

εὐυμνία (euhymnia)

εὔφθογγος (euphthongos)

εὐφόρμιγξ (euphorminx)

εὔφωνος (euphonos)

εὔχορδος (euchordos)

εὐῳδὸς (euodos)

ἐφύμνιον (ephymnion)

Ἐχέμβροτος (Echembrotus)

ἑώρα (eora)

Z

ζυγὸς (zygos)

H

ἡγεμών (hegemon)
ἡδύκωμος (hedykomos)
ἦθος (ethos)
ἡμιόλιος (hemiolios)
ἡμιτόνιον (hemitonion)
ἡμιχόριον (hemichorion)
Ἡρακλείδης ὁ Ποντικὸς (Heracleides Ponticus)
Ἠριγόνη (Erigone)
ἡρμοσμένος (hermosmenos)
Ἡσύχιος (Hesychius)
ἠχεῖον (echeion)
ἦχος (echos)

Θ

Θαλήτας (Thaletas)
Θάμυρις (Thamyris)
Θεόφραστος (Theophrastus)
θερμαστρὶς (thermastris)
θέσις (thesis)
Θέων Σμυρναῖος (Theon of Smyrna)
θήρειος αὐλὸς (thereios aulos)
θηρεπωδὸς (therepodos)
θίξις (thixis)
Θράσυλλος (Thrasyllus)
θρεττανελὸ (threttanelo)
θρηνητικὸς αὐλὸς (threnetikos aulos)
θρῆνος, θρηνῴδημα, θρηνῳδία (threnos, threnodema, threnodia)
θυροκοπικὸν (thyrokopikon)

I

ἰάλεμος (ialemos)

ἰαμβικὴ (iambike)
ἰαμβικὸν (iambikon)
ἰαμβὶς (iambis)
ἴαμβος (iambus)
ἰαμβύκη (iambyke)
Ἴβυκος (Ibycus)
ἴγδις (igdis)
ἰδοῦθοι (idouthoi)
ἱεράκιον μέλος (hierakion melos)
Ἱέραξ (Hierax)
ἱεραοιδὸς (hieraoedos)
ἱεραύλης (hieraules)
ἱεροσαλπικτὴς (hierosalpiktes)
ἴθυμβος (ithymbos)
ἰθύφαλλοι (ithyphalloi)
ἱλαρῳδία, ἱλαρῳδὸς (hilarodia, hilarodos)
ἱμαῖος (himaeos)
ἰόβακχος (iobacchos)
ἴουλος (ioulos)
ἱπποφορβὸς (hippophorbos)
Ἰσμηνίας (Ismenias)
ἰσοτονία, ἰσότονοι (isotonia, isotonoi)
ἰσόφθογγος (isophthongos)
ἰσόχορδος (isochordos)
Ἱστιαῖος (Histiaeus)
Ἴων ὁ Χῖος (Ion of Chios)
ἰωνικὸν (Ionikon)
Ἰώνιος ἁρμονία, τόνος (Ionios harmonia, tonos)

K

καθαπτὸν (kathapton)
καλαβρισμὸς (kalabrismos)
καλαθίσκος (kalathiskos)
καλαμαύλης (calamaules)
κάλαμος (calamus)
καλλαβὶς (kallabis)

355

καλλίνικος (kallinikos)
καλλίουλος (kallioulos)
καλλίχορος (kallichoros)
καλύκη (kalyke)
καμπὴ (kampe)
κανὼν (canon)
καρικὸν μέλος (Karikon melos)
καρπαία (karpaea)
καρυᾶτις (Karyatis)
καστόριον (kastorion)
Καστορίων ὁ Σολεὺς (Kastorion of Soli)
καταβαυκάλησις (katabaukalesis)
κατάδειν (katadein)
κατακελευσμὸς (katakeleusmos)
κατάληξις (katalexis)
κατάληψις (katalepsis)
καταλογὴ (kataloge)
καταπεπλασμένον (katapeplasmenon)
καταπλοκὴ (kataploke)
καταπνεόμενα (katapneomena)
καταπύκνωσις (katapycnosis)
κατασπάσματα (kataspasmata)
κατασπασμὸς (kataspsamos)
καταστροφὴ (katastrophe)
κατατροπὰ (katatropa)
καταύλησις (kataulesis)
καταχόρευσις (katachoreusis)
κατεπάδειν (katepadein)
κατηχὴς (kateches)
κατήχησις (katechesis)
κάττυμα (kattyma)
κεκλασμένα, μέλη (keklasmena, mele)
κέλαδος (kelados)
κελευστοῦ ὄρχησις (keleustou orchesis)
κέρας (keras)
κεράστης (kerastes)

κερατουργὸς (keratourgos)
κερατόφωνος (keratophonos)
κεραύλης (keraules)
κερνοφόρος (kernophoros)
κεχυμένα, μέλη (kechymena, mele)
κηπίων (kepion)
Κηφισόδοτος (Kephisodotus)
κίδαρις (kidaris)
κιθάρα (kithara)
κίθαρις (kitharis)
κιθάρισις, κιθαριστικὴ (kitharisis, kitharistike)
κιθαριστήριος (kitharisterios)
κιθαριστὴς (kitharistes)
κιθαρῳδία, κιθαρῳδικὸς νόμος (kitharodia, kitharodikos nomos)
κιθαρῳδὸς (kitharodos)
κινδαψὸς (kindapsos)
Κινησίας (Kinesias)
κίνησις (kinesis)
κινούμενοι (kinoumenoi)
κινύρα (kinyra)
Κλεονείδης (Cleoneides)
κλεψίαμβος (klepsiambos)
Κλονᾶς (Clonas)
κνισμὸς (knismos)
κοιλία (koelia)
κοκκυσμὸς (kokkysmos)
κόλλαβος (kollabos)
κολλοβὸς (kollobos)
κολοφωνία (kolophonia)
κόμμα (comma)
κομμάτιον (kommation)
κομμὸς (commos)
κομπισμὸς (kompismos)
Κόννος (Konnus)
κόρδαξ (kordax)
Κόριννα (Corinna)
Κορύβαντες (Korybantes)
κορυθαλίστριαι (korythalistriai)

κορυφαῖος (koryphaeus)
κορώνισμα (koronisma)
κόχλος (kochlos)
κραδίας νόμος (kradias nomos)
Κράτης (Krates)
κρεγμὸς (kregmos)
κρέκειν (krekein)
κρέμβαλον (krembalon)
Κρέξος (Krexus)
κρητικὸς (Kretikos)
κρόταλα (krotala)
κροῦμα (krouma)
κρουπέζιον (kroupezion)
κρουσίθυρον (krousithyron)
κροῦσις (krousis)
κρουστὰ (krousta)
Κτησίβιος (Ktesibius)
κύκλιος (cyclios)
κύμβαλα (cymbala)
κώδων (kodon)
κῶλον (kolon)
κωμάρχιος νόμος (komarchios no-
    mos)
κωμαστικὴ (komastike)
κῶμος (komos)

Λ

Λαμπροκλῆς (Lamprocles)
Λάμπρος (Lamprus)
Λᾶσος ὁ Ἑρμιονεὺς (Lasus of Her-
    mione)
λεῖμμα (leimma)
Λείψανα Ἑλληνικῆς Μουσικῆς (Re-
    mains of Greek Music)
λέξις (lexis)
λέων (leon)
λῆψις (lepsis)
λῆψις διὰ συμφωνίας (lepsis dia
    symphonias)

λίβυς αὐλὸς (Libys aulos)
λιγυηχὴς (ligyeches)
λιγύθροος (ligythroos)
Λιμένιος (Limenius)
λίνος (linos)
Λίνος (Linus)
λινῳδία (linodia)
λιτυέρσης (lityerses)
λιχανοειδὴς (lichanoeides)
λιχανὸς (lichanos)
λογῶδες μέλος (logodes melos)
λόκριος ἁρμονία (Locrios harmo-
    nia)
λομβρότερον (lombroteron)
λύδιος ἁρμονία (Lydios harmonia)
Λυκάων (Lycaon)
λύρα (lyra)
λυρογηθὴς (lyrogethes)
λυροφοῖνιξ (lyrophoenix)
λυρῳδία, λυρῳδὸς (lyrodia, lyro-
    dos)
Λύσανδρος (Lysandrus)
λυσιῳδὸς (lysiodos)

M

μαγάδιον (magadion)
μάγαδις (magadis)
μαγὰς (magas)
μαγῳδὸς (magodos)
μακρὸν (makron)
μακτρισμὸς (maktrismos)
μαλακὸς (malakos)
μανερὼς (maneros)
μανὸς, μανότης (manos, manotes)
Μαρσύας (Marsyas)
μεθαρμογὴ (metharmoge)
Μελάμπους (Melampous)
Μελανιππίδης (Melanippides)

μελεάζειν (meleazein)
μελίγηρυς (meligerys)
μέλισμα (melisma)
μελογραφία (melographia)
μελοποιεῖν (melopoeein)
μελοποιΐα (melopoeia)
μέλος (melos)
μελουργεῖν (melourgein)
μέλπειν, μελπῳδός (melpein, mel-
    podos)
μελύδριον (melydrion)
μελῴδημα (melodema)
μελῳδία (melodia)
μελῳδός (melodos)
μέση (mese)
μεσοειδής (mesoeides)
μεσόκοπος, αὐλὸς (mesokopos,
    aulos)
Μεσομήδης (Mesomedes)
μεσόπυκνοι (mesopycnoi)
μέσος (mesos)
μεταβολή (metabole)
μετάβολος (metabolos)
μετακατατροπὰ (metakatatropa)
μεταρχὰ (metarcha)
Μέτελλος (Metellus)
μετρική (metrike)
μέτρον (metron)
μῆνες (menes)
μηνίαμβος (meniambos)
μητρῷα (metroa)
Μίδας (Midas)
μικτὸς (miktos)
μίμαυλος (mimaulos)
μιμητική (mimetike)
Μίμνερμος (Mimnermus)
μινυρισμὸς (minyrismos)
μίξις (mixis)
μιξολύδιος ἁρμονία (Mixolydios
    harmonia)

μίτος (mitos)
μογγὰς (mongas)
μόθων (mothon)
μολοσσικὴ (molossike)
μολοσσὸς (molossos)
μολπὴ (molpe)
μοναυλία (monaulia)
μοναύλιον (monaulion)
μόναυλον μέλος (monaulon melos)
μόναυλος (monaulos)
μονὴ (mone)
μονόχορδον (monochordon)
μονῳδία (monodia)
μορφασμὸς (morphasmos)
μοῦσα (Mousa)
Μουσαῖος (Musaeus)
μουσεῖον (mouseion)
μουσεῖος (mouseios)
μουσίζειν (mousizein)
μουσικεύεσθαι (mousikeuesthai)
μουσικὴ (mousike)
μουσικὸς (mousikos)
μουσόθετος (mousothetos)
μουσοποιὸς (mousopoeos)
μουσοτέχνης (mousotechnes)
μουσοτραφὴς (mousotraphes)
μουσοῦμαι (mousoumai)
μουσούργημα (mousourgema)
μουσουργὸς (mousourgos)
μυρμηκιὰ (myrmekia)
Μυρτὶς (Myrtis)

N

νάβλας (nablas)
νευρὰ (neura)
νηνία (nenia)
νηνίατον (neniaton)
νήτη (nete)
νητοειδὴς (netoeides)

νιβατισμός (nibatismos)
νίγλαρος (niglaros)
Νικόμαχος ὁ Γερασηνὸς (Nicomachus of Gerasa)
νόμιον (nomion)
νόμος (nomos)

Ξ

Ξάνθος (Xanthus)
Ξενόδαμος (Xenodamus)
Ξενόκριτος (Xenocritus)
ξιφισμός (xiphismos)
ξυλόφωνον (xylophonon)

Ο

ὀδοντισμός (odontismos)
ὀδός (hodos)
οἶκτος (oektos)
οἰτόλινος (oetolinos)
ὄκλασμα (oklasma)
ὀκτάσημος (oktasemos)
ὀκτάχορδον (octachordon)
ὀλιγοχορδία (oligochordia)
ὅλμος (holmos)
ὀλολυγμός (ololygmos)
ὀλοφυρμός (olophyrmos)
Ὄλυμπος (Olympus)
ὁμοιότροπος (homoeotropos)
ὁμότονα (homotona)
ὁμότονοι, φθόγγοι (homotonoi,
phthongoi)
ὁμοφωνία, ὁμόφωνοι (homophonia, homophonoi)
ὀμφαλός (omphalos)
ὀνομασία, ὀνοματοθεσία (onomasia, onomatothesia)
ὀξύβαφοι (oxybaphoi)
ὀξυηχής (oxyeches)

ὀξύπυκνος (oxypycnos)
ὀξύς (oxys)
ὀξύτονος (oxytonos)
ὄργανον (organon)
ὄρθιος (orthios)
ὅρμος (hormos)
ὅρος (horos)
ὀρσίτης (orsites)
Ὀρφεύς (Orpheus)
ὄρχησις, ὀρχηστική (orchesis,
orchestike)
ὀρχήστρα (orchestra)
ὄστρακον (ostrakon)
οὖλος (oulos)
οὖπιγγος (oupingos)

Π

Παγκράτης (Pankrates)
πάθος (pathos)
παιάν, παίων (paean, paeon)
παιδικός (paedikos)
παλινῳδία (palinodia)
πάμφωνος (pamphonos)
πανδούρα (pandoura)
πανδούριον (pandourion)
Πάππος ὁ Ἀλεξανδρινὸς (Pappus
of Alexandria)
παράβασις (parabasis)
παραδιάζευξις (paradiazeuxis)
παρακαταλογὴ (parakataloge)
παράκρουσις (parakrousis)
παραμέση (paramese)
παράμουσος (paramousos)
παρανήτη (paranete)
παρανιέναι (paranienai)
παραπλασμός (paraplasmos)
παρασημαντικὴ (parasemantike)
παρασκήνιον (paraskenion)
πάραυλος (paraulos)

παραφωνία, παράφωνοι φθόγγοι (paraphonia, paraphonoi phthongoi)
παράχορδος (parachordos)
παραχορήγημα (parachoregema)
παρελκυσμὸς (parhelkysmos)
παρθένεια (partheneia)
παρθένιος (parthenios)
παριαμβὶς (pariambis)
παρίαμβος (pariambos)
Πάριον Χρονικὸν (Parion Chronikon)
πάροδος (parodos)
παροιμιακὸς (paroemiakos)
παρυπάτη (parhypate)
Παχυμέρης (Pachymeres)
παχὺς (pachys)
πεῖρα (peira)
πεντάσημος (pentaseinos)
πεντάχορδον (pentachordon)
πεντεκαιδεκάχορδον σύστημα (pentekaedecachordon systema)
περιάδειν (periadein)
περίοδος (periodos)
περισπώμενος (perispomenos)
περιστόμιον (peristomion)
περιφερὴς (peripheres)
περιφορὰ (periphora)
περσικὸν (Persikon)
πεττεία (petteia)
πῆκτις (pektis)
πήληξ (pelex)
πῆχυς (pechys)
πινακὶς (pinakis)
Πίνδαρος (Pindarus)
πλαγία γλῶσσα (plagia glossa)
πλαγίαυλος (plagiaulos)
πλάσμα (plasma)
πλάστιγξ (plastinx)
πλάτος (platos)

Πλάτων (Platon)
πλῆκτρον (plectron)
πλοκὴ (ploke)
Πλούταρχος (Plutarchus)
πνεῦμα (pneuma)
πνοὴ (pnoe)
ποδίκρα (podikra)
ποδισμὸς (podismos)
ποδοψόφος (podopsophos)
ποίημα (poeema)
ποίησις (poeesis)
ποιητὴς (poeetes)
ποικίλος, ποικιλία (poekilos, poekilia)
ποίφυγμα (poephygma)
πολεμικὸν (polemikon)
πολλαπλοῦν (pollaploun)
πολυαρμόνιον (polyharmonion)
Πολυδεύκης (Polydeukes, Pollux)
Πολύειδος (Polyeidus)
πολυκέφαλος νόμος (polykephalos nomos)
Πολύμνηστος (Polymnestus)
πολύτροπος (polytropos)
πολύφθογγος (polyphthongos)
πολύφωνος (polyphonos)
πολυχορδία (polychordia)
πολύχορδον (polychordon)
πόππυσμα (poppysma)
Πορφύριος (Porphyrius)
ποῦς (pous)
Πρατίνας (Pratinas)
προαναβολὴ (proanabole)
προανάκρουσμα (proanakrousma)
πρόασμα (proasma)
προαύλημα (proaulema)
προαυλία, προαύλιον (proaulia, proaulion)
προκελευσματικὸς (prokeleusmatikos)

Πρόκλος (Proclus)
πρόκρουμα (prokrouma)
πρόκρουσις, πρόληψις (prokrousis, prolepsis)
προκρουσμὸς, προλημματισμὸς (prokrousmos, prolemmatismos)
προνόμιον (pronomion)
Πρόνομος (Pronomus)
προοίμιον (prooemion)
πρόποδα μέλη (propoda mele)
προσανιέναι (prosanienai)
προσαυλεῖν (prosaulein)
προσαύλημα (prosaulema)
προσαύλησις (prosaulesis)
πρόσθεσις (prosthesis)
προσλαμβανόμενος (proslambanomenos)
προσμελῳδεῖν (prosmelodein)
προσόδιον (prosodion)
πρόσοδος (prosodos)
πρόσχορδος (proschordos)
πρόσχορος (proschoros)
προσῳδία (prosodia)
προσῳδὸς (prosodos)
Πρόφραστος (Prophrastus)
προῳδὸς (proodos)
πρύλις (prylis)
πταῖσμα (ptaesma)
πτερὸν (pteron)
πτιστικὸν, πτισμὸς (ptistikon, ptismos)
Πτολεμαῖος (Ptolemaeus)
πτῶσις (ptosis)
Πυθαγόρας (Pythagoras)
Πυθαγόρας ὁ Ζακύνθιος (Pythagoras of Zante)
πυθαύλης (pythaules)
Πύθερμος (Pythermus)
πυθικὸν (pythikon)
πυθικὸς αὐλὸς (Pythikos aulos)

πυθικὸς νόμος (Pythikos nomos)
Πυθοκλείδης (Pythocleides)
Πυθόκριτος (Pythocritus)
πυκνὸν (pycnon)
Πυλάδης (Pylades)
πυρρίχη (pyrrhiche)

P

ραπαύλης (rapaules)
ραψῳδὸς (rhapsodos)
ρητόν, ἄλογον (rheton, alogon)
ρόμβος (rombos)
ρόπτρον (roptron)
ρυθμικὴ (rhythmike)
ρυθμογραφία (rhythmographia)
ρυθμοειδὴς (rhythmoeides)
ρυθμοποιΐα (rhythopoeia)
ρυθμὸς (rhythmos)

Σ

Σακάδας (Sakadas)
σάλπιγξ (salpinx)
σαμβύκη (sambyke)
Σαπφώ (Sappho)
Σείκιλος (Seikilus)
σεῖστρον (seistron)
σημασία (semasia)
σημεῖον (semeion)
σιγμὸς (sigmos)
σίκιννις (sikinnis)
σικιννοτύρβη (sikinnotyrbe)
σίμαι (simai)
σιμὴ (sime)
σιμίκιον (simikion)
σιμῳδία, σιμῳδὸς (simodia, simodos)
Σιμωνίδης (Simonides)
σιφνιάζειν (siphniazein)

σκάζων (skazon)
σκηνικὸς (skenikos)
σκινδαψὸς (skindapsos)
σκόλιον (scolion)
σκυτάλιον (skytalion)
σκὼψ (skops)
σοβὰς (sobas)
Σουΐδας (Suidas)
Σοφοκλῆς (Sophocles)
σπάδιξ (spadix)
Σπένδων (Spendon)
σπονδαύλης (spondaules)
σπονδαύλιον μέλος (spondaulion melos)
σπονδειάζων τρόπος (spondeiazon tropos)
σπονδειακὸς αὐλός, τρόπος (spondeiakos aulos, tropos)
σπονδειασμὸς (spondeiasmos)
σπονδεῖον (spondeion)
σπονδεῖος (spondeios)
στάσιμον (stasimon)
στάσις (stasis)
Στησίχορος (Stesichorus)
στιγμή (stigme)
στίξις (stixis)
στοιχεῖον (stoecheion)
Στρατόνικος (Stratonicus)
στρόβιλος (strobilos)
στρόμβος (strombos)
στροφή (strophe)
συβήνη (sybene)
συβωτικὸν (sybotikon)
συγκροτητικαὶ γλῶτται (synkrotetikai glottai)
σύγκρουσις (synkrousis)
συγχορδία (synchordia)
συγχορεία (synchoreia)
συγχορευτὴς (synchoreutes)
σύγχορος (synchoros)

συζυγία (syzygia)
συλλαβὴ (syllabe)
σύλληψις (syllepsis)
συμμετρία (symmetria)
συμπλοκὴ (symploke)
συμφωνία, σύμφωνος (symphonia, symphonos)
συνάγειν (synagein)
συναυλία (synaulia)
συναφὴ (syn(h)aphe)
συνεχὴς (syneches)
συνημμένος (synemmenos)
συνηρμοσμένος (synermosmenos)
συνήχησις (synechesis)
σύνθεσις (synthesis)
σύνθετος (synthetos)
σύνταγμα (syntagma)
σύντονος (syntonos)
συνῳδία, συνῳδὸς (synodia, synodos)
σύριγγες (syrinxes)
συρίγγιον (syringion)
σύριγμα (syrigma)
συριγμὸς (syrigmos)
σύριγξ (syrinx)
σύρμα (syrma)
συρτὸς (syrtos)
σύστασις (systasis)
σύστημα (systema)
σφραγὶς (sphragis)
σχῆμα (schema)
σχίσμα (schisma)
σχιστὰς (schistas)
σχοινίων νόμος (schoenion nomos)
σχοινοτενὴς (schoenotenes)

T

τάξις (taxis)
τάσις (tasis)

τελαμών (telamon)

τέλειος, ὑπερτέλειος αὐλός (teleios, hyperteleios aulos)

Τελεσίας (Telesias)

τελεσιάς (telesias)

Τελέσιλλα (Telesilla)

Τελέστης (Telestes)

τελευτή (teleute)

τερετισμός, τερέτισμα (teretismos, teretisma)

Τέρπανδρος (Terpandrus)

τεταρτημόριον (tetartemorion)

τετράγηρυς (tetragerys)

τετράγωνος (tetragonos)

τετρακτύς (tetraktys)

τετράκωμος (tetrakomos)

τετραοίδιος (tetraoedios)

τετράσημος (tetrasemos)

τετράχορδον (tetrachordon)

τεχνῖται Διονύσου (technitai Dionysou)

Τηλεφάνης (Telephanes)

τήνελλα (tenella)

Τιμόθεος (Timotheus)

τιτύρινος αὐλός (tityrinos aulos)

τίτυρος (tityros)

τομή (tome)

τονή (tone)

τόνος (tonos)

τόπος (topos)

τορεύειν ᾠδήν (toreuein oden)

Τόρηβος (Torebus)

τρῆμα (trema)

τρίγωνον (trigonon)

τριημιτόνιον (trihemitonion)

τριηραύλης (trieraules)

τριμελής καὶ τριμερής νόμος (trimeles and trimeres nomos)

τριποδιφορικὸν μέλος (tripodiphorikon melos)

τρίπους (tripous)

τρίσημος (trisemos)

τρίτη (trite)

τριτημόριον (tritemorion)

τρίχορδον (trichordon)

τρόπος (tropos)

τροχαῖος (trochaeos)

τρυγῳδοποιομουσική (trygodopoeomousike)

τυμβαύλης (tymbaules)

τύμπανον (tympanon)

τυρβασία (tyrbasia)

τύρβη (Tyrbe)

τυρρηνὸς αὐλός (Tyrrhenos aulos)

Τυρταῖος (Tyrtaeus)

Υ

Ὕαγνις (Hyagnis)

ὕδραυλις, ὕδραυλος (hydraulis, hydraulos)

ὑμέναιος (hymenaeos)

ὕμνος (hymnos)

ὑπαγωγεύς (hypagogeus)

ὑπάτη (hypate)

ὑπατοειδὴς τόπος (hypatoeides topos)

ὑπαυλεῖν (hypaulein)

ὑπεραιόλιος τόνος (Hyperaeolios tonos)

ὑπερβατὸν (hyperbaton)

ὑπερβολαιοειδὴς (hyperbolaeoeides)

ὑπερβολαίων, τετράχορδον (hyperbolaeon, tetrachordon)

ὑπερδιάζευξις (hyperdiazeuxis)

ὑπερδώριος τόνος (Hyperdorios tonos)

ὑπεριάστιος τόνος (Hyperiastios tonos)

363

ὑπερλύδιος τόνος (Hyperlydios tonos)
ὑπερμέση (hypermese)
ὑπερμιξολύδιος τόνος (Hypermixolydios tonos)
ὑπέρτονος (hypertonos)
ὑπερυπάτη (hyperhypate)
ὑπερφρύγιος τόνος (Hyperphrygios tonos)
ὑπηχεῖν (hypechein)
ὑποαιόλιος τόνος (Hypoaeolios tonos)
ὑπογύπωνες (hypogypones)
ὑποδιάζευξις (hypodiazeuxis)
ὑποδώριος ἁρμονία, τόνος (Hypodorios harmonia, tonos)
ὑποθέατροι αὐλοί (hypotheatroi auloi)
ὑποϊάστιος τόνος (Hypoïastios tonos)
ὑποκιθαρίζειν (hypokitharizein)
ὑποκρέκειν, ὑποτερετίζειν (hypokrekein, hypoteretizein)
ὑπολύδιος ἁρμονία, τόνος (Hypolydios harmonia, tonos)
ὑπολύριος (hypolyrios)
ὑπόρχημα (hyporchema)
ὑποσυναφὴ (hyposynaphe)
ὑποφρύγιος ἁρμονία, τόνος (Hypophrygios harmonia, tonos)
ὑφὲν (hyphen)
ὑφόλμιον (hypholmion)

Φ

φαλλικὸν (phallikon)
φάνδουρος (phandouros)
φερεκράτειος στίχος (Pherecrateios stichos)
Φερεκράτης (Pherecrates)

Φήμιος (Phemius)
φθόγγος (phthongos)
Φιλάμμων (Philammon)
φιληλιὰς (philhelias)
Φιλόδημος (Philodemus)
Φιλόλαος (Philolaus)
φιλόμουσος (philomousos)
Φιλόξενος (Philoxenus)
φιλόρρυθμος (philorrhythmos)
φιλότεχνος (philotechnos)
φιλῳδὸς (philodos)
φλύαξ (phlyax)
φοῖνιξ, φοινίκιον (phoenix, phoenikion)
φοιτητὴς (phoetetes)
φορβειὰ (phorbeia)
φόρμιγξ (phorminx)
φρύγιος ἁρμονία (Phrygios harmonia)
Φρῦνις (Phrynis)
Φρύνιχος (Phrynichus)
φυσαλλὶς (physallis)
φωνασκία (phonaskia)
φωνή (phone)
φῶτιγξ αὐλὸς (photinx aulos)

X

χαλαρὸς (chalaros)
χειροκαλαθίσκος (cheirokalathiskos)
χειρονομία (cheironomia)
χειρονόμος (cheironomos)
χειρουργία (cheirourgia)
χελιδόνισμα (chelidonisma)
χέλυς (chelys)
χιάζειν (chiazein)
χοραύλης (choraules)
χορδὴ (chorde)
χορδοτόνος (chordotonos)

χορεία (choreia)
χορεῖος (choreios)
χόρευμα (choreuma)
χορεύς (choreus)
χορηγός (choregos)
χορίαμβος (choriambos)
χορικός (chorikos)
χοροδιδάσκαλος (chorodidaskalos)
χοροκάλη (chorokale)
χοροκιθαυρεύς (chorokithareus)
χορολέκτης (chorolektes)
χορός (chorus)
χοροστάτης (chorostates)
χορῳδία (chorodia)
χρεῶν ἀποκοπὴ (chreon apokope)
χρῆσις (chresis)
χρησμῳδός (chresmodos)
χρόα (chroa)
χρόνος (chronos)
χρωματικὸν γένος (Chromatikon genos)
χωλίαμβος (choliambos)

χώρα (chora)

Ψ'

ψάλλειν, ψαλτικὰ ὄργανα (psallein, psaltika organa)
ψαλμὸς (psalmos)
ψαλτήρ, ψάλτης, ψάλτρια (psalter, psaltes, psaltria)
ψαλτήριον (psalterion)
ψάλτιγξ (psaltinx)
Ψελλός, Μιχαὴλ (Psellus, Michael)
ψιθύρα (psithyra)
ψιλὸς (psilos)
ψόφος (psophos)

Ω

ᾠδεῖον (odeion)
ᾠδὴ (ode)
ᾠδὸς (odos)
'Ωλὴν (Olen)
ὠσχοφορικὰ (oschophorika)

Note: *The drawings of the instruments are by Eleni G. Chariclidou.*

PLATES

PLATE I
Cypriot double-aulos player.
c. 600 B.C.; New York, Cesnola Collection

PLATE II

Maenad playing the double aulos.
Volute-crater, 410 B.C.; Taranto, Museo Nazionale Archeologico.

PLATE III
Barbiton player (reveller and girl).
Skyphos, 490 B.C.; Paris, Louvre.

PLATE IV
Kitharodos.   Amphora, c. 490 B.C., Berlin.
New York, Metropolitan Museum of Art

PLATE V

Muse playing the kithara (or phorminx?).
445 B.C.; Lugano, Private Collection.

PLATE VI
Linus and Iphicles at lyra lesson.
Skyphos, c. 470 B.C.; Schwerin Staatliche Museum.

PLATE VII
    Pronomus Vase (detail).
    Pronomus the aulete.
    5th to 4th cent. B.C.; Napoli, Museo Nazionale Archeologico.

PLATE VIII
Muse playing the trichordon.
Mantineia-Base; First half 4th cent. B.C.
Athens, National Archaeological Museum.

PLATE IX
The harpist of Keros.
Statuette. Athens, National Archaeological Museum.

PLATE X
Maenad playing the tympanon.
Stamnos, 420 B.C.
Napoli, Museo Nazionale Archeologico.

N